UMI ANNUAL COMMENTARY

PRECEPTS FOR LIVING®

MISSION STATEMENT

*W*e are called
of God to create, produce, and distribute
quality Christian education products;
to deliver exemplary customer service;
and to provide quality Christian
educational services, which will empower
God's people, especially within the Black
community, to evangelize, disciple,
and equip people for serving Christ,
His kingdom, and church.

Urban Ministries, Inc.
The African American Christian Publishing
& Communications Co.

UMI ANNUAL SUNDAY SCHOOL LESSON COMMENTARY
PRECEPTS FOR LIVING® 2013–2014
INTERNATIONAL SUNDAY SCHOOL LESSONS
VOLUME 16
UMI (URBAN MINISTRIES, INC.)

Melvin Banks Sr., Litt.D., Founder and Chairman
C. Jeffrey Wright, J.D., CEO

All art: Copyright © 2013 by UMI.
Bible art: Fred Carter

All proper names mentioned in this publication are fictional unless otherwise indicated.
Item No.: 1-2014. ISBN-13: 978-1-60997-869-3. ISBN-10: 1-60997-869-2.

PFL Large Print Item No.:1-2614. ISBN-13: 978-1-60997-872-3, ISBN-10: 1-60997-872-2

Publisher: UMI (Urban Ministries, Inc.), Chicago, IL 60643. To place an order, call us at 1-800-860-8642, or visit our www.urbanministries.com.

Get the Precepts for Living® eBook!

Are you among those reading books using a Kindle, iPad, NOOK, or other electronic reader? If so, there's good news for you! UMI (Urban Ministries, Inc.) is keeping up with the latest technology by publishing its annual Sunday School commentary, *Precepts for Living®*, in the leading eBook formats: Kindle (Amazon), NOOK (Barnes & Noble), and iBooks (Apple).

To buy an eBook copy of *Precepts for Living®*, visit our website at urbanministries.com/precepts to find download links and step-by-step instructions.

If you've purchased *Precepts for Living®* for your e-reader, be sure to leave a rating and a review at the iTunes or Amazon store sites to tell others what you think. Also, spread the word on your favorite social networking sites, and follow *Precepts for Living®* on Facebook and Twitter (with the handle @precepts4living).

PRECEPTS
FOR
LIVING®

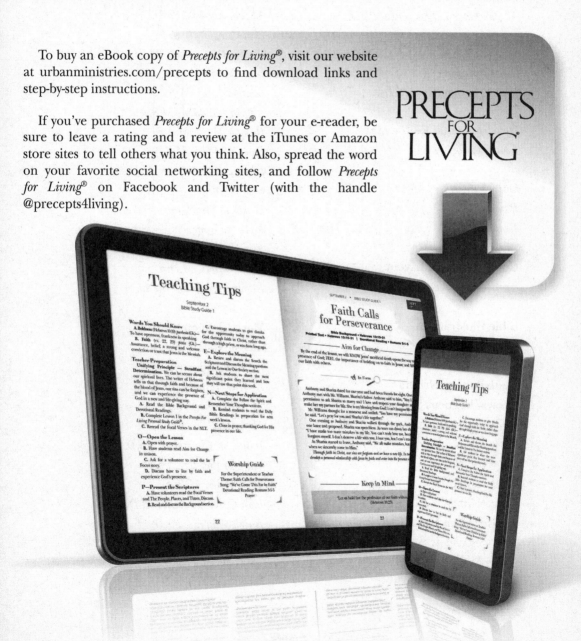

CONTRIBUTORS

Editor
A. Okechukwu Ogbonnaya, Ph.D.

Associate Director of Adult Content Development
John C. Richards, Jr., M.Div.

Developmental Editor
Linda Taylor, M.A.

Copy Editors
Pamela Graves
Benton Sartore

Cover Design & Layout
Trinidad D. Zavala, B.A.

Bible Illustrations
Fred Carter

Contributing Writers
Essays/In Focus Stories
Melvin E. Banks Sr., Litt.D.
Eugene A. Blair
Aja Carr, M.T.S.
Prathia Hall, Ph.D.
Jennifer King, M.A.
A. Okechukwu Ogbonnaya, Ph.D.
John C. Richards, Jr., M.Div.
Robert Smith, Ph.D.

Bible Study Guide Writers
Allyson Abrams, Ph.D.
Lisa Crayton, B.A.
Rukeia Draw-Hood, Ph.D.
Jean Garrison, M.A.
Jennifer King, M.A.
Angela Lampkin, M.S.
Ramon Mayo, M.A.
Beverly Moore, M.S.
John C. Richards, Jr., M.Div.
Amy Rognile
Elizabeth Simington
LaTonya Summers
Kim Varner, M.Div.
Faith Waters, M.Div.
Rigoberto Weekes, M.Div.

More Light on the Text
Allyson Abrams, Ph.D.
J. Ayodeji Adewuya, Ph.D.
Rukeia Draw-Hood, Ph.D.
Richard Gray, Ph.D.
Kevin Hrebik, D.Min.
Judith St. Clair Hull, Ph.D.
Vanessa Lovelace, Ph.D.
Tony Myles, M.B.A.
John C. Richards, Jr., M.Div.
Ralph Watkins, Ph.D.
Kelly Whitcomb, Ph.D.

Dear Precepts Customer,

It is our privilege to present the 2013–2014 *Precepts For Living*®. As you encounter God's Word through these lessons, we anticipate that you will find this resource to be indispensable.

Precepts For Living® comes to you in three versions: the Personal Study Guide (the workbook), the App version, and a large print edition. You will also notice that the biblical text for each lesson includes the New Living Translation in addition to the King James Version. This contemporary translation will enhance your textual understanding when you compare it side by side to the classic English translation. It is very helpful in illuminating your understanding of the text.

Precepts For Living® is designed to be a witness through our learning and sharing more of the Bible. Our intent is to facilitate innovative ways for pursuing a deeper understanding and practice of God's Word. One of the ways we strive to do this is by highlighting the larger narrative of God's work in salvation as a key part of understanding each biblical passage. We believe it is important to help you understand not only the particulars of the text but also the broad extent of God's revelation to us as well. This panoramic approach enhances our ability to witness to others about the saving power of Jesus Christ.

This year we explore the themes of creation, justice, tradition, and community. Each year of Bible study offers great potential for a more intimate and transformative walk with God.

We want to continually refine *Precepts For Living*® as we endeavor to meet our customers' needs. We are always looking for ways to enhance your study of the Bible, and your comments and feedback are vital in helping us. If you have questions or suggestions, we encourage you to please e-mail us at precepts@urbanministries.com or mail your comments to UMI, *Precepts For Living*®, PO Box 436987, Chicago, IL 60643-6987.

May God draw you closer to the fullness of life with Him through this book.

God's blessings to you,

A. Okechukwu Ogbonnaya

A. Okechukwu Ogbonnaya, Ph.D.
Editor

Uncovering the Benefits of Precepts

It is a great privilege to participate in Christian education and play a significant role in the spiritual formation of fellow Christians in our churches. *Precepts for Living®* is a resource that is designed to help you lead others toward greater knowledge and practice of following Jesus Christ. To that end, please take full advantage of the substantive offerings provided to you in this year's commentary. From the standpoint of your vocation as a teacher, it is very important to be aware of the great responsibility that goes along with your position. James 3:1 reminds us that we have such a great opportunity in front of us that we run the risk of greater judgment if we are derelict in our duties. In the Gospels, Jesus is often referred to as "teacher." Being a teacher means participating in one of the church's greatest tasks, one that the ancient church called "catechesis." This is a strong word that helps us understand the great influence we have when we help our students learn about God's Word. While this word is often associated with particular denominations and with a form of teaching that relies upon a systematic question-and-answer format, the central meaning of the word is teaching. It carries with it the idea of imparting the entirety of the faith to Christians. While many Sunday School teachers might not be familiar with this word, the truth is that every time we help other learn about God's Word and ways, we are participating in this great task of the church that has been with us from the beginning. Our participation in catechesis is central to the life of the church. Unfortunately, though, this gets lost amid other concerns. As a teacher, you have an opportunity to energize or revitalize this aspect of your church's ministry. Reflect on how you have prepared for the challenge.

What is the goal when you use *Precepts for Living®* to open up the riches of the Bible to your students? It is beyond the mere acquisition of "spiritual data." Certainly we want our students to grow in knowledge, but the knowledge we seek to pass on does not solely comprise Bible facts but includes a larger sense of comprehension where the information and doctrine conveyed is oriented toward a faithful life of discipleship. The People, Places, and Times; Background; In Depth; and More Light on the Text sections are there to help you provide insight and understanding of the text. But the sections include more than a simple compilation of information. In each lesson, you will also see In Focus stories and Lesson in Our Society and Make It Happen sections serving as catalysts for applying the biblical text to life situations. It is very important that we as teachers pass on knowledge that will enable our students to deepen their devotion to God in an upward focus and encourage them to better embody that devotion in a way that makes their lives a living witness to the world. Our hope from every lesson should be to inspire students to become the best living examples of the Scriptures with the understanding that their lives may be the only Bible some people ever read.

To best take advantage of this commentary, utilize the essays highlighting notable African Americans to emphasize quarterly themes and enhance the classroom experience.

We believe this commentary is a great tool to help form fully devoted followers of Christ, and we invite you to wholeheartedly partake in all of the resources provided here. May God be glorified as you play your part in this great task of the church!

Creative Teaching

• **Energizing the Class.** If the class does not seem as enthusiastic or energy is low, after you open with prayer, have everyone stretch to the sky or outward. Then tell the class to shake off the low energy, and open up their hands to receive the love of God that is right there. You can always have a 30-second meet-and-greet time. This usually helps to wake people up so you can begin class on a higher energy level.

• **Two Teachers in One Class—Bring Out the Best in Both.** Taking turns works in some classes, but in others it creates tension and favorites. Encourage teachers to study together, and then divide the segments of the lesson. Perhaps one will teach the introduction while the other teaches a section of the text. Encourage them to also become a true team with each contributing throughout the lesson.

• **Remember.** Everyone cannot read or write on the same level. Use different teaching techniques and styles when teaching. How you learn affects how you teach, so be open and willing to learn and teach through various media.

• **Avoid Study in Isolation.** People often "get it" when they are involved with more than talking about the lesson. Why not allow the class to see the connections themselves? Try using a chart to have adult students work in pairs or groups to compare and contrast Bible people such as David and Solomon or Ruth and Orpah, Naomi's daughters-in-law. To help the students get started, suggest specific categories for comparisons such as lifestyles, families, or public ministry. As class members search the Scriptures, they will learn and remember much more than if you told them about either person individually.

• **Group Studies.** Have the class form groups, and have each group read the Scripture lesson and a section of the Background for the text. Have each group create a two-minute skit about the Scripture to share with the class. Encourage the groups to use their imaginations and energy. You may want to have at least one "leader" in a group if you have more than two or three reserved people in your class.

• **Volunteers.** Many classes begin with reading the lesson. When class members have studied, this activity is more "bringing minds" together than about the actual lesson. Still some classes can benefit from dramatic and creative reading of Bible passages at any point in the lesson. When the passage under study lends itself, assign parts to volunteers. This need not be formal—standing up isn't even critical. This strategy works best in passages that have a story such as the conversation between Moses and his father-in-law, Jethro, or Paul confronting the merchants in Thessalonica. Assign one person to each speaking character in the Bible text. Feel free to be creative with giving the class roles as "the crowd." Make sure to assign a narrator who will read the nonspeaking parts. It is fun, it is fast, and it makes for memorable Bible reading.

• **Alternatives.** Select one or two people from the class to read the Scripture lesson with enthusiasm and drama. Ask a few people to develop a newspaper or magazine headline with a brief story that explains the lesson. Have another group write the headlines and a story that will be used in a cell phone video. (Let the class know that they should bring their cell phones—with video recording—so most people can share in this activity.)

- **Materials.** You may want to have large sheets of paper, markers, glue or tape, newspapers, and magazines available on a weekly basis for the various activities.

- **Additional Methods.** Write the theme on a large poster board or sheet of paper, and ask each person to write a word or draw a picture that best describes the theme. Read the themes aloud, and discuss any of the pictures before you begin your class discussion or activities. If you have a very large class or time is limited, only select a few words or pictures for discussion. You can either lead the discussion or invite members of the class to do so.

- **Web sites.** Connect with us by logging on to www.urbanministries.com. Email us at precepts @urbanministries.com, and send us some of your favorite Teaching Tips for ages 18 and older that you want to share with others. If yours is selected, we will post them under our Teaching Tips sections for Precepts. If you have ice-breaker activities, please submit them as well. Your submissions should be no longer than 125 words.

- **Closing.** At the end of the lesson, give your class the assignment of looking for scenes from films or television, advertisements, or parts of songs that either demonstrate the coming week's In Focus story, Lesson in Our Society section, or Make It Happen section. Encourage them to be creative and to come up with an explanation of how their contribution helps make the truth of the lesson come to life.

- **Prayer.** Have a Prayer Request Board for people to write their prayer requests on each Sunday. You may want to make this a weekly activity. Have someone read the prayer request and let the class decide which prayer requests they will pray for during the week. One Sunday School teacher has his class write their prayer requests on sheets of paper and place them in the middle of the floor once a year. He then shares with the class that he will write them all down in a prayer journal that he keeps and pray over them at least once a week. Be creative and create your own prayer journal or prayer tradition(s) within your class.

Questions Related to the Heritage Profiles:

1. Why are some people chosen over others to be recognized for their achievements?

2. When reading the Heritage Profiles, what contemporary person comes to mind? A family member or friend can be a part of your decision.

3. Have you ever been recognized for a special achievement? How did you feel, and who have you lifted up to receive a special award in your church, community, or family? Why?

4. List three things from the Heritage Profiles you believe are important for others to know.

5. What similarities do you see between the historical figure and your life? If there are none, share ways the person's life may have made an impact on your life and on future generations.

6. List three characteristics that stand out about the Heritage Profiles that you think are either positive or negative. List three characteristics about your life that you believe are either positive or negative. Compare the lists and write a short paragraph about the similarities and/or differences.

Remember that creative teaching can maximize your students' learning experience.

TABLE OF CONTENTS

2012–2016
SCOPE & SEQUENCE–CYCLE SPREAD

	FALL	WINTER	SPRING	SUMMER
1 YEAR 2012–13	**FAITH** **A Living Faith** Psalm 46 1 Corinthians 13:1–13 Hebrews Acts	**GOD: JESUS CHRIST** **Jesus Is Lord** Ephesians Philippians Colossians	**HOPE** **Beyond the Present Time** Daniel Luke Acts 1, 2 Peter 1, 2 Thessalonians	**WORSHIP** **God's People Worship** Isaiah Ezra Nehemiah
2 YEAR 2013–14	**CREATION** **First Things** Genesis Exodus Psalm 104	**JUSTICE** **Jesus and the Just Reign of God** Luke James	**TRADITION** **Jesus' Fulfillment of Scripture** Zechariah Malachi Deuteronomy Matthew	**COMMUNITY** **The People of God Set Priorities** Haggai 1, 2 Corinthians
3 YEAR 2014–15	**HOPE** **Sustaining Hope** Jeremiah Habakkuk Ezekiel Isaiah	**WORSHIP** **Acts of Worship** Psalm 95:1–7 Daniel Matthew Mark Luke John Ephesians Hebrews James	**GOD: THE HOLY SPIRIT** **The Spirit Comes** Mark John Acts 1 Corinthians 12–14 1, 2, 3 John	**JUSTICE** **God's Prophets Demand Justice** Amos Micah Isaiah Jeremiah Ezekiel Psalms Zechariah Malachi
4 YEAR 2015–16	**COMMUNITY** **The Christian Community Comes Alive** Matthew John 1 John	**TRADITION** **Sacred Gifts and Holy Gatherings** Leviticus Numbers Deuteronomy	**FAITH** **The Gift of Faith** Mark Luke	**CREATION** **Toward a New Creation** Genesis Psalms Zephaniah Romans

Creation's Groaning

by John C. Richards, Jr.

"In the beginning God created the heaven and the earth" (Genesis 1:1, KJV).

Mountains are wondrous to behold. While residing in Pasadena, California, I was amazed at the fact that I could look out of my window and see snow-capped mountains. I'd then step outside and walk to Greek class on my seminary's campus in shorts and a T-shirt, enjoying the 80-degree weather below the mountains. How could this be? I could see the snow, but the cold air seemed isolated on the mountains' lofty peaks. Growing up along the coastland in Georgia, I'd never been exposed to mountainous terrain like this. The way the mountains towered over the Los Angeles area, it was as if they demanded reverence, respect, and, dare I say, admiration.

Yet even in all their splendor and majesty, the mountains didn't just appear by chance. They were formed as part of God's creative work. Theologians call this "*creatio ex nihilo*," a mysterious Latin phrase meaning "creation out of nothing." Before these mountains were formed, God was there: Father, Son, and Spirit (see Psalm 90:2), ready to set in motion a series of events that would include humanity's creation, fall, sinful bondage, and redemption through Christ Jesus. Paul later tells believers at Rome that this creation, having been adversely affected by the fall, has been "groaning" (from Romans 8:22, NIV) for the redemption offered through Christ. What a wonderful word picture! Those snow-capped mountains I saw on that clear day in Pasadena were groaning. They were telling me a story. They reminded me of the redemptive work of our Creator.

Our cover art reflects this truth. It tells a story. Let the structures below the mountains remind us that we live surrounded by God's creative work. The same God who formed magnificent mountains was caring enough to form us (see Amos 4:13) and create us in His image (see Genesis 1:27). And He cared enough for us to send His Son to fulfill the righteous requirement so we may be saved (see Romans 8:3–4). The mere fact that the Potter would become the very clay He shaped in the beginning is mind-blowing (see John 1:14).

Scripture records several breathtaking experiences on mountaintops. Abraham experienced provision in the form of a ram in the bush (see Genesis 22). Moses received confirmation in the form of God's commandments (see Exodus 31). Jesus was transfigured and confirmed by the Father before a select group of his disciples (see Matthew 17). In fact, in the same way Moses received the commandments of the Lord on top of Mount Sinai, Jesus' disciples experienced the revelation of Christ written on the tablets of their hearts (see Hebrews 8:10). In a very real sense, these mountains declared God's glory.

As we explore the themes of "Creation—First Things" and "Justice—Jesus and the Just Reign of God" for September and December 2013, and "Tradition—Jesus' Fulfillment of Scripture" and "Community—The People of God Set Priorities" for March and June 2014, we want you to consider the splendid design of God. We want you to think about God's plan—from beginning to end. In forming

the mountains and seas, and crowning His work by forming mankind, evidence of His love is visible around us daily. In doing so, we hope you realize that the Creator of heaven and earth causes "all things to work together for good to them that love God..." (from Romans 8:28, KJV, author's paraphrase). When you realize this, you begin to prioritize your life. The Kingdom of God becomes the driving force for everything you do. And that's just the way Jesus wants it (see Matthew 6:33).

Bara is the Hebrew word for "create," used in the Old Testament. *Kitzo* is the Greek word for "create," used in the New Testament. It's no coincidence that the only time the two words are used in Scripture reference God. After all, God is the only one who can create. Humans have attempted to re-create. We've attempted to duplicate. We've attempted to simulate. Creating is special, though, reserved for the Creator. The psalmist declares that God can even create in humans a clean heart (see Psalm 51:10). A heart that forgives. A heart that is slow to anger. A heart that isn't easily offended. A heart that cares for the poor and disenfranchised. Most of all, He can create a heart that becomes the dwelling place of His Spirit. Humans may have perfected the art of heart transplants, but there is One who knows how to create a new heart—from scratch. Continue to create, oh God. Your creation longs for Your touch.

Source:
Luz, Ulrich. *Matthew 8-20: A Commentary.* Minneapolis, MN: Fortress Press, 2001. 398.

John Richards is the Associate Director of Adult Content Development at UMI. He holds a Master of Divinity from Fuller Theological Seminary in Pasadena, California.

First Things

God's creative work is seen throughout the stories found in Genesis and Exodus. The quarter begins with the creation of the world and of human beings, explores the creation of a nation that began with God's promises to Abraham and Sarah and their heirs, and then studies the stories of the Hebrew people on their journey out of captivity toward freedom.

UNIT 1 • FIRST DAYS

This is a five-lesson unit that explores Israel's earliest stories. The first lesson is a hymn that affirms God's creation. The next two lessons focus on God as the Creator of the universe and humanity. The fourth lesson concentrates on God's promises to Noah and the establishment of an everlasting covenant. The fifth lesson explores the scattering of the nations.

Lesson 1: September 1, 2013
God Creates
Psalm 104:5–9, 24–30

All humans have some basic needs that must be supplied to sustain their daily lives. The psalmist tells the reader that God's hands are full to overflowing with the resources needed by everything He created.

Lesson 2: September 8, 2013
God's Image: Male and Female
Genesis 2:18–25

Finding a suitable companion with whom one can share life can be a struggle, but it can also bring great joy. According to Genesis 2, God created Eve as a partner for Adam.

Lesson 3: September 15, 2013
Knowledge of Good and Evil
Genesis 3:8b–17

Everyone at times has given in to lust or greed instead of making a right choice. Genesis 3 informs readers that when temptation confronts them, God gives them the freedom to make choices.

Lesson 4: September 22, 2013
An Everlasting Covenant
Genesis 9:8–17

A natural disaster can cause great anxiety over the safety and welfare of loved ones. God said that the rainbow would remind Him of the covenant to protect all living creatures.

Lesson 5: September 29, 2013
God Scatters the Nations
Genesis 11:1–9

Sometimes leaders make plans that will take those they serve in a harmful direction. In Genesis 11, the participants learn that God is aware of misguided plans and will intervene for the greater good of creation.

UNIT 2 • FIRST NATION

This is a four-lesson unit that develops the promise made to Abraham by God. The first two lessons tell of the promise of land and children to Abraham and Sarah. Lesson 3 sheds light on the blessing promised to Abraham's lineage. The final lesson outlines the blessing being passed to Jacob.

Lesson 6: October 6, 2013
A Promise of Land
Genesis 15:7–21

Many people hope to leave an inheritance for their children. God's promise to Abraham was the promise of creating a special relationship—a chosen nation—with Abraham and Sarah's heirs.

Lesson 7: October 13, 2013
A Promise to Sarah
Genesis 17:15–17, 18:9–15, 21:1–7

We often rejoice at the birth of a new member in the family or community. Abraham and Sarah saw their child as evidence of God's faithfulness in keeping the promise to create a nation.

Lesson 8: October 20, 2013
A Blessing for Ishmael and Isaac
Genesis 21:13–14, 17–21, 26:2–5, 12–13

The circumstances surrounding one's birth can affect a child's identity and self-worth. Despite the circumstances surrounding their births, God promised to create great nations through Ishmael and Isaac.

Lesson 9: October 27, 2013
The Blessing Passes to Jacob
Genesis 28:1, 10–22

When people feel insecure, they look for a place of security and the assurance of not being alone. God assures Jacob of His presence and promises that through Jacob and his offspring, all the families of the earth will be blessed.

UNIT 3 • FIRST FREEDOM

This is a four-lesson unit that explores the power of God to save Israel from oppression. The first and second lessons look at how God prepares and actually delivers Israel from bondage. Lessons three and four develop the story of Israel's beginning as a freed nation.

Lesson 10: November 3, 2013
Preparation for Deliverance
Exodus 3:7–17

When people are called to a new challenge, they must overcome their fears. Before Moses could lead the people to freedom, God repeatedly assured Moses of God's persistent help in all the trials to come.

Lesson 11: November 10, 2013
Beginning of Passover
Exodus 12:1–14

People who are living under oppression hunger for freedom. The freedom God promises to the Hebrew people will create a new beginning in their relationship with God—a beginning they will commemorate for generations to come.

Lesson 12: November 17, 2013
Beginning of Freedom
Exodus 14:21–30

People may find themselves in seemingly impossible circumstances while seeking freedom. God created a way out when there was no way.

Lesson 13: November 24, 2013
Beginning of the Tabernacle
Exodus 40:16–30, 34, 38

In the midst of a difficult transition, people look for security and guidance. While the Israelites were on their way to the Promised Land, God instructed the people to create the tabernacle—a place where they could always find God's presence and guidance.

Setting the Stage!

"And I will put enmity between thee and the woman, and between thy seed and her seed; it shall bruise thy head, and thou shalt bruise his heel"

(Genesis 3:15, KJV).

Christian Education in Action

Book	Author	Audience	Purpose	Key People
Psalm	King David wrote 73 psalms; Asaph (12); the sons of Korah (9); Solomon (2); Heman (with the sons of Korah); Ethan and Moses each wrote one; 51 are anonymous	The Hebrew people	Written to provide poetry for the expression of praise, worship, and confession to Almighty God	David, Asaph
Genesis	Not identified, but tradition suggests Moses	The Hebrew people	To trace the beginnings of history	Adam, Eve, Noah, Abraham, Isaac, Jacob, Esau, Sarah, Rebekah, Leah, Rachel, Ishmael
Exodus	Not identified, but tradition suggests Moses	The Hebrew people	To give an account of God's faithfulness in delivering His people from Egypt	Moses, Aaron, Pharaoh, Children of Israel
Matthew	Matthew (Levi)	The Jews	To prove that Jesus is the Messiah, the eternal King	Jesus, Mary, Joseph, John the Baptist, the disciples, the religious leaders, Caiaphas, Pilate, Mary Magdalene

Book	Author	Audience	Purpose	Key People
Mark	John Mark—not one of the 12 disciples—joined Paul on his first missionary journey (Acts 13:13)	Christians in Rome, where he wrote the Gospel	To present the person, work, and teachings of Jesus	Jesus, the 12 disciples, Pilate, the Jewish religious leaders
Luke	Luke—a doctor (Colossians 4:14), a Greek, and Gentile Christian; he was a close friend and companion of Paul	Theophilus ("one who loves God"), Gentiles, and people everywhere	To present an accurate account of the life of Christ and to present Christ as perfect human Savior	Jesus, Elizabeth, Zechariah, John the Baptist, Mary, the disciples, Herod the Great, Pilate, Mary Magdalene
John	John—one of the 12 disciples, leader of the early Christian community in Jerusalem (Acts 15:6; Galatians 2:9)	Gentile Christians	To represent the Christian faith in relation to the person of Christ as its center	Jesus, the disciples, John the Baptist, the religious leaders

Easton, George Matthew. *Illustrated Bible Dictionary, and Treasury of Biblical History, Biography, Geography, Doctrine, and Literature.* London: T. Nelson and Sons, 1897.

Life Application Study Bible, New Living Translation. Wheaton, IL: Tyndale House Publishers, Inc. 1062, 1766, 1867, 1936, 2120, 2261, 2444.

Pfeifer, Charles F., Howard F. Vos, John Rea, eds. *Wycliffe Bible Dictionary.* Peabody, Mass.: Hendrickson Publishers, Inc. 1998. 713.

Through the Tempest!

"But the children of Israel walked upon dry land in the midst of the sea; and the waters were a wall unto them on their right hand, and on their left"

(Exodus 14:29, KJV).

WILLIAM STILL
(October 7, 1821–July 14, 1902)
Underground Railroad Leader and Reformer

One of the legendary leaders of the Underground Railroad was a freeborn Black man named William Still. His father, Levin Steel, was a former slave from Maryland. After buying his freedom, Steel went to New Jersey and waited for his wife, Sidney, to join him. After her second attempt to escape, Sidney managed to join her husband with all but two of their children. To avoid recapture, the family changed its name to Still, and the mother's name to Charity. Later, William was born, the youngest of eighteen children.

As a boy, William helped his father on the family farm. In his early twenties, he left the farm and a few years later went on to Philadelphia, arriving with only five dollars in his pocket. Having had very few educational opportunities as a boy, William taught himself to read and write.

In 1847, William married Letitia George, with whom he later had four children—two boys and two girls. In 1847 he also became secretary of the Pennsylvania Society for the Abolition of Slavery. At that time the Society consisted of a few white members who had little experience with the practical needs of runaway slaves. William, remembering his family's struggles to become free, became such a helpful member of the Society that in 1851, he was elected its chairman. He later became director of the General Vigilance Committee of Philadelphia, managing its finances and funding Harriet Tubman's numerous raids. He established a network of safe houses from the upper part of the South to Canada. He kept a careful record of each fugitive so family and friends could later locate them in their newfound freedom. For a while, William hid his records in a cemetery, eventually publishing them in a book, *The Underground Railroad*, in 1872.

As a leading conductor of the Underground Railroad, William used his large house as a station. He kept it stocked with food and clothing for the frightened runaways for fourteen years. About 649 slaves were helped in their escape to freedom. William even helped John Brown's widow and daughter when they passed through Philadelphia. In his classic book, William accounts for about 800 escaped slaves, including 60 children, who were helped during an eight-year period. Black churches offered extensive aid, and while some few white churches offered help, most were hostile to runaways. Unfortunately, spies of both races were often present, looking for an opportunity to sell out escaped slaves for money. Even so, the system worked so well that the slave hunters came up with the term "Underground Railroad." Often, while pursuing slaves, the trackers would lose all trace of the runaways. In their frustration and bewilderment, some suggested there must be an underground railroad the fugitives were escaping to, and although it was spoken in bitter sarcasm, the term came into popular use.

As runaways arrived at Underground Railroad stations in his network, William Still personally interviewed them. His meticulous records, along with the accounts of other observers of the runaway phenomenon, show that thousands of slaves vanished daily from the plantations as the numbers of field workers steadily dwindled. He helped dispel the notion that runaway slaves were aided chiefly by white abolitionists and Quakers by documenting the aid that black churches, institutions, and especially ex-runaways gave to themselves and each other.

A very dramatic example of the courage and creativity of those wanting to flee slavery is that of Henry "Box" Brown. Henry was sealed in a box with water and biscuits for sustenance. It took two days by steamboat, wagon, and rail before he arrived at William Still's office. After emerging from the box, Henry sang a psalm: "I waited patiently for the Lord, and He heard my prayer."

The story of Margaret Garner is another illustration of dramatic uncertainties which often confronted fugitives. One snowy night, Margaret, her husband, their four children, and eleven other slaves from various plantations crowded into a sled drawn by two horses taken from one of the slaveholders. In the morning, they reached a small town and split up into smaller groups. One group was led to safe hiding places until nightfall, when they were conducted to the Underground Railroad and escaped to Canada. Unfortunately, Margaret's group was discovered. Margaret, who had vowed never to be returned to slavery, immediately grabbed a sharp knife and killed her youngest baby. She would have killed her other children and herself had she not been stopped by the slave trackers. After a trial, Margaret, her husband, and the next youngest child were ordered back to their owners. While on a boat returning them to the plantation, Margaret and her baby fell overboard. The baby drowned, and two years later, Margaret died of typhoid fever, asking her husband to wait for his freedom before marrying again. She believed Black people would one day be free.

William Still also found time to help organize an association to collect data on Black people. He set up an orphanage for the children of Black soldiers and sailors in Philadelphia, and helped organize the first YMCA for Black men. He went into the stove and later, coal business and obtained a modest fortune. He remained active in helping his people develop their potential and gain more civil rights until his death in 1902.

Sources: Russell L. Adams, *Great Negroes Past and Present* (Afro-Am Publishing Co., Inc., Chicago, 1969), p. 31; Wm. Still Underground R. R. Foundation, Inc., 1998; Charles L. Blockson, *The Underground Railroad* (Prentice Hall Press, New York, 19870, pp. 217, 229, 233, 135; Dumas Malone, *Dictionary of American Biography* (Charles Scribner's Sons, New York, 1936), Vol. 9, Part 2, pp. 22-23.

Teaching Tips

Words You Should Know

A. Rebuke (Psalm 104:7) *gearah* (Heb.)—To express sharp, stern disapproval of; reprove; reprimand.

B. Bound (v. 9) *gebuwl* (Heb.)—Boundary, territory, border, landmark, or limit.

Teacher Preparation

Unifying Principle—Everything We Need. Every human has needs that must be met for his survival and, through His creation, God has made provision for them all.

A. Set aside time to pray that you will teach in a way that students will meet the Aim for Change.

B. Study Psalm 104 in its entirety, using a commentary and concordance.

C. Complete the companion lesson in the *Precepts For Living Personal Study Guide®*.

O—Open the Lesson

A. Begin today's lesson with prayer.

B. Read the Aim for Change and the Keep in Mind verse.

C. Initiate discussion by telling students that Labor Day is Monday, September 2. Ask students to share how the day can be used to honor God for His creation, which makes us prosperous and strong.

D. Have a volunteer read the In Focus story. Ask students, "How did God make provision for all of our needs through His creation?"

P—Present the Scriptures

A. Have volunteers take turns reading through the Focal Verses.

B. To clarify the verses, use The People, Places, and Times; Background; Search the Scriptures; At-A-Glance outline; In Depth; and More Light on the Text.

E—Explore the Meaning

A. Divide the class into three groups, assigning to each group one of the following sections to explore: Discuss the Meaning; Lesson in Our Society; and Make It Happen.

B. Make sure to relate the Aim for Change and the Keep in Mind verse to the three sections.

N—Next Steps for Application

A. Encourage students to begin a prayer journal.

B. Close with prayer, thanking God for creating resources that supply our needs.

Worship Guide

For the Superintendent or Teacher
Theme: God Creates
Song: "He's Got the Whole World in His Hands"
Devotional Reading: Matthew 6:25–34

God Creates

Bible Background • PSALM 104
Printed Text • PSALM 104:5–9, 24–30 | Devotional Reading • MATTHEW 6:25–34

Aim for Change

By the end of the lesson, we will: DESCRIBE God's creative power and provision; APPRECIATE the wonder of God's Creation; and PRAISE God for the resources available for us.

In Focus

When Gale lost her job last year, her joy went with it. At first, she was happy to spend a couple of months with her children. Then she began her job search, expecting to be employed within a month. Thirteen months later, she was staring at a pile of disconnection and collection notices. It seemed that the more she prayed, the worse her situation became.

Since she couldn't pay her bills, she decided to take her last five-dollar bill to buy a fast food value meal. Inside the restaurant, she ran into a former coworker who remembered Gale as "the Cake Lady." Gale used to share homemade cakes with the employees. The woman explained that her wedding was coming up, and she was considering a $1,200 estimate from a cake designer she didn't know. She offered the job to Gale since she knew her work, then wrote a $600 check for a deposit.

At that moment, Gale realized she'd been praying for a temporary fix for her problem, and God gave her a permanent solution. She went to her car, retrieved a folder full of cake order forms, and handed some to the woman to pass out at work. Gale praised God on the way home for giving her the talent to make the money she needed.

God has already given us everything we need. In today's lesson, we will praise God for resources available to us.

Keep in Mind

"O LORD, how manifold are thy works! in wisdom hast thou made them all: the earth is full of thy riches" (Psalm 104:24).

"O LORD, how manifold are thy works! in wisdom hast thou made them all: the earth is full of thy riches" (Psalm 104:24).

Focal Verses

KJV **Psalm 104:5** Who laid the foundations of the earth, that it should not be removed for ever.

6 Thou coveredst it with the deep as with a garment: the waters stood above the mountains.

7 At thy rebuke they fled; at the voice of thy thunder they hasted away.

8 They go up by the mountains; they go down by the valleys unto the place which thou hast founded for them.

9 Thou hast set a bound that they may not pass over; that they turn not again to cover the earth.

104:24 O LORD, how manifold are thy works! in wisdom hast thou made them all: the earth is full of thy riches.

25 So is this great and wide sea, wherein are things creeping innumerable, both small and great beasts.

26 There go the ships: there is that leviathan, whom thou hast made to play therein.

27 These wait all upon thee; that thou mayest give them their meat in due season.

28 That thou givest them they gather: thou openest thine hand, they are filled with good.

29 Thou hidest thy face, they are troubled: thou takest away their breath, they die, and return to their dust.

30 Thou sendest forth thy spirit, they are created: and thou renewest the face of the earth.

NLT **Psalm 104:5** You placed the world on its foundation so it would never be moved.

6 You clothed the earth with floods of water, water that covered even the mountains.

7 At your command, the water fled; at the sound of your thunder, it hurried away.

8 Mountains rose and valleys sank to the levels you decreed.

9 Then you set a firm boundary for the seas, so they would never again cover the earth.

104:24 O LORD, what a variety of things you have made! In wisdom you have made them all. The earth is full of your creatures.

25 Here is the ocean, vast and wide, teeming with life of every kind, both large and small.

26 See the ships sailing along, and Leviathan, which you made to play in the sea.

27 They all depend on you to give them food as they need it.

28 When you supply it, they gather it. You open your hand to feed them, and they are richly satisfied.

29 But if you turn away from them, they panic. When you take away their breath, they die and turn again to dust.

30 When you give them your breath, life is created, and you renew the face of the earth.

The People, Places, and Times

The Book of Psalms. *Tehillim,* the Hebrew name for the book of Psalms, means "praises." The book is made up of 150 chapters, each one written as a lyrical piece to be sung to musical instruments. The Jewish church used it as a hymnbook in the temple. Seventy-three of the psalms are credited to David, making him the most prolific psalmist. Other composers include Asaph, Ethan the Ezrahite, Herman the Ezrahite, Moses, Solomon, and the Sons of Korah. Psalms is broken up into five divisions. Psalm 104, our lesson text, is taken from the fourth division. It is not clear who wrote Psalm 104, but some scholars believe David is its author.

David. David's life was so rich that it's no wonder he wrote most of the psalms. He was Jesse's youngest son, he was a shepherd, he was anointed as king of Israel, and he defeated the giant Goliath with a stone and slingshot (see 1 Samuel 17). And all of this was before his adulthood! Though he had many triumphs, David had just as many trials, and his range of emotions is captured in the psalms. He wrote Psalm 3 when his son Absalom rebelled against him. Psalm 51 was one of confession, written after his adulterous relationship with Bathsheba and the murder of her husband. He wrote Psalm 142 while hiding from Saul in a cave. David was an ancestor of Jesus Christ, and he died at 70 years old.

Background

It is possible that the Israelites were in captivity during the time Psalm 104 was written. Most people held against their will focus on the things they do not have—freedom, security, and happiness. While in bondage, captives complain, cry out to God, and shake their fists in anger. However, because some scholars attribute this psalm to David, the purpose would be different, for David lived long before the Israelites went into captivity. If David was indeed the author, he did just the opposite of raising his fists in anger when faced with difficult situations. In Psalm 104, he gave an account of the things that he knew could not be taken from him. He focused his attention on God's creation, emphasizing that it is God who creates, sustains, provides, and preserves. With Psalm 104, David affirms that God has provided all our needs through His creation.

At-A-Glance

1. God Orders (Psalm 104:5–9)
2. God Works (vv. 24–26)
3. God Provides (vv. 27–30)

In Depth

1. God Orders (Psalm 104:5–9)

It is said that God is a God of order, and the first portion of our lesson text proves it. To "order" means to attend to the arrangements of items. The way in which items are arranged is an indication of their size, importance, or when each will be dealt with. David boasted that God is so creative that He hung the earth on its own axis, and no matter how heavy it is or what shock it absorbs, it cannot fall or be moved. Then, God covered it and "the waters stood above the mountains." But, because God's greatest creation—man—could not live in such a place, God reprimanded the waters and they fled to more suitable places, like the valleys. At God's rebuke, a boundary was formed that water could not cross over so that man could live.

2. God Works (vv. 24–26)

Throughout the Bible, God endorses work. Work *is* good. God created so much that verse 24 reads "the earth is full of thy riches." God was so productive that He didn't just create the oceans for show, but He filled them with great and small creatures, both swimming and creeping kinds. In time, humans, the crown of creation, created boats and ships to use these waters as passageways for merchants. His work produced work! He also emphasizes the importance of balance. There can't be all work and no play. David mentioned the leviathan, a sea monster of immense size and power, that has no other duty than to play in the vast waters it calls home.

3. God Provides (vv. 27–30)

According to Scripture, God's provision is bountiful and seasonable. Verse 27 reads that "these wait all upon thee; that thou givest them their meat in due season." The *Matthew Henry Commentary on the Whole Bible* asserts in its discussion of Genesis 1 that God's creation patiently waits for His provision because of the natural instinct He put in it. His creation knows that He is bountiful and open-handed (v. 28), and they gather what He gives and are satisfied. Because they desire no more than what God sees fit for them, they have no need to complain or be dissatisfied. They recognize that if God hides His face from them (i.e., ignores or leaves them to themselves), they will be troubled. They are so dependent upon their Creator that they cannot take their next breath without Him. When, at God's bidding, they give up their existence, others come behind them as God recreates and replenishes.

Search the Scriptures

1. Why did God set a bound over the waters (Psalm 104:9)?

2. What happens when God sends forth His Spirit (v. 30)?

Discuss the Meaning

1. How does this text illustrate God's creative power and provision?

2. Using the text, identify resources God made available to us through His creation.

Lesson in Our Society

In a downturned economy, it is easy to focus on what we have lost, things we cannot obtain, and the hopelessness we might feel. In Psalm 104, David chose to focus on God's creation and the riches thereof. We will do well to challenge ourselves to identify resources we can use to produce what we need. Provision is all around us.

Make It Happen

This week, challenge yourself to focus on what you have rather than on what you do not. Challenge yourself to see God the way David characterizes Him—bountiful, attentive, and open-handed. He has not forgotten you or your family. While you wait for Him, make daily gratitude lists and thank Him for what you do have. Then, pray for wisdom to use what you have to get what you need.

Follow the Spirit

What God wants me to do:

_____

_____

_____

_____

Remember Your Thoughts

Special insights I have learned:

_____

_____

_____

_____

More Light on the Text

Psalm 104:5–9; 24–30

Anyone who studies the psalms quickly learns that commentators sort them into types, e.g., lament, praise, thanksgiving, trust, and so on. Psalm 104 belongs in the category of creation psalms, or "Songs of Creation" in Walter Brueggemann's words, which also includes Psalms 8, 33, and 145. Brueggemann further lists these as "Orientation" psalms among his general psalm rubric of "Orientation–Disorientation–Reorientation." As such, they not only do not contain complaints or crying out to God, but "in a variety of ways articulate the joy, delight, goodness, coherence, and reliability of God, God's creation, [and] God's governing law" (*The Message of the Psalms*, 19). Psalm 104 is also a hymn of praise and has been paired with the similarly structured Psalm 103—the former praising the Creator-King and the latter praising the Redeemer-King, according to Willem VanGemeren (*Psalms, Proverbs, Ecclesiastes, Song of Songs*, 657).

5 Who laid the foundations of the earth, that it should not be removed for ever. 6 Thou coveredst it with the deep as with a garment: the waters stood above the mountains.

The first portion of our lesson, verses 5–9, comprises what VanGemeren describes as the "Material Formation of the Earth" (*Psalms, Proverbs, Ecclesiastes, Song of Songs*, 658), which

comes after the psalm's introduction, praising God's royal, kingly splendor in verses 1–4. John Goldingay separates this portion of the lesson as God's "original activity" from the second portion (vv. 24–30), which is His "ongoing activity" (*Baker Commentary on the Old Testament, Vol. 3*, 181). Another commentator calls our two sections "creating life" and "providing for life" (Mays, *Interpretation: A Bible Commentary for Teaching and Preaching. Psalms*, 335). In verse 5, God builds the earth like a skilled engineer with eternal permanence in mind. The writer alternates voices from third person to addressing God directly in verse 6, then back to third person in verses 8–9. Focusing here on the third day of creation (cf. Genesis 1:9–10), this account of creation is more poetic than the Genesis account. Whether creatively or descriptively reported, it seems clear that water completely covered our globe during its formation.

7 At thy rebuke they fled; at the voice of thy thunder they hasted away. 8 They go up by the mountains; they go down by the valleys unto the place which thou hast founded for them. 9 Thou hast set a bound that they may not pass over; that they turn not again to cover the earth.

The language stresses God's creative and all-powerful authority and uses nature's greatest sounds to illustrate His incomparable power. Rushing water can be incredibly powerful and destructive, as amply demonstrated whenever a sudden flood destroys roads, houses, and anything else in its path—yet, like a timid child, all the water of the earth obeys the thunderous voice of its creator God. A line from a popular song titled "My Redeemer Lives" by Nicole C. Mullins memorably captures the verse's message, "Who taught the sun where to stand in the morning? And who told the ocean you can only come this far?" (cf. Job 38:8–11).

24 O LORD, how manifold are thy works! in wisdom hast thou made them all: the earth is full of thy riches.

This second portion of our lesson, verses 24–30, comprises what VanGemeren describes as the "Glory of Animal Creation" (vv. 24–26) and "Spiritual Sustenance of Earth" (vv. 27–30) (*Psalms, Proverbs, Ecclesiastes, Song of Songs,* 658). In verses prior to this portion (vv. 10–18), the psalm writer elaborates on God's intentional interconnectedness of creation, e.g., water first finding its place and then becoming a resource for all of creation, sustaining life and fruitfulness, each part of which in turn becomes food, seed, or supply for myriads of needs. Then everything is refreshed and replenished by rain, God's "celestial sprinkler" system (Goldingay, *Baker Commentary on the Old Testament,* 187).

Everything God does—all His many "works" (cf. v. 13) are wonderful, magnificent, and excellent in every way; individually or collectively, they reveal His wisdom, power, creativity, and glory—but humanity is His crowning achievement. Even though man is not specified here, he is eminently included among God's "works" (see Proverbs 8:22–31).

25 So is this great and wide sea, wherein are things creeping innumerable, both small and great beasts. 26 There go the ships: there is that leviathan, whom thou hast made to play therein.

From the perspective of ancient writers, both ships on the sea (see Proverbs 30:19; Isaiah 33:21) and the great sea creatures (see Job 41:1; Psalm 74:14; Isaiah 27:1) were marvels that particularly revealed to them God's boundless creative ability. This verse uses a literary device called synecdoche, which is when a part is used to represent the whole—e.g., from homeless box to penthouse suite, representing all residences. So it is that ships on the great sea and beasts of all kinds in the sea represent all of creation.

27 These wait all upon thee; that thou mayest give them their meat in due season. 28 That thou givest them they gather: thou openest thine hand, they are filled with good.

God is the source and sustainer; He is the maker and the maintainer—everything comes from Him and everything depends on Him, including and especially mankind.

29 Thou hidest thy face, they are troubled: thou takest away their breath, they die, and return to their dust. 30 Thou sendest forth thy spirit, they are created: and thou renewest the face of the earth.

In Hebrew, "breath" is *ruach* (**RU-akh**), and means wind, breath, mind, or spirit. It is the same word used in Genesis 1:2, "The Spirit [*ruach*] of God moved upon the face of the waters," as well as Genesis 7:22 referring to all the creatures taken aboard the Ark, "All in whose nostrils was the breath [*ruach*] of life." *Ruach* is also used for both man and animals in Ecclesiastes 3:21.

A quick look at the verbs in the last four verses (vv. 27–30) gives an overview of all God does: He *gives* food to all, He *opens* His hand and *fills* creation with good things, He *hides* His face, He *takes* away breath/life [*ruach*], He *sends* His Spirit [*ruach*], and He *renews* everything. Consider Goldingay's unique translation of verses 29–30: "You hide your face, they panic; You gather up their breath, they perish; they return to their dirt; you send out your spirit, they are created; you renew the face of the ground" (*Baker Commentary on the Old Testament,* 193). Interestingly, in Genesis 2:7, when God "breathed into his [man's] nostrils the *breath* of life" (emphasis added), the

Hebrew uses *neshamah* (**nesh-a-MA**), which is essentially an interchangeable synonym for *ruach*. In Isaiah 42:5, God is described as "He that giveth breath [*neshemah*] unto the people . . . and spirit [*ruach*] to them." Also in Job 34:14, both Hebrew words are used side by side to indicate either man's life or death, "If he gather unto himself his and his spirit [*ruach*] and his breath [*neshamah*]." Both *neshamah* and *ruach* are used for the English "breath" of life in Genesis 7:22.

The essence of the passage is that God is both giver and sustainer of the very breath and spirit within all living things—He alone gives, sustains, and takes life away.

Something noteworthy about creation through the eyes of faith is that it was not a one-time event that was then left to its own devices or random evolutionary winds of fate. Our God is an interactive God; He spoke creation into existence in the beginning as an expression of Himself (Romans 1:20) and He continues to actively maintain every part, especially tending like a loving father to His most unique creation of all, the *homo sapiens* who were made in His image and likeness (Genesis 1:26–27, 5:1, 9:6). Mankind, earth, and our entire universe are a divinely inspired, divinely created, and divinely maintained ecosystem that no other theory or philosophy other than Christian creationism wholly explains, much less celebrates.

Sources:
Blue Letter Bible. BlueLetterBible.org. http://www.blueletterbible.org/ (accessed July 8, 2012).
Brueggemann, Walter. *The Message of the Psalms: A Theological Commentary.* Minneapolis: Augsburg Publishing House, 1984. 15–49.
Goldingay, John. *Baker Commentary on the Old Testament, Vol. 3: Psalms 90–150.* Grand Rapids, MI: Baker Academic, 2008. 178–199.
Henry, Matthew. *Matthew Henry Commentary on the Whole Bible.* Genesis 1. http://www.biblestudytools.com/commentaries/matthew-henry-complete/genesis/1.html (accessed July 25–27, 2012).
Mays, James L. *Interpretation: A Bible Commentary for Teaching and Preaching. Psalms.* Louisville: John Knox Press, 1994. 331–337.
Mullins, Nicole C. "My Redeemer Lives." http://www.lyricsmode.com/lyrics/n/nicole_c_mullins/my_redeemer_lives.html (accessed December 19, 2012).
Smith, William. *Smith's Bible Dictionary.* Peabody, MA: Hendrickson Publishers, Inc., 2000. 137, 539–541.
VanGemeren, Willem A. *Psalms, Proverbs, Ecclesiastes, Song of Songs. The Expositor's Bible Commentary, Vol. 5.* Edited by Frank E. Gaebelein. Grand Rapids, MI: Zondervan, 1985. 657–664.
Word in Life Study Bible (NKJV). Nashville: Thomas Nelson Publishers, 1993. 908–909.

Say It Correctly

Manifold. **MAN**-i-fold.
Leviathan. le-**VI**-a-than.
Innumerable. in-**NOO**-mer-ab-ul.

Daily Bible Readings

MONDAY
God Knows Our Every Need
(Matthew 6:25–34)

TUESDAY
The Greatness of the Creator
(Psalm 104:1–4)

WEDNESDAY
Nourishment for All Creatures
(Psalm 104:10–17)

THURSDAY
The Cycle of Days and Seasons
(Psalm 104:18–23)

FRIDAY
The Exalted God of Creation
(Psalm 97:1–9)

SATURDAY
Praise God, the Creator
(Psalm 104:31–35)

SUNDAY
God, Our Creator and Sustainer
(Psalm 104:5–9, 24–30)

Teaching Tips

September 8
Bible Study Guide 2

Words You Should Know

A. Adam (Genesis 2:7) *adem* (Heb.)—The first man; created by God, in God's image. God made Adam from the dust of the ground, breathing the breath of life into his nostrils.

B. Woman (v. 23) *issa* (Heb.)—The first woman; created by God to be a companion for Adam, the first man. Adam named her Woman because God made her from one of Adam's ribs.

Teacher Preparation

Unifying Principle—Love and Marriage. Finding a suitable companion with whom one can share life can be a struggle, but it can also bring great joy. How does one find a suitable partner? According to Genesis 2, God created Eve as a partner for Adam.

A. Pray for your students that God will bring clarity to this lesson.

B. Study and meditate on the entire text.

C. Prepare to share examples of relationships; include family ties and friendships.

O—Open the Lesson

A. Open with prayer.

B. After prayer, introduce today's subject, Aim for Change, and the Keep in Mind verse. Discuss.

C. Have a volunteer read the In Focus story. Ask the following: "Why did God create relationships?"

D. Have students share testimonies about good relationships.

P—Present the Scriptures

A. Have volunteers read the Focal Verses.

B. Now use The People, Places, and Times; Background; Search the Scriptures; At-A-Glance outline; In Depth; and More Light on the Text to clarify the verses.

E—Explore the Meaning

A. To answer questions in the Discuss the Meaning, Lesson in Our Society, and Make It Happen sections, divide the class into groups. Assign one or two questions to each group, depending on the class size.

B. Have each group select a representative to report their responses to the rest of the class.

N—Next Steps for Application

A. Summarize the lesson.

B. Close with prayer and praise God for giving us relationships.

Worship Guide

For the Superintendent or Teacher
Theme: God's Image:
Male and Female
Song: "Breathe on Me, Breath of God"
Devotional Reading: Psalm 8

God's Image: Male and Female

Bible Background • GENESIS 1–2; 5:1–2
Printed Text • GENESIS 2:18–25 | Devotional Reading • PSALM 8

Aim for Change

By the end of the lesson, we will: KNOW how and why God created human companionship; APPRECIATE that God takes an active role in creating loving partnerships; and IDENTIFY spiritual practices that honor strong family bonds.

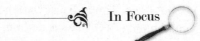 In Focus

"There used to be a time," the singer on the radio says as she sings about her dislike for being alone. Sharon knew that feeling all too well. Being new to the Dallas area, she was apprehensive about moving but understood what it could mean for her career. As she sank down onto the floor of her empty living room, her furniture located on a moving van stuck in winter storms somewhere in the Midwest, she identified with the singer's feelings of being alone. She noticed a church within walking distance from her new place. Perhaps she should attend one of their services. Maybe not, she convinced herself; she did not know anyone.

The knock on her door interrupted her thoughts. "Who is it?" she asked. It was her neighbors with a pot of soup and freshly baked bread, asking if they might join her. She hesitantly opened her door. They saw her empty living room, apologized, and invited her over to their place. At their apartment they ate, laughed, talked, and made plans for the weekend to show Sharon the neighborhood.

Companions were created by God for people to be in relationship with one another. As representatives of the body of Christ, the church has an obligation to become inclusive, for the Word of God teaches that man should not be alone.

Keep in Mind

"And the LORD God said, It is not good that the man should be alone; I will make him an help meet for him" (Genesis 2:18).

"And the LORD God said, It is not good that the man should be alone; I will make him an help meet for him" (Genesis 2:18).

Focal Verses

KJV **Genesis 2:18** And the LORD God said, It is not good that the man should be alone; I will make him an help meet for him.

19 And out of the ground the LORD God formed every beast of the field, and every fowl of the air; and brought them unto Adam to see what he would call them; and whatsoever Adam called every living creature, that was the name thereof.

20 And Adam gave names to all cattle, and to the fowl of the air, and to every beast of the field; but for Adam there was not found an help meet for him.

21 And the LORD God caused a deep sleep to fall upon Adam, and he slept: and he took one of his ribs, and closed up the flesh instead thereof;

22 And the rib, which the LORD God had taken from man, made he a woman, and brought her unto the man.

23 And Adam said, This is now bone of my bones, and flesh of my flesh: she shall be called Woman, because she was taken out of Man.

24 Therefore shall a man leave his father and his mother, and shall cleave unto his wife: and they shall be one flesh.

25 And they were both naked, the man and his wife, and were not ashamed.

NLT **Genesis 2:18** Then the LORD God said, "It is not good for the man to be alone. I will make a helper who is just right for him."

19 So the LORD God formed from the ground all the wild animals and all the birds of the sky. He brought them to the man to see what he would call them, and the man chose a name for each one.

20 He gave names to all the livestock, all the birds of the sky, and all the wild animals. But still there was no helper just right for him.

21 So the LORD God caused the man to fall into a deep sleep. While the man slept, the LORD God took out one of the man's ribs and closed up the opening.

22 Then the LORD God made a woman from the rib, and he brought her to the man.

23 "At last!" the man exclaimed. "This one is bone from my bone, and flesh from my flesh! She will be called 'woman,' because she was taken from 'man.'"

24 This explains why a man leaves his father and mother and is joined to his wife, and the two are united into one.

25 Now the man and his wife were both naked, but they felt no shame.

The People, Places, and Times

Adam. The first man; created by God, in God's image. God made Adam from the dust of the ground, breathing the breath of life into his nostrils. God gave Adam the responsibility for the created order.

Woman. The first woman; created by God to be a companion to Adam, the first man.

The book of Genesis. The book of beginnings: The beginning of the creation of the universe (Genesis 1); the creation of the world and living things (Genesis 1–2); the creation of mankind (Genesis 1–2).

Background

The book of Genesis is the first book of the Bible and the first book of the Pentateuch.

The Pentateuch is the first five books of the Old Testament. The Jewish label for these books is "Torah," which means teaching, while English Bibles refer to these books simply as the "Law."

Written by Moses, the leader of the enslaved Hebrew people (Exodus 1), the book of Genesis is a book about beginnings—the beginning of the universe, the beginning of creatures, the beginning of mankind, and the beginning of God's activity in the life of the world. "In the beginning God created . . ." (Genesis 1:1) "And God said . . . and God made . . . and God blessed . . . and God saw . . ." (Genesis 1 and 2).

At-A-Glance

God Provides Companionship (Genesis 2:18–25)

In Depth
God Provides Companionship (Genesis 2:18–25)

Adam named all of the creatures God had placed before him, but felt he was alone. God recognized this, placed Adam in a deep sleep, and created a companion for him. Unlike the animals and birds God created from the ground, Adam's companion was created from one of his ribs. Adam named his companion Woman because she was "bone of my bones, and flesh of my flesh" (Genesis 2:23).

The creation of Woman introduced mankind to the concept of friendship. According to *The American Heritage Dictionary,* a friend is "a person whom one knows, likes, and trusts." Adam knew Woman because "the LORD God had taken from man, made he a woman, and brought her unto the man" (Genesis 2:22). Adam liked Woman because

he said, "This is now bone of my bones, and flesh of my flesh" (Genesis 2:23). Adam trusted Woman "because she was taken out of Man" (Genesis 2:23). This first pair was also the first marriage; the text indicates that part of God's purpose for humans includes the marital union of man and woman.

Moreover, the Bible illustrates other friendships that are not unique to male and female relationships. There was the bond between Jonathan and David recorded in 1 Samuel 18. "And it came to pass, when he had made an end of speaking unto Saul, that the soul of Jonathan was knit with the soul of David, and Jonathan loved him as his own soul. And Saul took him that day, and would let him go no more home to his father's house. Then Jonathan and David made a covenant, because he loved him as his own soul. And Jonathan stripped himself of the robe that was upon him, and gave it to David, and his garments, even to his sword, and to his bow, and to his girdle" (1 Samuel 18:1–4). The book of Proverbs teaches one how to be a friend: "A man that hath friends must shew himself friendly: and there is a friend that sticketh closer than a brother" (Proverbs 18:24). The Bible describes mankind's friendship with Jesus Christ, provided we are obedient to Jesus' commandments (John 15:14). Humans were not created to live in isolation but in community. Companionship is one vital dimension for human flourishing.

Search the Scriptures

1. Why does God say it is not good to be alone (Genesis 2:18)?

2. When should man and woman compete with one another (v. 24)?

Discuss the Meaning

God created in pairs so the creations would be dependent on one another. Human dependency begins with an acquaintance, which leads to a friendship, which leads to a relationship. Relationships are with one another and with God. How might this impact your relationships moving forward?

Lesson in Our Society

Those of us who are healthy, have strong family ties, and are regularly connected to a church family can take companionship for granted. There are people among us who are shut in and shut out because of illness, incarceration, low self-esteem, or poverty. Their circumstances exclude them from continuous human contact. With the popularity of social media, they are ignored and shut out because they do not have the existing technology, negating their efforts to maintain face-to-face contact.

Make It Happen

Commit to regularly telephone and visit with a person who is shut in. If they desire, show the person the existing technology and how to use it. If your church has a prison ministry, become involved. If your church is located in an inner city, become involved with the community. Be genuine and display the love of Jesus.

Follow the Spirit

What God wants me to do:

_____

_____

_____

_____

Remember Your Thoughts

Special insights I have learned:

_____

_____

_____

_____

_____

More Light on the Text

Genesis 2

18 And the LORD God said, It is not good that the man should be alone; I will make him an help meet for him.

Here we see the combination of the name "LORD God." The personal name for the God of Israel is represented by the four-letter consonants YHWH or *Yahweh*, also called the Tetragrammaton, while the name *El/Elohim* was used for God throughout the ancient Near East. The Hebrew word for "Lord" or master, *adonai* (**aw-dah-NAHY**), is substituted for the Tetragrammaton in English translations of the Bible in all capital letters to reflect the ancient Jewish tradition of not pronouncing the name of Israel's deity out of deference. Ancient Jewish scholars inserted the vowels "a-o-a" in *adonai* between the consonants to remind the readers to substitute *adonai* when they read YHWH aloud.

God was concerned for the man's social well-being and declared that the man (Heb. *adam*, **aw-DAWM**) should not be alone. Technically the man was not alone; God, along with the other heavenly beings (Genesis 3:22), was present with him. The announcement serves more as an explanation for why God made the other creatures. The verb *asah* (**ah-SAW**) means "to do" or "make." God is depicted as making the creatures by hand in chapter 2, in contrast to chapter 1, where God spoke and Creation came into existence.

19 And out of the ground the LORD God formed every beast of the field, and every fowl of the air; and brought them unto Adam to see what he would call them: and whatsoever Adam called every living creature, that was the name thereof.

The Hebrew verb for "form" or "fashion" is *yitser* (**yits-ZER**). The Lord God formed all of the living creatures (Heb. *nephesh chay*, **neh-FESH khah-E**) in the field and in the air out of the soil or earth (Heb. *adamah*, **ad-aw-MAW**). The image of God in 2:18–19 is as a potter at the wheel spinning and molding the creatures into shape. The prophet Isaiah drew upon this analogy to connote the relationship between God and the people (Isaiah 64:8). Isaiah expressed that we are all intimately related to God as living creatures formed by Him.

God brought the creatures to the man to name them. This included the beasts of the field and the birds of the air. The Hebrew noun *chay* (**khah-E**) means "living thing" or "animal" and conveys a wild beast that has not yet been tamed or domesticated. It also contrasts the difference between the man and the animals.

20 And Adam gave names to all cattle, and to the fowl of the air, and to every beast of the field; but for Adam there was not found an help meet for him.

The Hebrew for "help meet" is *ezer kenegdo* (**ay-zer ke-NEG-doh**) and without the preposition, *ke* means "help" or "succor" in front of or opposite to. However, with the preposition, the translation is "a help corresponding to him"; in other words, equal and adequate to himself. A more literal translation would be a help (over) against him. The esteemed medieval Jewish commentator Rashi noted that if a man was worthy, he would have a partner (*ezer*) who was a help to him. However, if he

was not worthy, she would be his adversary (*kenegdo*).

By naming the animals, the man asserted his authority or dominion over them, but this also included a caretaker role. Also implicit in this verse is that by naming the creatures, the man would find one with whom he would be compatible. The man's expectations probably rose and fell with each presentation of a new creature to name and define its function. The Hebrew verb "find" (*matsa*, **maw-TSAW**) means to "attain to" or "find," as in a thing sought. However, he did not find the one that he was seeking or that God intended for him—one that corresponded to him.

21 And the LORD God caused a deep sleep to fall upon Adam, and he slept: and he took one of his ribs, and closed up the flesh instead thereof.

The Hebrew noun *tsela* (**TSEH-law**) is translated "rib" or "side." The term is translated "rib" in verse 21. However, the exact meaning is unknown. God had determined that in order to create a help meet compatible with the man, He would have to take a different route. The new creature would have to consist of substance taken directly from the man. God closed (Heb. *sagar*, **saw-GAR**) the place where the rib was taken, leaving it as if nothing had occurred. God is the surgeon *par excellence* who performs the task with precision and finesse.

22 And the rib, which the LORD God had taken from man, made he a woman, and brought her unto the man.

The verb in Hebrew translated in verse 22 as "made" is not the same verb as in verses 18–19 that describes God as making or forming. The verb here is *banah* (**baw-NAW**) and means "to build," as in a house or to perpetuate or establish a family (Ruth 4:11), or to "fashion," as in to give a particular shape or form. The latter is applicable to verse 22. God fashioned or shaped the rib into the form of the being that was the opposite of the man. The act of forming or shaping objects conjures images of simpler, plainer creations. However, to fashion suggests a higher form of creation where the creator has paid more attention to the details. One can imagine God being especially intentional about getting just the right partner for the man this time.

The understanding of "to build" in place of "made" is also appropriate as the creation of one like the man would be the necessary piece for beginning to build up the human family.

23 And Adam said, This is now bone of my bones, and flesh of my flesh: she shall be called Woman, because she was taken out of Man.

The man's response to the new creation was pure joy. He had finally found one like him who was made of bone (Heb. *etsem*, **eh-TSEM**) and flesh (Heb. *basar*, **baw-SAWR**). As if to emphasize that this creation was the one who would finally bring him the companionship he sought, he named her Woman (Heb. *ishshah*, **ish-SHAW**) because she was created from the side of the man (Heb. *ish*). This song of praise celebrated the culmination of God's creative acts in the garden. What God declared was not good in verse 18 (Heb. *lo-tov*) had been remedied in verse 23.

The creation of the woman introduced gender difference. In 1:27 God created male and female, biological and physiological sexual categories. Man and woman are characterized by masculine and feminine gender roles in 2:23.

24 Therefore shall a man leave his father and his mother, and shall cleave unto his wife: and they shall be one flesh.

The Hebrew verb *azab* (**aw-ZAB**) means "to leave," "forsake," or "loose." For the man to leave his parents explains why males abandon or reject their kin to marry and start new families with their female partners. The Hebrew word for woman, *ishshah* (**ish-SHAW**), is the same word for wife.

The Hebrew word for "cleave," also cling or keep close, is *dabaq* (**daw-BAK**). It represents here the sexual union of the man and his wife. The differences inferred by gender are muted by the unity of the man and woman. The separateness of the two when God took the man's bone and flesh to create the woman has now been reunited through their becoming husband and wife. The two becoming one flesh (Heb. *basar*, **baw-SAWR**) symbolizes this union.

25 And they were both naked, the man and his wife, and were not ashamed.

We come into this world naked. Children have no inhibitions about being naked. Parents will often permit toddlers to walk around in nothing but a diaper. Caretakers think nothing of bathing children together in the same tub. The fact that adults don't make an issue of this allows children to feel comfortable and free in their nakedness. The nakedness of the man and woman represented their childlike innocence at the time of their creation. They were not ashamed (Heb. *bosh*, **boosh**) of being naked (Heb. *arome*, **aw-ROME**). This lack of shame attested to their lack of sin at this point. They could look upon each other without any need to cover or hide themselves. After the fall, God clothes them when their sin brings about shame (Genesis 3:20).

Sources:

Gibson, John C. L. *OT Daily Study Bible Series. Genesis, Vol. 1.* Philadelphia: Westminster John Knox Press, 1981.

Speiser, E. A. *The Anchor Bible, Vol. 1 Genesis: A New Translation with Introduction and Commentary.* New York: Doubleday, 1962.

Say It Correctly

Cleave. **CLEEVE**.
Naked. **NAY**-ked.
Ashamed. uh-**SHAYM**-d.

Daily Bible Readings

MONDAY
Living Creatures of Every Kind
(Genesis 1:20–25)

TUESDAY
Made in the Image of God
(Genesis 1:26–31)

WEDNESDAY
Formed from the Dust
(Genesis 2:1–9)

THURSDAY
In the Likeness of God
(Genesis 5:1–5)

FRIDAY
Made a Little Lower than God
(Psalm 8)

SATURDAY
Created in the Likeness of God
(Ephesians 4:17–24)

SUNDAY
Created Male and Female
(Genesis 2:18–25)

Notes

_____

_____

_____

_____

Teaching Tips

Words You Should Know

A. Serpent (Genesis 3:13) *nawkhawsh* (Heb.)—Also known as Satan; called "the great dragon . . . that old serpent" (Revelation 12:9).

B. Enmity (v. 15) *aybaw* (Heb.)—Deep-rooted hatred or irreconcilable hostility.

Teacher Preparation

Unifying Principle—Choices and Consequences. Everyone at times has given in to lust or greed instead of making a right choice. Why do humans make poor choices? Genesis 3 informs readers that when temptation confronts them, God gives them the freedom to make choices.

A. Pray for your students.

B. Read and meditate on all the Scriptures from the Bible Background and the Devotional Reading sections.

C. Reread the Focal Verses in two or more translations (NLT, ESV, NIV, etc.).

O—Open the Lesson

A. Open with prayer, including the Aim for Change.

B. After prayer, have a volunteer read the In Focus story.

C. Have your students read the Aim for Change and Keep in Mind verses in unison.

D. Discuss.

E. Tie in the In Focus story with the Aim for Change and Keep in Mind verses.

P—Present the Scriptures

A. Have volunteers read the Focal Verses.

B. Now use The People, Places, and Times; Background; and Search the Scriptures to clarify the verses.

E—Explore the Meaning

A. Have volunteers summarize the Discuss the Meaning, Lesson in Our Society, and Make It Happen sections.

B. Connect these sections to the Aim for Change and the Keep in Mind verses with the Lesson in Our Society and Make It Happen sections.

N—Next Steps for Application

A. Summarize the lesson.

B. Close with prayer and praise God for leading us to make right choices.

Worship Guide

For the Superintendent or Teacher
Theme: Knowledge of Good and Evil
Song: "We'll Understand It Better By and By"
Devotional Reading:
Deuteronomy 30:11–20

Knowledge of Good and Evil

SEPT 15th

Bible Background • GENESIS 1–2
Printed Text • GENESIS 3:8b–17 | Devotional Reading • DEUTERONOMY 30:11–20

Aim for Change

By the end of the lesson, we will: IDENTIFY ways in which sin creates barriers to healthy relationships with God and others; EXPRESS sorrow and repentance for wrongdoing; and SEEK God's help in discerning right from wrong.

 In Focus

Teenagers often say, "My parents don't understand me." So they try to work everything out on their own. When they do things this way, they generally run into problems that could have been avoided if they had only talked to someone about what they were thinking.

Kizzy was struggling with her grades. Her parents were in a bitter divorce and didn't seem to have much time for her. She felt she couldn't talk to her parents about the situation because they were having their own problems. So she started missing school altogether. It was getting close to the end of the semester when grades would be sent home to her parents. Somehow she had to get her grades before her parents did. There was no other way to fix this problem but to continue to hide the evidence of the problem. Or so she thought.

She had become withdrawn and introverted. Eventually her parents found out, and she was in a lot of trouble. After talking to her parents, she regretted not talking to them in the beginning.

Sin destroys and leads to broken relationships. In today's lesson, we see the consequences of sin and the provisions God makes for His creation.

Keep in Mind

"And the LORD God said, Behold, the man is become as one of us, to know good and evil: and now, lest he put forth his hand, and take also of the tree of life, and eat, and live for ever: Therefore the LORD God sent him forth from the garden of Eden, to till the ground from whence he was taken" (Genesis 3:22–23).

"And the LORD God said, Behold, the man is become as one of us, to know good and evil: and now, lest he put forth his hand, and take also of the tree of life, and eat, and live for ever: Therefore the LORD God sent him forth from the garden of Eden, to till the ground from whence he was taken" (Genesis 3:22–23).

Focal Verses

KJV **Genesis 3:8b** And Adam and his wife hid themselves from the presence of the LORD God amongst the trees of the garden.

9 And the LORD God called unto Adam, and said unto him, Where art thou?

10 And he said, I heard thy voice in the garden, and I was afraid, because I was naked; and I hid myself.

11 And he said, Who told thee that thou wast naked? Hast thou eaten of the tree, whereof I commanded thee that thou shouldest not eat?

12 And the man said, The woman whom thou gavest to be with me, she gave me of the tree, and I did eat.

13 And the LORD God said unto the woman, What is this that thou hast done? And the woman said, The serpent beguiled me, and I did eat.

14 And the LORD God said unto the serpent, Because thou hast done this, thou art cursed above all cattle, and above every beast of the field; upon thy belly shalt thou go, and dust shalt thou eat all the days of thy life:

15 And I will put enmity between thee and the woman, and between thy seed and her seed; it shall bruise thy head, and thou shalt bruise his heel.

16 Unto the woman he said, I will greatly multiply thy sorrow and thy conception; in sorrow thou shalt bring forth children; and thy desire shall be to thy husband, and he shall rule over thee.

17 And unto Adam he said, Because thou hast hearkened unto the voice of thy wife, and hast eaten of the tree, of which I commanded thee, saying, Thou shalt not eat of it: cursed is the ground for thy sake; in sorrow shalt thou eat of it all the days of thy life.

NLT **Genesis 3:8b** So they hid from the LORD God among the trees.

9 Then the LORD God called to the man, "Where are you?"

10 He replied, "I heard you walking in the garden, so I hid. I was afraid because I was naked."

11 "Who told you that you were naked?" the LORD God asked. "Have you eaten from the tree whose fruit I commanded you not to eat?"

12 The man replied, "It was the woman you gave me who gave me the fruit, and I ate it."

13 Then the LORD God asked the woman, "What have you done?"

"The serpent deceived me," she replied. "That's why I ate it."

14 Then the LORD God said to the serpent, "Because you have done this, you are cursed more than all animals, domestic and wild. You will crawl on your belly, groveling in the dust as long as you live.

15 And I will cause hostility between you and the woman, and between your offspring and her offspring. He will strike your head, and you will strike his heel."

16 Then he said to the woman, "I will sharpen the pain of your pregnancy, and in pain you will give birth. And you will desire to control your husband, but he will rule over you."

17 And to the man he said, "Since you listened to your wife and ate from the tree whose fruit I commanded you not to eat, the ground is cursed because of you. All your life you will struggle to scratch a living from it."

The People, Places, and Times

Garden. The beautiful garden made by God for Adam and Eve. The word "Eden" refers to a well-watered place, suggesting a luxuriant park. The word translated "garden" does not typically refer to vegetable plots but to orchards or parks containing trees.

Cool of the day. Akkadian terminology has demonstrated that the word translated "day" also has the meaning "storm." This meaning can also be seen for the same Hebrew word for "day" in Zephaniah 2:2. It is at times connected to the deity coming in a storm of judgment. If this is the correct rendering of the word in this passage, Adam and Eve heard the thunder of the Lord moving about in the garden in the wind of the storm.

Background

God created the heaven and the earth and the Holy Spirit moved on the waters (Genesis 1:1–2). He created the light and the firmament (vv. 3–8), separated the waters (vv. 9–13), made the sun, moon, and stars (vv. 14–19), and created man in His image (vv. 26–28). God then planted a garden in Eden, where He placed the man and took care of him (vv. 29–31). God made the trees to grow, including the tree of life and the tree of knowledge of good and evil (2:8–9). God told the man he may eat freely of every tree in the garden except the tree of knowledge of good and evil (vv. 16–17). Then, God made a help meet for the man because it was not good for man to be alone. The Lord God caused a deep sleep to fall on Adam. Performing the first surgery, God took one of Adam's ribs and made a woman (vv. 18–25). They were given only one prohibition, but we see in today's lesson that they failed to obey God and began to experience life under the curse.

At-A-Glance

1. Hiding from and Breaking God's Heart (Genesis 3:8–9)
2. Broken Fellowship Caused by Sin (vv. 10–13)
3. The First Judgment upon Sin (vv. 14–17)

In Depth

1. Hiding from and Breaking God's Heart (Genesis 3:8–9)

God came walking into the garden, a word that reveals His calmness and slowness to anger. He came in the cool of the day as opposed to the night, when it is natural to be more fearful. He came looking for man, taking the first steps toward a journey of redemption for His people. Man did what sin makes people do—he hid. Sin causes us to be ashamed, guilty, and fearful. Fear immediately attacked Adam and Eve after eating the forbidden fruit. The security of having fellowship with the almighty Lord God was gone. They felt they had to hide and could no longer trust the security they once had with their Creator.

God asked the question not because He didn't know where Adam was; He asked the question as if to ask, "What condition are you in? Adam, have you done what I told you not to do? Adam, where are you?"

2. Broken Fellowship Caused by Sin (vv. 10–13)

Adam answered the Lord God with a confession of guilt. "I was afraid, because I was naked." God asked the question to which He already knew the answer: "Who told you you were naked? I didn't tell you." God knew what had happened but was gently reminding man of his disobedience.

Adam tried to place blame on his wife. He allowed her to take the lead and persuade him to do what God told him not to do. As if God was partly to blame, he reminded God where he got the woman.

The woman blamed the serpent, but she was the one who sinned. Now she stood alone. Though Satan's subtlety may draw us into sin, that does not justify us in sin. Though he is the tempter, we are the sinners; indeed, it is our own lust that draws us aside and entices us. Finally, after pointing the finger and blaming someone else, she confessed, "I did eat."

3. The First Judgment upon Sin (vv. 14–17)

God began to reveal the consequences of sin to the serpent. He is to be forever looked upon as a vile and despicable creature: "Upon thy belly thou shalt go, no longer upon feet, or half erect, but thou shalt crawl along, thy belly cleaving to the earth," an expression of a very abject miserable condition (*Matthew Henry's Commentary on the Whole Bible*, Psalm 44:25).

God assumed all responsibility for the sorrow the woman would endure because of her disobedience. God mercifully allows her to bring forth children—which will give her great joy—although she will do so in great pain. The usage of the word "desire" was for the woman to rule over her husband or demand of her husband, but because of her disobedience, he shall rule over her.

Adam's sin changed everything for him and mankind. Adam himself was not cursed as the serpent was (v. 14), but God cursed the ground that Adam would have to till in order to eat and live. Adam was still above the ground, but now he would have to toil and sweat just to survive. If only he had been obedient to God and not yielded to temptation!

Search the Scriptures

1. Why did God call out to Adam and ask, "Where art thou?" Did He not know where Adam was (Genesis 3:9)?
2. Why was Adam punished (v. 17)?

Discuss the Meaning

God placed His children in a perfect environment accompanied by His holy presence. In a perfect place, sin was still an option. Adam and the woman committed their own sin. They suffered their own consequences, which affected all of mankind. What causes you to hide from God?

Lesson in Our Society

Sin affects everyone. When we sin, we sin against God. That sin is passed down from generation to generation and destroys people, families, and communities. God sent His Son to save us from our sin. However, we have a part to play—we must accept Him as Lord and Savior. Just as God provided for His children in the Garden of Eden, He has also made provisions for us. The first provision is Jesus Christ, His only begotten Son.

Make It Happen

The growing trend in technology offers us many good things but carries with it the potential for distracted lives that wind up neglecting God and giving more attention to the things of the world. As Christians, we must pursue a deeper relationship with God our Father so we may bring glory to Him. Let's ask God to give us discernment so we will do right instead of wrong.

Follow the Spirit

What God wants me to do:

_____

_____

_____

_____

Remember Your Thoughts

Special insights I have learned:

_____

_____

_____

_____

More Light on the Text

Genesis 3:8b–17

8b: And Adam and his wife hid themselves from the presence of the LORD God amongst the trees of the garden.

God came down to Adam and Eve in the cool of the day (Genesis 3:8), literally at "the wind of the day" (Heb. *leruach haiyom*, **le-roo-akh ha-i-yowm**) or in the evening breeze. This probably was the time that Adam and Eve engaged in the acts of their religious worship, at which God was always present. At the usual time for worship, God came again to fellowship with Adam and Eve, but instead of being in the place of worship, they were hidden among the trees! They knew that when they heard the Lord coming, He would want to be with them. What a tragic consequence sin brings.

The author's attention to the hiding place of Adam and Eve is significant—they hid among the trees. In Genesis 1 and 2, trees play a central role in portraying Adam and Eve's changing relationship with God. God's bountiful provision is manifested in the fruit trees. However, in chapter 3, a tree was the instrument of temptation that lured Adam and Eve into sin and then became the place where the rebellious man and woman sought to hide from God. Cast out of the garden, Adam and Eve were barred from making their way back to the tree of life (v. 24). Later in Deuteronomy, a tree is described as the place of the punishment of death (Deuteronomy 21:22–23), but that is not the end of the story! The tree is also the place of the gift of life (Galatians 3:13), and as John shows in the book of Revelation, the leaves of the "tree of life" in the new heaven will be for the healing of the nations (Revelation 22:2).

9 And the LORD God called unto Adam, and said unto him, Where art thou?

God made his first move to counter sin: He confronted the participants and demanded an explanation. God is like a gentle and loving Father seeking out His own. We hear the heartfelt cry of an anguished Creator who did not come with denunciation but with disappointment. God knew where they were, but He also knew a gulf had been made between Himself and humankind, a gulf that He Himself would have to bridge. God's question was intended to prompt Adam to consider his wrongdoing. It is interesting to note that the order of trial is the opposite of the order of temptation: Adam, having been giving the responsibility of watching over the garden, was first to be confronted.

10 And he said, I heard thy voice in the garden, and I was afraid, because I was naked; and I hid myself.

Adam was evasive. Instead of saying where he was, he gave the excuse that God's voice made him afraid. The immediate consequences of sin are evident. First, sin brings alienation. God's peaceful voice and presence suddenly instilled fear in Adam. Second, sin brings shame. In aiming to be like God, Adam and Eve were now in a state of the greatest wretchedness and nakedness. They knew their own covering was completely inadequate, and they were embarrassed before God. Adam and Eve knew that their attempt to cover themselves failed. Third, sin brings fear and judgment. Having been deceived by Satan, Adam and Eve were now exposed to that death and punishment from which God had promised them an exemption. The effects of sin remain the same even today. Alienation from God, shame, fear, and judgment were the first consequences of that first sin and remain so to the present time.

11 And he said, Who told thee that thou wast naked? Hast thou eaten of the tree, whereof I commanded thee that thou shouldest not eat?

God confronted Adam's problem squarely. God sharpened the fact of the crime by following up with two rhetorical questions. The first question showed that Adam didn't need to be told of his shame because he was already experiencing guilt for his crime—a true guilt that came from a violated conscience. With the second question, Adam's nakedness was linked to his transgression concerning the tree. The "tree" is no longer identified as the tree of knowledge but the tree that God had commanded them not to eat from (2:16–17). God knew the answers to these questions. Together these questions explained to Adam that his sense of shame arose from his defiance of God's command. This was a sin problem and Adam's shame, fear, or self-understanding could not be addressed until the sin problem was addressed. God asked those questions and, in doing so, allowed Adam to

make the best of a bad situation by repenting right then and there. Adam, however, did not own up to his sin and repent before God.

12 And the man said, The woman whom thou gavest to be with me, she gave me of the tree, and I did eat.

Adam was obliged to acknowledge his transgression, but he did so in such a way as to shift the blame from himself to God and the woman—"the woman whom THOU gavest to be with me" (emphasis added, Heb. *immadi*, **i-MA-di**, literally, "to be my companion"). Despite his culpability, the man pointed to the woman as the real offender. Adam probably thought that since he did not pluck the fruit, he was guiltless; hence he said, "She gave me of the tree."

How few genuinely confess their sin or acknowledge their guilt! In the same manner as Adam, people continue to make excuses for their crimes by blaming the strength and subtlety of the tempter, the natural weakness of their own minds, society, or the unfavorable circumstances and environment in which they are placed. People plead these things as excuses for their sins and, in doing so, they preclude the possibility of repentance. Until a person takes responsibility for his or her sins and acknowledges that he or she alone is guilty, the person remains unhumbled and, consequently, cannot be saved.

13 And the LORD God said unto the woman, What is this that thou hast done? And the woman said, The serpent beguiled me, and I did eat.

When God questioned the woman, she blamed the serpent. Although she admitted that she was deceived (and, unlike Adam, she could rightly claim to be the victim of deception), she still passed the blame as though she had done nothing wrong.

34

14 And the LORD God said unto the serpent, Because thou hast done this, thou art cursed above all cattle, and above every beast of the field; upon thy belly shalt thou go, and dust shalt thou eat all the days of thy life: 15 And I will put enmity between thee and the woman, and between thy seed and her seed; it shall bruise thy head, and thou shalt bruise his heel.

The tempter was not asked why he deceived the woman. God only had words of condemnation for the serpent, whereas the man and woman received God's continued concern and provision in the midst of their punishment. The serpent had no excuse; therefore, God pronounced sentence on him first. There is a clear tie between the serpent's actions and the punishment that follows. It is important to know that God does not render judgment arbitrarily or capriciously; there is always a correspondence between the crime committed and the nature of the judgment. The curse upon the serpent did not necessarily suggest that the snake had previously walked with feet and legs as the other land animals. The emphasis lies in the snake's "eating dust," an expression that elsewhere carries the meaning of total defeat (cf. Isaiah 65:25; Micah 7:17).

There will not only be a perpetual enmity between the woman and the serpent but also between their "seeds." The word "enmity" (Heb. *eybah*, **ay-BAW**) in this context and other passages suggests a long-lasting, intense hostility, such as is experienced among nations and which results in warfare (cf. Numbers 35:21–22; Ezekiel 25:15, 35:5). The human race and the offspring of the serpent will be forever at loggerheads. Although the same verb "bruise" is used to describe the actions of both progenitors, the location of the blow distinguishes the severity and success of the attack. The impact delivered by the offspring of the woman at the "head" of the serpent is mortal, while the serpent will only deliver a non-mortal blow to the "heel." The Hebrew word for "seed" (Heb. *zera*, **zeh-RAH**), better translated as "offspring," is a messianic reference to Jesus (Galatians 3:16). The curse upon the serpent includes its final destruction by a descendant of the woman. The serpent was instrumental in the undoing of the woman; in turn, the woman will ultimately bring down the serpent through her offspring (the Messiah who would conquer sin and death). The relationship between the promise in verse 15 and the judgment pronounced on the woman in verse 16 is striking. Childbirth is again to be the means through which the serpent would be defeated and by which Adam and Eve's forfeited blessing would be restored. In the pain of childbirth is the reminder of the hope that lay in God's promise. Birth pangs are not merely a reminder of the futility of the Fall; they are also a sign of an impending joy. Ultimately God will destroy "that old serpent" (Revelation 12:9) for his deception of the nations (Revelation 20:2, 7–10).

16 Unto the woman he said, I will greatly multiply thy sorrow and thy conception; in sorrow thou shalt bring forth children; and thy desire shall be to thy husband, and he shall rule over thee.

As part of her judgment, the womanly and wifely sorrow of Eve was to be intensified, and in particular the pains of labor were to be multiplied (cf. Jeremiah 31:8). In Scripture, the pains of childbirth are symbolic of the severest anguish both of body and mind (cf. Psalm 48:6; Micah 4:9–10; John 16:21; 1 Thessalonians 5:3; Revelation 12:2). What the woman once was to do as a blessing in being a marriage partner and having children became tainted by the curse. It is in those moments of life's greatest blessings of marriage and children that the woman would sense most clearly the painful consequences of her disobedience to God.

As part of the judgment on the woman, her desire is to be with her husband. The word "desire" (Heb. *teshuqath*, **tes-HU-kat**) can also mean "longing." The woman was created and given to Adam as a help meet (2:18), and her relation to the man from the first was one of dependence. It was the reversal of these roles that led to the Fall (3:17). The husband was now to rule. As a result of the Fall, the marriage vow "to love and to care" becomes "to desire and to dominate." As such, the "rule" here may refer to the harsh exploitative subjugation which, unfortunately, often characterizes the plight of women in many societies and associations. Although the New Testament recognizes the theological significance of the fallen relationship between men and women due to the Fall, Christians must strike a healthy balance between who we are in Christ (Galatians 3:28) and what we continue to be as a result of the Fall (Colossians 3:18; 1 Peter 3:1).

17 And unto Adam he said, Because thou hast hearkened unto the voice of thy wife, and hast eaten of the tree, of which I commanded thee, saying, Thou shalt not eat of it: cursed is the ground for thy sake; in sorrow shalt thou eat of it all the days of thy life.

Adam, being the last to transgress, was brought up last to receive his sentence: The "good land" provided by the Creator (chs. 1–2) was cursed. Adam should have been following God's word, but he followed his wife's word and broke God's specific command (2:15–17). As man's judgment, Adam and future generations could no longer "freely eat" of the produce of the land. One must note throughout chapters 2 and 3 man's ongoing relationship with his Creator by means of the theme of "eating." At first, God's blessing and provision for man are noted in the words, "Of every tree of the garden thou mayest freely eat" (2:16). In chapter 3, it was specifically over the issue of "eating" that the tempter raised doubts about God's goodness in His care for Adam and Eve (3:1–3). Finally, the act of disobedience in chapter 3 is simply described as she "did eat" and "he did eat" (v. 6). It is not surprising, then, to find that the description of the judgment on the man includes eating: He is to eat in sorrow all the days of his life. Henceforth the fertility of the ground shall be greatly impaired. All the fruits of man's toil are often destroyed by landslides, erosion, insects, drought, land floods, etc. The current earth is not what God intended. Man's sin changed everything. Anxiety and difficult toil are the laboring man's portion. The earth was no longer completely good. Death had entered. Even the ground had changed.

Sources:

"Enmity." *The New Unger's Bible Dictionary.* Unger, Merrill, R. K. Harrison, Howard Vos, and Cyril Barber. Chicago: Moody Publishers, 2006.

"Garden." *Cambridge Advanced Learner's Dictionary & Thesaurus.* Cambridge Dictionaries Online. http://dictionary.cambridge.org/dictionary/british/ (accessed June 21, 2012).

Henry, Matthew. *Matthew Henry Commentary on the Whole Bible.* Genesis 3. http://www.blueletterbible.org/commentaries/comm_view.cfm?AuthorID=4&contentID=630&commInfo=5&topic=Genesis (accessed June 22, 2012).

Henry, Matthew. *Matthew Henry's Commentary on the Whole Bible.* Psalm 44. http://www.blueletterbible.org/commentaries/comm_view.cfm?AuthorID=4&contentID=1167&commInfo=5&topic=Psalms (accessed June 22, 2012).

Henry, Matthew. *Matthew Henry's Commentary on the Whole Bible.* James 1. http://www.blueletterbible.org/commentaries/comm_view.cfm?AuthorID=4&contentID=1832&commInfo=5&topic=James (accessed June 23, 2012).

Walton, John H., Victor H. Matthews, and Mark W. Chavalas. *Bible Background Commentary: Old Testament.* Downers Grove, IL: IVP Academic, 2000.

Say It Correctly

Serpent. **SIR**-pent.
Enmity. **EN**-mit-ee.
Conception. con-**SEP**-shun.

Daily Bible Readings

MONDAY
Obeying God's Voice
(Exodus 19:3–8)

TUESDAY
The Blessing in Obedience
(Deuteronomy 11:26–32)

WEDNESDAY
Choosing the Life of Obedience
(Deuteronomy 30:11–20)

THURSDAY
Obeying God Above All
(Acts 5:27–42)

FRIDAY
The Enticement to Disobey
(Genesis 3:1–7)

SATURDAY
The Punishment for Disobedience
(Genesis 3:20–24)

SUNDAY
The Consequences of Disobedience
(Genesis 3:8b–17)

Notes

_____

_____

_____

_____

Teaching Tips

Words You Should Know

A. Covenant (Genesis 9:9) *beyrith*, (Heb.)—Literally "cutting," the term applied to various transactions between God and man, and between man and his fellow man.

B. Creature (v. 10) *nefesh* (Heb.)—This means a "breathing creature." In the Old Testament, "creature" is a general term for any animal, though it can be used in other contexts to mean "soul," "self," or "person."

Teacher Preparation

Unifying Principle—Never Again. A natural disaster can cause great anxiety over the safety and welfare of loved ones. How can loved ones be assured of God's protection in the future? God said that the rainbow would remind Him of the covenant to protect all living creatures.

A. Pray for your students.

B. Read and meditate on all the Scriptures from the Bible Background and the Devotional Reading sections.

C. Reread the Focal Verses in two or more translations (NLT, ESV, NIV, etc.).

O—Open the Lesson

A. Open with prayer, including the Aim for Change.

B. After prayer, have a volunteer read the In Focus story.

C. Have your students read the Aim for Change and Keep in Mind verse in unison.

D. Discuss and allow time to hear student testimonies.

P—Present the Scriptures

A. Have volunteers read the Focal Verses.

B. Now use The People, Places, and Times; Background; and Search the Scriptures to clarify the verses.

E—Explore the Meaning

A. Have volunteers summarize the Discuss the Meaning, Lesson in Our Society, and Make It Happen sections.

B. Connect these sections to the Aim for Change and the Keep in Mind verse with the Lesson in Our Society and Make It Happen sections.

N—Next Steps for Application

A. Summarize the lesson.

B. Allow students to share how the lesson impacted them.

C. Close with prayer and praise God for keeping His promises.

Worship Guide

For the Superintendent or Teacher
Theme: An Everlasting Covenant
Song: "Wonderful Peace"
Devotional Reading: Isaiah 54:9-14

An Everlasting Covenant

Bible Background • GENESIS 8:20–9:7
Printed Text • GENESIS 9:8–17 | Devotional Reading • ISAIAH 54:9–14

Aim for Change

By the end of the lesson, we will: EXPLORE the covenant God made with Noah after the flood; DELIGHT in signs of God's grace; and IDENTIFY promises of God on which we can stake our lives.

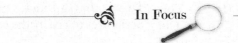 In Focus

Children look forward to promises their parents make to them, especially when the promises are something they consider good. Talhia was anxiously awaiting her father's arrival after he got home from work. He had given her responsibilities she needed to complete before his arrival home.

She had only completed most of the assignments. She worried that her dad would be upset with her for not completing all her assignments. She wondered if they were still going to be able to go to the park as he promised.

Reluctantly, she opened the door for her father when she heard him pull in the driveway. She still had a glimmer of hope because he had not said going to the park was contingent on all of the assignments being complete.

Dad was very exhausted after work. He asked Talhia if she had completed her assignments. She regretfully admitted that she tried to and was close to finishing, but she had not completed everything. Dad said that although he was tired, he wanted to keep his promise.

God is also a promise keeper. In today's lesson, we learn that He never fails!

Keep in Mind

"And I will establish my covenant with you, neither shall all flesh be cut off any more by the waters of a flood; neither shall there any more be a flood to destroy the earth" (Genesis 9:11).

"And I will establish my covenant with you, neither shall all flesh be cut off any more by the waters of a flood; neither shall there any more be a flood to destroy the earth" (Genesis 9:11).

Focal Verses

KJV **Genesis 9:8** And God spake unto Noah, and to his sons with him, saying,

9 And I, behold, I establish my covenant with you, and with your seed after you;

10 And with every living creature that is with you, of the fowl, of the cattle, and of every beast of the earth with you; from all that go out of the ark, to every beast of the earth.

11 And I will establish my covenant with you; neither shall all flesh be cut off any more by the waters of a flood; neither shall there any more be a flood to destroy the earth.

12 And God said, This is the token of the covenant which I make between me and you and every living creature that is with you, for perpetual generations:

13 I do set my bow in the cloud, and it shall be for a token of a covenant between me and the earth.

14 And it shall come to pass, when I bring a cloud over the earth, that the bow shall be seen in the cloud:

15 And I will remember my covenant, which is between me and you and every living creature of all flesh; and the waters shall no more become a flood to destroy all flesh.

16 And the bow shall be in the cloud; and I will look upon it, that I may remember the everlasting covenant between God and every living creature of all flesh that is upon the earth.

17 And God said unto Noah, This is the token of the covenant, which I have established between me and all flesh that is upon the earth.

NLT **Genesis 9:8** Then God told Noah and his sons,

9 "I hereby confirm my covenant with you and your descendants,

10 and with all the animals that were on the boat with you—the birds, the livestock, and all the wild animals—every living creature on earth.

11 Yes, I am confirming my covenant with you. Never again will floodwaters kill all living creatures; never again will a flood destroy the earth."

12 Then God said, "I am giving you a sign of my covenant with you and with all living creatures, for all generations to come.

13 I have placed my rainbow in the clouds. It is the sign of my covenant with you and with all the earth.

14 When I send clouds over the earth, the rainbow will appear in the clouds,

15 and I will remember my covenant with you and with all living creatures. Never again will the floodwaters destroy all life.

16 When I see the rainbow in the clouds, I will remember the eternal covenant between God and every living creature on earth."

17 Then God said to Noah, "Yes, this rainbow is the sign of the covenant I am confirming with all the creatures on earth."

The People, Places, and Times

Covenant. A covenant is a formal agreement between two parties. The principal section of a covenant is the stipulations, which may include requirements for either party or both. In this covenant, God took stipulations upon Himself rather than imposing them on Noah and his family. Unlike the later covenant with Abraham and those that build on the covenant with Abraham, this covenant did not entail election or new revelation. It was also made with every living creature, not just people.

Rainbow Significance. The designation of the rainbow as a sign of the covenant does not suggest that this was the first rainbow ever seen. The function of a sign is connected to the significance attached to it. In like manner, circumcision is designated as a sign of the covenant with Abraham, yet that was an ancient practice not new with Abraham and his family. In the Gilgamesh Epic, the goddess Ishtar identified the lapis lazuli (deep blue semiprecious stones with traces of gold-colored pyrite) of her necklace as the basis of an oath by which she would never forget the days of the Flood. An 11th century Assyrian relief shows two hands reaching out of the clouds, one hand offering blessing, the other holding a bow. Since the word for rainbow is the same word as that used for the weapon, this is an interesting image.

Background

Leaving the Ark, Noah made a sacrifice to God. Noah received God's grace, walked with God in obedience and righteousness, was preserved from judgment, entered a new age with people's wickedness temporarily removed, and responded with worship.

After Noah made the sacrifice, God promised never to curse the ground in this way again. The continuity of seasons is evidence of God's forbearance.

God instructed Noah to be fruitful and increase in number and fill the earth (vv. 1, 7) just as He told Adam (1:28). And Noah, like Adam, was to have dominion over animals (9:2; cf. 1:26, 28). Also, both were given food to eat (9:3; cf. 1:29, 2:16) with one prohibition (9:4, cf. 2:17).

With Noah's new beginning came a covenant. It was necessary now to have a covenant with obligations for mankind and a promise from God. Because of the Flood's destruction of life, people might think that God views life as cheap and assume that taking life is a small matter. This covenant shows that life is sacred and that man is not to destroy man, who is made in the image of God.

In essence, then, this covenant was established to ensure the stability of nature. It helped guarantee the order of the world. People would also learn that human law was necessary for the stability of life and that wickedness should not go unchecked as it had before. So human government was brought in.

At-A-Glance

1. The Author, Recipients, and the Covenant (Genesis 9:8–11)
2. The Sign of the Covenant and the Rainbow (vv. 12–16)

In Depth

1. The Author, Recipients, and the Covenant (Genesis 9:8–11)

God is a covenant God. Some scholars believe this is the second covenant He makes with mankind—the first being marriage. Although the church doesn't talk about this covenant as much as the Abrahamic covenant laid out a few chapters later in Genesis (cf. Genesis 12), it's an unparalleled display of God's grace.

God promised to Noah, his sons, their descendants, and every living thing that there would never again be a flood to destroy all mankind. God had drowned the world once, and though He foresaw the future wickedness of it, He promised that He would never drown it again. If the flowing of the tides should last for several days instead of just a few hours each day, what desolation that would cause! And how destructive would the clouds be if such showers as we have sometimes seen were continued for days or weeks at a time! But God shows what He could do in wrath and yet reveals what He will do in mercy.

2. The Sign of the Covenant and the Rainbow (vv. 12–16)

God assures us of His promises: He created the rainbow (v. 13); it shall be seen in the cloud (v. 14) so that seeing shall be the token of the covenant (vv. 12, 15). God did not need a reminder; He gave the rainbow for the sake of His people. As God looks upon the bow, He remembers the covenant and so should we, that we also may be ever mindful of the covenant with faith and thankfulness.

The rainbow is one of those natural wonders that leave us speechless when it appears in the sky, almost out of nowhere. It is literally a reflection of light on water droplets that causes the phenomenon. But it should also cause a phenomenon in our hearts. Our hearts should be warmed when we see this reminder of God's grace in the sky. It's a promise sealed in a multi-colored bow across the sky.

The rainbow also delivers another message to us: the storm is over. The flooding in our lives have subsided. We are safe now. It pictures the greatest instrument of God's grace in the Cross of Christ. In it, God took the storms, floods, and rain in our lives and placed it on His Son, so that the Prince of peace could bring us peace.

Search the Scriptures

1. With whom did God make the covenant (Genesis 9:8–10)?

2. What is the purpose of the rainbow in the cloud (vv. 13–15)?

Discuss the Meaning

God provides for all our needs by even making provisions for our fears. We may hear about and even see things that frighten us, but God reminds us through the rainbow of His love for us and His promise to us. What kind of things in your life make you fearful?

Lesson in Our Society

So often we hear about natural disasters and hundreds of people dying and being affected by the events. We can't help but feel concern for ourselves and others. We pray that our families and loved ones remain safe from the destruction. In the meantime, we must remind each other of the covenant God made to His people and trust that He will never forget.

Make It Happen

As we continually hear of alarming situations, we must remain prayerful and hopeful, knowing God does provide for His people. God teaches us to "trust in the LORD with all thine heart; and lean not unto thine own understanding" (Proverbs 3:5). So we must rely on the hope in which He has given us.

Follow the Spirit

What God wants me to do:

_____

_____

_____

_____

Remember Your Thoughts

Special insights I have learned:

_____

_____

_____

_____

More Light on the Text

Genesis 9:8–17

8 And God spake unto Noah, and to his sons with him, saying, 9 And I, behold, I establish my covenant with you, and with your seed after you; 10 And with every living creature that is with you, of the fowl, of the cattle, and of every beast of the earth with you; from all that go out of the ark, to every beast of the earth.

Divine sovereignty is in view as God took the initiative and spoke to Noah and his sons. "Noah" (Heb. *Noach*, **no-AKH**) means rest. After the destruction of the world by the Flood, Noah became the seminal head of God's new creation because he and his family were the only ones saved from the watery death. Possibly to ensure that man would not be in abject fear of Him, God spoke to Noah and made a "covenant" (Heb. *beriyth*, **ber-eeth**, meaning divine ordinance with signs or pledges) with him. Surviving the great Flood, Noah had been through an ordeal. God wanted to assure him that he could now live out his life in peace and rest. God's anger with the world had been appeased and man could now be at peace as well. God's pledge was extended not only to Noah but also to all of his "seed" (Heb. *zera*, **zeh-RAH**, meaning successive generations).

11 And I will establish my covenant with you, neither shall all flesh be cut off any more by the waters of a flood; neither shall there any more be a flood to destroy the earth.

In establishing His covenant with Noah, God made the covenant both universal and unconditional. Noah was not asked to do anything in order for the covenant to remain in force. By including every living creature in the covenant, we are reminded of God's instructions to Adam and Eve to reproduce and multiply and cover the earth (Genesis 1:28–30). Here, God promised that water will never again be the cause for the destruction of all mankind or the earth.

12 And God said, This is the token of the covenant which I make between me and you and every living creature that is with you, for perpetual generations: 13 I do set my bow in the cloud, and it shall be for a token of a covenant between me and the earth.

So that Noah would know His word is good, God gave a "token" (Heb. *owth*, **oth**), meaning a distinguishing mark or miraculous sign. This sign is His "bow" (Heb. *qesheth*, **keh-SHETH**). This bow, in the usual treatment of the Hebrew word, is God's bow of war, but here He gives His bow a new use and a new meaning. The bow or rainbow will be a reminder to Him of His covenant with Noah and the earth never again to destroy it with water.

14 And it shall come to pass, when I bring a cloud over the earth, that the bow shall be seen in the cloud: 15 And I will remember my covenant, which is between me and you and every living creature of all flesh; and the waters shall no more become a flood to destroy all flesh.

It is noteworthy that nothing happens outside of God's permissive will. God brought the cloud and determined that the rainbow would be seen in that cloud. God will see it, but man will be permitted to witness the rainbow as well. Each time we see a rainbow, we are to be reminded that God has made a covenant to never again destroy the earth with a great flood. God is faithful and true to His word—a word that remains universal in its application, extending to all flesh, human and non-human.

16 And the bow shall be in the cloud; and I will look upon it, that I may remember the everlasting covenant between God and every living creature of all flesh that is upon the earth.

The rainbow usually appears when particles of moisture in a "cloud" (Heb. *anan*, **aw-NAWN**) interact with the rays of the sun, usually after a storm. It is comforting to know that the storm of God's wrath that once resulted in a universal Flood will always be quieted when He looks upon His token of peace, the rainbow.

17 And God said unto Noah, This is the token of the covenant, which I have established between me and all flesh that is upon the earth.

Once more God's covenant is confirmed. This is the seventh time God stated it. He will not forget. In the completeness of God's promise, Noah and all mankind can be assured that God is in control and mindful of all that is occurring on the earth.

Sources:

Cambridge Advanced Learner's Dictionary & Thesaurus. Cambridge Dictionaries Online. http://dictionary.cambridge.org/dictionary/british/ (accessed October 8, 2012).

Coffman, James Burton. *Commentary on Genesis.* Abilene, TX: Abilene Christian University Press, 1974.

"Covenant." *The New Unger's Bible Dictionary.* Unger, Merrill, R. K. Harrison, Howard Vos, and Cyril Barber. Chicago: Moody Publishers, 2006.

Dunn, James D. G. and John W. Rogerson. *Commentary on the Bible.* Grand Rapids, MI: Wm. B. Eerdmans Publishing Company, 2003.

Henry, Matthew. *Matthew Henry Commentary on the Whole Bible.* Genesis 9. http://www.biblestudytools.com/commentaries/matthew-henry-complete/genesis/9.html (accessed October 7, 2012).

Mays, James L., ed. *HarperCollins Bible Commentary.* San Francisco: HarperOne, 1988, 2000.

Walton, John H., Victor H. Matthews, and Mark W. Chavalas. *Bible Background Commentary: Old Testament.* Downers Grove, IL: IVP Academic, 2000.

Zuck, Roy. *The Bible Knowledge Commentary.* Wheaton, IL: Victor Books, 1983.

Say It Correctly

Covenant. **COV**-en-ant.
Offspring. **OFF**-spring.
Livestock. **LYVE**-stock.

Daily Bible Readings

MONDAY
An Invitation to Covenant with God
(Genesis 6:11–22)

TUESDAY
Doing All the Lord Commands
(Genesis 7:1–10)

WEDNESDAY
Preserved in the Ark
(Genesis 7:11–24)

THURSDAY
Waiting for the Waters to Subside
(Genesis 8:1–12)

FRIDAY
A Sacrifice Pleasing to God
(Genesis 8:13–22)

SATURDAY
God's Covenant with All Humanity
(Genesis 9:1–7)

SUNDAY
Remembering the Everlasting Covenant
(Genesis 9:8–17)

Teaching Tips

September 29
Bible Study Guide 5

Words You Should Know

A. Go to (Genesis 11:3) *yahab* (Heb.)—To grant, permit, and come now.

B. Confound (v. 7) *balal* (Heb.)—To mix, mingle, and confuse.

Teacher Preparation

Unifying Principle—The Proud Brought Low. We all want to hear God say "well done" about how we've used what He has given us. But using those gifts to get glory rather than glorifying God sets us up for disaster.

A. Pray that God enables you to teach in a way that students will meet the Aim for Change.

B. Use a commentary and concordance to study Genesis 11 in its entirety.

C. Complete the companion lesson in the *Precepts For Living Personal Study Guide®*.

O—Open the Lesson

A. Start today's lesson with prayer.

B. Initiate discussion by asking students to tell you what they know about the tower of Babel.

C. Solicit volunteers to read the In Focus story, and have students discuss it.

D. Ask students to humbly acknowledge any futile attempts to be like God.

P—Present the Scriptures

A. Give students time to read through the Focal Verses.

B. Use The People, Places, and Times; Background; Search the Scriptures; At-A-Glance outline; In Depth; and More Light on the Text to clarify the verses.

E—Explore the Meaning

A. Divide students into three groups, assigning each one of the following sections: Discuss the Meaning, Lesson in Our Society, and Make It Happen. Tell each group to select a representative to share the group's responses.

B. Make sure to relate the Aim for Change and the Keep in Mind verse to the three sections.

N—Next Steps for Application

A. Encourage students to look at their own lives and identify ways they've taken matters into their own hands. Admonish them to cast their cares on Him.

B. Have students write a paragraph summary of today's lesson.

C. Close with prayer, thanking God for not letting us get in the way of His plans for us.

Worship Guide

For the Superintendent or Teacher
Theme: God Scatters the Nations
Song: "Great is Thy Faithfulness"
Devotional Reading:
2 Chronicles 34:22–28

God Scatters the Nations

Bible Background • GENESIS 11
Printed Text • GENESIS 11:1–9 | Devotional Reading • 2 CHRONICLES 34:22–28

—————— Aim for Change ——————

By the end of the lesson, we will: DISCUSS the misguided theology of the plan to build the tower of Babel; humbly ACKNOWLEDGE futile attempts to be like God; and IDENTIFY personal "towers of Babel" that we attempt to construct today.

 In Focus

John hated the school district where he lived, but the community was affordable. The problem was the crime rate at the high school his daughter, Lauren, just started was higher than its graduation rate. The schools on the South Side were better. They had more resources and better books, and their students were not "wanded" or patted down by security before football games.

John could not bear to hear any more of the stories Lauren told when she came home. After praying for a month with no change, John decided to take matters into his own hands. He found a nice, small house for himself and his daughter. There, Lauren would be able to attend Southside High. It didn't matter that the rent was double what he paid on the West Side; John could not afford to jeopardize Lauren's academic success. When his rental application was turned down because of poor credit, John cried. Didn't God care about his child's needs? John realized the answer to that question when, a month later, he heard the news of a pipe bomb explosion at Southside High School that fatally injured two students.

Sometimes God has to confuse us to protect us. In today's lesson, we learn that a failed attempt at something can be God's sovereign grace at work.

—————— Keep in Mind ——————

"So the LORD scattered them abroad from thence upon the face of all the earth: and they left off to build the city" (Genesis 11:8).

"So the LORD scattered them abroad from thence upon the face of all the earth: and they left off to build the city" (Genesis 11:8).

Focal Verses

KJV **Genesis 11:1** And the whole earth was of one language, and of one speech.

2 And it came to pass, as they journeyed from the east, that they found a plain in the land of Shinar; and they dwelt there.

3 And they said one to another, Go to, let us make brick, and burn them thoroughly. And they had brick for stone, and slime had they for morter.

4 And they said, Go to, let us build us a city and a tower, whose top may reach unto heaven; and let us make us a name, lest we be scattered abroad upon the face of the whole earth.

5 And the LORD came down to see the city and the tower, which the children of men builded.

6 And the LORD said, Behold, the people is one, and they have all one language; and this they begin to do: and now nothing will be restrained from them, which they have imagined to do.

7 Go to, let us go down, and there confound their language, that they may not understand one another's speech.

8 So the LORD scattered them abroad from thence upon the face of all the earth: and they left off to build the city.

9 Therefore is the name of it called Babel; because the LORD did there confound the language of all the earth: and from thence did the LORD scatter them abroad upon the face of all the earth.

NLT **Genesis 11:1** At one time all the people of the world spoke the same language and used the same words.

2 As the people migrated to the east, they found a plain in the land of Babylonia and settled there.

3 They began saying to each other, "Let's make bricks and harden them with fire." (In this region bricks were used instead of stone, and tar was used for mortar.)

4 Then they said, "Come, let's build a great city for ourselves with a tower that reaches into the sky. This will make us famous and keep us from being scattered all over the world."

5 But the LORD came down to look at the city and the tower the people were building.

6 "Look!" he said. "The people are united, and they all speak the same language. After this, nothing they set out to do will be impossible for them!

7 Come, let's go down and confuse the people with different languages. Then they won't be able to understand each other."

8 In that way, the LORD scattered them all over the world, and they stopped building the city.

9 That is why the city was called Babel, because that is where the LORD confused the people with different languages. In this way he scattered them all over the world.

The People, Places, and Times

Brickmaking. Buildings in the ancient world were constructed using bricks made of clay or a claylike mixture of mud and straw. Scholars suggest that there were likely two ways of making bricks. One way—the easiest—was to pack clay into a mold and let it dry in the sun. The Hebrews probably used this method in Egypt and later in the Promised Land. But the Babylonian method was more advanced—they used kilns to make their bricks harder and more durable. Their bricks were also larger and flatter, so they could support more weight. It was probably the Babylonians' ancestors who built the tower of Babel.

Shinar. Its name means "country of two rivers," as it was a tract of land between the Tigris and Euphrates Rivers. It is reported that Shinar was a plain country where brick was used for stone and slime for mortar. The country was later called Chaldea. Babel (Babylon) was its capital.

Tower of Babel. Only mentioned once in the Bible, this tower was built of brick and slime. It is reported that it had the shape of a pyramid and was built in seven receding stages. The first, second, and third stories were twenty-six feet high, and the other four were sixteen feet. Scholars assert that there may have been a fifteen-foot ark or tabernacle on the seventh story, nearly covering it. The entire height of the tower, with a three-foot platform (to support its weight and height), would have been 160 feet, but without the platform, 157 feet.

Background

Genesis 9 closes the curtain on Noah's life, letting us know he lived 350 years after the Flood. One may be tempted to skip over Genesis 10, as it appears to be another long genealogical account of names and places. But Genesis 10 sets the stage for the rest of the book's chapters. It shows us how God repopulated the earth, tells us who the main characters are and the roles they'll play, and unfolds God's plan for all people of the world. In our lesson text, we see how God carried the Gospel to all the world by scattering a bold group of people.

At-A-Glance

1. The People Exalt Themselves
(Genesis 11:1–4)
2. The Lord Brings Down the People
(vv. 5–9)

In Depth

1. The People Exalt Themselves (Genesis 11:1–4)

What peace there must have been! After the Flood, all was in unison. With one language, one would think it'd be easier to care for and love one another. Perhaps the place where the people lived grew to be too small for them, so they agreed to split up. The text records that some journeyed from the east and found a tract of land in a country called Shinar. With the Tigris and Euphrates flowing through it, there was much clay and slime. In Babel, the country's capital, the people used brick to build up the city so that it became a great place of wealth. Its city walls were thick, and some of its private homes had as many as twenty-six rooms and several courtyards. Babel is noted for its developments of medicine, mythology, linguistics, mathematics, and astronomy. No wonder they thought they could build a tower to heaven!

2. The Lord Brings Down the People (vv. 5–9)

Who better than God knows the power of oneness and creating something from an image? When He saw the people operating under the same principles but with misguided motives, He had to intervene. He confused their language so they could not understand each other then He scattered them to different parts of the earth. God is a righteous and omnipotent judge who thwarted this attempt at grandiosity, but

He also used it for a greater good. After the world had been destroyed by the Flood, only Noah's family remained. After a while, as the population began to grow, they not only stayed in one geographic location, but they also began to think too much of themselves. We do not know if all the people would have stayed on that one spot, but it is interesting to consider whether the rest of the world might have been uninhabited if their efforts had been successful. But the Lord saw this group of bold people who built a city, and He scattered them so that eventually the earth was repopulated.

Search the Scriptures

1. What did the people say to one another (Genesis 11:3–4)?

2. How did God respond to their work (vv. 7–8)?

Discuss the Meaning

1. Why didn't God choose another intervention to stop the people from building the tower? Why do you think He chose to give them different languages?

2. What do you think about God using the very thing the people were afraid of as His judgment (i.e., v. 4 records that they were afraid of being scattered)?

Lesson in Our Society

What the tower of Babel's builders did not realize is that they had already made a name for themselves. They'd turned Babel into a very prosperous place. But they wanted something grander—a stairway to heaven. If the United States does nothing else, our country is already great, but no, we're striving to become greater. To date, our national debt is more than $15.5 trillion. What else will result from our aspirations to legendary greatness?

Make It Happen

Are you overstepping your bounds, living beyond your means, or taking matters into your own hands? If so, your challenge this week is to get help. Find a credit counseling agency to deal with your finances, a pastor or advisor to help you trust God again, or a therapist to help you learn how to be content.

Follow the Spirit

What God wants me to do:

_____

_____

_____

_____

Remember Your Thoughts

Special insights I have learned:

_____

_____

_____

_____

More Light on the Text
Genesis 11:1–9

While most are familiar from childhood with the story of the tower of Babel, one wonders whether most could articulate exactly why God was displeased with the tower's construction and chose to intervene as He did. In this portion of Scripture, God's big-picture thinking and His faithful, unchanging nature are juxtaposed against a faithless people's vain imaginations and plans. This is a classic story of man's plans for God coming into sharp conflict with God's plans for man.

The previous chapter of Genesis contains a genealogy of Noah's descendants after the Flood. The problem, which soon became apparent, was that sin also survived the Flood.

1 And the whole earth was of one language, and of one speech. 2 And it came to pass, as they journeyed from the east, that they found a plain in the land of Shinar; and they dwelt there.

The first verse is a key background statement setting up the coming events. Unfortunately, there is no way to know what language (Heb. *saphah*, **sa-FA**) was once universal.

Scholars agree that the ancient "land of Babylonia," also known as Chaldea, is in southern Mesopotamia; most versions call it Shinar (see 10:10, 14:1, 9). Some think it significant that the author of Genesis noted an eastward movement, which they see as having a dark similarity with Adam and Eve heading east out of the Garden of Eden (3:24) and Cain moving east of Eden after killing Abel (4:16).

3 And they said one to another, Go to, let us make brick, and burn them thoroughly. And they had brick for stone, and slime had they for morter. 4 And they said, Go to, let us build us a city and a tower, whose top may reach unto heaven; and let us make us a name, lest we be scattered abroad upon the face of the whole earth."

Tourists in Israel are often told a legend that once an angel was carrying a huge load of stones overhead, but the bag broke and the stones littered the nation, where they remain to this day. Unlike the plethora of stones available in Palestine, however, stones in the new region were rare, so the travelers learned local construction methods. John Walton writes, "This combination of baked brick and bitumen mastic made for waterproof buildings as sturdy as stone" (*The NIV Application Commentary,* 372).

The towers in Mesopotamia, called ziggurats, would have differed from those in Israel, which were mostly defensive watchtowers. Among the thirty or so ruins of ziggurats that archaeologists have found in the region, all share similar features. They tended to resemble pyramids, were usually dedicated to deities, had outer ramps or stairs leading to the peak, ranged in size from sixty to 200 feet per side, and were considered sacred places reserved for the gods. The idea was to make it easy for the gods to visit humans, via the convenient stairway, and bless and interact with them.

Just making bricks and building a city, and even building towers, were neither evil nor uncommon practices. The problem—and offense to God—was in the motivation and purpose. The people wanted to 1) reach into the sky, and 2) become famous or, as other versions word it, make a name for themselves. Ironically, albeit infamously, they succeeded in both endeavors.

5 And the LORD came down to see the city and the tower, which the children of men builded. 6 And the LORD said, Behold, the people is one, and they have all one language; and this they begin to do: and now nothing will be restrained from them, which they have imagined to do. 7 Go to, let us go down, and there confound their language, that they may not understand one another's speech.

As much or more can be gained from studying God's reaction than the people's actions. Similar to God judging the world harshly via the Flood because of systemic unbridled evil in the world (6:5), so it seems that the events at hand represented a more serious heart of evil than at first meets the eye. William LaSor writes, "Whether the descendants of Seth have become corrupt or something demonic has entered the world, the point is that a new level has been reached in the rampant spread of evil" (*Old Testament Survey*, 82). LaSor notes that just as cancer doctors attack the disease with the strongest treatment possible, so God sweepingly judged sin at the Fall, and He intended to wipe out sin with the Flood, pushing the restart button on humanity with Noah. With plans in full motion to erect the tower, God saw the people's hearts and recognized a familiar saturation of evil. In short, man was in rebellion mode again, even if the narrative is not sufficiently specific. Enough blanks can be filled in by God's comprehensive response.

Walton observes that the fact people did not want to scatter would not have been such a terrible thing. Even today, families continually lament that they are so spread out from one another. The whole problem was with the ziggurat, which was the ultimate symbol of Babylonian religion. As mankind subdued the earth, his error was to begin to subdue the gods, to humanize them. In Walton's words, "with the development of urbanization people began to envision their gods in human terms" (*The NIV Application Commentary*, 377). In other words, they not only tried to bring their gods down to earth, they also tried to make them into their own image. As Walton notes, the sin here "went beyond mere idolatry; it degraded the nature of God by portraying him as having [human] needs" (Ibid.).

Thus, we must trust that God's response was appropriate for the level and extent of the willful, idolatrous, cancerous ignorance in the people's hearts. "This will only lead to unmitigated disaster," was His judgment, and He put a swift and irreversible end to it.

8 So the LORD scattered them abroad from thence upon the face of all the earth: and they left off to build the city. 9 Therefore is the name of it called Babel; because the LORD did there confound the language of all the earth: and from thence did the LORD scatter them abroad upon the face of all the earth.

Some commentators say that God scattered the people because His original plan was for mankind to spread out over the earth (1:28), and they rebelled against the master plan. God filling the earth, however, was to be through reproduction, not simply forcing them to spread out, which would not increase population. The people scattering was the natural, inevitable result of them no longer being able to communicate.

The name of the tower, Babel meant confusion or mixing, and it was also the source of the word "Babylon" (e.g., Genesis 10:10; 2 Kings 17:24, 20:14; Micah 4:10), which was the metropolis of Babylonia, the whole of which was often referred to as Babylon (e.g., Psalm 87:4, 137:1; Isaiah 14:4). In Ezra 5:13 (KJV), King Cyrus of Persia was referred to as "king of Babylon," and the same for the Persian king Artaxerxes in Nehemiah 13:6. The ruins of Babylon today are found near Al Hillah, Iraq, about fifty-five miles south of Baghdad.

God does not condemn building cities or towers, but He does condemn spiritually fatal thinking that obstinately insists on humanizing God and refusing to recognize Him as the one, eternal, sovereign, supreme God. Man's plan without God is to take matters into his own hands, to make his own master plan, to create his own name and fortune, and worst of all, to create his own humanized gods. Everything is up to man; he is responsible for the entire universe. Tired of waiting on God, he forfeits God's blessing and grabs what he can grab and does what he can do under his own finite power. God's plan for man, in contrast, is to trust Him, to let Him take care of humanity and the universe, to follow His plan, to let Him lead and guide, and to let Him work out His plan for His people who are called by His great name.

Sources:

Blue Letter Bible. BlueLetterBible.org. http://www.blueletterbible.org/ (accessed July 2, 2012).

Henry, Matthew. *Matthew Henry Commentary on the Whole Bible.* Genesis 11. http://www.biblestudytools.com/commentaries/matthew-henry-complete/ (accessed July 25–27, 2012).

LaSor, William Sanford, David Allan Hubbard, and Frederic William Bush. *Old Testament Survey: The Message, Form, and Background of the Old Testament.* Grand Rapids, MI: Wm. B. Eerdmans Publishing Company, 1982. 81–86.

Sailhamer, John H. "Genesis." *The Expositor's Bible Commentary with the New International Version: Genesis, Exodus, Leviticus, Numbers, Vol. 2.* Edited by Frank E. Gaebelein. Grand Rapids, MI: Zondervan, 1985. 102–105.

Smith, William. *Smith's Bible Dictionary.* Peabody, MA: Hendrickson Publishers, Inc., 2000. 26–27, 71–72, 622.

Walton, John H. Genesis. *The NIV Application Commentary.* Grand Rapids, MI: Zondervan, 2001. 371–378.

Word in Life Study Bible (NKJV). Nashville: Thomas Nelson Publishers, 1993. 30.

Say It Correctly

Babel. **BA**-bel.
Shinar. **SHI**-nar.
Bitumen. bi-**TU**-men.

Daily Bible Readings

MONDAY
Dark Counsel Lacking Knowledge
(Job 38:1–7)

TUESDAY
Limited Knowledge and Influence
(Job 38:12–18)

WEDNESDAY
The Expanse beyond Human Control
(Job 38:28–38)

THURSDAY
Overshadowed by God's Greatness
(Job 40:6–14)

FRIDAY
The Wrath of the Lord
(2 Chronicles 34:14–21)

SATURDAY
A Humble and Penitent Heart
(2 Chronicles 34:22–28)

SUNDAY
Human Achievement without God
(Genesis 11:1–9)

Notes

_____

_____

_____

Teaching Tips

October 6
Bible Study Guide 6

Words You Should Know

A. Inherit (Genesis 15:7) *yarash* (Heb.)—To take possession of.

B. Covenant (v. 18) *beriyth* (Heb.)—Agreement between God and man.

Teacher Preparation

Unifying Principle—A Lasting Inheritance. God promised and confirmed to Abram that he and Sarah's heirs would inherit land.

A. Pray for your students and that God will bring clarity to this lesson.

B. Study and meditate on the entire text.

C. Prepare a PowerPoint presentation showing signs people see as they drive or walk along the streets. Discuss the meaning of the signs.

D. Then, discuss the importance of having a will and what it should contain.

O—Open the Lesson

A. Open with prayer, including the Aim for Change.

B. After prayer, introduce today's subject of the lesson.

C. Have your students read the Aim for Change and Keep in Mind verse in unison. Discuss.

D. Share your presentation.

E. Ask: "Do you recall receiving an inheritance from someone in your family? Do you still have that inheritance?" Allow volunteers to share their responses.

F. Now have a volunteer summarize the In Focus story. Discuss.

G. Then ask, "Why is it so hard to trust God to keep His promises?" Discuss.

P—Present the Scriptures

A. Have volunteers read the Focal Verses.

B. Now use The People, Places, and Times; Background; Search the Scriptures; At-A-Glance outline; In Depth; and More Light on the Text to clarify the verses.

E—Explore the Meaning

A. Have volunteers summarize the Discuss the Meaning and Lesson in Our Society.

B. Connect these sections to the Aim for Change and the Keep in Mind verse.

N—Next Steps for Application

A. Summarize the lesson and review the Make It Happen section.

B. Close with prayer and praise God for the eternal inheritance He promised to give all believers.

Worship Guide

For the Superintendent or Teacher
Theme: A Promise of Land
Song: "A Charge to Keep I Have"
Devotional Reading: Hebrews 11:8–16

55

A Promise of Land

Bible Background • GENESIS 12:1–7; 13; 15:7–21; 17:8
Printed Text • GENESIS 15:7–21 | Devotional Reading • HEBREWS 11:8–16

Aim for Change

By the end of the lesson, we will: DISCUSS the significance of God's covenant with Abraham; TRUST God to keep His promises; and TELL others about the inheritance God promises to give to believers.

In Focus

OCT
6th

Mariam's parents always treated her special. Her father gave her the best of everything in life. He promised her, "I'll always take care of you." Her life began to change when her father was injured on his job as a firefighter. At first he was able to get disability checks, but soon they stopped. He applied for Social Security Disability but was denied. The financial strain affected his relationship with his wife. They argued all the time.

Her parents divorced when Mariam was thirteen years old. Her father disappeared, and no one knew where he went. For many years, Mariam wondered what happened to her father, and became very angry and bitter.

One day, Miriam received a letter from a lawyer who represented her father's estate. He had recently died and left all of his estate to her. Mariam contacted the lawyer and discovered that her father had been living on the West Coast, where he found a doctor who helped him recover from his injuries. It allowed him to secure a job as a fire safety trainer for corporations. Her father expressed in his will that he wanted to take care of Mariam as he had promised. All of it was now hers.

All believers will receive an inheritance from God. In today's lesson, we will examine the inheritance God promised Abraham and Sarah.

Keep in Mind

"In the same day the LORD made a covenant with Abram, saying, Unto thy seed have I given this land, from the river of Egypt unto the great river, the river Euphrates" (Genesis 15:18).

"In the same day the LORD made a covenant with Abram, saying, Unto thy seed have I given this land, from the river of Egypt unto the great river, the river Euphrates" (Genesis 15:18).

Focal Verses

KJV **Genesis 15:7** And he said unto him, I am the LORD that brought thee out of Ur of the Chaldees, to give thee this land to inherit it.

8 And he said, LORD God, whereby shall I know that I shall inherit it?

9 And he said unto him, Take me an heifer of three years old, and a she goat of three years old, and a ram of three years old, and a turtledove, and a young pigeon.

10 And he took unto him all these, and divided them in the midst, and laid each piece one against another: but the birds divided he not.

11 And when the fowls came down upon the carcases, Abram drove them away.

12 And when the sun was going down, a deep sleep fell upon Abram; and, lo, an horror of great darkness fell upon him.

13 And he said unto Abram, Know of a surety that thy seed shall be a stranger in a land that is not theirs, and shall serve them; and they shall afflict them four hundred years;

14 And also that nation, whom they shall serve, will I judge: and afterward shall they come out with great substance.

15 And thou shalt go to thy fathers in peace; thou shalt be buried in a good old age.

16 But in the fourth generation they shall come hither again: for the iniquity of the Amorites is not yet full.

17 And it came to pass, that, when the sun went down, and it was dark, behold a smoking furnace, and a burning lamp that passed between those pieces.

18 In the same day the LORD made a covenant with Abram, saying, Unto thy seed have I given this land, from the river of Egypt unto the great river, the river Euphrates:

NLT **Genesis 15:7** Then the LORD told him, "I am the LORD who brought you out of Ur of the Chaldeans to give you this land as your possession."

8 But Abram replied, "O Sovereign LORD, how can I be sure that I will actually possess it?"

9 The LORD told him, "Bring me a three-year-old heifer, a three-year-old female goat, a three-year-old ram, a turtledove, and a young pigeon."

10 So Abram presented all these to him and killed them. Then he cut each animal down the middle and laid the halves side by side; he did not, however, cut the birds in half.

11 Some vultures swooped down to eat the carcasses, but Abram chased them away.

12 As the sun was going down, Abram fell into a deep sleep, and a terrifying darkness came down over him.

13 Then the LORD said to Abram, "You can be sure that your descendants will be strangers in a foreign land, where they will be oppressed as slaves for 400 years.

14 But I will punish the nation that enslaves them, and in the end they will come away with great wealth.

15 (As for you, you will die in peace and be buried at a ripe old age.)

16 After four generations your descendants will return here to this land, for the sins of the Amorites do not yet warrant their destruction."

17 After the sun went down and darkness fell, Abram saw a smoking firepot and a flaming torch pass between the halves of the carcasses.

18 So the LORD made a covenant with Abram that day and said, "I have given this land to your descendants, all the way from

19 The Kenites, and the Kenizzites, and the Kadmonites,

20 And the Hittites, and the Perizzites, and the Rephaims,

21 And the Amorites, and the Canaanites, and the Girgashites, and the Jebusites.

the border of Egypt to the great Euphrates River—

19 the land now occupied by the Kenites, Kenizzites, Kadmonites,

20 Hittites, Perizzites, Rephaites,

21 Amorites, Canaanites, Girgashites, and Jebusites."

The People, Places, and Times

Abram. Abram grew up in the Euphrates River town of Ur, in what is now southern Iraq. For unknown reasons, his father, Terah, decided to move his entire extended family to Canaan (Genesis 11:31). Terah stopped halfway to Canaan. He settled some six hundred miles upriver in the busy caravan town of Haran, on Turkey's side of the border with Syria. After Terah died, God told Abram to finish the trip to Canaan (12:1–3). God also promised to make him into a great nation, even though he and Sarai had no children. Abram obeyed God and moved his family and herds southward to Canaan, an area now known as Israel (12:4–5).

Canaan. A name of the country west of the Jordan and the Dead Sea, and between those waters and the Mediterranean. The name means "belonging to the land of the red purple." It was a land in which the Canaanites and Phoenician traders trafficked in red-purple dye obtained from the spiny warm-water shellfish called murex on the Mediterranean coast. The land is now known as Palestine. The Canaanites engaged in nature worship and had prostitute goddesses and many other gods. The land was given by God to Abram and the Children of Israel (12:7; Exodus 6:4).

Background

Abram was a descendent of Shem, Noah's son. His father, Terah, moved the family from Ur to Haran, which was near Canaan. Terah never completed the journey to Canaan. God directed Abram at seventy-five years old to pack up and move his family, servants, and possessions to Canaan (12:1–5). He promised to grow Abram's family and make them a great nation. By faith, Abram obeyed God and traveled to Canaan. God appeared to Abram in Canaan and promised to give the land to his offspring (12:7). His wife, Sarai, was sixty-six years old at this time.

A severe famine in the land caused Abram to take his family to Egypt to live for a while. He made Sarai lie and tell the Egyptians she was his sister (12:10–13). Abram feared they would see how beautiful she was and kill him to keep her there for Pharaoh. They were treated very kindly and given animals and servants by Pharaoh. Later, serious diseases afflicted Pharaoh and his household because of the lie Sarai and Abram told (12:17–20). Pharaoh sent them out of Egypt. Abram was more wealthy than when he came to Egypt.

Both Abram and his nephew, Lot, had acquired many livestock. The land in Canaan could not sustain both their livestock and possessions. To avoid conflict among the herders, Abram let Lot choose land to live on. Lot chose to live near the wicked city of Sodom because it had good pasture and a dependable water supply. After Lot departed, God once again promised Abram the land and innumerable offspring (13:14–17). Abram moved his family and possessions to Hebron.

A war broke out amongst the kings in the area, including the king of Sodom—he would eventually flee and retreat (14:8–10). All the possessions and food of Sodom and Gomorrah were seized, along with Lot. Abram assembled 318 trained men and went to rescue Lot (14:14–16). Abram rescued Lot and the other captives. He also recovered all their goods and possessions.

At-A-Glance

1. Abram's Uncertainty
(Genesis 15:7–11)
2. God's Promise (vv. 12–16)
3. God's Covenant Confirmed
(vv. 17–21)

In Depth

1. Abram's Uncertainty (Genesis 15:7–11)

Abram had just defeated four kings and rescued his nephew Lot and others (ch. 14), yet God needed to encourage him. It is unclear why Abram was so afraid. Abram may have feared that the nations whose kings he had just defeated would rise up and come against him and his family. God reassured Abram that he had no need to fear (15:1). Moreover, God promised to protect Abram from all his enemies because He was his "shield." God also promised to reward Abram for trusting Him. But a personal relationship with God was Abram's greatest reward.

Abram heard God's reassuring words but still complained about being childless. He was upset that his chief servant, Eliezer, was his only heir (15:2–3). If a husband and wife were childless, it was legally permissible to adopt a slave or servant as a conditional heir. God told Abram, "Look now toward heaven, and tell the stars, if thou be able to number them: and he said unto him, So shall thy seed be. And he believed in the LORD; and he counted it to him for righteousness" (15:5–6). Abram is the "father of all them that believe" (Romans 4:11).

God also said to Abram, "I am the LORD that brought thee out of Ur of the Chaldees, to give thee this land to inherit it" (15:7). God's covenant with Abram was announced and confirmed (12:1–4, 13:14–17, 15:1–7). But Abram still wanted confirmation and assurance that he would possess the land of Canaan (15:8). God requested that Abram bring a "heifer of three years old, and a she goat of three years old, and a ram of three years old, and a turtledove, and a young pigeon" (15:9). Abram cut the animals into two pieces, except for the birds (v. 10; Leviticus 1:17).

2. God's Promise (vv. 12–16)

Abram fell into a deep sleep, and a frightening great darkness came over him. God spoke to Abram while he was asleep. He foretold the captivity of the Israelites by the Egyptians for over 400 years (v. 13; Exodus 12:40). They would be mistreated until God punished the Egyptians. Ultimately, the Israelites would be released and leave with great possessions from the Egyptians (Exodus 11:2–3, 12:35–36). These events would occur after Abram's death at the age of 175.

Just as the Israelites were dwelling in Canaan before their captivity, they would dwell there again after four generations (Genesis 15:16). A generation was the age of a man when his first son was born. This meant a generation for Abram was one hundred years. It would take 400 years because all the wicked Amorite people had to be cast out of the land after God passed judgment on them.

3. God's Covenant Confirmed (vv. 17–21)

"A smoking furnace, and a burning lamp" passed between the animal pieces (v. 17). This represented the presence of God. Often God's presence was manifested through fire (Exodus 3:2, 14:24, 19:18). A covenant was confirmed by the slaughtering and cutting of animals in two halves between which the two parties walked. It was a symbolic act meaning that if either broke the covenant, it would be with them like it was with the slaughtered animal.

God gave Abram a sign as assurance that the covenant was real and trustworthy. This covenant was an unconditional divine promise to fulfill the grant of the land. When the smoking furnace and burning lamp passed through the animal pieces, this ratified the covenant.

Today, we do not need to see smoke or fire to be assured of God's promises. We have the Word of God and our testimonies. We can remember that Jesus, who was the offspring of Abraham, promised to give us a lasting inheritance if we put our trust in Him. He has prepared a city for us to live in with Him for eternity. The New Jerusalem, a holy city, awaits us (Revelation 21:2).

Search the Scriptures

1. What did God promise Abram and his descendants (15:7, 16)?

2. How did God ratify the covenant He made with Abram (v. 17)?

Discuss the Meaning

Abram wanted proof or assurance from God that His promise would be fulfilled. God confirmed His promise by telling Abram about future events. Why is it so difficult to trust God's promises without having proof?

Lesson in Our Society

People often make promises they have no intention of keeping. This cultivates an environment of mistrust. We learn to trust people based on their word. God proved He is trustworthy because He has fulfilled every promise made. It sometimes can be difficult to trust the promises of God. What are some of God's promises for your life that seem impossible to believe? What impact does God's promise of an inheritance for His children have on your faith?

Make It Happen

Abraham is the "father of all them that believe" (Romans 4:11), and that makes all Christians his heirs. God promised an inheritance to those who put their trust in Him. We will live in a city, the New Jerusalem (Revelation 21:2). God will dwell there with His people. This week, share with unbelievers God's promises so they too can one day dwell in that holy city with God.

It would be wonderful to inherit lots of money, houses, and land from someone. In reality, it may not happen. If it does, it will not last. With the exception of eternal life in heaven or hell, nothing lasts forever.

Follow the Spirit

What God wants me to do:

_____

_____

_____

_____

Remember Your Thoughts
Special insights I have learned:

_____

_____

_____

_____

More Light on the Text
Genesis 15:7–21

Like the prophet that Abram was (20:7), he "saw" a conversation with God in a vision (Heb. *machazeh*, **makh-az-EH**, used only four times in the Old Testament), which started with verse 1 of this chapter and during which he queried God about his offspring (vv. 2–3). This was his fourth of eight conversations with the Almighty. This time, God promised that he would have a child, not by adoption or other legal means, but a biological child (v. 4), and that his descendants—literally "seed" (Heb. *zera*, **ZEH-rah**)—would be as uncountable as the stars (v. 5). Later, God would promise that they would also be as numberless as the sand of the seashore (22:17).

The much-quoted verse 6 says that Abram "believed in the LORD," for which God credited him with "righteousness." Abram had just become the father of faith (see also Romans 4:1–3; Galatians 3:6–9; Hebrews 11:8–10)! John Walton writes, "Recognized righteousness becomes the basis for blessing" (*The NIV Application Commentary,* 422). Similarly, John Sailhamer notes, "Only after he had been counted righteous through his faith could Abram enter into God's covenant" (*The Expositor's Bible Commentary,* 129).

In our lesson, God will make an eternal promise regarding a key aspect of that covenant: land, aptly named the "Promised Land."

7 And he said unto him, I am the LORD that brought thee out of Ur of the Chaldees, to give thee this land to inherit it.

Soon God will speak similar words to Moses just prior to making another major covenant with him at Mount Sinai (Exodus 20:2). God's deliverance, bringing them "out of Ur of the Chaldees," will mirror His coming deliverance of the Hebrews "out of the land of Egypt, out of the house of bondage." Both are spoken as reminders of God's sovereignty and divine power of salvation, but more than that, they are identifying characteristics—God alone has intervened on behalf of His people; it is God alone who delivers His people from bondage and sin.

8 And he said, LORD God, whereby shall I know that I shall inherit it? 9 And he said unto him, Take me an heifer of three years old, and a she goat of three years old, and a ram of three years old, and a turtledove, and a young pigeon. 10 And he took unto him all these and divided them in the midst, and laid each piece one against another: but the birds divided he not.

Abram's honest question was met with an odd answer consisting of not only bringing five animals but also cutting three of them in half—the heifer, goat, and ram (all normally acceptable as sacrifices)—and laying out the halves opposite each other. Inexplicably, he did not divide the two birds. Little is known about this ancient ritual, which seems to be a way of ratifying a covenant or taking a blood oath—similar to today's signing of contracts or having something notarized. One verse, Jeremiah 34:18, reveals a similar scenario; a few ancient texts also reference similar rituals.

11 And when the fowls came down upon the carcasses, Abram drove them away.

Commentators agree that this probably refers to divine protection from Israel's enemies, which Abram's faith provided as he drove away those who would devour. A parallel reference might be made with Matthew 24:28–30, during which vultures descend on carcasses. In both instances, the birds of prey immediately precede a darkening of the sun, which then precedes a future redemption. It is possible that this refers to the coming of Christ, the protecting Shepherd, the One who returns and redeems, as referenced in the Matthew passage.

12 And when the sun was going down, a deep sleep fell upon Abram; and, lo, an horror of great darkness fell upon him.

Adding to the mysterious imagery is the fact that this series of events happened while Abram was in the modern equivalent of an induced coma. At this point, he saw terrible, future events that would happen to his flesh-and-blood descendants, namely Egypt's enslavement of the Hebrews. It is noteworthy that this is the only time God spoke to Abram in such a manner; all seven of his other encounters with the Lord were when he was fully awake.

13 And he said unto Abram, Know of a surety that thy seed shall be a stranger in a land that is not theirs, and shall serve them; and they shall afflict them four hundred years; 14 And also that nation, whom they shall serve, will I judge: and afterward shall they come out with great substance. 15 And thou shalt go to thy fathers in peace; thou shalt be buried in a good old age. 16 But in the fourth generation they shall come hither again: for the iniquity of the Amorites is not yet full.

With overlapping references such as this, God reaffirmed the earlier connection in verse 7 with the future enslavement in Egypt and the coming deliverance. A connection with the Exodus and its typology-rich deliverance inherently makes a connection with Christ, who delivers any who believes from their slavery to sin. By following Abram's example of faith, believers instantly become his spiritual descendants, who collectively are as numerous as the stars by now!

17 And it came to pass, that, when the sun went down, and it was dark, behold a smoking furnace, and a burning lamp that passed between those pieces.

Here, the ritual was complete with the symbolic "smoking furnace" ("firepot" in many versions) and "burning lamp" passing between the halves of the severed animals. While there is room for interpretation of the symbolism, the explanation that seems best suited for the context is that the smoking furnace or firepot represents judgment, and the burning lamp represents the light of the world—both of which could represent either God's presence or Christ. Sailhamer's view is, "God walking through the parts represents his presence with his people" (*The Expositor's Bible Commentary*, 130). This was God's response to Abram's question in verse 8—He sealed His promises with His own presence and fiery, brilliant nature.

18 In the same day the LORD made a covenant with Abram, saying, Unto thy seed have I given this land, from the river of Egypt unto the great river, the river Euphrates: 19 The Kenites, and the Kenizzites, and the Kadmonites, 20 And the Hittites, and the Perizzites, and the Rephaims, 21 And the Amorites, and the Canaanites, and the Girgashites, and the Jebusites.

The borders of the Promised Land seem to be the same as for the Garden of Eden (2:10–14). Walter Brueggemann believes the description fits a later time in Israel's history: "It can be claimed that verses 18–21 describe the actual borders of the monarchy at its high point under Solomon (cf. 1 Kings 4:24)" (*Genesis, Interpretation Bible Commentary*, 150).

For believers today, the old lessons of faith and patience exemplified by Abram still apply because the object of our faith, God, has not changed. "God is always impressed with faith," says Walton (441). What God starts, God will finish, even if He does not operate on our timetable. The Old Testament prophet Habakkuk writes, "Though it tarry, wait for it; because it will surely come, it will not tarry" (Habakkuk 2:3). Similarly, in the New Testament, Apostle Peter asserts, "The Lord is not slack concerning his promise" (2 Peter 3:9; see also Philippians 1:6; 1 Thessalonians 5:24).

Sources:
Bible Study Tools. www.BibleStudyTools.com. "Old Testament Hebrew Lexicon—King James Version." http://www.biblestudytools.com/lexicons/hebrew/kjv (accessed July 10, 2012).
Blue Letter Bible. BlueLetterBible.org. http://www.blueletterbible.org/ (accessed July 5, 2012).
Brueggemann, Walter. *Genesis. Interpretation Bible Commentary.* Atlanta: John Knox Press, 1982. 148–150.
Gill, John. www.BibleStudyTools.com. *John Gill's Exposition of the Bible.* Genesis 15. http://www.biblestudytools.com/commentaries/gills-exposition-of-the-bible/genesis-15/ (accessed July 18, 2012).
Life Application Bible (NRSV). Wheaton, IL: Tyndale House, 1989. 29–30.
Sailhamer, John H. "Genesis." *The Expositor's Bible Commentary with the New International Version: Genesis, Exodus, Leviticus, Numbers, Vol. 2.* Edited by Frank E. Gaebelein. Grand Rapids, MI: Zondervan, 1985. 126–131.
Unger, Merrill F. *Unger's Bible Dictionary.* Chicago: Moody Press, 1985, 170–171, 224–225.
Walton, John H. *Genesis. The NIV Application Commentary.* Grand Rapids, MI: Zondervan, 2001. 420–441.
Youngblood, Ronald F., ed. *Nelson's New Illustrated Bible Dictionary.* Nashville: Thomas Nelson Publishers, 1995.

Say It Correctly

Amorite. **AM**-oh-rite.
Kennizite. **KEE**-nuh-zite.
Kadmonite. **KAD**-muh-nite.
Rephaim. **REF**-ih-yum.
Girgashite. **GUR**-gah-shite.
Jebusite. **JEB**-you-site.

Daily Bible Readings

MONDAY
The Faith of Abraham
(Hebrews 11:8–16)

TUESDAY
The Call of Abram
(Genesis 12:1–7)

WEDNESDAY
Settling in the Land
(Genesis 13:8–18)

THURSDAY
The Land and the Covenant
(Genesis 17:1–8)

FRIDAY
The Covenant Recounted and Renewed
(Joshua 24:1–13)

SATURDAY
The Covenant Remembered
(Psalm 105:1–11)

SUNDAY
The Covenant with Abraham
(Genesis 15:7–21)

Teaching Tips

October 13
Bible Study Guide 7

Words You Should Know

A. Sarai (Genesis 17:15) *Saray* (Heb.)—A princess.

B. Sarah (v. 15) *Sarah* (Heb.)—Noblewoman.

Teacher Preparation

Unifying Principle—A Promise Kept. We often rejoice at the birth of a new member in the family or community. What does a birth mean to a family or community? Abraham and Sarah saw their child as evidence of God's faithfulness in keeping the promise to create a nation.

A. Pray for your students and that God will bring clarity to this lesson.

B. Read and study Genesis 12–21, using several translations and commentaries.

C. Prepare a blank list entitled "Promises of God" to hand out to students.

O—Open the Lesson

A. Open with prayer, including the Aim for Change.

B. Ask a volunteer to read the In Focus story.

C. Have the students discuss how the characters responded to strife and what it must have been like for them as they waited for God to fulfill His promise.

P—Present the Scriptures

A. Ask another two students to read The People, Places, and Times and Background sections.

B. Read the Focal Verses aloud with the class.

C. Do an exposition of the Focal Verses using the In Depth section.

E—Explore the Meaning

A. Have the class answer the questions in the Discuss the Meaning section.

B. Ask a volunteer to read Lesson in Our Society and ask the class to discuss, "Have you ever waited for a promise of God to be fulfilled? How did you maintain your trust in God while waiting?"

N—Next Steps for Application

A. Read the Make It Happen section and ask the class to spend the next week recording the promises God has kept on the "Promises of God" sheet you hand out.

B. Share with the class how God has fulfilled the promise of salvation for all of you. Have the students write this down as their first promise from God.

C. Close with a prayer for each student to be able to remember all that God has done for him or her and to thank Him.

Worship Guide

For the Superintendent or Teacher
Theme: A Promise to Sarah
Song: "El Shaddai"
Devotional Reading: Isaiah 51:1–6

A Promise to Sarah

Bible Background • GENESIS 17, 18, 21
Printed Text • GENESIS 17:15–17, 18:9–15, 21:1–7
Devotional Reading • ISAIAH 51:1–6

Aim for Change

By the end of the lesson, we will: SUMMARIZE God's promise to Sarah; APPRECIATE life as a gift of God; and THANK God for His faithfulness to the faith family across generations.

In Focus

Amelia and Derek never thought that when they said "I do" seven years ago, they would ever face a problem like this one.

OCT
13th

"If you go to full term, the baby could be stillborn," the doctor said gravely.

"But is there at least a chance of our daughter being born all right?" asked Derek.

"Very small."

"What do we do, Derek?" Amelia pleaded with her husband.

"We've got to pray about this," Derek resolved.

Amelia and Derek had always thought there wouldn't be any problems once they started a family. They had waited because they wanted to make sure they were mature enough to be parents, but now it seemed their first child wasn't going to survive.

"I think we should go full term," Amelia finally said after she and Derek had arrived home. "I know the situation looks bleak, but we've prayed about having kids and we believed God was going to bless us to be parents."

Amelia and Derek put their faith in God's promise, and not only was their daughter born healthy, but they are now in the process of adopting a son.

Sometimes a situation may look just as impossible as it did for Abraham and Sarah. However, today's lesson teaches that no matter the circumstances, God keeps His promises.

Keep in Mind

"For Sarah conceived, and bare Abraham a son in his old age, at the set time of which God had spoken to him" (Genesis 21:2).

"For Sarah conceived, and bare Abraham a son in his old age, at the set time of which God had spoken to him" (Genesis 21:2).

Focal Verses

KJV **Genesis 17:15** And God said unto Abraham, As for Sarai thy wife, thou shalt not call her name Sarai, but Sarah shall her name be.

16 And I will bless her, and give thee a son also of her: yea, I will bless her, and she shall be a mother of nations; kings of people shall be of her.

17 Then Abraham fell upon his face, and laughed, and said in his heart, Shall a child be born unto him that is an hundred years old? and shall Sarah, that is ninety years old, bear?

18:9 And they said unto him, Where is Sarah thy wife? And he said, Behold, in the tent.

10 And he said, I will certainly return unto thee according to the time of life; and, lo, Sarah thy wife shall have a son. And Sarah heard it in the tent door, which was behind him.

11 Now Abraham and Sarah were old and well stricken in age; and it ceased to be with Sarah after the manner of women.

12 Therefore Sarah laughed within herself, saying, After I am waxed old shall I have pleasure, my lord being old also?

13 And the LORD said unto Abraham, Wherefore did Sarah laugh, saying, Shall I of a surety bear a child, which am old?

14 Is any thing too hard for the LORD? At the time appointed I will return unto thee, according to the time of life, and Sarah shall have a son.

15 Then Sarah denied, saying, I laughed not; for she was afraid. And he said, Nay; but thou didst laugh.

21:1 And the LORD visited Sarah as he had said, and the LORD did unto Sarah as he had spoken.

NLT **Genesis 17:15** Then God said to Abraham, "Regarding Sarai, your wife—her name will no longer be Sarai. From now on her name will be Sarah.

16 And I will bless her and give you a son from her! Yes, I will bless her richly, and she will become the mother of many nations. Kings of nations will be among her descendants."

17 Then Abraham bowed down to the ground, but he laughed to himself in disbelief. "How could I become a father at the age of 100?" he thought. "And how can Sarah have a baby when she is ninety years old?"

18:9 "Where is Sarah, your wife?" the visitors asked.

"She's inside the tent," Abraham replied.

10 Then one of them said, "I will return to you about this time next year, and your wife, Sarah, will have a son!"

Sarah was listening to this conversation from the tent.

11 Abraham and Sarah were both very old by this time, and Sarah was long past the age of having children.

12 So she laughed silently to herself and said, "How could a worn-out woman like me enjoy such pleasure, especially when my master—my husband—is also so old?"

13 Then the LORD said to Abraham, "Why did Sarah laugh? Why did she say, 'Can an old woman like me have a baby?'

14 Is anything too hard for the LORD? I will return about this time next year, and Sarah will have a son."

15 Sarah was afraid, so she denied it, saying, "I didn't laugh." But the LORD said, "No, you did laugh."

21:1 The LORD kept his word and did for Sarah exactly what he had promised.

2 For Sarah conceived, and bare Abraham a son in his old age, at the set time of which God had spoken to him.

3 And Abraham called the name of his son that was born unto him, whom Sarah bare to him, Isaac.

4 And Abraham circumcised his son Isaac being eight days old, as God had commanded him.

5 And Abraham was an hundred years old, when his son Isaac was born unto him.

6 And Sarah said, God hath made me to laugh, so that all that hear will laugh with me.

7 And she said, Who would have said unto Abraham, that Sarah should have given children suck? for I have born him a son in his old age.

2 She became pregnant, and she gave birth to a son for Abraham in his old age. This happened at just the time God had said it would.

3 And Abraham named their son Isaac.

4 Eight days after Isaac was born, Abraham circumcised him as God had commanded.

5 Abraham was 100 years old when Isaac was born.

6 And Sarah declared, "God has brought me laughter. All who hear about this will laugh with me.

7 Who would have said to Abraham that Sarah would nurse a baby? Yet I have given Abraham a son in his old age!"

The People, Places, and Times

Childlessness. The culture of Abraham and Sarah was a patriarchal one in which inheritance was handed down from father to son. Therefore, it was of the utmost importance for a woman to have children because "childlessness threatened the very perpetuation of the political and economic structure of [their] society" (Redford, *The Pentateuch*, 74). If a wife was barren, she was of little worth and considered cursed. There were a few options for childless couples—they could adopt a servant or have children by surrogacy. If a wife made her servant a surrogate for her husband, the child would actually belong to the wife. Although this was the custom, surrogacy was not without its troubles, as Scripture illustrates in the rancor among Sarah, her maid Hagar, and Abraham.

Bedouin tent. The Bedouins are a nomadic people who have been desert dwellers for thousands of years. They live in tents, allowing them to break camp whenever they need to move. Abraham lived the nomadic lifestyle and would have lived in a tent like the Bedouins. The tents in Bible times were larger than the tents of today. Abraham's tent would have had at least two sections. The front section was where the men lived and received guests. When it was warm, this section could be opened. The section for women was separated from the men by a curtain made of goat hair. Some tents had a third section for servants or cattle.

Background

In His initial message, God told Abraham, who was still called Abram, to leave his home (Genesis 12:1). He promised to make Abram a great nation, make his name great, and make him a blessing to the entire world (vv. 2–3). Once in Canaan, God spoke to Abram a second time, saying He would give the land to Abram's descendants (12:7). In the third communication, God was more specific about what part of Canaan He would give to Abram's offspring, who would be "like the dust of the earth" (13:16, NIV). Genesis 15 encompasses God's fourth communication with Abram. 1) God said Abram's heir would be from his own flesh, and his descendants would be as numerous as the stars (vv. 4–5). 2) God reiterated that Canaan would belong to Abram (v. 7) through his descendants, who would endure four hundred years of enslavement (vv. 12–17) before taking possession. 3) God was even more specific about the land Abram's offspring would possess (vv. 18–21). Today's lesson text begins in the midst of God's fifth communication with Abram. Twenty-four years had passed since God made His initial promise to Abram, and God was explicit about the details of the promise. God changed Abram's name to Abraham to reflect that he would be the father of many nations. There would be kings in his lineage, God would always be their God, and Canaan would be their land forever (17:4–8). As a sign of this covenant, Abraham and all the males in his house were circumcised and, thereafter, each male would be circumcised at eight days old (vv. 9–14).

At-A-Glance

1. Sarah's Part in the Promise
(Genesis 17:15–17)
2. The Promise Confirmed (18:9–15)
3. The Promise Kept (21:1–7)

In Depth

1. Sarah's Part in the Promise (Genesis 17:15–17)

Each time God spoke with Abraham in the past, He never mentioned Sarai. We know that she was barren (16:1), which would have made God's covenant impossible. Abraham was perplexed by the situation. "O Sovereign LORD, what good are all your blessings when I don't even have a son? Since you've given me no children, Eliezer of Damascus, a servant in my household, will inherit all my wealth. You have given me no descendants of my own, so one of my servants will be my heir" (from Genesis 15:2–3, NLT). However, God reassured His servant that his heir would be of his flesh. This would have been devastating news for Sarai.

Because of her barrenness, Sarai would have believed surrogacy was her only recourse. Imagine the hurt and shame she already carried being exacerbated by her incapability to provide the child of the promise. She decided to help God's promise by suggesting Abraham sleep with her maid, Hagar. From their union, Ishmael was born (16:15). However, God never needs our help to accomplish His promises; we need only to obey and wait in faith. God had a plan and the power to bring it to pass. The child of the promise would come through Sarai, who would now be called Sarah, for she would be the "mother of many nations" (17:16, NLT). Sarai and Sarah both mean "princess," but the latter has the added distinction of noblewoman, the "wife of a king of noble birth" (Vine). The name change signifies that Sarah's life had changed directions. God was not only moving her from barrenness but also into nobility. Kings would be among her descendants. Abraham laughed to himself at the notion that he and Sarah, both advanced in age, could actually conceive a child. Instead of Abraham's laughter denoting disbelief as some believe, perhaps the sentiment is amazement because "Abraham never wavered in believing God's promise. In fact, his faith grew stronger, and in this he brought glory to God. He was fully convinced that God is able to do whatever he promises" (Romans 4:20–21, NLT).

2. The Promise Confirmed (18:9–15)

After finding out Sarah was included in the promise, Abraham was still in a waiting position—the perfect opportunity for faith to grow. In the meantime, three heavenly guests—God and two angels (Genesis 19:1)—pay him a visit and confirm the promise. After eating and resting, the guests inquired after Sarah, who, as was the custom, had gone back to her part of the tent after serving the men. She overheard the Lord say, "I will return to you about this time next year, and your wife, Sarah, will have a son!" (from 18:10, NLT). Judging from her reaction, Abraham probably had not told her she was included in God's promise. Sarah, of course, thought this claim to be impossible and laughable. After all, she and Abraham were extremely advanced in age, she was beyond her childbearing years, and even if she had been a younger woman, she was still barren. Sarah was not aware that God had heard what she believed to have been a quiet comment to herself.

God appeared to be speaking only to Abraham when He asked him why Sarah laughed. He was, however, also addressing Sarah. To be told that all the years of hurt and shame would soon be over would have been unfathomable were it not for God. "Is anything too hard for the LORD? I will return about this time next year, and Sarah will have a son" (18:14, NLT). In the Complete Jewish Bible, the word for Lord here is *Adonai*, which means "Master," someone with total authority. As *Adonai*, God has complete possession of His servant and is solely responsible for the "provision and protection" (Stone, *Names of God*) of His servant, and whatever He says will happen. Therefore, whenever God makes a promise, it, in essence, is already done. A servant of God need only trust, obey, and wait faithfully.

3. The Promise Kept (21:1–7)

God certainly kept His promise because Sarah became pregnant and gave birth exactly at the time He had ordained (21:2). It was now twenty-five years since God had called Abraham to leave his home. As God commanded, Abraham named their son Isaac (17:19) and circumcised the boy at eight days old as a sign of the covenant. Isaac's name means "he laughs," and Sarah did laugh again, but this time it was evidence of her joy, not disbelief. "And Sarah declared, 'God has brought me laughter. All who hear about this will laugh with me. Who would have said to Abraham that Sarah would nurse a baby? Yet I have given Abraham a son in his old age!'" (21:6–7, NLT). One can gather that the pain of all the years of her barrenness was nothing compared to the depth of Sarah's gratitude. "When mercies have been long deferred, they are the more welcome when they come" (Henry). And we can rejoice with her because if God would accomplish the impossible for her, He would accomplish the same for all who put their faith in Him. Deferred promises are never denied promises.

Search the Scriptures

1. What did God promise Sarah (Genesis 17:16)?

2. What was God's response to Sarah's laughter (18:13–14)?

Discuss the Meaning

If God already knew that Sarah was part of His promise to Abraham, why do you think He waited to tell him? What is the purpose of delayed promises?

Lesson in Our Society

Many of us face hardships daily, yet we continue to press on because God has promised us that He will never forsake us and that

He is working for our good. But what if the promises of God seem to take too long? The story of Abraham and Sarah encourages us to remain hopeful because no matter how bleak the situation, God will keep His word. After all, He has already kept His ultimate promise because through Abraham and Sarah, He provided the way to salvation, Jesus Christ.

Make It Happen

We focus so much on waiting for a promise from God that we forget all He has already done. The next week, take time each morning to prayerfully write down at least three promises God has already kept for you. At the end of the week, set aside time to thank God for His faithfulness. Hang this list of promises where you can see it every day to help you remember to be thankful.

Follow the Spirit

What God wants me to do:

_____

_____

_____

_____

Remember Your Thoughts

Special insights I have learned:

_____

_____

_____

_____

More Light on the Text

Genesis 17:15–17, 18:9–15, 21:1–7

15 And God said unto Abraham, As for Sarai thy wife, thou shalt not call her name Sarai, but Sarah shall her name be. 16 And I will bless her, and give thee a son also of her: yea, I will bless her, and she shall be a mother of nations; kings of people shall be of her.

According to Jewish tradition, Sarah was one of the most beautiful women in the world, but to be barren in a patriarchal society was to be considered almost worthless. However, God elevated Sarah to be the mother of the Jewish people. When we read the ancestry lists in Scripture, heirs are assumed to come through the father; the mother is seldom mentioned. But here we see that the promised child came not just through Abraham, but also through Sarah. Both Sarai and Sarah have the same meaning—princess—but this renaming emphasizes that nations and kings will come from the descendants of the marriage of Sarah and Abraham. Sarai is the older form of the word, and this renaming is meant to emphasize to Abraham that Sarah was his God-given wife and as such, the promised nation would come through her as well as through him.

17 Then Abraham fell upon his face, and laughed, and said in his heart, Shall a child be born unto him that is an hundred years old? and shall Sarah, that is ninety years old, bear?

The Hebrew for "laughed" is *tsachaq* (**tsaw-KHAK**). Laughter was a theme throughout the promised birth of Isaac. Was God playing a joke on Abraham? It had been thirteen years since Ishmael was born. Is a man who is a hundred years old even capable of having sex? And not only was Sarah 90 years old, but she had demonstrated her inability to bear children when she was younger. The Hebrew word for "laughed" does not tell us what was going on in Abraham's mind. Was he laughing at the incongruity of a child coming from a union of himself with Sarah? Or was his laugh scornful, demonstrating his lack of belief in God's ability to bring this about? We see in Abraham's situation that God is going to bring about the fulfillment of His promise only when it is obviously impossible from a human standpoint. This is often the way God works in our lives. It is only when we have come to the end of our own resources that He demonstrates His ability to do all that He has promised.

18:9 And they said unto him, Where is Sarah thy wife? And he said, Behold, in the tent. 10 And he said, I will certainly return unto thee according to the time of life; and, lo, Sarah thy wife shall have a son. And Sarah heard it in the tent door, which was behind him.

Now we make a jump in the biblical story. After the visit of the Lord to Abraham in chapter 17, Abraham immediately circumcised Ishmael and all the other males in his household. Chapter 18 begins with another visit from the Lord, shortly after the first. This time God communicated through three beings that appeared as men who were traveling through the region. Abraham graciously entertained these strangers. After Sarah quickly made a meal according to Abraham's instructions, she kept in the background, as was the custom. But in this home full of rivalry and jealousy between wife and concubine, motherhood and barrenness, Sarah hid behind the curtain to listen in on the conversation of the men. However, the men visiting with Abraham were no ordinary men. One was probably the Lord Himself (an earthly appearance of God before the incarnation of our Savior, called a "theophany"), and

the other two were definitely angels. We are told in Hebrews 13:2 that we should be sure to practice hospitality to strangers just as Abraham did because, although he did not know it, he was entertaining angels.

After Abraham indicated that Sarah was inside the tent, the holy Spokesman made a promise that He would return "according to the time of life" (v. 14, Heb. *attah chiyel*, **at-TAW khee-ALE**). This was understood to mean in the spring of the year, when life is returning. At this moment, God was appearing to Abraham and Sarah in the form of a man, but when He returned, it was to be *hinneh* (**hin-NAY, "**behold" or "lo") in the form of the fulfillment of His promise—a son.

11 Now Abraham and Sarah were old and well stricken in age; and it ceased to be with Sarah after the manner of women.

We are reminded again that Abraham and Sarah were both physically beyond the years of childbearing. In fact, Sarah had ceased to be "after the manner of women," a euphemism for menopause.

12 Therefore Sarah laughed within herself, saying, After I am waxed old shall I have pleasure, my lord being old also?

Sarah was feeling dried up with age, and rightly assumed that Abraham was also. The Hebrew word for pleasure is *eden* (**AY-den**), which comes from the word for the Garden of Eden, the garden of pleasure, and here implies sexual pleasure. Evidently, it had been years since Abraham and Sarah had enjoyed sex together. And the thought of having a baby was also delightful to her who had longed for a child for so many years.

13 And the LORD said unto Abraham, Wherefore did Sarah laugh, saying, Shall I of a surety bear a child, which am old? 14 Is any thing too hard for the LORD? At

the time appointed I will return unto thee, according to the time of life, and Sarah shall have a son.

Sarah was laughing within herself at the thought of having sex and having a baby at her age. Evidently, Abraham had never shared with her the previous message from God (17:15–16). He must have continued to have some doubts. So the Lord asked two rhetorical questions, not expecting any answers: "Wherefore did Sarah laugh?" and "Is any thing too hard for the LORD?" Of course, nothing is too hard for the Lord. The Hebrew for "hard" is *pele* (**PEH-leh**) and means much more than difficult; it means that nothing is too miraculous, too marvelous, or too wonderful for God to do. So, in verse 14, God repeated that He would fulfill the promise He made in verse 10, word for word.

15 Then Sarah denied, saying, I laughed not; for she was afraid. And he said, Nay; but thou didst laugh.

Sarah was caught in the act. God revealed that He knew exactly what she was thinking. And He also knew that her denial was because she was afraid—God understood how she felt, even though He made sure she knew that He could see her heart.

21:1 And the LORD visited Sarah as he had said, and the LORD did unto Sarah as he had spoken. 2 For Sarah conceived, and bare Abraham a son in his old age, at the set time of which God had spoken to him.

Chapter 19 tells the parenthetical narrative of Sodom and Gomorrah. Then, chapter 20 recounts another disappointing story regarding Abraham. In chapter 12, Abraham passed Sarai as his sister, and Pharaoh took her into his harem. Now Abraham repeated this same awful behavior—passing Sarah as his sister to Abimelech, king of Gerar. Perhaps God was protecting Abraham and

Sarah from conceiving babies with these foreign kings through her barrenness. Not only did God cause infertility in the households of these foreign kings, but it appears that the ability of the kings to engage in sex was also interrupted.

Finally, when it was God's time, Sarah conceived a son with Abraham. In the first verse are four phrases that emphasize the work of God in fulfilling His promises to Abraham and Sarah. "The LORD visited" and "the LORD did" speak of God's actions in fulfilling the promises; "as he had said" and "as he had spoken" refer to His promises that were spoken to Abraham and Sarah. Verse 2 gives us the specifics as to how God fulfilled His promise—Sarah became pregnant and gave birth to a son at just the time that God had promised. The Hebrew word for this timeliness is *ittiy* (**it-TEE),** and it echoes the words of the promise in 17:21 and 18:14. This reminds us of the old adage from our ancestors, "God may not come when you want Him to, but He always comes on time."

3 And Abraham called the name of his son that was born unto him, whom Sarah bare to him, Isaac. 4 And Abraham circumcised his son Isaac being eight days old, as God had commanded him.

Here we see the theme of laughter again as Abraham named the child as God commanded (17:19). The Hebrew pronunciation of the name Isaac is *Yitschaq* (**yits-KHAWK**), meaning laughter. In this case, it was not the laughter of scorn, nervousness, or mockery, but the laughter of pure joy. And in another example of obedience, Abraham personally circumcised Isaac on the eighth day of his life (v. 12).

5 And Abraham was an hundred years old, when his son Isaac was born unto him. 6 And Sarah said, God hath made me to

laugh, so that all that hear will laugh with me. 7 And she said, Who would have said unto Abraham, that Sarah should have given children suck? for I have born him a son in his old age.

Sarah was again laughing, but this time we see a very happy mother who had waited many years to finally have a child. She had endured so much, but finally she took her place as the mother of the child of promise. No longer were people laughing at her barrenness; now they were joining her in the laughter of joy. Jewish tradition interprets the seventh verse to mean that all the mothers of infants passed their children to Sarah, and she nursed every one to proudly prove her maternal accomplishment and ability. God had given Sarah this wonderful gift of the promised son, and she was so happy she was bubbling over with laughter. And that is just how God works to fulfill His promises to us. He usually does things in totally different ways than we expect, but He gives abundantly to us and answers our prayers.

Sources:
Abu-Rabi'a, Aref, Dr. *Bedouin Century: Education and Development Among the Negev Tribes in the Twentieth Century*. New York: Berghahn Books, 2001. 1.

Beers, V. Gilbert. *The Victory Journey Through the Bible*. Colorado Springs: Cook Communications Ministries, 1996. 22.

BibleGateway.com. *The Holy Bible*, New Living Translation. Wheaton, Illinois: Tyndale House, 2007 (accessed July 24, 2012).

Bible Study Tools. www.BibleStudyTools.com. "Old Testament Hebrew Lexicon—King James Version." http://www.biblestudytools.com/lexicons/hebrew/kjv/sarah-3.html, http://www.biblestudytools.com/lexicons/hebrew/kjv/saray.html (accessed July 27, 2012).

Garrett, Duane and Walter C. Kaiser, Jr. *NIV Archaeological Study Bible: An Illustrated Walk Through Biblical History*. Grand Rapids, MI : Zondervan, 2005.

Henry, Matthew. "Genesis." *Matthew Henry's Commentary on the Whole Bible, Vol. 1 (Genesis to Deuteronomy)*. Genesis 18, 19, 22. http://www.ccel.org/ccel/henry/mhc1.Gen.xviii.html, http://www.ccel.org/ccel/henry/mhc1.Gen.xix.html, http://www.ccel.org/ccel/henry/mhc1.Gen.xxii.html (accessed July 20, 2012).

"Housing: Nomadic Tents." Architecture of the Bible. http://www.bible-architecture.info/Housing.htm (accessed July 28, 2012).

Janzen, J. Gerald, Fredrick Carlson Holmgren, and George Angus Fulton Knight. *Abraham and All the Families of the Earth: A Commentary on the Book of Genesis 12–50*. Grand Rapids, MI: Wm. B. Eerdmans Publishing Company, 1993.

Jeansonne, Sharon Pace. *The Women of Genesis: From Sarah to Potiphar's Wife*. Minneapolis: Augsburg Fortress, 1990.

Kroeger, Catherine Clark and Mary J. Evans. *The IVP Women's Bible Commentary*. Downers Grove, IL: InterVarsity Press, 2002.

Mathews, Kenneth A. *Genesis 11:27–50:26, Vol. 1B. The New American Commentary*. Nashville: Broadman and Holman Publishers, 2005.

Redford, Doug. *The Pentateuch, Vol. 1, Genesis to Deuteronomy*. Cincinnati, OH: Standard Publishing, 2008. 74.

"Sarah." *Vine's Complete Expository Dictionary of Old and New Testament Word*s. Vine, W. E. http://www.blueletterbible.org/lang/lexicon/lexicon.cfm?Strongs=H8283&t=KJV. (accessed July 26, 2012).

Stern, David H. *The Complete Jewish Bible*. Jewish New Testament Publications, 1988. http://www.biblegateway.com/passage/?search=Genesis%2018&version=CJB (accessed July 29, 2012).

Stone, Nathan. *Names of God*. Chicago: Moody Publishers, 2010. 61–65.

Strong, James. Free Bible Study Tools. *Strong's Concordance with Greek and Hebrew Lexicon*. http://www.tgm.org/bible.htm (accessed July 24, 2012).

Strong, James. *Strong's Concordance with Hebrew and Greek Lexicon*. http://www.eliyah.com/lexicon.html (accessed October 10, 2012).

Ten Names of God Rose Publishing e-Chart. Rose Publishing, 2008. www.rose-publishing.com (accessed July 29, 2012).

Say It Correctly

Circumcised. **SIR**-cum-sized.
Rhetorical. re-**TOR**-i-cal.
Theophany. the-**OFF**-an-ee.

Daily Bible Readings

MONDAY
A Childless Wife
(Genesis 11:27–32)

TUESDAY
A Beautiful Wife
(Genesis 12:10–20)

WEDNESDAY
A Threatened Wife
(Genesis 16:1–6)

THURSDAY
The Promise of a Covenant
(Genesis 17:18–22)

FRIDAY
Dispelling the Competition
(Genesis 21:8–14)

SATURDAY
Mourning a Beloved Wife
(Genesis 23:1–6)

SUNDAY
Bearing a Child of Promise
(Genesis 17:15–17; 18:9–15; 21:1–7)

Notes

_____

_____

_____

_____

Teaching Tips

Words You Should Know

A. Bondwoman (Genesis 21:13) *amah* (Heb.)—A maidservant or a female slave.

B. Opened (v. 19) *paquach* (Heb.)—Made to be observant.

C. Waxed great (26:13) *gadal* (Heb.)—Implies being made large in body, mind, and property.

Teacher Preparation

Unifying Principle—Sibling Rivalry. The circumstances surrounding one's birth can affect a child's identity and self-worth. Where does a child find his or her identity and self-worth? Despite the circumstances surrounding their births, God promised to create great nations through Ishmael and Isaac.

A. Pray and ask God to bring clarity to this lesson.

B. Read Genesis 21 and 26 in their entirety.

C. Note various examples of sibling rivalry that occur in the Bible.

O—Open the Lesson

A. Open with prayer.

B. Ask the class to read the Keep in Mind verses in unison.

C. Ask a volunteer to read the In Focus story.

D. Ask your students to give examples of sibling rivalry that occur in the Bible. Have them share their lists with the class.

E. Ask students to share examples of sibling rivalry from their own lives.

P—Present the Scriptures

A. Ask for two or three volunteers to read the Focal Verses.

B. Now use The People, Places, and Times; Background; Search the Scriptures; At-A-Glance outline; In Depth; and More Light on the Text to clarify the verses.

E—Explore the Meaning

A. Divide the students into small groups and ask each group to talk about the Discuss the Meaning question. When the class reassembles, have a representative from each group report their group's response to the entire class.

B. Connect this section to the Aim for Change and the Keep in Mind verses.

N—Next Steps for Application

A. Ask for a volunteer to summarize the lesson.

B. Ask for a volunteer to close the class in prayer.

Worship Guide

For the Superintendent or Teacher
Theme: A Blessing for
Ishmael and Isaac
Song: "Standing on the Promises"
Devotional Reading: Hebrews 11:17–22

A Blessing for Ishmael and Isaac

Bible Background • GENESIS 15:1–6; 16; 17:1–14, 18, 20–27; 21:9–21; 26:1–25
Printed Text • GENESIS 21:13–14, 17–21, 26:2–5, 12–13
Devotional Reading • HEBREWS 11:17–22

Aim for Change

By the end of the lesson, participants will: EXPLORE the implications of the blessing God gave to Isaac and Ishmael; CONFESS any jealousies that stand in the way of loving God and neighbor as believers should; and PRAY for world peace, including peace among people of all faiths.

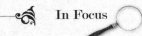 **In Focus**

Carol slowly opened the envelope. She already knew what was inside. Since age 13, Carol's father sent her a birthday card and enclosed a $100 check. Her father had never really been a part of her life, and a part of her resented this annual token "gift" from him.

Carol was the oldest of his three daughters; her younger half-sisters, Vivian and Shirley, lived with her dad and his new wife, their mother. Carol's father and her mom had dated in high school. When Carol's mother became pregnant, her father broke all ties. He sent regular child support payments, but rarely visited Carol, even though they lived in the same city. If they happened to bump into one another at stores or on the street, he would say hello and then claim to have to hurry off somewhere.

OCT 20th

When she graduated from high school, he had sent a note congratulating her and a check. Friends told her that he attended the graduations of both her sisters and had showered each one with floral bouquets. In a few months, Carol would graduate from college with honors. She already knew that her father would have some excuse for not attending. She knew there would probably be another note and a check.

In today's lesson, we will see how the circumstances of birth can cruelly separate siblings. Only through the loving kindness of God do justice and fairness come into fruition.

Keep in Mind

"In all that Sarah hath said unto thee, hearken unto her voice; for in Isaac shall thy seed be called. And also of the son of the bondwoman will I make a nation, because he is thy seed" (from Genesis 21:12–13).

"In all that Sarah hath said unto thee, hearken unto her voice; for in Isaac shall thy seed be called. And also of the son of the bondwoman will I make a nation, because he is thy seed" (from Genesis 21:12–13).

Focal Verses

KJV **Genesis 21:13** And also of the son of the bondwoman will I make a nation, because he is thy seed.

14 And Abraham rose up early in the morning, and took bread, and a bottle of water, and gave it unto Hagar, putting it on her shoulder, and the child, and sent her away: and she departed, and wandered in the wilderness of Beersheba.

21:17 And God heard the voice of the lad; and the angel of God called to Hagar out of heaven, and said unto her, What aileth thee, Hagar? fear not; for God hath heard the voice of the lad where he is.

18 Arise, lift up the lad, and hold him in thine hand; for I will make him a great nation.

19 And God opened her eyes, and she saw a well of water; and she went, and filled the bottle with water, and gave the lad drink.

20 And God was with the lad; and he grew, and dwelt in the wilderness, and became an archer.

21 And he dwelt in the wilderness of Paran: and his mother took him a wife out of the land of Egypt.

26:2 And the LORD appeared unto him, and said, Go not down into Egypt; dwell in the land which I shall tell thee of:

3 Sojourn in this land, and I will be with thee, and will bless thee; for unto thee, and unto thy seed, I will give all these countries, and I will perform the oath which I sware unto Abraham thy father;

4 And I will make thy seed to multiply as the stars of heaven, and will give unto thy seed all these countries; and in thy seed shall all the nations of the earth be blessed;

5 Because that Abraham obeyed my voice, and kept my charge, my commandments, my statutes, and my laws.

NLT **Genesis 21:13** "But I will also make a nation of the descendants of Hagar's son because he is your son, too."

14 So Abraham got up early the next morning, prepared food and a container of water, and strapped them on Hagar's shoulders. Then he sent her away with their son, and she wandered aimlessly in the wilderness of Beersheba.

21:17 But God heard the boy crying, and the angel of God called to Hagar from heaven, "Hagar, what's wrong? Do not be afraid! God has heard the boy crying as he lies there.

18 Go to him and comfort him, for I will make a great nation from his descendants."

19 Then God opened Hagar's eyes, and she saw a well full of water. She quickly filled her water container and gave the boy a drink.

20 And God was with the boy as he grew up in the wilderness. He became a skillful archer,

21 and he settled in the wilderness of Paran. His mother arranged for him to marry a woman from the land of Egypt.

26:2 The LORD appeared to Isaac and said, "Do not go down to Egypt, but do as I tell you.

3 Live here as a foreigner in this land, and I will be with you and bless you. I hereby confirm that I will give all these lands to you and your descendants, just as I solemnly promised Abraham, your father.

4 I will cause your descendants to become as numerous as the stars of the sky, and I will give them all these lands. And through your descendants all the nations of the earth will be blessed.

5 I will do this because Abraham listened to me and obeyed all my requirements, commands, decrees, and instructions."

26:12 Then Isaac sowed in that land, and received in the same year an hundredfold: and the LORD blessed him.

13 And the man waxed great, and went forward, and grew until he became very great.

26:12 When Isaac planted his crops that year, he harvested a hundred times more grain than he planted, for the LORD blessed him.

13 He became a very rich man, and his wealth continued to grow.

The People, Places, and Times

Hagar. Hagar was an Egyptian girl who lived as a slave in the household of Abraham and Sarah. Although the Bible does not tell us, it is reasonable to assume that Hagar may have been a part of a generous dowry paid to Abraham by Pharaoh (12:10–20). Giving slaves was a widely accepted practice. If this theory is correct, then it is easy for us to see that Hagar was at a distinct advantage among Sarah and the other Hebrew women. She had come from Egypt, a land that was economically, socially, and politically advanced. Now she was the property of a nomadic tribeswoman. She was both a foreigner and a slave among a people whose living conditions must have seemed quite primitive to her.

Concubines. In the ancient world, it was not unusual for men in power to have both wives and concubines. Concubines served many of the same roles as wives. The primary difference was their inability to actually marry the man. Often, this was a socioeconomic issue. If the concubine was a slave, then she could not marry her master.

Reasons for the practice of concubinage are numerous. Poor families could find financial relief by selling their daughters (Exodus 21:7–11; Judges 19:1). A concubine was often used to provide male heirs for a barren wife (Genesis 16:15–16) and often for multiplying both the available family workforce and the family wealth and status. Concubinage was also used to solidify political relationships between nations. Royal wives were sometimes inherited by succeeding kings (2 Samuel 12:8). We read of concubinage in the early Israelite history. Though they did not have the same status as the wife, concubines were not to be mistreated (Exodus 21:7–11) and were protected from being violated by other men (Genesis 35:22, 49:3–4). The sons of concubines were often treated as co-heirs with the sons of wives.

Background

Not only does God make promises, He can be counted on to keep them. God promised Abraham that not only would he have a son, God would also "make thy seed as the dust of the earth: so that if a man can number the dust of the earth, then shall thy seed also be numbered" (from 13:16). Abraham was already an old man when God made this promise, and his wife, Sarah, was past childbearing age. More than ten years went by and still Abraham had no child. So it is not that surprising that Abraham had grown doubtful. Instead of trusting God to do what He said He would, Abraham foolishly listened to his wife, Sarah. She proposed that Abraham take her Egyptian slave, Hagar, as a concubine and father children through her. Hagar became pregnant and the domestic situation between the two women became so hostile that Hagar ran away.

Hagar was intercepted by the angel of the Lord on her way back to Egypt. The angel, perhaps a pre-incarnate presence of Jesus, told Hagar, "Return to thy mistress [Sarah], and submit thyself under her hands. . . . I will multiply thy seed exceedingly, that it shall not be numbered for multitude" (from 16:9–10).

Hagar believed that God would keep His promise to her, and she returned to Abraham and Sarah. Perhaps Hagar understood that if God could be with her in the wilderness, He could be with her in having to submit to Sarah. This is a wonderful reminder to us. We often want to run away from our problems, but God wants to demonstrate His power in the midst of our problems. When her son was born, Hagar obeyed the instructions she had received from the angel and named him Ishmael, which means "God hears."

At-A-Glance

1. God's Promise for Ishmael
(Genesis 21:13–14)
2. God's Protection and Provision for
Ishmael (vv. 17–21)
3. God's Promise for Isaac
(26:2–5, 12–13)

In Depth

1. God's Promise for Ishmael
(Genesis 21:13–14)

When a son was finally born to him, Abraham was 99 years old. It had been 24 years since he had obeyed the call of God and left his homeland of Haran (12:1–3). After he separated from his nephew, Lot, Abraham enjoyed the favor of God, including his defeating the eastern alliance of kings. God made a formal covenant with this faithful servant that specified three particular promises. First, Abraham would father a child of his own body (15:4). Second, Abraham was told what will become of his offspring for the next several generations (vv. 12–16). Finally, he would come to possess a specific land (vv. 18–21).

Abraham's reliance on God did waver, however. Instead of trusting God, Abraham placed his trust in himself. He attempted to produce the heir God had promised by taking Sarah's slave, Hagar, as a concubine and fathering a child with her. Not surprisingly, this only led to hurt and heartache for all three of them. Abraham was not unlike present-day Christians. We sometimes lose faith when God does not "show up" when we want Him to. Rather than rely on Him and wait on Him, we grow anxious and turn instead to our own limited abilities.

2. God's Protection and Provision for Ishmael (vv. 17–21)

The strain of the relationships in Abraham's household became apparent during the celebration held for Isaac's weaning. During the festivities, Sarah saw Ishmael, now a teenager, mocking her son Isaac. Sarah was outraged. All the resentment she felt toward Hagar and Ishmael spilled out. She demanded that Abraham expel Hagar and Ishmael from the encampment. We must remember that even the slaves within the tribal group enjoyed the food, shelter, and protection of the camp. Now Sarah demanded that these vital means of survival be removed from Hagar and Ishmael. Sarah's motivation was clear: Ishmael must not share in any part of her son Isaac's inheritance. This is especially heartbreaking when we consider that God had already made a promise to Sarah and Abraham concerning the inheritance that would be given to Isaac.

Of course, the idea of sending Ishmael away made Abraham very unhappy as he had, no doubt, grown to love his firstborn son. However, God instructed Abraham to "hearken unto her voice." God reminded Abraham "in Isaac shall thy seed be called" (v. 12). God reminded Abraham that Ishmael was the product of his and Sarah's impatience, while Isaac was the child of God's promise.

Because God is a promise keeper, He offered Abraham this reassurance: "And also of the son of the bondwoman will I make a nation, because he is thy seed" (v. 13).

The continued presence of Hagar and Ishmael placed a psychological strain on Sarah, however, and she wanted the discomfort to end. Sarah's desire for a "quick fix" should remind us of ourselves. We want our problems and worries to end—quickly! We often take actions that are not motivated by love but by our own selfishness. It is in these dark and difficult times that we must draw near to God and seek His wisdom and strength. It is only when we follow direction from God that we can we get through those dark and bitter experiences. As He did with Abraham and Sarah, God has made us promises. He has promised us freedom from stress and worry (Philippians 4:6–7; Psalm 91:1; Matthew 11:29), hope (Psalm 33:18; Colossians 1:27; 1 Peter 1:3), forgiveness (1 John 1:9; Psalm 103:12; Isaiah 1:18), and eternal life (John 3:16, 36, 4:14). Our realization of God's promises is predicated upon our obedience to Him.

It would appear that Ishmael was a casualty in the domestic strife between his parents; however, verses 21–27 make it clear that God had not forgotten His promise to Abraham, and that He fully intended to protect and provide for Abraham's firstborn son. After Abraham expelled Hagar and Ishmael, they quickly ran out of water. Verse 17 lets us know that the omniscient God was aware of everything going on, including their distress: God heard Ishmael crying. Once again God revealed Himself to Hagar and repeated His promise to provide for her son. He would, God assured Hagar again, "make him a great nation" (v. 18). Here we see that not only was God concerned about Ishmael's immediate needs (water and shelter), He had plans for Ishmael's future as well. God had no intention of allowing Abraham's firstborn son to die in the desert. He may not be the "promised child," but we see that God loved Ishmael as much as He loved Isaac. In verse 19, we read that God "opened her eyes, and she saw a well of water." Distress often has a blinding effect on us. Everything appears dark when we are troubled, and often we cannot clearly see our situation. As God ministered to Hagar in the desert, she was able to see what she could not see before: a well. This is a powerful reminder that we must continue to praise God even when we are at our wit's end. Thanking Him and praising Him is our "eye-opener."

3. God's Promise for Isaac (26:2–5, 12–13)

In the opening of Genesis 26, there was a famine in the land. This led Isaac, now a grown man, to seek out a safe haven for his tribe in a larger city where they would have a better chance of finding a regular food source. Gerar is located on the coast of the Mediterranean Sea in the territory belonging to the Philistine people. Isaac would have needed the permission of Abimelech, the Philistine king, to set up residency for his people. At some point, Isaac must have also considered moving his people forward into Egypt because we read that God appeared to him and told him not to go there.

Now God transferred to Isaac the blessings that He had given to Abraham. It is important to note that the promises were conditional and were preceded by God's warning to Isaac not to travel south into Egypt. Instead, God told Isaac to settle in a land that He would provide for him. God then transferred the future promises that He had laid out for Abraham to Isaac.

Not only would God be with Isaac, but He would bless him and give him a land for himself and his offspring. The continuation of God's promise to Isaac also included the establishment of the same covenant He had made with his father Abraham. God promised to multiply Isaac's offspring and give them the land. The culmination of the promise was that through Isaac, all of the nations would be blessed because Abraham had obeyed and kept God's commandments. Interestingly, we see in the entire remainder of the Bible the fulfillment of these promises made to Abraham and then to Isaac.

Search the Scriptures

1. Concerning Ishmael's future, what did God promise to Abraham and to Hagar (Genesis 21:13, 18)?

2. What were some of the blessings that God promised to Isaac (26:2–5)?

Discuss the Meaning

The strain between Sarah and Hagar was tremendous. When Sarah reached a breaking point, she demanded that her husband banish Hagar and Ishmael. What did this say about Sarah's consideration of her husband's feelings toward his son?

Lessons in Our Society

God offers constant reassurance to those who love Him. His promises are certain, but they require our complete obedience to Him and to His word. When we disobey God, we only invite dire consequences and difficulties into our lives. Rather than God's will being done in our lives, we often waste time trying to supplant His will with our ways. As He did for Abraham, God can work through any circumstances in our lives to bring His promises to fulfillment. Most of us have had the unhappy experience of making an agreement only to find that it profited us far less than we had hoped for and been led to expect. Just the opposite is true with God's promises. The more we learn of them, the richer the blessings they contain.

Make It Happen

Many of us know of situations of hurt and resentment within our own families. We know about fathers who have no relationships with their children, and siblings who have not spoken with one another in years. The causes for these estrangements are numerous, but the result is the same: bitterness and brokenness. Think about some of those situations in your family. Pray and ask God to use you to help reconcile family members.

Follow the Spirit

What God wants me to do:

_____

_____

_____

_____

Remember Your Thoughts

Special insights I have learned:

_____

_____

_____

_____

More Light on the Text

Genesis 21:13–14, 17–21, 26:2–5, 12–13

21:13 And also of the son of the bondwoman will I make a nation, because he is thy seed.

Abraham cared for both Ishmael and Hagar and did not want to abandon them, but God said it must be done. When Sarah talked Abraham into sleeping with her maid, she made a mess of many things. That's just what happens when we take matters into our own hands and do things our way instead of God's way. But God had compassion for Hagar, Ishmael, and all the Arab children that would be Ishmael's descendants. This, too, is the way God works. We may mess up His best plans, but He always knew the mistakes we'd make and is able to bring blessings in spite of it all. This is our wonderful God of grace and compassion.

The previous verse (v. 12) reminds us that Isaac was Abraham's seed, and in this verse the same Hebrew word for "seed" is used: *zera* (**ZEH-rah**), which can be translated as posterity. God created the Jewish people from Isaac, but He also created the Arab people from Ishmael's descendants. God created many nations from Abraham's descendants—both from Sarah and from Hagar. The Hebrew word for nation is *gowy* (**GO-ee**) and can be translated as people or nation. And as time passed, more nations branched off from Isaac's and Ishmael's descendants.

14 And Abraham rose up early in the morning, and took bread, and a bottle of water, and gave it unto Hagar, putting it on her shoulder, and the child, and sent her away: and she departed, and wandered in the wilderness of Beersheba.

Abraham made lots of mistakes, but we also see that when God gave him a direct command, he obeyed immediately, such as when he circumcised all the males in his household (17:23) and even more dramatically, when he started on the path to sacrifice Isaac (22:1–18). So Abraham got up early in the morning to send Hagar and Ishmael away from their home. This was a very difficult task for Abraham, but he did what he could to care for Hagar and Ishmael. Obeying God is not easy if we have already disrupted His perfect plans.

Hagar wandered about in the wilderness, having no home and no refuge. The first part of the place name Beersheba refers to a well, which was there, but Hagar didn't see it until it was supernaturally revealed to her. Beersheba (Heb. *Ber Sheba,* **be-AYR SHEH-bah**) means "well of the oath."

17 And God heard the voice of the lad; and the angel of God called to Hagar out of heaven, and said unto her, What aileth thee, Hagar? fear not; for God hath heard the voice of the lad where he is.

The Hebrew meaning for Ishmael (*Yishmael,* **yish-maw-ALE**) is "God will hear," and God heard Ishmael's cries. When Sarah initially sent the very pregnant Hagar away (16:6–11), God's eyes were upon her as she desperately stumbled about in the wilderness. God spoke to her, giving her the name for her son. Hagar had already experienced God's loving care for her and her son even before he was born. And now that she and Ishmael (probably about seventeen years old at this time) were exiled from their home, God was still watching over them both.

The angel of the Lord asked Hagar what was wrong. Surely God knew, but there is nothing more comforting than to have someone who knows you are suffering ask, "How are you?" This question lets us know that someone cares about how we are feeling. In His great compassion, God let Hagar know that He was aware of her desperate situation. Although the Ishmaelites were not God's chosen people, still God cares for them and for all who feel like outsiders.

18 Arise, lift up the lad, and hold him in thine hand; for I will make him a great nation. 19 And God opened her eyes, and she saw a well of water; and she went, and filled the bottle with water, and gave the lad drink.

This promise to Hagar and Ishmael was very similar to the promise made to Abraham in Genesis 12:2. God had promised to make Abraham into a great nation, and here He was making a similar promise to Ishmael as Abraham's descendant. But God made far greater promises to His chosen people, the Jews (12:2–3, 17:7–8, 18:18, 22:16–18), and these were the promises to Isaac, the son of both Abraham and Sarah.

God opened Hagar's eyes to see the well, so she quickly got water for her son, who was dehydrated almost to the point of death. Hagar knew exactly how to take care of Ishmael at this point.

20 And God was with the lad; and he grew, and dwelt in the wilderness, and became an archer. 21 And he dwelt in the wilderness of Paran: and his mother took him a wife out of the land of Egypt.

God enabled Ishmael to grow and become a man in his wilderness home. Becoming a skillful archer was necessary in this environment. Paran today is known as the Sinai Peninsula. It is hot and desert-like and is the bridge between Egypt and Israel. This was the wilderness that the Israelites wandered in for 40 years. It is now a part of Egypt—that part of the African continent that borders Israel. Bedouin herders still live in this area and are the descendants of Ishmael.

26:2 And the LORD appeared unto him, and said, Go not down into Egypt; dwell in the land which I shall tell thee of: 3 Sojourn in this land, and I will be with thee, and will bless thee; for unto thee, and unto thy seed, I will give all these countries, and I will perform the oath which I sware unto Abraham thy father; 4 And I will make thy seed to multiply as the stars of heaven, and will give unto thy seed all these countries; and in thy seed shall all the nations of the earth be blessed.

And now we shift the story to Isaac, son of Abraham and Sarah, the son of promise. By this time, both Abraham and Sarah had died and Isaac had married Rebekah. Abraham had been constantly on the move, a nomad traveling from one country to the next. He was a man of action with many dramatic things happening in his life.

But God called Isaac to a quiet life. He commanded him to stay right where he was. The Hebrew for "sojourn" is *guwr* (**goor**), meaning to remain, to be a stranger or a guest. Although Isaac was called to remain where he was, he was still a stranger in the land, just as God called Abraham to be. God moves in the lives of each individual in different ways. For those whose lives seem very quiet, God may still be leading, and it was to seemingly unremarkable Isaac that God first made the promise, "I will be with thee" (v. 3). This is the promise that we hear God make again and again to His people (Jacob, Moses, Joshua, Gideon, and to us today).

God chose Abraham to be the head of the family that became His chosen people, and He restated the promises to Isaac in these verses. The promise to multiply his descendants (Heb. *rabah,* **raw-BAW**) means to increase, to nourish. This was something God was doing, something that He was causing to happen. The word "countries" is plural (Heb. *erets,* **EH-rets**). The plural assumes that the chosen people would be replacing a number of small nations or city-states. God gave these nations plenty of time to repent—hundreds of years until Joshua led God's people in conquering the land. Although many people were dispossessed of their lands by the Hebrew people, this was necessary so that God could bless all the nations of the earth, because it was through the chosen people that God sent the Savior.

"Bless" is a word that is often tossed around by Christians without really thinking of what it means. The Hebrew word is *barak* (**baw-RAK**), and when we bless God, it means that we figuratively kneel in adoration to Him. But when He blesses us, it means that He provides benefits to us. In sending Jesus Christ through the family of Abraham and Isaac, God has given everyone the most wonderful blessing of all.

5 Because that Abraham obeyed my voice, and kept my charge, my commandments, my statutes, and my laws.

In 22:1–18, God gave Abraham the most awful test—the command to sacrifice Isaac, the son of God's promise to him and to Sarah. We know the story of how at the very last minute God provided a ram in the bush for the sacrifice (v. 13), but Abraham's total obedience was proved. Then in verse 18, we read the same words as we see here—because Abraham obeyed God's voice, God chose his descendants to be His people and to bless all the nations through Jesus, who came through his lineage.

12 Then Isaac sowed in that land, and received in the same year an hundredfold: and the LORD blessed him. 13 And the man waxed great, and went forward, and grew until he became very great.

God blessed Isaac immediately. In the very first year, he harvested one hundred times as much as he had sown, a miraculous crop that could only be due to the blessing of the Lord. Isaac became a wealthy man

with an abundance of crops and large herds of sheep and goats. His phenomenal success continued as is evident in the Hebrew, which repeats the thought of the multiplication three times—"waxed great," "went forward," and "grew until he became very great."

Sources:
"Concubine." BibleStudyTools.com. http://www.biblestudytools.com/dictionaries/bakers-evangelical-dictionary/concubine.htm (accessed July 15, 2012).

Janzen, J. Gerald, Fredrick Carlson Holmgren, and George Angus Fulton Knight. *Abraham and All the Families of the Earth; A Commentary on the Book of Genesis 12–50.* Grand Rapids, MI: Wm. B. Eerdmans Publishing Company, 1993.

Mathews, Kenneth A. *Genesis 11:27–50:26, Vol. 1B. The New American Commentary.* Nashville: Broadman and Holman Publishers, 2005.

Strong, James. *Strong's Concordance with Greek and Hebrew Lexicon.* http://www.eliyah.com/lexicon.html (accessed October 10, 2012).

Say It Correctly

Posterity. pos-**TER**-i-tee.
Ramifications. ram-i-fi-**CAY**-shuns.

Daily Bible Readings

MONDAY
The Promise of Many Descendants
(Genesis 15:1–6)

TUESDAY
A Child Born in Affliction
(Genesis 16:7–16)

WEDNESDAY
The Symbol of the Covenant
(Genesis 17:9–14)

THURSDAY
Abraham's Test of Faith
(Genesis 22:1–8)

FRIDAY
Abraham's Obedience Blessed
(Genesis 22:9–18)

SATURDAY
The Blessed of the Lord
(Genesis 26:26–31)

SUNDAY
Blessing Two Family Branches
(Genesis 21:13–21; 26:2–5, 12–13)

Notes

_____

_____

_____

_____

Teaching Tips

October 27
Bible Study Guide 9

Words You Should Know

A. Jacob (Genesis 28:1, 10, 16, 20) *Yaaqob* (Heb.)—He takes by the heel, he supplants.

B. Place (vv. 11, 16, 17) *Maqowm* (Heb.)— Place, post, shrine.

C. Bethel (v. 19) *Beyth-El* (Heb.)—House of God.

Teacher Preparation

Unifying Principle—Vision and Dreams. When people feel insecure, they look for a place of security and the assurance of not being alone. Where and with whom can they find sanctuary? God assures Jacob of His presence and promises that through Jacob and his offspring, all the families of the earth will be blessed.

A. Pray for your students and that God will bring clarity to this lesson.

B. Read and study Genesis 24–28, using several translations and commentaries.

O—Open the Lesson

A. Open with prayer, including the Aim for Change.

B. After prayer, ask a volunteer to read the In Focus story.

C. Have the students discuss why they think each character had a different level of confidence in the assurance of God's presence.

P—Present the Scriptures

A. Ask two students to read The People, Places, and Times and Background sections.

B. Do an exposition of the Focal Verses using the In Depth section.

E—Explore the Meaning

A. Have the class answer the questions in the Discuss the Meaning section.

B. Ask a volunteer to read Lesson in Our Society and ask the class to discuss: "In what ways have you seen the presence of God in your life?"

N—Next Steps for Application

A. Ask the class to write down the areas in their lives in which they need to invite God, along with three actions to implement the invitation.

B. Close with a prayer of thanks for the presence of God in your lives.

Worship Guide

For the Superintendent or Teacher
Theme: The Blessing Passes to Jacob
Song: "Blessed Assurance"
Devotional Reading: John 4:1–15

The Blessing Passes to Jacob

Bible Background • GENESIS 28
Printed Text • GENESIS 28:1, 10–22 | Devotional Reading • JOHN 4:1–15

Aim for Change

By the end of the lesson, we will: INTERPRET the meaning of Jacob's vision; CHERISH God's presence in our personal experiences; and INVITE God's presence into our everyday activities.

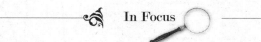 In Focus

"Honey, maybe you should reconsider leaving," said Layla's mother as she watched her daughter pack.

"Ma, I've been praying for a long time and I believe this is the path God wants me to take."

When her mother took ill ten years ago, Layla put off her mission trip and moved back into her mother's house to take care of her. However, even after her mother had received a clean bill of health from the doctor, Layla stayed and continued to put her dream of helping orphans on hold. But now she really felt the Lord nudging her to go. "What if something happens? I'll be all alone," her mother cried.

OCT 27th

"Oh Ma, don't cry," Layla said as she hugged her mother. "I don't know what the future holds, but I do know God is with me. If we have submitted our lives to Him, He promised to keep us. Guess who taught me that when she was sick?"

"I did." Layla's mother could only laugh.

"See, God was with you through your illness and He continues to be with you. We're never alone. And I, for one, am glad about that."

For whatever reason, many of us may feel like we are alone. But just as God assured Jacob of His presence and promises, He promises to always be with us.

Keep in Mind

"And, behold, I am with thee, and will keep thee in all places whither thou goest, and will bring thee again into this land; for I will not leave thee, until I have done that which I have spoken to thee of" (Genesis 28:15).

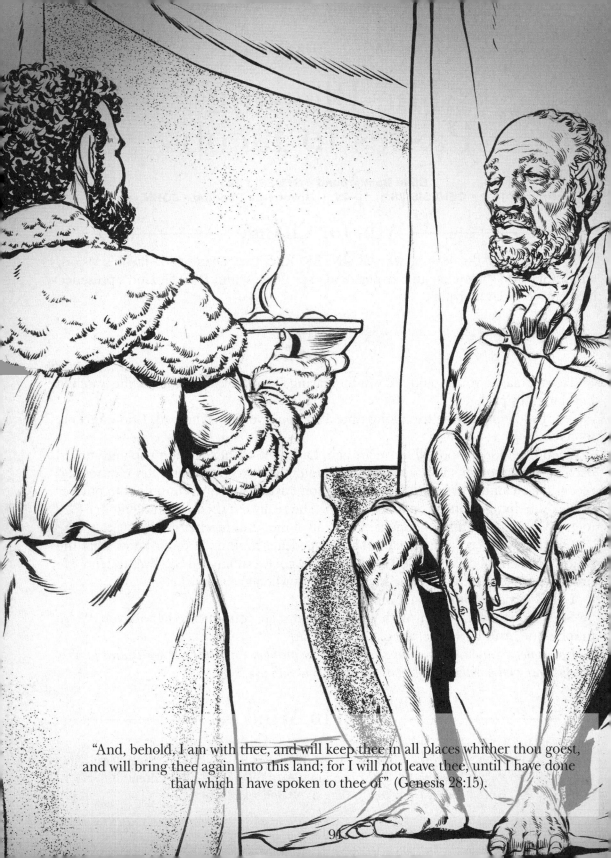

"And, behold, I am with thee, and will keep thee in all places whither thou goest, and will bring thee again into this land; for I will not leave thee, until I have done that which I have spoken to thee of" (Genesis 28:15).

Focal Verses

KJV **Genesis 28:1** And Isaac called Jacob, and blessed him, and charged him.

28:10 And Jacob went out from Beersheba, and went toward Haran.

11 And he lighted upon a certain place, and tarried there all night, because the sun was set; and he took of the stones of that place, and put them for his pillows, and lay down in that place to sleep.

12 And he dreamed, and behold a ladder set up on the earth, and the top of it reached to heaven: and behold the angels of God ascending and descending on it.

13 And, behold, the LORD stood above it, and said, I am the LORD God of Abraham thy father, and the God of Isaac: the land whereon thou liest, to thee will I give it, and to thy seed;

14 And thy seed shall be as the dust of the earth, and thou shalt spread abroad to the west, and to the east, and to the north, and to the south: and in thee and in thy seed shall all the families of the earth be blessed.

15 And, behold, I am with thee, and will keep thee in all places whither thou goest, and will bring thee again into this land; for I will not leave thee, until I have done that which I have spoken to thee of.

16 And Jacob awaked out of his sleep, and he said, Surely the LORD is in this place; and I knew it not.

17 And he was afraid, and said, How dreadful is this place! this is none other but the house of God, and this is the gate of heaven.

18 And Jacob rose up early in the morning, and took the stone that he had put for his pillows, and set it up for a pillar, and poured oil upon the top of it.

NLT **Genesis 28:1** So Isaac called for Jacob, blessed him.

28:10 Meanwhile, Jacob left Beersheba and traveled toward Haran.

11 At sundown he arrived at a good place to set up camp and stopped there for the night. Jacob found a stone to rest his head against and lay down to sleep.

12 As he slept, he dreamed of a stairway that reached from the earth up to heaven. And he saw the angels of God going up and down the stairway.

13 At the top of the stairway stood the LORD, and he said, "I am the LORD, the God of your grandfather Abraham, and the God of your father, Isaac. The ground you are lying on belongs to you. I am giving it to you and your descendants.

14 Your descendants will be as numerous as the dust of the earth! They will spread out in all directions—to the west and the east, to the north and the south. And all the families of the earth will be blessed through you and your descendants.

15 What's more, I am with you, and I will protect you wherever you go. One day I will bring you back to this land. I will not leave you until I have finished giving you everything I have promised you."

16 Then Jacob awoke from his sleep and said, "Surely the LORD is in this place, and I wasn't even aware of it!"

17 But he was also afraid and said, "What an awesome place this is! It is none other than the house of God, the very gateway to heaven!"

18 The next morning Jacob got up very early. He took the stone he had rested his head against, and he set it upright as a memorial pillar. Then he poured olive oil over it.

19 And he called the name of that place Bethel: but the name of that city was called Luz at the first.

20 And Jacob vowed a vow, saying, If God will be with me, and will keep me in this way that I go, and will give me bread to eat, and raiment to put on,

21 So that I come again to my father's house in peace; then shall the LORD be my God:

22 And this stone, which I have set for a pillar, shall be God's house: and of all that thou shalt give me I will surely give the tenth unto thee.

19 He named that place Bethel (which means "house of God"), although it was previously called Luz.

20 Then Jacob made this vow: "If God will indeed be with me and protect me on this journey, and if he will provide me with food and clothing,

21 and if I return safely to my father's home, then the LORD will certainly be my God.

22 And this memorial pillar I have set up will become a place for worshiping God, and I will present to God a tenth of everything he gives me."

The People, Places, and Times

Jacob. Jacob was the younger of the twin sons of Rebekah and Isaac, who was the son of Abraham and Sarah. Jacob and his brother, Esau, were always at odds with each other, even fighting in the womb (25:22). In fact, Jacob's name means "he takes by the heel or he supplants" because when he was born, he was grasping his brother's heel as if he wanted to take Esau's place as firstborn. Jacob had a trickster nature and was skillful at making schemes, as was illustrated when he later used Esau's weakness to trick him into selling his birthright. Jacob "was a plain man, dwelling in tents" (v. 27), meaning he was quiet (a trait that no doubt afforded him the opportunity to better observe people's actions and nature so he could better deceive them) and was more at ease in the home, "a man of the domestic domain, a man of culture." His character changed, however, after a divine encounter with an angel of God in which he wrestled with the "man" and was able to last until dawn (32:24–32). Jacob was then given the name Israel, which means "he struggles with God." He no longer was arrogant (32:9–10) and desired to make peace with Esau (33:1-20).

Background

When an aging Isaac was ready to bless Esau, he told his son to go hunt wild game and make a stew for him before he would bless him (27:3–4). Rebekah devised a plan for Jacob, a willing participant, to steal Esau's blessing. She instructed Jacob to put on his brother's clothes and goat's skin to mimic Esau's hairiness while she made the stew herself. Isaac, who was going blind, thought it was Esau who brought the stew, but it was Jacob. Isaac then blessed his younger son, saying, "Therefore God give thee of the dew of heaven, and the fatness of the earth, and plenty of corn and wine: Let people serve thee, and nations bow down to thee: be lord over thy brethren, and let thy mother's sons bow down to thee: cursed be every one that curseth thee, and blessed be he that blesseth thee" (27:28–29).

When Esau heard what Jacob had done, he plotted to kill his brother. To save both sons (Esau would have been put to death for murdering Jacob), Rebekah told Jacob to run away to her brother, Laban, then planted in Isaac's mind that it would be greatly bothersome to her if Jacob were to marry a local

Canaanite woman (v. 46) as Esau had already done (26:34–35).

At-A-Glance

1. A Solitary Place (Genesis 28:1, 10–11)
2. Jacob's Dream of God's Promise
   (vv. 12–15)
3. Jacob's Response to the Promise
   (vv. 16–22)

In Depth

1. A Solitary Place (Genesis 28:1, 10–11)

On the surface, Isaac was ordering Jacob to leave so that he could find a wife among his mother's people. The patriarch had sent his son away with the hope of the same blessing God had given Abraham (28:4). This was supposed to be a great journey, but in reality, it was probably a dreadful one because Jacob was running for his life. In addition to being afraid that his brother might come after him at any minute, Jacob was probably extremely lonely because he was away from home, traveling toward the unknown—the land of Haran. After a day's journey, Jacob settled down for the night in a solitary place with stones for his pillow. However, looks can be deceiving. "Place can also mean shrine. . . . The setting at night . . . corresponds to the later divine encounter in 32:22–33 (Jacob wrestling with an angel of God). . . . Jacob laying his head on one of the stones of the place becomes clearer in retrospect—the stone signifies a sacred space" (*HarperCollins Study Bible*). In essence, what looked like a lonely, unassuming place was the perfect setting for something divine to happen. Sometimes it is necessary to be in what appears to be a lonely time to be available for an encounter with God. In His earthly ministry, whenever Jesus went off by Himself, it was to communicate with the Father (Mark 1:35; Matthew 14:23, 26:36–46).

2. Jacob's Dream of God's Promise (vv. 12–15)

Jacob fell asleep and dreamed of a ladder upon which he saw the angels of God traveling between heaven and earth. This was a place where there was open communication with the divine. "The angels are active spirits . . . they rest not, day nor night, from service, according to the posts assigned them. They ascend, to give account of what they have done, and to receive orders; and then descend, to execute the orders they have received" (Henry). The ladder might also represent the "mediation of Christ" (Henry). "I am the way, the truth, and the life: no one man cometh unto the Father, but by me" (John 14:6). God, at the top of the ladder, identified Himself as the Lord God of Abraham and Isaac, One who was in relationship with Jacob's grandfather and father. Jacob would soon see that God was also seeking a relationship with him. Isaac had already sent Jacob away, claiming the blessing of Abraham for his son (28:3–5), but God confirmed that indeed what was promised to Abraham was now being passed to Jacob. The words of the blessing paralleled the words He had spoken to Abraham: "Thy seed shall be as the dust of the earth, and thou shalt spread abroad to the west, and to the east, and to the north, and to the south" (from 28:14, see also 13:14–17) and "in thee and in thy seed shall all the families of the earth be blessed" (from 28:14, see also 12:3). At the end of this encounter, God left Jacob with the reassurance that even in the lowest, most vulnerable time in his life, He was his protection, would never leave him, and would complete His promise.

3. Jacob's Response to the Promise (vv. 16–22)

When Jacob woke up, he made an assessment of what he had dreamed. He was in awe and afraid because, as he declared, he was on sacred ground. In response, Jacob rose early and built a shrine to God, anointed it with oil, and named the place Bethel, the "house of God." He thought that perhaps later, when he would return home, he could build a proper altar. He also anointed the place so that all who would come would know that they were in a place of worship, not just a place of almond trees ("Luz" means almond tree). As was the custom of the time, Jacob made a vow. In verse 20, Jacob said, "*If* God will be with me" (emphasis added), which gives the impression that Jacob was placing a condition on God before making his vow. However, "if" can also mean "given," as in "given the fact that God will be with me." In light of this, Jacob was affirming his belief that God would do as He had said and was interpreting what that promise meant to him in that moment. Although God's promise entailed the grander things of assurance for his descendants and blessings for all through his seed, Jacob was concerned with his immediate needs in his time of distress: food, clothes, and seeing his father again. Our visions may only extend as far as our finite minds can imagine, but God still does "exceeding abundantly above all that we ask or think, according to the power that worketh in us" (from Ephesians 3:20). Given that God would do those things, Jacob resolved that "the LORD will certainly be my God" (Genesis 28:21, NLT) and vowed to give God a tenth of everything he would gain.

Search the Scriptures

1. What are the details to God's promise to Jacob (Genesis 28:13–15)?

2. How did Jacob respond to the dream and God's promise (vv. 16–22)?

Discuss the Meaning

God informed Jacob that He would always be with him. In what ways has God shown He is with us? How can we invite God into all areas of our lives?

Lesson in Our Society

As we attend to our daily lives, we often feel alone in our life's journeys. When life's distresses—like illness, loss of a job, a broken heart, or death of a loved one—occur, we may begin to wonder if anyone is there. Is anyone concerned about our troubles? Is there any place to feel safe? The answer to every question is yes, God is always there. Just as He assured Jacob He was keeping him, we can be assured He is keeping us wherever we may go.

Make It Happen

God has promised to always be with us and to keep us, but sometimes we do not invite Him into every part of our lives. This week, begin to identify those areas in your life where you need to give God full disclosure. As you do this, think of at least three actions you can do to invite God into each area. Then, do them.

Follow the Spirit

What God wants me to do:

_____

_____

_____

_____

Remember Your Thoughts
Special insights I have learned:

_____

_____

_____

_____

More Light on the Text
Genesis 28:1, 10–22
From v. 1 And Isaac called Jacob, and blessed him, and charged him.

Perhaps now Isaac resigned himself to what his wife, Rebekah, told him was the Lord's will all along—that the older would serve the younger and that Jacob, not Esau, would receive the birthright. So Isaac sent Jacob on with blessing and instructions.

10 And Jacob went out from Beersheba, and went toward Haran. 11 And he lighted upon a certain place, and tarried there all night, because the sun was set; and he took of the stones of that place, and put them for his pillows, and lay down in that place to sleep.

In obedience to his father's command to seek a wife (v. 2) but also in compliance with his mother's counsel to evade the wrath of Esau, Jacob set out on his journey toward Haran. As he traveled on, he came to a place where he was obliged to stop all night because the sun had set. Jacob had probably intended to reach Luz, but he opted to stop and rest for the night. The words "he lighted upon a certain place" indicate the apparently accidental, yet divinely appointed, choice of this place for his night quarters, for the place had already been consecrated by one of Abraham's altars (12:8, 13:4). Jacob took some of the stones and made

them his pillow or head-place (Heb. *mraas-hah*, **MER-ah-ash-aw**).

12 And he dreamed, and behold a ladder set up on the earth, and the top of it reached to heaven: and behold the angels of God ascending and descending on it.

Jacob fell asleep and had a dream in which he saw a ladder (Heb. *cullam*, **sool-LAWM**) resting upon the earth, with the top reaching to heaven. Upon the ladder, he saw angels of God going up and down, and Jehovah Himself standing above it. What a much-needed, refreshing, and inspiring experience for Jacob! God showed up for him at the right time. Jacob was tired, lonely, and forlorn when he arrived at Bethel. He had no company to travel with, no place but the ground for a bed, and no pillow but a stone for his head, but he experienced God in a personal and unusual way. The doors at home, to his family, and to Beersheba were shut, but the window of heaven was wide open to him. God literally threw down a ladder of hope to a hopeless Jacob who was caught up with a problem of his own making. For a short while, God made accessible His presence, promise, and providence to Jacob. Although the etymology of the Hebrew word for "ladder" is not entirely certain, its symbolism is without doubt. It was a visible symbol of the real and uninterrupted fellowship between God in heaven and His people upon earth. Although a brief episode, it was nonetheless significant as it represents God's deliberate disclosure of His active involvement in the world and His astute intervention into people's lives. Nothing could be a more expressive emblem of the incarnation and its effects—Jesus Christ is the great ladder between heaven and earth, and between God and humanity (John 1:51).

13 And, behold, the LORD stood above it, and said, I am the LORD God of Abraham thy father, and the God of Isaac: the land whereon thou liest, to thee will I give it, and to thy seed.

The vision was not just about angels. The Lord "stood" (Heb. *natsab*, **naw-TSAB**) above the ladder. It was a personal revelation of Jehovah to Jacob. It manifested the presence of his covenant God, pointed out his mode of life wandering from place to place, and promised protection in all his ways. In proclaiming Himself to Jacob as the God of his fathers, "I am the LORD God of Abraham," God not only confirmed to him all the promises and the blessing of Abraham for which Isaac had prayed (vv. 3–4), but also assured him of God's protection on his dangerous journey and a safe return to his home (v. 14).

14 And thy seed shall be as the dust of the earth, and thou shalt spread abroad to the west, and to the east, and to the north, and to the south: and in thee and in thy seed shall all the families of the earth be blessed. 15 And, behold, I am with thee, and will keep thee in all places whither thou goest, and will bring thee again into this land; for I will not leave thee, until I have done that which I have spoken to thee of.

God confirmed to Jacob his destiny as the heir of God's promise to his forefathers. God reiterated His promise to Abraham and Isaac, relayed to Jacob the prosperity of his descendants, and reassured the fearful patriarch of His presence in the dangerous journey. The Lord will guide the poor, afflicted wanderer in seeking rest and bread. Jacob seems to have left home with a heavy heart and invoked divine protection; God showed him the communication that exists between heaven and earth, the guard of angels, and His ever-watchful eye looking down on man, whether waking or asleep. What then had Jacob to fear? No evil could happen to him while God was his guardian and strong defense. In this dream, the Lord completely dispelled Jacob's fears. But as the fulfillment of this promise to Jacob was still far off, God added the firm assurance, "I will not leave thee, until I have done [carried out] that which I have spoken to thee of."

16 And Jacob awaked out of his sleep, and he said, Surely the LORD is in this place; and I knew it not.

"The LORD is in this place; and I knew it not"—that is, God had made this place His particular residence. Jacob had gone to sleep, fearful, alone, and helpless. He had no idea that he was being specially cared for and watched over by Abraham's God. He thought he was exiled from the presence of the Lord, but good men often find Him in times and places where they do not expect. Surely his heavenly Father watches over him. Jacob acknowledged that this place had been consecrated to God.

17 And he was afraid, and said, How dreadful is this place! this is none other but the house of God, and this is the gate of heaven.

Jacob seems to wake up in two stages. As he awoke, a feeling of awe came upon him. Consequently, when he arose, he solemnly dedicated one of the stones and vowed to bring his tithes to the God who dwelt in this place (vv. 18–22). "House of God" (Heb. *bet elohim*; **bet e-lo-YIM**) anticipates the name Jacob was about to give to the place, "Bethel" (v. 19). "Gate of heaven" occurs only here in the Old Testament, but the concept that heaven, the divine abode, has one or more entrances is a familiar idea in ancient thought. The appearance of the ladder, the

Lord standing at its top, and the movement of the angels up and down must have left deep, solemn, and even awe-inspiring impressions on the mind of Jacob. It was an impression so strong that he declared, "How dreadful is this place!" As Jacob continued on his journey, he was to carry with him a holy awe of the gracious presence of God.

18 And Jacob rose up early in the morning, and took the stone that he had put for his pillows, and set it up for a pillar, and poured oil upon the top of it.

Jacob turned the *pillow* into a *pillar*. In the morning, Jacob erected the stone as a monument of the extraordinary vision which he had experienced in that place. The word "stone" here (Heb. *eben*, **eh-VEN**) could mean a heap of stones that is piled up for a memorial, hence the word *monument*. He poured oil on the top to consecrate it as a memorial of the mercy that had been shown him there, not as an idol or an object of divine worship (Exodus 30:26 ff.).

19 And he called the name of that place Bethel: but the name of that city was called Luz at the first.

He then gave the place the name Bethel, "house of God" (Heb. *bethel*, **BET-el**), whereas the town had been called Luz before. It appears that Jacob gave the name not to the place where the pillar was set up but to the town in the neighborhood in which he had received the divine revelation. He renewed it on his return from Mesopotamia (35:15). This is confirmed by 48:3, where Jacob, in the same manner as in 35:6–7, spoke of Luz as the place of this revelation.

20 And Jacob vowed a vow, saying, If God will be with me, and will keep me in this way that I go, and will give me bread to eat, and

raiment to put on, 21 So that I come again to my father's house in peace; then shall the LORD be my God: 22 And this stone, which I have set for a pillar, shall be God's house: and of all that thou shalt give me I will surely give the tenth unto thee.

The significance of this vow within the story of Jacob's life is underscored by its mention again at key points (31:13, 35:1–3, 7). This was no ordinary vow but a grand and solemn expression of Jacob's complete acceptance of the Lord to be his God. It was merely the echo and the thankful acknowledgment of the divine assurance, "I am with thee," which had been given immediately before. God had already made an unconditional promise to Jacob to watch over him and bring him back to this land (v. 15). As such, his vow was not designed to manipulate God or twist His arm. Jacob needed not do anything in return, but he offered to God an altar, a tithe (28:22), and a commitment. He did not ask for what God was already giving him—His presence, care, and guidance, including his safe return to the land (v. 15).

One thing is certainly clear from this episode: Jacob was gradually coming to the end of himself. Instead of relying on his abilities, he was to stop scheming and rely on God to supply his needs and protect him. The *if* in Jacob's vow did not imply doubt in God's promise but was the natural form of his taking God at His word: "If God is going to do so much for me, then I will do something for Him." In other words, if God, who had appeared to him, proved Himself to be God by fulfilling His promise, then Jacob would acknowledge and worship Him by making the stone into a house of God and by tithing all his possessions. Finally, the circumstances in which Jacob made his vow are very striking. Typically in the Old Testament, vows were made in situations of distress. Jacob's vow was no exception. He was in a distressed state, running away from home—something which could be considered equivalent to being under threat of death. But now he had received an unexpected revelation announcing his return to his country and guaranteeing him safety on the journey. What could be more natural than for Jacob to make a vow and pledge himself to worship God?

"This stone . . . shall be God's house," a monument of the presence of God among His people. It is recorded in 35:7 that Jacob built an altar and probably also dedicated the tenth to God.

Sources:

BibleGateway.com. *The Holy Bible*, New Living Translation. Wheaton, Illinois: Tyndale House, 2007. (accessed August 1, 2012).

Bible Study Tools. www.BibleStudyTools.com. "Old Testament Hebrew Lexicon—King James Version." http://www.biblestudytools.com/lexicons/hebrew/kjv/yaaqob.html, http://www.biblestudytools.com/lexicons/hebrew/kjv/maqowm.html, http://www.biblestudytools.com/lexicons/hebrew/kjv/beyth-el.html (accessed August 4, 2012).

HarperCollins Study Bible (NRSV). New York: Harper Collins Publishers, 2006. 35–55.

Henry, Matthew. "Genesis." *Matthew Henry's Commentary on the Whole Bible, Vol. 1 (Genesis to Deuteronomy)*. Genesis 29. http://www.ccel.org/ccel/henry/mhc1.Gen.xxix.html. (accessed August 1, 2012).

Strong, James. Free Bible Study Tools. *Strong's Concordance with Greek and Hebrew*. http://www.tgm.org/bible.htm (accessed August 5, 2012).

Unger, Merrill F., R. K. Harrison, Howard Vos, and Cyril Barber. *The New Unger's Bible Dictionary*. Chicago: Moody Publishers, 1988. 635, 644–646.

Daily Bible Readings

MONDAY
One Greater than Jacob
(John 4:1–15)

TUESDAY
The Plot to Gain a Blessing
(Genesis 27:1–10)

WEDNESDAY
Planning the Deception
(Genesis 27:11–17)

THURSDAY
A Blessing Gained through Deceit
(Genesis 27:18–29)

FRIDAY
Jacob Received God's Blessing
(Genesis 32:22–30)

SATURDAY
Jacob's Name Changed to Israel
(Genesis 35:9–15)

SUNDAY
God's Assurance for Jacob
(Genesis 28:1, 10–22)

Say It Correctly

Beersheba. beer-**SHEE**-buh.
Rebekah. ri-**BEK**-uh.

Teaching Tips

November 3
Bible Study Guide 10

Words You Should Know
A. Moses (Exodus 3:11) *mosheh* (Heb.)—Moses was chosen by God to lead the Children of Israel out of Egypt.

B. Pharaoh (v. 10) *paroh* (Heb.)—The Egyptian ruler to whom the Children of Israel were enslaved.

Teacher Preparation
Unifying Principle—Get Ready. When people are called to a new challenge, they must overcome their fears. How can the participants overcome their fears? Before Moses could lead the people to freedom, God repeatedly assured Moses of His persistent help in all the trials to come.

A. Pray for your students and that God will bring clarity to this lesson.

B. Study and meditate on the entire text.

C. Prepare to share examples of how God helps us to overcome our fears.

D. Complete the companion lesson in the *Precepts For Living Personal Study Guide*®.

O—Open the Lesson
A. Open with prayer, including the Aim for Change.

B. After prayer, introduce today's subject, Aim for Change, and Keep in Mind verses. Discuss.

C. Share your presentation.

D. Then ask, "Are you ready for new challenges?"

E. Share testimonies.

F. Now have a volunteer summarize the In Focus story. Discuss.

P—Present the Scriptures
A. Have volunteers read the Focal Verses.

B. Now use The People, Places, and Times; Background; Search the Scriptures; At-A-Glance outline; In Depth; and More Light on the Text to clarify the verses.

E—Explore the Meaning
A. To answer questions in the Discuss the Meaning, Lesson in Our Society, and Make It Happen sections, divide the class into groups. Assign one or two questions to each group, depending on the class size.

B. Have each group select a representative to report their responses to the rest of the class.

N—Next Steps for Application
A. Summarize the lesson.

B. Close with prayer and praise God for preparing us.

Worship Guide

For the Superintendent or Teacher
Theme: Preparation for Deliverance
Song: "Go Down, Moses"
Devotional Reading: Exodus 4:10–16

Preparation for Deliverance

Bible Background • EXODUS 3:7–17
Printed Text • EXODUS 3:7–17 | Devotional Reading • EXODUS 4:10–16

Aim for Change

By the end of the lesson, we will: EXPLAIN why Moses was hesitant to answer God's call; EXPLORE fears that hinder us from saying yes to the call of God; and PRAY for help in overcoming fears that prevent us from obeying God's call.

In Focus

Jeff wasn't raised in church, which is why his business associates didn't understand his love for gospel music. He listened nonstop, despite being a drug dealer. He loved the references to faith in God, hope, and God's love for all. He asked God if He really loved him despite what he did. If his associates knew of this conversation with God, he would be out of business.

Weeks later, lying in the hospital because someone tried to kill him, Jeff found himself wondering if that song "Never Would Have Made It" was true. Drifting off to sleep, he was gently awakened by a voice who lovingly called out his name. The voice told Jeff his career as a drug dealer was over. There was a new plan for his life. Jeff responded, "God, if that is really You, please reveal Yourself." From that moment forward, Jeff lived a life dedicated to Christ. He began to realize his perceived disqualifications were what really qualified him for ministry. He went on to change lives with the message of the Gospel.

When God calls us to serve Him, instead of dwelling on our inadequacies, our response should be, "Yes, Lord." This response is the basis of our belief that God can do anything with anyone. In today's lesson, we will explore Moses' call to serve God.

Keep in Mind

"Go, and gather the elders of Israel together, and say unto them, The LORD God of your fathers, the God of Abraham, of Isaac, and of Jacob, appeared unto me, saying, I have surely visited you, and seen that which is done to you in Egypt: and I have said, I will bring you up out of the affliction of Egypt unto the land of the Canaanites, and the Hittites, and the Amorites, and the Perizzites, and the Hivites, and the Jebusites, unto a land flowing with milk and honey" (Exodus 3:16–17).

"Go, and gather the elders of Israel together, and say unto them, The LORD God of your fathers, the God of Abraham, of Isaac, and of Jacob, appeared unto me, saying, I have surely visited you, and seen that which is done to you in Egypt: and I have said, I will bring you up out of the affliction of Egypt unto the land of the Canaanites, and the Hittites, and the Amorites, and the Perizzites, and the Hivites, and the Jebusites, unto a land flowing with milk and honey" (Exodus 3:16–17).

Focal Verses

KJV **Exodus 3:7** And the LORD said, I have surely seen the affliction of my people which are in Egypt, and have heard their cry by reason of their taskmasters for I know their sorrows;

8 and I am come down to deliver them out of the hand of the Egyptians, and to bring them up out of that land unto a good land and a large, unto a land flowing with milk and honey; unto the place of the Canaanites, and the Hittites, and the Amorites, and the Perizzites, and the Hivites, and the Jebusites.

9 Now therefore, behold, the cry of the children of Israel is come unto me; and I have also seen the oppression wherewith the Egyptians oppress them.

10 Come now therefore, and I will send thee unto Pharaoh, that thou mayest bring forth my people the children of Israel out of Egypt.

11 And Moses said unto God, Who am I, that I should go unto Pharaoh, and that I should bring forth the children of Israel out of Egypt?

12 And he said, Certainly I will be with thee, and this shall be a token onto thee, that I have sent thee: When thou hast brought forth the people out of Egypt, ye shall serve God upon this mountain.

13 And Moses said unto God, Behold, when I come unto the children of Israel, and shall say unto them, The God of your fathers hath sent me unto you; and they shall say to me, What is his name? what shall I say unto them?

14 And God said unto Moses, I AM THAT I AM; and he said, Thus shalt thou say unto the children of Israel, I AM hath sent me unto you.

15 And God said moreover unto Moses, Thus shalt thou say unto the children of

NLT **Exodus 3:7** Then the LORD told him, "I have certainly seen the oppression of my people in Egypt. I have heard their cries of distress because of their harsh slave drivers. Yes, I am aware of their suffering.

8 So I have come down to rescue them from the power of the Egyptians and lead them out of Egypt into their own fertile and spacious land. It is a land flowing with milk and honey—the land where the Canaanites, Hittites, Amorites, Perizzites, Hivites, and Jebusites now live.

9 Look! The cry of the people of Israel has reached me, and I have seen how harshly the Egyptians abuse them.

10 Now go, for I am sending you to Pharaoh. You must lead my people Israel out of Egypt."

11 But Moses protested to God, "Who am I to appear before Pharaoh? Who am I to lead the people of Israel out of Egypt?"

12 God answered, "I will be with you. And this is your sign that I am the one who has sent you: When you have brought the people out of Egypt, you will worship God at this very mountain."

13 But Moses protested, "If I go to the people of Israel and tell them, 'The God of your ancestors has sent me to you,' they will ask me, 'What is his name?' Then what should I tell them?"

14 God replied to Moses, "I AM WHO I AM. Say this to the people of Israel: I AM has sent me to you."

15 God also said to Moses, "Say this to the people of Israel: Yahweh, the God of your ancestors—the God of Abraham, the God of Isaac, and the God of Jacob—has sent me to you. This is my eternal name, my name to remember for all generations.

Israel, the LORD God of your fathers, the God of Abraham, the God of Isaac, and the God of Jacob, hath sent me unto you; this is my name for ever, and this is my memorial unto all generations.

16 Go, and gather the elders of Israel together, and say unto them, The LORD God of your fathers, the God of Abraham, of Isaac, and of Jacob, appeared unto me, saying I have surely visited you, and seen that which is done to you in Egypt:

17 and I have said, I will bring you up out of the affliction of Egypt unto the land of the Canaanites, and the Hittites, and the Amorites, and the Perizzites, and the Hivites, and the Jebusites, unto a land flowing with milk and honey.

16 "Now go and call together all the elders of Israel. Tell them, 'The LORD, the God of your ancestors—the God of Abraham, Isaac, and Jacob—has appeared to me. He told me, "I have been watching closely, and I see how the Egyptians are treating you.

17 I have promised to rescue you from your oppression in Egypt. I will lead you to a land flowing with milk and honey—the land where the Canaanites, Hittites, Amorites, Perizzites, Hivites, and Jebusites now live."'"

The People, Places, and Times

Children of Israel. The people of Israel whose ancestors are Abraham, Isaac, and Jacob. God had established a covenant relationship with these ancestors. The covenant is an agreement based on faith.

Moses. His name literally means "drawn out." A Hebrew woman gave birth to him. After Pharaoh issued a decree to kill male babies, the Hebrew woman placed him in a homemade basket on the river. One of Pharaoh's daughters found him and raised him as her own. God chose Moses to lead the Children of Israel from slavery to freedom.

Background

God heard the Israelites' pleas to be delivered and told Moses to go to Pharaoh and bring the Israelites out of slavery.

Now in the desert after fleeing Egypt, Moses was married and working with his father-in-law, Jethro. When God appeared and commissioned him to deliver the Israelites, Moses expressed doubts about his abilities and questioned God. God assured Moses that "certainly I will be with thee" (from Exodus 3:12). God told Moses what to say to the Israelites to assure them that God had indeed heard their cries for help. "Thus shalt thou say unto the children of Israel, I AM hath sent me unto you. . . . The LORD God of your fathers, the God of Abraham, of Isaac, and of Jacob" (from vv. 14–16).

At-A-Glance

1. God Hears the Israelites' Cries for Help (Exodus 3:7–9)
2. God Commands Moses to Go to Pharaoh (v. 10)
3. Moses Doubts His Abilities, God's Assurance (vv. 11–12)
4. God's Response to Moses (vv. 13–17)

In Depth

1. God Hears the Israelites' Cries for Help (Exodus 3:7–9)

God appeared to Moses in the form of a burning bush. God identified Himself to Moses with the statement, "I am the God of thy father, the God of Abraham, the God of Isaac, and the God of Jacob" (from 3:6).

God told Moses He was aware of the situation with the Israelites: "I have surely seen the affliction of my people which are in Egypt, and have heard their cry by reason of their taskmasters" (from v. 7). God shared with Moses His plan to come down to rescue the Israelites from the Egyptians and bring them to a land flowing with milk and honey. This divine encounter was specific to God's call to Moses but reveals the great truth that our afflictions are not unknown to God. God chooses many ways to address our afflictions and difficulties, but we can be assured that His eye is on us.

2. God Commands Moses to Go to Pharaoh (v. 10)

God commanded Moses to go to Pharaoh: "Come now therefore, and I will send thee unto Pharaoh" (from v. 10). God directed Moses to "bring forth my people the children of Israel out of Egypt" (from v. 10). God's commands are not always in line with our way of pursuing life. Sometimes God's commands present challenges to us and require us to move in directions that contrast with our plans or current station in life. In today's lesson, we see Moses given a command that must have been far from any plans Moses had for the future, but they were God's plans for him and beyond what Moses could have imagined.

3. Moses Doubts His Abilities, God's Assurance (vv. 11–12)

Moses objected to God's directive. He wondered aloud what authority he would have to speak with Pharaoh. He did not know how to persuade the Israelites to follow him, and this was the beginning of his attempts to negotiate his way out of this seemingly impossible task. Before we are too hard on Moses, we should ask ourselves, "What would I have done if God had said this to me?" Perhaps we should even consider whether we are negotiating with God about our life today, rather than asking Him about the plans He has for us.

Moses received assurance from God that he would not be alone: "Certainly I will be with thee" (from v. 12). Whenever we face challenges in our lives, we need to remember God's faithfulness to us, presence with us, and power to deliver us. If He asks us to do something, He will bring it to pass.

4. God's Response to Moses (vv. 13–17)

"And God said unto Moses, I AM THAT I AM . . . I AM hath sent me unto you. . . . The LORD God of your fathers, the God of Abraham, the God of Isaac, and the God of Jacob . . . and seen that which is done to you in Egypt . . . I will bring you up out of the affliction" (from vv. 14–17). God's response to Moses did not provide answers in exactly the fashion he might have desired. Surely God's faithful presence with him was a source of assurance, but he would need to take as a matter of faith what God revealed to him about His name. And he knew that not only the Israelites would need convincing but probably Pharaoh as well. What do you do when you know the truth of God's word and plan? How much are you like Moses? How deep is your trust in the God who promises to be with you?

Search the Scriptures

1. Does God know about our trials (Exodus 3:7)?

2. How have you felt the presence of God when you have been sent out as His representative (v. 12)?

Discuss the Meaning

God is always present with us. God's presence is experienced both in and out of our comfort zone. God's best work occurs when we are afraid and discouraged. How has God operated like this in your life?

Lesson in Our Society

Fear and disobedience contradict one's faith. Disobedience implies that one does not totally believe and trust in the promises of God. Moses' life is an example of God's preparation process. Before one achieves success, one must experience failure. Failure is the vehicle to keep going and to not give up. Failure strengthens faith in God. Failure leads to unconditional trust in God's promises. Obedience and trust promote a can-do attitude. Fear produces an unwillingness to trust God.

Make It Happen

Seek an opportunity to participate with a ministry in your church that you normally financially support. If your church does not have such ministries, look within the community. Some ideas to consider are to become a Big Brother/Big Sister or volunteer at soup kitchens, homeless shelters, nursing homes, or with at-risk youth.

Follow the Spirit

What God wants me to do:

_____

_____

_____

_____

Remember Your Thoughts

Special insights I have learned:

_____

_____

_____

_____

More Light on the Text

Exodus 3:7–17

7 And the LORD said, I have surely seen the affliction of my people which are in Egypt, and have heard their cry by reason of their taskmasters; for I know their sorrows.

The Hebrew word for affliction (*ani,* **aw-NEE**) means to be made lowly or oppressed by the rich and powerful. God acknowledged that He had not only seen the affliction of the Israelites but also heard their cries—He was completely aware of their suffering. The Hebrew term for cry (*tsaaq,* **tsaw-AK**) means to cry out in distress. Like the hymn "Have a Little Talk with Jesus," God will "hear our faintest cry; answer by and by." We can take comfort in knowing that God both hears and responds to our cries of distress.

God explained that He was the God of Moses' ancestors and author of the covenant with Abraham, Isaac, and Jacob that had made the Israelites His people. Because they are His people, God knows all about their troubles. The Hebrew word for "know" (*yada,* **yaw-DAH**) is rich with meaning. Its significance ranges from having learned something, being knowledgeable from experience, being acquainted with someone, to sexual intercourse. However, in this situation, it refers to God's intimate, thorough awareness of the circumstances of His people.

106

8 And I am come down to deliver them out of the hand of the Egyptians, and to bring them up out of that land unto a good land and a large, unto a land flowing with milk and honey; unto the place of the Canaanites, and the Hittites, and the Amorites, and the Perizzites, and the Hivites, and the Jebusites.

God was not content to just know about the suffering of His people, however; He decided to come down and act on their behalf. God descended (Heb. *yarad*, **yaw-RAD**) from His heavenly abode. God's plan was to deliver the Israelites from the Egyptians and place them under His own protection. The Hebrew word for "deliver" here is from the verb *natsal* (**naw-TSAL**) and means to be snatched away from danger.

God's plan also included delivering the Israelites from the land of Egypt and bringing them into the land He had promised to Abraham (Genesis 17:7–8). That land is the land of Canaan—modern-day Palestine—and is a land abundant with resources to help make the Israelites' lives less burdensome than their existence in Egypt.

9 Now therefore, behold, the cry of the children of Israel is come unto me: and I have also seen the oppression wherewith the Egyptians oppress them.

God repeated that the cries of the Children of Israel (Heb. *bene yisrael*, **ben-AY YIS-raw-ALE**) had risen to Him, and He had seen their oppression. The Hebrew root for "oppression" and "oppress" here is *lachats* (**lakh-ATS**) and means to squeeze or press. Its use here implies that the pressure on the Israelites by the Egyptians was like a vise tightening on them, prompting God to intervene.

10 Come now therefore, and I will send thee unto Pharaoh, that thou mayest bring forth my people the children of Israel out of Egypt.

The current Pharaoh, king of Egypt, did not know Joseph or care that this Israelite had saved Egypt from famine. He saw the proliferation of Joseph's descendants in his land as a threat to Egypt's national security, so he ordered their destruction. God commissioned Moses to go to Pharaoh and lead the Israelites out of Egypt. This passage is filled with action. The verbs "come" (Heb. *lekah*, **lay-KAW**), "send" (Heb. *shalach*, **shaw-LAKH**), and "bring or lead out" (*yatsa*, **yaw-TSAW**) denote movement and a sense of urgency in God's command to Moses. The adverb "now" (Heb. *attah*, **at-TAW**) at the beginning of the passage expresses the immediacy of God's command. God expected Moses to go to Pharaoh immediately, without any further delay.

11 And Moses said unto God, Who am I, that I should go unto Pharaoh, and that I should bring forth the children of Israel out of Egypt?

Moses' reply feigned humility. His rhetorical question implied that he was but a Hebrew servant or commoner whose humble status would not allow him to approach someone as powerful as Pharaoh. Or it may indicate his lack of confidence in going before Pharaoh, fearing the king's refusal to let the Israelites go, or worse, that he would be killed for returning to Egypt as punishment for having killed an Egyptian taskmaster (2:11–12).

12 And he said, Certainly I will be with thee; and this shall be a token unto thee, that I have sent thee: When thou hast brought forth the people out of Egypt, ye shall serve God upon this mountain.

God assured Moses that he would not be alone when he confronted Pharaoh. As proof, God offered to show Moses a sign (Heb. *oth*, **oth**) that He had sent him: Once Moses has brought the Israelites out of Egypt, he would bring them to the mountain where he was currently standing. The Hebrew term for "serve" (*abad*, **aw-BAD**) means to work for another or serve another by labor, such as a servant or slave. The ancient Egyptians considered the Pharaohs to be divine. Work on the magnificent building projects, including the grinding labor by the Israelites, was considered a privilege as it was service to the divine. However, the Israelites who currently served Pharaoh would soon serve God as God's servants.

13 And Moses said unto God, Behold, when I come unto the children of Israel, and shall say unto them, The God of your fathers hath sent me unto you; and they shall say to me, What is his name? what shall I say unto them?

God had already announced that He was the God of Abraham, Isaac, and Jacob—the Israelites' forefathers. That should have been sufficient evidence. Yet Moses feared being rejected by the Israelites, so he asked for God's personal name in case they challenged his authority to bring them out of Egypt. Ancient Near Eastern cultures, including ancient Israel, all had deities with names. The Hebrew Bible (Old Testament) mentions a few, such as the gods El and Baal, and the goddesses Anath, Asherah, and Astarte. Moses might have believed that knowing the personal name of the Hebrew God would cause the Israelites to view him as an insider. It is like belonging to a secret society that has a password to identify one as a member.

14 And God said unto Moses, I AM THAT I AM: and he said, Thus shalt thou say unto the children of Israel, I AM hath sent me unto you.

God's reply to Moses was, "I AM THAT I AM." The Hebrew phrase *ehyeh asher ehyeh* (**eh-YEH ash-ER eh-YEH**) is from the verb *hayah* (**haw-YAW**), meaning "to be." *Ehyeh* is first person, common singular and is literally translated, "I will be."

God revealed that His personal name is "I am who I am" or "I will be what (who) I will be." God seems to imply that His name is not important. What was important was that God would be sufficient for them. The essence of the divine being ("I will be what I will be") was to be there for them as He had been in the past and would be in the future.

15 And God said moreover unto Moses, Thus shalt thou say unto the children of Israel, the LORD God of your fathers, the God of Abraham, the God of Isaac, and the God of Jacob, hath sent me unto you: this is my name for ever, and this is my memorial unto all generations.

God didn't just reiterate the revelation that He was the God of Moses' father as well as the God of Abraham, Isaac, and Jacob. This time, God added His personal name, signified by the consonants YHWH (also referred to as the Tetragrammaton and represented in English Bibles as LORD, as the meaning of the verb *hayah* in v. 14). The King James Version combines the personal name with the impersonal name God.

God's personal name and the identification of God as the God of *their* fathers, *their* ancestors Abraham, Isaac, and Jacob, should satisfy the Israelites that God had sent Moses. God declared that this is the name He shall be known by forever (Heb. *olam*, **O-lawm**). The Hebrew word for "memorial" (*zeker*, **ZAY-ker**) signifies something by which someone is remembered. There would be no need to put a marker in the place where Moses encountered God, for His name would be a memorial for all generations.

16 Go, and gather the elders of Israel together, and say unto them, The LORD God of your fathers, the God of Abraham, of Isaac, and of Jacob, appeared unto me, saying, I have surely visited you, and seen that which is done to you in Egypt.

Moses' first task was to go and assemble (Heb. *asaph*, **AW-saf**) the elders before speaking to the rest of the community. In many traditional cultures, including traditional African cultures, reverence is given to elders (Heb. *zaqen*, **zaw-KANE**). Junior members of society often ask permission of senior members before speaking. God instructed Moses to tell the elders that the God of their fathers had appeared (Heb. *raah*, **raw-AW**) to him. The announcement of an appearance by God gave legitimacy to Moses' commission to the Israelites. Among the multiple meanings for the Hebrew term for "visit" (*paqad*, **paw-KAD**) is to take notice of or be concerned with. God sent Moses to tell the Israelites that He was aware of their suffering in Egypt and had come down to do something about it.

17 And I have said, I will bring you up out of the affliction of Egypt unto the land of the Canaanites, and the Hittites, and the Amorites, and the Perizzites, and the Hivites, and the Jebusites, unto a land flowing with milk and honey.

God repeated the plan for the Israelites given to Moses in verses 7–8. Now Moses was instructed to repeat the plan to the people.

It was the plan that would become the fulfillment of God's promise to their ancestors Abraham, Isaac, and Jacob, and it was about to unfold.

Sources:

Doumbia, Adama, and Naomi Doumbia. *The Way of the Elders: West African Spirituality & Tradition*. St. Paul, MN: Llewellyn Worldwide, 2004.

Draper, Charles W., Chad Brand, and Archie England, eds. *Holman Illustrated Bible Dictionary*. Grand Rapids, MI: Holman Reference, 2003.

Fretheim, Terence. *Exodus: Interpretation*. Louisville, KY: Westminster/John Knox Press, 2010.

Janzen, Waldemar. *Exodus: Believers Church Bible Commentary*. Harrisonburg, VA: Herald Press, 2000.

Myers, Allen C., John W. Simpson, Philip A. Frank, Timothy P. Jenney, and Ralph W. Vunderink, eds. *The Eerdmans Bible Dictionary*. Grand Rapids, MI: Wm. B. Eerdmans Publishing Company, 1996.

Radmacher, Earl D., Ronald B. Allen, and H. W. House, eds. *Nelson Study Bible* (NKJV). Nashville: Thomas Nelson Publishers, 2001.

Today's Parallel Bible (KJV/NIV/NASB/NLT). Grand Rapids, MI: Zondervan, 2000.

Say It Correctly

Canaanites. **KAY**-nan-ites.
Perizzites. **PER**-i-zits.
Hivites. **HI**-vits.

Daily Bible Readings

MONDAY
Oppression Under a New King
(Exodus 1:7–14)

TUESDAY
The King's Evil Plan
(Exodus 1:15–22)

WEDNESDAY
The Sparing of the Infant Moses
(Exodus 2:1–10)

THURSDAY
Moses Flees from Pharaoh
(Exodus 2:15–25)

FRIDAY
The People Worship God
(Exodus 4:27–31)

SATURDAY
Moses' Encounter with God
(Exodus 3:1–6)

SUNDAY
Moses' Commission from God
(Exodus 3:7–17)

Notes

_____

_____

_____

_____

Teaching Tips

Words You Should Know

A. Unleavened bread (Exodus 12:8) *matstsah* (Heb.)—Unfermented loaf or cakes with no yeast.

B. Passover (v. 11) *pesach* (Heb.)—It is a sparing, an exemption, an immunity (from penalty and calamity).

Teacher Preparation

Unifying Principle—Remember and Celebrate. People who are living under oppression hunger for freedom. What is the meaning of freedom? The freedom God promises to the Hebrew people will create a new beginning in their relationship with God—a beginning they will commemorate for generations to come.

A. Pray for clarity as you study the lesson.

B. Study the entire text, review More Light on the Text, and do additional research on the Passover.

C. Review the In Focus story and draw parallels relevant for today.

O—Open the Lesson

A. Open the lesson with prayer and ask students to especially intercede on behalf of those lost and oppressed by the enemy.

B. Introduce the lesson by asking students why it is important to commemorate religious and historical events in their lives. Ask which ones are important to them and why.

P—Present the Scriptures

A. Ask for a volunteer to read the lesson.

B. Lead students in answering the Search for the Scriptures, Discuss the Meaning, or any other questions that may arise from the study.

E—Explore the Meaning

A. Discuss parallels of bondage and freedom in today's context. How can the church be more instrumental in helping people become and remain free?

B. Look for the opportunities for students to personally or corporately commemorate milestones to pass on to the next generation.

N—Next Steps for Application

A. Encourage students to pray for opportunities to share Christ this week and target someone in their circle of influence to intercede for in prayer.

B. Encourage students to actively seek new ways to highlight God's deliverance in their lives.

Worship Guide

For the Superintendent or Teacher
Theme: Beginning of Passover
Song: "You Are the Living Word"
Devotional Reading: John 1:29–37

Beginning of Passover

Bible Background • EXODUS 12
Printed Text • EXODUS 12:1–14 | Devotional Reading • JOHN 1:29–37

―――――――――――― Aim for Change ――――――――――――

By the end of the lesson, we will: UNDERSTAND the historical events that lie behind the Jewish celebration of Passover; EMPATHIZE with those who are in need of deliverance; and IDENTIFY ways in which the church can participate in freeing those who need deliverance.

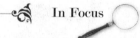 In Focus

For African Americans, the Emancipation Proclamation serves as our people's release from bondage. Black abolitionists, such as Frederick Douglass, and white allies in the North applied continuous pressure and called for an end to slavery.

However, as history records it, those instrumental in freeing the slaves were not as benevolent as often portrayed. President Abraham Lincoln's primary motive was to preserve the Union, not necessarily to free the slaves. As commander in chief, he still served God's purposes. On January 1, 1863, he issued the Emancipation Proclamation, which freed slaves in the rebel states as a ploy to get the South to surrender. This tactic was considered necessary to end the war.

The Civil War ended in 1865 with the Confederacy conceding defeat. More than 600,000 American lives were lost on both sides. In December 1865, the Thirteenth Amendment to the Constitution was ratified, abolishing slavery in the United States. With the end of the war, four million African Americans were free to start new lives.

Enslavement's impact is felt throughout generations. However, God sent His deliverance to our African American ancestors, and as we have progressed throughout history, we shall never forget God's faithfulness. In today's lesson, we will review the historical account of the first Passover, which set in motion freedom for the Children of Israel by God's mighty hand.

NOV 10th

―――――――――――― Keep in Mind ――――――――――――

"And this day shall be unto you for a memorial; and ye shall keep it a feast to the LORD throughout your generations; ye shall keep it a feast by an ordinance for ever" (Exodus 12:14).

"And this day shall be unto you for a memorial; and ye shall keep it a feast to the LORD throughout your generations; ye shall keep it a feast by an ordinance for ever" (Exodus 12:14).

Focal Verses

KJV **Exodus 12:1** And the LORD spake unto Moses and Aaron in the land of Egypt saying,

2 This month shall be unto you the beginning of months: it shall be the first month of the year to you.

3 Speak ye unto all the congregation of Israel, saying, In the tenth day of this month they shall take to them every man a lamb, according to the house of their fathers, a lamb for an house:

4 And if the household be too little for the lamb, let him and his neighbour next unto his house take it according to the number of the souls; every man according to his eating shall make your count for the lamb.

5 Your lamb shall be without blemish, a male of the first year: ye shall take it out from the sheep, or from the goats:

6 And ye shall keep it up until the fourteenth day of the same month: and the whole assembly of the congregation of Israel shall kill it in the evening.

7 And they shall take of the blood, and strike it on the two side posts and on the upper door post of the houses, wherein they shall eat it.

8 And they shall eat the flesh in that night, roast with fire, and unleavened bread; and with bitter herbs they shall eat it.

9 Eat not of it raw, nor sodden at all with water, but roast with fire; his head with his legs, and with the purtenance thereof.

10 And ye shall let nothing of it remain until the morning; and that which remaineth of it until the morning ye shall burn with fire.

11 And thus shall ye eat it; with your loins girded, your shoes on your feet, and your staff in your hand; and ye shall eat it in haste: it is the LORD's passover.

NLT **Exodus 12:1** While the Israelites were still in the land of Egypt, the LORD gave the following instructions to Moses and Aaron:

2 "From now on, this month will be the first month of the year for you.

3 Announce to the whole community of Israel that on the tenth day of this month each family must choose a lamb or a young goat for a sacrifice, one animal for each household.

4 If a family is too small to eat a whole animal, let them share with another family in the neighborhood. Divide the animal according to the size of each family and how much they can eat.

5 The animal you select must be a one-year-old male, either a sheep or a goat, with no defects.

6 "Take special care of this chosen animal until the evening of the fourteenth day of this first month. Then the whole assembly of the community of Israel must slaughter their lamb or young goat at twilight.

7 They are to take some of the blood and smear it on the sides and top of the doorframes of the houses where they eat the animal.

8 That same night they must roast the meat over a fire and eat it along with bitter salad greens and bread made without yeast.

9 Do not eat any of the meat raw or boiled in water. The whole animal—including the head, legs, and internal organs—must be roasted over a fire.

10 Do not leave any of it until the next morning. Burn whatever is not eaten before morning.

11 "These are your instructions for eating this meal: Be fully dressed, wear your sandals, and carry your walking stick in your

12 For I will pass through the land of Egypt this night, and will smite all the firstborn in the land of Egypt, both man and beast; and against all the gods of Egypt I will execute judgment: I am the LORD.

13 And the blood shall be to you for a token upon the houses where ye are: and when I see the blood, I will pass over you, and the plague shall not be upon you to destroy you, when I smite the land of Egypt.

14 And this day shall be unto you for a memorial; and ye shall keep it a feast to the LORD throughout your generations; ye shall keep it a feast by an ordinance for ever.

hand. Eat the meal with urgency, for this is the LORD's Passover.

12 On that night I will pass through the land of Egypt and strike down every firstborn son and firstborn male animal in the land of Egypt. I will execute judgment against all the gods of Egypt, for I am the LORD!

13 But the blood on your doorposts will serve as a sign, marking the houses where you are staying. When I see the blood, I will pass over you. This plague of death will not touch you when I strike the land of Egypt.

14 "This is a day to remember. Each year, from generation to generation, you must celebrate it as a special festival to the LORD. This is a law for all time."

The People, Places, and Times

Egypt. This country was the leading power of its age because of its positioning for sea traffic and the production and richness of its land due to the Nile River. In times of famine, Egypt's major cities of Pithom and Rameses further solidified its might through their stocked surplus of grain, storage of local and imported goods, and military equipment. These major cities were built on the backs of the Hebrew slaves, who became captives around 1500 B.C. after the ascension of a new king who conquered Egypt and did not know Joseph (1:8–11).

Background

God promised Abraham (Genesis 12:2–4, 15:5), Isaac (26:24), and Jacob (28:13–15) that from their lineage a great nation would come and that all the families of the earth would be blessed through them. This patriarchal line would go down in the history of humankind as the most detailed and celebrated of all families on earth and, ultimately, as the chosen lineage of Jesus Christ, God Incarnate.

God told Abraham in a vision about the years of hardship his people would endure in Egypt, but by His mighty hand God would deliver them (15:12–16).

Fast forward hundreds of years, God sent Moses as His mouthpiece to bring to pass the covenant He made with his ancestors. Citing his own shortcomings, Moses was a reluctant spokesman for God. However, God assured Moses that He was with him. With God's mighty hand, Moses would accomplish God's plan in the midst of what appeared to be formidable opposition.

Moses, having lived as the adopted son of Pharaoh's daughter, knew the inner workings of the palace. With God going before him and his brother Aaron at his side, Moses brought to Pharaoh the message of impending judgment on Egypt. Through signs and wonders in devastating plagues, God proved that His power trumps any earthly ruler. With the final and most deadly plague forthcoming, God would show His ability to protect His people and make a distinction between them and the Egyptians (11:7).

At-A-Glance

1. Instructions to Mark a New
   Beginning (Exodus 12:1–2)
2. Instructions to Prepare for Freedom
   (vv. 3–6)
3. Instructions for the Exit (vv. 7–12)
4. Instructions to Institute the Passover
   (vv. 13–14)

In Depth

1. Instructions to Mark a New Beginning (Exodus 12:1–2)

God set the stage for a final display of His great power. In the previous chapter (Exodus 11), God warned Moses and Aaron of the final plague He would bring upon Egypt. The Lord noted that "about midnight I will go out through Egypt" (11:4, NRSV) and strike down the firstborn of everything—from the throne of Pharaoh down to the slaves and even the animals. However, in the midst of this turmoil, the Lord would send great deliverance for those who heeded the directives given through Moses. What was about to take place would serve as the beginning of a new life for His people. The Lord called on them to mark the occasion as the beginning of the calendar year henceforth. For the descendants of Abraham, Isaac, and Jacob, this occasion also marks God's fulfillment of His covenant to them.

2. Instructions to Prepare for Freedom (vv. 3–6)

As God's representatives, Moses and Aaron gave the instructions to the elders, who were to prepare the Children of Israel for their promised exit from bondage. On the tenth day of the month, they were to gather everything needed for what would be the Passover sacrifice and the Feast of Unleavened Bread, which were to be celebrated in tandem (12:15–20, 23–28). The solemn assembly would serve as a reminder for generations of God's faithfulness.

God was very specific in His instructions. Each family of the twelve tribes of Israel was responsible for obtaining an animal for the occasion, which could either be a lamb or a goat but had to be a year-old male without blemish. If a household was too small to consume a lamb in its entirety, they were to join with a neighbor. The idea was to build community and fellowship in marking the end of this time of oppression. On the first Passover, known as the Egyptian Passover, the tribal leaders gathered on the 14th day of the month in a common meeting place "in the evening" (v. 6, other translations say "twilight") to slaughter the lamb or goat in preparation for the actual Passover. Future Passover celebrations would be offered up at the tabernacle and later the temple and, according to tradition, would occur at sundown (Deuteronomy 16:1–2; Ezekiel 45:18–21).

3. Instructions for the Exit (vv. 7–12)

After the slaughter of the Passover lamb or goat, the household leaders were to take the blood, dip a bunch of hyssop into it, and smear the lintels and sides of the doorposts of their homes (Exodus 12:22). When the Lord sent His judgment, the plague would "pass over" those homes marked with the blood: "For the LORD will pass through to smite the Egyptians; and when he seeth the blood upon the lintel, and on the two side posts, the LORD will pass over the door, and will not suffer the destroyer to come in unto your houses to smite you" (v. 23). It was very important for the Children of Israel to follow God's instructions to the detail. The blood had to be placed on the sides and above the doors, basically marking the threshold of the home as one belonging to Yahweh.

This same night, the Israelites were to cook and eat the flesh of the lamb or goat, roasting it by fire and eating it with unleavened bread and bitter herbs. The unleavened bread represented the release as they made their escape from their life of bondage. The bitter herbs were in memory of the pain and oppression of slavery. The lamb itself was a symbol of God's redemption through the blood; later, Jesus Christ would become the paschal (Passover) lamb who was slain for the sins of the world.

God gave specific instructions to leave no remnants of the past, as His people were set to obtain their freedom. In the same manner, we are to lay aside any weight or sin that so easily besets us and look to the Lord Jesus, the author and finisher of our faith (paraphrase of Hebrews 12:1–2). The Lord went on to instruct the Children of Israel to be alert and ready to move, knowing that soon after the final plague hit, their freedom would be at hand. Therefore, the Lord told them to eat fully dressed—"loins girded," "shoes on your feet," and "staff in your hand" (Exodus 12:11)—in order to make a hasty exit. God's final blow, showing His power and sovereignty, came through the death of every firstborn in the land of Egypt. With this plague, God distinguished Himself as the one true God over all other gods, setting His people apart as His chosen ones. By delivering His people with His mighty hand, the Lord executed judgment against Egypt for their arrogance and years of cruel oppression. We have the same assurance of God's deliverance from the enemy, as well as any adversity thereafter.

4. Instructions to Institute the Passover (vv. 13–14)

As God's judgment was released in Egypt, the blood of the sacrificed lamb served as the mark that sealed the Israelite homes and provided protection from the destroyer. The Lord warned them that as He saw the blood, He would "pass over" that home. Although they were in Egypt, they were still set apart from the coming destruction. In a similar manner, as Christians, we are *in* the world but not *of* the world. When we accept the gift of salvation purchased by the blood of Jesus, we are sealed unto the day of redemption (Ephesians 1:7, 4:30).

The Passover celebration is a memorial of God's great deliverance of His people. The Children of Israel were to leave behind their former way of living in servitude among the Egyptians and accept their true status as God's chosen people. They were to forever remind themselves and future generations of God's mighty hand. The Passover feast is celebrated in conjunction with the Feast of Unleavened Bread to commemorate their new beginnings as a nation, the new calendar year, the harvest, and their special spiritual connection to Yahweh. The Passover would go on to be one of the greatest celebrations of the Jewish people and continues in significance today. In Exodus 12 and throughout the Pentateuch, God would go on to provide further details of how this feast was to be implemented (Leviticus 23:4–8; Numbers 9:1–14, 28:16–31; Deuteronomy 16:1–8).

Search the Scriptures

1. How were the Children of Israel to set themselves apart from the Egyptians in advance of the final plague (Exodus 12:7, 12–13)?

2. How were the Children of Israel to prepare for their exit from Egypt (v. 11)?

Discuss the Meaning

What are the parallels between Pharaoh and Egypt; the devil as our captor and God as our Liberator; the world and our deliverance from sin; and the Passover lamb and Jesus Christ as our Passover lamb?

Lesson in Our Society

As believers in Jesus Christ, we have the answer for the world today. Our world continues to be in great turmoil. The world system encourages people to place their hope in all kinds of things that leave them disappointed and in despair. In the midst of our troubled times, we are to have the peace of God that surpasses all understanding. Through the light of Christ, we are to draw others unto Him. As we encounter people who are in trouble and searching for answers, it is a divine appointment for us to share our faith. Just as we are able to provide customer reviews and referrals when we experience a great product or service, our testimony serves as convincing proof that God in Christ is real and can deliver hope to the hopeless.

Make It Happen

Be intentional! Ask God to build up your faith and pray as the early church prayed for the boldness to share the Gospel of Jesus Christ. The Lord is always looking to show Himself strong through His people. We are, as Paul said in 2 Timothy 2:21, sanctified and set apart for the Master's use and prepared for every good work. Look for opportunities to be an agent of change for others to receive their deliverance from the bondage of sin and come into relationship with God in Christ.

Follow the Spirit

What God wants me to do:

_____

_____

_____

_____

Remember Your Thoughts

Special insights I have learned:

_____

_____

_____

_____

More Light on the Text

Exodus 12:1–14

1 And the LORD spake unto Moses and Aaron in the land of Egypt saying, 2 This month shall be unto you the beginning of months: it shall be the first month of the year to you.

Israel was to be delivered by God from bondage in Egypt. As a first step in growing His people into a nation, God instructed Moses and Aaron to designate that month as the first month of the new year—the start of a new beginning. According to 13:4, the month so assigned was called *Abib*, which would correspond to the middle of March on our contemporary calendar. The Jewish nation identified the month as Abib until the time of the Babylonian captivity. Then, following the Babylonian calendar, the name of the month was changed to *Nisan*. It is noteworthy that Moses and Aaron were simply instruments through whom God communicated His desire.

3 Speak ye unto all the congregation of Israel, saying, In the tenth day of this month they shall take to them every man a lamb, according to the house of their fathers, a lamb for an house.

After 400 years of captivity, the Israelites would have numbered in the millions and would have had thousands upon thousands of lambs. However, God here instructed that every man was to take *a* lamb, singular. The single lamb is a type, or foreshadowing, of the Lord Jesus Christ, who would give His life as an offering. The people were to choose the lamb on the tenth day of the month, four days before it was to be slaughtered. This also foreshadowed Jesus Christ, who would enter Jerusalem four days before He was to be offered upon Calvary's cross. The phrase, according to the house of their "fathers" (Heb. *ab*, **awb**, meaning head or founder of a household, group, family, or clan), was a common expression at the time.

4 And if the household be too little for the lamb, let him and his neighbor next unto his house take it according to the number of the souls; every man according to his eating shall make your count for the lamb.

For a household to be "too little," it needed to contain fewer than ten people. If that were the case, then the household was to join with the household of a near neighbor. The heads of the households were then to make a determination as to how much each member of a given family could eat. It is noteworthy that the first Passover was not an individualized exercise but was communal in nature. By making the determination as to how much each person could eat, the head of the household was to take note of the age, size, and other appropriate considerations.

5 Your lamb shall be without blemish, a male of the first year: ye shall take it out from the sheep, or from the goats.

Four days before it was to be slaughtered, a perfect male lamb without blemish was to be "taken out from" (Heb. *laqach*, **law-KAKH**, meaning to be taken hold of or separated) the rest of the herd. Again, this verse foreshadows the Lord Jesus Christ, who would be separated from His followers and His Father in order to be sacrificed for the sins of humanity. In various passages, Christ is identified as the Passover lamb (1 Corinthians 5:7) and the Lamb of God (John 1:29). Christ, as the only begotten Son of God, was seen by God as completely perfect and without "blemish" (Heb. *tamiym*, **taw-MEEM**, meaning flawless). Like the lamb of this first Passover, Christ was not sacrificed as an infant but was permitted to grow into a young adult so that, like the year-old lamb, He would be in the prime of His life and at the zenith of His strength.

6 And ye shall keep it up until the fourteenth day of the same month: and the whole assembly of the congregation of Israel shall kill it in the evening.

Four days after separating the lamb from the rest of the herd, the whole "assembly" (Heb. *qahal*, **kaw-HAWL**, meaning horde or mass of people) was to come together and slaughter the lambs. This verse represents the very first time the people of Israel are identified as a "congregation" (Heb. *edah*, **ay-DAW**, meaning gang, company, or community). The mass slaughter of the innocent lambs foretold the way in which the future nation of Israel would come together and take the life of Jesus Christ as God's sacrificial lamb. The slaughter was to take place in the "evening" (Heb. *'ereb*, **EH-reb**, meaning late afternoon or sunset) and is usually thought to have occurred sometime between three and six o'clock. According to Matthew 27:46, Christ was sacrificed at the ninth hour, which would have been three o'clock in afternoon. The sacrifice was to be performed by the head of each household, who acted on behalf of the entire nation. This was to be understood as a communal act, just as Christ was to be offered up for all of mankind.

7 And they shall take of the blood, and strike it on the two side posts and on the upper door post of the houses, wherein they shall eat it. 8 And they shall eat the flesh in that night, roast with fire, and unleavened bread; and with bitter herbs they shall eat it.

The blood of the shed lamb was then taken to the front door of each home, where it was used to mark the home so the angel of death would see the blood and pass over it. Michael Esses, a converted Jewish rabbi, suggests that in "striking" (Heb. *Nathan*, **naw-THAN**, meaning to be put upon) the two side posts and the upper lintel of the house with the blood, the action would have formed the sign of the cross. Then the flesh of the lamb was to be roasted with fire and consumed that night. Safe from the destruction in the blood-smeared house, the Israelites would have been partaking of the lamb's flesh as the angel of death passed over them. This act would have foreshadowed the Last Supper, where Christ shared that His body was offered up and "eaten" (Heb. *akal*, **aw-KAL**, meaning devoured or consumed) for the sins of all humanity. God was communicating a sense of urgency to the people of Israel as He gave instruction that unleavened bread and bitter herbs were also to be prepared and consumed with the lamb. At the appointed time, so rapid would be the deliverance of the Israelites from their bondage in Egypt that the bread for the meal would not have time to rise. The bitter herbs would later remind them of the cruelty of their bondage.

9 Eat not of it raw, nor sodden at all with water, but roast with fire; his head with his legs, and with the purtenance thereof.

In the pagan worship of Dionysus and Bacchus, raw meat was often consumed. This practice was forbidden in the newly forming nation of Israel. Nor was the flesh of the lamb to be "sodden" (Heb. *bashal*, **baw-SHAL**, meaning boiled or cooked) with water. Rather, the meat was to be roasted with fire. The entire being of the animal was to be cooked in the fire—its head and legs with the "purtenance" (Heb. *qereb*, **KEH-reb**, meaning entrails or innermost parts) included.

10 And ye shall let nothing of it remain until the morning; and that which remaineth of it until the morning ye shall burn with fire.

The Israelites were instructed to burn any meat that remained after they had eaten until "nothing of it" remained (Heb. *yatar*, **yaw-THAR**, meaning to save over or preserve); in other words, it was completely consumed. No effort was to be made by the people to try and save any of the flesh for a later time. God would now need to be trusted to meet any need for food.

11 And thus shall ye eat it; with your loins girded, your shoes on your feet, and your staff in your hand; and ye shall eat it in haste: it is the LORD's passover. 12 For I will pass through the land of Egypt this night, and will smite all the firstborn in the land of Egypt, both man and beast; and against all the gods of Egypt I will execute judgment: I am the LORD.

So urgent was to be the deliverance from Egyptian captivity that the Israelites were to eat in haste (Heb. *chippazown*, **khip-paw-ZONE**, meaning hurriedly or with a sense of trepidation) and be fully clothed, wearing their shoes and coat with a walking stick in hand. As He executed His judgment over Egypt, God intended to "smite" (Heb. *nakah*, **naw-KAW,** meaning to attack and destroy) all the firstborn males and animals in the nation, and He would do His work that very night. In killing all the firstborn, God was demonstrating that He alone is God by exacting "judgment" (Heb. *shephet*, **SHEH-fet**) on the false gods of Egypt. By including the animals in this judgment, God was seeking to undermine the Egyptian belief that animals could be deified and worshipped in the same manner that God alone was to be worshipped. A deified Pharaoh or calf and bulls made of bronze could not hold equal status with the only living God.

13 And the blood shall be to you for a token upon the houses where ye are: and when I see the blood, I will pass over you, and the plague shall not be upon you to destroy you, when I smite the land of Egypt. 14 And this day shall be unto you for a memorial; and ye shall keep it a feast to the LORD throughout your generations; ye shall keep it a feast by an ordinance for ever.

In passing through the land of Egypt, God was executing His judgment on that nation. By passing over the homes sprinkled with the blood of the lamb, however, God was showing His mercy. Only the blood of Christ could satisfy the wrath of God against sin. God promised the Israelites that when He saw the blood sprinkled on their homes, He would act with compassion, hold back the "plague" (Heb. *negeph*, **NEH-ghef**, meaning the striking or blow), and pass over them in mercy. However, where the blood was absent, God would destroy. In later years, in obedience to God's "ordinance" (Heb. *chuqqah*, **khook-KAW**, meaning fixed law or requirement), the Israelites would remember the night God passed over them, delivered them from

Egyptian bondage, and began establishing them as a holy nation.

Sources:
Coffman, James Burton. *Commentary on Exodus.* Abilene, TX: Abilene Christian University Press, 1974.
Dunn, James D. G. and John W. Rogerson. *Commentary on the Bible.* Grand Rapids, MI: Wm. B. Eerdmans Publishing Company, 2003.
"Egypt." Bible Encyclopedia. www.BibleEncyclopedia.com. http://bibleencyclopedia.com/egypt.htm (accessed July 31, 2012).
Esses, Michael. Jesus in Exodus. Grand Rapids, MI: Bridge Logos, 1977.
Gill, John. www.BibleStudyTools.com. *John Gill's Exposition of the Bible.* Exodus 12:1–14. http://www.biblestudytools.com/commentaries/gills-exposition-of-the-bible/exodus-12-introduction.html, http://www.biblestudytools.com/commentaries/gills-exposition-of-the-bible/exodus-12-1.html (accessed July 24, 2012).
Hebrew Greek Key Word Study Bible (KJV) 2nd ed. Chattanooga, TN: AMG Publishers, 1991. 1630, 1651
Mays, James L., ed. *HarperCollins Bible Commentary.* San Francisco: HarperOne, 1988, 2000.
"Passover." Bible Encyclopedia. www.BibleEncyclopedia.com. http://bibleencyclopedia.com/passover.htm (accessed July 23, 2012).
Public Broadcasting System. www.pbs.org. "The Civil War and Emancipation." http://www.pbs.org/wgbh/aiapart4/4p2967.html (accessed July 31, 2012).
Unger, Merrill, and Robert F. Ramey. *Unger's Bible Dictionary.* Chicago: Moody Press, 1981. 292, 352–354.
Unger, Merrill. *Unger's Bible Handbook.* Chicago: Moody Press, 1967. 84, 93.

Say It Correctly

Pithom. **PAHY**-thuhm.
Rameses. **RAM**-uh-seez.

Daily Bible Readings

MONDAY
The Lamb of God
(John 1:29–37)

TUESDAY
The Troubles Multiply
(Exodus 5:19–23)

WEDNESDAY
Broken Spirits and Closed Ears
(Exodus 6:2–9)

THURSDAY
The Final Plague
(Exodus 11)

FRIDAY
The First Passover
(Exodus 12:21–28)

SATURDAY
The Lord Delivered Israel
(Exodus 12:43–51)

SUNDAY
The Promise to Pass Over
(Exodus 12:1–14)

Notes

_____

_____

_____

_____

Teaching Tips

Words You Should Know

A. Wind (Exodus 14:21) *ruach* (Heb.)—Breath or spirit, the blast of God, divine miraculous power by which inanimate things begin to move.

B. Troubled (v. 24) *hamam* (Heb.)—To put in motion, impel, to drive to agitate, confound, put into commotion, to disturb, to put into flight, to disperse.

Teacher Preparation

Unifying Principle—From Despair to Deliverance. The participants may find themselves in seemingly impossible circumstances while seeking freedom. How can they safely reach freedom? God created a way out when there was no way.

A. Pray for lesson clarity.

B. Study and meditate on the entire text in different translations.

C. Reflect on seemingly impossible situations either in history, current events, or personal life as examples of God's divine intervention and deliverance.

O—Open the Lesson

A. Open with prayer. Ask students to write down situations in their lives that seem impossible right now.

B. Ask volunteers to share prayer requests for impossible situations.

C. Ask a volunteer to read the Aim for Change and In Focus story and discuss.

P—Present the Scriptures

A. Have volunteers read the Focal Verses.

B. Use The People, Places, and Times; Background; Search the Scriptures; At-A-Glance outline; In Depth; and More Light on the Text to clarify the verses.

C. Search for additional Scriptures on the promises of God that could be applicable to impossible situations.

E—Explore the Meaning

A. Divide students into groups of three or four, and divide the Discuss the Meaning, Lesson in Our Society, and Make It Happen sections.

B. Have students select a representative to report the groups' responses to the rest of the class.

N—Next Steps for Application

A. Write some take-away principles under the Follow the Spirit or Remember Your Thoughts section.

B. Close with prayer.

Worship Guide

For the Superintendent or Teacher
Theme: The Beginning of Freedom
Song: "Oh, Freedom"
Devotional Reading: Galatians 5:13–21

Beginning of Freedom

Bible Background • EXODUS 14
Printed Text • EXODUS 14:21–30 | Devotional Reading • GALATIANS 5:13–21

———————— Aim for Change ————————

By the end of the lesson, we will: DESCRIBE how God made a way for the Israelites when there seemed to be none; APPRECIATE the freedom we have in God's plan; and LIST ways to promote freedom for those who are oppressed.

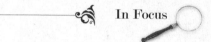 In Focus

Linda knew bad relationships. She was a magnet for them. But this guy, Darryl, was the worst she had ever met. He only called on weekends, never introduced her to his family, and never spent any significant holidays with her. It bothered her that his relationship status on a popular social media network was "It's Complicated." But he asked her to do a lot. Although they weren't living together, she cooked for him, did his laundry when he took business trips, and kept his personal calendar. She didn't feel like she was getting anything in return. But, for some reason, she felt stuck.

One day, she got fed up. She decided to move on. For the next month, Darryl tried to convince her he had changed. He did things to entice her to return. Linda had changed, though. She'd met a godly man, Joe, who knew how to treat her right. A year later they wed. The theme for the wedding was "Out of Egypt, Into Our Promise"—to commemorate the struggle they'd both been through with past relationships.

God sometimes grants us release from oppressive situations that do not bring Him glory. In today's lesson, we will see the Lord provide the Children of Israel with deliverance over their enemies that could only come from His mighty hand.

———————— Keep in Mind ————————

NOV 17th

"Thus the LORD saved Israel that day out of the hand of the Egyptians; and Israel saw the Egyptians dead upon the sea shore" (Exodus 14:30).

"Thus the LORD saved Israel that day out of the hand of the Egyptians; and Israel saw the Egyptians dead upon the sea shore" (Exodus 14:30).

Focal Verses

KJV **Exodus 14:21** And Moses stretched out his hand over the sea; and the LORD caused the sea to go back by a strong east wind all that night, and made the sea dry land, and the waters were divided.

22 And the children of Israel went into the midst of the sea upon the dry ground: and the waters were a wall unto them on their right hand, and on their left.

23 And the Egyptians pursued, and went in after them to the midst of the sea, even all Pharaoh's horses, his chariots, and his horsemen.

24 And it came to pass, that in the morning watch the LORD looked unto the host of the Egyptians through the pillar of fire and of the cloud, and troubled the host of the Egyptians,

25 And took off their chariot wheels, that they drave them heavily: so that the Egyptians said, Let us flee from the face of Israel; for the LORD fighteth for them against the Egyptians.

26 And the LORD said unto Moses, Stretch out thine hand over the sea, that the waters may come again upon the Egyptians, upon their chariots, and upon their horsemen.

27 And Moses stretched forth his hand over the sea, and the sea returned to his strength when the morning appeared; and the Egyptians fled against it; and the LORD overthrew the Egyptians in the midst of the sea.

28 And the waters returned, and covered the chariots, and the horsemen, and all the host of Pharaoh that came into the sea after them; there remained not so much as one of them.

29 But the children of Israel walked upon dry land in the midst of the sea; and the

NLT **Exodus 14:21** Then Moses raised his hand over the sea, and the LORD opened up a path through the water with a strong east wind. The wind blew all that night, turning the seabed into dry land.

22 So the people of Israel walked through the middle of the sea on dry ground, with walls of water on each side!

23 Then the Egyptians—all of Pharaoh's horses, chariots, and charioteers—chased them into the middle of the sea.

24 But just before dawn the LORD looked down on the Egyptian army from the pillar of fire and cloud, and he threw their forces into total confusion.

25 He twisted their chariot wheels, making their chariots difficult to drive. "Let's get out of here—away from these Israelites!" the Egyptians shouted. "The LORD is fighting for them against Egypt!"

26 When all the Israelites had reached the other side, the LORD said to Moses, "Raise your hand over the sea again. Then the waters will rush back and cover the Egyptians and their chariots and charioteers."

27 So as the sun began to rise, Moses raised his hand over the sea, and the water rushed back into its usual place. The Egyptians tried to escape, but the LORD swept them into the sea.

28 Then the waters returned and covered all the chariots and charioteers—the entire army of Pharaoh. Of all the Egyptians who had chased the Israelites into the sea, not a single one survived.

29 But the people of Israel had walked through the middle of the sea on dry ground, as the water stood up like a wall on both sides.

waters were a wall unto them on their right hand, and on their left.

30 Thus the LORD saved Israel that day out of the hand of the Egyptians; and Israel saw the Egyptians dead upon the sea shore.

30 That is how the LORD rescued Israel from the hand of the Egyptians that day. And the Israelites saw the bodies of the Egyptians washed up on the seashore.

The People, Places, and Times

The Red Sea. Also known as the Reed Sea, Papyrus Sea, Papyrus Lake, or Papyrus Marsh. It is a body of water between Africa and the Arabian peninsula, ranging in width from 100 to 175 miles, and 1,350 miles in length extending from the Indian Ocean to the Suez Gulf. It is over 7,200 feet deep. Its northern end splits into two gulfs, the Gulf of Suez and the Gulf of Akabah. Based on the account in Exodus, it is believed that the Children of Israel crossed from the north.

Background

With the final plague striking down all the firstborn in the land of Egypt (with exception of those covered by the blood of the lamb), God forced Pharaoh's hand. As He promised, the Children of Israel were released from captivity. The Israelites did not leave Egypt empty-handed, however; God gave them great favor and they were able to plunder their captors and go out with much wealth (12:35–36). By the strength of God's hand, the Israelites were free. God led them on a roundabout route to their destination, for He knew that if they went through the way of the Philistines, they would turn back to Egypt (13:17). God directed them into the wilderness toward the Red Sea and prepared them for battle (v. 18). He instructed Moses to have the people camp in front of Pihahiroth between Migdol and the sea in front of Baalzephon, and for them to encamp by the sea (14:1–2). God warned Moses that He would harden Pharaoh's heart, which would

cause him to come after them. However, what would seem to be impossible would be God's most brilliant display of His power. God went on to let Moses know how He would gain glory for Himself over this self-proclaimed god, and all the Egyptians would know that He is the Lord (v. 4).

At-A-Glance

1. God's Great Deliverance
(Exodus 14:21–25)
2. God's Great Triumph (vv. 26–30)

In Depth

1. God's Great Deliverance
(Exodus 14:21–25)

In the previous verses of chapter 14, Pharaoh did exactly as God warned. Pharaoh's heart was hardened and he and his officials wondered why they had released the Israelites from their service, so they went in hot pursuit (vv. 5–8). As Pharaoh and his army drew closer to the camp, the Israelites became afraid. They thought this was the end and that their short-lived freedom was a fluke—the army was closing in on one side and an impassable body of water lay on the other. They lamented to Moses, "Why did you bring us out here to die in the wilderness? Weren't there enough graves for us in Egypt? What have you done to us? Why did you make us leave Egypt?" (from v. 11, NLT). As God's representative, Moses spoke a reassuring word to them that the Lord would deliver them. "Don't be afraid. Just stand still and watch the LORD rescue you today. The Egyptians you see today will never be seen again. The LORD himself will fight for you. Just stay calm" (from vv. 13–14, NLT). Since their departure from Egypt, God led the Children of Israel via a pillar of cloud by day and pillar of fire by night. As they moved, He was with them. God made His presence known going before and behind His people so that their enemies could not come near them (vv. 19–22).

God instructed Moses to use what he had been using from the beginning of this journey of freedom to show forth God's mighty hand: "Pick up your staff and raise your hand over the sea" (from v. 16, NLT). Moses lifted his staff and God divided the sea, providing dry ground for passage. What a mighty display of power! God provided a wall of water that served as protection for the Israelites as they passed through. In their arrogance, the Egyptians thought that they too had safe passage and went into the divided sea after them. Pharaoh and his chariots met face to face with Yahweh. Through the pillar of fire and cloud, the Lord "troubled" or "agitated" the Egyptians (v. 24). In His awesome power, God confused the enemy to the point where they could not even steer their chariots. The Egyptians were well aware of the fact that they had met a force they could not fight. The Egyptians called out that the Lord was fighting for His people, so they sought to flee from the presence and power of God (v. 25). What a great assurance to know that God will fight for His people—but we must stand still and see the salvation of the Lord. When we are in the will of God, no force is too strong. Nothing is too hard for the Lord.

2. God's Great Triumph (vv. 26–30)

After all the Children of Israel passed through the divided waters of the Red Sea

and the Egyptians made their way to the middle, God was not finished doing the miraculous. He then instructed Moses to once again stretch forth his hand over the waters to bring them back into place. As Moses lifted his hands, the water walls came crashing down over the Egyptians. God brought the deliverance He promised. In triumph, the Children of Israel were finally free. They watched their enemies drown in the Red Sea—chariots, horses, and all. There were no survivors. The Children of Israel passed through on dry land; not a life was lost. The Lord showed His faithfulness to His covenant through this event, proving why He is Jehovah Sabaoth (The Lord of Hosts) and Jehovah Shammah (The Lord Is There). The great deliverance from Egypt would be the reference point of God's character for His people throughout the generations. Moses would pen a song in honor of God and His mighty acts (ch. 15). God ordained feasts so that all the succeeding generations could celebrate and remember God's faithfulness (12:14–20, 23:14–19; Leviticus 23; Deuteronomy 16). David and other psalmists would write songs to chronicle this great deliverance for future generations (e.g. Psalm 105).

Search the Scriptures

1. What happened to the Red Sea when Moses drew back his hand (Exodus 14:21, 26)?

2. Who was able to pass on dry ground (vv. 22, 29)?

Discuss the Meaning

1. What does it mean to you to know that the Egyptians recognized that God was fighting on behalf of the Israelites?

2. What does it mean to you to know that the Children of Israel saw their enemies

destroyed? How would you respond differently in your own Red Sea experience?

Lesson in Our Society

God is faithful to His word! Through His great display of power, He delivered the Children of Israel by His mighty hand. Imagine what our world would be like if we truly believed that God would do such a display today in our communities to deliver us from violence and oppression. God is no respecter of persons; He is the same yesterday, today, and forever. He left this story as a testament of His greatness. Today, Yahweh continues to prove He is the same God who shows us His care and mercy, including forms of deliverance beyond our imagination.

Make It Happen

We have a mighty vehicle through the power of prayer to bring God's will on earth as it is in heaven. Begin to seek the mind of the Lord in what He wants to do in and through you to impact your community for His glory. As you pray, believe God for concepts, ideas, vision, and favor to bring His will to pass.

Follow the Spirit

What God wants me to do:

_____

_____

_____

_____

Remember Your Thoughts

Special insights I have learned:

_____

_____

_____

_____

More Light on the Text

Exodus 14:21–30

21 And Moses stretched out his hand over the sea; and the LORD caused the sea to go back by a strong east wind all that night, and made the sea dry land, and the waters were divided.

The body of water before Moses was the Red Sea (sometimes called the Reed Sea), identified by name in 13:18 and 15:4. This particular lake region was a seawater inlet of the Indian Ocean and would change its shape and size as often as floods and droughts altered the landscape around it. For this reason, many theologians and archaeologists today have differing opinions on where this miracle specifically occurred.

It's also worth noting that the name of the Lord in this passage is *Yehovah* (**yeh-HO-va**), sometimes pronounced as "Jehovah" and indicating the proper name of the one true God. Although it may not stand out this way in our translation, to the Jewish culture at the time, it meant that in a land of false gods and human tyrants, the only real Lord was the one who was saving them.

22 And the children of Israel went into the midst of the sea upon the dry ground: and the waters were a wall unto them on their right hand, and on their left.

The inconsistency of the Red Sea's geography coupled with the dramatic miracle of this particular story has caused some to doubt its validity. However, outside of the Bible's own credibility, a *Los Angeles Times* article entitled "Research Supports Bible's Account of Red Sea Parting" (3/14/92) states: "Sophisticated computer calculations indicate that the biblical parting of the Red Sea, said to have allowed Moses and the Israelites to escape from bondage in Egypt, could have occurred precisely as the Bible describes it. Because of the peculiar geography of the northern end of the Red Sea, researchers report Sunday in the Bulletin of the American Meteorological Society, a moderate wind blowing constantly for about 10 hours could have caused the sea to recede about a mile and the water level to drop 10 feet, leaving dry land in the area where many biblical scholars believe the crossing occurred."

23 And the Egyptians pursued, and went in after them to the midst of the sea, even all Pharaoh's horses, his chariots, and his horsemen.

The beginning of Israel's freedom created such an emotional reaction in Pharaoh that he sent his entire army to recapture them. In the previous generation, Egypt's ruler saw that the Israelites outnumbered the Egyptians (1:9). It's probable that even after tightening control by killing off babies and oppressing the Israelites into hard labor, Pharaoh found the Jewish nation was growing in size again. Jacob's family first came to Egypt with a total of seventy people (v. 5), yet by the book of Numbers, a national census conducted after the Exodus lists 603,550 men above the age of twenty (Numbers 1:45–56). If each man was married and had at least two children, the Jews could have numbered around 2.5 million people when they left Egypt. It's possible to imagine even a greater number since ancient cultures often had larger families,

which may have meant more than 3.5 million people if every household had at least four children. It's no wonder that Pharaoh sent all he had to recapture his slave labor force.

24 And it came to pass, that in the morning watch the LORD looked unto the host of the Egyptians through the pillar of fire and of the cloud, and troubled the host of the Egyptians,

For four centuries, the Israelites had lived in a pagan culture that believed in many different gods. The concept of one God watching over them may have been confusing to many, including the Egyptians who were about to experience the other end of the same miracle meant to bless the Jews. Since both the pillar of fire and the pillar of cloud are listed, it's likely this was the morning watch where a transition was taking place.

God looked down from both and observed all that was happening with such silence that His sheer presence threw the Egyptian army into a panic. In the original language, the word for "troubled" is *hamam* (**ha-MAM**). This indicates that there was noise, movement, and confusion to the point that the people felt something was breaking into their comfort and about to consume them. This confusion not only vexed the Egyptians but also made them fear for their lives.

25 And took off their chariot wheels, that they drave them heavily: so that the Egyptians said, Let us flee from the face of Israel; for the LORD fighteth for them against the Egyptians.

The Egyptians stood before the manifestation of God in the sky, not realizing He is everywhere and would begin addressing them from even the very wheels of their chariots. The theological term for this is "omnipresence," which means that God is everywhere at all times. Psalm 139:7–12 explores this in detail, "Whither shall I go from thy spirit? or whither shall I flee from thy presence? If I ascend up into heaven, thou art there: if I make my bed in hell, behold, thou art there. If I take the wings of the morning, and dwell in the uttermost parts of the sea; even there shall thy hand lead me, and thy right hand shall hold me. If I say, Surely the darkness shall cover me; even the night shall be light about me. Yea, the darkness hideth not from thee; but the night shineth as the day: the darkness and the light are both alike to thee."

Christians may better grasp this concept today, but it remains a difficult concept to internalize. Pharaoh's army experienced it firsthand when God removed their ability to use their chariots, causing them to have to pursue the Israelites on foot. In doing so, they unknowingly made it easier for the Lord to perform the offensive move of stopping them all at once.

26 And the LORD said unto Moses, Stretch out thine hand over the sea, that the waters may come again upon the Egyptians, upon their chariots, and upon their horsemen.

One of the benefits of following God is that He involves people in His work. By using Moses to perform this miracle, the Lord shared His work with a human and showed His favor to the people and their prophet. Although the Lord would later let Israel face pagan armies in battle, He first fought for them through one man. This concept is most fully revealed in Jesus Christ and further magnified when Christians are referred to in 1 Peter 2:9: "But ye are a chosen generation, a royal priesthood, an holy nation, a peculiar people; that ye should shew forth the praises of him who hath called you out of darkness into his marvellous light."

27 And Moses stretched forth his hand over the sea, and the sea returned to his strength when the morning appeared; and the Egyptians fled against it; and the LORD overthrew the Egyptians in the midst of the sea.

Freedom is a gift from God but often needs to be received. When Israel first experienced God's protection during the Passover, they had to mark their homes with the blood of a lamb and remain in their houses (ch. 12). As they arrived at the Red Sea, God required further participation from them, including trusting His instructions without explanation in a violent situation. As Moses brought the walls of the sea back together, God was showing His people that only by moving forward could a real release from slavery be achieved. Had any of the Jews stopped short during the crossing and demanded that all of their questions be answered, they would have become consumed by discipline instead of experiencing freedom.

28 And the waters returned, and covered the chariots, and the horsemen, and all the host of Pharaoh that came into the sea after them; there remained not so much as one of them.

Stories of the Israelites' success against those who stood against them or God grew among neighboring nations. In Joshua 2:9–11, a woman in the pagan city of Jericho told the Jewish spies that they had heard about how the Lord has blessed His people, and they had a great fear of God and His people because of it. As bodies of Egyptian soldiers showed up on the coastlines, surely the surrounding nations heard the story of how Israel's God had defeated the entire Egyptian army. This one act of deliverance became a defining moment for the Jews and everyone who heard of them—this was a powerful

God who was protecting His people. It also created a shift in awareness that political and national power means nothing when standing against God. Showing the Jews the death of their human oppressors may very well be why God shows us the elimination of Satan in the final chapters of Revelation—sometimes to claim freedom, we have to realize that a history of slavery doesn't eliminate freedom in our future.

29 But the children of Israel walked upon dry land in the midst of the sea; and the waters were a wall unto them on their right hand, and on their left.

The word "land" doesn't appear in the original biblical text, which originally would state *yabbashah tavek yam* (**yab-BA-shaw ta-VEK yam**), or "upon dry in the midst of the sea." Simply put, the Bible says the Israelites walked on something that was dry while surrounded by walls of water on each side. Some have argued that this allows for the possibility of a slab of ice that God provided for His people to walk across before dropping it and allowing the water to consume the Egyptians. Others maintain a more traditional understanding that the Israelites literally walked on dry ground and could peer into the walls of water around them that were full of aquatic life. What is clear is that the miracle was favorable for the Jews and unfavorable for their pursuers.

30 Thus the LORD saved Israel that day out of the hand of the Egyptians; and Israel saw the Egyptians dead upon the sea shore.

The idea of being "saved" is something that even today, Jewish people have a different understanding of than Christians. In this passage, the original word, *yasha* (**ya-SHEH**), means that a form of physical liberation or deliverance took place. The Jews would come

to expect that a Messiah would do this again for them in this type of tangible, political way. However, Jesus would reestablish that the core element of being saved is something internal: reconciliation related to Christ the King, who will in the end bring about a physical deliverance as well.

Nonetheless, God left no doubt in this moment that He has tremendous power to bless those who trust Him and protect them from anyone who would persecute them. Unfortunately, life is not made up of one miracle after another—remember that the Jews had waited for 400 years for deliverance from slavery in Egypt. It's tempting to resent why the victorious moments don't seem to outnumber the defeated ones unless we remember God's original plan as contained in Genesis 1–2 and which won't be fully redeemed until Revelation 21–22. No matter how long the world is around in its present state, it's nothing compared to the eternity ahead. It's our challenge to maintain a reverent awe before the Lord in the down moments by recognizing that, whether or not a dramatic miracle occurs, we have the ultimate miracle coming on the last day that time even matters.

Sources:

Associates For Scriptural Knowledge. www.askelm.com. "More on Crossing the Red Sea." http://www.askelm.com/secrets/sec102.htm (accessed August 10, 2012).

Bible Study Tools. www.BibleStudyTools.com. *International Standard Bible Encyclopedia.* "Red Sea." http://www.biblestudytools.com/encyclopedias/isbe/red-sea.html (accessed August 3, 2012).

Collins, J. John. *A Short Introduction to the Hebrew Bible.* Minneapolis: Fortress Press, 2007. 81.

Hebrew Greek Key Word Study Bible (KJV) 2nd ed. Chattanooga, TN: AMG Publishers, 1991. 1609, 1659.

Maugh, Thomas H. "Research Supports Bible's Account of Red Sea Parting: Weather: Gulf of Suez's geography would make it possible, meteorologist and oceanographer say." *Los Angeles Times.* http://articles.latimes.com/1992-03-14/news/mn-3138_1_red-sea (accessed August 4, 2012).

Unger, Merrill F. *Unger's Bible Dictionary.* Chicago: Moody Press, 1981. 914.

Say It Correctly

Akabah. **AH**-kuh-buh.
Suez. **SOO**-ez.
Arabian. uh-**RAY**-bee-an.

Daily Bible Readings

MONDAY
Called to Live in Freedom
(Galatians 5:13–21)

TUESDAY
Setting Apart the Firstborn
(Exodus 13:11–16)

WEDNESDAY
Guided by Pillars of Cloud and Fire
(Exodus 13:17–22)

THURSDAY
Pharaoh's Change of Heart
(Exodus 14:5–9)

FRIDAY
The Lord Will Fight for You
(Exodus 14:10–14)

SATURDAY
Guarded from the Approaching Enemy
(Exodus 14:15–20)

SUNDAY
The Lord Saved Israel that Day
(Exodus 14:21–30)

Notes

Teaching Tips

Words You Should Know

A. Tabernacle (Exodus 40:17) *mishkan* (Heb.)—Dwelling place.

B. Commanded (v. 16) *tsavah* (Heb.)—To give orders or lay charge upon.

C. Glory (v. 34) *kabowd* (Heb.)—Honour, splendor.

Teacher Preparation

Unifying Principle—Traveling Light. After the Israelites left Egypt, they felt insecure and afraid as they traveled to the Promised Land. God commanded Moses and the people to build the tabernacle, so they would always feel God's presence and guidance.

A. Pray and ask for God's help with the lesson.

B. Review Exodus 39:32–40:38.

C. Prepare a PowerPoint presentation showing pictures of holy oil, water, fire, thunder and lightning, clouds, and doves—all things that represent God's presence in Scripture.

O—Open the Lesson

A. Open with prayer, including the Aim for Change.

B. After prayer, introduce the subject of today's lesson.

C. Have your students read the Aim for Change and Keep in Mind verse in unison. Discuss.

D. Show the PowerPoint presentation and ask, "Can you identify any other symbols of God's presence?"

E. Now have a volunteer read the In Focus story. Discuss.

P—Present the Scriptures

A. Have volunteers read the Focal Verses.

B. Now use The People, Places, and Times; Background; Search the Scriptures; At-A-Glance outline; In Depth; and More Light on the Text to clarify the verses.

E—Explore the Meaning

A. Have volunteers summarize the Discuss the Meaning and Lesson in Our Society sections.

B. Connect these sections to the Aim for Change and the Keep in Mind verse.

N—Next Steps for Application

A. Summarize the lesson and review the Make It Happen section.

B. Close with prayer and praise God for His continual presence and guidance.

Worship Guide

For the Superintendent or Teacher
Theme: Beginning of the Tabernacle
Song: "Lord Prepare Me"
Devotional Reading: Hebrews 9:11–15

NOV
24th

Beginning of the Tabernacle

Bible Background • EXODUS 40:16–30, 34, 38
Printed Text • EXODUS 40:16–30, 34, 38 | Devotional Reading • HEBREWS 9:11–15

———————— Aim for Change ————————

By the end of the lesson, we will: DISCUSS the significance and purpose of the tabernacle; SENSE God's presence in our lives; and THANK God for His abiding presence.

In Focus

Patrice was placed in foster care when she was 10 years old after her parents died in a car accident. She frequently felt alone and abandoned. Neither of her parents' families desired to have her live with them. Patrice's foster family did not include her in any of their family gatherings. When she turned 18, Patrice aged out of the system. She lived in a homeless shelter until she went to college. She graduated from college with honors and obtained a high-paying job as a Certified Public Accountant. Yet, Patrice still felt alone.

One day, a package was delivered to her home from her Aunt Betty. She had been cleaning her closet and found a box of items that belonged to Patrice's mother. Aunt Betty thought Patrice should have her mother's journal and gold cross necklace. Patrice spent a week reading the journal. She discovered that her mother had a deep faith in Christ and trusted Him to guide her. The cross necklace was a gift from a friend who wanted her to always remember that God was present with her at all times. Patrice took the necklace and wore it all the time. It helped her feel close to her mother and remember God was with her.

Even when we do not feel God's presence, He is still with us. In today's lesson, God commands the people to build the tabernacle so they could feel His presence and guidance.

———————— Keep in Mind ————————

"For the cloud of the LORD was upon the tabernacle by day, and fire was on it by night, in the sight of all the house of Israel, throughout all their journeys" (Exodus 40:38).

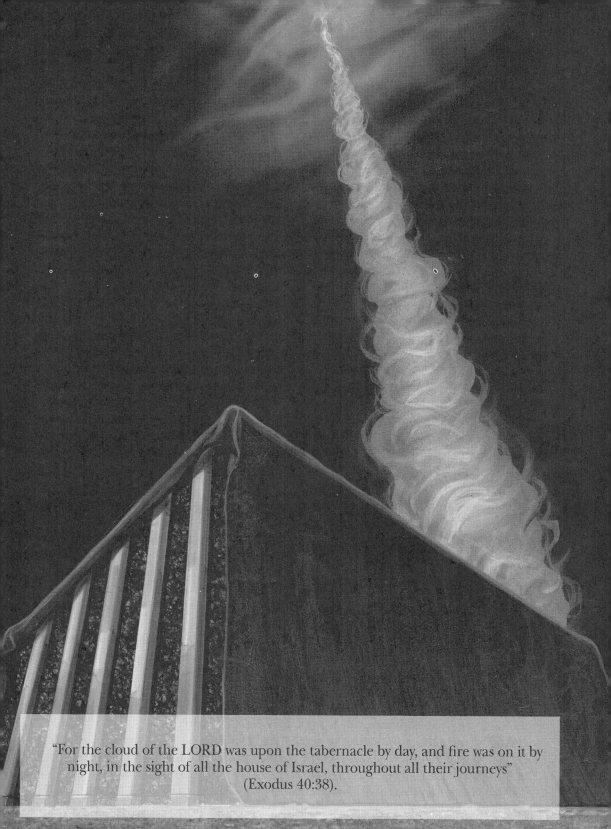

"For the cloud of the LORD was upon the tabernacle by day, and fire was on it by night, in the sight of all the house of Israel, throughout all their journeys" (Exodus 40:38).

Focal Verses

KJV **40:16** Thus did Moses: according to all that the LORD commanded him, so did he.

17 And it came to pass in the first month in the second year, on the first day of the month, that the tabernacle was reared up.

18 And Moses reared up the tabernacle, and fastened his sockets, and set up the boards thereof, and put in the bars thereof, and reared up his pillars.

19 And he spread abroad the tent over the tabernacle, and put the covering of the tent above upon it; as the LORD commanded Moses.

20 And he took and put the testimony into the ark, and set the staves on the ark, and put the mercy seat above upon the ark:

21 And he brought the ark into the tabernacle, and set up the vail of the covering, and covered the ark of the testimony; as the LORD commanded Moses.

22 And he put the table in the tent of the congregation, upon the side of the tabernacle northward, without the vail.

23 And he set the bread in order upon it before the Lord; as the LORD had commanded Moses.

24 And he put the candlestick in the tent of the congregation, over against the table, on the side of the tabernacle southward.

25 And he lighted the lamps before the LORD; as the LORD commanded Moses.

26 And he put the golden altar in the tent of the congregation before the vail:

27 And he burnt sweet incense thereon; as the LORD commanded Moses.

28 And he set up the hanging at the door of the tabernacle.

29 And he put the altar of burnt offering by the door of the tabernacle of the tent of the congregation, and offered upon it the

NLT **Exodus 40:16** Moses proceeded to do everything just as the LORD had commanded him.

17 So the Tabernacle was set up on the first day of the first month of the second year.

18 Moses erected the Tabernacle by setting down its bases, inserting the frames, attaching the crossbars, and setting up the posts.

19 Then he spread the coverings over the Tabernacle framework and put on the protective layers, just as the LORD had commanded him.

20 He took the stone tablets inscribed with the terms of the covenant and placed them inside the Ark. Then he attached the carrying poles to the Ark, and he set the Ark's cover—the place of atonement—on top of it.

21 Then he brought the Ark of the Covenant into the Tabernacle and hung the inner curtain to shield it from view, just as the LORD had commanded him.

22 Next Moses placed the table in the Tabernacle, along the north side of the Holy Place, just outside the inner curtain.

23 And he arranged the Bread of the Presence on the table before the LORD, just as the LORD had commanded him.

24 He set the lampstand in the Tabernacle across from the table on the south side of the Holy Place.

25 Then he lit the lamps in the LORD's presence, just as the LORD had commanded him.

26 He also placed the gold incense altar in the Tabernacle, in the Holy Place in front of the inner curtain.

27 On it he burned the fragrant incense, just as the LORD had commanded him.

28 He hung the curtain at the entrance of the Tabernacle, burnt offering and the meat offering; as the LORD commanded Moses.

30 And he set the laver between the tent of the congregation and the altar, and put water there, to wash withal.

40:34 Then a cloud covered the tent of the congregation, and the glory of the LORD filled the tabernacle.

40:38 For the cloud of the LORD was upon the tabernacle by day, and fire was on it by night, in the sight of all the house of Israel, throughout all their journeys.

29 and he placed the altar of burnt offering near the Tabernacle entrance. On it he offered a burnt offering and a grain offering, just as the LORD had commanded him.

30 Next Moses placed the washbasin between the Tabernacle and the altar. He filled it with water so the priests could wash themselves.

40:34 Then the cloud covered the Tabernacle, and the glory of the LORD filled the Tabernacle.

40:38 The cloud of the LORD hovered over the Tabernacle during the day, and at night fire glowed inside the cloud so the whole family of Israel could see it. This continued throughout all their journeys.

The People, Places, and Times

Egypt. Joseph had been a high official in Egypt under Pharaoh. Joseph's family, the seventy descendants of Jacob, had been permitted to move to Egypt to escape a terrible famine in Canaan (Genesis 45:9–10). After Joseph's death, a new Pharaoh came to power who enslaved the growing population of Israelites. God raised up Moses to lead the people out of slavery (Exodus 3–4), but Pharaoh refused to let the Israelites go. God sent ten plagues, which destroyed the Egyptians' crops, herds, and families. God instituted the first Passover the night of Israel's release. After Pharaoh released them, he changed his mind and decided to pursue them. God miraculously enabled the Israelites to cross the Red Sea to safety (14:15–31), but Pharaoh's army drowned. The Israelites were free and on their way to the Promised Land.

Ark of the Covenant. The Ark of the Covenant was a box measuring 3¾ feet long, 2¼ wide, and 2¼ feet high. It was made of acacia wood overlaid with pure gold. Acacia trees flourished in the area and were fairly common in Old Testament times. The wood was very hard and good material for building furniture.

The Ark of the Covenant represented God's covenant with Israel's people. It was located in the most holy place of the tabernacle, behind a curtain to hide it from view. Only the high priest could enter the most holy place and then only once a year, on the day of atonement. The Ark contained the tablets of the Ten Commandments, a pot of manna, and later other items as instructed by God. God commanded Moses to keep an omer (two quarts) of manna as a reminder of the way He provided for the Israelites in the wilderness (16:31–34). The cover of the Ark of the Covenant was called the "mercy seat" or "atonement cover." The mercy seat had a gold lid.

Background

The purpose of the book of Exodus is to record the events of Israel's deliverance from Egypt and development as a nation. The book begins with a short account of how the

Israelites became slaves in Egypt (ch. 1) then goes on to expound on Moses' birth, life, and call by God. Moses was used by God to lead the people out of slavery in Egypt to freedom in the Promised Land (5:1–18:27). God guided the Israelites while they were in the wilderness by a cloud in the day and a pillar of fire by night. This was a visible sign that God was present and guiding them along the way.

The Israelites promised to obey God's commands as given to Moses (20:1–17, 24:3). Moses spent time in the presence of God for forty days and forty nights. God gave Moses specific directions concerning the building of the tabernacle (chs. 25–31), and the people carried them out exactly (chs. 35–39).

At-A-Glance

1. The Tabernacle Assembled
(Exodus 40:16–30)
2. God's Presence Fills the Tabernacle
(vv. 34, 38)

In Depth

1. The Tabernacle Assembled
(Exodus 40:16–30)

God had spoken to Abram about his offspring in Genesis 15:13–14, "Then the LORD said to Abram, 'You can be sure that your descendants will be strangers in a foreign land, where they will be oppressed as slaves for 400 years. But I will punish the nation that enslaves them, and in the end they will come away with great wealth'" (NLT). Just as God predicted, the Israelites were enslaved and mistreated in Egypt for many years. He then used Moses to lead them out of Egypt. When the Israelites left Egypt, the Egyptians gave them silver and gold jewelry and clothing (Exodus 12:35–36).

Just before the Israelites left Egypt, God instituted the Passover (12:1–20). Passover is a sacred holiday when the Israelites celebrate their deliverance from Egypt and remember what God has done for them. A year had passed after the institution of the Passover when God commanded Moses and the people to erect the tabernacle (25:8). It would be a temporary dwelling place where the Israelites would always feel God's presence.

Moses followed every detail in the construction of the tabernacle (40:16) so it would be built precisely as God required. The pieces placed inside included: the Ark of the Covenant (symbolizing God's covenant with the Israelites); mercy seat (symbolizing God's presence among His people); curtain (symbolizing humanity's separation from God due to sin); table that held the bread of the presence (symbolizing the spiritual nourishment God offers His people); candlestick (lighting the holy place for the priests); altar of incense (burning incense that symbolized acceptable prayers); altar for the burnt offerings (symbolizing how sacrifice restored one's relationship with God); laver (symbolizing the need for spiritual cleansing). The tabernacle was the place where God would come to be present with Israel in a special way.

2. God's Presence Fills the Tabernacle
(vv. 34, 38)

God blessed Moses and the people with His presence as He filled the tabernacle with His glory. This cloud was the same as the pillar of cloud that went before the Israelites when they came out of Egypt. It led them through the Red Sea and appeared at Mount Sinai. Now it appeared in a different form, more expanded, so as to cover the tabernacle inside and out.

This cloud had an uncommon brightness and a glorious stream of light which no eye could behold. God's glory also would later fill Solomon's temple at the dedication (1 Kings 8:10–11). It was a symbol of Christ, with the brightness of His Father's glory, dwelling in and filling the tabernacle. So great was the splendor, Moses was not able to minister.

The Israelites were given the pillar of cloud by day and a pillar of fire by night as assurance of God's presence with them. The cloud and fire also acted as a means of guidance. Whenever the cloud or fire moved, the people moved. If the cloud or fire stopped, the people did as well. The pillar became the compass that helped the Israelites as they traveled toward the Promised Land.

Search the Scriptures

1. What was used to screen the Ark of the Covenant? Why (Exodus 40:20–21)?

2. What symbols did God give the Israelites to represent His presence (v. 38)?

Discuss the Meaning

God instructed the people to create the tabernacle, a place where they could always find His presence and guidance. People always want to feel secure and have guidance for their lives. Who or what do you turn to for security?

Lesson in Our Society

Sometimes in life we all face difficult transitions. It may be moving to a different state, taking another job, getting married or divorced, going back to college, etc. In the midst of transitions, we seek guidance from family, friends, or church leaders. We want to know that we are making the right decision. What criteria can be used to decide if the guidance given to us is reliable and trustworthy? How do we determine if God is with us?

Make It Happen

Every day when we wake up, we need to seek God's presence. We do not have to go to a tabernacle or church every time we want to enter into God's presence. His presence is with us through the Holy Spirit, who is our source for security and guidance. Begin to worship and praise God for always being with us. If we sing and offer thanksgiving, God's glory will fill the place where we are dwelling.

Follow the Spirit

What God wants me to do:

_____

_____

_____

_____

Remember Your Thoughts

Special insights I have learned:

_____

_____

_____

_____

More Light on the Text

Exodus 40:16–30, 34, 38

16 Thus did Moses: according to all that the LORD commanded him, so did he.

In the context of this passage, Moses did everything God commanded of him. The full description of the dedication ceremony in the prior verses is found in Leviticus 8–9, and the remainder of this passage addresses Moses overseeing the assembly of the tabernacle. The problem is that while Moses would at times be known for his obedience, he also struggled with reckless moments where his insistence on doing things his way or adding additional action beyond what God asked strained his relationship with the Lord. Numbers 20–21 and the latter chapters of Deuteronomy show that this inconsistency led to him not being allowed to enter the Promised Land. No one is perfect, but the Lord can work wonders if the intention of our heart is to fully do what He has commanded.

17 And it came to pass in the first month in the second year, on the first day of the month, that the tabernacle was reared up.

This is a historic moment for the Jews and a revelation for all people to recognize that God longs to dwell among His people. The word for tabernacle is *mishkan* (**MISH-khan**) and refers to a dwelling place, typically thought to be a tent. Genesis 1–2 and 3:8 display the original intent for our relationship with God being personal, and the great lesson of the tabernacle is that the Lord hasn't given up on that concept. From the scattered accounts of Him talking with people to this intentional transition, our Creator longs to be among His creation. John 1:14 says that Jesus "dwelt" or "tabernacled" among us. The tabernacle served as God's dwelling place for five hundred years until it was replaced by the temple during the reign of Solomon. It was the Lord's way of showing that once His people were redeemed, they could be free from sin and more fully enjoy an intentional relationship with Him.

18 And Moses reared up the tabernacle, and fastened his sockets, and set up the boards thereof, and put in the bars thereof, and reared up his pillars.

There's no irony in such a sound structure being assembled in the middle of nowhere, for the physical features of the tabernacle

represented divine truths. Even the wood that came from the acacia trees had a relatively enduring and incorruptible makeup that symbolized what the Jews had survived and later how Christ would endure sin and persecution for our sake. The acacia tree was unattractive outwardly and only grew in adverse environments, such as the wilderness. The metaphor of these trees making up the pillars and boards of the tabernacle spoke in ways that the Jews probably didn't fully understand. The prophet Isaiah wrote of the coming Messiah, "For he shall grow up before him as a tender plant, and as a root out of a dry ground: he hath no form nor comeliness; and when we shall see him, there is no beauty that we should desire him" (Isaiah 53:2).

19 And he spread abroad the tent over the tabernacle, and put the covering of the tent above upon it; as the LORD commanded Moses.

God was essentially the designer of the tabernacle, and Moses was the general contractor. This created a twofold purpose between divinity and humanity, starting by first weaning the people away from worshipping what they could see. The Jews had lived in a culture where people set up visible objects of worship, such as snakes and animals, yet the tabernacle would be a visible tent that housed the presence of an invisible God. The immediate purpose of the tabernacle was to give the Jews the assurance that the Lord was with them even though they couldn't see Him. The later symbolism of this would reveal the role of the Holy Spirit in the lives of believers, for He indwells those who are born again even though we cannot see Him. These distinct designations keep worship relational versus transactional, allowing people to see God through reverence and awe so that they might one day see Him face to face (Revelation 21–22). Jesus said: "God is a Spirit: and they that worship him must worship him in spirit and in truth" (John 4:24).

20 And he took and put the testimony into the ark, and set the staves on the ark, and put the mercy seat above upon the ark.

Moses once again personally handled the *eduwth* (**AY-dooth**) or "testimony" of the Ten Commandments that were written on tablets of stone. He'd eventually hand this type of ministry to priests, even though he's later counted as being among them (Psalm 99:6). The Ark was a gold-plated chest that contained the tablets of the Ten Commandments, or "testimony," making it one of the most significant objects involved in worship. The mercy seat (atonement cover) was the lid to the Ark of the Covenant, where God would manifest His presence.

21 And he brought the ark into the tabernacle, and set up the vail of the covering, and covered the ark of the testimony; as the LORD commanded Moses.

In building the tabernacle, Moses again showed the uniqueness of his ministry. He served in the roles of a prophet and a priest, taking special instructions from God to the people while talking with the Lord on their behalf. He likewise served the initial office of sharing the Law, as well as giving instructions for worship so people could have a right relationship with the Lord. By setting the wheels in motion through these endeavors, Moses again showed himself to be a foreshadowing of what Jesus would fulfill. This is one reason why Moses appears during the Transfiguration of Christ (Matthew 17:3).

22 And he put the table in the tent of the congregation, upon the side of the tabernacle northward, without the vail.

According to 25:23–24, the table was made of acacia wood and covered with gold. Chairs aren't mentioned because eating standing up symbolizes readiness to action. Exodus 12:11 records God's instruction to the people to eat as if they were ready to go when God called them out of Egypt, showing that eating at the table of the Lord is more than a place of worship or fellowship but of preparation for action. Ephesians 6:13 offers the same challenge to withstand evil and remain standing as one who has taken up the full armor of God. It's no accident that this was the first object a priest encountered when entering the holy place.

23 And he set the bread in order upon it before the LORD; as the LORD had commanded Moses.

The bread on the table had many purposes, including being an offering to the Lord as well as food for priests. There were twelve loaves of bread, one for each tribe of Israel. Fresh loaves were baked each Sabbath and placed on the table, and the old loaves were eaten by the priests. Just as one might offer a financial tithe that blesses God by blessing His church, so does providing for ministers serve as an expression of gratitude to the Lord. The bread of the presence also indicated God's desire for a relationship with humanity, later underscored in how Jesus was a friend of sinners and ate with them (Mark 2:13–17) and His self-description as the "bread of life" (John 6:35). God also wants to satisfy our hunger, and spending time with Him or experiencing salvation is likened to a banquet spread across a table (Luke 14:7–14; Revelation 19:7–10).

24 And he put the candlestick in the tent of the congregation, over against the table, on the side of the tabernacle southward.

Each element in the tabernacle had a specific role in context that will be culminated in eternity. The candlestick or lampstand offered illumination in this otherwise darkened tent since there were no windows or places to let in light. The candlestick had an ornate base with six branches and a center shaft, each ending with a cup that looked like an open almond flower. This "menorah" has become a recognizable symbol of Judaism, but it also is shown to be the person of Jesus Christ, who is known as the "light" of the world (John 8:12) and the illumination of heaven (Revelation 21:23, 22:5).

The concept of a "congregation" is also different than what some may think today. The phrase *mowed* (**mow-AID**) indicates an appointed time or place for a significant meeting. Christ later expanded this idea by showing His followers that church is a community and identity versus a place, but for the time being, a congregation was thought of in this circumstantial sense.

25 And he lighted the lamps before the LORD; as the LORD commanded Moses.

Moses was to build and arrange everything in the tabernacle according to God's instructions, but others would take over certain roles. Eventually the high priest would be responsible to make sure the lamps were always lit to brighten the holy place (Leviticus 24:3). The opened petals contained a wick and oil lamp that were attended to by a priest every morning and every evening (Exodus 30:7).

26 And he put the golden altar in the tent of the congregation before the vail.

The golden altar was a gold-plated wooden structure that was used to offer incense before the Lord. It stood in front of a vail (veil) or curtain that separated the holy place from the most holy place, and measured around three feet high. It had rings on the corners so that the priests could insert poles in the rings when carrying it.

27 And he burnt sweet incense thereon; as the LORD commanded Moses.

The incense burned on this altar symbolized prayer as a sweet smell, reminding people that the tabernacle was a place where people could approach the Lord. The priests were to burn incense every morning on the altar so that all day the people would smell its fragrance and remember to pray. This particular incense includes the four spices of stacte, onycha, galbanum, and frankincense—a recipe that was to be kept sacred among the people (30:34–38). It isn't surprising to see this played out in the Bible's descriptions of heaven, for Revelation 8:3–4 mentions an altar of incense in heaven that represents the prayers of God's people. Moses began this imagery by burning the first fragrant incense on the altar, just as the Lord commanded him.

28 And he set up the hanging at the door of the tabernacle.

Exodus 36:37 states that the tabernacle's entrance was covered by a screen woven with blue, purple, and scarlet thread that was mixed with fine white linen. This same material was used to create the curtains and veil, although each had a specific design. The hanging served as a divider between the outside and the entrance into the dwelling, stretching across the eastern side and standing ten cubits (fifteen feet) high and hung on five pillars. It separated the tabernacle courtyard and the holy place.

29 And he put the altar of burnt offering by the door of the tabernacle of the tent of the congregation, and offered upon it the burnt offering and the meat offering; as the LORD commanded Moses.

The altar of burnt offering was also made of acacia wood overlaid with bronze (38:1–7) with a horn (like an animal horn) protruding up from each corner. When the priest offered a sacrifice upon it, the four horns were sprinkled with the blood of the sin offering, reminding the people that the consequence of sin is death (and eventually why the blood of Jesus would be needed for the once-and-for-all sacrifice on our behalf). Bible interpreters use different words to describe what is referenced in this passage as a "meat offering." According to Roy Lee DeWitt's book *Teaching from the Tabernacle*, the King James Bible uses the word "meat" because it was published when the word "meat" was used much like today we use the word "meal." The Hebrew word used in the passage is *minchah* **(min-CHAH)** and refers to a grain offering or a general "food" offering. It was a tribute offering to God that voluntarily recognized His goodness, while the burnt offering further recognized unintentional sin and general devotion to the Lord.

30 And he set the laver between the tent of the congregation and the altar, and put water there, to wash withal.

The priests used this bronze basin filled with water to wash their hands and feet before serving at the altar. It was located halfway between the altar of burnt offering and the holy place, a significant place for the priests to cleanse themselves before

approaching God. This practice is completed through Christ's work on the cross, although as we immerse ourselves in the Bible, we continue the practice of being transformed by the cleansing of our minds.

34 Then a cloud covered the tent of the congregation, and the glory of the LORD filled the tabernacle.

The cloud was a mystic symbol that reminded the people of God's presence. It was manifested when the Lord spoke with Moses on the mountain (24:15–16) and showed that God desired the people to hear from him (19:9). Its presence in the tabernacle displayed the active presence of the Lord and His desire to emanate His glory in a visible way. On this occasion, there was such majestic splendor about it that it "filled the tabernacle."

God's glory is described as *kabowd* (**ka-VODE**), revealing unique honor. This hints at abundance, splendor, dignity, and reputation unlike anyone else. The Lord didn't just stand apart from false gods but could cause even the most noble person to know why they needed to bow before Him.

38 For the cloud of the LORD was upon the tabernacle by day, and fire was on it by night, in the sight of all the house of Israel, throughout all their journeys.

The cloud of the Lord not only served a purpose in the tabernacle but also indicated when it was time for the Israelites to travel. Whenever the cloud lifted from the dwelling, they would recognize that to dwell with God meant to follow however and wherever He leads. It also indicates that the Lord may seem to leave, but He will return again—an obvious teaching magnified in the New Testament. Christ Himself will come again "with clouds" (Revelation 1:7). The Lord chose the cloud to not only symbolize Himself but also to show the nature of His commitment to us both now and forevermore.

Sources:
Bible Knowledge Accelerator. www.Bible-history.com. "Golden lampstand." http://www.bible-history.com/tabernacle/TAB4The_Golden_Lampstand.htm (accessed July 16, 2012).
Bible Study Tools. www.BibleStudyTools.com. "Old Testament Hebrew Lexicon—King James Version." http://www.biblestudytools.com/lexicons/hebrew/kjv (accessed July 21, 2012).
DeWitt, Ray Lee. *Teaching from the Tabernacle*. Grand Rapids, MI: Baker Publishing Group, 1989.
Gill, John. www.BibleStudyTools.com. *John Gill's Exposition of the Bible*. Exodus 40. http://www.biblestudytools.com/commentaries/gills-exposition-of-the-bible/Exodus-40.html (accessed July 21, 2012).
International EMECS Center. "Red Sea." http://www.emecs.or.jp/guidebook/eng/pdf/16redsea.pdf.
Life Application Bible (NRSV). Wheaton, IL: Tyndale House, 1989. 151–157.
Sweet, John. www.Spiritualfoundations.com. *Spiritual Foundations, Vol. II—Old Testament Foreshadowings*. "The Grain and Drink Offerings." http://www.spiritualfoundations.com/Vol2OldTestament/Chapter11VolII.htm (accessed July 19, 2012).
The Tabernacle Place. www.the-tabernacle-place.com. "The Golden Altar of Incense." http://the-tabernacle-place.com/articles/what_is_the_tabernacle/tabernacle_altar_of_incense (accessed July 20, 2012).
Unger, Merrill F. *Unger's Bible Dictionary*. Chicago: Moody Press, 1985. 88, 1059–1066.

Say It Correctly

Tabernacle. **TA**-ber-na-kul.
Atonement. uh-**TONE**-ment.

Daily Bible Readings

MONDAY
Offering Our Possessions
(Exodus 35:4–9)

TUESDAY
Offering Our Skills
(Exodus 35:10–19)

WEDNESDAY
Stirred Hearts and Willing Spirits
(Exodus 35:20–29)

THURSDAY
Skills for Every Kind of Work
(Exodus 35:30–35)

FRIDAY
An Overabundance of Offerings
(Exodus 36:2–7)

SATURDAY
Blessing the Faithful Workers
(Exodus 39:32–43)

SUNDAY
God Affirms the Completed Work
(Exodus 40:16–30, 34, 38)

Notes

Jesus and the Just Reign of God

This quarter has three units centering on the overall theme of "justice." God's power is proclaimed through the person of Jesus Christ, resulting in Christians being empowered to live under God's rule.

UNIT 1 • GOD SENDS JESUS

This is a five-lesson study. The Gospel of Luke is the biblical context for these lessons. Lesson 1 presents readers with the prophecy regarding the birth of Jesus. Lesson 2 recounts Mary's response to the angel's announcement concerning her future. In Lesson 3, Zacharias prophesies concerning his son, John, who would be the forerunner of the Lord. Lesson 4 recalls the Christmas story of Jesus' birth. In Lesson 5, Jesus is presented as the Messiah and a light to the Gentiles.

Lesson 1: December 1, 2013
Jesus' Birth Foretold
Luke 1:26–40

People are always amazed and often perplexed when unexpected things happen in their lives. Mary responded at first with surprise and then with dedication to the angel's announcement about the birth of her baby.

Lesson 2: December 8, 2013
Mary's Song of Praise
Luke 1:46–56

People usually respond with great joy when good things happen to them. Mary responded from the depths of her soul by praising her God of justice for receiving such a wonderful gift.

Lesson 3: December 15, 2013
Zacharias Prophesies about His Son John
Luke 1:57–58, 67–79

When a baby is born, parents usually have high expectations for their new child. Zacharias prophesied that his son John would prepare the way for the God of justice.

Lesson 4: December 22, 2013
Jesus Is Born
Luke 2:1–17

New parents marvel at the miracle of birth. The angels announced to the shepherds the most miraculous birth of all—Jesus, Savior, Messiah, and Lord.

Lesson 5: December 29, 2013
Jesus Is Presented in the Temple
Luke 2:25–38

All people desire to live in freedom. Simeon and Anna anticipated the presentation of the baby Jesus in the Temple because they recognized Jesus as the just fulfillment of the prophecy of the coming Messiah.

UNIT 2 • JESUS USHERS IN THE REIGN OF GOD

This is a four-lesson unit. These lessons continue the study from the Gospel of Luke. The first lesson encourages us to honor the

Sabbath. The second lesson challenges us to live as God's people. The third lesson instructs us concerning Jesus' teachings about relationships. The fourth lesson looks at Jesus' teachings concerning compassion for the poor.

Lesson 6: January 5, 2014
Honoring the Sabbath
Luke 6:1–11

Often, rules and limitations set by others make it difficult for us to help one another. Jesus, who is Lord of the Sabbath, teaches that acts of mercy and justice should be practiced all the time.

Lesson 7: January 12, 2014
How to Live as God's People
Luke 6:17–31

People experience both love and hate from others around them. Jesus teaches that justice does not always appear in the way people treat one another, but His followers are to love people regardless of what they do or say to them.

Lesson 8: January 19, 2014
Jesus Teaches about Relationships
Luke 14:7–18a, 22–24

Homogeneity is the standard by which people invite others to social events. Jesus has a message of social justice that reverses the custom and compels His followers to welcome all people.

Lesson 9: January 26, 2014
Jesus Teaches Compassion for the Poor
Luke 16:19–31

Selfishness motivates the attitudes and behaviors of many people. Jesus tells the story of Lazarus and the rich man to teach His followers to put their selfish desires aside so they can help the poor.

UNIT 3 • LIVE JUSTLY IN THE REIGN OF GOD

This four-lesson unit is a study of the book of James. Lesson 1 provides a challenge for us to hear and do the Word. Lesson 2 is an admonishment for us to treat everyone equally and not show preference for those who "have" at the expense of those who "have not." In Lesson 3, James encourages believers to show their faith by their works. The final lesson contains a challenge for believers to control their speech.

Lesson 10: February 2, 2014
Hear and Do the Word
James 1:19–27

People often talk about what will help others, but they do not take action. James says that those who are both hearers and doers of the Word practice justice.

Lesson 11: February 9, 2014
Treat Everyone Equally
James 2:1–13

People show partiality toward others for a variety of reasons. James reminds his followers of the importance of justice practiced through taking care of the poor and loving our neighbors as ourselves.

Lesson 12: February 16, 2014
Show Your Faith by Your Works
James 2:14–26

People often make great declarations of faith but show no evidence of them in their actions. James states that faith, which by itself is dead, becomes active when carried out through works of justice.

Lesson 13: February 23, 2014
Control Your Speech
James 3:1–12

Often, people speak without thinking about the impact their words will have on others. James speaks of justice within the context of controlling a person's tongue because both blessings and curses can come from the same mouth.

GOD'S JUSTICE

The moral arc of the universe bends at the elbow of justice.

-Martin Luther King, Jr.

Teaching That Changes Lives

by Dr. Melvin E. Banks Sr., Litt.D.

The goal of teaching is transformation. Human beings change as their life situations change. And since we believe the purpose of God's Word is to help us know and do God's will, we believe Bible study materials should enable people to come to grips with their life needs—the situations they encounter every day. Unless the teachers of Bible study curriculum are sufficiently knowledgeable of those needs, they will not be able to raise the right issues and help students see the relevance of that truth to their lives. Any person conversant with Scripture may be able to expound the text. But exposition alone does not get us to application and obedience.

There are learning principles which are widely accepted in educational circles of which teachers must be cognizant. Such principles must be adapted to the unique lifestyles of the learners. Teaching as transformation is seen in the manner Jesus communicated with the woman of Samaria, as recorded in Chapter 4 of John's Gospel. Notice how Jesus led this woman from one degree of spirituality to another, from her sin to the Savior.

1. JESUS SECURED THE WOMAN'S ATTENTION.

The objective of teaching is to communicate the Word of God in such a way that students are able to grasp its truth, then embrace it to the extent that it becomes an integral part of their lives. But learning does not take place until the attention of the mind has been obtained.

Attention and learning readiness are achieved when students grasp the importance and relevance of the material to their lives. To secure the attention and readiness of the Samaritan woman, Jesus first affirmed her self-identity and worth by asking her for a drink of water. Since Jews never spoke to Samaritans, the mere fact of His speaking to her communicated to the woman that He respected her. By addressing her in public and as a Samaritan, Jesus conveyed to the woman what He thought of her and other Samaritans.

But Jesus went further. He requested from her a drink of water. In so doing, Jesus totally disarmed the woman and eliminated any misgivings or apprehension she may have had concerning Him. She now knew that this Jew accepted her. She would now have an attentive ear to accept whatever He subsequently said.

The affirmation Jesus showed this woman reveals a basic principle: anyone wishing to be effective in communicating the truth about Jesus must have a caring and affirming attitude for the people to be taught. Students must grasp that the teacher really cares about them. I suspect that one of the drawbacks of public education today is that students perceive that some teachers are there only to receive a paycheck. Or when Sunday School teachers habitually show up late (or not at all), the perception is conveyed to students that the teacher has no real interest in them. Jesus possessed and communicated a concern for the Samaritan woman that won her heart.

By asking the woman for a drink of water, Jesus began His conversation right where her knowledge and interest lay. He did not begin with some lofty theological issue about which she knew very little. Instead, He discoursed with her about water. She knew what water was and could relate to it because she used it every day. He began on her level and at her point of need. She had come to the well to fetch water for her household use. Water was on her mind—water for cooking, cleaning, drinking, and bathing. So building upon what she knew, He now offered her water that was not in the well. Jesus went from the KNOWN to the UNKNOWN.

In the same way, to communicate with students, provoking interest in learning is more readily achieved when we begin where the students are—at their point of need. That is not to say one begins and ends with the student's felt need. That is, a class designed to teach the Bible does not become reduced to a discussion of hot topics as an end in itself. Rather, we begin with felt needs in order to provoke interest in a subject about which they know very little. Example: Since adults encounter problems on the job, in the community, with family members, and even in their personal lives, lessons which begin in one of those areas will usually find student interest high.

2. JESUS PROMISED TO SATISFY HER FELT NEED.

Next, Jesus promised the woman a source of water that made coming to the well unnecessary. In so doing, the Christ peaked her interest. Jesus told her that the water in the well was temporary and ineffective in quenching the deeply felt spiritual thirst she was experiencing. He assured her that He could give water that was not in the well. This promise to satisfy a deeply felt need really turned her on. She declared, "Sir, give me this water..." (John 4:15, NIV).

In a similar way, the teacher who promises students that their keenly felt need will be satisfied through a study of the Word of God will find greater interest. Of course, to sustain interest, the subsequent class discussion must live up to the promise.

Example: A news clipping of someone who reflects a lonely lifestyle could be followed by a short brainstorming session of how people cope with loneliness. That could lead into a lesson dealing with God's faithfulness to His children, how He never leaves or forsakes us.

3. JESUS PRESENTED NEW INFORMATION IN AN INTERESTING WAY.

By building on the knowledge the woman already possessed, Jesus presented her with the new information: He could give her water that was not in the well. To clarify what He meant by water "not in the well," Jesus engaged the woman in dialogue. The new information she needed to hear was about eternal life, where and how to worship God, and about Jesus' own identity. Though He started the conversation with water, He did not end there. Jesus knew He was sent to represent His Father, to present words of eternal life. He would have compromised His mission had He allowed the dialogue to dissipate into frivolous chatter.

But secondly, Jesus knew that in order to truly communicate this information, He had to present it in a form she could understand and relate to. His statements provoked questions from her. By answering the woman's questions, Jesus clarified the truth for her.

Perhaps no other signal reveals a person's readiness to learn than a question. The communication went two ways—between Him and her, and her to Him. On other occasions, Jesus engaged His listeners by brainstorming: "Who do people say the Son of Man is?" (Matthew 16:13). Or, presenting a "case study," "What do you think? There was a man who had two sons. . . ." (Matthew 21:28, NIV). On one occasion, He set a child among them as a visual aid. On another occasion, He invited the audience to take a look at the birds, the lilies, the sheep, etc. All of this was to clarify truth for His listeners. Likewise, we do well when we vary teaching techniques to communicate the content of the Bible so listeners will clearly understand.

4. JESUS APPLIED THE NEW TRUTH TO THE SPIRITUAL NEED

Jesus was not satisfied in just presenting new information to the woman. He knew she needed to see the relationship of His identity to her own life situation. So Jesus invited her to call her husband. Applying truth to life is one of the critical components of effective teaching. Unless students can see the relationship of the Bible, written thousands of years ago, to the issues and problems they face today, the relevance of the Scriptures will appear very remote.

Indeed, it is very remarkable how in reading and studying the Scriptures, one can see how each book is directed at a specific need among the people of God. Matthew was written to help Jews understand that the arrival of Jesus was a fulfillment of Old Testament prophecies concerning the Messiah. Paul's epistles to the Corinthians were written to answer questions they had about Christian life. This is especially true of the epistles, but is discernible in all the Bible books. So exploring how Scripture relates to life is imbedded within the Bible itself as well as in the learning needs of students.

5. JESUS MOTIVATED THE WOMAN TO ACT ON WHAT SHE KNEW.

The action the woman took reinforced her new convictions. She left her water pot to spread the news in the village. It was as though the woman said, "Now that I believe You could be the Messiah, let me do something with this information. Let me go tell people back in the town." Immediately, therefore, she dropped her water pot, and ran back into the city to tell the townspeople to come investigate this Stranger in town. "Could this be the Messiah?" she asked them.

The teacher who motivates students to take action from the study of the Scriptures has indeed been effective. That's because the ultimate objective of Bible study is not just to increase knowledge, but to impact a person's behavior, to motivate them to DO the will of God (1 John 2:17). This is accomplished best, not just from lecturing or exhorting them to obey, but by guiding them to DISCOVER the information themselves from the Word, by impacting the EMOTIONS through worship of God, and by providing opportunities to TAKE ACTION—to implement the truth to be learned.

That is what UMI (Urban Ministries, Inc.) aims to accomplish in its Bible study materials. These principles are imbedded into the lessons.

The African American Church and the Freedom Movement

by Rev. Dr. Prathia Hall, Ph.D.

The history of African American people is absolutely amazing. Consider the tortuous events filled with brutality and pain which tore our African ancestors away from our homeland and planted us on American soil. It is reasonable to ask, "How have we survived?" The experience has included excruciating pain. The journey has also included capture, kidnap, shackles, chains, neck braces, and leg irons. During the traumatic Middle Passage, our ancestors were packed like sardines in a can, spoon-like on top of each other with insufficient breathing space. One can also consider how they were defiled and humiliated even before they arrived at the slave docks of the Southeastern United States.

The African continent was seriously depopulated. Millions died having been literally worked to death after a few short years. This was followed by 244 years of chattel slavery, segregation, discrimination, and the ugly and deadly reign of terror that was lynching. These events of human shame and pain are correctly characterized as the African holocaust.

Many Americans do not wish to remember this gruesome history. They believe it divides Americans and encourages racial hostility. Yet if we do not know our history, we will fail to understand much of our contemporary life. Both Black and White Americans need to be aware of our racial history. If we learn the important lessons of the past, we can work to prevent repetition in the future. When we know the truth, the truth shall set us free.

It is very necessary to learn how we survived as a people. Indeed, had God not been with us, we would have been destroyed. Most researchers agree that African American churches have been essential to the survival of African American people. The Black church has functioned as the primary institutional advocate for our people. Further, when we examine closely the history of the Black church within the framework of the history of Black people in the United States, we find both histories interwoven in very interesting ways. Indeed, the church's own struggle for existence was identical with the African American freedom struggles because the church actually emerged from the people's struggle for identity and existence.

Religion was one of the aspects of African life which the oppressors attempted to destroy. During the breaking-in process, Africans were separated from their original regional and tribal groups so that they could not speak their African languages, use their African names, or practice their African religions. The early African American sociologist E. Franklyn Frazier believed that the process of kidnap, capture, and breaking-in was so profoundly traumatic that the slaves were totally stripped of their African cultural heritage. Therefore, they retained no memory of their African way of life, including their religious faith. Most contemporary scholars believe that Frazier was wrong; African people found a variety of ways to keep their faith alive. As slaves in the Caribbean and in South America, Blacks continued to practice African beliefs and mingled them with the Roman Catholic traditions to which they were introduced on this side of the Atlantic.

New research and archaeological digs of old plantations and cemetery excavations have revealed evidence that slaves in the United States practiced their African beliefs in secret, in the slave quarters and in the woods, far from the eyes and ears of the slaveholders. Current research helps to explain the relation of African American Christianity to Africans and the factors that make African American Christianity different in many ways from European American Christianity.

Africans from different regions and tribes were able to piece together some of what the slaveholders attempted to destroy. These African religious beliefs had many similarities to Christianity. Africans believed in a supreme God who was Creator and Ruler of everything in the universe. They also believed in other divine creatures who were emissaries for good or evil and were involved directly in the lives of human beings. Africans believed that all life was sacred. They possessed a powerful and vibrant spirituality and worshiped God with their bodies and souls in sacred dance. These beliefs and practices were compatible with Christian beliefs and practices and over a period of time were merged through the experience of slavery to form African American Christianity.

We learn a great deal more about African American Christian churches and their relation to the African American freedom struggle when we examine the process by which the African slaves were introduced to Christianity. Slaveholders did not want their slaves to convert to Christianity if it meant they would have to set the slaves free. Slaveholders feared that Christianity would make the slaves bold and rebellious, stirring their deep longing for freedom. The most evil and destructive obstacle to the process of evangelization was the claim by many slaveholders that Blacks did not have souls and could not go heaven; therefore, they should not be Christianized. Those slaveholders who did permit missionaries to preach to the slaves held the belief that Christianity would make the Africans better slaves. Some of these preachers preached a distorted version of the Gospel that claimed that God had ordained slavery.

The process of evangelization that led to the creation of the Black churches was very complex and very difficult. Despite the attempts to use religion to control slaves, planters greatly feared that Christianity could not be trusted to function as a tool of oppression if the slaves were able to examine, understand, and interpret it for themselves. Consequently, laws were passed which prohibited religious meetings by Black people. It was against the law to teach a Black person to read or write. Punishment for breaking these laws was very severe. Andrew Bryan, a Black pastor, preached to slaves and organized the first African Baptist Church in Savannah, Georgia. He and the church members were arrested and whipped by slave patrols, even when they had passes for worship. The pattern of harassment and abuse continued as more slaves embraced the new faith and interpreted it through their experience of slavery.

Christian faith, under such conditions, became itself an act of rebellion. The earliest form of congregational life was what Frazier called the "invisible institution." Under cover of night, Black women and men would "steal away" to the brush arbor, praise houses, or secret praying ground in the woods. There, they heard what they called "real preaching," as opposed to what the White preachers offered. They were able to sing, shout, and cry to God. They interpreted the Scriptures, claimed the Exodus as their own, and analyzed the Christianity of the slaveholders, finding it to be false.

We can see then that the life of the Black church was formed as a part of the struggle for the survival of Black people. The church had to fight for the right to exist in much the same way African American people had to fight. The invisible institution was the place where freedom struggles were carried out. Slaves not only sang, prayed, preached, and danced in the praise house meetings, they also plotted escape and rebellion. The spirituals expressed their Christian theology and gave them solace in pain. They also contained code language by which they could communicate plans to escape by way of the Underground Railroad—a network of helpful friends, White and Black, who would feed and hide them along their escape route. "Steal Away to Jesus" was one of the popular code songs.

Independent Black churches were organized in the North and large cities in the South where free Blacks lived. These churches became the heartbeat of the Black movement for the abolition of slavery. Frederick Douglass, the Reverend Henry Highland Garnett, and many other preachers and leaders, including such women as Maria Stewart, Harriet Tubman, and Sojourner Truth, often proclaimed the message of God-ordained freedom from the pulpits of these churches. Mr. Gayraud Wilmore calls these Black churches "the Black Church Freedom Movement." They taught what Peter Paris called "the prophetic principle" of the equality of all human beings before God. This foundational belief and practice distinguished the Black Christian churches from the White Christian churches more profoundly than their styles of worship. The Black churches continued to grow and develop as places of worship, centers of religious education, and the heart of the freedom movement.

The Black churches followed the concept of the African worldview, which understood the religious and the political, the sacred and the secular, to be integrated in the pattern of life. The church was the center of the lives of Black people. Schools were organized and operated in the churches, including famous historically Black colleges. Social agencies, banks, insurance agencies, and civil rights organizations were organized in and by the Black churches. Following emancipation, the African American church became the center of the work of racial uplift.

This pattern of church leadership in the social, civil, and economic development struggles of the Black community continues today. However, many churches have become less active; this was even true during the Civil Rights Movement of the 1950s and 1960s. The movement was led by churches, but it did not have support from all of them; some advocated a less activist, more accommodating approach.

We can see from this brief historical survey that the roots of the Black church are planted firmly in the struggles of Black people for survival, emancipation, freedom, and social development. The path to independent existence for the Black church was a path of great suffering and turmoil. The roots of the faith struggle and the freedom struggle are tied by an inseparable connection. This formation of history compels the African American church.

TOUSSAINT L'OUVERTURE
(1743–1803)
Slave Revolt Leader

Francois–Dominique Toussant L'Ouverture was one of the most important leaders of the slave revolt of St. Domingue (later called Haiti). The insurrection later led to the independence of Haiti. His father, Gaou-Guinou, was the son of an African king. Toussaint labored as a slave on a sugar plantation. He learned French, Latin, geometry, and the Roman Catholic religion.

The Spanish brought slaves to St. Domingue in 1512. The French came in 1630 and controlled the western side of St. Domingue. Through use of free slave labor, their territory became the richest colonial possession. They were able to send abundant supplies of sugar, indigo, and cotton back to France. By the end of the 17th century, there were at least 2,000,000 Blacks, 50,000 mulattoes, and 20,000 Frenchmen. Outnumbering their masters by such a large margin created a very uneasy balance on the island. Sadly, class and caste systems deeply divided these groups, creating feelings of arrogance on one hand and bitterness on the other. In contrast, France was filled with the talk of freedom, equality, and fraternity. While in France the people fought to obtain the rights of man, on the island the French ruled the slaves with cruelty and no thought of dealing fairly with the Haitians. The slaves produced great wealth for the French while enduring harsh treatment, and the mulattoes, while permitted to own land, had no recognized social or political position. The lofty ideals of the French Revolution found no root in the hearts of the French overseers.

On August 1, 1789, a voodoo priest named Boukmann held a meeting with various leaders. Francois–Dominique Toussant L'Ouverture was invited because of his reputation for wisdom and respect for his level of education. Plans were laid for a revolt. On August 9, the sound of hundreds of drums signaled the beginning of the attack. Thousands of slaves swept through village after village, burning property and killing French people. More than 6,000 coffee plantations and 200 sugar refineries were destroyed but the French fought back and killed the slave leader, Boukmann.

Toussaint became the leader of the slaves. At the same time, France had declared war on Spain and England. Toussaint shrewdly joined the Spanish and fought the French again. The Spanish equipped Toussaint's rebels, who drove 3,000 French soldiers from the northern and eastern parts of the island. He later left the Spanish and fought his way

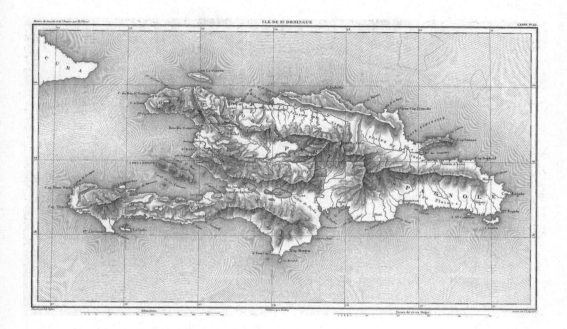

through French territory, overcoming the enemy forces in town after town. His many victories won him the nickname of L'Ouverture (the Opener). He then established himself as governor-general of St. Domingue and began to develop the island's natural resources and foreign trade. Showing that he was not blinded by bitterness, he began trade with France and sent his two sons to study in Paris. He saw the revolt as directed against the institution of slavery rather than against the French people.

In the meantime, Napoleon had conquered much of Europe and was determined to recapture St. Domingue and all its rich resources. He had 86 ships built to carry 22,000 soldiers back to the island. In February 1802, the powerful armada arrived. Captain-General LeClerc was the commander and declared that all plantations be returned to their former French owners and that slavery be reinstituted. LeClerc attacked Cap Francois, which was burned by Henri Christophe, one of Toussaint's governors. Realizing the futility of having to continually face further insurrections, LeClerc declared an end to slavery. He offered Christophe a generalship in the French army. Toussaint was captured in June 1802 and sent to France. He died there in prison on April 7, 1803.

St. Domingue again erupted in a bloody revolt. The slaves and mulattoes drove the French into the sea. St. Domingue was proclaimed a republic and given the Indian name of Haiti. Haitian independence was declared on January 1, 1804.

Toussaint L'Ouverture was an extraordinary leader who worked to free the slaves. He was a champion of freedom and independence.

(Source: Russell Adams, *Great Negroes Past and Present*, Chicago: Afro-Am, pp. 16-19.)

Teaching Tips

Words You Should Know

A. Hail (Luke 1:28) *cairay* (Gk.)—To be cheerful, rejoice. A salutation conveying a wish for the welfare of the person addressed (Luke 1:28); continued among our Saxon forefathers in "Joy to you" and "Health to you."

B. Virgin (v. 10) *parthenos* (Gk.)—Either a marriageable maiden or a young married woman, a pure virgin (2 Corinthians 11:2).

Teacher Preparation

Unifying Principle—Surprised and Expectant. People are always amazed and often perplexed when unexpected things happen in their lives. How can Christians handle these unanticipated events that occur? Mary responded at first with surprise and then with dedication to the angel's announcement about the birth of her baby.

A. Pray for your students.

B. Read and meditate on all the Scriptures from the Background and the Devotional Reading sections.

C. Reread the Focal Verses in three or more translations (NLT, ESV, NIV, etc.).

O—Open the Lesson

A. Open with prayer, including the Aim for Change.

B. After prayer, have a volunteer read the In Focus story and relate it to the lesson.

C. Have a volunteer read the Aim for Change and Keep in Mind verse.

P—Present the Scriptures

A. Have volunteers read the Focal Verses.

B. Now use The People, Places, and Times; Background; and Search the Scriptures to bring clarity to the verses.

E—Explore the Meaning

A. Have volunteers summarize the Discuss the Meaning, Lesson in Our Society, and Make It Happen sections.

B. Connect these sections to the Aim for Change and the Keep in Mind verse with the Lesson in Our Society and Make It Happen sections.

N—Next Steps for Application

A. Summarize the lesson.

B. Allow for students to share how the lesson impacted them.

C. Close with prayer and praise God for keeping His promises.

Worship Guide

For the Superintendent or Teacher
Theme: Jesus' Birth Foretold
Song: "O Holy Night!"
Devotional Reading: Psalm 89:1–7

Jesus' Birth Foretold

Bible Background • LUKE 1:5–25
Printed Text • LUKE 1:26–40 | Devotional Reading • PSALM 89:1–7

——————— Aim for Change ———————

By the end of the lesson, we will: REVIEW the foretelling of Jesus' birth; REFLECT on the unexpected and perplexing events of our lives; and DEDICATE ourselves to the purposes of God.

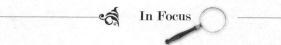

In Focus

Months had passed since Dad announced to the boys they were going to have a new addition to the family. The boys were so excited because Damon, the oldest of the boys, wanted a sister. One day he told his parents he had been asking God to give him a sister.

After that prayer, his parents found out they were expecting. His mom and dad had just come back from seeing the doctor. Dad told the boys he wanted to tell them something. He said, "Looks like God has answered your prayers. Mom is expecting!"

Damon and his brother, Brandon, were so happy. Damon declared, "I know it is a girl because that's what I asked God for."

Sure enough, on February 12 in the wee hours of the morning, Damon's prayers were answered and his sister was born. With great excitement, Damon ran to his mom's hospital room. As soon as he saw his mom, he asked, "What is she?"

Everyone laughed and agreed—the little baby girl was an answer to prayer.

With God, nothing shall be impossible. In today's lesson, we are reminded of the events prior to the birth of Jesus. We should forever be grateful!

——————— Keep in Mind ———————

"And behold, thou shalt conceive in thy womb, and bring forth a son, and shalt call his name JESUS" (Luke 1:31).

"And behold, thou shalt conceive in thy womb, and bring forth a son, and shalt call his name JESUS" (Luke 1:31).

Focal Verses

KJV **Luke 1:26** And in the sixth month the angel Gabriel was sent from God unto a city of Galilee, named Nazareth,

27 To a virgin espoused to a man whose name was Joseph, of the house of David; and the virgin's name was Mary.

28 And the angel came in unto her, and said, Hail, thou that art highly favoured, the Lord is with thee: blessed art thou among women.

29 And when she saw him, she was troubled at his saying, and cast in her mind what manner of salutation this should be.

30 And the angel said unto her, Fear not, Mary: for thou hast found favour with God.

31 And, behold, thou shalt conceive in thy womb, and bring forth a son, and shalt call his name JESUS.

32 He shall be great, and shall be called the Son of the Highest: and the Lord God shall give unto him the throne of his father David:

33 And he shall reign over the house of Jacob for ever; and of his kingdom there shall be no end.

34 Then said Mary unto the angel, How shall this be, seeing I know not a man?

35 And the angel answered and said unto her, The Holy Ghost shall come upon thee, and the power of the Highest shall overshadow thee: therefore also that holy thing which shall be born of thee shall be called the Son of God.

36 And, behold, thy cousin Elisabeth, she hath also conceived a son in her old age: and this is the sixth month with her, who was called barren.

37 For with God nothing shall be impossible.

NLT **Luke 1:26** In the sixth month of Elizabeth's pregnancy, God sent the angel Gabriel to Nazareth, a village in Galilee,

27 to a virgin named Mary. She was engaged to be married to a man named Joseph, a descendant of King David.

28 Gabriel appeared to her and said, "Greetings, favored woman! The Lord is with you!"

29 Confused and disturbed, Mary tried to think what the angel could mean.

30 "Don't be afraid, Mary," the angel told her, "for you have found favor with God!

31 You will conceive and give birth to a son, and you will name him Jesus.

32 He will be very great and will be called the Son of the Most High. The Lord God will give him the throne of his ancestor David.

33 And he will reign over Israel forever; his Kingdom will never end!"

34 Mary asked the angel, "But how can this happen? I am a virgin."

35 The angel replied, "The Holy Spirit will come upon you, and the power of the Most High will overshadow you. So the baby to be born will be holy, and he will be called the Son of God.

36 What's more, your relative Elizabeth has become pregnant in her old age! People used to say she was barren, but she has conceived a son and is now in her sixth month.

37 For nothing is impossible with God."

38 Mary responded, "I am the Lord's servant. May everything you have said about me come true." And then the angel left her.

39 A few days later Mary hurried to the hill country of Judea, to the town

40 where Zechariah lived. She entered the house and greeted Elizabeth.

38 And Mary said, Behold the handmaid of the Lord; be it unto me according to thy word. And the angel departed from her.

39 And Mary arose in those days, and went into the hill country with haste, into a city of Juda;

40 And entered into the house of Zacharias, and saluted Elisabeth.

The People, Places, and Times

The Annunciation. In what many scholars believe to be the year 5 B.C., Mary, a virgin betrothed to Joseph, was living in Nazareth, a city in Galilee. The angel Gabriel came to her with a message from God, announcing that she was to be the mother of the long-expected Messiah by the power of the Holy Spirit (1:26–38; cf. Romans 1:3).

Elisabeth (Elizabeth in NLT). The wife of Zacharias (Zechariah in NLT) and mother of John the Baptist. She was a descendant of Aaron, Moses' brother and the first high priest of Israel. She remained childless until well advanced in years. For five months she concealed her pregnancy, but the angel Gabriel revealed it to Mary as an assurance to her of her own miraculous pregnancy (Luke 1:36–37). Mary visited her cousin, Elisabeth, and they exchanged congratulations and praised God together. Mary stayed with her for three months (vv. 39–56).

Background

Luke introduces us to two major players—an exemplary couple named Zacharias and Elisabeth, who had received the grace of God in large measure. In the time of Herod, king of Judea, there was a priest named Zacharias who belonged to the priestly division of Abijah; his wife, Elisabeth, was also a descendant of Aaron. Both of them were upright in the sight of God, observing all the Lord's commandments and regulations blamelessly.

But they had no children because Elisabeth was barren, and they were both well along in years (vv. 5–7). In any culture, infertility is an aching disappointment and for some an almost unbearable stress. But the burden cannot be compared to that borne by childless women in ancient Hebrew culture, where barrenness was considered a disgrace—even a punishment. Barrenness carried a moral stigma because, in Jewish thinking, it was not the fate of the righteous. Elisabeth called her barrenness her "reproach" (v. 25).

At-A-Glance

1. Christ's Birth Announced
(Luke 1:26–38)
2. Mary Visited Elisabeth (vv. 39–40)

In Depth

1. Christ's Birth Announced (Luke 1:26–38)

We have here an account of the mother of our Lord; though we are not to pray to her, we ought to praise God for her. The angel Gabriel who had previously visited Zechariah, now visits Mary. The angel's address, "Hail, thou that art highly favoured . . . blessed are thou among women" (v. 28), means that Mary was chosen and favored by God to have the honor of birthing the Messiah, something Jewish mothers have so long desired. And look who God decided to choose. She was a teenage virgin. She didn't grow up in a royal household. She wasn't from the religious center of life, Jerusalem, but the small town of Nazereth. God indeed chooses the weak things of this world to confound the mighty (see 1 Corinthians 1:27).

The angel's wondrous salutation and appearance troubled Mary. Unlike Zechariah, who appeared to be afraid of the angel's presence, her trouble may have been attributed to the fact that God would choose someone as lowly as her for such a great task. Whatever the case, the angel assured her that she had found favor with God and would become the mother of a son whose name she should call Jesus, the Son of the Highest. Mary then asked the next logical question: How is this possible? The angel's reply can be summed up in his final words: "For with God nothing shall be impossible." With that understanding, Mary responds to the angel's words with gratefulness. Her reply to the angel was full of faith and humility.

As Mary did here, we must guide our desires by the Word of God. In all conflicts, let us remember that with God, nothing is impossible. As we read and hear His promises, let us turn them into prayers, saying, "Behold the willing servant of the Lord. May it be to me according to Your word."

2. Mary Visited Elisabeth (vv. 39–40)

Mary was young (perhaps just 13 or 14) and now pregnant. She probably did not talk to anyone about the news she had received from heaven, though she surely needed to talk to someone. She knew no person in the world she could freely converse with about it but her cousin, Elisabeth, and therefore she hurried to her.

When she arrived, Elisabeth greeted Mary with a prophecy—already knowing of Mary's pregnancy: "The babe leaped in her womb; and Elisabeth was filled with the Holy Ghost" (1:41). This would have been a great encouragement to Mary.

Search the Scriptures

1. Who sent the angel Gabriel (Luke 1:26)?
2. Who is Elisabeth to Mary (v. 36)?

Discuss the Meaning

Living day-to-day life, sometimes we lose focus as to the purpose God has for us. God has given His children many promises. It is important for us to read and study His Word to know Him and the promises He has for His people. "As he spake by the mouth of his holy prophets, which have been since the world began . . . to give light to them that sit in darkness and in the shadow of death, to guide our feet into the way of peace" (Luke 1:70, 79). How might you regain a proper perspective of God's purposes for you?

Lesson in Our Society

Today, many people have babies together without being married. We celebrate the birth of the children with the parents as though we are following the way of the Lord. How often do we stop to consider the guidelines God has set for us? Fornication is sin! We should marry before having sex. This is God's way. Let us not conform to this world. Let us take a stand for righteousness' sake.

Make It Happen

God has given us guidelines to follow to give an accurate representation of Him. We should be mindful to live in such a way that Jesus' light in us is most dominant in any circumstance. Will your excitement for what the Lord has done be seen by others in the way you live?

Follow the Spirit

What God wants me to do:

_____

_____

_____

_____

Remember Your Thoughts

Special insights I have learned:

_____

_____

_____

_____

More Light on the Text

Luke 1:26–40

26 And in the sixth month the angel Gabriel was sent from God unto a city of Galilee, named Nazareth, 27 To a virgin espoused to a man whose name was Joseph, of the house of David; and the virgin's name was Mary.

The story of Mary and Joseph begins in the region of Galilee and the town of Nazareth, which was where Jesus grew up. In Elisabeth's sixth month, God sent Gabriel to Mary to announce that she would miraculously bear a child who would be Israel's Messiah. Luke calls Nazareth a *polis* (**PA-lis**), which is often translated "city," but it was a small "town" (NIV) or "village." Its relatively unimportant size contrasts with Jerusalem, where Gabriel's previous appearance to Zacharias had taken place at the temple (v. 19). Galilee bordered Gentile nations; therefore, it was sometimes called Galilee of the Gentiles. The entire

nation was under subjugation to the mighty Roman empire. Nazareth, in particular, was a despised city, considered inferior by the rest of Israel (John 1:46). The city and its citizens were disparaged and were the object of deep prejudice both by Jews and Romans. Yet God had a vessel of choice, by name Mary, in this unlikely place. Here we learn an important lesson that God is no respecter of persons or places. Also, we must refrain from our quickness to judge places, cities, or nations, as we are apt to do.

God sent a message to a virgin (Gk. *parthenos*, **par-THE-nos**) in Nazareth (Mary) as readily as he did to a priest in Jerusalem (Zacharias). In the Greek translation of the Old Testament (commonly referred to as the Septuagint or LXX), *parthenos* means "girl," with chastity implied. A stress on chastity or virginity occurs in Leviticus 21:13–14; Deuteronomy 22:23, 28; and 2 Samuel 13:2. When used with place names, it referred to non-pollution with idolatry. When used with the description of Mary, it meant that she had not yet had sexual relations. Mary's question in verse 34, and the reference in verse 27 to her being "espoused" or pledged to be married, make this clear. Since betrothal often took place soon after puberty, Mary may have been in the early part of her teenage years. Betrothal was similar to what we would call an "engagement," but it was legally binding and to break it off was considered "divorce." According to Jewish custom and tradition, only divorce or death could sever betrothal; and in the latter event the girl, though unmarried, would be considered a widow. Mary had already committed to marry Joseph, but she had not had sexual relations with him. In the betrothal period, sexual contact was considered adultery and resulted in stoning.

The phrase "house of David" explains that the child would be born in David's line. David was Israel's greatest king, and God promised to David that his kingdom would be everlasting (2 Samuel 7:16). The everlasting kingdom of David is fulfilled in Jesus.

28 And the angel came in unto her, and said, Hail, thou that art highly favoured, the Lord is with thee: blessed art thou among women. 29 And when she saw him, she was troubled at his saying, and cast in her mind what manner of salutation this should be.

The angel greeted Mary and proclaimed that she was highly favored, or literally, "having been much graced (by God)." "Highly favoured" translates the Greek word *kecharit-omene* (**ke-khar-ee-TO-me-ne**), which has the same root as the words for "greetings" (*chaire*, **KHA-ee-reh**), and "grace of favour" (*charin*, **KHAR-een**, v. 30). Mary is "highly favoured" because she is the recipient of God's grace. But Mary was troubled, or more accurately, she was *greatly* troubled by the words of the angel. The Greek word *diatarasso* (**dee-at-ar-AS-so**) means to be confused or greatly perplexed. In contrast to Zacharias, who doubted the angel's words and required some sign before he could believe, Mary was perplexed but did not express doubt. Her terror at the sudden appearance of the angel—who probably appeared to her as a young man clad in garments of a strange dazzling whiteness—was not unfounded. Her perplexity was most natural considering the sudden, unexpected appearance of an angel and the weight of the message the angel conveyed. She did not understand how God could so greatly favor a person like herself. Mary probably never dreamed she was anyone special. How could she, so ordinary and humble, do anything special for God? That is the essence of grace. What a striking example Mary was! Mary's favor was only by the grace of God. God reversed the human

expectations in Mary's situation, for He was willing to use the lowest in that time to be the bearer of a king. Today God continues to use the poor, the powerless, the helpless, and the weak (2 Corinthians 12:9).

30 And the angel said unto her, Fear not, Mary: for thou hast found favour with God. 31 And, behold, thou shalt conceive in thy womb, and bring forth a son, and shalt call his name JESUS. 32 He shall be great, and shall be called the Son of the Highest: and the Lord God shall give unto him the throne of his father David: 33 And he shall reign over the house of Jacob for ever; and of his kingdom there shall be no end.

The mighty work God foretold He would do through John the Baptist's ministry would be surpassed by an even greater work through His Son's ministry. Whereas John would be "great in the sight of the Lord" (1:15), Jesus would be great without qualification (v. 32) and would be "called the Son of God" (v. 35). An even more important tie between the accounts is that the whole significance of John's ministry, as pointed out in verse 17, is found in his preparation for the One coming after him who was more powerful than he (3:16).

34 Then said Mary unto the angel, How shall this be, seeing I know not a man? 35 And the angel answered and said unto her, The Holy Ghost shall come upon thee, and the power of the Highest shall overshadow thee: therefore also that holy thing which shall be born of thee shall be called the Son of God. 36 And, behold, thy cousin Elisabeth, she hath also conceived a son in her old age: and this is the sixth month with her, who was called barren. 37 For with God nothing shall be impossible.

Mary's question, "How shall this be?" was probably due to being puzzled rather than a question that arose from doubt or distrust. She was not asking for some sign or proof as Zacharias did (1:18). There is a world of difference between her request and that of Zacharias. Hers stemmed from her faith; the question of Zacharias stemmed from his lack of faith.

She was simply asking for more information. She was single and had never known a man sexually. How could she possibly bear a child? Mary's statement that she had not been with a man reveals the miraculous action of God that took place in Jesus' conception through the Holy Spirit. God's divine actions reveal that nothing is impossible for Him. If a woman is able to have a child despite not having sexual relations, God is able to do anything.

To assuage any lingering apprehensions that Mary might have had, the angel informed her of another seemingly impossible situation: Elisabeth's pregnancy in her old age. Elisabeth was in her sixth month of pregnancy, again bearing testimony to the fact that nothing is impossible with God.

38 And Mary said, Behold the handmaid of the Lord; be it unto me according to thy word. And the angel departed from her.

Mary's response to the angel was that she was only a servant of the Lord, which reveals her humility and further strengthens the reason why she had been chosen to bear the Messiah of Israel. Mary was a servant of God and would follow the words of God. No one could have asked for, or given, any better response. What a marvelous testimony to the magnificence of Mary! Her attitude of servanthood recalls that of Hannah in 1 Samuel 1:11, where the LXX also has *doule* (**DOO-lay**), meaning "servant." Her servanthood consisted of a submission to God that characterized genuine believers in Scripture and should characterize believers today (cf. Luke 1:48).

How do we respond to the words of God even when they seem impossible? Do we accept them with faith, remembering that we are humble servants of God? Or do we reject the words of God as impossible? Mary's trusting submission is a worthy example for believers today.

39 And Mary arose in those days, and went into the hill country with haste, into a city of Judah; 40 And entered into the house of Zacharias, and saluted Elisabeth.

After the departure of the angel, Mary paid a memorable visit to Elisabeth. She probably went so she and Elisabeth could encourage and share with each other. They both had similar situations. God had acted upon both their bodies, performing a miracle for both. Mary in particular could be encouraged, for Elisabeth was already six months pregnant, visible evidence that God had already acted upon her miraculously. It should be noted that Mary knew about Elisabeth's miraculous conception, but Elisabeth did not know about Mary's conception. This provides an important context for understanding Elisabeth's prophetic pronouncements that follow.

Sources:
Hughes, R. Kent. *Luke (Volume One): That You May Know the Truth.* Preaching the Word. Wheaton, IL: Crossway, 1998.
Keener, Craig S. *The IVP Bible Background Commentary: New Testament.* Downers Grove, IL: IVP Academic, 1994.
Unger, Merrill F., R. K. Harrison, Howard Vos, and Cyril Barber. *The New Unger's Bible Dictionary.* Chicago: Moody Publishers, 1988.

Say It Correctly

Gabriel. **GAY**-bree-elle.
Zacharias. za-kah-**RAY**-ahs.

Daily Bible Readings

MONDAY
A Covenant with David
(Psalm 89:1–7)

TUESDAY
God's Faithfulness and Steadfast Love
(Psalm 89:19–24)

WEDNESDAY
The Highest of Earthly Kings
(Psalm 89:26–34)

THURSDAY
A Promise for a Distant Future
(2 Samuel 7:18–29)

FRIDAY
A Child Named Immanuel
(Isaiah 7:10–15)

SATURDAY
Elizabeth's Blessing
(Luke 1:41–45)

SUNDAY
The Announcement to Mary
(Luke 1:26–40)

Notes

Teaching Tips

Words You Should Know

A. Blessed (Luke 1:48) *makaridzo* (Gk.)—To pronounce as fortunate or happy.

B. Mercy (v. 50) *elehos* (Gk.)—Divine or human compassion, tender mercy.

Teacher Preparation

Unifying Principle—Jubilant. People usually respond with great joy when good things happen to them. What is the origin of such joyful responses? Mary responded from the depths of her soul by praising her God of justice for receiving such a wonderful gift.

A. Pray for your students.

B. Read and meditate on all the Scriptures from the Bible Background and the Devotional Reading sections.

C. Reread the Focal Verses in three or more translations (NLT, ESV, NIV, etc.).

O—Open the Lesson

A. Open with prayer, including the Aim for Change.

B. After prayer, have a volunteer read the In Focus Scripture, Psalm 111.

C. Have a volunteer read the Aim for Change and Keep in Mind verse.

D. Discuss and allow time to hear student testimonies.

P—Present the Scriptures

A. Have volunteers read the Focal Verses.

B. Now use The People, Places, and Times; Background; and Search the Scriptures to bring clarity to the verses.

E—Explore the Meaning

A. Have volunteers summarize the Discuss the Meaning, Lesson in Our Society, and Make It Happen sections.

B. Connect these sections to the Aim for Change, and the Keep in Mind verse with the Lesson in Our Society and Make It Happen sections.

N—Next Steps for Application

A. Summarize the lesson.

B. Allow students to share how the lesson impacted them.

C. Close with prayer and praise God for keeping His promises.

Worship Guide

For the Superintendent or Teacher
Theme: Mary's Song of Praise
Song: "Sweeter Than the Day Before"
Devotional Reading: Psalm 111

Mary's Song of Praise

DEC
8th

Bible Background • LUKE 1:36–45
Printed Text • LUKE 1:46–56 | Devotional Reading • PSALM 111

—— Aim for Change ——

By the end of the lesson, we will: EXPLORE themes of justice in Mary's song of praise; APPRECIATE the deepest meanings of praise in response to God; and DEVELOP new ways of praising God.

 In Focus

Joe's mom was a singer at heart. She'd grown up singing in the local church in their small hometown. She even spent some time touring with some Motown artists in the late 1970s. Joe was impressed by the pictures that arrayed their home in St. Louis. His mom had pictures with all the greats. From Aretha Franklin to Gladys Knight, their home looked like a "who's who" of the music industry.

Now his mother served as the music director of the same church she had grown up in. She was passionate about her work at the church, and it showed. The choir had won several competitions nationwide and the church's album was one of the top sellers in the gospel genre. Despite that, Joe was sure that his mom missed singing with so many celebrities on tour.

"Mom, don't you miss your time with Motown?" he asked.

"Yes, son, but all the glitz and glamour pales in comparison to worshiping God. When I'm singing to Him, I feel—well, I feel at home."

After receiving the Good News, Mary broke out in a song. In today's lesson, we discover the importance of praising God in response to His divine grace in our lives.

—— Keep in Mind ——

"And my spirit hath rejoiced in God my Saviour" (Luke 1:47).

"And my spirit hath rejoiced in God my Saviour" (Luke 1:47).

Focal Verses

KJV **Luke 1:46** And Mary said, My soul doth magnify the Lord,

47 And my spirit hath rejoiced in God my Saviour.

48 For he hath regarded the low estate of his handmaiden: for, behold, from henceforth all generations shall call me blessed.

49 For he that is mighty hath done to me great things; and holy is his name.

50 And his mercy is on them that fear him from generation to generation.

51 He hath shewed strength with his arm; he hath scattered the proud in the imagination of their hearts.

52 He hath put down the mighty from their seats, and exalted them of low degree.

53 He hath filled the hungry with good things; and the rich he hath sent empty away.

54 He hath helped his servant Israel, in remembrance of his mercy;

55 As he spake to our fathers, to Abraham, and to his seed for ever.

56 And Mary abode with her about three months, and returned to her own house.

NLT **Luke 1:46** Mary responded, "Oh, how my soul praises the Lord.

47 How my spirit rejoices in God my Savior!

48 For he took notice of his lowly servant girl, and from now on all generations will call me blessed.

49 For the Mighty One is holy, and he has done great things for me.

50 He shows mercy from generation to generation to all who fear him.

51 His mighty arm has done tremendous things! He has scattered the proud and haughty ones.

52 He has brought down princes from their thrones and exalted the humble.

53 He has filled the hungry with good things and sent the rich away with empty hands.

54 He has helped his servant Israel and remembered to be merciful.

55 For he made this promise to our ancestors, to Abraham and his children forever."

56 Mary stayed with Elizabeth about three months and then went back to her own home.

The People, Places, and Times

Mary, the virgin. The mother of Christ, the wife of Joseph, modeled faith for the church—the faith that realized the birth of Christ in her life and fostered her discipleship. Faith is belief in addition to trust that leads to total dependence on Christ and then bursts into activity, producing a life of service.

Background

We take up Mary's story with her immediate decision to visit her aged, barren relative Elisabeth, who, as Gabriel had just revealed to Mary, was pregnant and six months along

(1:36). Her pregnancy was miraculous, but we must never confuse how vastly different it was from the miracle occurring within Mary. Barren Elisabeth was not a virgin, and Zacharias was the natural father of her child. Nevertheless, what a surge of joy swept through Mary as she heard the shocking good news about the miracle in Elisabeth's womb, for it bore parallel testimony to God's power.

Luke matter-of-factly reports Mary's response: "At that time Mary got ready and hurried to a town in the hill country of Judea" (v. 39, NIV). Mary made hasty arrangements with her parents (Did she tell them? We do not know.) and rushed the 80 to 100 miles south to the countryside of Judea, a three- or four-day journey. Her haste indicates eagerness. She could not wait to get there. There were no leisurely teenaged conversations along the way. As she hurried along, she thought long and deep of their crossed destinies, as she and Elisabeth were both in miraculous pregnancies. And then she was there, unannounced, silhouetted in the old couple's doorway.

There was a strong human joy in the meeting of these two expectant mothers— one in the flower of youth, the other's bloom long gone. These two were to become innocent co-conspirators, soul-sisters in the divine plot to save the lost. They would share their hearts as few humans ever have. Through their birthing pain, sweat, blood, and mothering, the world would receive its greatest blessing.

At-A-Glance

1. God is the Subject of Her Song, Her Savior is Worthy (Luke 1:46–50)
2. God Helped His People (vv. 51–56)

In Depth
1. God is the Subject of Her Song, Her Savior is Worthy (Luke 1:46–50)

Mary had just experienced a wonderful visit with her cousin Elizabeth. So great, in fact, that upon Mary's arrival, the baby leaped in Elizabeth's womb. Elizabeth then praised God for what He was doing in having Mary visit her (Luke 1:42–45).

In response to Elizabeth's words, Mary recited a song that praised God's favor on her and her people. God alone was the center of her praise. The *Magnificat*, as the

song is called, consists almost entirely of Old Testament allusions and quotations. In fact, the *Magnificat* closely resembles the song of Hannah in 1 Samuel 2:1–10. Both open in similar exultation of the Lord. Luke's Gospel is full of lowly people; from the shepherds that find themselves stableside for his birth to the inclusion of women and children, his account encourages us that God is concerned about the lowly. Mary says as much when she declares that God has regarded her lowly estate. And she closes her song with the soon-to-be consummated reality of God exalting the lowly and bringing low the strong and proud.

This points to the redemptive work of Christ and accurately reflects the paradoxical nature of the kingdom of God. In order to lead, we must serve; in order to be elevated, we must first be brought low. The kingdom of God values humility over pride. It values the poor in spirit over those rich in their religious practices. The last are first; the least are the greatest, and Mary is a wonderful reflection of this truth.

Mary saw herself as part of the godly remnant that had served Yahweh. She knew she had been chosen by God and was privileged with carrying the Savior of the world. She called God "my Saviour," showing an intimate acquaintance with Him. She spoke of His faithfulness (v. 48), power (v. 49), holiness (v. 49), and mercy (v. 50).

2. God Helped His People (vv. 51–56)

This is the language of vindication through judgment; often in the Old Testament, God's "arm" would save His people and "scatter" their (His) enemies. Mary wove together the language of various psalms. The principle that God exalts the humble and casts down the proud was common in the Old Testament. "Filled the hungry" comes from

Psalm 107:9. God wasn't looking for a group of rebellious peasants to bring this to pass (as many Jews who were considered Zealots believed). Rather, God Himself would enter creation as a vulnerable child.

D.L. Moody has said, "Christ sends none away empty but those who are full of themselves." Who would that include? Mary gives us an idea in her song: the proud, the rich and self-sufficient, and rulers, all who demonstrate some level of behavior that is not God-honoring. That's the message here. As Christians, we need to constantly evaluate our lives to ensure that we are not full of pride. We should never reach a point where our self-sufficiency removes the necessity of God in our daily lives, for He is our source. Finally, should we be blessed to have a leadership role, we should do so in humility, knowing we are under the authority of God. Our text closes recalling God's faithfulness to the Children of Israel. God had promised to be faithful to His people Israel forever because of the eternal covenant He had made by oath with their forefathers (e.g., Deuteronomy 7:7–8).

Search the Scriptures

1. How long is God's mercy on those who fear Him (Luke 1:50)?
2. How did He scatter the proud (v. 51)?

Discuss the Meaning

Mary believed what Gabriel said. She believed that the virgin birth was possible and would happen. She trusted her whole life to God's promise. What does it mean to trust God's promises today, great or small?

Lesson in Our Society

It is so much easier to follow than to lead. We have a tendency to look around and see what the rest of the world is doing and then follow suit. It is time for God's people to appropriately represent Him in the way we live. Our reflection of Christ should show up in the way we obey our God and in the way we encourage one another to do the same.

Make It Happen

When we study God's Word, we are reminded of His promises. Our faith is shown in the way we obey God. Let's take a closer look at how we express praise to God in our actions. Mary's obedience gave praise to God! In the upcoming week, begin to follow Mary's lead and praise God in the way you obey Him.

Follow the Spirit

What God wants me to do:

_____

_____

_____

_____

Remember Your Thoughts

Special insights I have learned:

_____

_____

_____

_____

More Light on the Text
Luke 1:46–56

Mary's song in Luke 1:46–56 is commonly referred to as the *Magnificat*. It has several striking features. First, it is filled with Old Testament concepts and phrases and seems to have been modeled on Hannah's prayer in 1 Samuel 2:1–10. Second, the song reveals Mary's deep piety and knowledge of the Old Testament, a familiarity with the Scriptures that was not unusual at that time. Third, in its essence, the song reveals a God who vindicates the downtrodden and ministers to the hungry (cf. 1 Samuel 2:5), makes the poor to sit with the nobles (v. 8), judges those who arrogantly oppose God (vv. 3, 7, 10; cf. Luke 1:51, 53), and topples the nobles from their places of power (Luke 1:52). Mary's song can be divided into four parts: (1) verses 46–48 praise God for what He has done for Mary, a theme that continues into the first part of the next section; (2) verses 49–50 mention God's power, holiness, and mercy; (3) verses 51–53 show God's sovereign action in reversing certain social conditions; and (4) verses 54–56 recall God's mercy to Israel.

46 And Mary said, My soul doth magnify the Lord, 47 And my spirit hath rejoiced in God my Saviour. 48 For he hath regarded the low estate of his handmaiden: for, behold, from henceforth all generations shall call me blessed.

Mary responded to Elisabeth's Spirit-inspired utterances in a song. The word "magnify" (Gk. *megalynei*, **meg-al-OO-ne-i**) literally means "to enlarge." Here it ascribes greatness to God. To magnify means to make something appear larger than what it already is in order to have a better and proper perception. Think of a magnifying glass that a child uses to see an ant. The ant is small, but when the child looks through the glass, the ant seems large. Yet God cannot appear larger because He is already bigger than we could ever imagine. Magnifying demands that we enlarge our *picture* of God. We oftentimes have a picture of God that is too small and contrived, so we need to magnify Him so we can have a better and bigger picture of Him.

The song is an expression of praise for what God had done to Mary. It opens with the declaration of her intention to magnify God in song (v. 46), which parallels the affirmation that she had found joy in God who, enabling her in a miraculous way to become pregnant with the child of messianic hopes, had now intervened as Savior (v. 47). This happy state existed because God had regard for the afflicted state of His servant (v. 48). It was not that Mary had some personal and individual affliction; her affliction was simply that of God's people awaiting His saving intervention on their behalf. Hannah's affliction had been childlessness (1 Samuel 1:11); for God's people it may be spoken of as the lack of that child who was to be the messianic deliverer (Isaiah 9:6). The Messiah is a symbol of liberation, freedom, and salvation to the Israelites. They believe that the coming of the Savior means God is saving them from oppression. This Savior bestowed grace on Mary, and she responded with humility. She restated that she was only a servant of the Lord. Mary was one of the lowest and most powerless people in that world, yet God used her to bring salvation to all. The grace God had given her was more than she deserved, and so Mary praised the Lord with a humble heart.

Although it has been noted above that the song has some similarity to Hannah's song in 1 Samuel 2:1–10, it is equally noted that that there is a striking difference between the two songs. Whereas Hannah proclaimed triumph over her enemies, Mary proclaimed God and His glorious mercy to humanity. She proclaimed the salvation of God, a salvation wrought through the promised Messiah, her Savior. How different are modern-day songs! Mary's song was not self-centered. She was not praising herself. The Lord was the subject of her song, her praise and rejoicing.

The greatness of the work of God is that it is a universal blessing to all; Jesus came so all people would be blessed. God blesses all because He is mighty and holy. He did a mighty work in the life of Mary that affected all people everywhere for all time. The King has come and will bring salvation.

49 For he that is mighty hath done to me great things; and holy is his name. 50 And his mercy is on them that fear him from generation to generation.

Mary proclaimed God's power. She was in awe of "he that is mighty," the One whose great power had touched her life. The word "mighty" (*megala*, **meg-AL-a**) recalls "magnify" (*megalynei*, **meg-al-OO-ne-i**) in verse 46. Mary proclaimed God's holiness: "holy is his name"; that is, God is to be set apart as different from all others. His very nature, His very being, is different. God is both pure being and pure in being, perfect being and perfect in being, holy in name and holy in being. In this context, God's holiness has overtones of power and may be defined as His transcendent mightiness. Verse 50 echoes Psalm 103:17, affirming what God was accomplishing in Mary: This act of God's mercy is for generation upon generation of those who fear Him. God's mercy is His active faithfulness to His covenant with Israel.

Mary proclaimed God's mercy. There were at least two thoughts in Mary's mind—what God had done in her life and what God had done in history. God has done mighty works through history, and God continues to do mighty works even into our own time. He has shown His mighty power, and God will take Israel by the hand and lead them to salvation.

Mary was lowly and humble in her heart, and thus she was able to hear the word of the Lord, obey it, and receive His grace. She is an example of those whom God wishes to use. God does not use the rich, powerful, and full because often they are arrogant, trusting too much in themselves. Those who are needy, hungry, and weak are open to hearing the word of the Lord; they will be humble servants and follow the word of the Lord.

51 He hath shewed strength with his arm; he hath scattered the proud in the imagination of their hearts. 52 He hath put down the mighty from their seats, and exalted them of low degree. 53 He hath filled the hungry with good things; and the rich he hath sent empty away.

Mary proceeded from adoration to celebration. She saw into the future and proclaimed what the Messiah's coming would accomplish. She prophetically spoke as though the future had become the past, as though the child yet to be born had already lived and done His mighty work in the world. She recognized the strength of God's "arm" which, in old days, had wrought such mighty things for Israel. Mary showed that God will reverse the order of things on earth.

At the end of time, the Lord will scatter the proud "in the imagination of their hearts." Although the Greek word *dianoia* (**dee-AN-oy-ah**), translated "imagination," may ordinarily refer to a mode of thinking, its combination with *kardias* (**kar-DEE-as**), "heart," connotes arrogance or pride in human thoughts, intents, or attitudes. The Lord will dethrone the mighty and exalt the humble. The mighty are those who sit in positions of power, authority, and influence over others. Third, those who are rich only in the things of this world will be stripped of all their earthly goods and sent away empty. And those who have nothing of this world, but who put their trust in God, will receive all the good things that God will provide.

54 He hath helped his servant Israel, in remembrance of his mercy; 55 As he spake to our fathers, to Abraham, and to his seed forever. 56 And Mary abode with her about three months, and returned to her own house.

Mary recognized that the salvation her Son would bring is rooted in God's covenant with Abraham. Mary recalled what God had done both for the nation and its patriarchs. She mentioned two specific helps God provided for His people. First, God remembered His mercy. Israel desperately needed God's mercy and deliverance. In Jesus' day, God's people were enslaved by the Romans. They were desperate both in their need and search for deliverance, so desperate that many were turning to false messiahs to escape their predicament. Some were even finding their security in the Roman state and in humanistic answers instead of God. It was at such a time Mary proclaimed the Lord had remembered His mercy. Second, and more importantly, God had remembered His promise of the Messiah made to Abraham. The promise had now been fulfilled. God had sent the Messiah, the Savior of the world.

Sources:

Cambridge Advanced Learner's Dictionary & Thesaurus. Cambridge Dictionaries Online. http://dictionary.cambridge.org/dictionary/british/ (accessed July 25, 2012).

Keener, Craig S. *The IVP Bible Background Commentary: New Testament.* Downers Grove, IL: IVP Academic, 1994.

Say It Correctly

Magnificat. mag-**NI**-fi-kat.
Messiah. mes-**EYE**-ah.

Daily Bible Readings

MONDAY
My Heart Exults in the Lord
(1 Samuel 2:1–10)

TUESDAY
O Magnify the Lord with Me
(Psalm 34:1–8)

WEDNESDAY
Give Thanks to the Lord
(Psalm 100)

THURSDAY
Bless the Compassionate Lord
(Psalm 103:13–22)

FRIDAY
Praise the Gracious and Merciful Lord
(Psalm 111)

SATURDAY
The Lord Reigns for All Generations
(Psalm 146)

SUNDAY
God Has Done Great Things
(Luke 1:46–56)

Teaching Tips

Words You Should Know

A. Prophesy (Luke 1:67) *propheteuo* (Gk.)—To speak forth by divine inspiration, to predict; sometimes with the idea of foretelling future events pertaining especially to the kingdom of God.

B. Dayspring (v. 78) *anatole* (Gk.)—A rising of the sun and stars; the dawn.

Teacher Preparation

Unifying Principle—Opening the Way. While parents wait to see what their child becomes, Zacharias proclaimed that his child would open the way for Christ.

A. Set aside time to pray that you will teach in a way that students will meet the Aim for Change.

B. Study Luke 1 in its entirety, using a commentary and concordance.

O—Open the Lesson

A. Begin today's lesson with prayer.

B. Read the Aim for Change and Keep in Mind verses.

C. Initiate discussion by asking students if they believe that today's parents can forecast what their children will become, as Zacharias did. Have them explain their answers.

P—Present the Scriptures

A. Have volunteers take turns reading through the Focal Verses.

B. To clarify the verses, use The People, Places, and Times; Background; Search the Scriptures; At-A-Glance outline; In Depth; and More Light on the Text.

E—Explore the Meaning

A. Divide the class into three groups, assigning to each one of the following sections to explore: Discuss the Meaning, Lesson in Our Society, and Make It Happen. Tell each group to select a representative to share their responses.

B. Make sure to relate the Aim for Change and the Keep in Mind verses to the three sections.

N—Next Steps for Application

A. Encourage students to find verses to pray for today's youth. Isaiah 54:13 is a great verse, and the book of Proverbs is full of them.

B. Close with prayer, thanking God for the example Zacharias showed through his prophetic utterances about his son.

Worship Guide

For the Superintendent or Teacher
Theme: Zacharias Prophesies about
His Son John
Song: "Hark, the Herald Angels Sing"
Devotional Reading: Luke 1:59–66

Zacharias Prophesies about His Son John

Bible Background • LUKE 1
Printed Text • LUKE 1:57–58, 67–79 | Devotional Reading • LUKE 1:59–66

Aim for Change

By the end of the lesson, we will: REVIEW the story of Zacharias' prophecy concerning his son, John the Baptist; GAIN an appreciation for prophecy and reflect on expectations we have for the next generation; and ADDRESS the justice modeled in Zacharias' prophecy.

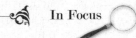

In Focus

Horace woke up and found his two sons texting on their cell phones. As a child, his Saturday mornings were spent cutting grass, trimming bushes, and washing his parents' cars. Now, his sons had become too entitled and selfish. Horace decided that they needed to be humbled, so he drove them to a homeless shelter to serve less-fortunate people.

The teens complained, and Horace told them they'd appreciate the experience after the visit. "I want you both to realize just how blessed you really are."

When they got out of the car, one of the boys ran over to an elderly man who had fallen off the curb. The other son used his cell phone to call for help. Horace helped lift the man to a bench.

They waited with him for the paramedics, and the man praised Horace's sons. "It's really good to see two young men who actually care." The boys left that experience with a new perspective.

We should never underestimate the power of our positive words; we must know that speaking favorably over today's youth will help effect change.

Keep in Mind

"And thou, child, shalt be called the prophet of the Highest: for thou shalt go before the face of the Lord to prepare his ways; To give knowledge of salvation unto his people by the remission of their sins" (Luke 1:76–77).

"And thou, child, shalt be called the prophet of the Highest: for thou shalt go before the face of the Lord to prepare his ways; To give knowledge of salvation unto his people by the remission of their sins" (Luke 1:76–77).

Focal Verses

KJV **Luke 1:57** Now Elisabeth's full time came that she should be delivered; and she brought forth a son.

58 And her neighbours and her cousins heard how the Lord had shewed great mercy upon her; and they rejoiced with her.

1:67 And his father Zacharias was filled with the Holy Ghost, and prophesied, saying,

68 Blessed be the Lord God of Israel; for he hath visited and redeemed his people,

69 And hath raised up an horn of salvation for us in the house of his servant David;

70 As he spake by the mouth of his holy prophets, which have been since the world began:

71 That we should be saved from our enemies, and from the hand of all that hate us;

72 To perform the mercy promised to our fathers, and to remember his holy covenant;

73 The oath which he sware to our father Abraham,

74 That he would grant unto us, that we being delivered out of the hand of our enemies might serve him without fear,

75 In holiness and righteousness before him, all the days of our life.

76 And thou, child, shalt be called the prophet of the Highest: for thou shalt go before the face of the Lord to prepare his ways;

77 To give knowledge of salvation unto his people by the remission of their sins,

78 Through the tender mercy of our God; whereby the dayspring from on high hath visited us,

79 To give light to them that sit in darkness and in the shadow of death, to guide our feet into the way of peace.

NLT **Luke 1:57** When it was time for Elizabeth's baby to be born, she gave birth to a son.

58 And when her neighbors and relatives heard that the Lord had been very merciful to her, everyone rejoiced with her.

1:67 Then his father, Zechariah, was filled with the Holy Spirit and gave this prophecy:

68 "Praise the Lord, the God of Israel, because he has visited and redeemed his people.

69 He has sent us a mighty Savior from the royal line of his servant David,

70 just as he promised through his holy prophets long ago.

71 Now we will be saved from our enemies and from all who hate us.

72 He has been merciful to our ancestors by remembering his sacred covenant—

73 the covenant he swore with an oath to our ancestor Abraham.

74 We have been rescued from our enemies so we can serve God without fear,

75 in holiness and righteousness for as long as we live.

76 "And you, my little son, will be called the prophet of the Most High, because you will prepare the way for the Lord.

77 You will tell his people how to find salvation through forgiveness of their sins.

78 Because of God's tender mercy, the morning light from heaven is about to break upon us,

79 to give light to those who sit in darkness and in the shadow of death, and to guide us to the path of peace."

The People, Places, and Times

Zacharias. Was also from a priestly family and was a descendant of Aaron. He was a priest ministering in the temple when an angel came to him and promised a son. His son, John, was born to him and Elisabeth in their old age.

Luke. The author of the third Gospel and the book of Acts. He was born in Antioch, learned medicine, and was known as "the beloved physician" (Colossians 4:14). He was the Apostle Paul's friend and companion on a few of his missionary journeys, including visiting Macedonia, Philippi, Caesarea, and Jerusalem. He probably died a martyr.

Background

Chapter 1 begins with Luke informing readers that his only purpose in writing this book was to make a record of Jesus' birth so we would know the truth. With pleasure, he recounted the story of Zacharias and Elisabeth—a priest and his old barren wife. Zacharias was working in the temple when the angel Gabriel came to announce that Elisabeth would give birth to a son. When Zacharias questioned Gabriel's words, his voice was taken away so he could not speak until his son was born. Elisabeth hid herself for five months.

In the sixth month of Elisabeth's pregnancy, Luke took us to Mary's house, a close relative of Elisabeth. There, Mary also received a visit from Gabriel with the same announcement—she, too, would bear a son. But her pregnancy would not result from relations with a man but through the overshadowing of the Holy Spirit. Unlike Zacharias, Mary believed Gabriel. She then went to visit Elisabeth, where she stayed for three months.

At-A-Glance

1. Praises for Elisabeth (Luke 1:57–58)
2. Promises for Jesus (vv. 67–75)
3. Prophecies for John (vv. 76–79)

In Depth

1. Praises for Elisabeth (Luke 1:57–58)

While female friends, neighbors, and relatives gave birth to their babies, Elisabeth gave up hope that she would ever bear a child. Barren and now aged, she could have easily been the baby shower organizer, the babysitter, and the shoulder to cry on as mothers complained about the terrible twos and the turbulent teens. What she wouldn't have given to be called "mom."

Then, just as the others were becoming menopausal and grandmothers, Elisabeth became pregnant. Imagine how she had to reserve her strength and preserve her health to carry a child to full term at her age. Now, imagine the joy and awe she felt the day she delivered a healthy baby. What great mercy the Lord showed her, and Luke records that her neighbors and cousins—all of whom she had supported—came to praise her for the birth of her beautiful boy.

Interestingly, the description of John's birth is limited to these two verses. Maybe it's better that way. John would later recall in his adult ministry, "[Jesus] must increase, but I must decrease" (John 3:30). In that text, John's disciples were concerned about Jesus' increasing popularity and John's status. John appropriately understood his role in God's redemptive plan, and our text here hints at this fact. There's no extended biography on John because his life is engulfed by a greater story—the Gospel of Christ. So we have two verses here. Elizabeth was full term and she brought forth a son.

When we think about our ministries today are we able to say the same thing? Is Jesus increasing in our congregation or are we increasingly becoming man-centered and personality driven? It may be time to retain the narrative here. Our lives and our service, although important, are but a few sentences in the grand scheme of God's plan. Lord, let us continually decrease so You may increase and Your glory may cover the earth.

2. Promises for Jesus (vv. 67–75)

Zechariah was previously told that his son would be filled with the Spirit (Luke 1:15). Afterward, his wife was filled with the Spirit (Luke 1:41). Finally, it was his turn.

Zacharias had nine months of silence to think about all the things he would say when his time came to speak. Imagine how frustrating it must have been to not be able to hear his own voice, to utter a simple prayer, or to tell his wife how beautiful she looked pregnant. He endured more than 270 days of scribbling requests, grunting to emphasize what he used to easily say, and gesturing with his hands. He made it through the whole delivery of his son's birth. What a great day it would be when he was no longer handicapped. There would be so many things to talk about. But on the day his son was born, Zacharias opened his mouth—not to praise himself, his wife, or his son—but to bless Jesus, the child still to be born.

3. Prophecies for John (vv. 76–79)

What parent doesn't have high hopes for his child? There aren't too many parents who look over their newborns and envision visiting them in prison when they get older. Most parents visualize their children as scholars, professionals, and stars. Zacharias was no different. He had endured years of his wife's barrenness and months of silence, so surely he wondered what kind of child John

would be. Knowing he had not suffered in vain, Zacharias declared an affirmation of Gabriel's earlier promise, "And thou, child, shalt be called the prophet of the Highest." Zacharias needed only to look to Hebrew Scripture for further evidence of John's future: John was to be the servant who would prepare the way of the Lord (Isaiah 40:3). John would be the prophet to call the people of Israel to repentance. Even with his limited understanding of the entire story, Zacharias spoke life over his son, proclaiming his purpose and establishing him as the forerunner for Christ.

Search the Scriptures

1. Why did the neighbors rejoice with Elisabeth (Luke 1:58)?

2. Whom did Zacharias praise when his son was born (v. 68)?

Discuss the Meaning

1. How does Zacharias' prophecy model justice?

2. Zacharias was silent for months. There were plenty of things he could have said. What do you think about his first words?

Lesson in Our Society

We live in a society that prides itself upon its right to exercise freedom of speech. Though we can freely say whatever we think and feel, today's lesson demonstrates that we ought to exercise our right to remain silent. What if we were arrested every time we spoke against the Lord? Zacharias' ability to speak was taken away from him when he verbalized unbelief. Growing up, we are taught how and when to speak. Spiritual maturity is evidenced by those who know how and when *not* to speak.

Make It Happen

This week, challenge yourself to practice something you learned when you were a child—to only speak if you have something nice to say. Enjoy a week without complaining, cursing, or criticizing. It should be a week of positivity.

Follow the Spirit

What God wants me to do:

_____

_____

_____

_____

Remember Your Thoughts

Special insights I have learned:

_____

_____

_____

_____

More Light on the Text

Luke 1:57–58, 67–79

57 Now Elisabeth's full time came that she should be delivered; and she brought forth a son.

Elisabeth was the second cousin of Mary, the mother of Jesus. Both of their babies had divine origins, for the angel Gabriel stood before Zacharias in the temple just as he stood before Mary. Zacharias and Elisabeth differed from Mary in that they were very old and the idea of having a child seemed like a lost cause. The promise did come true, and even in the womb their baby was already filled with the Holy Ghost and leapt with joy in response to hearing the voice of Mary when she visited (Luke 1:15, 44). For three months, Mary and Elisabeth spent time together, likely preparing the home for the baby. Just after Mary left, the baby was born.

58 And her neighbours and her cousins heard how the Lord had shewed great mercy upon her; and they rejoiced with her.

The Jewish custom for welcoming babies was full of music, food, and celebration. Family and neighbors would gather for a party and wait to hear if a boy or girl was born, anxiously hoping that it was the former in the event that it might be the Messiah. For this reason, boys took on a greater significance for families than girls. One theologian states that if a boy was born, the musicians would start playing, the people would all dance, and everyone would have a big party; if a girl was born, the musicians would leave, and there would be no great celebration. This may be why the word "mercy" (Gk. *eleos*, **eh-LEE-ose**) is used. It indicates a unique kindness or good will toward someone who is afflicted.

67 And his father Zacharias was filled with the Holy Ghost, and prophesied, saying . . .

To be filled with the Holy Ghost (Gk. *pneuma*, **NOO-ma**) during this time was a rare gift, unlike how all Christians would experience this after Pentecost. Zacharias was a priest from the line of Aaron and was the first person God spoke to through an angel about his baby's birth. He'd been divinely struck mute since this happened due to his unbelief. Now that the events had come to pass, God blessed Zacharias with Himself and the return of his voice.

68 Blessed be the Lord God of Israel; for he hath visited and redeemed his people.

Biblical prophecies often begin with praises of who God is and then move into a personal application or promise. Zacharias' praise is called the *Benedictus,* a Latin term to describe his praise to God. Even though he could have been angry at God for the punishment of not being able to speak for nine months, he instead celebrated who the Lord is and what He was about to do. This song can be divided into two sections, including an initial burst of thanksgiving that then leads into an address from Zacharias to his son. All of it reveals his personal thrill at seeing his household take part in the great purpose of God to save all people.

69 And hath raised up an horn of salvation for us in the house of his servant David.

The Jews commonly saw a horn as a symbol of strength, so a "horn of salvation" means a mighty Savior. God is described this way in Psalm 18, so by sharing similar sentiments here, Zacharias provides another link to the Trinity through the birth of Jesus. People likewise viewed the reign of David as a time when Israel held power to defend itself against its enemies. The coming Messiah would again put the Jews in a place of prominence, but in a divine, spiritual sense versus merely a political one.

This is the meaning behind what true salvation (Gk. *soteria,* **sow-TAY-ree-ah**) is. Deliverance is more than protection from physical oppression; it also affects internal and ethical issues like humanity's sin. The Messiah would present both to Christians, but in stages: personal transformation that would lead to an eternal dwelling with God when the kingdom of God arrives in fullness.

70 As he spake by the mouth of his holy prophets, which have been since the world began.

Zacharias affirmed that all that was taking place was in accordance with God's promises to His people in the past. In each verse that follows, Zacharias tracked a chronology of different core events the Jews experienced in waiting for their Messiah. In doing so, Zacharias simultaneously fulfilled his roles as a priest and prophet by pouring out worship toward the Lord and instructing others to remember their people's story.

71 That we should be saved from our enemies, and from the hand of all that hate us.

By sending someone like John the Baptist who would prepare the way for the Messiah, God declared that the people had not been forgotten. They endured the scorn of surrounding nations as well as their Roman oppressors but never were without the promise that God would one day save them. Just as He visited His people when they were captive in Egypt (Exodus 3:16, 4:31) and then continued to send them numerous prophets throughout succeeding generations, it was time for the Lord to supernaturally save His people from all that stood against them. It began with John, who would remind them of their sin so that Christ alone would be shown to be the Savior.

72 To perform the mercy promised to our fathers, and to remember his holy covenant.

A covenant (Gk. *diatheke,* **dee-ah-tha-KAH**) meant a unique arrangement that was valid between a superior party and a lesser party. The one with more power or authority would initiate the arrangement, finalize the terms, and then validate things through a symbolic sacrifice. God always played the stronger role, and Israel the yielding role.

73 The oath which he sware to our father Abraham.

Abraham was considered to be the father of the Jews since the Lord pledged that out of his offspring the whole world would be blessed. Something promised centuries earlier was being fulfilled in their midst, revealing that God is distinct in establishing His lordship over time while also binding Himself into moments of history. The passing of time in no way dims the promises He's made, including more than 45 signs in the Old Testament that identify the Messiah.

74 That he would grant unto us, that we being delivered out of the hand of our enemies might serve him without fear.

For more than 400 years before this time, the Lord had withheld speaking through another prophet. During that time, the Jewish nation had been constantly oppressed by foreign enemies. Zacharias now proclaimed that the Messiah will come and his son will prepare the way. The hope was that this would lead to deliverance from their oppressors, but the Lord God of Israel had deeper plans than temporary relief from bullies. Israel was a chosen people full of the potential to save the whole world through their Savior.

75 In holiness and righteousness before him, all the days of our life.

It is a privilege to be able to join God in what He's doing. To be able to do so, however, requires that we prepare our hearts so when the Lord moves, we are ready. The call to holiness and righteousness helps to prepare us to be in God's presence. Being holy means we set ourselves apart for Him, allowing our righteousness to form after being delivered from sin. John would prepare the people for the former, while Jesus would make the latter possible.

76 And thou, child, shalt be called the prophet of the Highest: for thou shalt go before the face of the Lord to prepare his ways.

Isaiah 40:3 speaks about the forerunner of the Messiah, and John himself would later own this truth and claim it publicly (John 1:23). Zacharias knew this pattern as a priest, for just as Aaron was Moses' mouthpiece (Exodus 7:1), so would John be a messenger to prepare people for salvation and the kingdom of heaven. He would preach repentance by calling people to open their hearts to the Lord.

77 To give knowledge of salvation unto his people by the remission of their sins,

Psalm 56:13 states, "For thou hast delivered my soul from death: wilt not thou deliver my feet from falling, that I may walk before God in the light of the living?" Zacharias said the Messiah would not just reveal sins but actually purify people of their sins. This freedom is more than being delivered out of the hands of enemies—it involves forgiveness of what we've done wrong and the sin nature that corrupts us, and then it enables us to have a relationship with God.

78 Through the tender mercy of our God; whereby the dayspring from on high hath visited us.

The ability to even know that John would be a prophet who would prepare the way for the Messiah was a sign that Zacharias was speaking under divine guidance, knowing things that only the Holy Ghost could have revealed to him. By speaking even now about Jesus, whom he didn't know, Zacharias revealed his relationship to the God he did know. There is also a backdrop for this statement from Isaiah 60:1–2 that says, "Arise, shine; for thy light is come, and the glory of the LORD is risen upon thee. For, behold, the darkness shall cover the earth, and gross darkness the people: but the LORD shall arise upon thee, and his glory shall be seen upon thee."

79 To give light to them that sit in darkness and in the shadow of death, to guide our feet into the way of peace.

Jesus Christ is more than the giver of salvation, and John the Baptist was more than His forerunner. Each offered a light in the darkness that humanity needed to find the way back to a peace that only the Lord can provide. Christ is the morning Light and rising Sun (Malachi 4:2). Through John the Baptist, this light began to break into the darkness of sin, increasing until the Messiah shone it in perfect brilliance through His character, teachings, and mission.

Part of knowing God involves discovering things that we were utterly in the dark about before. Revelation 21:23 reveals that the light of the Lamb, Christ Himself, will shine so brightly that there will be no need for a sun. That type of illumination is more than physical, for He can begin it even now in your life.

Sources:
Blue Letter Bible. BlueLetterBible.org. http://www.blueletterbible.org/commentaries/comm_view.cfm?AuthorID=1&contentID=7140&commInfo=25&topic=Luke&ar=Luk_1_57 (accessed August 28, 2012).
Smith, William. *Smith's Bible Dictionary*. Peabody, MA: Hendrickson Publishers, Inc., 2000. 137, 366–67, 539–41.
Word in Life Study Bible (NKJV). Nashville: Thomas Nelson Publishers, 1993. 167, 755.

Say It Correctly

Zacharias. za-ka-**RI**-as.
Prophesied. **PRA**-fa-sid.

Daily Bible Readings

MONDAY
What Will This Child Become?
(Luke 1:59–66)

TUESDAY
John's Call to Repentance
(Luke 3:1–6)

WEDNESDAY
What Then Should We Do?
(Luke 3:7–14)

THURSDAY
One More Powerful than John
(Luke 3:15–20)

FRIDAY
The Baptizer of Jesus
(Matthew 3:13–17)

SATURDAY
A Prophet and More
(Luke 7:18–27)

SUNDAY
A Prophet of the Most High
(Luke 1:57–58, 67–79)

Teaching Tips

DEC 22nd

Words You Should Know

Decree (Luke 2:1) *dogma* (Gk.)—Doctrine, ordinance. The rules and requirements of the law of Moses, carrying a suggestion of severity and threatened judgment.

Espoused (v. 5) *mnesteuo* (Gk.)—To be promised in marriage; engaged.

Manger (v. 7) *phatne* (Gk.)—Stall, a compartment for one domestic animal in a barn or shed.

Teacher Preparation

Unifying Principle—A Bundle of Joy. What kind of child is conceived by no earthly means, whose birth is announced by angels, and whose whereabouts are pinpointed by a star? Though born meagerly—in a stall alongside animals—nothing could overshadow Jesus' majesty.

A. Review the Aim for Change.

B. Use a commentary and concordance to study Luke 2 in its entirety.

O—Open the Lesson

A. Open today's lesson by including the Aim for Change in your prayer.

B. Ask your students to identify how they will incorporate worship into the holiday.

C. Give students a few minutes to read the In Focus story, and discuss.

P—Present the Scriptures

A. Allow a few minutes for the students to read through the Focal Verses.

B. So they can gain a better understanding of the verses, have volunteers read The People, Places, and Times; Background; Search the Scriptures; At-A-Glance outline; In Depth; and More Light on the Text sections.

E—Explore the Meaning

A. Assign the following sections to groups of students to explore: Discuss the Meaning and Lesson in Our Society. Have each group share their responses.

B. Encourage students to memorize the Keep in Mind verse.

N—Next Steps for Application

A. Encourage your students to incorporate worship into their daily lives with a morning, noon, or evening devotion.

B. Have students identify ways they can worship (i.e., reciting psalms, singing hymns, or bowing on knees).

Worship Guide

For the Superintendent or Teacher
Theme: Jesus Is Born
Song: "Away in a Manger"
Devotional Reading: Galatians 4:1–7

Jesus Is Born

Bible Background • LUKE 2
Printed Text • LUKE 2:1–17 | Devotional Reading • GALATIANS 4:1–7

———————— Aim for Change ————————

By the end of the lesson, we will: REVIEW the story of Joseph and Mary's journey to Bethlehem and Jesus' birth; REFLECT on the meaning of the Messiah in contemporary times; and IDENTIFY the saving work of Jesus in the world today.

————————— In Focus —————————

Janelle knew Christmas was about more than buying gifts for her three children, but it didn't feel good not having the money to do so. She couldn't believe it was Christmas Eve and her checking account was negative. Desperately, she applied for and was turned down for an advance loan. She cried when she learned that the Christmas toy giveaways had just ended. There was nothing left for her to do but tell the kids the truth. "Tomorrow, there'll be no need to go downstairs and look under the tree," she told them sadly.

Without asking why, her six-year-old son said, "That's okay, Mommy. Jesus is only the gift we need." That made Janelle cry even harder.

On Christmas morning, Janelle's children were all snuggled in bed with her when they heard a knock on the door. There, they found Janelle's mother with a car full of gifts. "I know your mom said you weren't getting anything for Christmas, but I've brought a surprise for all of you."

How do you think Janelle responded to her mother's gifts? Do you think it made her want to worship God? While no gift can compare to Jesus, make sure you remember to worship Him this Christmas.

———————— Keep in Mind ————————

"And she brought forth her firstborn son, and wrapped him in swaddling clothes, and laid him in a manger; because there was no room for them in the inn" (Luke 2:7).

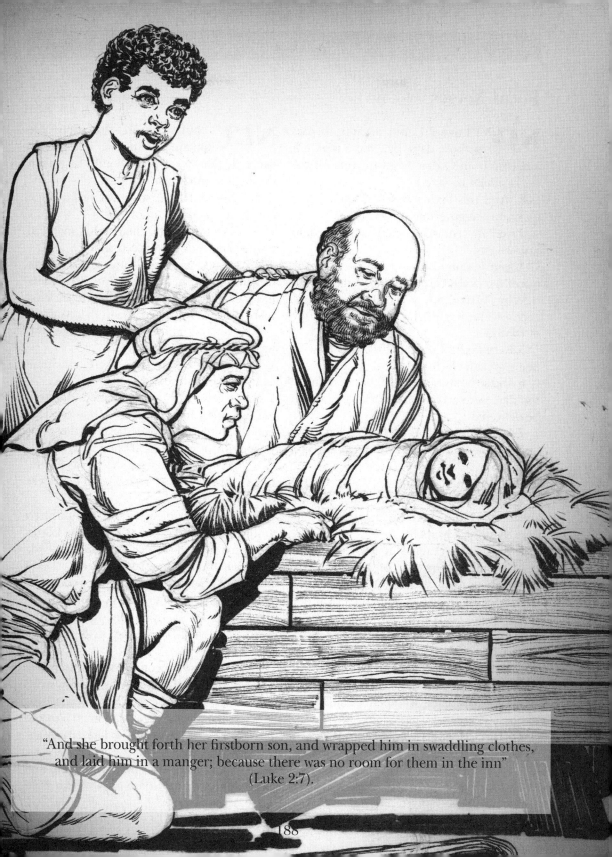

"And she brought forth her firstborn son, and wrapped him in swaddling clothes, and laid him in a manger; because there was no room for them in the inn" (Luke 2:7).

Focal Verses

KJV **Luke 2:1** And it came to pass in those days, that there went out a decree from Caesar Augustus that all the world should be taxed.

2 (And this taxing was first made when Cyrenius was governor of Syria.)

3 And all went to be taxed, every one into his own city.

4 And Joseph also went up from Galilee, out of the city of Nazareth, into Judaea, unto the city of David, which is called Bethlehem; (because he was of the house and lineage of David:)

5 To be taxed with Mary his espoused wife, being great with child.

6 And so it was, that, while they were there, the days were accomplished that she should be delivered.

7 And she brought forth her firstborn son, and wrapped him in swaddling clothes, and laid him in a manger; because there was no room for them in the inn.

8 And there were in the same country shepherds abiding in the field, keeping watch over their flock by night.

9 And, lo, the angel of the Lord came upon them, and the glory of the Lord shone round about them: and they were sore afraid.

10 And the angel said unto them, Fear not: for, behold, I bring you good tidings of great joy, which shall be to all people.

11 For unto you is born this day in the city of David a Saviour, which is Christ the Lord.

12 And this shall be a sign unto you; Ye shall find the babe wrapped in swaddling clothes, lying in a manger.

13 And suddenly there was with the angel a multitude of the heavenly host praising God, and saying,

14 Glory to God in the highest, and on earth peace, good will toward men.

NLT **Luke 2:1** At that time the Roman emperor, Augustus, decreed that a census should be taken throughout the Roman Empire.

2 (This was the first census taken when Quirinius was governor of Syria.)

3 All returned to their own ancestral towns to register for this census.

4 And because Joseph was a descendant of King David, he had to go to Bethlehem in Judea, David's ancient home. He traveled there from the village of Nazareth in Galilee.

5 He took with him Mary, his fiancée, who was now obviously pregnant.

6 And while they were there, the time came for her baby to be born.

7 She gave birth to her first child, a son. She wrapped him snugly in strips of cloth and laid him in a manger, because there was no lodging available for them.

8 That night there were shepherds staying in the fields nearby, guarding their flocks of sheep.

9 Suddenly, an angel of the Lord appeared among them, and the radiance of the Lord's glory surrounded them. They were terrified,

10 but the angel reassured them. "Don't be afraid!" he said. "I bring you good news that will bring great joy to all people.

11 The Savior—yes, the Messiah, the Lord—has been born today in Bethlehem, the city of David!

12 And you will recognize him by this sign: You will find a baby wrapped snugly in strips of cloth, lying in a manger."

13 Suddenly, the angel was joined by a vast host of others—the armies of heaven—praising God and saying,

14 "Glory to God in highest heaven, and peace on earth to those with whom God is pleased."

189

15 And it came to pass, as the angels were gone away from them into heaven, the shepherds said one to another, Let us now go even unto Bethlehem, and see this thing which is come to pass, which the Lord hath made known unto us.

16 And they came with haste, and found Mary, and Joseph, and the babe lying in a manger.

17 And when they had seen it, they made known abroad the saying which was told them concerning this child.

15 When the angels had returned to heaven, the shepherds said to each other, "Let's go to Bethlehem! Let's see this thing that has happened, which the Lord has told us about."

16 They hurried to the village and found Mary and Joseph. And there was the baby, lying in the manger.

17 After seeing him, the shepherds told everyone what had happened and what the angel had said to them about this child.

The People, Places, and Times

Joseph. A just man from the lineage of David. He lived in Nazareth in Galilee. Before marrying Mary, he thought to leave the relationship when she told him she was pregnant. But then he received angelic communication that his fiancée was indeed pregnant with a child by the Holy Spirit. He chose to remain with her and raise the child.

Shepherds. Palestinian shepherds had lives characterized by danger, hardship, and exposure to extreme heat and cold. Their equipment consisted of a cloak made of sheepskin and fleece which could be turned inside out for protection from the cold, a scrib or wallet for food and money, a staff with a crook to manage the flock and to be used as a weapon against foes, and a sling. The shepherd's occupation required great watchfulness, especially at night.

Background

It is true that what the enemy means for evil, God allows for good. At the exact time Joseph and Mary were settling, waiting for the arrival of their firstborn child, Rome made a decree for a regional census. With Mary so close to her due date, the couple must have wondered how they would make the 90-mile trek from Nazareth to Bethlehem. But God was working behind the scenes. To fulfill His promise, Jesus had to be born in Bethlehem, the City of David. What better way to get His parents there than by a decree that required the couple to go back to their hometowns to pay taxes?

Homecomings are celebrated with much fanfare, but not this one. The census caused Bethlehem to be so overpopulated that every inn was decorated with *No Vacancy* signs. Breathtaking contractions caused Mary to stop at the only place she could find to deliver her son—a stable. Imagine Mary pushing between gulps of air in a smelly stable and grunting alongside noisy cows, horses, and pigs. She must've laughed to keep from crying, considering she brought forth the promised Child and had nowhere to lay Him but a feeding trough for a makeshift crib.

At-A-Glance

1. Going Back (Luke 2:1–6)
2. Coming Forth (vv. 7–12)
3. Spreading Out (vv. 13–17)

In Depth

1. Going Back (Luke 2:1–6)

Joseph and Mary had probably prepared a place for the baby in their home, chosen His first outfit, and made sure they had a well-practiced first-century version of Lamaze breathing ready for Mary's labor and delivery. Then Caesar issued a decree—every man had to go to his hometown to be taxed.

This seemingly random tax was all a part of God's plan. For Bethlehem held a special place in Scripture. It was King David's hometown and was from where the expected Messiah was to hail (Micah 5:1; cf. Matthew 2:1). The tax wasn't necessarily a Caesar thing, but a God thing. It caused two people who lived in Nazareth to journey to Bethlehem in a prophecy-fulfilling moment in history.

Maybe they were expecting to be back in Nazareth in time for the birth. How in the world would they make a three-day journey to Bethlehem and get back so Mary could deliver their child in the comfort of their own home? What a dilemma! Considering they were carrying the promised child, one whose birth was announced by angels, surely God would make a way.

Guess what happened when the couple got to Bethlehem? Mary's contractions began. With no rooms in any of the inns, the couple was forced to seek shelter in a barn. There in a stall, the first witnesses to the Messiah's birth were animals.

2. Coming Forth (vv. 7–12)

A manger seemed like a strange place, but it was all they had. As we read this text today, it's possible that God was sending a subtle message here. Isaiah 1:3 records: "The ox knows its owner, and the donkey its master's crib, but Israel does not know, my people do not understand." These same animals in this manger knew their owner. They knew that He had put on flesh and was lying before them in a manger.

Far from the outfit she picked out at home, Mary wrapped Jesus tightly in a cloth. Considering many things in the stall for use as a bed, she settled upon a feeding trough.

While the Messiah and His parents slept, some shepherds were in a field keeping watch over their sheep. The evening started out as routine as any other—the shepherds brought the sheep back to the fold. They made sure none of the flock was missing by passing them "under the rod" (a counting mechanism used) as they entered the entrance of the enclosure. If any of the sheep had strayed, the shepherds would have searched until it was found, which would have made for a long night!

Then, out of nowhere, an angel appeared to the shepherds, causing them to be afraid. However, the angel brought them Good News of great joy, telling them about Jesus' birth and bidding them to go see for themselves.

3. Spreading Out (vv. 13–17)

If the shepherds doubted that what they saw and heard was true, the host of praising angels was enough to make them eager enough to check it out. If heaven was excited about this newborn Savior, the least the shepherds could do was verify the sign they'd been given. They went quickly to Bethlehem. Imagine how they felt as they came upon Mary, Joseph, and the Babe lying in a manger. How wonderful it is to find that God's words are true, that something is just as God told you it would be. As witnesses, they had to tell somebody, anybody, and everybody! Not just about a child who was born or the hope of expectant parents—but the Good News of the birth of the Savior of all people.

Search the Scriptures

1. What caused Joseph and Mary to go back to Bethlehem (Luke 2:1–4)?

2. Whom did the angels tell to go see Jesus (vv. 8–12)?

Discuss the Meaning

1. How did God use the census to fulfill His promise?

2. What made the shepherds go tell everyone about the birth of Jesus?

Lesson in Our Society

We live in a society where people think that God's promises are easy to obtain. They say, "What God has for me is for me," until they come upon hardship. Then they say, "I must've heard God wrong." Almost every God-given promise is shrouded by problems. The path from Egypt led straight to the Red Sea. The Promised Land had giants in it. Jesus' birth was redirected by a census that caused a series of unfortunate events. We must learn to persist and endure if we are ever going to be witnesses of the greater things of God.

Make It Happen

What promise has God made to you? Make a list of the obstacles you're enduring and remember Mary and Joseph. Know that each obstacle gets you closer to the promise. Praise God in advance for the birth of the promise He's entrusted to you.

Follow the Spirit

What God wants me to do:

_____

_____

_____

_____

Remember Your Thoughts

Special insights I have learned:

_____

_____

_____

_____

More Light on the Text

Luke 2:1–17

1 And it came to pass in those days, that there went out a decree from Caesar Augustus that all the world should be taxed.

The phrase "those days" refers to an era of oppression under the Roman empire. Caesar Augustus was born Gaius Octavius, the grandnephew of Julius Caesar. Because Julius Caesar had legally adopted Octavius as his son, Octavius took the name "Caesar" from Julius, which in later years became a name almost equal to "emperor." The term "Augustus" in Latin means "worthy of reverence," which kept in step with how the Romans used titles with overtones of pagan divinity. He reigned as emperor for 41 years from 27 B.C. to A.D. 14, a time of political security and lavish building projects. Augustus restored 82 temples in Rome alone and became an object of worship in the state religion, although he emphasized a return to worship the old gods that had made Rome great. This is the scene into which the one true Messiah was born.

2 (And this taxing was first made when Cyrenius was governor of Syria.)

Taxing the whole world took place regionally, and everyone in power tended to receive some form of a profit from it. The Greek verb used for this process of taxing is *apographa* (a-pa-gra-FA), which also means to "enroll" or "register," as in an official listing of citizens. The census is here called a "taxing" because once everyone was accounted for, they could be more accurately taxed. Additionally, Augustus wanted to know whether the population of his empire was growing, and he was especially interested in all the nations that Rome had absorbed. This "first" or "prior" census (taxing) was distinguished from the later one Luke mentions in Acts 5:37.

3 And all went to be taxed, every one into his own city.

Even people who lived far away from their home city had to travel to their ancestral birthplace for this type of census. A Roman census document, dated A.D. 104, was discovered in Egypt and showed such a command. In another document from A.D. 119, an Egyptian man identified himself by citing his name, the names of his parents and grandparents, his original village, age, profession, a physical scar above his left eyebrow, his wife's name and age, his father's name, his son's name and age, and the names of other relatives living with him. These types of documents offer insight into what Joseph would have had to share during the census.

4 And Joseph also went up from Galilee, out of the city of Nazareth, into Judaea, unto the city of David, which is called Bethlehem;

(because he was of the house and lineage of David:)

The trip from Nazareth to Bethlehem is about 90 miles, going upward to an elevation of 2,300 feet above sea level. In this sense, Joseph "went up" on a journey that was a significant undertaking of multiple days of travel and expense. Luke mentions the territories they crossed as a reference point for Jews who would also recognize that Bethlehem is an area first mentioned in Genesis 35:19, then 48:7, Judges 12:8–10, and Ruth 1:1–19. Bethlehem was a small, humble village, but Micah prophesied that the Messiah would be born there (Micah 5:2). He would be the "Son of David," and Bethlehem was where David had been born and raised (1 Samuel 16:1).

5 To be taxed with Mary his espoused wife, being great with child.

Joseph is mentioned as being a descendant of David, but there remains a question whether Mary was. No mention is made of this, and yet she went with Joseph even though there is no overt reason why other than their marriage. Mary is described as being espoused to Joseph, which is the state of betrothal or engagement, so intertwined with marriage that to break it off would also be considered divorce. Matthew 1:24 seems to clarify since it reveals that Joseph took Mary as his wife before Jesus was born. There's also the matter of the controversial pregnancy that would have left Mary under fire had she remained home while Joseph made the trek to Bethlehem.

6 And so it was, that, while they were there, the days were accomplished that she should be delivered.

It's not necessarily true that Jesus was born the moment Joseph and Mary arrived in Bethlehem. The text reveals that "while they were there" the birth took place, which may have been several days. The census allowed Mary to be in the prophesied place of the Messiah's birth, whether she knew to be there or not. The self-centered decree of Caesar Augustus was used by the true Lord of the universe to fulfill prophecy.

7 And she brought forth her firstborn son, and wrapped him in swaddling clothes, and laid him in a manger; because there was no room for them in the inn.

Since the census affected all of Joseph's family, there were likely many family members there taking part in a type of reunion. There is also no indication that Mary had any help in giving birth, for the text indicates that she brought forth her own baby, wrapped Him in clothes herself, and placed Him in the manger. Given the exhaustion of childbirth on the heels of a long trip to Bethlehem, the miraculous birth may have appeared quite common.

8 And there were in the same country shepherds abiding in the field, keeping watch over their flock by night.

Shepherds made little money and were on the low end of the social scale for many reasons. Due to long periods of time out in the fields with sheep, they couldn't keep up with the ceremonial cleansing rituals that Orthodox Jewish leaders demanded. And beyond that, they often smelled bad. Although their profession was necessary to the era and honored at some level by the Jews, the general population likely saw them as second-class people.

9 And, lo, the angel of the Lord came upon them, and the glory of the Lord shone round about them: and they were sore afraid.

One interpretation of Micah 4:8 is that the Messiah would first be presented at the "tower of the flock." Tradition identifies this as a shepherd's village just outside of Bethlehem called *Beit Sahur* where the temple offerings were chosen from among the flocks. The shepherds mentioned in the text may have been in this location or near it, which opens up another possibility of fulfilled prophecy when the angels selected these shepherds as the first recipients of the Good News.

10 And the angel said unto them, Fear not: for, behold, I bring you good tidings of great joy, which shall be to all people.

God's glory appeared with this unnamed angel as a brilliant light, just as it had in other passages (Isaiah 60:1; Ezekiel 1:28, 10:4; Matthew 17:5). The shepherds were absolutely terrified, just as Zacharias and Mary were afraid when they saw the angel. The angel said to the shepherds the same thing that was said to others: "Fear not." It would seem that until you have a fear of God, you won't hear the invitation to no longer be afraid of Him.

11 For unto you is born this day in the city of David a Saviour, which is Christ the Lord.

The pronouncement of Jesus' birth was presented as a gift not only to everyone but also to these particular people. Most groups of shepherds during that era would include a mixture of ages and backgrounds, from those who had been shepherding their whole life to others in training. It may have also included girls who hadn't yet had a physical transition into womanhood, for once they did they would go home and serve alongside their mothers. This announcement to those on the margins of society is indicative of God's concern for all of us, including those most of us may ignore.

12 And this shall be a sign unto you; Ye shall find the babe wrapped in swaddling clothes, lying in a manger.

The angel promised a tangible sign to validate the claims, which follows a pattern all throughout the Bible of how God promised something, pledged to do it within certain circumstances, and then offered visible proof that He would follow through. The virgin birth itself was a sign (Isaiah 7:14), but in this instance the focus was on Jesus and not His mother. While she had used the common clothes and feeding trough to care for her baby, these natural elements would become supernatural markers for the shepherds.

13 And suddenly there was with the angel a multitude of the heavenly host praising God, and saying,

The angel was suddenly joined by a great multitude of angels. The Greek word for "host" is *stratia,* which refers to an army, a band of soldiers, or a troop of angels. These weren't cute little angel cherubs with fat cheeks, but military-level angels. As heavenly soldiers, they understood the amazing event taking place at that moment on earth, so they proclaimed it.

14 Glory to God in the highest, and on earth peace, good will toward men.

The angels fathomed the enormity of what was happening and couldn't help but invite others to respond. The phrase "Glory to God in the highest" means to force yourself to a new place of worship in response to who God is. It's as if heaven itself cracked open for a brief moment and our shadowy world had light and song.

15 And it came to pass, as the angels were gone away from them into heaven, the shepherds said one to another, Let us now go even unto Bethlehem, and see this thing which is come to pass, which the Lord hath made known unto us.

This experience overwhelmed the shepherds. By dropping everything to go in search of the baby in the manger, they prioritized finding Him over watching their own flocks. The angels didn't divinely transport them to Jesus but left them with the freedom to respond.

16 And they came with haste, and found Mary, and Joseph, and the babe lying in a manger.

The Bible contains the names of several people about whom we know very little. In contrast, these shepherds were among the first to see the face of Jesus, and yet they remain unnamed. These unnamed shepherds will forever have the honor of being the first ones outside of the holy family to hear of the birth of Jesus. God ordained it for them, which perhaps is how they mysteriously found Christ in the middle of the night during a busy census season. They found Him asleep in a manger, just as the angel had said.

17 And when they had seen it, they made known abroad the saying which was told them concerning this child.

Just as the shepherds risked losing their flocks by looking for Jesus, so they now risked being scorned as they tried to tell others. In a sense, they did on a human level what the angels did on a divine level—singing praises to God for His wonderful works. The shepherds' public praise and sharing of all they'd seen, heard, and experienced is meant to inspire us to share ours.

Sources:
Faithhelper.com. "Is Bible God's Words?" http://www.faithhelper.com/ntrel3.htm (accessed September 11, 2012).
Potter, D. S. "Life, Death and Entertainment in the Roman Empire." UNRV History. http://www.unrv.com/book-review/life-death-entertainment.php (accessed September 12, 2012).
Smith, William. *Smith's Bible Dictionary.* Peabody, MA: Hendrickson Publishers, Inc., 2000. 137, 322–23, 386, 617–18.

Say It Correctly

Bethlehem. **BETH**-li-hem.
Nazareth. **NA**-za-reth.
Cyrenius. **CY**-ren-ee-us.

Daily Bible Readings

MONDAY
A Child Dedicated to the Lord
(1 Samuel 1:21–28)

TUESDAY
Blessing the Children of Israel
(Numbers 6:22–27)

WEDNESDAY
Hope for the Coming One
(Isaiah 9:1–5)

THURSDAY
A Ruler from Bethlehem and Judah
(Micah 5:1–5)

FRIDAY
God's Blessings on David's Descendants
(Psalm 18:46–50)

SATURDAY
The Fullness of Time
(Galatians 4:1–7)

SUNDAY
The Birth of Jesus in Bethlehem
(Luke 2:1–17)

Notes

Teaching Tips

Words You Should Know

A. Devout (Luke 2:25) *eluabes* (Gk.)—Reverencing God, pious.

B. Glory (v. 32) *doxa* (Gk.)—The kingly majesty of the Messiah.

C. Redemption (v. 38) *lutrosis* (Gk.)—Ransoming, deliverance.

Teacher Preparation

Unifying Principle—Dreams Come True. We all have hopes and dreams that we pray will one day become reality. God can fulfill those desires through Jesus Christ, just as it was done for Simeon and Anna.

A. Pray and seek God's help in presenting this lesson.

B. Bring pictures or a PowerPoint presentation of things people dream of acquiring, such as a mansion, cars, jewelry, etc.

O—Open the Lesson

A. Open with prayer.

B. Have your students read the Aim for Change and Keep in Mind verses. Discuss.

C. Ask, "What dreams do you have? What do these items represent?" Share your pictures.

D. Ask, "What promises of God can we look forward to being fulfilled as we live holy lives?" Discuss.

P—Present the Scriptures

A. Have volunteers read the Focal Verses.

B. To clarify the Focal Verses, use The People, Places, and Times; Background; Search the Scriptures; At-A-Glance outline; In Depth; and More Light on the Text.

E—Explore the Meaning

A. Have volunteers answer the Discuss the Meaning question.

B. Summarize the Lesson in Our Society and Make It Happen sections.

C. Discuss the Search the Scriptures section.

D. Connect these sections to the Aim for Change and the Keep in Mind verses.

N—Next Steps for Application

A. Tell students to write some take-away principles under the Follow the Spirit or Remember Your Thoughts section.

B. Close with prayer and praise God for enabling them to live holy lives that glorify Him.

Worship Guide

For the Superintendent or Teacher
Theme: Jesus Is Presented
in the Temple
Song: "Emmanuel"
Devotional Reading: Isaiah 49:8–13

Jesus Is Presented in the Temple

Bible Background • LUKE 2:25–38
Printed Text • LUKE 2:25–38 | Devotional Reading • ISAIAH 49:8–13

———————— Aim for Change ————————

By the end of the lesson, we will: EXPLORE Jesus' presentation in the Temple; EXPRESS our feelings about the phrase, "This child is set for the fall and rising again of many" (from Luke 2:34); and DECIDE how we might walk in holiness.

DEC
29th

———— In Focus ————

Irene Barnes and her husband, Darnell, were experiencing hard times. Darnell worked for over thirty years as a teacher in Chicago. Because of budget cuts, however, he was laid off. Irene worked part-time. Their expenses always exceeded their monthly income. They had to sell their home and moved in with their oldest son, Timothy. Timothy's sister, Jasmine, was upset that their parents had not come to live with her in New Jersey.

Irene told Jasmine she was hoping for a promotion and wanted to remain in Chicago. Jasmine refused to listen and stopped speaking to her parents. They prayed to be reconciled with her. The Barnes' pastor encouraged them to continually believe God would resolve the matter.

Ten years later, Irene was diagnosed with cancer. Her husband and children wanted to have a special birthday party for her. Jasmine and her family came to celebrate her life. Irene hugged them tightly and said, "I knew God would bring us together again."

We all have hopes and dreams that only God can fulfill. In today's lesson, we will examine how God fulfilled the dreams of Simeon and Anna.

———————— Keep in Mind ————————

"For mine eyes have seen thy salvation, Which thou hast prepared before the face of all people" (Luke 2:30–31).

"For mine eyes have seen thy salvation, Which thou hast prepared before the face of all people" (Luke 2:30–31).

Focal Verses

KJV Luke 2:25 And, behold, there was a man in Jerusalem, whose name was Simeon; and the same man was just and devout, waiting for the consolation of Israel: and the Holy Ghost was upon him.

26 And it was revealed unto him by the Holy Ghost, that he should not see death, before he had seen the Lord's Christ.

27 And he came by the Spirit into the temple: and when the parents brought in the child Jesus, to do for him after the custom of the law,

28 Then took he him up in his arms, and blessed God, and said,

29 Lord, now lettest thou thy servant depart in peace, according to thy word:

30 For mine eyes have seen thy salvation,

31 Which thou hast prepared before the face of all people;

32 A light to lighten the Gentiles, and the glory of thy people Israel.

33 And Joseph and his mother marvelled at those things which were spoken of him.

34 And Simeon blessed them, and said unto Mary his mother, Behold, this child is set for the fall and rising again of many in Israel; and for a sign which shall be spoken against;

35 (Yea, a sword shall pierce through thy own soul also,) that the thoughts of many hearts may be revealed.

36 And there was one Anna, a prophetess, the daughter of Phanuel, of the tribe of Aser: she was of a great age, and had lived with an husband seven years from her virginity;

37 And she was a widow of about fourscore and four years, which departed not from the temple, but served God with fastings and prayers night and day.

38 And she coming in that instant gave thanks likewise unto the Lord, and spake of

NLT Luke 2:25 At that time there was a man in Jerusalem named Simeon. He was righteous and devout and was eagerly waiting for the Messiah to come and rescue Israel. The Holy Spirit was upon him

26 and had revealed to him that he would not die until he had seen the Lord's Messiah.

27 That day the Spirit led him to the Temple. So when Mary and Joseph came to present the baby Jesus to the Lord as the law required,

28 Simeon was there. He took the child in his arms and praised God, saying,

29 "Sovereign Lord, now let your servant die in peace, as you have promised.

30 I have seen your salvation,

31 which you have prepared for all people.

32 He is a light to reveal God to the nations, and he is the glory of your people Israel!"

33 Jesus' parents were amazed at what was being said about him.

34 Then Simeon blessed them, and he said to Mary, the baby's mother, "This child is destined to cause many in Israel to fall, but he will be a joy to many others. He has been sent as a sign from God, but many will oppose him.

35 As a result, the deepest thoughts of many hearts will be revealed. And a sword will pierce your very soul."

36 Anna, a prophet, was also there in the Temple. She was the daughter of Phanuel from the tribe of Asher, and she was very old. Her husband died when they had been married only seven years.

37 Then she lived as a widow to the age of eighty-four. She never left the Temple but stayed there day and night, worshiping God with fasting and prayer.

him to all them that looked for redemption in Jerusalem.

38 She came along just as Simeon was talking with Mary and Joseph, and she began praising God. She talked about the child to everyone who had been waiting expectantly for God to rescue Jerusalem.

The People, Places, and Times

Firstborn. Jewish families had to adhere to strict ceremonies after the birth of a child. If the child was a male, he had to be circumcised and named on the eighth day. God made a covenant with Abraham and commanded that, as a sign of the covenant, every male should be circumcised (Genesis 17:10–14). This included children, as well as slaves and foreigners before they could become Jewish citizens or take part in Passover. Moses made circumcision a legal requirement (Leviticus 12:3).

There was also a redeeming of the firstborn when the child was one month old. In memory of the death of Egypt's firstborns and the preservation of the firstborn of Israel, all the firstborn of Israel belonged to God (Exodus 13:2, 11–16). The offering of five shekels was given to the priest to redeem the child from God.

Background

The Gospel of Luke was written to affirm both Christ's divinity and humanity. Luke, a Greek physician, wrote the book around A.D. 60. He was very detailed in recording events and dates. This enabled him to connect Jesus to events and people in history. Luke 1 records the story of the birth of John and foretells the birth of Jesus. Chapter 2 opens with the decree from Caesar Augustus that a census be conducted. This required all people to go to their hometown to be registered. Joseph and Mary traveled to Judea, to the city of Bethlehem, to register. There, Jesus was born.

After the announcement to the shepherds in verses 8–20, Luke skipped ahead eight days to the circumcision and naming of Jesus (v. 21). He would be given the name Jesus, just as the angel had told Mary and proclaimed to Joseph in a dream (Luke 1:31; Matthew 1:21). Mary was required to undergo a purification ceremony 40 days after the birth of her son (v. 22; Leviticus 12:1–4). The purification ceremony included a sacrifice of a lamb and a pigeon, but exceptions were made for those who were poor. Mary and Joseph were living in poverty, so they could only offer two pigeons (or doves) (v. 24). Jesus was also presented to the Lord as the firstborn.

At-A-Glance

1. Simeon's Hope (Luke 2:25–32)
2. Simeon's Prophecy (vv. 33–35)
3. Anna's Devotion (vv. 36–38)

In Depth

1. Simeon's Hope (Luke 2:25–32)

Simeon was a "just and devout" Israelite, indeed a rare one who was filled with the Holy Spirit. Even though he was nearing the end of his life, Simeon believed God's promise through the Holy Spirit that he would not die before seeing Christ. Simeon believed the Old Testament prophecies and waited expectantly for "the consolation of Israel," the Messiah. We, too, should faithfully trust God's promises in His Word.

On the very day Mary and Joseph brought Jesus to the temple to be dedicated, Simeon was guided by the Holy Spirit to go to the temple. In the outer court, Simeon encountered the baby Jesus. Simeon knew immediately who the baby was without a word from the parents. He held the baby Jesus in his arms and praised God for allowing him to see the Messiah. His faith had been rewarded. Imagine what this must have meant for Simeon!

Simeon's song of praise is called the *Nunc Dimittis*, which are the first two words in the Latin translation. The phrases he used were inspired by the Spirit and came in part from Isaiah 40–55. Simeon was ready to peacefully enter into eternal rest since he had beheld the Savior of all people, Jew and Gentile. Jesus would be "the glory of thy people Israel" because He was born a Jew and was first sent to them. Jesus would be "a light to lighten the Gentiles" by dispelling the darkness of sin and revealing a new way of life and salvation to those who had been excluded from God's covenant.

2. Simeon's Prophecy (vv. 33–35)

Jesus' parents were amazed at what Simeon said. Simeon had spoken prophecies that were similar to those given by angels, Zacharias, and Elisabeth; now the Holy Spirit was confirming the previous prophecies. In stark contrast to the wonderful praises and prophecy offered earlier, Simeon gave Mary a foreshadowing of what price she and her Son would have to suffer on behalf of humanity.

His word to Mary foretold that Jesus would have to die on the Cross for the salvation of the world, and Mary would have to suffer the pain of seeing Jesus rejected and crucified. We see Simeon's prophecy fulfilled in the crucifixion story in all of the Gospels.

Most of the Israelites overlooked or ignored the significance of Jesus' birth, life, and ministry and disregarded or rejected His identity as the Messiah. Those who acknowledge Jesus as the Messiah and accept Him as Lord and Savior shall be given a new life now and in eternity.

3. Anna's Devotion (vv. 36–38)

While Simeon was with Jesus and His parents, Anna came into the temple area. Anna was the daughter of Phanuel, of the tribe of Asher, a prophetess and widow. She devoted herself to attending worship services in the temple. Anna fasted and prayed night and day. She was completely devoted to God. What example and challenge does she present for us?

Anna was over 84 years old when the baby Jesus was presented in the temple. Anna was so filled with joy when she saw the Messiah that she broke forth in praise. Like Simeon, she rejoiced in the fulfillment of the divine promises of God. Her faithfulness had been rewarded. She then went about sharing the Good News with others. We, too, have to live by faith and strive for holiness. God will always honor His promises to those who remain faithful.

Search the Scriptures

1. Who did Simeon identify Jesus as (Luke 2:32)?

2. What did Anna say Jesus would do for Jerusalem (v. 38)?

Discuss the Meaning

What are your thoughts on the phrase, "This child is set for the fall and rising again of many" (from Luke 2:34)? Many people do not think about the importance and necessity of a personal relationship with Jesus Christ. Some reject Christ while others accept Him as Lord and Savior. It is a personal decision that affects our eternal destination.

Lesson in Our Society

Both Simeon and Anna lived holy lives as they faithfully served God. They were old when the promises of God were fulfilled concerning the Messiah. Simeon and Anna could have easily given up hope of ever seeing the Messiah in their lifetime. Yet they never doubted. We, too, can live holy lives as we await the fulfillment of God's promises. Every day we have to make a decision to trust and serve God no matter the circumstances we face.

Make It Happen

God is calling us to a life of holiness. Our age doesn't matter. Whether young or old, God wants us to live as an example for others. How do we live holy lives? We can devote time to praying, fasting, and reading the Word. The Holy Spirit will help to sustain us. Our devotion and service to God can draw others to Him.

Follow the Spirit

What God wants me to do:

_____

_____

_____

_____

Remember Your Thoughts

Special insights I have learned:

_____

_____

_____

_____

_____

More Light on the Text

Luke 2:25–38

A main focal point in this portion of Scripture is the Jewish law. In the verses just prior, Mary and Joseph meticulously followed the law in every aspect of Jesus' life: circumcision, naming (v. 21), forty days of purification (v. 22), presentation to the Lord (vv. 22–23), and offering a sacrifice (v. 24, see also v. 39). Also drawing attention to Mary and Joseph's faithful adherence to the law, Luke introduced "two pious figures who, under divine inspiration, testify to the significance of Jesus," in Walter Liefeld's words (*Matthew, Mark, Luke. The Expositor's Bible Commentary*, 848). Perhaps also because of the Jewish tradition of two witnesses for critical matters (Deuteronomy 19:15), the Holy Spirit coordinated Simeon's and Anna's appointments with the Messiah just when Jesus' parents brought Him to the temple for dedication to God.

25 And, behold, there was a man in Jerusalem, whose name was Simeon; and the same man was just and devout, waiting for the consolation of Israel: and the Holy Ghost was upon him.

Luke cites four qualifications for Simeon, whose name means "God hears," clearly establishing him to be a reliable witness in the eyes of traditional Jews. Liefeld observes,

"It is appropriate that the Spirit who is the Consoler was upon one who awaited the consolation" (*Matthew, Mark, Luke. The Expositor's Bible Commentary*, 849). Naturally, Luke used the still-relevant Old Testament expression of the Holy Spirit being "upon" someone (e.g. Numbers 11:17; Judges 3:10; 1 Samuel 10:6), and similarly, referencing Jesus, "The spirit of the LORD shall rest upon him" (from Isaiah 11:2).

26 And it was revealed unto him by the Holy Ghost, that he should not see death, before he had seen the Lord's Christ.

The same Spirit who was "upon" Simeon told him he would see the Lord's Christ (Gk. *Christos*, **khre-STOS**, literally "anointed") before he died. The vast majority of the New Testament's usages of *Christos* are translated as "Christ." In John 1:41 and 4:25, the apostle used a different Greek word for Messiah (*messias*, **mes-SE-as**), but then in parentheses immediately clarified that he was referring to *Christos*—"which is, being interpreted, the Christ" and "which is called Christ," respectively.

27 And he came by the Spirit into the temple: and when the parents brought in the child Jesus, to do for him after the custom of the law, 28 Then took he him up in his arms, and blessed God, and said,

Clearly, Simeon's was a divinely guided appointment or, as some say, a divine coincidence. Modern readers can only imagine what it would have been like to hold the infant Jesus in their arms, especially realizing He was the long-awaited Messiah. Simeon's poignant moment of blessing or praise (Gk. *eulogeo*, **eu-lo-GE-oh**) seems the perfect response to such a powerful, intimate meeting. In effect, he uttered a solemn poem of consecration (a psalm or song).

29 Lord, now lettest thou thy servant depart in peace, according to thy word.

The fact that Simeon had been told he would see the Messiah before he died and that he surrendered his life in his prayer indicate that he was elderly. God had kept His word; Simeon's life was now complete; he could depart in peace. If only more of us could similarly depart or "be dismissed" with no unfinished business.

30 For mine eyes have seen thy salvation, 31 Which thou hast prepared before the face of all people.

While Luke used the word "Messiah," Simeon used the metaphor "thy salvation." Liefeld writes, "To see Jesus is to see salvation embodied in him" (*Matthew, Mark, Luke. The Expositor's Bible Commentary*, 849). The phrase about this salvation being prepared "before the face of all people" or "in the sight [or presence] of all people" in other versions, such as the NIV (cf. Isaiah 52:10; Psalm 98:3), implies the universality of the Gospel—that is, God's salvation is intended for all mankind (see Isaiah 42:6, 49:6). This thought is immediately reinforced and specified in the next verse.

32 A light to lighten the Gentiles, and the glory of thy people Israel.

Luke chose an interesting word for "lighten" (Gk. *apokalypsis*, **a-po-KA-lu-pses**), which means "revelation" and became the name of John's book (cf. Romans 16:25; Galatians 1:12; Ephesians 3:3). First Corinthians 1:7 has the same word referring to the second "coming" of Christ, and 1 Peter 1:7 uses the same word for His second "appearing."

The prophet's prayer, in David Jeffrey's insightful words, "has been part of daily prayers since the fourth century. . . . Simeon's benedictional praise poem has . . . become a 'sign to many' for two millennia" (*Luke*, 47–48).

33 And Joseph and his mother marvelled at those things which were spoken of him. 34 And Simeon blessed them, and said unto Mary his mother, Behold, this child is set for the fall and rising again of many in Israel; and for a sign which shall be spoken against.

As part of Simeon's anointed poetic consecration of the Messiah, he included a sobering thought, good and bad news. The "fall" and "rising again" of many indicates "downfall" from the Greek *ptosis* (**PTO-ses**), used elsewhere only in Matthew 7:27, and "resurrection" (of the dead) from the Greek *anastasis* (**a-NA-sta-ses**), used 42 times in the New Testament, only two of which do not use the actual word "resurrection" (cf. Acts 26:23).

35 (Yea, a sword shall pierce through thy own soul also,) that the thoughts of many hearts may be revealed.

Luke's choice of words for "sword" was a large broadsword; surely there is no greater "major sword to the heart" than for a parent to have to bury his or her child. Mary will have joys as the mother of the Messiah but will also experience a unique pain.

36 And there was one Anna, a prophetess, the daughter of Phanuel, of the tribe of Aser: she was of a great age, and had lived with an husband seven years from her virginity.

Anna, which means "favor," the second pious character to testify to Jesus' significance, was an elderly widow and "prophetess"—a familiar figure in both the Old and New Testaments (e.g. Exodus 15:20; Judges 4:4; Acts 2:17). Luke seems to list her

tribal roots to bolster her authenticity as a Jewish witness.

37 And she was a widow of about fourscore and four years, which departed not from the temple, but served God with fastings and prayers night and day. And she coming in that instant gave thanks likewise unto the Lord, and spake of him to all them that looked for redemption in Jerusalem.

That Anna "departed not from the temple" may be some hyperbole to indicate that many were familiar with her as a holy woman; clearly, the temple was her life. As with Simeon, the Spirit led the prophetess by divine appointment to be present at the precise moment that Mary and Joseph brought baby Jesus to the temple. Also, like Simeon, she both gave thanks and, considering her extreme devotion, offered a heartfelt speech for onlookers. Unlike Simeon's blessing, the verb Luke chose for Anna's public giving of thanks is not used elsewhere in the New Testament—*anthomologeomai* (**an-tho-mo-lo-GE-o-me**). Compare her waiting for Israel's redemption to that of Joseph of Arimathea (Luke 23:51). J. C. Ryle perceptively comments, "When we read of Anna's consistency and holiness and prayerfulness and self-denial, we cannot but wish that many daughters of the Christian church would strive to be like her" (*Luke. The Crossway Classic Commentaries* 44).

Summary

Jesus' orientation and grounding in the Mosaic Law from childhood (cf. Galatians 4:4–5) enabled Him later "to oppose flawed and hollow practices in the name of the Law of Moses," in the words of Fred Craddock (*Luke: Interpretation: A Bible Commentary for Teaching and Preaching*, 38). Thus He proved Simeon's prophetic words that many would speak against Him (Luke 2:34), and He would reveal the evil thoughts of many (v. 35). Indeed, through the ages, Jesus has continued to draw critics and reveal men's true thoughts, even while Simeon and Anna continue to testify that the Messiah brought salvation to all mankind. As Jesus Himself once pointedly asked, "Who do you say I am?" (Matthew 16:15, NIV). Surely this is the question of the ages!

Sources:

Bible Study Tools. www.BibleStudyTools.com. "Old Testament Hebrew Lexicon—King James Version." http://www.biblestudytools.com/lexicons/hebrew/kjv (accessed August 9, 2012).

Blue Letter Bible. BlueLetterBible.org. http://www.blueletterbible.org/ (accessed July 13, 2012).

Craddock, Fred B. *Luke: Interpretation: A Bible Commentary for Teaching and Preaching*. Louisville: John Knox Press, 1990. 28–40.

Jamieson, Robert, A. R. Fausset, and David Brown. www.BibleStudyTools.com. *Commentary Critical and Explanatory on the Whole Bible*. http://www.biblestudytools.com/commentaries/jamieson-fausset-brown/luke/luke-2.html?p=5. (accessed August 10, 2012).

Jeffrey, David Lyle. *Luke*. Grand Rapids, MI: Brazos Press, 2012. 45–48.

Liefeld, Walter L. *Matthew, Mark, Luke. The Expositor's Bible Commentary, Vol. 8*. Edited by Frank E. Gaebelein. Grand Rapids, MI: Zondervan, 1984. 848–850.

Life Application Bible (NRSV). Wheaton, IL: Tyndale House, 1989. 1734–1745.

Ryle, J. C. *Luke. The Crossway Classic Commentaries*. Wheaton, IL: Crossway, 1997. 41–45.

Say It Correctly

Simeon. **SIM**-ih-un.
Phanuel. fuh-**NOO**-uhl.
Aser. **AY**-zer.

Daily Bible Readings

MONDAY
Parents Committed to the Law
(Luke 2:21–24)

TUESDAY
Circumcising on the Eighth Day
(Leviticus 12:1–5)

WEDNESDAY
Offering a Sacrifice to the Lord
(Leviticus 12:6–8)

THURSDAY
Consolation for Israel
(Isaiah 40:1–5)

FRIDAY
The Lord's Comfort and Compassion
(Isaiah 49:8–13)

SATURDAY
A Light to the Nations
(Isaiah 42:1–7)

SUNDAY
Jesus' Presentation in the Temple
(Luke 2:25–38)

Notes

Teaching Tips

Words You Should Know

A. Sabbath (Luke 6:1) *sabbaton* (Gk.)—The seventh day of each week, which was a sacred festival; on the Sabbath the Israelites were required to abstain from all work.

B. Do good (v. 9) *agathopoieo* (Gk.)—To do something that helps or profits others.

Teacher Preparation

Unifying Principle—Living with Justice and Mercy. Often, rules and limitations set by others make it difficult for us to help one another. What causes us to want to help others? Jesus, who is Lord of the Sabbath, teaches that acts of mercy and justice should be practiced all the time.

A. Read the Bible Background and Devotional Readings.

B. Complete Lesson 6 in the *Precepts For Living Personal Study Guide®*.

O—Open the Lesson

A. Open with prayer.

B. Have students read Aim for Change in unison.

C. Ask for a volunteer to read the In Focus story. Discuss.

P—Present the Scriptures

A. Ask for volunteers to read the Focal Verses and The People, Places, and Times. Discuss.

B. Read and discuss the Background section.

C. Encourage students to look for ways to practice mercy and justice by meeting people's needs.

E—Explore the Meaning

A. Review and discuss the Search the Scriptures and Discuss the Meaning questions and the Lesson in Our Society section.

B. Ask students to share the most significant point they learned and how to use that point this week.

N—Next Steps for Application

A. Complete the Follow the Spirit and Remember Your Thoughts sections.

B. Remind students to read the Daily Bible Readings in preparation for next week's lesson.

C. Close in prayer, thanking God for His presence in our lives.

Worship Guide

For the Superintendent or Teacher
Theme: Honoring the Sabbath
Song: "Hosanna"
Devotional Reading: John 5:2–17

Honoring the Sabbath

Bible Background • LUKE 6:1–11
Printed Text • LUKE 6:1–11 | Devotional Reading • JOHN 5:2–17

———————————— Aim for Change ————————————

By the end of the lesson, we will: KNOW the Sabbath laws and their conflicts with human need; FEEL an appreciation for the priority of human needs being met; and DECIDE to live in such a way that we honor the Sabbath from Jesus' perspective.

——————————— In Focus ———————————

Tasha walked by the church every Sunday afternoon while the deacons were giving out food from the food pantry. She was afraid to get in line or ask for help because she knew the rule: Only those who attended service were allowed to receive assistance from the pantry. Her quiet disappointment did not escape the notice of Doris, however. Doris had been working in the food pantry for about a month. She always saw Tasha and wanted to reach out to her, but she felt limited by the rules. This particular Sunday, Doris was overwhelmed with compassion. She knew she needed to do something to help Tasha. So she filled a box with groceries and gave it to Tasha along with a warm embrace.

Tears started to roll down Tasha's cheek. She finally opened her mouth to say, "Thank you so much. I know the rules. I want to make it to the services, but Sunday morning is the only time the state allows me to visit my children."

Doris looked at her with a look of reassurance. "We will always be here for you."

Jesus placed more of a priority on meeting human needs than on rules and limitations. In this lesson, we will learn how to practice acts of mercy and justice all the time.

———————————— Keep in Mind ————————————

"Then said Jesus unto them, I will ask you one thing; Is it lawful on the sabbath days to do good, or to do evil? to save life, or to destroy it?" (Luke 6:9).

"Then said Jesus unto them, I will ask you one thing; Is it lawful on the sabbath days to do good, or to do evil? to save life, or to destroy it?" (Luke 6:9).

Focal Verses

KJV **Luke 6:1** And it came to pass on the second sabbath after the first, that he went through the corn fields; and his disciples plucked the ears of corn, and did eat, rubbing them in their hands.

2 And certain of the Pharisees said unto them, Why do ye that which is not lawful to do on the sabbath days?

3 And Jesus answering them said, Have ye not read so much as this, what David did, when himself was an hungred, and they which were with him;

4 How he went into the house of God, and did take and eat the shewbread, and gave also to them that were with him; which it is not lawful to eat but for the priests alone?

5 And he said unto them, That the Son of man is Lord also of the sabbath.

6 And it came to pass also on another sabbath, that he entered into the synagogue and taught: and there was a man whose right hand was withered.

7 And the scribes and Pharisees watched him, whether he would heal on the sabbath day; that they might find an accusation against him.

8 But he knew their thoughts, and said to the man which had the withered hand, Rise up, and stand forth in the midst. And he arose and stood forth.

9 Then said Jesus unto them, I will ask you one thing; Is it lawful on the sabbath days to do good, or to do evil? to save life, or to destroy it?

10 And looking round about upon them all, he said unto the man, Stretch forth thy hand. And he did so: and his hand was restored whole as the other.

11 And they were filled with madness; and communed one with another what they might do to Jesus.

NLT **Luke 6:1** One Sabbath day as Jesus was walking through some grainfields, his disciples broke off heads of grain, rubbed off the husks in their hands, and ate the grain.

2 But some Pharisees said, "Why are you breaking the law by harvesting grain on the Sabbath?"

3 Jesus replied, "Haven't you read in the Scriptures what David did when he and his companions were hungry?

4 He went into the house of God and broke the law by eating the sacred loaves of bread that only the priests can eat. He also gave some to his companions."

5 And Jesus added, "The Son of Man is Lord, even over the Sabbath."

6 On another Sabbath day, a man with a deformed right hand was in the synagogue while Jesus was teaching.

7 The teachers of religious law and the Pharisees watched Jesus closely. If he healed the man's hand, they planned to accuse him of working on the Sabbath.

8 But Jesus knew their thoughts. He said to the man with the deformed hand, "Come and stand in front of everyone." So the man came forward.

9 Then Jesus said to his critics, "I have a question for you. Does the law permit good deeds on the Sabbath, or is it a day for doing evil? Is this a day to save life or to destroy it?"

10 He looked around at them one by one and then said to the man, "Hold out your hand." So the man held out his hand, and it was restored!

11 At this, the enemies of Jesus were wild with rage and began to discuss what to do with him.

210

The People, Places, and Times

Sabbath. The Jewish day of rest. It is based on God's act of resting on the seventh day after creation. Its observance has been practiced by Jewish people from the time of Moses. Keeping the Sabbath was a very critical issue in separating Jews from Gentiles and maintaining purity. It was so important that the Jewish leaders created 39 laws to make sure they were not violating the Sabbath. There were multiple laws on what constituted work on the Sabbath, and these laws were hotly debated by the Pharisees and other religious groups in first-century Palestine.

Pharisees. One of the major religious groups in first-century Palestine. Religious leaders known for their zealous obedience to God's law. They also became major opponents of Jesus. The name *Pharisee* carries the connotation of separatists and may indicate their devotion to avoiding things that would make them unclean. They believed in a twofold law: the written and the oral Torah or tradition. This tradition is what usually brought them into arguments with Jesus. One of these traditions regarded the keeping of the Sabbath.

Man with Withered Hand. The man with a withered hand was the recipient of healing from Jesus. His hand was deformed and, as a result, he could not use it to do anything—especially to work. This is significant in the story because the main argument between the Pharisees and Jesus was whether He was working on the Sabbath by healing the man with a withered hand—a man who was disabled and more than likely could not do any work on *any* day, including the Sabbath. Jesus' healing helped to make work and many other things in life possible for this man. It was truly an act of justice and mercy.

Background

Sabbath observance was one of the marks of being a true Jew in first-century Palestine. As a result, what constituted true Sabbath observance was a hot topic of discussion. In its true definition, keeping the Sabbath meant ceasing activity, and the most conservative Jews attempted to live out this definition. The problem was there was no set definition of what was meant by "work." The Pharisees and other religious leaders constantly debated the definition of "work" and recorded many guidelines in order to help people in their observance of the Sabbath. Many ordinary things were considered to be violations of the Sabbath, including such things as lighting a lamp. Unfortunately, many of these extra laws became a direct violation of human need.

Jesus and His disciples were meeting their needs when they walked into a field and began to pluck the grains of wheat and rub them in their hands in order to break them up so they could eat them. The two actions of plucking and rubbing were defined by conservative Pharisees as harvesting and threshing: two actions forbidden on the Sabbath because they were "work." Jesus explained to the Pharisees that the Sabbath is not an end in itself but was created to meet our needs as human beings. In saying this, Jesus asserted His sovereignty over the Sabbath. Next, He healed a man with a withered hand and challenged the Pharisees by asking whether it was lawful to do harm or to do good on the Sabbath. The question stumped them. Jesus redefined Sabbath law with two guidelines: justice and mercy.

At-A-Glance

1. Jesus Meets Human Needs on the Sabbath (Luke 6:1–4)
2. Jesus is Lord of the Sabbath (v. 5)
3. Jesus Shows Justice and Mercy on the Sabbath (vv. 6–10)
4. Jesus Shows the True Meaning of the Sabbath (v. 11)

In Depth

1. Jesus Meets Human Needs on the Sabbath (Luke 6:1–4)

In the first verses of Luke 6, Jesus and His disciples experienced one of the most basic human needs: hunger. In order to meet this need, Jesus broke one of the Pharisees' Sabbath-keeping rules, and this caused the Pharisees to question His actions. Jesus responded by pointing out a similar situation that David and his friends faced when they were on the run from Saul. David and his men were hungry and the only bread available was the shewbread that was displayed in the tabernacle. This bread was holy and was not to be eaten by anyone except the priests—and only after new bread replaced it every week. Abiathar the priest gave them this bread to meet their needs, showing that human needs are more of a priority than keeping rules. Jesus went a step further in meeting human needs by settling the debate on whether it was lawful to heal on the Sabbath when He healed the man with the withered hand. By doing this, He showed that it is lawful to "do good" on the Sabbath and not to "do evil," to "save life" and not to "destroy it" (v, 9).

2. Jesus is Lord of the Sabbath (v. 5)

Jesus responded to the Pharisees' question with the story of David and his men eating the shewbread. This story not only justified Jesus' actions in plucking grain and eating on the Sabbath, it also described who Jesus is. The particular story of David and his men eating shewbread occurred while they were on the run from Saul. At the time, David was the anointed king of Israel, although he had not yet been crowned king. Through this story, Jesus illustrated how He is the rightful King of Israel, although He is not King yet. Therefore His interpretation of keeping the Sabbath is superior because He has authority as the rightful King of God's people. His actions on this particular Sabbath and His guidelines for interpretation of the Sabbath are correct because He is Lord of the Sabbath.

3. Jesus Shows Justice and Mercy on the Sabbath (vv. 6–10)

The key values to properly observe the Sabbath are justice and mercy. Jesus showed justice and mercy toward His disciples by allowing them to pluck, rub, and eat the grain as they passed through a field on the Sabbath. It was right and just to allow them to do it since they had a genuine need. Not only that, but the law actually allowed them to do it (Deuteronomy 23:24–25). It was merciful to sympathize with their hunger. Jesus showed justice and mercy to the man with the withered hand by healing him on the Sabbath. The man received healing because it is right to do good and to save life no matter what day it is. The man received healing because of Jesus' mercy toward him.

4. Jesus Shows the True Meaning of the Sabbath (v. 11)

The Pharisees believed that strict observance of the Sabbath was a way to merit God's favor. At the time, they believed if the Jewish people stayed ceremonially pure, then God would come and give them their land and break the yoke of Roman oppression.

They thought that keeping the Sabbath was a means to that end, so they devised many rules as a means of getting there. Jesus turned this concept on its head. He asked them whether it was right to do good or evil on the Sabbath, to save life or destroy it. The Pharisees had nothing to say because they knew the answer: Do good. In other words, Jesus claimed that the Sabbath was a means and not an end. The Pharisees had it all wrong. The Sabbath was a means to attain the end of doing good and showing justice and mercy. This is what people need. Sabbath was not designed to oppress people but to liberate them and set them free.

Search the Scriptures

1. What is shewbread (Luke 6:4)?

2. What made it lawful for the disciples to pluck grain on the Sabbath (v. 5)?

3. Explain how Jesus' healing of the man was not in violation of the Sabbath (vv. 9–10).

Discuss the Meaning

1. How can we meet human needs in our daily lives? Are there any "rules" that keep us from meeting others' needs and showing them justice and mercy?

2. Jesus says that He is "Lord also of the sabbath." How can we make Him Lord over the Sabbath *and* every other aspect of our lives?

Lessons in Our Society

There are numerous rules and limitations in our society that keep us from meeting human needs. Many times we will be challenged on whether to follow the rules or to follow justice and mercy. As followers of Christ, our allegiance is to the one who is not only Lord of the Sabbath, but also Lord over the universe and every aspect of our lives. It is through following His example that we can meet human needs and overcome the rules and limitations that can become barriers to doing so. Jesus shows us that human needs are a priority over religious rule keeping. God's justice and mercy should be our guidelines when it comes to doing good and making a difference in the lives of others.

Make It Happen

It can be hard to see the importance of human needs around us. Many times we are caught up in religious rule-keeping instead of the more important matter of showing justice and mercy to others. As followers of Jesus, we can learn from His example and bless those who are near us in tangible ways. We can choose to place ourselves in situations where human needs will be hard to ignore. We can volunteer at a soup kitchen or homeless shelter. We can also choose to ask more insightful questions of our brothers and sisters in Christ to assess any needs that they may have. Then we can ask God for compassion to take action on the needs that He brings our way.

Follow the Spirit

What God wants me to do:

_____

_____

_____

_____

Remember Your Thoughts

Special insights I have learned:

_____

_____

_____

_____

More Light on the Text
Luke 6:1–11

Starting in the previous chapter, an uneasy tension had quickly grown between Jesus and the Pharisees. Scripture records several Sabbath controversies (Mark 1; Luke 6; 13; John 5; 9). The Sabbath generated much debate because it had roots in the Ten Commandments, was a weekly issue, and involved multiple details of what was or was not permissible. This subject was a hot topic of debate among rabbis and teachers in Jesus' time (39 activities were prohibited on the Sabbath), and the dispute continued unabated long after His time. Indeed, it continues to the present with some Christians insisting that Sunday worship violates Jewish Sabbath laws. Even among those who worship on Sunday, there is disagreement over what constitutes a day of rest—which is not far removed from the Pharisees' obsession over what constituted work on the Sabbath.

1 And it came to pass on the second sabbath after the first, that he went through the corn fields; and his disciples plucked the ears of corn, and did eat, rubbing them in their hands. 2 And certain of the Pharisees said unto them, Why do ye that which is not lawful to do on the sabbath days?

Luke noted that this was a separate Sabbath from the prior event in chapter 5. Gleaning by hand and not using tools ("sickle," Deuteronomy 23:25) in someone else's field was permissible. The problem was the day of the week, which suddenly made all aspects of what they were doing violations—they were reaping, threshing, winnowing, and preparing food!

3 And Jesus answering them said, Have ye not read so much as this, what David did, when himself was an hungred, and they which were with him; 4 How he went into the house of God, and did take and eat the shewbread, and gave also to them that were with him; which it is not lawful to eat but for the priests alone?

Always on the lookout for a good teaching opportunity, Jesus saw that the Pharisees were in need of a Bible lesson. His illustration involved David, also a leader with followers, and a similar controversy of the relationship between ritual law and moral law (1 Samuel 21:1–6; cf. Exodus 25:30). His clear implication was that these teachers of the law had misunderstood their own scriptures. Today, it would be similar to Thomas Jefferson explaining the Constitution to the U.S. Supreme Court justices.

5 And he said unto them, That the Son of man is Lord also of the sabbath.

The silence from the Pharisees was golden in the sense that they did not have a good answer. Jesus' response informed them simultaneously that He is divine and has the authority to speak to the issue, that He had not authored their myriad aberrations of the fourth commandment, and that because He created the original concept of the Sabbath, He understood better than they what was or was not permissible. We find Jesus, in J. C. Ryle's words, "clearing the day of God from the rubbish of human traditions" (*Luke. The Crossway Classic Commentaries*, 75).

6 And it came to pass also on another sabbath, that he entered into the synagogue and taught: and there was a man whose right hand was withered.

It would have been Jesus' custom from childhood to teach at the synagogue. Doctor Luke noted details that other Gospel writers did not—for example, that it was the man's right hand (in those days anyone left-handed

214

was seen as weak or handicapped), and that it was withered. Robert Stein describes this as "either paralysis or atrophy" (*Luke*, 189)—in other words, his primary hand was useless.

7 And the scribes and Pharisees watched him, whether he would heal on the sabbath day; that they might find an accusation against him.

These stuffy rabbis, law professors, and leaders of the Jewish people shamelessly trailed Jesus everywhere, like paparazzi or news media hounding presidential candidates. They were on the prowl for any infraction or (literally) to "find an accusation" (Heb. *kategoreo*, **ka-te-go-RE-o**). Per Stein, this meant "a legal accusation that could be used in court against Jesus" (*Luke. The New American Commentary,* 189); today, a formal charge.

8 But he knew their thoughts, and said to the man which had the withered hand, Rise up, and stand forth in the midst. And he arose and stood forth.

Man's heart is hopelessly and helplessly evil (cf. Genesis 6:5, 8:21; Jeremiah 17:9). As the divine Son of man, Jesus "possessed a prophetic awareness of men's thoughts" (Stein, 190). As if to build the drama, He had the man stand up so everyone could get a good look at what was about to happen. Interestingly, in John Phillip's words, the Pharisees "had withered hearts that were as shriveled as the hand of the cripple" (*Exploring the Gospel of Luke,* 109)—He would have healed them, too, had they only reached out to Him.

9 Then said Jesus unto them, I will ask you one thing; Is it lawful on the sabbath days to do good, or to do evil? to save life, or to destroy it?

Jesus knew this was another perfect moment for a Bible quiz. His rhetorical question was clear—when given two extremes, good/evil, save/destroy, which is "lawful"? Similar to today's phrase, "To not decide is to decide," evil is the default when good is withheld. If you have the ability and opportunity to do something good but do not do it, you actually do evil (cf. James 4:17). David Jeffrey notes "the law was intended to serve rather than to encumber the children of the covenant" (*Luke*, 86).

10 And looking round about upon them all, he said unto the man, Stretch forth thy hand. And he did so: and his hand was restored whole as the other.

Luke's narrative eye for detail captured Jesus' stage presence as He looked around prior to the healing, as if to make sure He had everyone's attention. At the command of the Lord of the Sabbath, the man's hand was restored and made whole again right before their eyes.

11 And they were filled with madness; and communed one with another what they might do to Jesus.

Instead of being amazed, impressed, or happy for the man; instead of allowing Jesus' good deed to rebuke their pettiness and self-centeredness—these leaders and teachers were irate! They were "out of their minds with anger," writes Jeffrey, not because of the good deed, but they were "enraged at being outwitted" (*Luke*, 89). Then, like the original sore losers, they agreed among themselves that something had to be done about this impudent Jesus. Who did He think He was?

As with the confrontation just prior in Luke 5:33–39, this one also illustrates the Pharisees' attempt to pour new wine (Jesus; new covenant) into old wineskins (Judaism; Mosaic covenant) and the resulting predictable problems (cf. 2 Corinthians 5:17). Darrell Bock observes, "Jesus is bringing about the new era in which we now share . . .

the new way means the end of the old way" (*Luke. The NIV Application Commentary,* 173).

The balanced take-away is that God's children are still to honor the Sabbath, as God has commanded, but acts of kindness, mercy, and justice take priority over the letter of the law (cf. Matthew 22:37–40). They can and should be done any time and, as the popular phrase goes, "twice on Sunday."

Sources:
Blue Letter Bible. BlueLetterBible.org. http://www.blueletterbible.org/ (accessed Friday, July 27, 2012).
Bock, Darrell L. *Luke. The NIV Application Commentary.* Grand Rapids, MI: Zondervan, 1996. 169–183.
Jeffrey, David Lyle. *Luke. Brazos Theological Commentary on the Bible.* Grand Rapids, MI: Brazos Press, 2012. 86–90.
Phillips, John. *Exploring the Gospel of Luke. The John Phillips Commentary Series.* Grand Rapids, MI: Kregel Academic and Professional, 2005. 108–110.
Ryle, J. C. *Luke. The Crossway Classic Commentaries.* Wheaton, IL: Crossway, 1997. 73–76.
Stein, Robert H. *Luke. The New American Commentary, Vol. 24.* Nashville: Holman Reference, 1992. 187–190.

Say It Correctly

Shewbread. **SHOW**-bread.
Synagogue. **SI**-na-gog.

Daily Bible Readings

MONDAY
God is Still Working
(John 5:2–17)

TUESDAY
A Day of Thanksgiving
(Psalm 92:1–8)

WEDNESDAY
A Day of Rest
(Exodus 16:22–30)

THURSDAY
A Day of Remembrance
(Deuteronomy 5:11–15)

FRIDAY
A Holy Convocation
(Leviticus 23:1–8)

SATURDAY
A Holy Day
(Jeremiah 17:19–27)

SUNDAY
Lord of the Sabbath
(Luke 6:1–11)

Notes

_____

_____

_____

Teaching Tips

Words You Should Know

A. Blessed (Luke 6:20–22) *makarios* (Gk.)—Fortunate, happy.

B. Love (v. 27) *agapao* (Gk.)—To welcome, entertain, be fond of, love dearly, be full of goodwill and exhibit the same.

Teacher Preparation

Unifying Principle—Living Justly with Others. People experience both love and hate from others around them. How are Christians to respond to those who hate them? Jesus teaches that justice does not always appear in the way people treat one another, but His followers are to love people regardless of what they do or say to them.

A. Read the Bible Background and Devotional Readings.

B. Complete Lesson 7 in the *Precepts For Living Personal Study Guide®*.

O—Open the Lesson

A. Open with prayer.

B. Have students read Aim for Change in unison.

C. Ask for a volunteer to read the In Focus story.

D. Discuss what it means to love our enemies and do good to those who hate us.

P—Present the Scriptures

A. Ask for volunteers to read the Focal Verses and The People, Places, and Times. Discuss.

B. Read and discuss the Background section.

C. Encourage students to follow Jesus' commands to love others and thank God for having His favor and blessing no matter how people treat them.

E—Explore the Meaning

A. Review and discuss the Search the Scriptures and Discuss the Meaning questions and the Lesson in Our Society section.

B. Ask students to share the most significant point they learned and how to use that point this week.

N—Next Steps for Application

A. Complete the Follow the Spirit and Remember Your Thoughts sections.

B. Remind students to read the Daily Bible Readings in preparation for next week's lesson.

C. Close in prayer, thanking God for His presence in our lives.

Worship Guide

For the Superintendent or Teacher
Theme: How to Live as God's People
Song: "Bow Down And Worship Him"
Devotional Reading:
Matthew 18:21–35

How to Live as God's People

Bible Background • LUKE 6:17–31
Printed Text • LUKE 6:17–31 | Devotional Reading • MATTHEW 18:21–35

—————— Aim for Change ——————

By the end of the lesson, we will: KNOW how to interpret the meanings of love and judgment; EXPLORE the difficult feelings associated with loving people who show total disdain for us; and DEVELOP prayers that express love for the enemy.

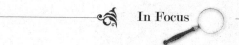

In Focus

Greg looked out on the lawn at all the trash and let out a deep sigh. "I'm tired of them knocking our trash cans over every week and I have to clean it up." Greg had a right to be upset. His neighbors, the Jacksons, had been a nuisance to his family since they moved in next door. It first started with the all-night parties and the loud music. Greg's dad had asked them to turn it down a notch, and after that, the Jacksons intentionally began to show hostility toward Greg and his family. Knocking down trash cans and taunting Greg's dad was not enough. The Jacksons' oldest son, Dayshawn, began to insult and threaten Greg at school. Greg's dad walked out onto the front porch and shook his head. "I guess they need a little more love."

Greg was fuming with anger. "A little more love? I think they need a little more fists, and Dayshawn is going to be the first to get his."

"No, son," interjected Greg's dad. "That may be how *they* do things, but *we* do things differently in this family."

As followers of Jesus, we are called to live a distinctive lifestyle marked by love. In this lesson, we will learn how to love others regardless of how they treat us.

> JAN
> 12th

—————— Keep in Mind ——————

"But I say unto you which hear, Love your enemies, do good to them which hate you" (Luke 6:27).

"But I say unto you which hear, Love your enemies, do good to them which hate you" (Luke 6:27).

Focal Verses

KJV **Luke 6:17** And he came down with them, and stood in the plain, and the company of his disciples, and a great multitude of people out of all Judaea and Jerusalem, and from the sea coast of Tyre and Sidon, which came to hear him, and to be healed of their diseases;

18 And they that were vexed with unclean spirits: and they were healed.

19 And the whole multitude sought to touch him: for there went virtue out of him, and healed them all.

20 And he lifted up his eyes on his disciples, and said, Blessed be ye poor: for yours is the kingdom of God.

21 Blessed are ye that hunger now: for ye shall be filled. Blessed are ye that weep now: for ye shall laugh.

22 Blessed are ye, when men shall hate you, and when they shall separate you from their company, and shall reproach you, and cast out your name as evil, for the Son of man's sake.

23 Rejoice ye in that day, and leap for joy: for, behold, your reward is great in heaven: for in the like manner did their fathers unto the prophets.

24 But woe unto you that are rich! for ye have received your consolation.

25 Woe unto you that are full! for ye shall hunger. Woe unto you that laugh now! for ye shall mourn and weep.

26 Woe unto you, when all men shall speak well of you! for so did their fathers to the false prophets.

27 But I say unto you which hear, Love your enemies, do good to them which hate you,

28 Bless them that curse you, and pray for them which despitefully use you.

NLT **Luke 6:17** When they came down from the mountain, the disciples stood with Jesus on a large, level area, surrounded by many of his followers and by the crowds. There were people from all over Judea and from Jerusalem and from as far north as the seacoasts of Tyre and Sidon.

18 They had come to hear him and to be healed of their diseases; and those troubled by evil spirits were healed.

19 Everyone tried to touch him, because healing power went out from him, and he healed everyone.

20 Then Jesus turned to his disciples and said, "God blesses you who are poor, for the Kingdom of God is yours.

21 God blesses you who are hungry now, for you will be satisfied. God blesses you who weep now, for in due time you will laugh.

22 What blessings await you when people hate you and exclude you and mock you and curse you as evil because you follow the Son of Man.

23 When that happens, be happy! Yes, leap for joy! For a great reward awaits you in heaven. And remember, their ancestors treated the ancient prophets that same way.

24 "What sorrow awaits you who are rich, for you have your only happiness now.

25 What sorrow awaits you who are fat and prosperous now, for a time of awful hunger awaits you. What sorrow awaits you who laugh now, for your laughing will turn to mourning and sorrow.

26 What sorrow awaits you who are praised by the crowds, for their ancestors also praised false prophets.

27 "But to you who are willing to listen, I say, love your enemies! Do good to those who hate you.

29 And unto him that smiteth thee on the one cheek offer also the other; and him that taketh away thy cloak forbid not to take thy coat also.

30 Give to every man that asketh of thee; and of him that taketh away thy goods ask them not again.

31 And as ye would that men should do to you, do ye also to them likewise.

28 Bless those who curse you. Pray for those who hurt you.

29 If someone slaps you on one cheek, offer the other cheek also. If someone demands your coat, offer your shirt also.

30 Give to anyone who asks; and when things are taken away from you, don't try to get them back.

31 Do to others as you would like them to do to you."

The People, Places, and Times

The Disciples. The word *disciple* means learner or student. It is most often used for students or followers of Jesus and only used in the Gospels and Acts. These students of Jesus were distinct from the multitudes that gathered when He preached and performed miracles. The Gospels refer to the Twelve and another larger group of unnamed disciples. Jesus spent intensive time with the Twelve; the other larger group of disciples did not spend as much time with Jesus but accepted and followed His teaching and practices.

The Plain. The plain or level place could have been one of two things: It could have been an actual plain or flat piece of land; it also could have been a level place on the side of the mountain. This word has confused scholars, as some have believed this passage is parallel to Matthew 5–7. If not parallel, then Jesus repeated some of the same sayings on a different occasion (which was often the case for an itinerant teacher).

Tyre and Sidon. Important cities on the coast of what is present-day Lebenon. In the Old Testament, they were powerful city-states and home to the Phoenicians. They were also known as the Sidonians—a Canaanite people who were not driven out by the Israelites when they entered the Promised Land. Instead, they remained on the coast and became powerful and rich through shipping and trading. Both cities were conquered by the Babylonians, Persians, Greeks, and Romans and consisted of mixed populations. The Greek woman in Mark 7:23–30 was a citizen of Tyre or Sidon.

Background

After spending all night in prayer and choosing the 12 apostles who would continue His ministry, Jesus descended to a plain where a group of disciples and a great multitude from all over the surrounding country were waiting for Him. They had traveled to hear this great teacher and be healed of their diseases and cured of evil spirits. Jesus came down with the Twelve and their presence symbolized the creation of a new Israel. Just like Israel had a set of laws that governed their behavior as a people, Jesus gave His disciples a set of "laws" that would govern their behavior. This set of laws is called the Sermon on the Plain.

The Sermon on the Plain is one of the most powerful passages in the entire Bible. In it, Jesus gives an agenda for God's kingdom, a set of rules and instructions for His people to live by. The first part of these instructions consists of four blessings and four woes. These blessings and woes are followed by more explicit instructions on loving our enemies and doing good to those who mistreat us. These instructions are general guidelines and do not cover every situation but can all be grouped under the golden rule: "Do to others as you would like them to do to you" (6:31, NLT).

At-A-Glance

1. God's People are Recipients of God's Blessings (Luke 6:17–23)
2. God's People Anticipate Future Rewards (vv. 24–26)
3. God's People are Called to Live a Distinctive Lifestyle (vv. 27–31)

In Depth

1. God's People are Recipients of God's Blessings (Luke 6:17–23)

The woes that Jesus pronounced in Luke 6:24–26 indicate that those whom we esteem highly in this life are not always the ones who have favor with God. Those who are already rich, well fed, laughing, and universally praised have no reason to be happy. They may not have the favor of God; therefore, Jesus pronounced grief on them. Their present condition does not attract God's favor.

In contrast, Jesus began His Sermon on the Plain by speaking blessings on those who follow Him, for often they are the ones whom society considers outcast and downtrodden. Jesus turns the world's categories of blessedness upside-down by stating that the poor, the hungry, the weeping, and the outcast are happy. Why are they happy? They are recipients of the kingdom and favor of God. It is not how much we possess or how many people praise us that matters. Our ultimate priority is receiving the praise of God. The pronouncements that Jesus uttered on the crowd of those who were poor, outcast, and disabled contain the empowerment needed to live the distinctive lifestyle that God calls us to live.

2. God's People Anticipate Future Rewards (vv. 24–26)

Those who are regarded as blessed in this world have no reason to rejoice, for they have experienced all that this life has to offer right now. The rich already have all the comfort they will ever receive. The well fed will be hungry. The laughing will be weeping. The universally praised will receive the fate of the false prophets of the Old Testament. They have their reward and have nothing to anticipate in the future.

In contrast, the people of God experience His present blessings because they anticipate His future rewards. They can be happy now because God will reward them in the future. They know that their position and status in this life is not their ultimate goal and destination. Jesus says that the poor have the kingdom of God, which is eternal. He says that the hungry are happy and blessed because they will be filled. The weeping will laugh. Those who are excluded and persecuted will receive a great reward since they are following in the footsteps of God's prophets. This is enough for them to not only be happy but to rejoice and leap for joy.

3. God's People are Called to Live a Distinctive Lifestyle (vv. 27–31)

By being recipients of God's blessing and anticipating future rewards as followers of Jesus, we are empowered to live a distinctive lifestyle marked by love. The definition of this love is to seek another's goodwill. What makes this so unique is that the seeking of another's goodwill encompasses everyone—including our enemies. This is fleshed out in Luke 6:27–31. Jesus' words to His followers are both countercultural and counterintuitive.

He commands us to do good to those who hate us, bless those who curse us, and pray for those who mistreat us. He commands us to turn the other cheek to those who strike us and to give to those who take from us.

Jesus also gives one last guideline that includes the previous commands and sums up the main way that His followers will live a distinctive lifestyle: "Do to others as you would like them to do to you" (v. 31, NLT). It is the guiding principle of seeking another's goodwill. If it were changed to "do to others as they have done to you," there would be room for retaliation and revenge. However, Jesus' command draws on our own desire for well-being so that we transfer that to our fellow man no matter what he has done to us. This is the main characteristic of living a distinctive lifestyle as a follower of Christ.

Search the Scriptures

1. What is the significance of people coming from Tyre and Sidon to hear Jesus (Luke 6:17)?

2. What is the kingdom of God (v. 20)?

3. What does it mean to bless those who curse us (v. 28)?

Discuss the Meaning

1. How are we as believers be empowered by God to love our enemies?

2. What can we do to cultivate joy about the future reward we will receive from God?

Lesson in Our Society

As followers of Jesus, we are called to live in an upside-down kingdom. We are not to follow the ways of this world. One of the ways that we live a distinctive lifestyle is by practicing love. Our love is not to only include those who love us—after all, that is very easy and how the world operates. Our love is to include those who are considered our enemies—this is the way of Jesus. We are empowered to live in this way because we already have the favor of God and will one day receive our reward from Him. That's why we can endure being mistreated and talked about. We know that this is not our final destination, and the world doesn't have the final say about who we are. We can love those who are considered unlovable because we are loved by God. We can show the world a different way to live and point the way to Jesus and His radical kingdom.

Make It Happen

It is easy to love those who love us. It is only natural to embrace people who embrace us. It is supernatural, however, to love those who hate us and mistreat us. Yet this is what we are called to do. Because we have the favor of God and His supernatural power, we can embrace and love our enemies. Consider having lunch or coffee with someone who is considered to be your enemy because of their religion, ethnicity, or political persuasion. Instead of posting up hateful or demeaning notes on social media, post prayers for those who are considered your enemies. Praise coworkers who criticize or gossip about you. Finally, pray for all those whom you find difficult to love.

Follow the Spirit

What God wants me to do:

_____

_____

_____

_____

Remember Your Thoughts
Special insights I have learned:

_____

_____

_____

_____

More Light on the Text
Luke 6:17–31

Luke's chapter just prior contains what has been called Jesus' Sermon on the Plain, which contrasts and compares with His longer Sermon on the Mount (Matthew 5–7)—both of which contain beatitudes (blessings). The unique portion that is detailed in our lesson also has been called Blessings and Woes or Jesus' Great Sermon. According to Darrell Bock, Jesus addressed the "disciple's ethical character and call," which is for each—then and now—to acquire God's love (*Luke*, 197). J. C. Ryle describes that love as "the grand characteristic of the Gospel" (*Luke*, 79).

In some ways, the teaching is in complete harmony with the Old Testament (Leviticus 19:18), but in other ways, it's just the opposite (Exodus 21:23–25), as our lesson affirms.

17 And he came down with them, and stood in the plain, and the company of his disciples, and a great multitude of people out of all Judaea and Jerusalem, and from the sea coast of Tyre and Sidon, which came to hear him, and to be healed of their diseases; 18 And they were vexed with unclean spirits: and they were healed. 19 And the whole multitude sought to touch him: for there went virtue out of him, and healed them all.

Of note here is the notion that Jesus "stood in the plain." Some translations render it,

"stood on a level place." The discourse that follows appears to mirror closely the material in Matthew's Gospel that has been deemed the Sermon on the Mount. Jesus could have given the same sermon at two very different locations, but even an elevated plateau above the sea of Galilee could be considered a "level place." Such a location would be ideal for the forthcoming healing of many that was to take place in the upcoming verses.

The people came to Jesus to hear Him and be healed. Luke may be stressing here the priority of the spoken word over the mighty works, especially in light of the fact that in a parallel account, Mark states that the people came because they heard (past tense) all that Jesus had done, rather than, as Luke states here, to hear him.

The word "virtue" (Gk., *dynamis*, **DOO-na-mis**) means strength, power, or ability. We derive the English word "dynamite" from it. It gives us a wonderful word picture of what kind of power Jesus had among the people of the first century.

20 And he lifted up his eyes on his disciples, and said, Blessed be ye poor: for yours is the kingdom of God. 21 Blessed are ye that hunger now: for ye shall be filled. Blessed are ye that weep now: for ye shall laugh.

Here begins Jesus' Sermon on the Plain. Much shorter than the Sermon on the Mount recorded in Matthew (30 verses compared to 107), Jesus goes through a series of blessings and woes, starting with the poor. The word "happy" may best express the Greek word translated "blessed" in this account (Gk., *markarioi*, **mar-KAY-rio**). When we think of the poor, we immediately think of those with material needs. But Luke here is thinking from a different perspective. King David calls himself poor throughout the Old Testament

(Psalm 40:17; 86:1), but as a king he had material wealth. Poor here is associated more with humility. It takes humility to experience the kingdom of God.

On the other hand, the hunger in this passage does appear to reference a physical hunger. And that hunger carries with it the promise to be filled—a theme we find in the Old Testament's treatment of a messianic banquet (cf. Isaiah 25:6–9; Psalm 107:33–39).

22 Blessed are ye, when men shall hate you, and when they shall separate you from their company, and shall reproach you, and cast out your name as evil, for the Son of man's sake. 23 Rejoice ye in that day, and leap for joy: for, behold, your reward is great in heaven: for in the like manner did their father unto the prophets.

We hardly think about being blessed or happy when others hate us, but this is precisely what Jesus' listeners heard. Little did they know that they would soon be hated for the message they proclaimed to the nations. They would soon be hated for Jesus' sake. In fact, when Luke wrote his Gospel, many Jewish Christians were already being expelled from the synagogue, so it was a reality for his First Century readers. Believe it or not, there was a time when the word "Christian" was a derogatory term (although it might seem that way today in some people's minds). Others would call Jesus' followers Christians, not as a form of identifying them, but to degrade them and hate them for their identification with Christ.

24 But woe unto you that are rich! for ye have received your consolation. 25 Woe unto you that are full! for ye shall hunger. Woe unto you that laugh now! for ye shall mourn and weep. 26 Woe unto you, when all men shall speak well of you! for so did their fathers to the false prophets.

Here we find a parallel list of woes that closely mirror the previous verses. Just as "poor" earlier in this passage was a reference to spiritual poverty, "rich" here means a sense of pride. It references someone who has a haughty spirit. Throughout Scripture, those with arrogant and haughty spirits are denounced (Proverbs 28:6, 11; Isaiah 32:9–14). The comfort felt in this prideful arrogance is waning and unsustainable.

Jesus then continues to discuss those addressed by these woes. Again, the source of their laughter is material and unlasting. The laughter is less about joy and more about looking down upon the fate of another. These people would eventually experience weeping and mourning. The tables would soon be turned. In fact, Luke goes on to record this very situation later in his account in the story of the rich man and Lazarus (Luke 16:19–31). We should be careful about the way we look at the fate of others and the attitude we display when another suffers a fate we feel that they "deserve."

27 But I say unto you which hear, Love your enemies, do good to them which hate you, 28 Bless them that curse you, and pray for them which despitefully use you.

It is important to note the opening word, "but," which serves to separate the verse from the woes listed just prior (vv. 24–26). The woes did not apply to the disciples, because Jesus counted them among those who both listened to His teachings and heard them—they had ears to hear (cf. Luke 8:8; 14:35; Romans 11:8). The teaching opens by zeroing in on the last beatitude (v. 22; cf. Matthew 5:38–48). Robert Stein observes, "Jesus' positive emphasis on loving your enemies is unique in its clarity as well as in the numerous examples given to explain what this love entails" (*Luke*, 206).

Love (Gk. *agapao*, **a-ga-pa-O**) means a genuine and selfless concern, to love dearly and sincerely (cf. Romans 12:14–21). To exhibit this love is to behave like Jesus, who not only defined humility and long-suffering but also was the epitome of compassion. Love means three things: to do good, to bless (Gk. *eulogeo*, **yu-lo-GE-o**), and to pray for one's enemies—which include three types: those who hate you, those who curse you, and those who abuse you. According to David Jeffrey, these exhorted or commanded actions in the face of evil "correspond formally to the four cardinal virtues—temperance, justice, prudence, fortitude" (*Luke*, 96).

Turning the cheek can be seen as overcoming evil with good (Romans 12:21); giving one's tunic or shirt in addition to one's cloak or coat can be seen as sacrificial giving in ministry, for example the selfless lifestyle of most missionaries; tangible blessings can be in the form of compassion or generosity, which ideally also include prayers over and above not seeking retribution for wrongs done. John Phillips notes, "Love looks with compassion on beggar and burglar alike" (*Exploring the Gospel of Luke*, 117).

Ultimately, the lesson involves trusting one's life to God's care, per Bock: "the disciple understands that God is watching over him or her" (*Luke*, 190). In addition to Jesus' own prayer of forgiveness for His crucifiers, another perfect example is Stephen praying for those who were stoning him to death—which prayer in Saul's presence ultimately bore fruit in his conversion (Acts 7:60, 9:1–19).

29 And unto him that smiteth thee on the one cheek offer also the other; and him that taketh away thy cloke forbid not to take thy coat also.

This verse illustrates the previous verse with concrete examples of actions and responses: If someone hits you or takes from you, don't hit back—in fact, allow another strike—and offer even more than is taken. Surely Jesus set the ultimate example of this with everything He silently endured during His trial and crucifixion. In Ryle's words, "He would have us concede much, submit to much, and put up with much rather than cause strife" (*Luke*, 81). Although he referred to a prophecy about Jesus, Stein maintains that striking on the cheek "involves insult more than injury (cf. Isaiah 50:6)" (*Luke*, 207).

30 Give to every man that asketh of thee; and of him that taketh away thy goods ask them not again.

Moving from the specific to the general, some believe this verse is intentional hyperbole to make a principled point, as Stein notes, "[It is] best to understand this as an overstatement for effect" (*Luke*, 208). This verse also uses theft as an example, the same as verse 29. This writer remembers well the response of someone he knew who had been robbed of more than $20,000 worth of valuables by three African American men, who later were convicted of the crime. Not satisfied with the justice served, his irate and racist verbal rampage afterward was aimed at an entire race—totally oblivious to the even bigger crime that he was committing afresh every day in his own heart.

The above points are restated in condensed form in verse 35, and the rest of the chapter has more examples of love in action.

31 And as ye would that men should do to you, do ye also to them likewise.

Luke summarized the entire teaching in a single sentence, which also is known and loved by most every person on the planet as the Golden Rule (cf. Leviticus 19:18)—which humanity saw incarnated in the life of Jesus, who embodied the heart of God (cf. Romans 5:8–10; Luke 6:36). Many have attempted to succinctly capture a definition; all are valuable contributions: "a practical governing principle" (Liefeld, 893); "one of the pinnacle points in Jesus' ethical teaching" (Bock, 190); "a precept of infinite wisdom" (Ryle, 80); "it is the law of love reduced to its simplest terms; even a child can understand it" (Phillips, 117). Essentially, observes Stein, "Christian love is not dependent on others' behavior" (*Luke*, 208).

A current and clear example of God's children being persecuted for their faith is the situation with the Chick-fil-A restaurant chain following the simple issuance of owner Dan Cathy's belief in traditional marriage. The wave of vitriol that resulted was both undeserved (Chick-fil-A did not discriminate against anyone in any way) and full of hatred. Rather than respond in kind, Cathy simply turned the other cheek and allowed the homosexual activists to viciously pummel his restaurants in the media and in protests. If even one activist nationwide noticed that forgiveness and tolerance were returned for evil and intolerance and had second thoughts about the character of Christians, then Cathy was vindicated before God.

St. Francis of Assisi (1181–1226) forever embodied the words of this verse with this line in his famous poem, "Where there is hatred, let me sow love," which is a direct reference to this passage. Another way to say it using the theme words from our lesson would be, "Where there is injustice, let me sow justice." As Bock words it, "To the one who pardons comes pardon; to the one who gives come gifts from God's hand" (*Luke*, 195). By the same token, he writes, "By failing to love, we fail to reveal the loving and merciful character of God" (198). Remember, you might well be the only Bible the person in front of you is reading—what take-home lesson will that person receive from you?

Sources:
Blue Letter Bible. BlueLetterBible.org. http://www.blueletterbible.org/ (accessed Tuesday March 29, 2012).
Bock, Darrell L. Luke. *The NIV Application Commentary*. Grand Rapids, MI: Zondervan, 1996. 190–198.
Liefeld, Walter L. "Luke." *The Expositor's Bible Commentary with the New International Version: Matthew, Mark, Luke, Vol. 8*. Edited by Frank E. Gaebelein. Grand Rapids, MI: Zondervan, 1984. 889–894.
Jeffrey, David Lyle. Luke. *Brazos Theological Commentary on the Bible*. Grand Rapids, MI: Brazos Press, 2012. 86–96.
Phillips, John. *Exploring the Gospel of Luke. The John Phillips Commentary Series*. Grand Rapids, MI: Kregel Publications, 2005. 108–117.
Ryle, J. C. Luke. *The Crossway Classic Commentaries*. Wheaton, IL: Crossway, 1997. 73–76.
Stein, Robert H. Luke. *The New American Commentary, Vol. 24*. Nashville: Holman Reference, 1992. 187–190.

Say It Correctly

Tyre. **TIRE**.
Sidon. **SI**-den.

Daily Bible Readings

MONDAY
Judged by the Righteous God
(Psalm 7:7–17)

TUESDAY
The Righteous and Upright
(Proverbs 11:3–11)

WEDNESDAY
Enslaved to God
(Romans 6:16–23)

THURSDAY
Living as God's Servants
(1 Peter 2:11–17)

FRIDAY
Forgiveness and Mercy
(Matthew 18:21–35)

SATURDAY
Blessings and Woes
(Luke 6:20–26)

SUNDAY
Do Not Judge
(Luke 6:27–42)

Notes

Teaching Tips

Words You Should Know

A. Humble (Luke 14:11, NLT) *tapeinoo* (Gk.)—To make low.

B. Exalt (v. 11, NLT) *hupsoo* (Gk.)—To rise to dignity, honor, and happiness.

Teacher Preparation

Unifying Principle—Welcoming All People. Homogeneity is the standard by which people invite others to social events. What inhibits Christians' ability to invite those who are different from them? Jesus has a message of social justice that reverses the custom and compels His followers to welcome all people.

A. Pray and ask God's help with the lesson.

B. Review Luke 14 and Psalm 147.

C. Bring pictures of people from different races, nationalities, and religions.

O—Open the Lesson

A. Open with prayer, including the Aim for Change.

B. Introduce today's lesson title.

C. Let students read the Aim for Change and Keep in Mind verse.

D. Post your pictures in front of the class on the blackboard.

E. Have the class read the In Focus Story silently, then discuss. Ask, "Why do we invite certain people to our churches while excluding others?" Discuss.

F. Ask, "What can we do to become more inclusive within our churches?" Discuss.

P—Present the Scriptures

A. Have volunteers read the Focal Verses.

B. Use The People, Places, and Times; Background; Search the Scriptures; At-A-Glance outline; In Depth; and More Light on the Text to clarify the verses.

E—Explore the Meaning

A. Divide the class into groups to answer questions in the Discuss the Meaning, Lesson in Our Society, and Make It Happen sections. Tell the students to select a representative to report their responses.

B. Connect these sections to the Aim for Change and the Keep in Mind verse.

N—Next Steps for Application

A. Tell the class to write some take-away principles they learned in the Remember Your Thoughts section.

B. Close with prayer and praise God that Jesus welcomes all to come be a part of His kingdom.

Worship Guide

For the Superintendent or Teacher
Theme: Jesus Teaches about
Relationships
Song: "Don't Stay Away"
Devotional Reading: Psalm 147:1–11

Jesus Teaches about Relationships

Bible Background • LUKE 14:7–18a, 22–24
Printed Text • LUKE 14:7–18a, 22–24 | Devotional Reading • PSALM 147:1–11

—————————— Aim for Change ——————————

By the end of the lesson, we will: EXPLORE Jesus' teachings about humility and exaltation; EVALUATE attitudes and behavior towards those who are disenfranchised; and SEEK ways to invite people who do not normally participate in the local church.

 In Focus

Every Saturday, Derrick volunteered at the local community center in San Antonio. One day, Derrick asked the director if he could start offering counseling services to the people they served. He was a professional family counselor. The director felt it was a great idea and helped Derrick get started. Many families came in for counseling since Derrick had already established relationships with the people.

JAN 19th

Derrick noticed that the families he counseled often spoke of the importance of their faith in helping them make the transition. He had the permission of the director to give the families a list of individual faith communities in the area.

One Sunday, an Asian family visited Derrick's church while he was away on vacation. The family told him that they had not felt welcomed in his church and would not be returning. During the welcoming of visitors, the members ignored them and made rude comments. Derrick apologized to the family.

Some churches are not open to welcoming people from outside their race or culture. In today's lesson, we will see how Jesus challenges us to love and welcome all people.

—————————— Keep in Mind ——————————

"For whosoever exalted himself shall be abased; and he that humbleth himself shall be exalted" (Luke 14:11).

"For whosoever exalted himself shall be abased; and he that humbleth himself shall be exalted" (Luke 14:11).

Focal Verses

KJV **Luke 14:7** And he put forth a parable to those which were bidden, when he marked how they chose out the chief rooms; saying unto them.

8 When thou art bidden of any man to a wedding, sit not down in the highest room; lest a more honourable man than thou be bidden of him;

9 And he that bade thee and him come and say to thee, Give this man place; and thou begin with shame to take the lowest room.

10 But when thou art bidden, go and sit down in the lowest room; that when he that bade thee cometh, he may say unto thee, Friend, go up higher: then shalt thou have worship in the presence of them that sit at meat with thee.

11 For whosoever exalteth himself shall be abased; and he that humbleth himself shall be exalted.

12 Then said he also to him that bade him, When thou makest a dinner or a supper, call not thy friends, nor thy brethren, neither thy kinsmen, nor thy rich neighbours; lest they also bid thee again, and a recompence be made thee.

13 But when thou makest a feast, call the poor, the maimed, the lame, the blind:

14 And thou shalt be blessed; for they cannot recompense thee: for thou shalt be recompensed at the resurrection of the just.

15 And when one of them that sat at meat with him heard these things, he said unto him, Blessed is he that shall eat bread in the kingdom of God.

16 Then said he unto him, A certain man made a great supper, and bade many:

17 And sent his servant at supper time to say to them that were bidden, Come; for all things are now ready.

NLT **Luke 14:7** When Jesus noticed that all who had come to the dinner were trying to sit in the seats of honor near the head of the table, he gave them this advice:

8 "When you are invited to a wedding feast, don't sit in the seat of honor. What if someone who is more distinguished than you has also been invited?

9 The host will come and say, 'Give this person your seat.' Then you will be embarrassed, and you will have to take whatever seat is left at the foot of the table!

10 "Instead, take the lowest place at the foot of the table. Then when your host sees you, he will come and say, 'Friend, we have a better place for you!' Then you will be honored in front of all the other guests.

11 For those who exalt themselves will be humbled, and those who humble themselves will be exalted."

12 Then he turned to his host. "When you put on a luncheon or a banquet," he said, "don't invite your friends, brothers, relatives, and rich neighbors. For they will invite you back, and that will be your only reward.

13 Instead, invite the poor, the crippled, the lame, and the blind.

14 Then at the resurrection of the righteous, God will reward you for inviting those who could not repay you."

15 Hearing this, a man sitting at the table with Jesus exclaimed, "What a blessing it will be to attend a banquet in the Kingdom of God!"

16 Jesus replied with this story: "A man prepared a great feast and sent out many invitations.

17 When the banquet was ready, he sent his servant to tell the guests, 'Come, the banquet is ready.'

18a And they all with one consent began to make excuse.

14:22 And the servant said, Lord, it is done as thou hast commanded, and yet there is room.

23 And the lord said unto the servant, Go out into the highways and hedges, and compel them to come in, that my house may be filled.

24 For I say unto you, That none of those men which were bidden shall taste of my supper.

18a But they all began making excuses.

14:22 After the servant had done this, he reported, 'There is still room for more.'

23 So his master said, 'Go out into the country lanes and behind the hedges and urge anyone you find to come, so that the house will be full.

24 For none of those I first invited will get even the smallest taste of my banquet.'"

The People, Places, and Times

Pharisees. A Jewish religious group that strictly followed the Old Testament laws as well as their own religious traditions. They outwardly obeyed God's laws to look pious, but their hearts were filled with pride and greed. The Pharisees were admired by the people and influential in the synagogues. They believed in a bodily resurrection and eternal life, as well as in angels and demons.

Both John the Baptist and Jesus often denounced the Pharisees. This religious group believed salvation came from perfect obedience to the law and was not based on forgiveness of sins. They did not accept God's message of mercy and grace. Therefore, they rejected Jesus' claim to be the Messiah.

Hospitality. The Old Testament teachings expected the Israelites to serve as hosts and practice hospitality. It was seen as godly, righteous behavior (Genesis 18:2–8). Hospitality was also encouraged among the early Christians (Titus 1:8). It was mainly focused on strangers in need or foreigners who had no community ties and needed immediate food and lodging. The poor, orphans, or widows lacked the provisions that came with inheriting land, the means to make a living, and the protection of a family. It was expected that such people's needs would be fully provided by the one taking them into his home.

In the ancient world, to share a meal with someone was a gesture of intimacy that created a bond of fellowship. Consider, for example, God's meal with the elders of Israel (Exodus 24:1–11), the Lord's Supper (Mark 14:17–26), and Peter's meal with the Gentiles (Acts 10:48–11:3). All these communicated a message of intimacy and unity. Jesus was dependent on the hospitality of others as He traveled through towns ministering (Luke 9:58, 10:38). While partaking of meals in the homes of others, Jesus united Himself to the lost as he shared meals with sinners, tax collectors, and Pharisees alike (Mark 2:15; Luke 14:1, 19:1–10).

Background

Jesus was always in conflict with the Pharisees for their teachings and hypocrisy. In Luke 12, Jesus warned the people against false doctrine (vv. 1–3). The teachings of the empty ritualists, the Pharisees, were nothing but a sham and hypocrisy. Jesus used the parable of the rich fool to express a warning against covetousness (vv. 16–21). He wants us to seek the spiritual benefits of the kingdom rather than the material goods of the world.

In chapter 13, Jesus taught on repentance and judging (13:1–5). This was in direct contradiction to the Pharisees' teaching that salvation comes from strict obedience to the law, not forgiveness of sins. On His way to Jerusalem, Jesus was warned by the Pharisees that Herod Antipas wanted to kill Him. However, the Pharisees said this to frighten Him into leaving the area. Jesus told them to tell Herod that His life's purpose was predetermined, and no one could change it. He wept over the condition of the people in Jerusalem (vv. 31–35).

In chapter 14, Jesus was invited to a Pharisee leader's house for a meal on the Sabbath (v. 1). This was not the first time He had been invited to a Pharisee's house (7:36). On this occasion, the Pharisees and lawyers present invited Jesus to the Sabbath meal to watch if He would say or do something so they could arrest Him. A man with dropsy was present, and Jesus questioned the Pharisees about the lawfulness of healing a man on the Sabbath. There was no response, and Jesus healed him (14:2–4). This was not in violation of Sabbath laws, just the Pharisees' interpretation of them.

At-A-Glance

1. The Places of Honor (Luke 14:7–11)
2. The Invitations (vv. 12–14)
3. The Parable of the Great Banquet (vv. 15–18, 22–24)

In Depth

1. The Places of Honor (Luke 14:7–11)

Not only were the Pharisees watching Jesus, He was also watching them. He noticed how the guests chose the best seats at the table (v. 7). The places of honor were the middle seats where the most important guests sat. Some felt it was vital that they sit in the places

of honor. This gave the symbolic status of being important.

Jesus told them a parable about going to a feast and *not* taking the most honorable seat (vv. 8–10) in order to teach the wisdom of humility. Jesus warned His listeners not to take the places of honor because someone very important may be a guest, and the host would then have to ask you to move to another seat. That would be embarrassing. It is wiser to sit at the lower end of the table or most inferior seat to show a humble attitude. When the host arrives, he may ask you to move up to a more honorable place at the table. Then others will admire your humility and think more highly of you.

"For whosoever exalted himself shall be abased; and he that humbleth himself shall be exalted" (v. 11). We should not boast or think more highly of ourselves in comparison to others. God and others will humble us. This can lead to public embarrassment and disgrace. We should humbly use the gifts God has given us to help others and give all glory to God for His grace and goodness. Then God will honor us.

2. The Invitations (vv. 12–14)

Jesus observed the behavior of His host and gave some advice. He suggested that when a host has a special meal, he should not invite only friends, family, or rich neighbors, for they can reciprocate the invitation or grant favors. Instead, he should invite the poor, needy, and the sick because they have no way to repay. They have no property or place in society, but they will pray God's blessings upon the host for such kindness and hospitality.

The New Testament's understanding of "hospitality" means "love of a stranger." This means inviting those who have no means to repay or host us in return. Sharing a meal is how we can show we accept others as our equals and bond in fellowship.

3. The Parable of the Great Banquet (vv. 15–18, 22–24)

The parable of the great banquet is a continuation of the concept of hospitality discussed in verses 12–14. One of the guests mentions the feast "in the kingdom of God" (v. 15). This could be related to the mention of the resurrection of the just in verse 14. The parable relates the story of a man who gave a banquet and invited many people. The custom was to send two invitations: one in advance to announce the party, then the second to let the guests who had accepted know the preparations had been completed (v. 17). In the parable, when the second invitation was given, many gave excuses for why they could not attend. To replace those people who refused to come, the host invited those in the streets of the city—the poor, needy, sick, and transient (vv. 21–23).

Jesus was using this parable to relate kingdom principles. The self-righteous (unbelieving Jews), especially the Pharisees, made excuses to get out of attending the great supper of salvation provided by God. They rejected Jesus' claims of being the Messiah and the need for His death on the Cross for the forgiveness of sins. Since they refused to accept the invitation, the invitation was extended to other people (disenfranchised of Israel and Gentiles) to replace the original guests (unbelieving Jews, v. 24). All those who accept will be welcomed into God's kingdom.

Search the Scriptures

1. What did Jesus teach about seeking places of honor (Luke 14:10–11)?

2. Who will be invited to the great banquet in God's kingdom (vv. 21, 23)?

Discuss the Meaning

If God's kingdom shall be composed of people from every nation, race, culture, and socioeconomic group, why are churches sometimes the most segregated places in our communities? What needs to be done to change our beliefs and attitudes about welcoming all people into our churches?

Lesson in Our Society

One of the greatest obstacles to reaching the disenfranchised is our misconception about others. Some of it may be our feelings of superiority. Or, we just do not want "those types of people" in our congregations. Whatever the reasoning, it is not acceptable to Christ. He wants us to practice hospitality and welcome all people. After all, His kingdom will be composed of people from "every kindred, and tongue, and people, and nation" (Revelation 5:9).

Make It Happen

This week, evaluate what is hindering you from inviting others to your church. Pray and ask God to forgive you for letting it stop you from witnessing and welcoming others. Discuss with your church leader and other members how to show hospitality and reach out to the disenfranchised in your communities. This can include community parties, health clinics, food programs, door-to-door witnessing, community concerts, etc.

Follow the Spirit

What God wants me to do:

_____

_____

_____

_____

Remember Your Thoughts

Special insights I have learned:

_____

_____

_____

_____

More Light on the Text

Luke 14:7–18a, 22–24

7 And he put forth a parable to those which were bidden, when he marked how they chose out the chief rooms; saying unto them,

A key term in this passage is "bidden" (Gk. *kaleo*, **kal-EH-o**), which is also the word for "invite," "summon" and "call." The root for the verb "to invite" or "call" appears ten times in the lesson. Jesus was speaking of those who were called to be His disciples and to whom He was giving instructions in the form of a parable, as well as those literally invited to dinner as guests.

Jesus was at a dinner with the disciples when He commanded them to observe where guests at a feast were choosing to sit. Jesus called forth imagery from the wisdom tradition found in the proverbs (cf. Proverbs 25:6–7) to teach the disciples about how one who is called should act humbly. He began the parable with a reference to the seating order at chief rooms (Gk. *protoklisia*, **pro-tok-li-SEE-ah**) or places of honor at a banquet.

8 When thou art bidden of any man to a wedding, sit not down in the highest room; lest a more honourable man than thou be bidden of him.

The custom in antiquity was that the most distinguished (Gk. *entimos*, **EN-tee-mos**) guests at a dinner or feast arrived late

and reclined at the space at the table (Gk. *kataklino*, **kat-ak-LEE-no**) closest to the host. Jesus admonished the disciples not to be like the other guests vying to sit in the places of honor before all the other guests arrived because someone of higher social status might still come.

Jesus' choice of a wedding banquet is also a metaphor for the kingdom of God. On another occasion, Jesus taught a parable about a king who held a wedding reception for his son as an image of the heavenly feast (Matthew 22:1–14).

9 And he that bade thee and him come and say to thee, Give this man place; and thou begin with shame to take the lowest room.

Honor and shame were very real concepts in the ancient Near East. Honor has a positive value for males, and modesty (Gk. *aischyne*, **ahee-SKHOO-nay**) has a positive value for women. Shame is a negative value for men and represents a loss of manliness. The man forced to move from the privileged seat at the head of the table down to the lowest (Gk. *eschatos*, **ES-khat-os**) end in front of all the other guests would not only be shamed by being relocated, but also because he had assumed a position in society to which he did not belong.

10 But when thou art bidden, go and sit down in the lowest room; that when he that bade thee cometh, he may say unto thee, Friend, go up higher: then shalt thou have worship in the presence of them that sit at meat with thee.

By contrast, Jesus commanded the disciples not to follow the example of the other guests but to do the unexpected and show humility by sitting at the farthest end of the banquet table. The expectation was that the host would seat the honored guests who arrived late at the front of the table near himself. However, the one who invited them has the prerogative to seat the guests wherever he chooses and may invite the guest with the lowest social status to move up to the higher (Gk. *anoteros*, **an-O-ter-os**) place of honor.

The Greek word for "worship" is *doxa* (**DOX-ah**) and means "glory." It is a term usually reserved for God. However, in the Hebrew and Greco-Roman context, it means the enhancement of one's reputation or social status. The act of seating the guest of more modest stature at the higher end would signal to the other guests that this person had moved up the ranks and was now worthy of honor.

11 For whosoever exalteth himself shall be abased; and he that humbleth himself shall be exalted.

From a worldly perspective, Jesus appears to be teaching that those who lift up or exalt themselves (Gk. *hupsoo*, **hoop-SO-o**) will be abased or lowered. The Greek word for "abased" is *tapeinoo* (**tap-i-NO-o**) and means to be geographically at a low point, or in human terms, a loss of esteem or status. In a culture where honor was such a coveted designation, a loss of honor would be a significant blow to one's standing in the community. In contrast, those who humble themselves shall have their status elevated. The real lesson Jesus was trying to impart to the disciples is that in God's kingdom, God will bring about a reversal of human social constructs. The ones considered among the lowest socially will be exalted or lifted up, and those who have enjoyed the highest social position, either as a result of the family they were born into or wealth acquired legitimately or through wile, will be lowered.

12 Then said he also to him that bade him, When thou makest a dinner or a supper, call not thy friends, nor thy brethren, neither thy kinsmen, nor thy rich neighbours; lest they also bid thee again, and a recompence be made thee.

Jesus next turned His attention to the host. One scholar noted that the host, like the guests, was more concerned with social status than the needs of those lower on the social rung. Jesus addressed this by advising him that when he prepared dinner, he should not exclusively invite his friends, siblings, extended family members, or neighbors who had an exceeding abundance of material wealth and would be obligated to invite him to dinner in kind. The Greek word for "recompence" (*antapodoma*, **an-tap-OD-om-ah**) means repayment. In the ancient world, gift giving was reciprocal and built relationships between the giver and receiver, therefore creating solidarity. However, a poor person could not repay a rich person who invited the poor person to dine, a fact that would have been obvious to the host.

13 But when thou makest a feast, call the poor, the maimed, the lame, the blind.

In a reversal of societal expectations, Jesus commanded His host to instead invite the poor, the physically disabled, and the blind. The poor, maimed, lame, and blind were members of society who were dependent on public generosity for their welfare and did not have the financial resources to repay their host. Jesus counseled the host that he should extend an invitation to society's outcasts. Jesus was very concerned with those pushed to the margins of society because of their economic disadvantage, uncleanness, or physical disability.

14 And thou shalt be blessed; for they cannot recompense thee: for thou shalt be recompensed at the resurrection of the just.

Jesus told the host if he invited the least to his home for dinner, he would be blessed. In the 1980s, performing "random acts of kindness" became popular. The idea was that individuals or groups would perform spontaneous selfless acts without expecting to receive recognition or reward in return. It could be something as small as putting coins in an expiring meter just as the officer is about to write a parking ticket, or as major as paying someone's hospital bill. The Greek word for "blessed" (*makarios,* **mak-AR-ee-os**) denotes a state of happiness. People who performed random acts of kindness believed that the blessing or happiness they derived from the act was repayment enough. Jesus' message is that performing such acts of kindness without the expectation for reward would not only bless the individual here on earth, but he or she would receive a heavenly reward at the resurrection of the just (cf. Daniel 12:2–3).

15 And when one of them that sat at meat with him heard these things, he said unto him, Blessed is he that shall eat bread in the kingdom of God.

Jesus' remarks on the resurrection of the just prompted one of the guests to comment that one would be happy to eat bread in the kingdom of God. The Greek word for "bread" (*artos,* **AR-tos**) means literally the bread one eats, and figuratively, the sustenance provided by God. The guest was implying that on the occasion of the resurrection of the just, one would enjoy his or her fill of food, thus experiencing a state of happiness. His remark allowed Jesus to introduce a parable on the great messianic banquet in the kingdom (Gk. *basileia,* **bas-il-I-ah**) of God.

16 Then said he unto him, A certain man made a great supper, and bade many.

Jesus began the parable of the kingdom by telling the story of a man who prepared a lot of food for an evening meal (Gk. *deipnon,* **DIPE-non**) and invited enough people to share it with him. This would have been a man of great wealth. Perhaps because of his status, he took for granted that an invitation from him would have been positively received, such as the above reference to Matthew 22:1–10.

17 And sent his servant at supper time to say to them that were bidden, Come; for all things are now ready.

The man sent his servant (Gk. *doulos,* **DOO-los**) to tell the invited guests that preparations were ready (Gk. *hetoimos,* **het-OY-mos**) and it was time to come eat. It is inferred that they had already received their invitations, and the time had come to accept. The summons by the servant reflects an ancient upper-class Jewish and Roman practice as a courtesy to the guests. Some scholars suggest that the parable refers to salvation, and Jesus is saying that the kingdom of God is at hand. The gracious host is God, who extended the invitation of salvation first to Israel, then to the rest of the nations.

18a And they all with one consent began to make excuse.

To say that all the guests rejected the summons to dinner with one accord or as one (Gk. *mias,* **MI-as**) voice implies that an entire group of people rejected the offer of salvation. We should be careful not to interpret this literally to suggest that, for example, all Jewish people or all wealthy people rejected salvation. The main point is that those to whom the invitation was first extended refused it. Therefore, salvation was extended to others, and finally to those least expected to be included. This is not so hard to imagine. Sometimes the people whom we believe have the most need for a helping hand will refuse because of who is offering assistance.

22 And the servant said, Lord, it is done as thou hast commanded, and yet there is room.

The host was left with a table overflowing with food and no guests. There was no Tupperware or refrigerator in which to pack and store the food for later use. The host was left to commanding (Gk. *epitasso*, **ep-ee-TAS-so**) his servant to summon those with whom the host would ordinarily not have dined. Yet, even after the servant had gone all around the streets and countryside, there were still not enough people to fill the seats at the table. This demonstrates that even when the Gospel message is universalized and extended to all peoples and nations, it does not always fall upon receptive ears.

23 And the lord said unto the servant, Go out into the highways and hedges, and compel them to come in, that my house may be filled.

The master (*kyrios*, **KOO-ree-os**) compelled the servant to search everywhere for anyone to bring to his house. The Greek word for "compel" (*anagkazo*, **an-ang-KAD-so**) in this situation means to do something with urgency. It implies an impending situation that required immediate attention. God will do everything possible to reach each person because time is of the essence.

24 For I say unto you, That none of those men which were bidden shall taste of my supper.

Jesus concluded the parable by saying that the original guests who declined the invitation will have passed on the opportunity to share in the man's meal. Likewise, if we who are called refuse the opportunity to follow Jesus and become His disciples, we will not taste (Gk. *geumai*, **GHYOO-om-ahee**) or experience the messianic banquet that is to come.

Sources:
Bauer, Walter, William F. Arndt, F. Wilbur Gingrich, and Frederick W. Danker. *A Greek-English Lexicon of the New Testament and Other Early Christian Literature, Second Edition.* Chicago: University of Chicago Press, 1979.
Bible Study Tools. www.BibleStudyTools.com. Bakers Evangelical Dictionary. "Hospitality." http://www.biblestudytools.com/dictionaries/bakers-evangelical-dictionary/hospitality.html (accessed August 20, 2012).
Bible Study Tools. "Hupsoo—New Testament Greek Lexicon—King James Version." http://www.biblestudytools.com/lexicons/greek/kjv/hupsoo.html (accessed August 16, 2012).
Bible Study Tools. "Tapeinoo—New Testament Greek Lexicon—King James Version." http://www.biblestudytools.com/lexicons/greek/kjv/tapeinoo.html (accessed August 16, 2012).
Craddock, Fred B. Luke: *Interpretation: A Bible Commentary for Teaching and Preaching.* Louisville: John Knox Press, 1990, 169–183.
Freeman, David. "Poor, Poverty." *Anchor Bible Dictionary.* New York: Doubleday, 1992, 403–424.
Gilmore, David, ed. *Honor and Shame and the Unity of the Mediterranean.* Washington, DC: American Anthropological Association, 1987.
Gill, John. www.BibleStudyTools.com. "John Gill's Exposition of the Bible. Luke 14." http://www.biblestudytools.com/commentaries/gills-exposition-of-the-bible/luke-14.html (accessed August 26, 2012).
Life Application Bible (NRSV). Wheaton, IL: Tyndale House, 1989. 1781–1786.
Marshall, I. Howard. *The Gospel of Luke. New International Greek Testament Commentary.* Grand Rapids, MI: Wm. B. Eerdmans Publishing Co., 1978.
Mauss, Marcel. *The Gift: Forms and Functions of Exchange in Archaic Societies.* Cohen & West, 1954.

Say It Correctly

Recompensed. re-**KAM**-pents.
Resurrection. re-ze-**REK**-shun.

Daily Bible Readings

MONDAY
The Danger of Self-Exaltation
(Isaiah 14:12–20)

TUESDAY
Humble Yourself Before the Lord
(James 4:7–12)

WEDNESDAY
God Gives Grace to the Humble
(1 Peter 5:1–7)

THURSDAY
God Gathers the Outcasts
(Psalm 147:1–11)

FRIDAY
God Lifts the Poor and Needy
(Psalm 113)

SATURDAY
God Shows No Partiality
(Romans 2:1–11)

SUNDAY
Honor and Disgrace
(Luke 14:7–18a, 22–24)

Notes

Teaching Tips

Words You Should Know

A. Rich (Luke 16:19) *plousios* (Gk.)—Wealthy, abounding with.

B. Beggar (v. 20) *ptochos* (Gk.)—Poor and helpless; one who in his abjectness needs lifting.

Teacher Preparation

Unifying Principle—Compassion and Generosity at the Gate. Selfishness motivates the attitudes and behaviors of many people. How does selfishness blind Christians to the needs of others? Jesus tells the story of Lazarus and the rich man to teach His followers to put their selfish desires aside so they can help the poor.

A. Pray for clarity as you study the lesson.

B. Study the entire text, review More Light on the Text, and do additional research on the Passover.

O—Open the Lesson

A. Open the lesson with prayer and ask a student to especially intercede on behalf of those who are impoverished and the rich. Ask, "Why do we need to pray for both?"

B. Show contrasting images of the rich and the poor in today's world. How are they treated differently? Discuss.

C. Review Aim for Change, and reflect on how you consider the poor of the world. How does this lesson impact you personally?

P—Present the Scriptures

A. Ask for a volunteer to read the lesson.

B. Lead students in answering the Search the Scriptures, Discuss the Meaning, or any other questions that may arise from your study.

C. Incorporate corresponding Scriptures that further illuminate the text to add to the discussion.

E—Explore the Meaning

A. Have students create a skit using the lesson in today's context. Ask who would be the rich man and Lazarus today.

B. Discuss why Jesus would use this parable to explain how God views justice for the poor.

N—Next Steps for Application

A. Read the Lesson in Our Society and Make It Happen sections aloud.

B. Encourage your students pray for opportunities to individually share Christ this week by giving to those less fortunate domestically or abroad.

Worship Guide

For the Superintendent or Teacher
Theme: Jesus Teaches Compassion
for the Poor
Song: "Please Don't Pass Me By"
Devotional Reading: Luke 19:1–10

Jesus Teaches Compassion for the Poor

Bible Background • LUKE 16:19–31
Printed Text • LUKE 16:19–31 | Devotional Reading • LUKE 19:1–10

————— Aim for Change —————

By the end of the lesson, we will: REVIEW the story of the rich man and Lazarus; DISCUSS our feelings about compassion toward the poor; and CONSIDER involving our congregation in developing a project that addresses selfishness and has a positive effect on everyone's attitudes and actions toward the poor.

In Focus

Jay has lived a very privileged life. His family always took pride in sponsoring events to help the less fortunate, but at the dinner table he often heard both his grandfather and father say that people who are in poverty live that way because they are lazy and worthless.

Then one day while walking downtown, Jay ran into Clarence, a former corporate attorney for a major energy company. Having achieved his dream, Clarence thought he had it all until disaster struck—on his watch, the company came under a major federal investigation, which cost him his career. Clarence lost everything and was homeless, living on the street. Jay knew Clarence through his father, so when Jay saw him, he was in shock. After exchanging some pleasantries, Jay asked what happened to him. All Clarence could muster up was "one bad decision and I lost everything." Jay slipped some money into Clarence's pocket as well as his business card. Jay was in tears when he left Clarence.

Oftentimes, even as Christians, we can carry the wrong attitude toward the poor. In today's lesson, Jesus demonstrates through a parable God's compassion and rewards for the poor.

JAN
26th

————— Keep in Mind —————

"He that is faithful in that which is least is faithful also in much: and he that is unjust in the least is unjust also in much" (Luke 16:10).

"He that is faithful in that which is least is faithful also in much: and he that is unjust in the least is unjust also in much" (Luke 16:10).

Focal Verses

KJV **Luke 16:19** There was a certain rich man, which was clothed in purple and fine linen, and fared sumptuously every day:

20 And there was a certain beggar named Lazarus, which was laid at his gate, full of sores,

21 And desiring to be fed with the crumbs which fell from the rich man's table: moreover the dogs came and licked his sores.

22 And it came to pass, that the beggar died, and was carried by the angels into Abraham's bosom: the rich man also died, and was buried;

23 And in hell he lift up his eyes, being in torments, and seeth Abraham afar off, and Lazarus in his bosom.

24 And he cried and said, Father Abraham, have mercy on me, and send Lazarus, that he may dip the tip of his finger in water, and cool my tongue; for I am tormented in this flame.

25 But Abraham said, Son, remember that thou in thy lifetime receivedst thy good things, and likewise Lazarus evil things: but now he is comforted, and thou art tormented.

26 And beside all this, between us and you there is a great gulf fixed: so that they which would pass from hence to you cannot; neither can they pass to us, that would come from thence.

27 Then he said, I pray thee therefore, father, that thou wouldest send him to my father's house:

28 For I have five brethren; that he may testify unto them, lest they also come into this place of torment.

29 Abraham saith unto him, They have Moses and the prophets; let them hear them.

NLT **Luke 16:19** Jesus said, "There was a certain rich man who was splendidly clothed in purple and fine linen and who lived each day in luxury.

20 At his gate lay a poor man named Lazarus who was covered with sores.

21 As Lazarus lay there longing for scraps from the rich man's table, the dogs would come and lick his open sores.

22 Finally, the poor man died and was carried by the angels to be with Abraham. The rich man also died and was buried,

23 and his soul went to the place of the dead. There, in torment, he saw Abraham in the far distance with Lazarus at his side.

24 The rich man shouted, 'Father Abraham, have some pity! Send Lazarus over here to dip the tip of his finger in water and cool my tongue. I am in anguish in these flames.'

25 But Abraham said to him, 'Son, remember that during your lifetime you had everything you wanted, and Lazarus had nothing. So now he is here being comforted, and you are in anguish.

26 And besides, there is a great chasm separating us. No one can cross over to you from here, and no one can cross over to us from there.'

27 Then the rich man said, 'Please, Father Abraham, at least send him to my father's home.

28 For I have five brothers, and I want him to warn them so they don't end up in this place of torment.'

29 But Abraham said, 'Moses and the prophets have warned them. Your brothers can read what they wrote.'

30 The rich man replied, 'No, Father Abraham! But if someone is sent to them

30 And he said, Nay, father Abraham: but if one went unto them from the dead, they will repent.

31 And he said unto him, If they hear not Moses and the prophets, neither will they be persuaded, though one rose from the dead.

from the dead, then they will repent of their sins and turn to God.'

31 But Abraham said, 'If they won't listen to Moses and the prophets, they won't listen even if someone rises from the dead.'"

The People, Places, and Times

Hades. Also known as *Sheol* or "place of the dead" in the Old Testament, it is the region of departed spirits for those who died. Its meaning translated denotes the underworld and was believed to be the immediate state between death and resurrection. In Jesus' parable, it is an impassible gulf or chasm that separates the lost from the righteous.

Abraham's Bosom. Believed to be the compartment of Hades for those who died in right standing with God due to their faith and obedience to the law. In the Talmud, a collection of rabbinic commentary of the Hebrew Bible, it is mentioned as the place where the soul rests after death. It is a place of privilege for Abraham's righteous children.

Background

The book of Luke features more parables than any of the other Gospels. Jesus used these illustrations to convey key principles of kingdom living. Early on in Luke 16, Jesus told the parable of the dishonest manager to make the point that to be true kingdom believers, we cannot serve God and wealth (v. 13). After hearing this parable, the Pharisees—because of their own position of power and wealth—ridiculed Jesus in an attempt to discredit Him before the people. In response, Jesus told the Pharisees that they were good at appearing righteous, but their hearts were not. In their minds, their great wealth showed that they were blessed by God, but Jesus pointed out that they were

only wealthy through dishonest gain. Jesus declared that the kingdom of God runs counter to the dominant culture. The Pharisees relished their wealth and power, but Jesus warned them that they fell short of God's standards. He further bruised their egos by letting them know that God reads the heart, so it was useless to justify themselves based on their works (v. 15).

At-A-Glance

1. A Picture of Life (Luke 16:19–21)
2. A Picture of the Afterlife (vv. 22–26)
3. A Picture of a Final Plea (vv. 27–31)

In Depth

1. A Picture of Life (Luke 16:19–21)

In opening this parable, Jesus gave a vivid contrast between the rich man and Lazarus, a poor beggar. He didn't give the rich man a name but gave great detail about his way of life. The rich man was dressed in purple and fine linen, showing his outward wealth and his ability to afford the best. He also noted that the rich man didn't just eat well, but that he "fared sumptuously every day," a signal to the hearer that this man did not eat to live but lived to eat. In this context, the ability to buy and enjoy rich foods was a symbol of wealth and abundance. Jesus sought to drive home the stark contrast between the beggar and the rich man as He was speaking to an audience who could relate to each character—they had seen plenty of very wealthy people and plenty of poor and destitute people.

Next, Jesus introduced Lazarus, a homeless beggar who stayed at the gate. As a part of the lowest social caste, he relied on the mercy and kindness of others to even receive crumbs to eat. Unlike the rich man, his existence was truly survival mode. He was unhealthy and malnourished; his clothes were tattered and worn; he lived in constant pain from sores that covered his body. Because he was an outcast, the only touch he experienced was from the dogs that would lick his wounds. Lazarus lived in a constant state of need. Jesus took great time and care to set up this story to communicate a message that is consistent with God's love and care for the poor and His disdain for those who would mistreat them. In establishing the Children of Israel as a nation, God always made provision for the care of the poor, widows, orphans, those enslaved due to debt, and foreigners (Exodus 22:21–24; Leviticus 23:22; Deuteronomy 15:4–8, 11). God commands His people to be a blessing to those in need and to show the same compassion He has shown. Their abundance was never meant to be hoarded but to be given freely so that no one would be in lack.

2. A Picture of the Afterlife (vv. 22–26)

In this parable, both Lazarus and the rich man died. Jesus then gave a glimpse of the afterlife. Some scholars argue whether or not Jesus meant to give a portrait of the afterlife or was simply telling a story, but He convincingly made the point that there is existence of the soul after death. Lazarus died and was carried away by angels to Abraham's bosom, which, according to Jewish tradition, was the place of rest for those who died in the faith of Abraham. According to early rabbis, Abraham's bosom was believed to be "paradise." According to tradition, Abraham sits at the gate to welcome the Children of Israel.

While Lazarus was carried away by angels, Jesus let the listeners know that the rich man was buried and went to hell. To add insult to injury, the rich man looked up and could see Lazarus in heaven. While the rich man was in torment, the very man he had scoffed and ignored on earth was now in comfort at Abraham's side. Thinking he could use his influence as a descendant of Abraham, the rich man sought to draw upon his lineage to receive mercy. In his continued arrogance, the rich man pleaded with Abraham to allow Lazarus to serve him by providing relief from his agony. Jesus gave us dramatic detail of the rich man's torment as he sought to receive just a drop of water because of the intense heat of the flames. Abraham reminded the rich man of the life he lived on earth and how he had everything while Lazarus had lived in lack, constant pain, and shame. Now the roles had been reversed: Lazarus was in comfort and the rich man was in agony. One could argue that the rich man had a lot of nerve wanting Lazarus to relieve his agony when he showed no compassion to Lazarus while on earth, but God shows us through Jesus that He will always care for the poor, and the selfish will receive their just reward (Psalm 147:6). Abraham spoke to the rich man, noting that there was a gulf or chasm that separated them and that no one could pass between.

Hannah provided a similar picture in her prayer about God's justice for the poor: "They that were full have hired out themselves for bread; and they that were hungry ceased . . . He raiseth up the poor out of the dust, and lifteth up the beggar from the dunghill, to set them among princes, and to make them inherit the throne of glory: for the pillars of the earth are the LORD's, and he hath set the world upon them" (1 Samuel 2:5, 8).

3. A Picture of a Final Plea (vv. 27–31)

Jesus closed out this parable with the rich man making a final appeal to Abraham on behalf of those he left behind. Still arrogant, the rich man asked for Lazarus to be sent back among the living to warn his brothers of the torment to come if they do not make things right (i.e., repent). In both Jewish and Hellenistic traditions, there was a belief that the dead are able to make appeals on behalf of the living; this is why, in Catholic traditions, people pray to patron saints. However, Abraham responded that the rich man's brothers should listen to Moses and the prophets who already gave warnings and calls to repentance. The rich man continued to plead with Abraham, saying that someone coming from the grave who had experienced the afterlife would be more believable. It is interesting that the rich man did not offer himself up to return to reach his brothers; apparently Lazarus would be a more credible witness. The rich man was convinced that if someone from the dead preached to them what is to come, they would change their ways and repent. But his request was denied. Abraham responded: "If they hear not Moses and the prophets, neither will they be persuaded, though one rose from the dead" (from v. 31). In short, Jesus taught His listeners then—and us today—that if the Word of God delivered through the power of the Holy Spirit is not enough to convince and draw men and women to repentance, nothing else is available. Likewise, for application in this age, it is our responsibility as Christians to go and make disciples, covering the earth with the Word of truth. Then, at the judgment, no one will be able to say he didn't hear the Gospel or have the opportunity to receive the gift of salvation through Jesus Christ. There is

no other sacrifice for sin and no other way to the Father but through Jesus Christ (Hebrews 10:26–31; John 14:6; Romans 10:9–13).

Search the Scriptures

1. Where did Lazarus and the rich man go when they died? What was different about their passing (Luke 16:22–23)?

2. Who did the rich man appeal to for relief from his torment (v. 24)?

3. What did the rich man want Lazarus to do to help his brothers (vv. 27–28)?

Discuss the Meaning

1. What was the significance of Lazarus receiving comfort after his death versus the rich man's fate after his death?

2. What does this parable say about how we should view our lives and the value we place on the things we have on this side of life?

3. How should we view those who are poor and in need? How can we also help the rich who may be poor in spirit?

Lesson in Our Society

Even in our churches, we often measure people by what they do, what they have, and who they know rather than their display of Christ-like character. This is not the way of the kingdom. We live in a self-centered, entertainment-driven, over-stimulated world where we are raising a generation of young people who have no regard for the sacrifices made to enjoy the freedoms we have today. In striving for a better life, we have forgotten that it was in our struggle that we banded together as a people and that this is the very foundation of our dignity—the heart of compassion to look at each other as brother and sister. Today's lesson reminds us that God does not want us to shut our eyes, close our ears, and cover our mouths when we see social injustices. We have a mandate from our Lord to care for the poor, the disenfranchised, and the marginalized. In the end, God will see to it that those who honor the poor honor Him and will be richly rewarded.

Make It Happen

Pray and ask God how you can individually and corporately be an agent of change to provide for the poor. Begin to pray and intercede for those who have abundance to have a heart for God so that they come alongside to advance the kingdom through wise use of their resources. Seek out opportunities to be a blessing to someone in need and to not pass by someone on the street who is hungry or in need of clothes or shelter. As we give and share with the least of these, we do it as unto the Lord, and He is pleased. Examine how you can be proactive in helping to change the attitudes about the poor in your community and help young people to be sensitive to the needs of others. Go beyond your comfort zone to extend a helping hand.

Follow the Spirit

What God wants me to do:

_____

_____

_____

_____

Remember Your Thoughts

Special insights I have learned:

_____

_____

_____

_____

More Light on the Text
Luke 16:19–31

This is the second of two consecutive teachings by Jesus on the subject of wealth (cf. the parable of the shrewd manager, vv. 1–13). The first was about choosing which master to serve, God or money; the other is about choosing between selfishness and compassion. These follow a lengthy section of the Gospel containing parables and teachings on a variety of subjects that Jesus dispensed as His Passion loomed in front of Him. This set of parables in Luke 16 is directed at the Pharisees. The type of story has been called a "reversal" (also a double-edged parable) and makes use of a frequently used plot, multiple versions of which existed in Jesus' time.

A related lesson on the rich fool is found in Luke 12:13–21; another on riches and the kingdom is found in 18:18–30. Clearly, wealth in general is an important subject that Jesus visited from multiple perspectives.

19 There was a certain rich man, which was clothed in purple and fine linen, and fared sumptuously every day.

Purple was a royal color in Jesus' time, such as the purple "kingly" robe mockingly tossed around His bleeding body to match his "crown" of thorns (John 19:2, 5). Lydia was a dealer in such purple cloth (Acts 16:14). Fine linens refer to high-quality undergarments made in Egypt. The ESV and RSV both have "feasted sumptuously," although "fared" (Gk. *euphraino*, **yu-FRI-no**) essentially means to celebrate or make merry, as in "eat, drink, and be merry" (Luke 12:19), which clearly includes feasting. A familiar concept in any time period, the set-up of the parable clearly is a person living in the lap of luxury and enjoying the finest of everything.

20 And there was a certain beggar named Lazarus, which was laid at his gate, full of sores, 21 And desiring to be fed with the crumbs which fell from the rich man's table: moreover the dogs came and licked his sores.

Unique among all of Jesus' parables, here He named one of His characters. That He named the poor man and left the rich man unnamed underscores the most important figure in the story since, normally, the rich would be named and the poor would be nameless. Also unique is Dr. Luke's use of "sores," meaning ulcerations, in one of the few instances in Scripture with the single use of a Greek or Hebrew word not repeated elsewhere (Gk. *helkoo*, **hel-KO-o**). That the man was "full of sores" indicates a truly pitiful state.

22 And it came to pass, that the beggar died, and was carried by the angels into Abraham's bosom: the rich man also died, and was buried; 23 And in hell he lift up his eyes, being in torments, and seeth Abraham afar off, and Lazarus in his bosom. 24 And he cried and said, Father Abraham, have mercy on me, and send Lazarus, that he may dip the tip of his finger in water, and cool my tongue; for I am tormented in this flame.

In the reversal, angels escorted the once lowly Lazarus to Abraham's bosom or side (Gk. *kolpos*, **KOL-pos**), which is the ultimate contentment for believing Jews (cf. Matthew 8:11)—"a poetic description of heaven,"

writes Philips, adding, "at death we are not left to find our own way home" (*Exploring the Gospel of Luke*, 220). For other uses of the same Greek word, Jesus was in the Father's bosom (John 1:18), and John leaned on Jesus' bosom (John 13:23). No one really knows what happens on the other side, but it is comforting that Jesus provided a picture of a gracious escort. For those who manage to escape judgment for their evil deeds in this life, it is also comforting to know that they will not escape ultimate justice. Paul tells us that those believers who fall asleep are with Christ (2 Corinthians 5:8; Philippians 1:23). In contrast, biological Jews are not guaranteed a place at Abraham's bosom by their bloodline alone—rather, along with the rest of unrepentant humanity, they also will face divine judgment.

Lazarus' reunion with Abraham contrasted with his previous life with dogs for company. Meanwhile, the rich man's former luxury not only ended but was replaced with torment—an even more serious condition than Lazarus' former humiliation. Another aspect of Lazarus' new reality of blessing was his joining with the patriarchs of the faith (cf. John 8:39), much like the modern future hope of being rejoined with loved ones as well as saints who passed before. The reversal continued with Lazarus' future in heaven compared with the rich man's polar opposite future in hell (Gk. *hades*, **HA-das**), which is the "lower parts of the earth" (Ephesians 4:9). Craddock describes this as the "flames of Hades" (*Luke*, 196). In life, the rich man was blessed and Lazarus suffered, but both temporarily. In death, Lazarus was blessed and the rich man suffered, now eternally (cf. the contrasts of the poor versus the rich in the Beatitudes, Luke 6:20–26). Whatever hell actually looks like, clearly there is terrible torment, and fire is a perfect depiction.

25 But Abraham said, Son, remember that thou in thy lifetime receivedst thy good things, and likewise Lazarus evil things: but now he is comforted, and thou art tormented.

Like the rich man in the parable, the rich Pharisees lived for themselves, not God; they followed their own wisdom, not God's. They were godless materialists—a timeless, transcultural phenomena often conducted in the name of religion. Misusing Scripture for their own benefit, they were the original prosperity preachers who scorned the poor who clearly must not be righteous or they, too, would be blessed. It is no wonder that they hated Jesus, because He exposed their wrong and self-centered interpretation of the Old Testament (see Deuteronomy 28:1–14; Psalm 1:3–4). Along with material preceding this parable, the story of Lazarus and the rich man is another example of their wrong and self-serving twisting of God's Word. Craddock writes: "Such a theology is called Deuteronomic, because in that book (and others of that tradition) the word is clear: obey God and you will be blessed in war, in the marketplace, in the field, and at home (Deuteronomy 28). Godliness is in league with riches; prosperity is the clear sign of God's favor" (*Luke*, 192).

Jesus' message to the Pharisees is clear: Just as the rich man was fatally wrong to ignore Lazarus and have no compassion on him, so the Pharisees were just as fatally wrong in their self-righteous and cold-hearted lifestyle. Other Old Testament laws pointed to having mercy on the poor and transients (e.g., Leviticus 19:9–10; Deuteronomy 15:7–11 even speaks of a gate like the rich man's). In fact, Isaiah 58:6–7 expressly directs the sharing of bread with the hungry, housing the homeless, and clothing the naked (cf. Matthew 25:35–36). Thus the Pharisees—like

prosperity preachers today—severely miss, to their peril, the point of material blessing. It is not earthly reward for human righteousness to be squandered in unrighteousness; rather, it is earthly seed to be generously sown in humility for heavenly reward. In Ryle's words, "Wealth is not a sign of God's favor; poverty is not a sign of God's displeasure" (*Luke*, 215).

26 And beside all this, between us and you there is a great gulf fixed: so that they which would pass from hence to you cannot; neither can they pass to us, that would come from thence.

Not only did Jesus state unequivocally that hell is real, but also that there is an unbridgeable, uncrossable chasm between—"No traffic moves between heaven and hell" (Philips, 221). The fate of the two men ends with an "utter and unchangeable finality" (Craddock, 192). Death visits ten out of ten people and strikes both the poor and the rich—for one, the trials end; for the other, the blessings end—for both, judgment begins. "Death is a great fact that everyone acknowledges but very few people take into account," states Ryle (*Luke*, 215), adding, "There are perhaps few more awful passages in the Bible than this" (216).

27 Then he said, I pray thee therefore, father, that thou wouldest send him to my father's house: 28 For I have five brethren; that he may testify unto them, lest they also come into this place of torment. 29 Abraham saith unto him, They have Moses and the prophets; let them hear them.

According to Craddock, the Pharisees "did not follow their own scripture, the 'Law and the Prophets' (v. 16); so they were no better than the rich man's brothers who 'have Moses and the Prophets' (v. 29)" (*Luke*, 421). The rich man found out the hard way just how far off was his and his family's interpretation of Scripture. Abraham informed him that the Scriptures would be sufficient to teach his brothers properly if only they would be willing to listen. Speaking through Abraham to the Pharisees via the parable, Jesus exposed both their flawed theology and their empty hearts.

30 And he said, Nay, father Abraham: but if one went unto them from the dead, they will repent. 31 And he said unto him, If they hear not Moses and the prophets, neither will they be persuaded, though one rose from the dead.

The rich man desperately believed that if his brothers only saw Lazarus alive, they would repent. Yet Jesus clearly stated that not even a dead person raised to life would persuade the hard-hearted (v. 31). Indeed, the Pharisees soon would personally witness this event twice, and their hearts not only would remain stone cold but would grow even more evil. Craddock writes: "The rejection of the risen Christ had its root in the misunderstanding of the true meaning of the Law and the Prophets" (*Luke*, 197). Everything Jesus did was true to Scripture and, most importantly, according to a proper understanding of it—about which He was intentional in teaching His disciples (24:25–27, 44–47).

Scholars speculate whether Jesus referred prophetically to the same Lazarus who would be the next person to be raised from the dead (John 11:43)—certainly, the name coincidence and the mention of resurrection in verse 31 make such an argument compelling. On the other hand, Lazarus was a common name in the day, and most scholars agree that Jesus was probably making reference to His own resurrection, which would forever seal the fate of the Pharisees and all like them— much like the fate of the heartless rich man.

This parable contains a strong warning to heed the Word when it brings conviction and to not harden your heart, because your decisions in life have consequences on the inevitable judgment day. Cast with a positive spin, per Stein, "Life is to be lived with eternity's values in view" (*Luke*, 421). Jesus made it clear that that the rich man's eternal demise came from his own decisions and hardness of heart—just as the Pharisees had consciously and selectively rejected the words of Moses and the prophets (Luke 16:29; cf. John 5:46). He may have prophesied about His own resurrection, knowing that not even that miracle of miracles would cause them to repent and change their ways.

A final note is that it was not the rich man's wealth that condemned him; it is not evil to be blessed with wealth. Rather, it was his lack of compassion that was his undoing. Like the rich fool mentioned earlier, he had no eternal wealth and lost his soul to the deceitfulness of temporal wealth (cf. Luke 12:21, 33, 16:11) and a crucially flawed misunderstanding of Scripture. In the New Testament, Jesus summarized the entire Old Testament in words that could not possibly be clearer—yet, most assuredly, many will continue to fatally miss the plain meaning: "Jesus said unto him, Thou shalt love the Lord thy God with all thy heart, and with all thy soul, and with all thy mind. This is the first and great commandment. And the second is like unto it, Thou shalt love thy neighbour as thyself. On these two commandments hang all the law and the prophets" (Matthew 22:37–40).

Sources:
Blue Letter Bible. BlueLetterBible.org. http://www.blueletterbible.org/ (accessed Tuesday, November 27, 2011).
Bock, Darrell L. *Luke*. The NIV Application Commentary. Grand Rapids, MI: Zondervan, 1996. 431–437.
Craddock, Fred B. *Luke: Interpretation: A Bible Commentary for Teaching and Preaching*. Louisville: John Knox Press, 1990. 192–198.
Hebrew Greek Key Word Study Bible (KJV) 2nd ed. Chattanooga, TN: AMG Publishers, 1991. 1755, 1758.

Jewish Encyclopedia. "Abraham's Bosom." http://www.jewishencyclopedia.com/articles/362-abraham-s-bosom (accessed August 23, 2012).

Liefeld, Walter L. "Luke." *The Expositor's Bible Commentary with the New International Version: Matthew, Mark, Luke, Vol. 8.* Edited by Frank E. Gaebelein. Grand Rapids, MI: Zondervan, 1984. 990–992.

Phillips, John. *Exploring the Gospel of Luke. The John Phillips Commentary Series.* Grand Rapids, MI: Kregel Publications, 2005. 219–222.

Ryle, J. C. *Luke. The Crossway Classic Commentaries.* Wheaton, IL: Crossway, 1997. 215–217.

Stein, Robert H. *Luke. The New American Commentary, Vol. 24.* Nashville: Holman Reference, 1992. 420 –427.

Unger, Merrill. *Unger's Bible Handbook.* Chicago: Moody Press, 1967. 531.

Unger, Merrill, and Robert F. Ramey. *Unger's Bible Dictionary.* Chicago: Moody Press, 1981. 13–14, 437, 467.

Say It Correctly

Lazarus. **LA**-za-rus, **LAZ**-rus.
Bosom. **BU**-zum.

Daily Bible Readings

MONDAY
An Open Hand to the Poor
(Deuteronomy 15:7–11)

TUESDAY
The Cry of the Poor and Afflicted
(Job 34:17–30)

WEDNESDAY
False Concern for the Poor
(John 12:1–8)

THURSDAY
I Will Give to the Poor
(Luke 19:1–10)

FRIDAY
Shrewdness and the Future
(Luke 16:1–9)

SATURDAY
Master of the Heart
(Luke 16:10–18)

SUNDAY
Comfort and Agony
(Luke 16:19–31)

Notes

_____

_____

_____

_____

Teaching Tips

Words You Should Know

A. Wrath (James 1:19) *orge* (Gk.)—Anger as a state of mind, indignation as an outburst of that state of mind with the purpose of revenge.

B. Meekness (v. 21) *prautes* (Gk.)—A condition of the mind and heart that demonstrates gentleness not in weakness but in power. A virtue of strength and character.

Teacher Preparation

Unifying Principle—Committed to Action. People often talk about what will help others, but they do not take action. What will help them take action? James says that those who are both hearers and doers of the Word practice justice.

A. Pray for clarity as you study the lesson.

B. Study the entire text review and More Light on the Text.

O—Open the Lesson

A. Open the lesson with prayer.

B. Introduce the lesson by asking students what they recall from a recent sermon and why it is important to be doers of the Word and not hearers only.

C. Review the Aim for Change and reflect on how this lesson relates to your own life.

P—Present the Scriptures

A. Ask for a volunteer to read the lesson.

B. Lead students in answering the Search the Scriptures, Discuss the Meaning, or any other questions that may arise from your study.

C. Incorporate corresponding Scriptures that further illuminate the text to add to the discussion.

E—Explore the Meaning

A. Discuss why it is important to study and apply the Scriptures for proper Christian living.

B. How can students, your class, and your church do more to take action and practice what is preached?

C. Discuss what true religion looks like in today's context.

N—Next Steps for Application

A. Read the Lesson in Our Society and Make It Happen sections aloud.

B. Encourage your students pray for opportunities to share Christ this week and target someone in their circle of influence to intercede in prayer.

Worship Guide

For the Superintendent or Teacher
Theme: Hear and Do the Word
Song: "O For a Faith
That Will Not Shrink"
Devotional Reading: 1 John 3:14–20

Hear and Do the Word

Bible Background • JAMES 1:19–27
Printed Text • JAMES 1:19–27 | Devotional Reading • 1 JOHN 3:14–20

——— Aim for Change ———

By the end of the lesson, we will: REVIEW the relationship that is expressed in the Scripture between hearing and doing the Word; EXPRESS our feelings about hearing and doing God's Word; and DEVELOP practical strategies for acting in accordance with what the Word says.

 In Focus

Alan professed to be a Christian and specifically sought to date women in the church. However, Alan's walk was very different from his talk. He always pursued a sexual relationship with women, and when he met one who obeyed the Word of God by living sexually pure, he would immediately end the relationship.

One day, Alan met Tracy, a beautiful young lady who loved the Lord. Alan really liked Tracy and told her that he could handle dating by her standards. After much prayer and conversation with others who knew Alan, Tracy decided that she would end the relationship because she did not discern that he was genuine in his intentions. Alan was devastated, and for the first time in his adult life, he turned to the Lord, sincerely asking for Jesus to come into his heart and change his life. Allowing some time to pass, rather than pursing a romantic relationship with Tracy, Alan sought to truly be her friend and brother in Christ.

Being a Christian requires a real commitment to godly living. In today's lesson, James calls attention to the need for believers to not just hear the Word of God but to do what it says as a proper reflection of God's presence and power in our lives.

FEB 2nd

——— Keep in Mind ———

"But be ye doers of the word, and not hearers only, deceiving your own selves" (James 1:22).

"But be ye doers of the word, and not hearers only, deceiving your own selves" (James 1:22).

Focal Verses

KJV **James 1:19** Wherefore, my beloved brethren, let every man be swift to hear, slow to speak, slow to wrath:

20 For the wrath of man worketh not the righteousness of God.

21 Wherefore lay apart all filthiness and superfluity of naughtiness, and receive with meekness the engrafted word, which is able to save your souls.

22 But be ye doers of the word, and not hearers only, deceiving your own selves.

23 For if any be a hearer of the word, and not a doer, he is like unto a man beholding his natural face in a glass:

24 For he beholdeth himself, and goeth his way, and straightway forgetteth what manner of man he was.

25 But whoso looketh into the perfect law of liberty, and continueth therein, he being not a forgetful hearer, but a doer of the work, this man shall be blessed in his deed.

26 If any man among you seem to be religious, and bridleth not his tongue, but deceiveth his own heart, this man's religion is vain.

27 Pure religion and undefiled before God and the Father is this, To visit the fatherless and widows in their affliction, and to keep himself unspotted from the world.

NLT **James 1:19** Understand this, my dear brothers and sisters: You must all be quick to listen, slow to speak, and slow to get angry.

20 Human anger does not produce the righteousness God desires.

21 So get rid of all the filth and evil in your lives, and humbly accept the word God has planted in your hearts, for it has the power to save your souls.

22 But don't just listen to God's word. You must do what it says. Otherwise, you are only fooling yourselves.

23 For if you listen to the word and don't obey, it is like glancing at your face in a mirror.

24 You see yourself, walk away, and forget what you look like.

25 But if you look carefully into the perfect law that sets you free, and if you do what it says and don't forget what you heard, then God will bless you for doing it.

26 If you claim to be religious but don't control your tongue, you are fooling yourself, and your religion is worthless.

27 Pure and genuine religion in the sight of God the Father means caring for orphans and widows in their distress and refusing to let the world corrupt you.

The People, Places, and Times

Dispersion. The descendants of the sons of Jacob were also known as "the twelve tribes" of Israel. This term was a symbolic reference to the Jews scattered abroad and living outside of Jerusalem. Jews were dispersed and settled in the civilized countries of the world at that time yet remained connected to the mother country.

Background

James, the half brother of Jesus, was among the early leaders of the church and was based in Jerusalem. Although the epistle of James is placed toward the end of the New Testament, it is actually the first letter of instruction written to the church—thus the first book written. The primary audience for this epistle was Christian Jews spread across the world due to persecution because of their faith in Christ.

The major theme of James' letter was to offer instruction for godly living in the midst of a self-indulgent world. This letter is viewed as a book of wisdom and instruction for Jewish believers. James appealed for his fellow believers to put outward actions with their inward faith. Scholars believe that James wrote this epistle in the mid 40s A.D. around the time of the council in Jerusalem. He was the first martyr of the church, executed in A.D. 62.

At-A-Glance

1. Behaving the Word (James 1:19–20)
2. Living by the Word (vv. 21–25)
3. Representing the Word (vv. 26–27)

In Depth

1. Behaving the Word (James 1:19–20)

In proverb fashion, James instructed believers to "be swift to hear, slow to speak, slow to wrath" (v. 19). This letter was written early in the church's life. The believers were facing persecution for their faith in Jesus Christ. As James offered up his instruction, he most likely used as basis from his own upbringing a combination of wisdom Scriptures such as Proverbs 10:19, 4:17, 19, and Ecclesiastes 5:2. Wisdom literature was captured by scribes and passed down orally as Jews met in the synagogues and talked in their homes. James took the practicality of the proverbs he learned and related them to his audience, who also would have heard such lessons as they were growing up. The purpose of reviving such language and instruction in the culture of his day was to usher in a new era, the reign of the kingdom of God, with wisdom from the old. He took

the time to remind them in the midst of persecution and rejection to be patient, seek God for His wisdom, trust God in the midst of trial, and act honorably to best represent their faith in Christ. Also, because his audience was scattered abroad and this letter was most likely written in Greek, James suspected that these believers might be influenced away from their Jewish roots. He wanted to remind them of those teachings that should influence their behavior, as well as incorporate Jesus' teachings on how to handle mistreatment and anger (Matthew 5:38–41, 47).

James reminded readers that anger does not produce the righteous living that God desires from His people (James 1:20). In the previous verses, he implored those who were lacking wisdom to ask God for it (vv. 5–6); Ecclesiastes 7:9 says, "Be not hasty in thy spirit to be angry: for anger resteth in the bosom of fools." It does not work in our favor or God's when we are unable to control our emotions. God is patient and longsuffering with us; therefore, we must do the same for others. Jesus Himself said that offense will come (Matthew 18:7), but it takes the wisdom of God to remain Spirit-led in the midst of adversity and trials. When we apply the principles James outlined to our behavior—being quick to hear, slow to speak, slow to wrath, remembering that anger does not produce what God desires—then we can make good decisions, keep our relationships intact, and glorify God.

2. Living by the Word (vv. 21–25)

James continued his discourse by providing additional instruction on managing one's emotions. He appealed to readers to put away worldly lifestyles and behaviors to welcome with humility and gladness the Word of God that had been planted inside them by the Holy Spirit. He emphasized that it is by receiving the truth as revealed through Jesus Christ, the living *logos*, that souls are saved. As the Word of God is planted into hearts, it brings about transformation into true kingdom living and God's ways of doing and being. Paul wrote in Romans 12:1–2 that Christians are not to be influenced or live by the patterns and dictates of the world's system but to be transformed by the renewing of our minds. Only then can we know what is the good, acceptable, and perfect will of God. Likewise, James, whose letter was a forerunner to Paul's writings, instructed believers to live above reproach. It was important to the early church leaders that Christians lived counter to their culture so as to best represent the power of God on earth. Key to successful reflection of God's love and grace is to bear the fruit of the Spirit (Galatians 5:22–23). To be doers of the word and not hearers only (v. 22) means to put the engrafted Word of God into practical application. Praise God for His mercy and grace when we fall short; therefore, we should be quick to own up to our mistakes, as John wrote in his epistle (1 John 1:9), and get back in alignment with God's Word. James said that if we are hearers of the Word and not doers, we only deceive ourselves; Paul warned, "Be not deceived; God is not mocked" (from Galatians 6:7).

James used an illustration in verses 23–24 to further drive home his point of how one can engage in self-deception about righteous living. When a person looks in a mirror, he or she sees an image for a moment, but when away from the mirror, the image is forgotten. The Word of God is our mirror to remind us that without Christ, our image is out of focus. Only when we look in the mirror of the Word and see the righteousness of Christ are we reminded what we are supposed to look like. The Word of God reminds us that we are in Christ but still growing into the knowledge of Him—which requires us to be diligent in study, fervent in prayer, and quick to obey. James went on to say that those who look into the perfect law of liberty, which is freedom in Christ, will live by the Word and be blessed.

3. Representing the Word (vv. 26–27)

James defined for his audience what real religion looks like by providing two contrasting images. He said that those who proclaim to be devout in their beliefs and actions but are unable to control their mouths only deceive themselves. The leaders in the synagogues were very good about practicing their piety to be seen by the masses as righteous. As keepers of the law, they lorded traditions and keeping of rituals over those of a lower social status. But, as Jesus pointed out in Luke 16:15, "Ye are they which justify yourselves before men; but God knoweth your hearts: for that which is highly esteemed among men is abomination in the sight of God." James emphasized that religion that does not reflect God's heart is in vain. In other words, it is not enough give outward expressions of devotion to God when one's lifestyle does not reflect one's words. Attending church every Sunday, paying tithes, and serving in ministry should be done out of loving obedience to God and in gratitude for salvation through Jesus Christ, but it is all for naught if there is no true transformation of the heart. Our works should express our love and reverence and not be mere duty. Quoting Isaiah, Jesus said of the Pharisees, "This people draweth nigh unto me with their mouth, and honoreth me with their lips; but their heart is far from me. But in vain they do worship me, teaching for doctrines the commandments of men" (Matthew 15:8–9; cf. Isaiah 29:13).

God does not want us to pay lip service to loving Him; He wants our love to be genuine and thus expressed in how we live and what we do. James further explained that "pure religion and undefiled before God and the Father is this, To visit the fatherless and widows in their affliction" (from James 1:27). God is always intentional in wanting His people to live selflessly by caring for the needs of others. Showing mercy to those who are marginalized is true religion—devotion to God—in practice. In the culture of the early church, those who had no one to care for them had no means to move out of their social station. The love of God is so great that He made provision for them through those called by His name. God always commanded His people to care for the least, and Jesus was intentional to bring His ministry to the poorest of the population.

James closed this part of the discourse by stressing that believers should keep themselves "unspotted" from the world, not allowing the world's way of living to be their marker. Only through active participation with the Holy Spirit can one live a life that is unspotted, unstained from the world. As John would later write in his epistle, "Love not the world, neither the things that are in the world. If any man love the world, the love of the Father is not in him" (1 John 2:15). As Christians, we are not to live according to the world's standards which run contrary to the Word of God; instead, we are to reflect the living Word, Jesus Christ, who came to do the will of Him who sent Him (John 5:30).

Search the Scriptures

1. How does James advise believers to behave (James 1:19)?

2. How does James recommend believers to use the Word of God (v. 22)?

3. What illustration does James use to describe how people can deceive themselves (vv. 23–24)?

Discuss the Meaning

1. Discuss what true religion looks like in today's context. How would James evaluate the body of Christ today? What would he say about how we treat widows and orphans?

2. How does one remain unspotted from the world in today's culture? Is it possible?

Lesson in Our Society

At one time or another we are all guilty of talking a good game when it comes to living according to godly principles, representing the best of Christ in our sphere of influence, being concerned about the world around us, and having great intentions on being more helpful to those in need. In today's lesson, James calls us to not just be hearers of the Word but also to carry it out in our everyday lives in word, thought, and deed. Oftentimes, we can get stuck because there is so much to be done; it can be an overwhelming task to change the world—let alone ourselves! When we embrace change in baby steps, taking one action at a time and doing it consistently, transformation takes place. Physics says that for every action there is a reaction; James teaches us to have a better reaction to the world around us.

Make It Happen

Really listen for God's instruction through the preached Word and in your time of personal devotion and Bible study. Take time to be quiet before the Lord and write down what He is speaking to you about through the Holy Spirit. As you listen, take steps to move in God's direction. Make a conscious effort to assess habits, behaviors, and actions that do not line up with the Word of God. Repent, and ask the Holy Spirit to help you act differently. Be patient with yourself. Trust that God has heard you and that His Word will change your heart if you yield to His way.

Follow the Spirit

What God wants me to do:

_____

_____

_____

_____

Remember Your Thoughts

Special insights I have learned:

_____

_____

_____

_____

More Light on the Text

James 1:19–27

19 Wherefore, my beloved brethren, let every man be swift to hear, slow to speak, slow to wrath: 20 For the wrath of man worketh not the righteousness of God.

James began by acknowledging that the ones to whom he was writing were also children of God the Father and righteous Judge. Therefore, there existed a bond of love between Him and them. It is from that sense of love that James admonished the believers (both Jews scattered around the known world and Gentiles who had put their faith in Christ) to remember, to "hear" (Gk. *akouo*, **a-KOO-o**, meaning to attend to, consider what is or has been said) the Word of God that had already been entrusted to them so that they would not fall under His judgment. James knew that a zealot-like fervor for rebellion was sweeping throughout the region, and many were being influenced by its call

for violence against Rome. He did not want those who followed Christ to be caught up in the hostility and anger in the same manner as those who did not belong to the risen Lord.

God's Word is powerful. It has the ability to change hearts and affect character, but it should not be shared hastily with others until its work in the hearer is evident. James also admonished believers to be slow to wrath (Gk. *orge*, **or-GAY**, meaning any violent emotion but especially anger), so that, by their lives and actions, they would demonstrate that a different message was at work in their hearts. James understood that man's anger inhibits the development of God's righteous work within him.

21 Wherefore lay apart all filthiness and superfluity of naughtiness, and receive with meekness the engrafted word, which is able to save your souls.

Evil flows from within us and expresses itself in our actions toward others. James instructed the believers to put off all "filthiness" (Gk. *rhuparia*, **hroo-par-EE-ah**, meaning to defile or dishonor) as though it were a dirty, useless garment. The work of righteousness would then begin to show itself and help to empower the believers to hold in check the "superfluity" (Gk. *perisseia*, pronounced **per-is-SI-ah,** meaning the wickedness remaining over in a Christian from his state prior to conversion) of "naughtiness" (Gk. *kakia*, **kak-EE-ah,** meaning malignity, malice, ill will, desire to injure). Such a state can only be accomplished in believers when they welcome the Word of God with true humility. God's Word then attaches itself to the very core fabric of our being and begins the work of transforming our evil nature into one pleasing to our righteous God and Savior.

260

22 But be ye doers of the word, and not hearers only, deceiving your own selves. 23 For if any be a hearer of the word, and not a doer, he is like unto a man beholding his natural face in a glass: 24 For he beholdeth himself, and goeth his way, and straightway forgetteth what manner of man he was.

James's admonition for believers, "be ye" (Gk. *ginomai*, **GHIN-om-ahee**, and carrying the implication to make sure that they are doers of the word), is to demonstrate to others how the Word of God is at work within them. They are to do this by the way they live before others and by making a habit of doing the Word. Living out the Word of God in this fashion also provides evidence for the believers that they are not pretending or playing at being righteous, thereby deluding themselves. By offering the analogy of one looking at his face in a glass, James wants believers to reflect on the fact that the best mirrors of the day were made out of Corinthian brass but the image reflected back was often distorted. It would have been easy then for the individual to look at the reflection of his "natural" (Gk. *genesis*, **GHEN-es-is,** meaning that of his origin) face, turn away, and forget what he looked like or what he had become.

25 But whoso looketh into the perfect law of liberty, and continueth therein, he being not a forgetful hearer, but a doer of the work, this man shall be blessed in his deed.

James contrasted the natural man with the spiritual man (see John 3:6). The Word of God, which produces the spiritual man, perfects the law and sets man free from his sinful nature or natural self. But in order for the Word of God to have its desired effect, believers need to "continueth" (Gk. *parameno*, **par-am-EN-o,** meaning to gaze or continue always near) in that Word. The act of gazing intently into the Word of God enables

believers to retain the image of what the Holy Spirit is producing within them.

Dunn and Rogerson (*Commentary on the Bible*, 1486) suggest that in drawing the contrast between the individual who views his image in a glass and then forgets what he looks like and the individual who lingers or gazes at his reflection in the glass, James was making the same type of analogy that Jesus made in His story of the two men who built houses—one on the sand and the other on rock (Matthew 7:24–27). The blessing for the believer is founded upon the actions that flow from the changed life that is the product of the Holy Spirit's work. This blessing manifests itself in the deeds of the believer that are a result of having built inwardly upon the solid ground of the Word of God.

26 If any man among you seem to be religious, and bridleth not his tongue, but deceiveth his own heart, this man's religion is vain.

For James, true religion is evidenced by the fruit that religion produces in the individual. A true believer, one who has permitted the Word of God to take root within, will not be like the zealots who made uncontrolled and impassioned speeches against Roman occupation. Instead, that person will "bridleth" (Gk. *chalingagogeo*, **khal-in-ag-ogue-EH-o,** meaning to hold in check or restrain) his tongue. The word that James used for "religious" (Gk. *threskos*, **THRACE-kos**) refers to giving scrupulous attention to the details of worship. This would include being careful of one's actions and one's speech when involved in religious activities. However, if one does not control his tongue when not engaged in religious activities, then that individual is only deceiving his own "heart" (Gk. *kardia*, **kar-DEE-ah,** meaning the center and seat of spiritual life). For that individual, religion is in "vain" (Gk. *mataios,* **MAT-ah-yos**), which means his religion is useless and of no purpose.

27 Pure religion and undefiled before God and the Father is this, To visit the fatherless and widows in their affliction, and to keep himself unspotted from the world.

James closed his counsel by explaining to believers that the type of religion that pleases God is both "pure" (Gk. *katharos,* **kath-ar-OS,** meaning free from corrupt desire, sin, and guilt) and "undefiled" (Gk. *amiantos,* **am-EE-an-tos,** meaning free from that by which the nature of a thing is deformed and debased, or its force and vigor impaired). The evidence that one possesses a religion that merits God's favor is found through the actions of visiting the fatherless and widows in times of distress, actions that reflect the work of the Holy Spirit on one's character. By encouraging believers to show concern for widows and the fatherless, James was reminding them that their heavenly Father identified Himself as the God of the fatherless and the widow (Psalm 68:5).

Sources:
Dunn, James D. G. and John W. Rogerson. *Commentary on the Bible.* Grand Rapids, MI: Wm. B. Eerdmans Publishing Company, 2003.
HarperCollins Study Bible (NRSV). New York: Harper Collins Publishers, 2006. 2052–2054.
Hebrew Greek Key Word Study Bible (KJV), 2nd ed. Chattanooga, TN: AMG Publishers, 1991. 1528, 1743, 1751.
Keener, Craig S. *The IVP Bible Background Commentary: New Testament.* Downers Grove, IL: IVP Academic, 1994.
Tasker, R. V. G. *The General Epistle of James: An Introduction and Commentary.* Grand Rapids, MI: Wm. B. Eerdmans Publishing Company, 1982.
Unger, Merrill. *Unger's Bible Handbook.* Chicago: Moody Press, 1967. 785–786.

Say It Correctly

Superfluity. su-per-**FLU**-it-ee.
Undefiled. un-**DE**-filed.

Daily Bible Readings

MONDAY
A People Who Will Not Listen
(Jeremiah 7:21–28)

TUESDAY
A Lamp to Lighten My Darkness
(2 Samuel 22:26–31)

WEDNESDAY
The Voice of the Living God
(Deuteronomy 5:22–27)

THURSDAY
Neither Add nor Take Away Anything
(Deuteronomy 4:1–10)

FRIDAY
Denying God by Actions
(Titus 1:10–16)

SATURDAY
Love in Truth and Action
(1 John 3:14–20)

SUNDAY
Hearers and Doers of the Word
(James 1:19–27)

Teaching Tips

Words You Should Know

A. Respect [of person] (James 2:1) *prosopolempsia (Gk.)*—Partiality.

B. Blaspheme (v. 7) *blaspemeo (Gk.)*—to speak reproachfully, rail at, revile, calumniate.

Teacher Preparation

Unifying Principle—Playing Favorites. People show partiality toward others for a variety of reasons. How can we avoid favoritism? James reminds Jesus' followers of the importance of justice practiced through taking care of the poor and loving their neighbors as themselves.

A. Pray for your students and that God will bring clarity to this lesson.

B. Study and meditate on the entire text.

C. Prepare to share examples of favoritisms and inadequate treatment of the poor.

O—Open the Lesson

A. Open with prayer, including the Aim for Change.

B. After prayer, introduce today's subject, the Aim for Change, and the Keep in Mind verse. Discuss.

C. Share your presentation.

D. Then ask, "How do we play favorites?"

E. Have a volunteer summarize the In Focus story. Discuss.

P—Present the Scriptures

A. Have volunteers read the Focal Verses.

B. Now use The People, Places, and Times; Background; Search the Scriptures; At-A-Glance outline; In Depth; and More Light on the Text to clarify the verses.

E—Explore the Meaning

A. To answer questions in the Discuss the Meaning, Lesson in Our Society, and Make It Happen sections, divide the class into groups. Assign one or two questions to each group, depending on the class size.

B. Have each group select a representative to report their responses to the rest of the class.

N—Next Steps for Application

A. Summarize the lesson.

B. Close with prayer and praise God for giving us relationships.

Worship Guide

For the Superintendent or Teacher
Theme: Treat Everyone Equally
Song: "Stand"
Devotional Reading: Romans 13:8–14

Treat Everyone Equally

Bible Background • JAMES 2:1–13
Printed Text • JAMES 2:1–13 | Devotional Reading • ROMANS 13:8–14

Aim for Change

By the end of the lesson, we will: REVIEW James's writings concerning partiality and ways to avoid it; EXPLORE the full meaning of the phrase, "Love your neighbor as yourself"; and INVESTIGATE ways we might discriminate against certain groups and find methods to instead demonstrate the love of God to those groups.

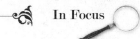 **In Focus**

Standing before the congregation in his freshly laundered white robe, Pastor Thomas "opened the doors" to the church for the call to salvation. It was communion Sunday, his favorite ritual of the church. Two men came down to the altar to give their lives to Jesus Christ. One was well dressed; the other man was unkempt. He obviously had not had a bath in weeks.

The custom Pastor Thomas had begun at the church was to have the congregation come and hug those who had just given their lives to Jesus Christ. With both men standing next to him and the unkempt man standing closest, Pastor Thomas knew he would have to hug him. Pastor Thomas's first thought was of his freshly laundered white robe. As he began to privately repent to Jesus, he turned to the man, welcomed him into the body of Christ, and fully embraced him, welcoming him to the church.

Partiality contradicts loving one's neighbor as oneself. The body of Christ should always genuinely embrace those not like us in order to show them God's love.

FEB
9th

Keep in Mind

"Hearken, my beloved brethren, Hath not God chosen the poor of this world rich in faith, and heirs of the kingdom which he hath promised to them that love him?" (James 2:5).

"Hearken, my beloved brethren, Hath not God chosen the poor of this world rich in faith, and heirs of the kingdom which he hath promised to them that love him?" (James 2:5).

Focal Verses

KJV **James 2:1** My brethren, have not the faith of our Lord Jesus Christ, the Lord of glory, with respect of persons.

2 For if there come unto you assembly a man with a gold ring, in goodly apparel, and there come in also a poor man in vile raiment;

3 and ye have respect to him that weareth the gay clothing, and say unto him, Sit thou here in a good place; and say to the poor, Stand thou there, or sit here under my footstool:

4 are ye not then partial in yourselves, and are become judges of evil thoughts?

5 Hearken, my beloved brethren, Hath not God chosen the poor of this world rich in faith, and heirs of the kingdom which he hath promised to them that love him?

6 But ye have despised the poor. Do not rich men oppress you, and draw you before the judgment seats?

7 Do not they blaspheme that worthy name by the which ye are called?

8 If ye fulfil the royal law according to the scripture, Thou shalt love thy neighbor as thyself, ye do well:

9 but if ye have respect to persons, ye commit sin, and are convinced of the law as transgressors.

10 For whosoever shall keep the whole law, and yet offend in one point, he is guilty of all.

11 For he that said, Do not commit adultery, said also, Do not kill. Now if thou commit no adultery, yet if thou kill, thou art become a transgressor of the law.

12 So speak ye, and so do, as they that shall be judged by the law of liberty.

13 For he shall have judgment without mercy, that hath shewed no mercy; and mercy rejoiceth against judgment.

NLT **James 2:1** My dear brothers and sisters, how can you claim to have faith in our glorious Lord Jesus Christ if you favor some people over others?

2 For example, suppose someone comes into your meeting dressed in fancy clothes and expensive jewelry, and another comes in who is poor and dressed in dirty clothes.

3 If you give special attention and a good seat to the rich person, but you say to the poor one, "You can stand over there, or else sit on the floor" –well,

4 doesn't this discrimination show that your judgments are guided by evil motives?

5 Listen to me, dear brothers and sisters. Hasn't God chosen the poor in this world to be rich in faith? Aren't they the ones who will inherit the Kingdom he promised to those who love him?

6 But you dishonor the poor! Isn't it the rich who oppress you and drag you into court?

7 Aren't they the ones who slander Jesus Christ, whose noble name you bear?

8 Yes indeed, it is good when you obey the royal law as found in the Scriptures: "Love your neighbor as yourself."

9 But if you favor some people over others, you are committing a sin. You are guilty of breaking the law.

10 For the person who keeps all of the laws except one is as guilty as a person who has broken all of God's laws.

11 For the same God who said, "You must not commit adultery," also said, "You must not murder." So if you murder someone but do not commit adultery, you have still broken the law.

12 So whatever you say or whatever you do, remember that you will be judged by the law that sets you free.

13 There will be no mercy for those who have not shown mercy to others. But if you have been merciful, God will be merciful when he judges you.

The People, Places, and Times

James. Half brother of Jesus Christ. Wrote a letter to believers whose behavior contradicted their faith in Jesus Christ.

Background

The epistle of James is a letter written by James to remind those who had become prosperous about their foundations in the faith. The prosperous believers were identified by James as having "faith in our glorious Lord Jesus Christ" (from James 2:1, NLT). James used some examples from daily life to remind them of the commitment of faith they had made to Jesus Christ. James used himself as an example by first identifying himself as "a servant of God and of the Lord Jesus Christ" (from 1:1). James chose two illustrations to demonstrate how partiality and ill treatment of the poor become stumbling blocks to believers and can contradict our faith in Jesus Christ.

At-A-Glance

1. Practicing Faith in Personal
Relationships (James 2:1–7)
2. Practicing Faith in Interpersonal
Relationships (vv. 8–13)

In Depth

1. Practicing Faith in Personal Relationships (James 2:1–7)

James, who has been identified as the half brother of Jesus Christ, wrote a letter of practicality to the believers. In this section, James addressed the moral behavior of believers toward the rich and the poor. James had just informed his readers what pure religion was all about. It was about serving those who are less fortunate—the orphans and the widows (James 1:27). Now it was time for him to look at some situations where professing Christians might not actually live out the faith in practice, and he begins here with the rich and the poor.

Some believers in this text were prosperous, even though the Bible does not specifically state their means of wealth. Using a story, James demonstrated how the believers were showing preference for the rich and how that contradicted the law of love. Throughout the Bible, Jesus teaches His followers to love their neighbors as themselves. By preferring the company of the rich and offering them special treatment, the believers were violating that command and were guilty of committing a sin against Jesus Christ.

These early Christians were rebuked for their behavior. Are we any different in our worship practices? Do we not reserve seats for special guests? If a homeless person walked into our church, we likely wouldn't sit him on the first row. James warns against esteeming one person over another, especially as it pertains to socioeconomic superiority. We would do well to heed his warning in our own respective worship settings.

2. Practicing Faith in Interpersonal Relationships (vv. 8–13)

James continued to show the believers their treatment of the poor also violated the law of love. "For the person who keeps all of the laws except one is as guilty as a person who has broken all of God's laws" (v. 10, NLT).

The kingdom James has just mentioned in verse 5 of this text now turns to the law of that kingdom in verse 8—that is, loving others as ourselves. Often called the Golden Rule, this is a prevailing theme in Jesus' ministry and in early Christian teaching. Our treatment of others is part of the way we live out our faith.

Here, James reminded the believers of Jesus' proclamation that the kingdom of heaven belongs to the poor. God will judge the believers on their treatment of the poor, especially if that treatment contradicts their faith statement. The believers were not showing love; instead, their behavior toward the poor was judgmental and would end in the believers themselves being judged by Jesus Christ: "So whatever you say or whatever you do, remember that you will be judged by the law that sets you free" (v. 12, NLT).

Search the Scriptures

1. How is faith practiced within our personal relationships (James 2:1–7)?

2. How is faith practiced within our interpersonal relationships (vv. 8–13)?

Discuss the Meaning

Favoritism is good treatment of people who are similar and ill treatment of those who are not. This behavior contradicts loving others as Jesus commanded. Loving ourselves and loving others is because God is love.

Lesson in Our Society

The word "love" is loosely used in our society. Real love is a reflection of God's love. The impact of love should be felt in healthy families, in acceptance of and compassion for others.

Love will conquer society's question of marriage. Love will decrease the murder rate. Love will stifle greed. Love will conquer racism and sexism. Love will conquer addictions. Love will end believers' segregated worship hour. Love will encourage doers of the Word. Love's motto will be, "Thy will be done" (Matthew 26:42).

Make It Happen

An active example of God's love is to initiate interfaith worship with a church of another ethnicity. Regularly commit to regular fellowship with one another. Encourage the study of God's Word together. Begin conversations on how the dynamics of the Bible sustain each group. Evangelize together to demonstrate that we are "all one in Christ Jesus" (Galatians 3:28).

Follow the Spirit

What God wants me to do:

_____

_____

_____

_____

Remember Your Thoughts

Special insights I have learned:

_____

_____

_____

_____

More Light on the Text

James 2:1–13

1 My brethren, have not the faith of our Lord Jesus Christ, the Lord of glory, with respect of persons.

The Palestine of James' day, like most societies of the time, showed special consideration to the wealthy by giving them special rank and status. Such favoritism was often shown in legal matters, but it even showed up in the Jewish synagogue, where people were often seated according to their rank in society. Here James continued his admonitions from chapter 1 by instructing believers that they are to emulate the Lord Jesus Christ with regards to how they treat and view other people. Like Paul's admonition to the Romans to "be not conformed to this world" (Romans 12:2), James was trying to help believers understand that they were no longer to have the world's attitudes. They, as followers of Christ, were not to show personal favoritism.

2 For if there come unto your assembly a man with a gold ring, in goodly apparel, and there come in also a poor man in vile raiment; 3 And ye have respect to him that weareth the gay clothing, and say unto him, Sit thou here in a good place; and say to the poor, Stand thou there, or sit here under my footstool: 4 Are ye not then partial in yourselves, and are become judges of evil thoughts?

James then gave an example of how believers might actually be showing favoritism toward people without even realizing it. By pointing at them "having respect" (Gk. *epiblepo*, **ep-ee-BLEP-o**) for the rich man over the poor man, James was drawing upon a common practice in the temples and courts of his society. In ancient Rome, the wearing of gold rings and fine robes spoke to membership in an elite class that always received favored treatment in Roman courts. Under Roman law, the poor could not bring accusations against people of higher class, and the penalties were often much harsher for the poor. Since the synagogue had become the place that served both as the house of prayer and as the community court, some of this same kind of favoritism was creeping in there as well. James counseled the believers against adopting such ways. The practice of showing such favoritism was strictly forbidden in Jewish law (cf. Leviticus 19:13), and it was contrary to the ideals established by the Lord Jesus Christ.

5 Hearken, my beloved brethren, Hath not God chosen the poor of this world rich in faith, and heirs of the kingdom which he hath promised to them that love him? 6 But ye have despised the poor. Do not rich men oppress you, and draw you before the judgment seats? 7 Do not they blaspheme that worthy name by the which ye are called?

There is a sense of bewilderment in James's voice as he asked believers how they could be guilty of despising the poor in the same fashion that the rich did. It was the rich who oppressed *them*. It was the rich who dragged *them* into court. James's hearers were well aware of the fact that the wealthy classes were most guilty of oppressing Christians by dragging them before the court authorities for punishment (see Acts 4:1–3 and 13:50 as examples). By "despising" (Gk. *atimato*, **at-im-AD-zo,** meaning to treat with contempt) the poor believers, they were showing by their actions that they had not really heard the Word of God. They were behaving just like the unsaved world around them, and that was unacceptable. God had chosen the "poor" (Gk. *ptochos*, **pto-KHOS,** meaning helpless, powerless to accomplish an end) to inherit His kingdom and to be rich in "faith" (Gk. *pistis*, **PIS-tis**, meaning a strong and welcome conviction or belief that Jesus is the Messiah). James then reminded his hearers that the godless people they were emulating were the same ones who "blaspheme" (Gk. *blasphemeo*, **blas-fay-MEH-o**, meaning to speak reproachfully of, rail at, or revile) the name of the very Lord to whom they had given themselves. James chose the phrase "worthy name" to refer to Christ because it was uncommon to use the name of God; other forms of expression were found. In choosing the phrase "worthy name" (Gk. *kalos*, **kal-OS**, meaning beautiful by reason of purity of heart and life, and hence praiseworthy), James reminded his listeners that they now belonged to Christ and should embrace his example with regard to how they lived and functioned in the world.

8 If ye fulfill the royal law according to the scripture, Thou shalt love thy neighbor as thyself, ye do well.

When Christ was asked to identify the greatest commandment, He told His listeners that they needed to love. First, they were to love God with all their hearts, souls, and minds, and then they were to love their neighbors in the same ways that they loved themselves (see Matthew 22:37–40). James called this the "royal" law because it was universally held in Jewish society that God's laws were higher than judicial laws; this law was a direct decree from God (see Leviticus 19:18) and was to be regarded as the highest, a law given by the King of kings Himself. The "neighbor" (Gk. *plesion*, **play-SEE-on**, meaning friend) to whom James was referring was anyone in need.

9 But if ye have respect to persons, ye commit sin, and are convinced of the law as transgressors.

The Jewish society of James' day viewed a neighbor only as a fellow Jew. But James was seeking to guide his listeners into an understanding that their view of what made one a neighbor had to be expanded. Anyone bearing the name of Christ and belonging to His kingdom was now to be included. Failure to follow the royal law would bring the "transgressor" (Gk. *parabates*, **par-ab-AT-ace**, meaning one who breaks God's law) under God's penalty.

10 For whosoever shall keep the whole law, and yet offend in one point, he is guilty of all. 11 For he that said, Do not commit adultery, said also, Do not kill. Now if thou commit no adultery, yet if thou kill, thou art become a transgressor of the law.

James drove home the point that the smallest transgression of God's law makes one guilty of violating the whole law. A chain with a broken link is just a broken chain or a piece of clothing that has a tear in it is just a damaged piece of clothing. James was trying to help his listeners understand that they were not to pick and choose when it comes to obeying God's commands. By choosing the imagery of someone who would not commit adultery but would kill, James might have had in mind the zealots who were so pious that they would never commit adultery but who also had no compunction about assassinating those they deemed worthy of death. God is not honored when we follow some of His commands and not others because we find some more acceptable than others.

12 So speak ye, and so do, as they that shall be judged by the law of liberty.

Finally, James cautioned his listeners to "speak" (Gk. *laleo*, **lal-EH-o**, meaning to use words in order to declare one's mind and disclose one's thoughts) and to "do" (Gk. *poieo*, **poy-EH-o**, meaning to carry out, to execute) as those who would be judged by the law of liberty, which was the standard that was set by the Lord Jesus Christ (see 1:25). James was again reminding believers that because they had taken Christ into themselves, the Spirit of Christ was at work transforming their nature into something that was pleasing and acceptable to a holy God. This transformation should show itself in their speech and actions.

13 For he shall have judgment without mercy, that hath shewed no mercy; and mercy rejoiceth against judgment.

Jewish teachers often defined God's character by two attributes: mercy and justice. Mercy (Gk. *eleos*, **EL-eh-os**) meant to show kindness or goodwill toward others, while justice (Gk. *krisis*, **KREE-sis**) meant condemnation. Both belong to the providence of God. James stated the truth that God's mercy will be shown to those who themselves show mercy, and God's condemnation will fall on anyone who does not show mercy. Believers who show kindness and goodwill toward others, then, need never fear being on the receiving end of God's judgment because Jesus has declared that the merciful will receive God's mercy (see Matthew 5:7).

Sources:

Draper, Charles W., Chad Brand, and Archie England, eds. *Holman Illustrated Bible Dictionary*. Grand Rapids, MI: Holman Reference, 2003.

Dunn, James D. G. and John W. Rogerson. *Commentary on the Bible*. Grand Rapids, MI: Wm. B. Eerdmans Publishing Company: 2003.

Keener, Craig S. *The IVP Bible Background Commentary: New Testament*. Downers Grove, IL: IVP Academic, 1994.

Myers, Allen C., John W. Simpson, Philip A. Frank, Timothy P. Jenney, and Ralph W. Vunderink, eds. *The Eerdmans Bible Dictionary*. Grand Rapids, MI: Wm. B. Eerdmans Publishing Company, 1996.

Radmacher, Earl D., Ronald B. Allen, and H. W. House, eds. *Nelson Study Bible* (NKJV). Nashville: Thomas Nelson Publishers, 2001.

Tasker, R. V. G. *The General Epistle of James: An Introduction and Commentary*. Grand Rapids, MI: Wm. B. Eerdmans Publishing Company, 1982.

Today's Parallel Bible (KJV/NIV/NASB/NLT). Grand Rapids, MI: Zondervan, 2000.

Say It Correctly

Raiment. **RAY**-ment.
Transgressors. trans-**GRES**-ors.

Daily Bible Readings

MONDAY
Judging Rightly and Impartially
(Deuteronomy 1:9–18)

TUESDAY
Judging on the Lord's Behalf
(2 Chronicles 19:1–7)

WEDNESDAY
Giving Justice to the Weak
(Psalm 82)

THURSDAY
Showing Partiality is Not Good
(Proverbs 28:18–22)

FRIDAY
God Shows No Partiality
(Acts 10:34–43)

SATURDAY
Put on the Lord Jesus Christ
(Romans 13:8–14)

SUNDAY
Faith and Favoritism
(James 2:1–13)

271

Teaching Tips

Words You Should Know

A. Faith (James 2:14) *pistis* (Gk.)—Belief and trust in God.

B. Works (v. 14) *ergon* (Gk.)—Behavior, actions. Works are character traits of faith.

Teacher Preparation

Unifying Principle—Live What You Believe. People often make great declarations of faith but show no evidence of them in their actions. What gives evidence of faith? James states that faith, which by itself is dead, becomes active when carried out through works of justice.

A. Pray for your students and that God will bring clarity to this lesson.

B. Study and meditate on the entire text.

C. Prepare to share examples of faith and the relationship between works and faith.

O—Open the Lesson

A. Open with prayer, including the Aim for Change.

B. After prayer, introduce today's subject, the Aim for Change, and the Keep in Mind verse. Discuss.

C. Share your presentation.

D. Ask, "Are you ready for new challenges?"

E. Share testimonies.

F. Have a volunteer summarize the In Focus story. Discuss.

P—Present the Scriptures

A. Have volunteers read the Focal Verses.

B. Now use The People, Places, and Times; Background; Search the Scriptures; At-A-Glance outline; In Depth; and More Light on the Text to clarify the verses.

E—Explore the Meaning

A. To answer questions in the Discuss the Meaning, Lesson in Our Society, and Make It Happen sections, divide the class into groups. Assign one or two questions to each group, depending on the class size.

B. Have each group select a representative to report their responses to the rest of the class.

N—Next Steps for Application

A. Summarize the lesson.

B. Close with prayer and praise God for preparing us.

Worship Guide

For the Superintendent or Teacher
Theme: Show Your Faith
by Your Works
Song: "Faith"
Devotional Reading: Luke 7:1–10

FEB
16th

272

Show Your Faith by Your Works

Bible Background • JAMES 2:14–26
Printed Text • JAMES 2:14–26 | Devotional Reading • LUKE 7:1–10

Aim for Change

By the end of the lesson, we will: REVIEW the connection James makes between faith and works; EXPRESS what it means to declare one's faith by performing good works; and CONSIDER a faith statement and identify how it may manifest itself through works.

In Focus

Everyone in Gloria's dorm spent their free time partying, with the main goal being to drink oneself into oblivion. All of her suitemates knew Gloria was a Christian because she continuously invited them to attend church with her.

One Saturday night, Gloria heard pounding at her door. When she answered, one of her suitemates was standing there sobbing hysterically. Gloria asked her what was wrong. Once inside her room, Gloria saw her bruises and torn clothing that was now only partially covering her body. She really wanted to ask her suitemate what had she gotten herself into, but instead, Gloria held her. Her suitemate spoke about the party at the fraternity and the drinking. Before she knew it, she had found herself in a dangerous, compromising position. As much as Gloria wanted to say she was lucky nothing worse had happened to her, she comforted her suitemate and told her about the love of Jesus Christ and how He never condemns us for the foolish decisions we make. That night, Gloria's suitemate gave her life to Jesus Christ.

Believers in Jesus Christ represent hope, love, and not condemnation. In today's lesson, we will learn about the relationship between faith and works.

Keep in Mind

"For as the body without the spirit is dead, so faith without works is dead also" (James 2:26).

"For as the body without the spirit is dead, so faith without works is dead also" (James 2:26).

Focal Verses

KJV **James 2:14** What doth it profit, my brethren, though a man say he hath faith, and have not works? can faith save him?

15 If a brother or sister be naked, and destitute of daily food,

16 And one of you say unto them, Depart in peace, be ye warmed and filled; notwithstanding ye give them not those things which are needful to the body; what doth it profit?

17 Even so faith, if it hath not works, is dead, being alone.

18 Yea, a man may say, Thou hast faith, and I have works: shew me thy faith without thy works, and I will shew thee my faith by my works.

19 Thou believest that there is one God; thou doest well: the devils also believe, and tremble.

20 But wilt thou know, O vain man, that faith without works is dead?

21 Was not Abraham our father justified by works, when he had offered Isaac his son upon the altar?

22 Seest thou how faith wrought with his works, and by works was faith made perfect?

23 And the scripture was fulfilled which saith, Abraham believed God, and it was imputed unto him for righteousness: and he was called the Friend of God.

24 Ye see then how that by works a man is justified, and not by faith only.

25 Likewise also was not Rahab the harlot justified by works, when she had received the messengers, and had sent them out another way?

26 For as the body without the spirit is dead, so faith without works is dead also.

NLT **James 2:14** What good is it, dear brothers and sisters, if you say you have faith but don't show it by your actions? Can that kind of faith save anyone?

15 Suppose you see a brother or sister who has no food or clothing,

16 and you say, "Good-bye and have a good day; stay warm and eat well"—but then you don't give that person any food or clothing. What good does that do?

17 So you see, faith by itself isn't enough. Unless it produces good deeds, it is dead and useless.

18 Now someone may argue, "Some people have faith; others have good deeds." But I say, "How can you show me your faith if you don't have good deeds? I will show you my faith by my good deeds."

19 You say you have faith, for you believe that there is one God. Good for you! Even the demons believe this, and they tremble in terror.

20 How foolish! Can't you see that faith without good deeds is useless?

21 Don't you remember that our ancestor Abraham was shown to be right with God by his actions when he offered his son Isaac on the altar?

22 You see, his faith and his actions worked together. His actions made his faith complete.

23 And so it happened just as the Scriptures say: "Abraham believed God, and God counted him as righteous because of his faith." He was even called the friend of God.

24 So you see, we are shown to be right with God by what we do, not by faith alone.

25 Rahab the prostitute is another example. She was shown to be right with God by her actions when she hid those messengers and sent them safely away by a different road.

26 Just as the body is dead without breath, so also faith is dead without good works.

People, Places, and Times.

Faith and Works. Faith is belief and trust in God and His Son, Jesus Christ. Works are character traits of faith. Character traits of faith are elements of unconditional submission to God and His Son, Jesus Christ: "You must clothe yourselves with tenderhearted mercy, kindness, humility, gentleness, and patience" (from Colossians 3:12, NLT). Works contain the love of God. God's love is displayed when we respond to the needs of others: "And whatever you do or say, do it as a representative of the Lord Jesus, giving thanks through him to God the Father" (v. 17, NLT).

Faith without Works. One still has a belief and trust in God and His Son, Jesus Christ. However, instead of one's actions displaying the love of God, the behavior reflects earthly, sinful things. "What good is it, dear brothers and sisters, if you say you have faith but don't show it by your actions? Can that kind of faith save anyone? Suppose you see a brother or sister who has no food or clothing, and you say, 'Good-bye and have a good day; stay warm and eat well'—but then you don't give that person any food or clothing. What good does that do?" (James 2:14–16, NLT).

Background

This is a continuation of James' letter to the believers on why the actual practice of one's faith in day-to-day living is more important than one's statement of faith. With the completion of teaching on the practice of faith, James shifted to the underlying principles of faith's lifestyle—the attitude of faith followed by actions of faith. James clearly states, "Faith by itself isn't enough. Unless it produces good deeds, it is dead and useless" (from James 2:17, NLT).

Believers' attitude of faith puts God's love in motion. God's love is shown when believers open their hearts to receive the poor and those who are not like them. "So you see, we are shown to be right with God by what we do, not by faith alone" (v. 24, NLT). James referred the believers to the Bible with two illustrations, one of Abraham and one of Rahab. Both believed *in* God, but their faith was made complete by their actions *for* God.

At-A-Glance

1. Usefulness of One's Faith
(James 2:14–17)
2. Faith Without Works is Dead
(vv. 18–19)
3. Acts of Faith (vv. 20–26)

In Depth

1. Usefulness of One's Faith
(James 2:14–17)

The authenticity of one's faith is determined by its usefulness. "Usefulness," as defined by the *American Heritage Dictionary*, is having a "beneficial use." A beneficial use for the believer is a statement of faith followed by actions of faith. The role model for the believer to emulate is Jesus Christ. "For even the Son of Man came not to be served but to serve others and to give his life as a ransom for many" (Matthew 20:28, NLT).

With service to others, believers represent God's love. While serving others, believers become aware of and develop compassion for those who are not like them. "Since God chose you to be the holy people he loves, you must clothe yourselves with tenderhearted mercy, kindness, humility, gentleness, and patience. . . . Above all, clothe yourselves with love, which binds us all together in perfect harmony" (Colossians 3:12, 14, NLT).

2. Faith Without Works is Dead (vv. 18–19)

Here, James creates a dialogue with someone who asserts that he has works without faith. On first glance, it would appear that the person in this passage holds the position James declares later in the text. James ultimately wants to get at the fact that faith is shown by the deeds of faith.

Here's the declarant's mistake in the text: He wants to assert the divisibility of one's faith and works. For James, the two can't be divided, which makes the following easier to digest: "Now someone may argue, 'Some people have faith; others have good deeds.' But I say, 'How can you show me your faith if you don't have good deeds? I will show you my faith by my good deeds'" (James 2:18, NLT).

3. Acts of Faith (vv. 20–26)

"I will show you my faith by my good deeds" (from James 2:18, NLT). James nows turns to the father of faith in the history of Israel—Abraham. He demonstrates how faith and works were both present in Abraham's life when he offfered his son as a sacrifice (see Genesis 22:1–18) and Rahab's life when she hid the two spies who were sent out by Joshua (Joshua 2). Abraham and Rahab both illustrate that one's faith is based on unconditional trust and obedience in God.

It isn't enough to hold right doctrine or truth, especially when it is not lived out practically. Abraham could have believed God was sovereign, but neglecting to obey when called to sacrifice his son would have told a different story. Instead, his actions supported his belief. Many Christians need to properly understand what James is getting at here. Living a life submitted to God isn't just about following rules and regulations; it's about living out your faith daily through your deeds. We can believe that the Christian life is about practicing patience toward others, but what happens when our patience is tested? It is through these tests that we move closer and closer to what James calls "perfect and complete, wanting nothing" (James 1:4).

Search the Scriptures

1. Does my faith convince others to desire a relationship with Jesus Christ (James 2:14)?

2. What is the difference between a statement of faith and an action of faith (v. 17)?

Discuss the Meaning

Faith in God is very important. God is pleased when believers worship Him. But is faith alone pleasing to God? How does one transition from a statement of faith to actions of faith (becoming a doer of God's Word)?

Lesson in Our Society

In today's society, with its increasing hostility toward Christians, believers need to do more than make a statement of faith. As followers of Jesus, believers need to put their statement of faith into action to display and represent God's love for all mankind. With an increasing disparity between the "haves and have nots," it is important now more than ever for believers to address the needs of the have nots and speak words of encouragement, hope, and love.

Make It Happen

The mindset of the believer must first be to serve. Some suggestions for serving are making regular visits with shut-ins, getting involved in a ministry that provides physical food and spiritual food, or perhaps creating a job training center (based on talent within one's congregation) that can address the needs of young people who lack their GED and need relevant job training.

Follow the Spirit

What God wants me to do:

_____

_____

_____

_____

Remember Your Thoughts

Special insights I have learned:

_____

_____

_____

_____

_____

More Light on the Text
James 2:14–26

Do Paul and James disagree on the subject of faith and works (cf. Ephesians 2:8–10; James 2:24)? Is Scripture inconsistent or, worse, contradictory? Are we justified by faith alone, or are works involved? Christians have wrestled with these questions ever since the first century. Martin writes, "These are among the most misunderstood passages in the New Testament" (*James, 1–2 Peter, Jude,* 28). Hopefully, today's lesson will help clarify and, perhaps, even resolve the issue for some.

14 What doth it profit, my brethren, though a man say he hath faith, and have not works? can faith save him?

It may be helpful to note that the literary construction of this part of James is one of a proposition supported by arguments and then summarized with conclusions. The proposition opens with a pair of rhetorical questions, the first of which basically says, "Suppose a man *says* he has faith." This is quite different from James wording it, "Suppose a man *has* faith." To actually have faith versus *saying* you have faith are two entirely different things. The second rhetorical question today would be worded, "This kind of faith—claimed faith without works—can't save him, can it?" Of course, the correct answer is no, as James will demonstrate.

15 If a brother or sister be naked, and destitute of daily food, 16 And one of you say unto them, Depart in peace, be ye warmed and filled; notwithstanding ye give them not those things which are needful to the body; what doth it profit? 17 Even so faith, if it hath not works, is dead, being alone.

The proposition continues with a hypothetical example, employing hyperbole with a "naked" brother or sister (Gk. *gymnos*, **gum-NOS**), indicating someone in dire straits or desperate need, reinforced with the supporting phrase "destitute of daily food." The common phrase "Depart in peace" means, in essence, "Go get what you need somewhere else, from someone else—but know that I care," or the popular "Go and be filled." Other similar responses might be "God helps those who help themselves," or the even colder "You got yourself into this mess, so you can just get yourself out of it." Such words come from a faith that is useless and dead (Gk. *nekros*, **ne-KROS**), which is the plain sense of the word; James was not pulling punches. "What good is a faith like that?" James asked. In other words, what good is a dead faith? Burdick writes, as if to respond, "Its seeming concern for the welfare of the poor is a worthless façade" (*Hebrews, James, 1, 2 Peter, 1, 2, 3 John, Jude, Revelation*, 183).

Salvation or justification, it can be said, is comprised of both hearing and doing; the same can be said of faith and works (cf. Matthew 7:24; 1 Thessalonians 1:3). The same is not true of the inverse, as if it were a formula, that hearing plus doing *results* in salvation, or that faith plus works *results* in the same (cf. Romans 10:9; James 1:23, 25, 2:14, 24). Just because something is true doesn't automatically mean the inverse is also true; that is, the fact that some roses are red does not also mean that red is only seen on some roses. Rather, genuine faith is a gift that comes from God (Ephesians 2:8) and works are a natural expression of such faith. Per Burdick, "Action is the proper fruit of living faith" (*Hebrews, James, 1, 2 Peter, 1, 2, 3 John, Jude, Revelation*, 182). Faith and works are two sides of the same coin.

For many, Paul and James have put faith and works at odds—and too often the argument has been framed as if one must make an either/or choice. Kistemaker writes, "To put the matter in different words, James explains the active side of faith and Paul the passive side" (*James and I–III John*, 87). In reality, they were talking about two types of faith—only one of which is alive, while the other is dead, incapable of saving anyone (cf. Galatians 5:6, 6:15; 1 Corinthians 7:19).

18 Yea, a man may say, Thou hast faith, and I have works: shew me thy faith without thy works, and I will shew thee my faith by my works. 19 Thou believest that there is one God; thou doest well: the devils also believe, **and tremble. 20 But wilt thou know, O vain man, that faith without works is dead?**

Having stated his proposition with rhetorical and hypothetical questions that beg an obvious answer, James next argued his case via a fictional debater. Person A has faith without deeds; Person B has faith with deeds. From Person A, James asked for evidence of the faith he claimed to possess, reminding him that even demons can make such claims. For Person B, the evidence of faith speaks for itself—the deeds are the evidence. In Burdick's words, "This epistle leaves no place for a religion that is mere mental acceptance of truth" (*Hebrews, James, 1, 2 Peter, 1, 2, 3 John, Jude, Revelation*, 182).

21 Was not Abraham our father justified by works, when he had offered Isaac his son upon the altar? 22 Seest thou how faith wrought with his works, and by works was faith made perfect? 23 And the scripture was fulfilled which saith, Abraham believed God, and it was imputed unto him for righteousness: and he was called the Friend of God.

It would be both normal and expected for any Jew talking about faith to mention Abraham. Both Paul (Romans 4:9) and James describe God calling Abraham righteous because of his faith. James here revisited the familiar details of Abraham's "works"—offering Isaac on the altar by faith—actively trusting God, even if it meant cooperating with God while He went against His own promise. Per Kistemaker, "Faith and action, then, are never separated. The one flows naturally from the other" (*James and I–III John*, 98).

James was saying that Abraham's obedient "work"—a tangible act of faith in putting Isaac on the altar and being willing to sacrifice even the son of promise at God's command—was a fulfillment of Scripture.

James referred to Genesis 15:6 (see also 2 Chronicles 20:7) when God reckoned as righteous Abraham's faith in the seemingly impossible covenant promise of countless generations born to an elderly couple. Abraham had faith, and God made a covenant with him because of it. Then Abraham proved his faith with the "work" of obeying God and being willing to sacrifice Isaac.

24 Ye see then how that by works a man is justified, and not by faith only.

Having made his proposition with questions, illustrations, and an example, and having presented an argument from the Old Testament, James made an early conclusion prior to making yet another argument from the Old Testament. It is this statement, which too many have pulled out of the context of his carefully constructed presentation, that has caused problems and confusion through the centuries. Such approaches to interpreting Scripture are simply poor hermeneutics. Earlier, James made a parallel argument, which also must remain within the context of his epistle, regarding being a hearer of the Word versus being a doer (1:22–25).

25 Likewise also was not Rahab the harlot justified by works, when she had received the messengers, and had sent them out another way?

James next appealed to an opposite type of character from the Old Testament for "Exhibit 2" of the argument part of his presentation. Some might feel as if they cannot relate to the head of the Jewish nation, the national shining star, Abraham. What about an example from the opposite side of society—would that be closer to home or at least more relatable? From Kistemaker, "Abraham demonstrated both faith and works, but so did Rahab—and she was a prostitute" (*James*

and I–III John, 99). This unlikely pair shared both differences and similarities. One was Hebrew, the other Gentile; one was called by God, the other originally destined for destruction; one was a man, the other a woman; one was the father of faith, the other a lowly prostitute; one went through a long-term process of interacting with God and proving his faith; the other only had hearsay to guide her quick thinking. For similarities, both were foreigners, both showed hospitality to strangers (Genesis 18:1–5; Joshua 2:1), and both became ancestors of Jesus (Matthew 1:2, 5). Rahab took her place in history next to Abraham because she had faith in God and acted on her faith—a simple but profound lesson that is completely transcultural for all believers.

26 For as the body without the spirit is dead, so faith without works is dead also.

James made his second parallel conclusion, creating a second passage that many after him will neatly clip from its clear context and use to make claims that do not square with either his complete argument or the whole counsel of God from both testaments. From Kistemaker, "What we have in this comparison [between Abraham and Rahab] is not a contrast of faith over against works. The point is that faith by itself is dead, much the same as the body without the spirit is dead" (*James and I–III John*, 101).

The concept of faith without works is so easy that even demons can do it. No lifestyle change is needed nor are sacrifices required. No compassion is necessary and no giving of time, treasure, or talent will be expected. Most Americans claim to be "Christian," but how many live Christian lives? Many attend church occasionally, or regularly, but what are they doing during the week? How much faith is being exercised for the millions who are "C. E." Christians—darkening the door-ways of churches only on Christmas and Easter? A modern adage holds that standing in a donut shop doesn't make one a donut, and walking into a garage doesn't turn some-one into a car. Perhaps Christians would do well to cease and desist from justifying their absence or lack of compassion and instead begin at once to incarnate the hands and feet and heart of Jesus in a cold, lonely, and desperate world. From Kistemaker, "Religion that is spiritual ministers to the need that is physical" (*James and I–III John*, 102).

Sources:
Blue Letter Bible. BlueLetterBible.org. http://www. blueletterbible.org/ (accessed Monday, December 17, 2011).
Burdick, Donald W. "James." *The Expositor's Bible Commentary with the New International Version: Hebrews, James, 1, 2 Peter, 1, 2, 3 John, Jude, Revelation, Vol. 12.* Edited by Frank E. Gaebelein. Grand Rapids, MI: Zondervan, 1981. 181–185.
Draper, Charles W., Chad Brand, and Archie England, eds. *Holman Illustrated Bible Dictionary.* Grand Rapids, MI: Holman Reference, 2003.
Kistemaker, Simon J. *James and I–III John. New Testament Commentary.* Grand Rapids, MI: Baker Publishing Group, 1986. 87–102.
Martin, R. A. and John H. Elliott. *James, 1–2 Peter, Jude. Augsburg Commentary on the New Testament.* Minneapolis: Fortress Press, 1982. 28–36.
Myers, Allen C., John W. Simpson, Philip A. Frank, Timothy P. Jenney, and Ralph W. Vunderink, eds. *The Eerdmans Bible Dictionary.* Grand Rapids, MI: Wm. B. Eerdmans Publishing Company, 1996.
Radmacher, Earl D., Ronald B. Allen, and H. W. House, eds. *Nelson Study Bible* (NKJV). Nashville: Thomas Nelson Publishers, 2001.
Today's Parallel Bible (KJV/NIV/NASB/NLT). Grand Rapids, MI: Zondervan, 2000.

Say It Correctly

Destitute. **DES**-te-toot.
Imputed. im-**PYUT**-ed.
Rahab. **RAY**-hab.

Daily Bible Readings

MONDAY
The Work of Faith with Power
(2 Thessalonians 1:3–12)

TUESDAY
Faith Distracted by Loving Money
(1 Timothy 6:6–12)

WEDNESDAY
Completing What's Lacking in Faith
(1 Thessalonians 3:4–13)

THURSDAY
An Example of Great Faith
(Luke 7:1–10)

FRIDAY
A Faith that Saves
(Luke 7:36–50)

SATURDAY
Living Your Life in Christ
(Colossians 2:1–7)

SUNDAY
Faith Demonstrated through Works
(James 2:14–26)

Teaching Tips

February 23
Bible Study Guide 13

Words You Should Know

A. We offend (James 3:2) *ptaio* (Gk.)—To cause someone to fall or stumble.

B. Boasteth great things (v. 5) *aucheo* (Gk.)—Haughty language that wounds.

Teacher Preparation

Unifying Principle—Bridle Your Tongue. Often people speak without thinking about the impact their words will have on others. How can Christians be sure that their words will benefit those who hear them? James speaks of justice within the context of controlling a person's tongue because both blessings and curses can come from the same mouth.

A. Pray and ask God to bring clarity to this lesson.

B. Read James 3 in its entirety.

C. If possible, use at least two modern translations to aid in your understanding.

O—Open the Lesson

A. Ask a volunteer to read the Keep in Mind verse.

B. Ask your students to give examples of an "untamed tongue." Get them started with "gossip." See how many examples they can come up with.

P—Present the Scriptures

A. Ask for two or three volunteers to read the Focal Verses.

B. Now use The People, Places, and Times; Background; Search the Scriptures; At-A-Glance outline; In Depth; and More Light on the Text to clarify the verses.

E—Explore the Meaning

A. Divide the students into small groups. Give each group an example of an "untamed tongue." Ask the groups to discuss ways they can intervene when they witness this type of speech.

B. When the class reassembles, have a representative from each group report their response to the entire class.

C. Connect this section to the Aim for Change and the Keep in Mind verse.

N—Next Steps for Application

A. Ask for a volunteer to summarize the lesson.

B. Ask for a volunteer to close the class in prayer.

Worship Guide

For the Superintendent or Teacher
Theme: Control Your Speech
Song: "I Speak Life"
Devotional Reading: Proverbs 18:2–13

FEB 23rd

Control Your Speech

Bible Background • JAMES 3:1–12
Printed Text • JAMES 3:1–12 | Devotional Reading • PROVERBS 18:2–13

—————————— Aim for Change ——————————

By the end of the lesson, we will: REVIEW James's teachings concerning how we speak to others; EXPRESS how it feels to be criticized and praised; and FIND ways to express praise and criticism in love despite the circumstances.

————————— In Focus —————————

Rashanna sat at the lunch table but didn't touch any of the meal in front of her. Her co-workers Kristine, C.J., and Shirley were recounting the BIG event in the accounting department. One of the other employees, Lauren, had been fired that morning. Lauren's boss had asked her to come into his office and closed the door. When Lauren finally came out of her supervisor's office, she was crying. She hastily gathered her personal belongings from her desk and left the building without speaking to anyone. Now at lunch, Kristine, C.J., and Shirley were sharing the office gossip about what really happened.

Rashanna looked at the nearby tables. Ordinarily the room was noisy, but today folks were huddled close together and speaking quietly. Kristine was speculating that Lauren's termination involved an office "romance." Rashanna was puzzled. Before today, Lauren had simply been a quiet and attractive co-worker. Now that something terrible had happened, she was the object of ugly office gossip and speculation.

In today's lesson, we will learn that engaging in gossip is never harmless. Such behavior is often cruel, and participation in it undermines our credibility as Christians.

————————— Keep in Mind —————————

"Out of the same mouth proceedeth blessing and cursing. My brethren, these things ought not so to be" (James 3:10).

"Out of the same mouth proceedeth blessing and cursing. My brethren, these things ought not so to be" (James 3:10).

Focal Verses

KJV **James 3:1** My brethren, be not many masters, knowing that we shall receive the greater condemnation.

2 For in many things we offend all. If any man offend not in word, the same is a perfect man, and able also to bridle the whole body.

3 Behold, we put bits in the horses' mouths, that they may obey us; and we turn about their whole body.

4 Behold also the ships, which though they be so great, and are driven of fierce winds, yet are they turned about with a very small helm, whithersoever the governor listeth.

5 Even so the tongue is a little member, and boasteth great things. Behold, how great a matter a little fire kindleth!

6 And the tongue is a fire, a world of iniquity: so is the tongue among our members, that it defileth the whole body, and setteth on fire the course of nature; and it is set on fire of hell.

7 For every kind of beasts, and of birds, and of serpents, and of things in the sea, is tamed, and hath been tamed of mankind:

8 But the tongue can no man tame; it is an unruly evil, full of deadly poison.

9 Therewith bless we God, even the Father; and therewith curse we men, which are made after the similitude of God.

10 Out of the same mouth proceedeth blessing and cursing. My brethren, these things ought not so to be.

11 Doth a fountain send forth at the same place sweet water and bitter?

12 Can the fig tree, my brethren, bear olive berries? either a vine, figs? so can no fountain both yield salt water and fresh.

NLT **James 3:1** Dear brothers and sisters, not many of you should become teachers in the church, for we who teach will be judged more strictly.

2 Indeed, we all make many mistakes. For if we could control our tongues, we would be perfect and could also control ourselves in every other way.

3 We can make a large horse go wherever we want by means of a small bit in its mouth.

4 And a small rudder makes a huge ship turn wherever the pilot chooses to go, even though the winds are strong.

5 In the same way, the tongue is a small thing that makes grand speeches. But a tiny spark can set a great forest on fire.

6 And the tongue is a flame of fire. It is a whole world of wickedness, corrupting your entire body. It can set your whole life on fire, for it is set on fire by hell itself.

7 People can tame all kinds of animals, birds, reptiles, and fish,

8 but no one can tame the tongue. It is restless and evil, full of deadly poison.

9 Sometimes it praises our Lord and Father, and sometimes it curses those who have been made in the image of God.

10 And so blessing and cursing come pouring out of the same mouth. Surely, my brothers and sisters, this is not right!

11 Does a spring of water bubble out with both fresh water and bitter water?

12 Does a fig tree produce olives, or a grapevine produce figs? No, and you can't draw fresh water from a salty spring.

The People, Places, and Times

The Book of James. Although there are four men named James mentioned in the New Testament, many scholars agree that the writer of the New Testament book is most probably the half-brother of Jesus (Matthew 13:55; Mark 6:3), also referred to as James the Just. Interestingly, James did not initially believe his brother's messianic claims (John 7:5), but it appears his conversion occurred following Jesus' Resurrection appearances (1 Corinthians 15:7). Once convinced, James fully embraced Christianity and became one of the leaders of the early church in Jerusalem.

James described his audience as "the twelve tribes which are scattered abroad" (James 1:1). From this we may reasonably conclude that what James teaches is applicable to all Christians. He was probably addressing the Jewish Christians who had fled persecution and were now living abroad in other countries. Acts 11:19 provides a description of how the Christians, who were persecuted in connection with Stephen, fled as far as Phoenicia, Cyprus, and Antioch. These exiled Christians quickly found themselves impoverished (James 5:1), victims of lawsuits (2:4–6), and oppressed by wealthy landlords (5:4). James encouraged the believers to continue to grow in their new faith, insisting that they not share their loyalty. They must either choose God or the world. James taught that their Christianity stemmed from a genuine religion, genuine faith, and genuine wisdom. He also emphasized that good actions will naturally flow from a Spirit-filled life.

Written in about A.D. 45, the book of James is probably the oldest book of the New Testament. According to the historian Josephus, James was martyred in approximately A.D. 62.

Background

During the time of this writing, religious leaders were no longer ignoring the new Christian church. Although they were still a part of Judaism, Christians were now being singled out, and the persecution of Christians had begun in earnest. Two other men named James mentioned in the New Testament (the apostle identified as the son of Zebedee and the brother of John, and the apostle identified as the son of Alphaeus) had been martyred. Similarly, Stephen had been stoned to death for his faith. In this increasingly hostile and dangerous atmosphere, it is not surprising that many Christians were abandoning the faith.

Internal strife was also taking place within the church. Christians were dealing with doctrinal arguments, false teachers, power struggles, gossip, and slander. The Christians were being encouraged to pursue self-fulfillment. During this time, many philosophers believed and taught the importance of knowledge for the sake of knowledge. Very little importance was placed on putting knowledge into practice. They mistakenly taught that the way to spiritual enlightenment was through knowledge. James wrote to combat this mind-set. Faith, not knowledge, is key. Our faith is rooted in our hearts; it is this faith that transforms us into "doers." Man, James insisted, must seek to attain the will of God. Only then can he bring about a change in his life and in the life of the church.

The remaining apostles, as they had been instructed to do, were off on missionary efforts. It was left to James, as leader of the Jerusalem church, to encourage the Christians and to provide much needed instruction to sustain them during this period of persecution. Like the excellent pastor he was, James taught the believers to keep their eyes on Christ, not their situation, and to continue to live lives that reflected Jesus Christ and His teachings.

At-A-Glance

1. Discipline of the Tongue
   (James 3:1–4)
2. Destructiveness of the Tongue
   (vv. 5–6)
3. Defiance of the Tongue (vv. 7–8)
4. Duplicity of the Tongue (vv. 9–12)

In Depth

1. Discipline of the Tongue (James 3:1–4)

In James 1 and 2, we are taught that Christians can be identified by the attitude they maintain during their suffering and by their obedience to God's will and His way. James next turned his attention to Christian speech. During James' time, rabbis and teachers abounded. All of them claimed to know the "truth." James understood that many of these men taught because of the esteem it brought them, not because they were called to teach. They viewed it as an occupation, not as a service to God. James was not discouraging qualified teachers. In fact, the Bible encourages the mature to teach (Hebrews 5:12–14). We must remember that not everyone is called to be a teacher. Sometimes "teachers" often misinform and mislead their listeners, who in turn misinform and mislead others (2 Peter 2:1–2). James warned that because teachers are responsible to their followers, they will be judged much more harshly for the errors they teach. The words we speak have a far deeper impact than we often realize. This is especially true in the body of the church. The spiritual health of the congregation is much better off when the leaders and teachers of the church, who use their speech to influence others, exercise spiritual maturity and godly control in this area. They must pray as David prayed, "I will take heed to my ways, that I sin not with my tongue" (from Psalm 39:1).

Next, James moved to the heart of the matter: the power of our words. What we say controls who we are. James went on to illustrate the power of the tongue and the awesome struggles to control this tiny member of our body, rather than have it control us. In chapter 1, James had warned that if our religion seems true but we are unable to control our speech, then our religion is in vain (v. 26). In the first illustration, James compared the tongue to a bit used to control a horse. In the second illustration, he compared the tongue to a ship's rudder. Both the bit and the rudder are small objects used to steer and control something far larger. They are seemingly unimportant, but their purpose is critical. Without a bit in the horse's mouth, the rider cannot control the massive animal beneath him and turn the horse when necessary. Without a rudder, the ship would float aimlessly.

In these illustrations, James was pointing out the importance of our words and the power they contain. Our ability to control our speech is an indication of our ability to control our desires, most especially our desire to please God. Whether truth or lie, a compliment or an insult, our words can have a profound impact on our lives and on the lives of others. This power is too much for us to handle. In the same way the horse needs the bit in his mouth and the rider to control him, and the ship needs the captain at the helm and rudder to keep the ship's course, we need Christ to control our speech.

2. Destructiveness of the Tongue (vv. 5–6)

James moved on to show the destructive potential of the tongue by describing how something as small as a "little fire" can rage out of control. This metaphor is especially meaningful to present-day believers who grew up with commercials stressing how a little match, when carelessly tossed away, could result in the destruction of an entire forest. Two very important ideas are contained here. First, our thoughtless and careless words are like a fire that consumes and destroys everything in its path (Proverbs 6:27). The hate-filled words of Adolf Hitler in Nazi Germany escalated and resulted in the murder of millions of people. Second, and equally important, just as the fire destroys as it spreads, the tongue affects all parts of our lives. An unrestrained tongue defiles our whole person.

Scripture tells us, "These six things doth the LORD hate: yea, seven are an abomination unto him: A proud look, a lying tongue, and hands that shed innocent blood, an heart that deviseth wicked imaginations, feet that be swift in running to mischief, a false witness that speaketh lies, and he that soweth discord among brethren" (Proverbs 6:16–19). Note that three of the seven involve what we say.

3. Defiance of the Tongue (vv. 7–8)

James now turned his attention to the difficulty in trying to tame the tongue. While all manner of birds, animals, reptiles, and creatures of the sea could be tamed, the human tongue is more difficult to control. This is affirmed when we read, "He that keepeth his mouth keepeth his life: but he that openeth wide his lips shall have destruction" (Proverbs 13:3). Examples of thoughtless, careless, and unkind speech include profanity, lying, gossiping, disclosing things that are told to us in confidence, and guessing and speculating about matters that we present to others as facts.

We are mistaken when we think that it is okay to say harsh or unkind things about others just because we preface it by saying things like, "Now, this is just between you and me." The greatest sign of integrity for Christians is not in what we say, but more often in what we do *not* say. Our refusal to speak negatively to or about others, even those who have hurt us, is a sign of spiritual maturity. Many churches and other organizations are adopting the following simple guideline for speaking to others: Before you speak to someone, ask yourself, "Is what I'm about to say true, necessary, and kind?" If the remark is not *all* three, then don't say it! This rule forces us to thoughtfully pause before we speak and then to put the feelings of others before our own. It insists that we recognize that others, like us, are children of the King. God loves them, and so must we.

4. Duplicity of the Tongue (vv. 9–12)

James pointed out the perverse ability of man to "bless" God and "curse" men with the same mouth. If we use our mouths for bad, it taints our ability to use them for good. How effective can a parent be if he screams at his children and calls them "stupid" one day then tries to encourage them the next? This duplicity was identified by Jesus when He said, "Either make the tree good, and his fruit good; or else make the tree corrupt, and his fruit corrupt: for the tree is known by his fruit. . . . for out of the abundance of the heart the mouth speaketh" (Matthew 12:33–34). Controlling our tongue is a constant and conscious effort. We have to be aware of it all day, every day.

What we say is a reflection of who we really are. Our words reveal our core beliefs and values. Sooner or later, what we really think and believe will come out in the things we say and do. Only by allowing the Spirit of the Lord to infill us can we control our tongues so we say things that build up, edify, strengthen, and encourage others. Without this infilling, our untamed tongues destroy, undermine, and cause immeasurable hurt. Christians are called to choose what we will say. We can choose to listen to the voice of God and do His will, or we can choose to put ourselves first and the care, concern, and love of others last.

Search the Scriptures

1. How does James tell us that teachers will be judged (James 3:1)?

2. In what ways does James say our lives are controlled by what we say (vv. 3–5)?

3. How does James describe the tongue (vv. 6–8)?

Discuss the Meaning

James used three metaphors for the tongue: a horse's bit, a ship's rudder, and fire. Why do you think he emphasizes the example of fire so much more than the other two?

Lessons in Our Society

What a wonderful gift speech is. Christians have the ability to exhort, coach, and build up other believers through our speech. Similarly, our words provide the vehicle to lovingly counsel the lost and to soothe and console the suffering and bereaved. This gift of speech is most perfectly employed when we speak words of truth and witness to others of God's saving plan. We must be very careful not to abuse this wonderful gift. Many Christians would never imagine causing someone physical harm. Yet this is exactly what we do when we say thoughtless, careless, and unkind things to or about others.

We verbally murder the character and reputations of others when our speech is unrestrained. Each day offers us a challenge to not only walk in the will and the way of our Lord, but also to speak in ways that glorify Him and all of His creation.

Make It Happen

It's never easy to listen to someone say unfair, incorrect, or mean-spirited things to us. Yet as Christians, we are never allowed to respond in kind. Our obligation is always to show a dying world that we are the children of a living God. We can only do this when our walk *and* our talk mirror those of our Savior. What comes out of our mouths must be loving. This means that our motivation to speak must be godly and intended to comfort, heal, and teach godly principles to others. Pray, and ask God to use your speech to as a vehicle for aid, comfort, and reconciliation.

Follow the Spirit

What God wants me to do:

_____

_____

_____

_____

Remember Your Thoughts

Special insights I have learned:

_____

_____

_____

_____

More Light on the Text

James 3:1–12

1 My brethren, be not many masters, knowing that we shall receive the greater condemnation.

The Greek word *didaskaloi* (**did-AS-kal-oy**), translated in the King James Version as "masters," means also "teachers." The teachers in this context were Jewish males, including the author, James, with expert training in the Scriptures. As such, they were authority figures held in high esteem. Some people wanted to become teachers to attain higher social status. However, those trained in the Scriptures were also charged with imparting to the community how to live according to God's will. Therefore, they were held to a higher standard. If they led the believers astray, they would be judged (Gk. *krima*, **KREE-mah**) more harshly than others.

2 For in many things we offend all. If any man offend not in word, the same is a perfect man, and able also to bridle the whole body.

The Greek word for "offend" is *ptaio* (**PTAH-yo**) and means to stumble. James acknowledged that as human beings we too often get tripped up and do or say things we don't intend to. But the person who has the ability to guard his speech achieves perfection in disciplining his entire body. The Greek word for "perfect" (*teleios*, **TEL-i-os**), when referring to human beings, does not mean without sin. Rather, it symbolizes the attainment of a virtue in a moral sense. For example, we often hear that "patience is a virtue." Anyone who has worked with children knows that they can test one's patience. However, the person who is able to deal with children without complaining or losing control of his temper is considered perfect in this sense.

A "bridle" (Gk. *chalinagogeo*, **khal-in-ag-OGUE-EH-o**) is literally a harness that fits over a horse's head. It has a bit that fits into the horse's mouth and reins that guide the animal in the direction it should go. Figuratively, to "bridle" one's speech means to show restraint.

3 Behold, we put bits in the horses' mouths, that they may obey us; and we turn about their whole body.

Horses were a common mode of transportation in the first century. Roman soldiers also used them in battles. People who ride horses use a bridle to control or guide the horse's movement. The horse responds to the tugging on the bit (Gk. *chalinos*, **khal-ee-NOS**) in its mouth by turning its whole body in the direction its rider wants it to go. Likewise, when we demonstrate the ability to control our speech, we display the discipline to govern other members of our body and guide them in the direction they should go.

4 Behold also the ships, which though they be so great, and are driven of fierce winds, yet are they turned about with a very small helm, whithersoever the governor listeth.

James furthered his argument on the importance of selecting teachers who have mastered the ability to guard their speech (and therefore their whole bodies) by using the example of a ship at sea being steered by something as small as a rudder. The Greek verb *metago* (**met-AG-o**) means to guide, to turn about, or to change direction. Similar to the horse, a large ship, which needs the power of strong winds in order to move it, is able to be steered this way or that by such a small thing as the rudder (Gk. *pedalion*, **pay-DAL-ee-on**).

5 Even so the tongue is a little member, and boasteth great things. Behold, how great a matter a little fire kindleth!

James finally got to the heart of his sermon: that something as small as the tongue (Gk. *glossa*, **GLOCE-sah**) can wield great power for good or evil. The forest fire metaphor is a good example of how a single spark can start a fire that can quickly burn out of control. If the right person is in control of speech, then he or she can guide others in the right way to go. Likewise, a single word by a person with no self-control can do damage that can take months or even years to repair.

6 And the tongue is a fire, a world of iniquity: so is the tongue among our members, that it defileth the whole body, and setteth on fire the course of nature; and it is set on fire of hell.

James returned again to the metaphor of the tongue represented by the teacher within the community whose speech could bring good or evil to bear. This verse is obscure and many scholars have found it difficult to interpret. The world of first-century Rome was far removed from our contemporary society, and many of the metaphors and images used in ancient writings such as the Bible are unfamiliar to today's readers.

The Greek word for "iniquity," also called unrighteousness, is *adikia* (**ad-ee-KEE-ah**) and means a deed violating law and justice, as in an unfair judge. A biased judge who hands down an unjust ruling negatively impacts the individual, his or her family, and the whole community. Or the tongue, with its potential for sin, represents a smaller version of the potential for all of humanity to sin.

7 For every kind of beasts, and of birds, and of serpents, and of things in the sea, is tamed, and hath been tamed of mankind.

James likened the tongue to a living being. However, in contrast to all the creatures of the land and sea which human beings are capable of restraining (Gk. *damazo*, **dam-ad-ZO**), humans appear to be incapable of taming the tongue.

8 But the tongue can no man tame; it is an unruly evil, full of deadly poison.

We might believe that James exaggerated the power of the tongue by comparing it to fires raging out of control. However, he took very seriously the power of someone in the authority position of a teacher to do great harm if he does not have the ability to control his speech. James referred to the tongue as "an unruly evil" (Gk. *kakon*, **kak-ON**). In the Greco-Roman context of the first century, the word "evil" meant to be foul or rotten down to the bone. It was an inward decay, somewhat like a cancer developing and spreading through one's body. Anyone who has ever been the victim of slander knows how lies left unchallenged can destroy careers and lives.

9 Therewith bless we God, even the Father; and therewith curse we men, which are made after the similitude of God.

It is ironic that the very same tongue we use to bless God is also used to curse others. The Greek word for "bless," *eulogon* (**YOO-log-on**), is from the same root as the word "eulogy" and means good words. To bless someone is to speak well of them or to praise them. In contrast, "to curse" (Gk. *kataraomai*, **kat-ar-AH-om-ahee**) someone means to doom or call down evil upon him or her. As creatures made in the image and likeness (Gk. *homoiosis*, **hom-OY-o-sis**) of God, we should have only good words for one another.

10 Out of the same mouth proceedeth blessing and cursing. My brethren, these things ought not so to be.

The Greek word for "mouth," *stoma* (**STOM-a**), refers both to the opening on the edge of the lips through which food enters, and speech, especially eloquent speech. It also means the point on a sword. Metaphorically, the tongue can be a sharp sword cutting down people with insults and imprecations. Or it can offer words of praise that lift up people. The notion that both virtuous and vile speech can come from the same source was anathema to James.

11 Doth a fountain send forth at the same place sweet water and bitter?

Fresh or living (Gk. *glukus*, **GLOO-koos**, literally "sweet") water is from a new or previously unused source. Bitter or brackish (Gk. *pikros*, **peek-ROS**) water is fresh water mixed with salt water, such as in river estuaries like Lake Pontchartrain in Louisiana. Living water is uncontaminated and refreshing; you wouldn't want to drink from brackish water that has not been treated to remove the salty taste. Those of us who grew up in urban areas have probably never encountered brackish water. However, those from rural areas likely learned as children not to drink such water. James rhetorically asked whether fresh and brackish water can come from the same source, knowing that his audience, who had come in contact with both types of water, would answer no.

12 Can the fig tree, my brethren, bear olive berries? either a vine, figs? so can no fountain both yield salt water and fresh.

Being an effective preacher requires delivering a message using illustrations your audience is familiar with. James did a commendable job demonstrating his point using metaphors, images, and illustrations from the world around his audience, such as the modes of travel to the methods of husbandry. Anyone who has ever cultivated or produced crops for food knows that a fig tree cannot yield olives any more than a grapevine can produce figs. This would be an aberration of nature. The fig tree can only produce figs and the olive tree only olives, as is their nature. Likewise, salt (Gk. *halykos*, **hal-yeek-OS**) water cannot yield sweet (fresh) water. James was making the point that a person with an evil disposition is not likely to be virtuous, as it is not in them to do so.

Sources:

Bauer, Walter, William F. Arndt, F. Wilbur Gingrich, and Frederick W. Danker. *A Greek-English Lexicon of the New Testament and Other Early Christian Literature, Second Edition.* Chicago: University of Chicago Press, 1979.

Bible Study Tools. www.BibleStudyTools.com. Bakers Evangelical Dictionary. "James." http://www.biblestudytools.com/dictionaries/bakers-evangelical-dictionary/James-theology (accessed October 1, 2012).

Davids, Peter H. *The Epistle of James. The New International Greek Testament Commentary.* Grand Rapids, MI: Wm. B. Eerdmans Publishing Company, 1982.

Got Questions Ministries. "Book of James." http://www.gotquestions.org/Book-of-James.html (accessed October 2, 2012).

HarperCollins Study Bible (NRSV). New York: Harper Collins Publishers, 2006. 2052–2058.

Say It Correctly

Similitude. si-**MI**-li-tood, -tyood.
Josephus. joe-**SEE**-fus.

Daily Bible Readings

MONDAY
Lying and Flattering Lips
(Psalm 12)

TUESDAY
Words that Intimidate
(1 Samuel 17:1–11)

WEDNESDAY
Words that Lead to Repentance
(2 Chronicles 15:1–12)

THURSDAY
Words that Lead to Mourning
(Nehemiah 1)

FRIDAY
Words that Lead to Worship
(Genesis 24:42–52)

SATURDAY
Words Guided by Wisdom
(Proverbs 18:2–13)

SUNDAY
Taming the Tongue
(James 3:1–12)

Notes

_____

_____

_____

_____

Jesus' Fulfillment of Scripture

The purpose of the spring quarter is to explore connections between Jesus and the Hebrew Scriptures. Each of the three units approaches this relationship from a different perspective.

UNIT 1 • JESUS AND THE DAVIDIC COVENANT
This is a four-lesson study. Lesson 1 studies the narrative of God's promise of a Davidic line that would sit on the throne forever. Lesson 2 looks at Matthew's Gospel as an interpretation of how God fulfills this promise in the birth of Christ. In Lesson 3, Peter's message on the day of Pentecost gives witness to Christ as God's promised Messiah. In Lesson 4, the scene takes place in the heavenly court of John's vision, where Christ is seated; the Lamb of Judah is on the eternal throne.

Lesson 1: March 2, 2014
An Eternal Kingdom
2 Samuel 7:4–16a
People value permanence and seek to build things that will outlast themselves. When David wanted to build a house for God, God promised to build a house for David—a dynasty, a tradition of royalty.

Lesson 2: March 9, 2014
Son of David
Psalm 89:35–37; Isaiah 9:6–7; Matthew 1:18–21

People have expectations and hopes regarding their descendants. What assurance do people have that their line of descendants will continue? As God promised David and as Isaiah prophesied, Matthew reports that the birth of Jesus fulfills the traditional expectation that a descendant of David would come as the Savior.

Lesson 3: March 16, 2014
Peter's Report
Psalm 110:1–4; Acts 2:22–24, 29–32

People need to understand the legacy they have received in order to perceive any value in it. Peter interpreted the coming of Jesus, which the followers witnessed, as His fulfillment of the prophecy for a savior descended from the line of David.

Lesson 4: March 23, 2014
Worthy is the Lamb
Revelation 5:6–13

When long-hoped-for dreams come about, people express their joy in celebration. The result of the fulfillment of the salvific tradition is the extravagant praise and worship of God by the multitude of the redeemed.

UNIT 2 • WHAT THE PROPHETS FORETOLD

This is a five-lesson unit. The unit opens with the story of Jesus' triumphal entry into Jerusalem followed by a lesson of His cleansing of the temple in conjunction with passages from Isaiah and Jeremiah. The next lesson moves to the scene after Jesus' trial in which the soldiers mock and beat Him. On Easter Sunday, the lesson celebrates the Resurrection and explores the significance of the "third day" as a Hebrew Scripture reference to deliverance. The final lesson of Unit II looks at the Emmaus Road story and the ways in which Jesus' life, death, and resurrection would fulfill Hebrew Scripture promises.

Lesson 5: March 30, 2014
Triumphant and Victorious
Zechariah 9:9; Matthew 21:1–11

People of every generation and from every country have traditional rituals for welcoming dignitaries or heads of state. The crowds who welcomed Jesus into Jerusalem spread out their cloaks on the road as a special gesture to recognize Him as the Messiah.

Lesson 6: April 6, 2014
Jesus Cleanses the Temple
Isaiah 56:6–7; Jeremiah 7:9–11; Mark 11:15–19

When an activity becomes rote, the original helpful intent and purpose may be lost and replaced by new, harmful ones. Jesus' angry action in the Temple called attention to the ways in which the priests and worshipers had lost sight of the tradition of God's dwelling place being a house of prayer for all peoples.

Lesson 7: April 13, 2014
A Messianic Priest-King
Jeremiah 23:5–6; Zechariah 6:9–14; John 19:1–5

People tend to lash out at perceived threats to established power. The perception of Jesus as a king, who would exercise political rule and power, seemingly made Him a threat to the existing Roman and Jewish powers.

Lesson 8: April 20, 2014
The Third Day
Hosea 6:1–3; Luke 24:1–12

Sometimes people do not recognize the accomplishment of long-held goals because they are achieved differently than what was expected. Jesus' forecast of His Resurrection on the third day alluded to the Hebrew Scripture theme (tradition) of deliverance in defiance of the horror of the Crucifixion.

Lesson 9: April 27, 2014
From Suffering to Glory
Isaiah 53:5–8; Luke 24:25–27, 44–47

Confusion, disappointment, and sorrow often result from not understanding fully what has happened. After Jesus explained His life, death, and resurrection within the context of Hebrew Scriptures, the two travelers on the road to Emmaus understood better what had occurred.

UNIT 3 • JESUS' USE OF SCRIPTURE

This four-lesson unit examines how Jesus utilized Scripture. Lesson 10 looks at Jesus' use of Scripture in confronting temptation. Lesson 11 helps the students understand Jesus' mission through His interpretation of the Law and the Prophets, and it offers His life as a pattern for Christian discipleship. Lesson 12 deals with Jesus' respect for tradition and also His warnings about its misuse. Lesson 13 is a study of the Great Commandment in its Hebrew Scripture context as well as its continued importance for Christian lives today.

Lesson 10: May 4, 2014
Jesus Resists Temptation
Deuteronomy 6:13–16; Matthew 4:4–11

In a world that offers people countless ways to satisfy their lusts and appetites, discipline is required to maintain high ethical and moral standards. Jesus' thorough knowledge of Scripture gave Him strength to withstand difficult temptations.

Lesson 11: May 11, 2014
Jesus' Mission on Earth
Luke 4:14–21

Many people wrestle with issues in finding, choosing, or accepting a job. Jesus' identity and mission were informed by the prophetic tradition of the Hebrew Scriptures.

Lesson 12: May 18, 2014
Jesus' Teaching on the Law
Matthew 15:1–11, 15-20

Traditions are powerful guides for determining actions and behavior. While Jesus was a firm believer in tradition, He warned against a misuse of tradition that makes "void the word of God" (Matthew 15:6).

Lesson 13: May 25, 2014
The Greatest Commandment
Leviticus 19:18; Deuteronomy 6:4–9; Mark 12:28–34

In societies that traditionally value individual achievement, it is assumed that people will look out for their best interests before those of others. When Jesus quoted Deuteronomy 6:4–5, He reminded the disputants that tradition had already determined which commandment was greatest. In addition, He said Christians are not far from the kingdom of God when the highest priority in their lives is to love God and neighbor.

Worship is a Heart Matter

"These people draweth nigh unto me with their mouth, and honoreth me with their lips; but their heart is far from me."

(Matthew 15:8 KJV)

The Purpose of Christian Education

by Rev. Eugene A. Blair

Liberty and liberation are important ideals for Africans and African Americans. The historical denial of this basic human right has become a rallying cry for people of color everywhere and in every generation. The Old and New Testaments speak of physical, moral, and spiritual freedom for those who believe. The Bible also speaks to us and says that our God understands the plight of the oppressed. The Christian church has a role to play in our understanding of God's plan of salvation and liberation for us as His people.

What is the purpose of Christian education?

Christian education in the African American church has three tasks. First, Christian education must enable people and groups to be active participants in their own spiritual journey. In order for our relationship with God to grow and deepen, we must be taught how to proclaim, celebrate, and live the Good News. The second task of Christian education is to teach us how to care for one another. We must be taught what it means to understand and experience the caring and healing spirit of Jesus Christ. We do this by developing within Christian communities supportive, open, and trusting relationships with each other in which we are free to love and be loved.

The third task of Christian education is our subject at hand: Christian liberation. The purpose of Christian education is to empower people and groups to respond to the call of Jesus Christ to be free. It is a teaching task, a call to become aware of the forces that oppress or dehumanize God's people. It is a call to show people and groups how to respond and take charge of their lives and situations and to develop the resources and skills necessary for their own liberation.

Liberty and the Liberator

For the purposes of Christian education, liberty and liberation have a great deal more to do with life than freedom from human physical bondage or slavery. Liberty is human freedom of the mind, heart, and soul. Liberation is the process people and groups engage in to secure that liberty. Christian education for Christian liberation fundamentally has to do with the purpose and quality of character and the personal and social life of individuals and groups. God's plan for each of our lives involves inner qualities as well as changes in outward behaviors. The liberation Christ gives to those who believe in Him and call upon His name is for both here and now and in the world to come.

Who frees us to live our lives in such a fashion?

It is none other than Jesus of Nazareth. Jesus came to show us that liberation has to do with our relationship with God and each other. He came to earth in human form, yet remained fully God and holy. He took upon Himself the sins of the world. He empowered us with His Spirit to live full, abundant, and fruitful lives under His name. We are no longer captives to sin, death, or human lies that enslave our souls and spirits. Christ came to "set at liberty those who are oppressed" (Luke 4:18, ESV).

Where does one begin such a life of liberty?

Such a transition from the old life to the new is made at Christian baptism. All Christian rituals of baptism in some way proclaim that baptism is an outward and visible sign of God's inward and invisible grace, working its power in the life of the baptized. We go down into the water as Christ went down into death. We are raised to new life as Christ was raised on the third day. We go forth to live a new faith, as ones who know and believe the Easter story: the tomb is empty, the grave is vacated, Christ is not there, He is risen! We are free!

Living a Liberated Life

In order to challenge people and groups to live this life of liberation, Christian education must be about the task of building character. Character can be defined as the depth of an individual's moral excellence and personal power. Character is an inner human quality that all of us possess. The question is, what kind of character? The goal of Christian education is to build up each person's character so they may live the liberated life we have been describing. The African American church must build character in five distinct ways.

Living Fruitful Lives

First, we must help people hear the call to fruitful living. Too many people measure the fruitfulness of their lives by their activities or possessions. But this is a false picture when we think about Christian maturity and liberation. Who you are is more important than what you do or what you own. Galatians 5:22–23 lists the fruit of the Spirit as love, joy, peace, patience, kindness, generosity, faithfulness, gentleness, and self-control. Bearing this fruit in one's life is the evidence that one walks in the Spirit. Those who have been liberated by the Spirit of Jesus Christ will walk like Christ. These fruits are the result of a godly attitude that reveals one's character. This is contrasted to the works of the flesh, which are deadly and dangerous to the moral and spiritual life of the believer.

Living Genuine Christian Love

The second task of character building has to do with genuine Christian love. Christian education must help believers unlearn wrong ideas about love. People have many different ideas and thoughts about love. Love is often confused with sex and sex with commitment. The radio fills the airways with songs about the hope, sorrow, joy, and tragedy of love. But usually all of these thoughts, ideas, and songs fall short of the deep, rich, and abiding qualities of love we learn about in Scripture (1 Corinthians 13). If Christian education is to liberate believers, it must liberate them from the woeful and lacking ideas about love today.

The Purity of Human Life

The third task of character building for Christian education is to help people and groups regain a sense of reverence for the purity of life and live by moral standards. Christians are free, but not from the moral teachings of the Scriptures. We must take a stand for God when and where Scripture requires such a stand. Many issues confront us as we seek to be God's light in the world—abortion, homosexuality, drugs, premarital sex, divorce and remarriage, and violence. While the world may seek freedom from all moral responsibility, Christian education must teach that our freedom in Christ allows us to live by biblical values. Jesus said, "Blessed are the pure in heart: for they shall see God" (Matthew 5:8).

Living With Integrity

One paraphrase of Psalm 101:3 is "I will walk with integrity of heart in my own house." Integrity is another quality of the Christian's character. To have integrity is to be morally whole and spiritually complete. It means to have unimpaired Christian vision and sound biblical judgment. To have integrity as a quality of one's heart means to be honest and sincere and to live before others in a blameless way. If people and groups are to be liberated for joyful Christian living, they must be taught how to nurture this quality of character called integrity. The task of Christian education is to show us how to be liberated from the ways of the world so we might live by the ways of our heart with integrity.

Living With Genuine Joy

Finally, Christian education has to teach people about joy. Christians are not immune to the human experience of suffering. Sickness, sorrow, death, and disappointment are a part of our everyday experience. But these events and realities do not have to define our experience. Life does not have the last word for us. God does. We read in James 1:2 to "consider it pure joy whenever you face trials of many kinds" (NIV). Christian joy is a hallmark of our faith. Christian joy is a character trait, a quality for living. This does not mean that we are always happy. But it does mean that we know who we are as God's children. Nothing can take away the joy of our relationship with God through Jesus Christ. In this we put our trust and hope. This world can toss us all about, but we are grounded in the joy of the Lord, our strength.

In conclusion, the church must view Christian education through the lenses of our times. We must be creative and open to new ways of doing ministry and reaching people. We must be aware that this generation is like no other. Cultural changes, technology, communication, and ways of relating as family, groups, and races all call for new ways to take the Word of God to the streets of our communities. In order for Christian education to be meaningful and liberating for African Americans, it must help people change their lives for the better. We must make the Church relevant not only for when we cross over to the other side, but we must make it relevant for the here and now—today.

Spirituals as Instruments of Survival for African Americans

by Jennifer King

More than 200 years after their creation, African American religious folk songs, or spirituals as they came to be known, remain with us and are still routinely performed in small churches as well as large concert settings. In traditional African American church settings, these songs continue to be a regular part of the musical repertoire. The impact of their lyrics on individuals varies widely. Many people find the jubilant and rejoicing spirit of many of the spirituals uplifting: "Every time I feel the spirit moving in my heart, I will pray!" Still others, like Frederick Douglass, who was himself a slave, found listening to spirituals too agonizing to bear. He wrote that these songs "breathed the prayer and complaint of souls boiling over with the bitterest anguish. Every tone was a testimony against slavery, and a prayer to God for deliverance from chains." Indeed, it is only the most bitter of anguish that inspires lyrics such as "Lord, how come me here?/I wish I never was born."

Perhaps the answer to why spirituals are received so differently lies in the paradox of their content. The spirituals are not "simple" religious songs; attempts to read them as such lead to misinterpretations of the invaluable way they assisted in the psychological survival of the enslaved Blacks who created them. Through the spirituals, the slaves created for themselves an expression of their religious and cultural beliefs that commented not

only on their particular circumstance, but their worldview as well. Specifically, the spirituals not only paid homage to a God who acknowledged their humanity and suffering but reaffirmed the sense of humanity, identity, and community that the institution of slavery labored to destroy.

The savagery of that "peculiar institution" that separated both close family members and kinsmen created a tremendous loss within the slave community. The slaves lost their homeland, families, language, and culture. This overwhelming loss gave way to intense desperation that was alleviated through the musical interpretation of certain biblical texts. In the only arena that was relatively free of White control—the performance of song—the enslaved Blacks created in the spirituals an expression for their religious and cultural beliefs that commented on their particular worldview.

These religious folk songs were most likely hymns with portions of sermons and prayers given during the worship. The spirituals certainly have as their topics God, heaven, Jesus, and salvation. We must remember, however, that the God of the slaves was a divine champion of the victims of injustice. This God of their fashioning allowed them, at least in song, to transcend the narrow limits of slavery.

While the dancing and drumming the slaves brought with them from Africa was often forbidden, White owners generally encouraged singing. The Whites did not foresee that when slaves began adopting specific biblical narratives as song lyrics, the Blacks would use them as vehicles to unify themselves by addressing one another in song, using lyrics that countered the racist assertions of their subhumanness.

The transmission of biblical information from the Whites to the slaves was a slow process. First, legal prohibitions prevented teaching slaves to read. The second problem was that the slave owners were divided on the question of religious training for their slaves. On one hand, their thought was that perhaps Christianizing the slaves would make them more obedient. After all, many of the Old Testament Scriptures proved that slavery was a recognized institution, and some of the New Testament Scriptures taught that slaves ought to "obey" their masters.

On the other hand, there was the growing concern that many of the biblical accounts could actually encourage rebellion and insurrection. This debate was ended largely through the evangelizing efforts of the Baptist, Methodist, and Presbyterian denominations throughout the South. Now that the slaves were able at last to attend gatherings, listening to Scripture readings, preaching, and singing alleviated the typical isolation among slaves. The religious gatherings provided a relief from the strict monitoring of movement from plantation to plantation and the monitoring of what slaves said to one another. Slave owners did not foresee that a people who had been so isolated from one another would seize the opportunity to use music as a medium for communicating between themselves.

The narrative accounts from the Old Testament, with their vast selection of heroes and adventures, and the easily identifiable themes of loss and displacement, suffering, and redemption, were especially appealing to the slaves. In these Scriptures, the slaves encountered a spiritual force with a proven track record of defending and liberating the underdog.

The attributes of this new God of the Bible were similar in nature and power to the African high gods worshiped by the slaves in their homeland. Because the slaves were already familiar with the concept of deity, their transfer of allegiance to the Christian God should not be surprising.

In addition to imbuing God with extraordinary presence, the slaves often indicated that their relationship with the Creator is less that of magnanimous guardian and benefactor, which many Whites perceived Him to be, and more of friend and confidante. The lyrics of one spiritual declares, "When I get to heaven, gonna be at ease/Me and my God gonna do as we please... Gonna chatter with the Father/argue with the Son/Tell 'em bout the world I just come from." This familiarity and intimacy with God allowed the slaves to view themselves very differently than their owners did. The singers' insistence that they were close enough to God to address Him so informally is an implicit argument that the singers were claiming for themselves a far more personal and privileged role with God than that held by Whites. Such songs also argued that the Blacks were not simply disposable property. Rather, such lyrics allowed them to view and identify themselves as God's "chosen."

As the slaves held themselves to be the elect of the Most High God, their songs insisted that God could be counted on to fight on their behalf and execute judgment upon those who merited destruction. Old Testament texts offered the slaves a continual affirmation that God is on the side of the oppressed. It is not surprising then that the African slaves identified so strongly with the oppression of the Children of Israel— the ultimate victims of loss. In the face of the harshness of chattel slavery endured by the Blacks, it stood to reason that the all-powerful God, who had so deftly delivered Israel out of bondage, could be counted on to deliver them from their captivity. A large body of spirituals reflects this affinity with the historical burdens suffered by the Israelites and other Old Testament heroes. The comparison between themselves and Old Testament narratives and heroes is constant in the spirituals: "Didn't my Lord deliver Daniel, and why not every man?"

These songs not only offered a hope of eventual salvation, they presented varying possibilities about the role of the vanquished sufferer while he waited for his deliverance. The Old Testament presented some enslaved people of God who took a proactive role in their deliverance, as in the case of Moses' demand that "Pharaoh let my people go." Still other songs insisted on patience and declared that salvation lay in resisting the temptation to fight and waiting for God to act on one's behalf. These songs urged a more passive approach to freedom. They called on the believer to be "laying down" one's burdens and "studying war no more."

The portrayals of Jesus in spirituals offered many of these same unique Black perspectives of God. The closeness and familiarity the spirituals claimed with God is also shared with His Son. In the lyrics "Nobody knows da trouble I sees, Nobody knows but Jesus," there was an insistence that only a people of true value and worth could be worthy of such special kinship with Jesus. Similarly, singing "Talk about a child that do love Jesus, here is one" was further evidence of heightened self-esteem.

Often in the songs, Jesus was presented as a New Testament Moses, a deliverer to whom the slaves could cry out for physical and spiritual deliverance (see Matthew 10:34): "King Jesus is my Captain/He is my all in all/He gives me grace to conquer/And take me home to rest." The repetition of the pronoun "my" intensifies the personalization of the relationship between the singer and Jesus.

It is not at all surprising that the slaves could so easily wholly identify with Jesus. The biblical account of His life closely mirrored the life of the enslaved Black. Jesus was innocent of any crimes, yet He was hated and persecuted by the authorities (who bore a curious resemblance to the slave holders in their religious hypocrisy).

The slaves sang of Jesus, not only because He could save their souls, but because He could reward and deliver them. The spirituals are replete with references to rewards for the longsuffering faithfulness of the believers. These rewards ran the gamut from the simple—long white robes, wings, harps, and golden slippers to trod upon streets of gold—to the spectacular: low swinging chariots accompanied by bands of angels, drinking from wells that never run dry, and perpetual rest in a kingdom that offered "no sorrow there."

The "heaven" of the spirituals expressed the slave's vision of a new home where simple pleasures would abound, relief from their suffering would be enjoyed, and where they would be recognized as worthy and welcome residents.

In addition to the rewards He offered, the Jesus contained in the lyrics of the spirituals held the key to their removal from the harsh conditions of slavery.

The creation and singing of spirituals allowed the slaves to recreate for themselves a new home. The creators of this music—those enslaved Blacks working in the cotton, rice, and tobacco fields of Georgia, the Carolinas, and Louisiana—had no way of knowing how to get back home, yet they knew the place and condition in which they found themselves was not home. The spirituals filled in the gaps of the tremendous losses these people suffered as slaves. In the spirituals, the African slaves literally sang their humanity into being. Through the spirituals, they created for themselves a God who loved, valued, and privileged them in a place that held them in such low esteem. The spirituals provided a mechanism by which the slaves, borrowing from the Bible, recreated a history for themselves that cast them as chosen sufferers, rather than captured chattel.

Just like the pattern of their singing, the spirituals contained a call and response. The enslaved Africans made a call for an understanding or an explanation of their horrific and seemingly hopeless situation: "Lord, How Come Me Here?" It was through their construction of this musical art form that they created for themselves a self-defining response which countermanded the master's insistence on their inferiority. In the skillfully poetic hands of the slaves, biblical texts took on a life of their own. The themes of loss, displacement, divine intervention, and deliverance were reinterpreted to allow for a universal adoption, better suited for the condition in which the slaves found themselves. These songs remain with us as proof of the slave's ability to react creatively, constructively, and responsively to the brutal realities of their new life.

Sources

Douglass, Frederick. *Narrative of the Life of Frederick Douglass. The Classic Slave Narratives.* New York: Penguin 1987.

Nelson, Angel. "The Spiritual." Christian History (10), 1991. p. 30.

Traditional African American Spiritual, "Every Time I Feel the Spirit."

Traditional African American Spiritual, "Lord, How Come Me Here?"

Traditional African American Spiritual, "Hold the Wind."

Traditional African American Spiritual, "Didn't My Lord Deliver Daniel?"

Traditional African American Spiritual, "Talk About a Child that Do Love Jesus."

Traditional African American Spiritual, "I'm Walking With Jesus."

Jennifer King holds a B.A. with honors in English and has served as Superintendent of Sunday School for Bay Area Christian Connection.

BARBARA JORDAN

(1936—1996)

(Attorney, congresswoman, educator)

The year was 1974, during the impeachment hearings of President Richard M. Nixon. The nation was electrified as it watched the televised speech of congresswoman Barbara Jordan. With powerful oratory, she delivered an impassioned, eloquent speech about the Watergate scandal, which had shamed Nixon and his presidency. A member of the Judiciary Committee, Jordan set a high moral tone during the impeachment proceedings with her drive to be fair.

Barbara Jordan was born February 21, 1936, in Houston, Texas. Her father, Benjamin Jordan, was a Baptist minister and warehouse laborer. Her mother, Arlyne, was a speaker at church functions and impressed upon Barbara the importance of skillful rhetoric. Her father gave Barbara and her two sisters a desire for academic success and discipline. Her grandfather, John, taught her how to enunciate words carefully.

While attending Phillis Wheatley High School, she received awards for debate and oratory. It was in high school that she began to feel racially segregated schools were immoral and developed a strong desire to do something about it. At a career-day event, she heard attorney Edith Sampson (who later became a judge) speak. It was then Jordan decided to become a lawyer. Before this, she didn't know a woman could even become a lawyer.

While attending Texas Southern University, a segregated university for Black Texans, Jordan established herself as a skilled debater. Graduating magna cum laude in 1956, she enrolled at Boston University Law School. She was happy to study in an integrated environment. She graduated in 1959 with a law degree, the only woman in a class of 128. Using her parents' living room, she set up a law practice while also working as assistant to a local county judge.

Jordan began to realize that politics could offer an opportunity to work for change, and began campaigning for John F. Kennedy and Lyndon B. Johnson for president and vice-president, respectively. She quickly became known for her oratory.

In 1962, Jordan ran for the Texas House of Representatives. She thought being Black and female were side issues which people would ignore. However, failing to attract White voters who made up the majority, she lost the election. In 1964 she tried and again lost. But in 1966, she won a seat in the State Senate, becoming the first African American woman in the Texas legislature.

She soon earned the respect of conservative and progressive legislators alike by being open-minded and dealing with issues fairly. In 1968 she was re-elected to a four-year term. During her six years as a state senator, Jordan was so skillful that half of the bills she submitted were enacted into law, including the Texas Fair Employment Practices Commission, and an expansion of minimum wage provisions covering domestics, farm laborers, and laundry workers. Her State Senate colleagues voted her outstanding freshman senator in response to her hard work and success.

In 1972, Jordan was elected to the U.S. House of Representatives, becoming the first African American congresswoman from the South. She served three terms in the U.S. Congress, forging alliances with conservatives and progressives, pushing through legislation that expanded voting rights to non-English-speaking residents and prohibited discrimination in industries that received public funding.

One of her most visible achievements was serving on the Judiciary Committee during the impeachment of President Richard Nixon in 1974.

At the Democratic Convention of 1976, Jordan delivered an impassioned keynote address and made an exciting impression upon everyone.

Some of Barbara Jordan's honors include: an autobiography, a woman of the year award, the Eleanor Roosevelt Humanities Award, and the Spingarn Medal. She was also chair of the U.S. Commission on Immigration Reform, holder of some 29 honorary doctorates, and a member of many corporate boards.

Teaching Tips

Words You Should Know

A. Tabernacle (2 Samuel 7:6) *mishkan* (Heb.)—A place to dwell.

B. Sheepcote (v. 8) *naveh* (Heb.)—The outdoor shelter for shepherds and/or their flocks.

Teacher Preparation

Unifying Principle—A Change of Plans. People value permanence and seek to build things that will outlast themselves. How do people seek to build a legacy? When David wanted to build a house for God, God promised to build a house for David—a dynasty, a tradition of royalty.

A. Pray and ask God to help you present this lesson to your students with clarity.

B. If possible, use at least two modern translations to aid in your understanding.

C. Read the Bible Background and Daily Bible Readings.

O—Open the Lesson

A. Open with prayer.

B. Ask the class to read the Keep in Mind verse in unison.

C. Ask a volunteer to read the In Focus story.

D. Have the students discuss plans they may have made for their lives and the events that forced them to change or abandon those plans.

P—Present the Scriptures

A. Ask for two or three volunteers to read the Focal Verses.

B. Now use The People, Places, and Times; Background; Search the Scriptures; At-A-Glance outline; In Depth; and More Light on the Text to clarify the verses.

E—Explore the Meaning

A. Ask for a volunteer to read The People, Places, and Times and then discuss.

B. Read and discuss the Background section.

N—Next Steps for Application

A. Ask for a volunteer to summarize the lesson.

B. Ask for a volunteer to close the class in prayer.

Worship Guide

For the Superintendent or Teacher
Theme: An Eternal Kingdom
Song: "The Lord's Prayer"
Devotional Reading: Psalm 98

An Eternal Kingdom

Bible Background • 2 SAMUEL 7:4–16a
Printed Text • 2 SAMUEL 7:4–16a | Devotional Reading• PSALM 98

———————— Aim for Change ————————

By the end of the lesson, we will: RECOGNIZE the significance of making God a major part of planning an inheritance for our descendants; FEEL the need to keep trusting God even when He denies our requests; and DECIDE to seek God's heart and to be in His presence.

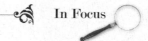

———————— In Focus ————————

Kristine and Shirley had been roommates in college. Later, when Shirley had her first job interview with an accounting firm, Kristine had taken her shopping; she had also styled Shirley's hair and rehearsed with her for the interview. When Kristine's mother passed away, it was Shirley who notified their friends and organized the repast.

When Kristine told Shirley that she was engaged, Shirley put a deposit on a room in the local community center so she could host an engagement party. She, and all of their friends, had assumed that Shirley would be the maid of honor at her best friend's wedding.

But this afternoon, when she and seven other ladies had met at Kristine's apartment to discuss wedding plans, Kristine announced that her sister, Valerie, would be her maid of honor. Shirley was devastated. As soon as the meeting ended, she grabbed her purse and hurried to her car. She didn't want the other women to see her crying.

Was Kristine fair in choosing her sister over her friend to be maid of honor? God's plans take precedence over our plans. In today's lesson, we will see that the plans God has for us are far greater than anything we can imagine.

———————— Keep in Mind ————————

"And thine house and thy kingdom shall be established for ever before thee" (from 2 Samuel 7:16).

"And thine house and thy kingdom shall be established for ever before thee"
(from 2 Samuel 7:16).

Focal Verses

KJV **2 Samuel 7:4** And it came to pass that night, that the word of the LORD came unto Nathan, saying,

5 Go and tell my servant David, Thus saith the LORD, Shalt thou build me an house for me to dwell in?

6 Whereas I have not dwelt in any house since the time that I brought up the children of Israel out of Egypt, even to this day, but have walked in a tent and in a tabernacle.

7 In all the places wherein I have walked with all the children of Israel spake I a word with any of the tribes of Israel, whom I commanded to feed my people Israel, saying, Why build ye not me an house of cedar?

8 Now therefore so shalt thou say unto my servant David, Thus saith the LORD of hosts, I took thee from the sheepcote, from following the sheep, to be ruler over my people, over Israel:

9 And I was with thee whithersoever thou wentest, and have cut off all thine enemies out of thy sight, and have made thee a great name, like unto the name of the great men that are in the earth.

10 Moreover I will appoint a place for my people Israel, and will plant them, that they may dwell in a place of their own, and move no more; neither shall the children of wickedness afflict them any more, as beforetime,

11 And as since the time that I commanded judges to be over my people Israel, and have caused thee to rest from all thine enemies. Also the LORD telleth thee that he will make thee an house.

12 And when thy days be fulfilled, and thou shalt sleep with thy fathers, I will set up thy seed after thee, which shall proceed out of thy bowels, and I will establish his kingdom.

NLT **2 Samuel 7:4** But that same night the LORD said to Nathan,

5 "Go and tell my servant David, 'This is what the Lord has declared: Are you the one to build a house for me to live in?

6 I have never lived in a house, from the day I brought the Israelites out of Egypt until this very day. I have always moved from one place to another with a tent and a Tabernacle as my dwelling.

7 Yet no matter where I have gone with the Israelites, I have never once complained to Israel's tribal leaders, the shepherds of my people Israel. I have never asked them, "Why haven't you built me a beautiful cedar house?"'

8 "Now go and say to my servant David, 'This is what the LORD of Heaven's Armies has declared: I took you from tending sheep in the pasture and selected you to be the leader of my people Israel.

9 I have been with you wherever you have gone, and I have destroyed all your enemies before your eyes. Now I will make your name as famous as anyone who has ever lived on the earth!

10 And I will provide a homeland for my people Israel, planting them in a secure place where they will never be disturbed. Evil nations won't oppress them as they've done in the past,

11 starting from the time I appointed judges to rule my people Israel. And I will give you rest from all your enemies.

"'Furthermore, the LORD declares that he will make a house for you—a dynasty of kings!

12 For when you die and are buried with your ancestors, I will raise up one of your descendants, your own offspring, and I will make his kingdom strong.

13 He shall build an house for my name, and I will stablish the throne of his kingdom for ever.

14 I will be his father, and he shall be my son. If he commit iniquity, I will chasten him with the rod of men, and with the stripes of the children of men:

15 But my mercy shall not depart away from him, as I took it from Saul, whom I put away before thee.

16a And thine house and thy kingdom shall be established for ever before thee:

13 He is the one who will build a house—a temple—for my name. And I will secure his royal throne forever.

14 I will be his father, and he will be my son. If he sins, I will correct and discipline him with the rod, like any father would do.

15 But my favor will not be taken from him as I took it from Saul, whom I removed from your sight.

16a Your house and your kingdom will continue before me for all time'"

The People, Places, and Times

Nathan. Nathan was a prophet and advisor to King David. His work with David is recorded in the books of Samuel, Kings, and Chronicles. The author of Chronicles twice mentions the "book of Nathan the prophet" (1 Chronicles 29:29; 2 Chronicles 9:29). Some Bible scholars believe that portions of Chronicles have been incorporated into the books of Samuel and Kings.

Although not much is written about him, Nathan's role was critical. It was through Nathan that God first delivered the Messianic promise of an eternal kingdom that would come through the lineage of David. Many scholars believe that Nathan may have had a significant role in designing the temple of Jerusalem. He seems to have been well acquainted with the inner workings of the royal household and appears in three key accounts recorded in the Old Testament. It was with Nathan that King David shared his plan to build a house for God (2 Samuel 7:4–17). Later, in what is probably the most dramatic biblical confrontation between a king and a prophet, Nathan boldly confronted David with his sins of adultery and murder (12:1–13). Finally, Nathan would diplomatically assist in making Solomon David's successor, in spite of the manipulations by David's oldest surviving son, Adonijah; thus, Nathan helped to ensure the line of dynastic succession and the genealogy of Jesus Christ, Son of David (1 Kings 1:10–45). About three centuries later, King Hezekiah seems to have been following instructions left by Nathan regarding the role of Levite musicians in the temple (2 Chronicles 29:25).

Background

Second Samuel 7 opens with King David enjoying a period of "rest from all the surrounding enemies" (v. 1, NLT). With the help and guidance of the Lord, David managed to subdue Israel's long-standing enemy, the ferocious Philistines. He captured Jerusalem and made it the center of all religious worship by bringing the Ark of the Covenant into the city. Like many Middle Eastern kings, David lived in a comfortable palace. Hiram, king of Tyre, had sent his carpenters and masons with the finest cedar trees to construct David's palace, which was, no doubt, beautiful. At this point, David had about half a dozen wives, so it is also reasonable to assume his home was quite large.

Despite this period of peace, David's mind was troubled. He shared with Nathan his unrest about living in a house of cedar—a wood that was highly valued—"while the ark of God remains in a tent" (v. 2, NIV). More than 400 years earlier, God had given the Children of Israel specific directions on building a tent of meeting, also called the tabernacle (Exodus 25:8–9). This was logical as Israel was in the wilderness and needed a place of worship that would be portable. God had never instructed His people to build a permanent dwelling place, yet David was distressed by the contrast with his own opulent palace and wanted to build a temple for the Lord.

At-A-Glance

1. God Responds to David's Desire
(2 Samuel 7:4–7)
2. God's Role in David's Present
(vv. 8–10)
3. God's Promise for David's Future
(vv. 11–13)
4. God's Covenant with David
(vv. 14–16)

In Depth

1. God Responds to David's Desire (2 Samuel 7:4–7)

It is understandable to believe that King David was feeling guilty living in a fine palace while the presence of God lived inside of a tent. David may have honestly believed that God should have a house that reflected His majesty and glory. So it is not surprising that he dreamt of building a fine temple to house the presence of God. David's motivations were sincere and unselfish, and we see the depth of this king's commitment to God. In fact, the writer of 2 Chronicles tells us that God praised King David for having the desire to honor Him in that way (2 Chronicles 6:7–

9). David was not asking God for anything; instead, he wanted to give back to God, who had given him everything. We should, like David, have a sincere desire to see God glorified and honored.

David shared this desire with the prophet Nathan. Without first consulting God, or even praying about it, Nathan agreed with David and told him that he, too, thought that building a temple was a good idea. At this point David felt affirmed in his desire, but failed to realize Nathan was relying on his own judgment, rather than obtaining God's approval. We must be careful to weigh our own desires—even those that seem godly—and ensure that they are in the will of God.

The same evening, Nathan heard from God. The Lord instructed the prophet to tell David that He never commanded anyone to build Him a house. It is important to notice here that God did not appear to be angry at David's wish to build the temple. Even as He refused to honor David's desire, God was gracious toward His beloved servant. Note that God spoke to Nathan *before* David acted on his plans, thus sparing him any embarrassment.

2. God's Role in David's Present (vv. 8–10)

God then instructed Nathan to remind David of His ever-present role in David's life and of all that He had done for the king. Of all the men in Israel, God had selected David, a young shepherd, to rule His people. We must remember that God had Samuel anoint the young David while there was still a king on the throne—Saul. God protected David as he spent years living in exile hiding from the wrath of Saul (e.g. 1 Samuel 18:12, 20:1, 31, 21:10). David's ascension from the fields to the throne was filled with danger and turmoil; however, the hand of God continually protected David. For about fifteen years, God delivered David from Saul's murderous jealousy and from the swords of his enemies.

In this way, David's story is a wonderful portrayal of what happens in our Christian walk when we follow God's lead. Just as God protected David from his internal enemies (King Saul and other dissidents living inside Israel's borders) and from the outside enemies (Philistines, Ammonites, and others), He protects the life of the believer. Jealousy, envy, strife, worry, bitterness, and lust are all internal enemies of our flesh. Our outside enemies are the influences of the world and the satanic attacks we must endure daily. These influences are only there to undermine the dominion that God intends for us to have in Christ.

3. God's Promises for David's Future (vv. 11–13)

God had been a constant presence in David's life, but His role was far from over. God entered into a covenant with David. This is one of the most important of all the biblical covenants because its fulfillment is in our Lord Jesus Christ.

God made specific promises. First, He promised David that He would "set up thy seed after thee" (v. 12). David would have successors from his body and others would be able to recognize them as the sons of David. This title, "Son of David," is used for Jesus numerous times in the New Testament. More importantly, God was promising that the descendants of David would always be recognized as a royal line. The right to reign and rule on earth will always belong to the "seed" of David. This promise was foreshadowed in Genesis when Jacob blessed his sons and prophesied that "the sceptre shall not depart from Judah, nor a lawgiver from between his feet, until Shiloh come; and unto him shall the gathering of the people be" (Genesis 49:10). Note that it is David's "seed" that will

build the Lord a house. Thus, we see that David's earnest desire to honor God will be fulfilled through his heir.

God also promised David a "throne of his kingdom for ever" (v. 13, cf. vv. 12, 16). This is a promise that someone from David's lineage will always sit on the throne. The use of the word "kingdom" implies that David will forever have both a reign and a realm. His heirs will not only have authority but also a place where that authority is recognized as legitimate.

4. God's Covenant with David (vv. 14–16)

God's promise to David of a hereditary monarchy is especially important when we realize that prior to this point in Israel's history, no king had been succeeded by his son. The previous king, Saul, died along with three of his sons (Jonathan, Abinadab, and Malchishua at the battle on Mount Gilboa, see 1 Samuel 31:3–6; 1 Chronicles 10:3–6). Saul's remaining son, Ishbosheth, was later killed by two of his own military officers. Mephibosheth, Saul's grandson and only living male descendant, came under the protection of David (because Mephibosheth was his dear friend Jonathan's son), but he never ascended to the throne.

Note that God did not promise that David's heirs would rule for a long time, but that "Your house and your kingdom will endure forever before me" (2 Samuel 7:16, NIV). We know of no other kingdom in the ancient Near East that endured as long as the Davidic dynasty, which lasted for more than four hundred years. When David's predecessor, Saul, did wrong, his kingdom was taken away from him. When the descendants of David displeased God, they would be spared because of this promise: "But my mercy shall not depart away from him, as I took it from Saul, whom I put away before thee" (v. 15).

The intimacy of the relationship between God and David's heir is contained in verse 14: "I will be his father, and he shall be my son." Here we see that God intended for Israel's king to be the official representative of the nation which God Himself already recognized as His son (Exodus 4:22; Deuteronomy 14:1). The father-son relationship requires discipline, a concept that was not new to Israel: "Know then in your heart that as a man disciplines his son, so the LORD your God disciplines you" (Deuteronomy 8:5, NIV).

David's reign is fulfilled in the reign of Jesus Christ. The first-century preaching of John the Baptist, the Twelve (Matthew 10:5–7), and Jesus' followers (Luke 10:1) offered Israel the opportunity to recognize and embrace Jesus as the Davidic King (Matthew 3:2). In rejecting Jesus, Israel failed to embrace its kingdom blessings (21:43). A considerable amount of time elapsed between the time that David was anointed as the king of Israel and his actual assumption of the throne following the death of Saul. Similarly, Jesus has already been anointed—at His resurrection and ascension—as the rightful, legal, and legitimate heir to the Davidic throne. Jesus' ultimate rule will begin when Satan is deposed (Revelation 20:2–3). Until that time, we have assurance that Jesus reigns right now at the right hand of God the Father.

Search the Scriptures

1. What past personal blessings did God tell Nathan to relay to King David (2 Samuel 7:8–9)?

2. What would be the consequences of David "commit[ing] iniquity"? (vv. 14–15)?

Discuss the Meaning

David's dream of building the temple had all of the earmarks of having come from the Lord, yet it did not. How can we be sure that our dreams are from the Lord and that they are part of His plan for our life?

Lessons in Our Society

How satisfied are we with what God has given us? Some of us own homes that are 25 or more years old, and we find ourselves constantly criticizing them and telling others how badly we want newer and nicer homes. If we drive a car that's ten years old, we yearn for the latest model luxury vehicle. As Christians, we want to be careful not to discount the blessings that God has given to each of us. We need to understand that God does not do blanket blessings. He blesses us individually, according to our needs and His purpose. Our relationship with our Creator is personal. We don't want to get sidetracked and distracted by material possessions. Our eyes must remain on Him and His will for our lives.

Make It Happen

When David dreamed of building a temple for God, he probably never imagined that God would have a problem with his plan. After all, David's motives were unselfish, and he wanted to honor God. Yet God did not accept David's plan. Instead, God had a plan for David. Each day, God has something new to tell us, and in doing so He reveals more about Himself. Pray, and ask God to help you remain open to His continual revelation.

Follow the Spirit

What God wants me to do:

_____

_____

_____

_____

Remember Your Thoughts

Special insights I have learned:

_____

_____

_____

_____

More Light On The Text

2 Samuel 7:4–16

4 And it came to pass that night, that the word of the LORD came unto Nathan, saying,

In verse 4 we see the typical way a portent was declared by the use of the prophetic formula, "the word of the LORD [Yahweh] came unto . . ." This formula occurs some 200 times in the Old Testament, especially in the books of Jeremiah and Ezekiel. The fact that the word came to Nathan at night may suggest that this word from God came to him in a dream or a vision, which was also typical of how God communicated in these times.

5 Go and tell my servant David, Thus saith the LORD, Shalt thou build me an house for me to dwell in?

This word that came to Nathan for David was in response to the opening of chapter 7 where David and Nathan had a conversation about David's desire to build a temple for God. David presumed that since he had a house and the Ark of the Covenant was residing in a tent, he should build a house for God. In that exchange, Nathan encouraged David, but Nathan had not consulted or heard from God. In verse 4, the word of the Lord came to Nathan in the form of this corrective. The interesting twist in verse 5 is that although God called David "my servant" (a term used to convey honor), it is followed by

God's rhetorical question to Nathan regarding David's plans, "Shalt thou build me an house for me to dwell in?" While this question was about David and his intentions, it was also about God challenging the very notion that He can be contained in a house. The pronoun "thou" (you) is, most likely, emphatic, indicating the negation concerns the person (David) rather than the action itself (the building of the temple).

6 Whereas I have not dwelt in any house since the time that I brought up the children of Israel out of Egypt, even to this day, but have walked in a tent and in a tabernacle. 7 In all the places wherein I have walked with all the children of Israel spake I a word with any of the tribes of Israel, whom I commanded to feed my people Israel, saying, Why build ye not me an house of cedar?

God had been always present with His people, so the need for a house, while not outright rejected, was here questioned. Robert Bergen summed it up this way: "Even in the absence of an impressive building that people could see, the Lord's presence among them was discernible, especially as he acted through the leaders 'whom I commanded to shepherd the people of Israel'" (*1, 2 Samuel*, 338).

8 Now therefore so shalt thou say unto my servant David, Thus saith the LORD of hosts, I took thee from the sheepcote, from following the sheep, to be ruler over my people, over Israel: 9 And I was with thee whithersoever thou wentest, and have cut off all thine enemies out of thy sight, and have made thee a great name, like unto the name of the great men that are in the earth. 10 Moreover I will appoint a place for my people Israel, and will plant them, that they may dwell in a place of their own, and move no more; neither shall the children of

wickedness afflict them any more, as before-time, 11 And as since the time that I commanded judges to be over my people Israel, and have caused thee to rest from all thine enemies. Also the LORD telleth thee that he will make thee an house.

As God had shown Himself to His people through His chosen leaders, God was now saying to David that his life had been a testimony to God's presence and power. God didn't need David to construct an impressive building for Him to dwell. "In fact it was not God's will for David to build Him a house; instead God would build a house for David" (*The Bible Knowledge Commentary*, 464).

God indicated to David that He had given him peace and victory over his enemies. God was trying to remind David that God had established him; he wasn't to establish God and His significance by building a place for God to dwell. Bergen states that the victories "which Yahweh had given to David (v. 9a) made the latter famous (v. 9b) and, at the same time, secured the land for God's people (v. 10a)" (*1, 2 Samuel*, 120).

That God "will appoint a place for my people" (v. 10) references what God had done and how He had shown Himself to His people by providing a place for them—a place of peace where they could live free from oppression and enemy attack.

12 And when thy days be fulfilled, and thou shalt sleep with thy fathers, I will set up thy seed after thee, which shall proceed out of thy bowels, and I will establish his kingdom. 13 He shall build an house for my name, and I will stablish the throne of his kingdom for ever.

"As for a temple, David would not be allowed to build it, but his son after him would have the honor of doing so" (*The Bible Knowledge Commentary*, 464). There is debate around the application and meaning of "and

I will stablish the throne of his kingdom for ever" (from v. 13). Did establishing a throne forever refer to David and his son, or to Jesus (as seen in Matthew 1:1)? "The Lord 'will raise up your offspring [Hebrew zera; literal; "seed"; see Gen 13:15] to succeed you' (v. 12). For the New Testament Christian community, this verse apparently was viewed as proof that Jesus was indeed the Messiah; God did indeed 'raise up' Jesus (see Acts 2:30; 13:23), thus legitimizing him as the messianic son of David" (*Bergan*, 340). One must remember that the New Testament Christians were taking their cue from Jesus, who claimed that He would build a temple (see Matthew 26:61, 27:40; Mark 14:58, 15:29; John 2:19–22). Jesus also claimed to have an eternal throne (see Matthew 19:28–29) while having an imperishable kingdom (see Luke 22:29–30; John 18:36). In the final analysis, the key here is God's sovereignty to act and establish not a house of cedar but a people who were loved by Him, led by Him, and given not a place, but a future.

14 I will be his father, and he shall be my son. If he commit iniquity, I will chasten him with the rod of men, and with the stripes of the children of men: 15 But my mercy shall not depart away from him, as I took it from Saul, whom I put away before thee. 16 And thine house and thy kingdom shall be established for ever before thee:

The reference to the father-son relationship once again presents commentators with a dilemma. Who was this referring to? Was it referring to David and his son, as it was believed that the Davidic king was the son of Yahweh, or was it referring to Jesus, the Son of God? Use of the term "son" was common in this period to represent at least three concepts: adoption, covenant, and royal grant. History suggests that the sins of David's descendants would bring punishment and alienation, but would not result in God's withdrawal of His love. In the end, God would establish David's "house," "kingdom," and "throne . . . forever." Therefore, we end up with God being a God of His word, doing what He said He would do. It wasn't about David or his son building a house for God; rather, it was about how God was going to build a "house" for His people through His Son.

Sources:
Anderson, A. A. *2 Samuel. Word Biblical Commentary. Vol. 11.* Nashville: Thomas Nelson Publishers, 1989. 118.
Bergen, Robert D. *1, 2 Samuel. The New American Commentary. Vol. 7.* Nashville: Holman Reference, 1996), 120. 338-340.
Concordia Self-Study Bible: NIV. St. Louis: Concordia Publishing House, 1986.
Walvoord, John F. and Roy B. Zuck, eds. *The Bible Knowledge Commentary: Old Testament.* Wheaton, IL: Chariot Victor Publishing, 1985. 464.

Say It Correctly

Sheepcote. **SHEEP**-coat.
Mephibosheth. meh-**FIB**-o-sheth.

Daily Bible Readings

MONDAY
The Lord is King
(Psalm 93)

TUESDAY
You are My Son
(Psalm 2)

WEDNESDAY
An Eternal Throne
(Psalm 45:1–9)

THURSDAY
God's Heritage
(Psalm 94:8–15)

FRIDAY
God's Steadfast Love and Faithfulness
(Psalm 98)

SATURDAY
The Messiah Will Reign Forever
(Revelation 11:15–19)

SUNDAY
A Throne Established Forever
(2 Samuel 7:4–16)

Teaching Tips

March 9
Bible Study Guide 2

Words You Should Know

A. Mercy (Mark 10:47) *eleheho* (Gk.)—An outward expression of compassion or pity.

B. Kingdom (Isaiah 9:7) *misraw* (Heb.)—Relating to dominion; to rule a kingdom.

Teacher Preparation

Unifying Principle—Family Connections. People have expectations and hopes regarding their descendants. What assurance do people have that their line of descendants will continue? As God promised David and as Isaiah prophesied, Matthew reported that the birth of Jesus fulfilled the traditional expectation that a descendant of David would come as the Savior.

A. Pray for your students, especially that God enables them to accept their family connections.

B. Prepare a display board or short PowerPoint presentation about a fictitious family's connections. Include photos, careers, achievements, and life mistakes.

O—Open the Lesson

A. Open with prayer.

B. Share your "Family Connections" board or presentation. Ask, "How does an ideal family look?"

P—Present the Scriptures

A. Invite students to read the Focal Verses aloud in both translations.

B. Read The People, Places, and Times; Background; and More Light on the Text.

E—Explore the Meaning

A. Have a student read the In Focus story.

B. Give students an opportunity to share about similar issues in their families—where folks just can't seem to get along.

N—Next Steps for Application

A. Have students draw two columns on a piece of paper—one labeled "Friend," the other "Unfriend."

B. Using the social media concept of choosing connections, have the students list a few relatives in each category.

C. Close with prayer, asking God to heal students' family connections.

Worship Guide

For the Superintendent or Teacher
Theme: Son of David
Song: "Friend of God"
Devotional Reading: Mark 10:46–52

318

Son of David

Bible Background • 1 SAMUEL 13:14; 2 SAMUEL 11–12; ACTS 13:22
Printed Text • PSALM 89:35–37; ISAIAH 9:6–7; MATTHEW 1:18–21
Devotional Reading • MARK 10:46–52

Aim for Change

By the end of the lesson, we will: EXPLAIN how our personal decisions can benefit or negatively affect our lives and the lives of others; FIND comfort in knowing that God's promises to us don't expire; and PLAN to live for a higher purpose as a selfless act for God and for generations to come.

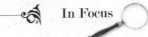 In Focus

Holding red pens, Marc and Sonia flipped through the pages of names on their wedding invitation lists. When they originally compiled their lists, they thought all the names would be easily accepted by both sides of their families. They were wrong.

Marc's dad refused to attend the event if Uncle Anthony stayed on the list. Marc's dad still held a grudge against his baby brother from a soured business deal that occurred over a decade earlier.

Then there was Sonia's mom, Katelyn. She was miffed that her twin sister, Rina, had been left off the list but her "crazy brother Perry" had been included. It didn't matter that Aunt Rina was a missionary in Africa and had no plans on attending. As the families squabbled, Marc and Sonia slipped away.

"How about eloping?" they said in unison.

Family matters. That's why it's so important to make God-honoring decisions that positively impact our lives today and the lives of our descendants. What decisions do you regret making? Ask God to show you how to make amends—starting today.

Keep in Mind

"And she shall bring forth a son, and thou shalt call his name JESUS: for he shall save his people from their sins. Now all this was done, that it might be fulfilled which was spoken of the Lord by the prophet" (from Matthew 1:21–22).

"And she shall bring forth a son, and thou shalt call his name JESUS: for he shall save his people from their sins. Now all this was done, that it might be fulfilled which was spoken of the Lord by the prophet" (from Matthew 1:21–22).

Focal Verses

KJV

Psalm 89:35 Once have I sworn by my holiness that I will not lie unto David.

36 His seed shall endure for ever, and his throne as the sun before me.

37 It shall be established for ever as the moon, and as a faithful witness in heaven.

Isaiah 9:6 For unto us a child is born, unto us a son is given: and the government shall be upon his shoulder: and his name shall be called Wonderful, Counsellor, The mighty God, The everlasting Father, The Prince of Peace.

7 Of the increase of his government and peace there shall be no end, upon the throne of David, and upon his kingdom, to order it, and to establish it with judgment and with justice from henceforth even for ever. The zeal of the LORD of hosts will perform this.

Matthew 1:18 Now the birth of Jesus Christ was on this wise: When as his mother Mary was espoused to Joseph, before they came together, she was found with child of the Holy Ghost.

19 Then Joseph her husband, being a just man, and not willing to make her a public example, was minded to put her away privily.

20 But while he thought on these things, behold, the angel of the Lord appeared unto him in a dream, saying, Joseph, thou son of David, fear not to take unto thee Mary thy wife: for that which is conceived in her is of the Holy Ghost.

21 And she shall bring forth a son, and thou shalt call his name JESUS: for he shall save his people from their sins.

NLT

Psalm 89:35 I have sworn an oath to David, and in my holiness I cannot lie:

36 His dynasty will go on forever; his kingdom will endure as the sun.

37 It will be as eternal as the moon, my faithful witness in the sky!

Isaiah 9:6 For a child is born to us, a son is given to us. The government will rest on his shoulders. And he will be called: Wonderful Counselor, Mighty God, Everlasting Father, Prince of Peace.

7 His government and its peace will never end. He will rule with fairness and justice from the throne of his ancestor David for all eternity. The passionate commitment of the LORD of Heaven's Armies will make this happen!

Matthew 1:18 This is how Jesus the Messiah was born. His mother, Mary, was engaged to be married to Joseph. But before the marriage took place, while she was still a virgin, she became pregnant through the power of the Holy Spirit.

19 Joseph, her fiancé, was a good man and did not want to disgrace her publicly, so he decided to break the engagement quietly.

20 As he considered this, an angel of the Lord appeared to him in a dream. "Joseph, son of David," the angel said, "do not be afraid to take Mary as your wife. For the child within her was conceived by the Holy Spirit.

21 And she will have a son, and you are to name him Jesus, for he will save his people from their sins."

The People, Places, and Times

Heavenly Bodies. In Psalm 89:36–37, David's enduring legacy is likened to that of the sun and moon. As David's seed, the birth of Jesus fulfilled the promise of an extraordinary lineage that would never expire. The significance was likely not lost on David. God made the sun, moon, and stars for specific purposes (Genesis 1:14–18; Psalm 104:19), and they serve as reminders of God's promises. For instance, in Joseph's dream, the sun, moon, and eleven stars (representing his brothers) bowed down to him—a prophetic dream signaling Joseph's future rule as second-in-command to Pharaoh (Genesis 37:9–11, 41:37–41, 42:6–9).

Background

Saul, Israel's first king, forfeited his throne due to sin and disobedience. The prophet Samuel informed Saul that God had stripped him of his office, saying, "But now your kingdom must end, for the LORD has sought out a man after his own heart" (1 Samuel 13:14, NLT). That man was David.

David was the youngest son of Jesse, a native of Bethlehem. While herding sheep, David had no idea that God planned for him to be not only a king of Israel, but *the* king whose descendant would prove to be the King of kings—Jesus.

During his reign, David learned that personal decisions can benefit or hinder his own life and the lives of others. His obedience to, and reliance on, God led to numerous military victories, as well as seasons of peace for his descendants, especially during his son Solomon's reign. Conversely, his sinful desire for Bathsheba caused him to commit adultery and then arrange her husband's murder. Those events contributed to the death of the child born from their adulterous union (2 Samuel 11, 12:1–18). God mercifully brings about the birth of Solomon from this adulterous relationship.

Despite David's mistakes and sins, he was quick to repent and seek God's mercy and forgiveness. Centuries later, he was still remembered as a man after God's heart (Acts 13:22). David's heart for God was rewarded with a promise of a perpetual kingdom. As God promised David and as Isaiah prophesied, Mathew reported that the birth of Jesus fulfilled the traditional expectation that a descendant of David would be coming as the Savior.

At-A-Glance

1. God's Promise (Psalm 89:35–37)
2. God's Purpose (Isaiah 9:6–7)
3. God's Plan (Matthew 1:18–21)

In Depth

1. God's Promise (Psalm 89:35–37)

After a period of rest, King David shared with the prophet Nathan a concern about the Ark of the Covenant's temporary dwelling. Nathan gave David the prophetic word and vision he had received: "If he [David's seed] commit iniquity, I will chasten him with the rod of men, and with the stripes of the children of men: But my mercy shall not depart away from him. . . . [T]hy throne shall be established for ever" (from 2 Samuel 7:14–16).

God's promise and David's response (v. 25) were uttered before David committed adultery or had Uriah killed, before Tamar was raped, before Absalom was killed, and before other grievous situations in David's life. Yet none of those events or others in ensuing years could break the promise of God. Rather, David's "kingdom will endure as the sun. It will be as eternal as the moon" (from Psalm 89:36–37, NLT).

The demonstration of God's grace in David's life is helpful for us. David, as flawed as he was, received God's mercy. Likewise, our flaws, though not excuses to continue in sin, make us prime candidates for God's mercy. Those of us who have put our trust in Jesus can stand on His promise to be with us always, even until the end of time (see Matthew 28:20).

2. God's Purpose (Isaiah 9:6–7)

God's promise to David of an everlasting kingdom reveals His eternal purpose for mankind. Isaiah prophesied that one descendant "will rule with fairness and justice from the throne of his ancestor David for all eternity" (from Isaiah 9:7, NLT). Jesus is *the* Davidic descendant purposed to forge the way for mankind to be forever united with God.

David could not have imagined the Christ child born of a virgin, sinless and uniquely qualified to bring God's salvation to mankind. Nonetheless, his selfless determination to live for God, despite his failings, made him an ideal ancestor.

Likewise, when we live for a higher purpose than earthly glory, possessions, or authority, we build a strong spiritual foundation on which our descendants can stand. Thanks to our faith in, and commitment to, Jesus Christ, they too can become heirs to the Davidic covenant and serve the "Wonderful Counselor, Mighty God, Everlasting Father, Prince of Peace" (Isaiah 9:6, NLT).

3. God's Plan (Matthew 1:18–21)

Matthew recorded that the birth of Jesus fulfilled the traditional expectation that a descendant of David would be coming as the Savior. This was God's plan determined centuries before Jesus was born and centuries after he called David "a man after his own heart" (from 1 Samuel 13:14). Before the plan could manifest, David and his descendants experienced many personal trials that seemed to contradict the promise of God. These, however, could not derail the promise, purpose, or plan of God.

Joseph's contemplation to divorce Mary because of her pregnancy, if carried out, could have changed the course of history. But his obedience through the instruction of God's servant—an angel mentioned in Matthew 1:20—ensured that God's plan stayed on track.

God places us in families for a divine purpose that supersedes the need for personal interactions. His ultimate goal is for us to live that others would know Christ (John 3:16).

Search the Scriptures

1. What did God swear to David, and why (Psalm 89:35–37)?

2. How did God change Joseph's mind about marrying Mary (Matthew 1:19–20)?

Discuss the Meaning

David's actions both positively and negatively impacted his descendants. How did his commitment to God ensure that generations to come would experience the mercy and love of God? How are you ensuring the same for your descendants?

Lesson in Our Society

There are times when a family experiences both the death of an aged loved one and the birth of a child within the same season. As grief and joy mingle together, how can believers share God's purpose for the continuation of a family line by offering both consolation and celebration at such times?

Make It Happen

David was able to trust God's promises despite his personal failings. What besetting sin causes you to doubt God's promises? Ask for God's help in overcoming the sin once and for all. Use a print or online concordance to locate Scriptures related to God's promises in that area and commit to memorizing them.

Follow the Spirit

What God wants me to do:

_____

_____

_____

_____

Remember Your Thoughts

Special insights I have learned:

_____

_____

_____

_____

More Light on the Text

Psalm 89:35–37

35 Once have I sworn by my holiness that I will not lie unto David.

Psalm 89 is a song of praise. In the first eighteen verses, the psalm writer praised the Lord for His covenant made years earlier with David, making his descendants heirs to the throne always. Verses 35–38 are the Lord's words affirming that promise. These verses are beautifully written as a "parallelism," a literary feature common in the psalms that uses similar words and phrases to convey the same idea or sentiment in two or more lines.

This particular passage is staged as a courtroom setting with the Lord as the defendant. The Lord swears (Heb. *shaba*, **shaw-BAH**) by His holiness (Heb. *kadash*, **kaw-DASH**) that this promise is guaranteed. To swear is to make an oath to tell the truth. In the United States, witnesses in courtrooms often must swear to tell the truth under the penalty of being jailed or paying a fine. As children, some of us would say "If I'm lyin', I'm flyin'" as evidence that our testament is the truth. The Hebrew for "I will not lie" is literally "If I lie." The Lord swears that what He has promised is assured because He cannot lie (Heb. *kazab*, **kaw-ZAB**); it is not in His character. Just as the children's oath means that if they are lying then the impossible (flying) will occur, the Lord is saying that, because He is holy, what He promised to David is the absolute truth.

36 His seed shall endure for ever, and his throne as the sun before me.

As if to emphasize the trustworthiness of the Lord's word in verse 35, the psalmist offered further testament to the promise to David. The Lord declared that David's seed (Heb. *zera*, **ZEH-rah**) shall endure (Heb. *hayah*, **haw-YAW**) forever (Heb. *olam*, **o-LAWM**). The verb translated "endure" in the King James Version is literally "to live" in Hebrew. David's seed or lineage shall always be in existence and his throne (Heb. *kisse*, **kis-SAY**) shall last as long as the sun exists. As a people who were confident that the sun shone each day, they could trust that David's descendants would reign as long. The two lines using similar language to express the continuity of David's line are an example of parallelism.

37 It shall be established for ever as the moon, and as a faithful witness in heaven.

Verse 37 continues this literary feature with the addition of the moon in parallel with the sun as a testament to the endurance of David's line. Just as the Lord placed the sun above, so also the Lord established (Heb. *kun*, **KOON**) the moon as a trustworthy (Heb. *aman*, **am-AN**) witness (Heb. *ed*, **ayd**). Not everyone called on to attest to the reliability of another's statement is dependable. Some witnesses are unreliable for various reasons, and some deliberately bear false witness. Recent studies have cast doubt on eyewitness accounts. However, the visibility of the sun and moon in the sky each day and evening as an assurance of the Lord's faithfulness surely resonated with the psalmist's audience that a descendant of David would remain on the throne.

Isaiah 9:6–7

6 For unto us a child is born, unto us a son is given: and the government shall be upon his shoulder: and his name shall be called Wonderful, Counseller, The mighty God, The everlasting Father, The Prince of Peace.

The first two lines of verse 6 are another example of parallelism. "A child is born" and "a son is given" convey the same idea, emphasizing the importance of this birth. The prophet Isaiah saw in a vision that this child had already been born and bore the government (Heb. *misrah*, **mis-RAW**) upon His shoulder. The word translated "government" in the King James Version (also New Living Translation and New International Version; "authority" in the New Revised Standard Version) means "rule" or "dominion." The passage uses Judean royal language found in the psalms (e.g. Psalm 2, 45:6) to refer to the enthronement of a descendant of David on the throne. The "royal psalms" sing of God's chosen earthly representative to implement His universal rule and sovereignty.

The various titles attributed to this future leader—Wonderful, Counselor, Mighty God, Everlasting Father, Prince of Peace—were words of praise bestowed on a king at his coronation. Implicit in these titles is the notion that the king or ruler was divine, or at least a representative of the divine. This ruler, whom God promised to Israel, is from the line of David, embodies God's presence with His people, and has His attributes. We can expect such a wonderful ruler to be discerning, protective, assuring, and able to bring the world peace forever.

7 Of the increase of his government and peace there shall be no end, upon the throne of David, and upon his kingdom, to order it, and to establish it with judgment and with justice from henceforth even for ever. The zeal of the LORD of hosts will perform this.

The Hebrew word for "increase" (*marbeh*, **mar-BEH**) also means abundance. Isaiah prophesied that with the ascension of David's descendant to the throne, his kingdom will be enlarged and peace will have no end (*kets*, **kates**). His government will be founded on justice (Heb. *mishpat*, **mish-PAWT**) and sustained by righteousness (Heb. *tzedekah*. **tsed-aw-KAW**) until the end of time (Heb. *ad*, **ad**). Justice is a term we usually associate with the act of deciding a case by a judge. A judge who is righteous executes right judgments. But we live in troublesome times, much like those during which the prophet Isaiah prophesied. Even so, we can be assured that there is a King on the throne who rules heaven and earth with righteousness now and forever. The Lord's "zeal" (Heb. *qinah*, **qin-AW**), also translated "jealousy," will bring about this vision because of His concern for the people and their welfare.

Matthew 1:18–21

18 Now the birth of Jesus Christ was on this wise: When as his mother Mary was espoused to Joseph, before they came together, she was found with child of the Holy Ghost.

Matthew referred to Jesus by His title "Christ" (Gk. *Christos*, **khris-TOS**), the Greek transliteration for the Hebrew "messiah" (*mashiah*, **maw-SHEE-akh**), which means the "anointed one." In the Old Testament, kings and priests were anointed with oil as a sign of their appointment as God's earthly representatives. Matthew's use of the title suggests that he believed that Jesus was the expected Messiah, the anointed one from the line of David, whom God sent into the world to bring salvation to His people.

Matthew emphasized the divinity of Jesus by describing His birth—He was born to a virgin named Mary, who was found to be with child through the aid of the Holy Spirit. The specialness of this birth is explained by the fact that she was "espoused" (Gk. *mnesteuo*, **mnace-TYOO-o**, also translated "betrothed," or "engaged") to Joseph, which meant she had been promised in marriage to him but had not yet been taken from her father's household to his family's household. This happened during the period of time between the engagement and the marriage ceremony, after which the relationship could be sexually consummated. During the time of being "espoused," young girls remained at their homes with other female relatives, and male relatives chaperoned them in public to protect their virginity from being taken before the marriage. If a male other than the girl's husband had sexual relations with her, it would bring dishonor to both her and her husband's family. Mary's visible pregnancy during this time of being espoused obviously suggested that she had sexual relations—and Joseph knew that it hadn't been with him.

19 Then Joseph her husband, being a just man, and not willing to make her a public example, was minded to put her away privily.

Joseph's discovery of Mary's condition left him with few options, none of which would bode well for Mary. He could expose her publicly (Gk. *deigmatiso*, **digh-mat-ID-zo**), which would bring great shame to her family and be an example to other families of what happens when unmarried daughters are not properly supervised. He could present evidence to the town elders of her lack of virginity before they had consummated their marriage and have her brought to the entrance of her father's house to be stoned to death (Deuteronomy 22:13–21). Or, he could end the engagement quietly. Joseph was a "just" (Gk. *dikaios*, **DIK-ah-yos**) man, which means he was a righteous man who was in a right relationship with God. Therefore, he chose the latter option.

20 But while he thought on these things, behold, the angel of the Lord appeared unto him in a dream, saying, Joseph, thou son of David, fear not to take unto thee Mary thy wife: for that which is conceived in her is of the Holy Ghost.

The angel who appeared to Joseph in a dream referred to him by his family name, "son of David," affirming Jesus' humanity and tracing His lineage to King David. The angel informed Joseph that he did not need to fear (Gk. *phobeo*, **fob-EH-o**) taking Mary as his wife. The angel assured Joseph that Mary had not been unfaithful to him; the child she was carrying had been conceived (Gk. *gennao*, **ghen-NAH-o**) by the Holy Spirit.

21 And she shall bring forth a son, and thou shalt call his name Jesus: for he shall save his people from their sins.

The angel's message confirmed all that was written in verse 18 about Jesus: The child Mary was carrying would be the Christ, the Messiah, promised from the line of David, who would bring salvation to His people. His name, Jesus (Gk. *Iesous*, **ee-ay-SOOCE**), the Greek transliteration of the Hebrew name *Yehoshua* (Heb. **yeh-ho-SHOO-ah**), shortened to Joshua, is Hebrew for "Yahweh saves" or "Yahweh is salvation."

Salvation from what? "Their sins." Sin (Gk. *hamartia*, **ham-ar-TEE-ah**) literally means to forfeit or have no part of something for having missed the mark. We fall short of God's standards, but through Jesus, the world is saved from their sins.

Sources:

Adeyemo, Tokunboh, ed. *Africa Bible Commentary*. 2nd edition. Grand Rapids, MI: Zondervan: 2010. 352–353, 714.

Bauer, Walter, William F. Arndt, F. Wilbur Gingrich, and Frederick W. Danker. *A Greek-English Lexicon of the New Testament and Other Early Christian Literature, Second Edition*. Chicago: University of Chicago Press, 1979.

Beers, V. Gilbert. *The Victor Handbook of Bible Knowledge*. Wheaton, IL: Victor Books, 1981. 212–213, 470–471.

Craven, Toni, and Walter Harrelson. "Excursus: Royal Psalms." *The New Interpreter's Study Bible: New Revised Standard Version with the Apocrypha*. Walter J. Harrelson, ed. Nashville: Abingdon Press, 2003. 767.

Draper, Charles W., Chad Brand, and Archie England, eds. *Holman Illustrated Bible Dictionary*. Grand Rapids, MI: Holman Bible Publishers, 2003. 391–392, 396.

Gilmore, David, ed. "The Shame of Dishonor." In "Honor and Shame and the Unity of the Mediterranean" (Special Publication of the American Anthropological Association; no. 22). Washington, D.C.: American Anthropological Association, July 1987, 136.

Sheppard, Gerald T. "Isaiah 1–39." *HarperCollins Bible Commentary*. James Luther Mays, ed. New York: Society of Biblical Literature, 1988. 542–570.

Stambor, Zak. "How reliable is eyewitness testimony?" *Monitor*, Vol. 37, No. 4, April 2006. American Psychological Association (http://www.apa.org/monitor/apr06/eyewitness.aspx. Accessed December 15, 2012).

Stuhlmueller, Carroll. "Psalms." *Harper's Bible Commentary*. James Luther Mays, ed. New York: Society of Biblical Literature, 1988.

Say It Correctly

Bathsheba. bath-**SHEE**-bah.
Absalom. **AB**-suh-luhm.

Daily Bible Readings

MONDAY
A Son Named Emmanuel
(Matthew 1:22–25)

TUESDAY
The King of the Jews
(Matthew 2:1–6)

WEDNESDAY
Is This the Son of David?
(Matthew 12:15–23)

THURSDAY
Hosanna to the Son of David
(Matthew 21:12–17)

FRIDAY
Whose Son Is the Messiah?
(Matthew 22:41–45)

SATURDAY
Following the Son of David
(Mark 10:46–52)

SUNDAY
The Son of David
(Psalm 89:35–37; Isaiah 9:6–7;
Matthew 1:18–21)

Teaching Tips

Words You Should Know

A. Foreknowledge (Acts 2:23) *prognosis* (Gk.)—A term denoting forethought; to know beforehand.

B. Witnesses (v. 32) *martoos* (Gk.)—Spectators, but also translated martyrs.

Teacher Preparation

Unifying Principle—Looking Forward and Looking Back. People need to understand the legacy they have received to perceive any value in it. How can people correlate tradition and legacy? Peter interpreted the coming of Jesus, which the followers witnessed, as Jesus' fulfillment of the prophecy for a Savior descended from the line of David.

A. Research the legacies (good or bad) a few well-known people have left their descendants, or brainstorm some of the legacies your family has received. Be prepared to discuss these.

B. Pray for students and their understanding of the importance of being people of their word.

O—Open the Lesson

A. Open with prayer.

B. Have volunteers read Aim for Change and the Keep in Mind verse.

C. Discuss your legacy research.

D. Read the In Focus Story. Ask for volunteers to share their struggles or successes with keeping their word.

P—Present the Scriptures

A. Invite students to read the Focal Verses.

B. Now use The People, Places, and Times and More Light on the Text to clarify the verses.

E—Explore the Meaning

A. Have volunteers summarize the Lesson in Our Society and Make It Happen sections.

B. Discuss why keeping one's word is so important.

N—Next Steps for Application

A. Ask students to think of one promise they've broken in the past week.

B. Have students brainstorm ways amends can be made in the situations discussed.

C. Close in prayer.

Worship Guide

For the Superintendent or Teacher
Theme: Peter's Report
Song: "He Rose Triumphantly"
Devotional Reading: Psalm 16:7–11

Peter's Report

Bible Background • PSALM 110; ACTS 2:22-36
Printed Text • PSALM 110:1–4; ACTS 2:22–24, 29–32
Devotional Reading • PSALM 16:7–11

Aim for Change

By the end of the lesson, we will: DISCUSS the importance of being people of our word; FIND comfort in knowing that no matter how tough things may get, God will keep His Word for our lives; and SHARE what we've learned about God's faithfulness to encourage others in tough times.

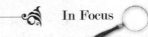 **In Focus**

"Girl, your dress is so not ready." Josie's voice ended in a chuckle that belied the seriousness of the situation.

Shirley counted to ten before speaking calmly into her smartphone. "Josie, you know I needed that for our church anniversary program this evening. What am I going to do now?"

"I'm sorry. Had things to do. Got to go, have a call." Josie hung up before Shirley could respond further.

Surely she's joking. Shirley could not believe her best friend would promise and then not deliver the dress she was altering for her.

Shirley picked up the phone to call her twin sister, Sheila, in hopes of borrowing an appropriate evening dress. As she dialed, she vowed to speak with Josie about her awful habit of breaking her promises. But not today. She needed time to pray about the situation, asking God to help her forgive her friend's lapse.

Breaking a promise causes a breach in our relationships and can result in additional stress or hard feelings for the person we've let down. In today's lesson, we learn that we shouldn't promise unless we know we can deliver.

Keep in Mind

"He seeing this before spake of the resurrection of Christ, that his soul was not left in hell, neither his flesh did see corruption" (Acts 2:31).

"He seeing this before spake of the resurrection of Christ, that his soul was not left in hell, neither his flesh did see corruption" (Acts 2:31).

Focal Verses

KJV **Psalm 110:1** The LORD said unto my Lord, Sit thou at my right hand, until I make thine enemies thy footstool.

2 The LORD shall send the rod of thy strength out of Zion: rule thou in the midst of thine enemies.

3 Thy people shall be willing in the day of thy power, in the beauties of holiness from the womb of the morning: thou hast the dew of thy youth.

4 The LORD hath sworn, and will not repent, Thou art a priest for ever after the order of Melchizedek.

Acts 2:22 Ye men of Israel, hear these words; Jesus of Nazareth, a man approved of God among you by miracles and wonders and signs, which God did by him in the midst of you, as ye yourselves also know:

23 Him, being delivered by the determinate counsel and foreknowledge of God, ye have taken, and by wicked hands have crucified and slain:

24 Whom God hath raised up, having loosed the pains of death: because it was not possible that he should be holden of it.

2:29 Men and brethren, let me freely speak unto you of the patriarch David, that he is both dead and buried, and his sepulchre is with us unto this day.

30 Therefore being a prophet, and knowing that God had sworn with an oath to him, that of the fruit of his loins, according to the flesh, he would raise up Christ to sit on his throne;

31 He seeing this before spake of the resurrection of Christ, that his soul was not left in hell, neither his flesh did see corruption.

32 This Jesus hath God raised up, whereof we all are witnesses.

NLT **Psalm 110:1** The LORD said to my Lord, "Sit in the place of honor at my right hand until I humble your enemies, making them a footstool under your feet."

2 The LORD will extend your powerful kingdom from Jerusalem; you will rule over your enemies.

3 When you go to war, your people will serve you willingly. You are arrayed in holy garments, and your strength will be renewed each day like the morning dew.

4 The LORD has taken an oath and will not break his vow: "You are a priest forever in the order of Melchizedek."

Acts 2:22 People of Israel, listen! God publicly endorsed Jesus the Nazarene by doing powerful miracles, wonders, and signs through him, as you well know.

23 But God knew what would happen, and his prearranged plan was carried out when Jesus was betrayed. With the help of lawless Gentiles, you nailed him to a cross and killed him.

24 But God released him from the horrors of death and raised him back to life, for death could not keep him in its grip.

2:29 Dear brothers, think about this! You can be sure that the patriarch David wasn't referring to himself, for he died and was buried, and his tomb is still here among us.

30 But he was a prophet, and he knew God had promised with an oath that one of David's own descendants would sit on his throne.

31 David was looking into the future and speaking of the Messiah's resurrection. He was saying that God would not leave him among the dead or allow his body to rot in the grave.

32 God raised Jesus from the dead, and we are all witnesses of this.

The People, Places, and Times

Miracles, Wonders, and Signs. These supernatural phenomena evident in Jesus' ministry set Him apart from workers of the occult and showcased God's power over the natural and spiritual realms. Scripture records just some of these, including that Jesus healed incurable diseases, raised at least two people from the dead, turned water into wine, and even walked on water. The Apostle John noted, "Jesus also did many other things. If they were all written down, I suppose the whole world could not contain the books that would be written" (John 21:25, NLT).

God as Counselor. In Scripture, God provided counsel to His people in diverse ways. In Old Testament times, prophets, counselors, and priests sought God's counsel on others' behalf. David noted that God counseled him and instructed his heart. This is the same work of the Holy Spirit seen in the New Testament. In John 14:16, the word "Comforter" can also be translated "Counselor." The Holy Spirit enables us to discern the will of God, offering divine counsel during life's trials. Because God is our Counselor, we can find comfort in knowing no matter how tough things get, God has plans for our lives that no one can cancel.

Background

King Melchizedek ruled the Old Testament city of Salem and was described in Genesis 14:18 as "the priest of the most high God." The term "most high God" was used to distinguish Jehovah God from the false gods the heathens served. Scripture's use of the term in connection with Melchizedek proves that he, like Abram, served the one true God.

Melchizedek encountered Abram returning from successful battles with several foreign kings and offered him a gift of bread and wine. Then, Melchizedek blessed Abram and God for helping Abram conquer his enemies. Abram responded by giving the king of Salem a tithe of everything he had won in the battles (vv. 19–20).

Abram's giving of tithes to someone other than God has prompted debate, causing many to wonder about the identity of Melchizedek as a possible Old Testament manifestation of Christ. While that is debatable, it seems certain that David's prophecy in Psalm 110:4 points to Jesus. Like Melchizedek, Jesus serves as both a Priest and King of the most high God. Moreover, Jesus is the only King whose reign will be everlasting.

Peter interpreted the coming of Jesus as fulfillment of the prophecy for a Savior descended from the line of David. Further, Peter stressed the fact that Jesus was not "abandoned to the realm of the dead" (Acts 2:31, NIV) as a way of proving that God keeps His promises.

At-A-Glance

1. Looking Forward (Psalm 110:1–4)
2. Looking Back (Acts 2:22–24)
3. Focus on the Future (vv. 29–32)

In Depth

1. Looking Forward (Psalm 110:1–4)

David was a warrior king who fought numerous bloody battles. He learned to overcome personal failures and remain steadfast before God. In turn, God gave David a glimpse of the legacy his progeny would enjoy. Looking forward, David could imagine that his generations would prosper so that a "priest for ever" could be born and rule. Down through the generations, no matter how tough times got, David's descendants could use that prophecy as a guide to help them understand the scope of their inheritance.

Similarly, we can look to the Word of God to discover the rich spiritual legacy we have in Christ. Knowing that we have a faith that can't be shaken, a Savior who can't be conquered, and a sure place in eternity with God can help us to better appreciate and share God's faithfulness. Tough times will come, but God has plans for us that no one can cancel.

2. Looking Back (Acts 2:22–24)

"I don't want to go there." How many times have we said that phrase in reference to something in our past that we did not want to revisit? But looking back has its benefits. Looking back reveals:

God's role in our lives. The Apostle Peter revealed that God worked through Jesus. Similarly, God works through us to touch others' lives.

God's foreknowledge of our trials. God is always with us, helping to work everything for our good (Romans 8:28).

God's victory over the enemy. Satan is defeated. Thus, God's victory is sure because Jesus lives. Of Jesus, Peter notes, "death could not keep him in its grip" (Acts 2:24, NLT). When we look back to the death, burial, and resurrection of Jesus, we find hope and strength to live a victorious Christian life.

3. Focus on the Future (vv. 29–32)

Later in Acts, the Apostle Peter reminds his listeners, "we are witnesses" (Acts 3:15, NLT). The significance was not lost on those who had seen him deny Jesus three times (Matthew 26:31–35, 69–75). Peter had vowed one thing, but he did not keep his word. However, as we enter our text on the day of Pentecost, we see that Peter received a new focus on the future. Strengthened by the Holy Spirit, he was able to speak boldly and embrace the legacy he received as a witness (Matthew 16:18).

People leave money, family heirlooms, and other legacies for their children. Peter interpreted Jesus' life and ministry, which His followers witnessed, as the fulfillment of the prophecy for a Savior descended from the line of David. One of the greatest legacies we can pass on to our descendants is an understanding of how they can receive the spiritual legacy Christ has made available, and why they should be faithful Christian witnesses from generation to generation.

Search the Scriptures

1. What did the Lord promise David (Psalm 110:1)?

2. How did David know about the resurrection of Christ (Acts 2:29–31)?

Discuss the Meaning

1. Why was it so important that Peter was a witness to Jesus' ministry and suffering?

2. How did Peter's initial failure and later success as a witness impact the tenet of the message he preached to others?

Lesson in Our Society

People receive financial inheritances and can spend them quickly when they don't understand the purpose of that inheritance and the sacrifice it took to ensure it. Similarly, the news is rife with reports of Christians who devalued their spiritual heritage in pursuit of money, fame, drugs, or other illusive riches. What are practical ways can we help others see the value of protecting their spiritual legacy for future generations?

Make It Happen

Peter became a man who kept his word. Begin each day this week asking for God's guidance to help you to only make those commitments He wants you to make. Keep track of the promises you make—and break. Why was it easy or difficult to keep your word? What did you discover about yourself and/or about God?

Follow the Spirit

What God wants me to do:

_____

_____

_____

_____

Remember Your Thoughts

Special insights I have learned:

_____

_____

_____

_____

More Light on the Text
Psalm 110:1–4

Long before the New Testament was written and well before any creeds or statements of faith had been hammered out, Jesus' disciples had obediently begun to preach the Gospel. As soon as Jesus ascended, these eyewitnesses began to tell people what they had seen and what they knew to be true. This earliest of these Gospels was called the *kerygma*, and it has been preserved in Peter's Pentecost sermon in today's lesson from Acts. But even before the *kerygma*, David long ago prophesied about the world-changing events to come.

1 The LORD said unto my Lord, Sit thou at my right hand, until I make thine enemies thy footstool. 2 The LORD shall send the rod of thy strength out of Zion: rule thou in the midst of thine enemies. 3 Thy people shall be willing in the day of thy power, in the beauties of holiness from the womb of the morning: thou hast the dew of thy youth.

The "right hand" of God is referenced in the Apostle's Creed as being Jesus' current position of exalted honor, occupied by no one else. In Old Testament times, this was an unparalleled honor. The New Testament makes prolific use of the phrase (e.g., Matthew 22:44; Mark 14:62; Luke 22:69). According to James Mays, Psalm 110 was the most quoted in the New Testament, adding, "In the early church it was regarded as the messianic text above all others" (*Psalms*, 350). John Goldingay states that it is "the twin of Psalm 2" (*Psalms*, 291) (cf. Psalm 89), which also is an enthronement or royal psalm used during the installation ceremony of a new king, adding, "The language of the oracle is symbolic and ideal because it speaks about the merging of a human political office and divine sovereignty" (352).

4 The LORD hath sworn, and will not repent, Thou art a priest for ever after the order of Melchizedek.

The promise of verses 1–3 merges with and reinforces the immutable oath here that the king will also be a priest. This was not the first time for such a dual role, but rather it was customary since the first priest-king, Melchizedek, who was the king of Salem in Abram's time (Genesis 14). What was significant was the eternal aspect, which clearly would not apply to any human priest or king.

Acts 2:22–24, 29–32

22 Ye men of Israel, hear these words; Jesus of Nazareth, a man approved of God among you by miracles and wonders and signs, which God did by him in the midst of you, as ye yourselves also know.

Among the apostles, the term "Jesus of Nazareth" was a common reference—all four Gospel writers as well as Peter and Paul used it freely, and it was on the inscription on Jesus' cross (John 19:19). "Wonders and signs" was another common phrase used extensively in Acts, but all three elements together, "miracles and wonders and signs," is much more rare—in fact there are only two other places in the New Testament where the three terms are used (2 Corinthians 12:12; Hebrews 2:4). Nicodemus epitomized the perfect response to Jesus' wonders, signs, and miracles: "No man can do these miracles that thou doest, except God be with him" (John 3:2). Other versions use "miraculous signs" (NLT) or just "signs" (NIV).

23 Him, being delivered by the determinate counsel and foreknowledge of God, ye have taken, and by wicked hands have crucified and slain: 24 Whom God hath raised up, having loosed the pains of death: because it was not possible that he should be holden of it.

There is enough packed in these two verses alone to comprise an entire lesson. Consider all the points: 1) With God's prior will and 2) foreknowledge, 3) Jesus was delivered by God 4) into wicked hands, who 5) killed Him, but 6) God raised Him, 7) relieving His agony 8) because death could not contain deity. Many books and endless discussions have resulted from these and similar verses about God's predestination and/or foreknowledge, which collectively raise countless ontological questions regarding human free will and divine sovereignty. Indeed, the entire debate between Calvinists and Arminians surely will continue unresolved on this side of eternity.

A quick review of the key words in the Greek points toward an illuminating comment from John MacArthur. Jesus was "delivered" up (Gk. *ekdotos*, **EK-do-tos**, meaning betrayed or given over to one's enemies) through God's "determinate" counsel (Gk. *horizo*, **ho-RE-zo**, meaning to define, determine, or appoint) and with God's "foreknowledge" (Gk. *prognosis*, **PROG-no-ses**, meaning foreordained or pre-arranged). MacArthur writes, "Together they indicate that Jesus Christ was delivered to death because God planned and ordained it . . . from all eternity" (*The MacArthur New Testament Commentary*, 63) (cf. Acts 4:27–28; 13:27–29; 2 Timothy 1:9; Revelation 13:8). In order to accomplish His purpose, God used evil men—without violating their free will and still holding them responsible for their sins. MacArthur concisely states, "Peter thus presents the total sovereignty of God alongside the complete responsibility of man" (63) (see Luke 22:22). John Calvin notes, "Peter rightly accused the whole nation of this evil deed . . . [but] their guilt was meant to lead them to repentance" (*Acts*, 37).

Verses 23–24 go together, as separating them divides the single thought: Israel rejected and killed Jesus *but* God raised Him from the dead. Death could not retain God in the flesh, who was the resurrection and the life (John 11:25) and whose resurrection guarantees our own.

29 Men and brethren, let me freely speak unto you of the patriarch David, that he is both dead and buried, and his sepulchre is with us unto this day. 30 Therefore being a prophet, and knowing that God had sworn with an oath to him, that of the fruit of his loins, according to the flesh, he would raise up Christ to sit on his throne; 31 He seeing this before spake of the resurrection of Christ, that his soul was not left in hell, neither his flesh did see corruption. 32 This Jesus hath God raised up, whereof we all are witnesses.

Essentially, Peter was comparing David with Christ. Even though he was both a king and prophet, David was also a human who died and decomposed, and his remains are still in his tomb. This would not have been the fate of the one he prophesied about in Psalm 16 who did not see decay (quoted in vv. 25–28). In contrast, even though He died, Jesus neither decomposed nor remained in His tomb. Instead, God raised Him up, as Jesus Himself had predicted to the Pharisees and which the disciples later remembered Him saying (John 2:18–22). He then symbolically sat on David's throne, as had been promised in 2 Samuel 7:11–16, seated at God's right hand. Peter emphasized that they were all eyewitnesses, which was extremely important at that time when other means of recording evidence were not available.

It is an understatement that God's thoughts are not our thoughts and His ways are not our ways. It is beyond the ability of even great thinkers to comprehend the many tensions and paradoxes contained with Scripture. As a wise theology professor once said, "Some things we simply have to hold together in tension," with the admonition against using "proof texts" to blindly defend only one side of a clear dichotomy contained in Scripture—present for reasons that are above man's pay grade, so to speak. As another wise person once noted, "It is better to fear a God you don't understand than one you do." Ironically, even though Israel could not have understood each and every detail of God's plan (any more than people today), had they embraced their collective guilt, they would have embraced their own Messiah—and He would have embraced them. He is Jesus the Christ, Son of God, Son of David, King and Priest, Lamb, King of kings, Lord of lords (1 Timothy 6:15; Revelation 7:14, 19:16).

Sources:
Beers, V. Gilbert. *The Victor Handbook of Bible Knowledge.* Wheaton, IL: Victor Books, 1981. 534.
Blue Letter Bible. BlueLetterBible.org. http://www.blueletterbible.org/ (accessed August 17, 2012).
Calvin, John. *Acts.* Alister McGrath and J. I. Packer, eds. Wheaton, IL: Crossway Books, 1995. 36–40.
Draper, Charles W., Chad Brand, and Archie England, eds. *Holman Illustrated Bible Dictionary.* Grand Rapids, MI: Holman Reference, 2003. 352.
Goldingay, John. "Psalms 90–150." *Psalms. Baker Commentary on the Old Testament, Wisdom, and Psalms, Vol. 3.* Louisville: John Knox Press, 2008. 290–297.
Hebrew Greek Key Study Bible (KJV), revised. Chattanooga, TN: AMG Publishers, 1994. 22.
Longenecker, Richard N. *John, Acts. The Expositor's Bible Commentary, vol. 9.* Frank E. Gaebelein, ed. Grand Rapids, MI: Zondervan, 1981. 277–279.
MacArthur, John. "Acts 1–12." *The MacArthur New Testament Commentary.* Chicago: Moody Publishers, 1994. 59–67.
Mays, James L. *Psalms. Interpretation: A Bible Commentary for Teaching and Preaching.* Louisville: Westminster John Knox Press, 1994. 351–355.

Say It Correctly

Melchizedek. mel-**KIZ**-a-dek.
Determinate. dih-**TUR**-muh-nit.

Daily Bible Readings

MONDAY
Protect Me, O God
(Psalm 16:1–6)

TUESDAY
Show Me the Path of Life
(Psalm 16:7–11)

WEDNESDAY
Freed from the Fear of Death
(Hebrews 2:14–18)

THURSDAY
The Power of the Resurrection
(Philippians 3:7–11)

FRIDAY
The Heavenly Call of God
(Philippians 3:12–16)

SATURDAY
Made Both Lord and Messiah
(Acts 2:33–36)

SUNDAY
Placed on David's Throne
(Psalm 110:1–4; Acts 2:22–24, 29–32)

Notes

_____

_____

_____

_____

Teaching Tips

Words You Should Know

A. Book (Revelation 5:7) *biblion* (Gk.)—A small book, a scroll, a written document.

B. Elders (v. 8) *presbyteros* (Gk.)—Pastors, bishops or overseers, and leaders or rulers of the flock.

Teacher Preparation

Unifying Principle—Victory Celebration. When long-hoped-for dreams come about, people celebrate their joy. How do people celebrate? The result of the fulfillment of the salvific tradition is the extravagant praise and worship of God by the multitude of the redeemed.

A. Read the Bible Background and Devotional Readings.

B. Complete Lesson 4 in the *Precepts For Living Personal Study Guide*®.

C. Reread the Focal Verses in a modern translation.

O—Open the Lesson

A. Open with prayer.

B. Discuss visions and dreams. Ask if anyone has ever had a vision. If so, get that person to share.

C. Have students divide into groups and share their victory stories.

D. Have students read Aim for Change and Make It Happen.

E. Connect the students' victory stories with victories as Christians in Christ Jesus.

P—Present the Scriptures

A. Read the Focal Verses and The People, Places, and Times. Discuss.

B. Have students discuss what it would be like to be on one's knees all day before God's throne—singing and worshiping.

C. Discuss what it means to be deserving of honor from others.

E—Explore the Meaning

A. Have students discuss what happens when they face adversity.

B. Discuss things that we as Christians do to overcome adversity.

N—Next Steps for Application

A. Have students celebrate those in the class who have achieved accomplishments.

B. Close in prayer, thanking God for His divine purpose for our lives.

Worship Guide

For the Superintendent or Teacher
Theme: Worthy is the Lamb
Song: "Agnus Dei"
Devotional Reading:
Matthew 9:35–10:1
Prayer

Worthy is the Lamb

**Bible Background • REVELATION 3:7; 5:5–13; 6:12–7:17; 22:16
Printed Text • REVELATION 5:6–13 | Devotional Reading • MATTHEW 9:35–10:1**

—————————— Aim for Change ——————————

By the end of the lesson, we will: RECOGNIZE that the God-given unlimited power believers possess is linked to total submission to His will; TRUST that even while living a life of obedience to God, troubles will come; and DECIDE to worship and praise God continuously, with zeal, through all of life's situations.

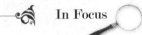

In Focus

Two brothers both wanted to be king when their father died. One brother, Alex, was very concerned about the people. He was always talking with the people of the province to see what he could do to make things better for them. He began to win their hearts because of the love he showed for them.

His older brother, Mafe, was a conceited person who wanted nothing more than power and servants to bow to him each day. He mocked people and never desired to do anything to make their communities better. He simply wanted the title and status of king.

Soon after, the current king died of old age. Mafe believed that since he was the oldest son, he would naturally ascend to the throne. Instead, the people of the province crowned Alex as their new king. The people said that Alex had the heart of a king and the love of the Lord. He was worthy of the honor of rulership.

We sometimes don't realize how many people want to be able to do what we do. However, if God has given us the assignment and the gift to match it, then we are the only ones worthy of doing the task.

—————————— Keep in Mind ——————————

"Saying with a loud voice, Worthy is the Lamb that was slain to receive power, and riches, and wisdom, and strength, and honour, and glory, and blessing" (Revelation 5:12).

"Saying with a loud voice, Worthy is the Lamb that was slain to receive power, and riches, and wisdom, and strength, and honour, and glory, and blessing" (Revelation 5:12).

Focal Verses

KJV **Revelation 5:6** And I beheld, and, lo, in the midst of the throne and of the four beasts, and in the midst of the elders, stood a Lamb as it had been slain, having seven horns and seven eyes, which are the seven Spirits of God sent forth into all the earth.

7 And he came and took the book out of the right hand of him that sat upon the throne.

8 And when he had taken the book, the four beasts and four and twenty elders fell down before the Lamb, having every one of them harps, and golden vials full of odours, which are the prayers of saints.

9 And they sung a new song, saying, Thou art worthy to take the book, and to open the seals thereof: for thou wast slain, and hast redeemed us to God by thy blood out of every kindred, and tongue, and people, and nation;

10 And hast made us unto our God kings and priests: and we shall reign on the earth.

11 And I beheld, and I heard the voice of many angels round about the throne and the beasts and the elders: and the number of them was ten thousand times ten thousand, and thousands of thousands;

12 Saying with a loud voice, Worthy is the Lamb that was slain to receive power, and riches, and wisdom, and strength, and honour, and glory, and blessing.

13 And every creature which is in heaven, and on the earth, and under the earth, and such as are in the sea, and all that are in them, heard I saying, Blessing, and honour, and glory, and power, be unto him that sitteth upon the throne, and unto the Lamb for ever and ever.

NLT **Revelation 5:6** Then I saw a Lamb that looked as if it had been slaughtered, but it was now standing between the throne and the four living beings and among the twenty-four elders. He had seven horns and seven eyes, which represent the sevenfold Spirit of God that is sent out into every part of the earth.

7 He stepped forward and took the scroll from the right hand of the one sitting on the throne.

8 And when he took the scroll, the four living beings and the twenty-four elders fell down before the Lamb. Each one had a harp, and they held gold bowls filled with incense, which are the prayers of God's people.

9 And they sang a new song with these words: "You are worthy to take the scroll and break its seals and open it. For you were slaughtered, and your blood has ransomed people for God from every tribe and language and people and nation.

10 And you have caused them to become a Kingdom of priests for our God. And they will reign on the earth."

11 Then I looked again, and I heard the voices of thousands and millions of angels around the throne and of the living beings and the elders.

12 And they sang in a mighty chorus: "Worthy is the Lamb who was slaughtered— to receive power and riches and wisdom and strength and honor and glory and blessing."

13 And then I heard every creature in heaven and on earth and under the earth and in the sea. They sang: "Blessing and honor and glory and power belong to the one sitting on the throne and to the Lamb forever and ever."

The People, Places, and Times

John. The beloved disciple who was one of the twelve apostles, son of Zebedee, and brother of James (also one of the Twelve). John was exiled to Patmos "for preaching the word of God and for [his] testimony about Jesus" (Revelation 1:9, NLT). Some events on the island of Patmos are reflected in the visions John describes in his book. John's separation from the mainland was quite intensely felt and thus expressed in his writings.

Patmos. A small, rocky, barren island in the Aegean Sea, about 56 miles (90 km) southwest of Ephesus. Roman political prisoners were the majority in exile on Patmos. The emperor Domitian had banished John to this island. This is where John received and recorded the revelation from God that is presented in this final book of the Bible.

Background

The Book of Revelation may have been written in A.D. 96 during the reign of Domitian. However, the date is disputed, and others think that it could have been written in A.D. 68 during the reign of Nero. The pivotal point in Revelation occurs in chapters 4 and 5. The final triumph of the Lamb is tied to the risen Lord's opening exhortation to the church and the judgments pronounced in chapters 2 and 3. These chapters warn the church about coming afflictions and God's ultimate triumph and give a historical and theological basis of the risen Lamb's authority over the church and the world. For the saving purposes of God, the Lamb is enthroned and empowered to carry out judgment in the world. Revelation points to future hope, and faithfulness and perseverance are called for from all. Readers are directed to focus on the glorious world to come.

At-A-Glance

1. Slaughtered But Still Standing
(Revelation 5:6–7)
2. Taking the Scroll (v. 8)
3. Power Belongs to You (vv. 9–12)
4. Victory Will Come (v. 13)

In Depth

1. Slaughtered But Still Standing (Revelation 5:6–7)

In this particular heavenly vision, John stood before an elder who told him not to weep, for "the Lion of the tribe of Judah" has prevailed (Revelation 5:5). John saw a Lamb, which looked as if it had been slain, standing at the center of the throne. This is a subtle reminder that because of His experience, we can trust Him when we face difficulty. Jesus' words in John 16:33 resonate here: "In the world ye shall have tribulation: but be of good cheer; I have overcome the world." Even though you get bruised, you can be healed of your wounds. Even though you may feel like you have lost the battle, when you trust God, you will still be standing in the end. Life has a way of hitting hard sometimes, but we must always know that we have the power to overcome through the Lord.

The lion and lamb also have biblical and cultural roots in the Hebrew Scriptures. The Lion of Judah recalls a promise that the Savior-King would come from the line of David (Genesis 49:9–10; Isaiah 11:1; Luke 2:4). Similarly, the presence of the slaughtered Lamb speaks of both Passover as well as the crucifixion of Christ (Exodus 12:1–13; Isaiah 53:6–7; John 1:29, 19:36). The throne and presence of elders represent the power and rule of God amidst the different beasts that visually link back to creation.

2. Taking the Scroll (v. 8)

Note that as soon as the Lamb took the scroll, the four living creatures and 24 elders fell down before Him. We should respond to the Lamb of God in a similar fashion. Once the Lamb took His place as the only One who could open the scroll, then the elders and creatures responded. Here we also see the first of three references to petitionary prayers in the Book of Revelation (6:10; 8:3–4). John may be accenting the importance of petitionary prayer here. There are times where we feel like our petitions are falling on deaf ears, but we're presented here with a great word picture of prayers rising before the lamb, like incense.

3. Power Belongs to You (vv. 9–12)

John witnessed the elders singing to the Lamb that He is worthy to take the scroll and open its seals. They opened their mouths to proclaim Jesus' sovereignty. Hearing this message in the middle of severe persecution must have been comforting for John's listeners. The church was small and insignificant at this time (from a worldly perspective), but the elders here proclaim that God's ransomed people would come from every tribe and language. What an encouragement for a persecuted people! The Lamb continues to ransom many today.

Note that Jesus didn't need permission from the singers, nor did He need them to tell Him that He was worthy—He already knew He was. Jesus' perfect obedience had yielded powerful results. We must be willing to be obedient and be used by God, while being assured that we will overcome.

4. Victory Will Come (v. 13)

John ended this chapter by informing us that every creature gave praise, honor, glory, and power forever and ever to the Lamb.

Jesus was anointed and empowered to accomplish God's will. The work that we do for the Lord isn't always easy, but when we trust God, submit to His will, and allow Him to guide us, it will bring us to a place of victory.

Search the Scriptures

1. Who was between the throne and the four living creatures and among the elders (Revelation 5:6)?

2. Who did the Lamb take the scroll from (v. 7)?

3. Who prostrated themselves before the Lamb (v. 8)?

4. What were they singing with a loud voice (v. 12)?

Discuss the Meaning

Have you ever been told that you were the only one who could do a certain job? Once you completed the task, what was the sentiment of the people who needed your assistance and those who supported your efforts? Many times there is one person who has been destined to complete a task on behalf of everyone. Once the assignment is completed, those who supported the project oftentimes will celebrate our success. But true success comes from knowing that what you had been gifted to do was completed and that for years to come many will be blessed because of you.

Lesson in Our Society

Sometimes in the church, we don't fully celebrate those who succeed. Storms come in the lives of many men and women of God. Christians pray their way through; they trust and depend on the Word of God. Victory comes into their lives but not without a struggle. When we, the body of Christ, see what others have gone through and where they have come from, we should celebrate what they have been able to do with the Lord.

Make It Happen

Remember that God has given you a purpose in life. You have been shaped to fulfill that purpose before you leave this earth. You want to be successful in accomplishing your purpose so that everyone whose blessing is connected to your destiny will receive what God has for them. You will receive your reward in heaven for all that you do to complete God's purpose in your life.

Follow the Spirit

What God wants me to do:

_____

_____

_____

_____

Remember Your Thoughts

Special insights I have learned:

_____

_____

_____

_____

More Light on the Text

Revelation 5:6–13

6 And I beheld, and, lo, in the midst of the throne and of the four beasts, and in the midst of the elders, stood a Lamb as it had been slain, having seven horns and seven eyes, which are the seven Spirits of God sent forth into all the earth.

As John turned to see the Lion, he instead saw a Lamb that looked slaughtered yet was standing tall. The Lamb was unique in appearance, having seven horns and seven eyes—traditionally, the former suggested power and the latter represented knowledge or wisdom.

The symbolism adds an apocalyptic element in its connection to the ministry of the "seven Spirits." This phrase is mentioned four times in the book of Revelation (1:4, 3:1, 4:5, 5:6); however, the full end times identity or purpose of the "seven Spirits" remains disputed. Common speculation includes that it is a reference to seven angelic spirits, a symbolism of completeness, or a recalling of the work of the Holy Spirit (Isaiah 11:2: "And the spirit of the LORD shall rest upon him, the spirit of wisdom and understanding, the spirit of counsel and might, the spirit of knowledge and of the fear of the LORD"). The latter may have the most weight since the word used for "Spirit" is *pneuma* (**NOO-ma**), which many times refers to the Holy Spirit—the third person of the Trinity.

7 And he came and took the book out of the right hand of him that sat upon the throne.

Heaven's throne is a primary fixture of symbolism throughout the book of Revelation. It shows God's power to rule (4:8) and character to be worshiped (4:10, 5:13, 7:10). It is the focal point of attack from the enemy (13:2) and where God reveals His sovereign authority to prevail (22:3). The Lamb's movement toward it hearkens back to how Christ unleashed the power of redemption when He was slain for our sins, making Him the only one worthy to bring people into His kingdom.

The book or scroll that the Lamb takes is atypical in that it has writing on the front and back (5:1). Symbolically, this meant that whatever is written on it is expansive—as if it is more than the book can contain. What is written in it remains unclear, but what is apparent is the Lamb takes this without any resistance from "the right hand of him that sat upon the throne."

By noting what happened before and after this moment, we can appreciate how God the Father, the Son, and the Spirit are all present with one another. The Lamb is in the center of the throne (v. 6); then, the Lamb approaches someone on the throne (v. 7). This means that the Lamb occupies the same space and position as the Father but remains distinct (John 10:30). The Spirit likewise shows that the three persons of the Trinity can coexist together as One or be distinctly manifest for a specific purpose, ministry, or revelation.

8 And when he had taken the book, the four beasts and four and twenty elders fell down before the Lamb, having every one of them harps, and golden vials full of odours, which are the prayers of saints.

The word John used to describe the "lamb" is *arnion* (**ar-NE-on**), which refers to a "little lamb." By no means does this appears to be a creature that would cause all of heaven to bow down before it. Nonetheless, the massive beasts and twenty-four elders fall down before Him—not because of His stature, but His holy authority to take the book from the one on the throne.

9 And they sung a new song, saying, Thou art worthy to take the book, and to open the seals thereof: for thou wast slain, and hast redeemed us to God by thy blood out of every kindred, and tongue, and people, and nation.

Christ's sacrifice created the means of redemption that makes it possible for all people in all generations from all nations to enter into the kingdom of heaven. Such a praise demanded a new song that respected the form and substance of the declaration. John would have been familiar with this type of praise. In the first century, high-ranking Roman leaders or emperors were welcomed into lands with similar praise. The difference is that, in this passage, praise is given not out of obligation but appreciation. The Lamb can open the seal, or *sphragis* (**sfra-GES**), as both God and mediator.

10 And hast made us unto our God kings and priests: and we shall reign on the earth.

Anyone who receives the offer of salvation and a new identity through Jesus Christ becomes part of His family. Because He is the king, we become "royal" in a heavenly sense. Our destiny to reign with Him is not through our own merit but because of His grace; our capacity to be a royal priesthood is only because we no longer need any mediator but Jesus Himself (2 Timothy 2:12; Hebrews 4:14–16; 1 Peter 2:9).

11 And I beheld, and I heard the voice of many angels round about the throne and the beasts and the elders: and the number of them was ten thousand times ten thousand, and thousands of thousands.

In Revelation 4:9–10, the living beings inspired the elders to worship because of the authority of God; however, here the praises of the elders about the redemption the Lamb offers inspire the angels. Such a cycle reveals that humanity and heaven are meant to work together and ultimately merge, especially when it comes to seeing and appreciating the different aspects of who God is. The number of angels couldn't be counted, for the Greek word *myrias* (**moo-re-AS**) is in this instance best translated "myriads of myriads."

12 Saying with a loud voice, Worthy is the Lamb that was slain to receive power, and riches, and wisdom, and strength, and honour, and glory, and blessing.

The angels spoke out with a loud voice, singing a chorus of praise together. While they don't know what it means to be redeemed like the elders do, they can with honesty declare the worthiness of Christ. The fact that there are seven specific praises symbolizes perfection (because the number seven is a number of perfection in the Bible). The Lamb is worthy to receive power, riches, wisdom, strength, honor, glory, and blessing. In 7:12, a similar sevenfold list of praise includes blessing, glory, wisdom, thanksgiving, honor, power, and might.

13 And every creature which is in heaven, and on the earth, and under the earth, and such as are in the sea, and all that are in them, heard I saying, Blessing, and honour, and glory, and power, be unto him that sitteth upon the throne, and unto the Lamb for ever and ever.

In many ways, the book of Revelation is a book of restoration. There's no mistake why every area of creation is mentioned here, be it angels from the inner realm of heaven or the creatures who live in the deepest parts of the earth or sea. It's as if, for a moment in time and eternity, everything and everyone recognizes the Lord for who He is, while at the same time realizing He is beyond understanding. Romans 1 declares that His great power is visible even now, but in that moment it will be a universal shout of praise.

Sources:
Blue Letter Bible. BlueLetterBible.org. http://www.blueletterbible.org/ (accessed November 10, 2012).
Dockery, David. *Holman Concise Bible Commentary*. Nashville: Holman Reference, 2011.
Draper, Charles W., Chad Brand, and Archie England, eds. *Holman Illustrated Bible Dictionary*. Grand Rapids, MI: Holman Bible Publishers, 2003.
Easton, M. G. *Easton's Bible Dictionary*. New York: Cosimo Classics, 2006.
Freedman, David Noel, Allen C. Myers, and Astrid B. Beck, eds. *Eerdman's Dictionary of the Bible*. Grand Rapids, MI: Eerdmans Publishing Co., 2000.

Daily Bible Readings

MONDAY
Sheep without a Shepherd
(Matthew 9:35–10:1)

TUESDAY
The One at God's Right Hand
(Psalm 80:8–19)

WEDNESDAY
The Lord Cares for the Flock
(Zechariah 10:1–5)

THURSDAY
The Wrath of the Lamb
(Revelation 6:12–17)

FRIDAY
Salvation Belongs to Our God
(Revelation 7:9–12)

SATURDAY
The Lamb Will Be Their Shepherd
(Revelation 7:13–17)

SUNDAY
Worthy is the Lamb
(Revelation 5:5–13)

Say It Correctly

Patmos. **PAT**-mas.
Domitian. dough-**MISH**-un.

Teaching Tips

Words You Should Know

A. King (Zechariah 9:9) *melek* (Heb.)— Royal; a supreme ruler.

B. Colt (Matthew 21:2) *polos* (Gk.)—The offspring of a horse or a donkey.

Teacher Preparation

Unifying Principle—Joy and Celebration. People of every generation and from every country have traditional rituals for welcoming dignitaries or heads of state. What is the most fitting way to celebrate the arrival of an honoree? The crowds who welcomed Jesus into Jerusalem spread out their cloaks on the road as a special gesture to recognize Him as the Messiah.

A. Read the Bible Background and Devotional Readings.

B. Conduct an online search and bring an inauguration web clip for the class to watch during the In Focus reading.

O—Open the Lesson

A. Open with prayer.

B. Have the class read Aim for Change in unison.

C. Ask for a volunteer to read the In Focus story and show the inauguration web clip.

D. Discuss how class members felt when the first African American president was inaugurated.

P—Present the Scriptures

A. Ask for volunteers to read the Focal Verses and The People, Places, and Times. Discuss.

B. Read and discuss the Background section.

E—Explore the Meaning

A. Review and discuss the Search the Scriptures and Discuss the Meaning questions and the Lesson in Our Society section.

B. Ask students to share why they felt Jesus' Triumphal Entry was necessary.

N—Next Steps for Application

A. Ask the students to examine areas in their lives where Christ is not King. Have them write down those areas and spend the next week thinking of ways to restore Christ to His rightful place.

B. Close in prayer.

Worship Guide

For the Superintendent or Teacher
Theme: Triumphant and Victorious
Song: "Hosanna"
Devotional Reading: Psalm 47
Prayer

Triumphant and Victorious

Bible Background • ZECHARIAH 9:9–10; MATTHEW 21:1–11
Printed Text • ZECHARIAH 9:9; MATTHEW 21:1–11 | Devotional Reading • PSALM 47

——————— Aim for Change ———————

By the end of the lesson, we will: EXPLAIN why so many gathered to acknowledge Jesus as Lord and King; EXPRESS a willingness to always honor Jesus through our everyday actions; and REPENT of the times when we have not given Jesus the honor due to Him.

MAR 30th

 ## In Focus

The crisp, cool air of January hit Jennifer's face as she stood on Pennsylvania Avenue with her girlfriends. They had made the cross-country trip from Los Angeles to Washington, D.C., to attend the inauguration of the President of the United States. The group of friends was certain that this was a once-in-a-lifetime opportunity. Though they didn't agree with all of the president-elect's policies, the country had just elected its first African American president, and they couldn't pass up the chance to see this historic event.

Around noon, the crowd began to swell. Jennifer suggested, "Let's move closer to the street. I want to get a better view." The women craftily moved through the audience. A few minutes later, a group of black SUVs slowly crept by. Jennifer screamed, "Mr. President! We love you!" And just like that, the moment was over. After a long pilgrimage, they had experienced what they wanted to experience—a life-transforming event and a story they could share with generations to come.

Events like this are generally reserved for prominent figures. In today's lesson, we learn the importance of Jesus' entry into Jerusalem and how it fulfilled a prophetic message from years past.

——————— Keep in Mind ———————

"And the multitudes that went before, and that followed, cried, saying, Hosanna to the son of David: Blessed is he that cometh in the name of the Lord; Hosanna in the highest" (Matthew 21:9).

"And the multitudes that went before, and that followed, cried, saying, Hosanna to the son of David: Blessed is he that cometh in the name of the Lord; Hosanna in the highest" (Matthew 21:9).

Focal Verses

KJV **Zechariah 9:9** Rejoice greatly, O daughter of Zion; shout, O daughter of Jerusalem: behold, thy King cometh unto thee: he is just, and having salvation; lowly, and riding upon an ass, and upon a colt the foal of an ass.

Matthew 21:1 And when they drew nigh unto Jerusalem, and were come to Bethphage, unto the mount of Olives, then sent Jesus two disciples,

2 Saying unto them, Go into the village over against you, and straightway ye shall find an ass tied, and a colt with her: loose them, and bring them unto me.

3 And if any man say ought unto you, ye shall say, The Lord hath need of them; and straightway he will send them.

4 All this was done, that it might be fulfilled which was spoken by the prophet, saying,

5 Tell ye the daughter of Sion, Behold, thy King cometh unto thee, meek, and sitting upon an ass, and a colt the foal of an ass.

6 And the disciples went, and did as Jesus commanded them,

7 And brought the ass, and the colt, and put on them their clothes, and they set him thereon.

8 And a very great multitude spread their garments in the way; others cut down branches from the trees, and strawed them in the way.

9 And the multitudes that went before, and that followed, cried, saying, Hosanna to the son of David: Blessed is he that cometh in the name of the Lord; Hosanna in the highest.

10 And when he was come into Jerusalem, all the city was moved, saying, Who is this?

11 And the multitude said, This is Jesus the prophet of Nazareth of Galilee.

NLT **Zechariah 9:9** Rejoice, O people of Zion! Shout in triumph, O people of Jerusalem! Look, your king is coming to you. He is righteous and victorious, yet he is humble, riding on a donkey—riding on a donkey's colt.

Matthew 21:1 As Jesus and the disciples approached Jerusalem, they came to the town of Bethphage on the Mount of Olives. Jesus sent two of them on ahead.

2 "Go into the village over there," he said. "As soon as you enter it, you will see a donkey tied there, with its colt beside it. Untie them and bring them to me.

3 If anyone asks what you are doing, just say, 'The Lord needs them,' and he will immediately let you take them."

4 This took place to fulfill the prophecy that said,

5 "Tell the people of Jerusalem, 'Look, your King is coming to you. He is humble, riding on a donkey—riding on a donkey's colt.'"

6 The two disciples did as Jesus commanded.

7 They brought the donkey and the colt to him and threw their garments over the colt, and he sat on it.

8 Most of the crowd spread their garments on the road ahead of him, and others cut branches from the trees and spread them on the road.

9 Jesus was in the center of the procession, and the people all around him were shouting, "Praise God for the Son of David! Blessings on the one who comes in the name of the LORD! Praise God in highest heaven!"

10 The entire city of Jerusalem was in an uproar as he entered. "Who is this?" they asked.

11 And the crowds replied, "It's Jesus, the prophet from Nazareth in Galilee."

The People, Places, and Times

Bethphage. Literally the "house of figs," Bethphage was a small village located near the Mount of Olives. Located east of Jerusalem on the way to Jericho, it was surrounded by a wall. Each of the Synoptic Gospels mentions this location in their respective Triumphal Entry accounts. It was there where Jesus' disciples obtained the donkey and colt for Him to ride into Jerusalem.

Mount of Olives. The Mount of Olives is one of three peaks of a mountain ridge bordering Jerusalem to the east. Its name derives from the fact that it is covered in olive trees. The peak is approximately two hundred feet higher than the Temple Mount in Jerusalem, which sits across the Kidron Valley, thus giving it a great view of Jerusalem. It was from this perspective that Jesus gave His discourse on the doomed city below (Mark 13:3). Some scholars believe this was the "high mountain" where the devil took Jesus to show Him all of the kingdoms of the world (Luke 4:5). It also served as the place where Jesus agonized over the task before Him prior to going to Calvary (Luke 22:39–46).

Messiah. Transliteration of the Hebrew word meaning "anointed one"; translated into Greek as *Christos* or "the Christ." Since apostolic times, the name Christ has become the proper name of Jesus, the person whom Christians recognize as the God-given Redeemer of Israel and the church's Lord. "Christ," or Messiah, is therefore a name suited to express both the church's link with Israel through the Old Testament and the faith that sees in Jesus Christ the worldwide scope of the salvation in Him. The Jews, however, thought that their Messiah would be a warrior-prince who would expel the hated Romans and usher in a kingdom in which Israel would be promoted to world dominion.

Background

A contemporary of Haggai, Zechariah began his prophetic career around 520 B.C., during the reign of King Darius. At fourteen chapters, the book of Zechariah is the longest book among the minor prophets. Though the first eight chapters of the book are dated, the ninth chapter mentions no dates. Most scholars believe a significant amount of time passed between the eighth and ninth chapters. Zechariah 9 begins a section of the text where God providentially saves and restores His people.

Matthew's Gospel is a theologically rich text, for Matthew was very intentional about pointing out the theological implications of Jesus' actions. The text in Matthew 21 follows this distinct pattern. In Matthew's account, this is Jesus' first appearance in the city of Jerusalem, though the city is mentioned earlier in the text (see Matthew 2:3). In that instance, King Herod and the inhabitants were troubled by the birth of Jesus. By the time we get to the later chapters in Matthew's Gospel, Jesus' reputation was growing. At the end of chapter 20, Jesus healed two blind men as a great crowd followed Him on His journey toward Jerusalem. Given this increased popularity, the lesson text now describes what has been deemed Jesus' Triumphal Entry.

At-A-Glance

1. A New King (Zechariah 9:9)
2. A Donkey for a King (Matthew 21:1–3)
3. The Prophecy Fulfilled (vv. 4–5)
4. The Crowds Worship the King (vv. 6–11)

In Depth

1. A New King (Zechariah 9:9)

The author began by exhorting the "daughter of Zion" and "daughter of Jerusalem" to rejoice (Zechariah 9:9). Here the former represented the inhabitants of Jerusalem, while the latter represented the nation of Israel as a whole. The prophet informed them that their King is on the way. And the King has three prevailing character traits: He is just, "[has] salvation," and arrives humbly (from v. 9). The messianic and eschatological properties of this passage are evident. Note that the King comes to Jerusalem after God's reign was established in surrounding Gentile communities, including Syria, Phoenicia, and Philistia.

The King had one characteristic that most would not associate with regal authority—humility. The new King would be meek and lowly as opposed to proud and haughty. He also would ride in on a donkey as opposed to a well-armored war horse. The Israelites were instructed not to trust in majestic war horses (see Isaiah 31:1).

2. A Donkey for a King (Matthew 21:1–3)

As Jesus and His disciples descended upon Jerusalem, they came to a small village called Bethphage (Matthew 21:1). It was here that Jesus made what probably seemed like strange requests. He asked two unnamed disciples to go into the village and retrieve a donkey and colt for him. When the owner of the donkey and the colt learned that Jesus requested them, he gave them freely and joyfully.

Jesus chose to ride on a colt, a symbol of humility, which made His Triumphal Entry and Crucifixion forever memorable. But the presence of a King on a colt did not keep the people from praising Him. They perceived a prophet among them and greeted Him as a King.

3. The Prophecy Fulfilled (vv. 4–5)

The previous verses in this passage complete the plan for Jesus' Triumphal Entry into Jerusalem. The prophet Zechariah's words foretold God's promise to fallen humanity. Historically, these words ran completely counter to the people's understanding of a kingly entrance. Kings were supposed to arrive with legions of bodyguards, officers, great riches, property, pomp, and circumstance. Chariots were the usual mode of transportation, or a king might ride on a mighty war horse. But the words of this prophecy gave the people a glimpse of the one to come, the one Matthew referenced in his text, a King who comes meekly.

4. The Crowds Worship the King (vv. 6–11)

As Jesus entered Jerusalem, the crowd threw down their coats and branches along the road and shouted praises to Him. Their actions honored Him, and they greeted Jesus with shouts and singing of the *hallel* psalms (Psalms 113–118) that were customary greetings to people journeying to Jerusalem for the Passover. However, the people knew Jesus was much more than just another traveler; they were honoring Him for the miracles they had seen Him perform. The throngs of people, the furor that the Messiah had come, and the deafening shouts of praise created a palpable momentum in the city. Leading the procession were children, not soldiers, who sang His praises and shouted His glory.

As the momentum grew, local religious leaders counseled Him to quiet the people. However, knowing His end was near, Jesus told them, "If these should hold their peace, the stones would immediately cry out" (from Luke 19:40). This peculiar response indicated that Jesus' kingship was not based on recognition from the people but on the foundations of the city and the temple which would declare His glory. Jesus was prophecy fulfilled, and no human proclamation could ultimately confirm or deny that truth.

The people of Jerusalem were excited and asked about Jesus' identity. Before this time, Jesus had not allowed anyone to publicly acknowledge Him as the Messiah. Most of Jesus' ministry had been done outside of Jerusalem to avoid agitating the Jewish leaders. But now these same people to whom He had ministered were leading the procession into the city, and the city dwellers wanted to know about this King who sat on a colt and not on a throne. The crowd replied that He was the prophet Jesus from Nazareth in Galilee. Some joined in the praise; others were disappointed when they saw Jesus enter the city without the majestic fanfare.

Search the Scriptures

1. How does the prophet Zechariah describe Jesus' Triumphal Entry (Zechariah 9:9)?

2. A grand entry into the city was common among those claiming to be the Messiah. How did Jesus' entry differ from what the Jews had previously witnessed (v. 9)?

3. What did the people say and do as Jesus entered Jerusalem? What was the significance of their words and actions (Matthew 21:8–9)?

4. What was the difference between the people of Jerusalem and the multitude who went before and after Jesus (vv. 10–11)?

Discuss the Meaning

1. In fulfilling His mission, Jesus was careful to look and act different from others professing to be Messiah. What character elements did Jesus possess that believers should imitate?

2. Jesus made a strange request of two of His disciples. When they arrived, everything was as He had said. How might the

disciples' faith inform us when we face tough decisions?

Lesson in Our Society

In today's society, it is very easy to be swept up in celebrity culture. We have a tendency to treat celebrities with a level of veneration that should be reserved for Jesus alone. We spend more time on gossip websites than we do in the Word of God. We concern ourselves with our follower count on social media websites. Getting a glimpse of the President of the United States at his inauguration brings a feeling of exhilaration. Unfortunately, church culture may not be exempt from this phenomenon. We treat special guests to special seats in our sanctuary, even though James warned against this (James 2:1). We show up in larger numbers when a celebrity pastor takes the platform at our church but are absent from other weekly services. Today's lesson should demonstrate that there is one King in our lives. He is to be worshiped and lifted above all others. If that isn't the case, then we should make the proper adjustment.

Make It Happen

Make an effort this week to remove something from your life that can become idolatrous. How many hours a day do you spend tracking cultural news? How about time spent online? Take a break from it. Set aside some time to reflect on whether it has hindered or enhanced your relationship with Jesus.

Follow the Spirit

What God wants me to do:

_____

_____

_____

Remember Your Thoughts

Special insights I have learned:

_____

_____

_____

_____

More Light on the Text

Zechariah 9:9

9 Rejoice greatly, O daughter of Zion; shout, O daughter of Jerusalem: behold, thy King cometh unto thee: he is just, and having salvation; lowly, and riding upon an ass, and upon a colt the foal of an ass.

After proclaiming a prediction against the nations in 9:1–8, Zechariah turned to the fate of Israel. In verses 9–17, he declared that the Lord will save His people by protecting them in battle and establishing peace among the nations. Whether the king who brings victory for Israel is a human king or the Lord Himself is unclear from the prophecy, but in either case, God is involved in delivering Israel and establishing peace. The addresses to the daughter of Zion and daughter of Jerusalem are synonymous because Zion was located in the southeastern part of Jerusalem. "Lowly" is *aniy* (**ah-NEE**) in Hebrew and can mean poor, humble, or even oppressed, indicating that this King is both just and righteous but also humble in status and attitude, as riding a work animal indicates.

Matthew 21:1–11

1 And when they drew nigh unto Jerusalem, and were come to Bethphage, unto the mount of Olives, then sent Jesus two disciples, 2 Saying unto them, Go into the village over against you, and straightway ye shall find an ass tied, and a colt with her: loose them, and bring them unto me. 3 And if any man say ought unto you, ye shall say, The Lord hath need of them; and straightway he will send them.

Jesus' ministry was coming to a close, and He and His disciples were about to enter Jerusalem for His final days. In the opening scene, they were in Bethphage on the Mount of Olives to the east of Jerusalem. The Mount of Olives figures in the Gospel as the location where Jesus prepared for His Triumphal Entry and the place where He was arrested (26:30). Although it was located outside the city, the temple was visible (*The Harper Collins Bible*, 783). In preparation for His entry into Jerusalem, Jesus told two disciples to get a donkey and its colt that they would find tied up in the village nearby, a reference to Zechariah 9:9, which prophesied that Israel's King would come riding on a donkey's colt. Jesus explained that the disciples should tell the owner of the donkeys that the Lord needed them.

4 All this was done, that it might be fulfilled which was spoken by the prophet, saying, 5 Tell ye the daughter of Sion, Behold, thy King cometh unto thee, meek, and sitting upon an ass, and a colt the foal of an ass.

Matthew interrupted the scene momentarily in order to explain that this event was a fulfillment of Zechariah's prophecy. Matthew both explicitly claimed this and provided a quotation blending Isaiah 62:11 and Zechariah 9:9 to remind the readers that the details of the scene were in alignment with the prophetic words. The New Testament writers often blended several verses or passages from different portions of Scripture in order to reveal that the events of the New Testament were fully in line with God's salvation history as prophesied. The significance of Jesus as God's chosen Savior is magnified by the fact that every word of the prophecy was fulfilled, including the appearance of both a donkey and its colt. Jesus, the Son of David, arrived in Jerusalem meek and riding a donkey. The Greek word *praus* (**prah-OOS**) can mean humble, meek, or gentle. The King James Version's rendering as "meek" probably best captures both nuances of gentleness and humility, indicating that the chosen Messiah is a King who is neither a warrior nor an arrogant ruler who had to show off His power. Though royal and God's chosen, He did not display behavior associated with a royal Messiah.

6 And the disciples went, and did as Jesus commanded them, 7 And brought the ass, and the colt, and put on them their clothes, and they set him thereon.

Matthew revealed that both Jesus' instructions to the disciples and Zechariah's prophecy were fulfilled. Jesus the Messiah was mounted on a donkey's colt as He was about to enter Jerusalem. Although this scene is also narrated by Mark and Luke (Mark 11:1–10; Luke 19:29–40), only Matthew indicated that there were two donkeys. Mark and Luke state that there was one donkey. It is possible that they were reading Zechariah 9:9 as it was intended in Hebrew poetic form, seeing the parallelism that puts two or more synonymous words or phrases parallel to each other but referring to one thing. This poetic device was often used throughout the books of Psalms and Proverbs to intensify or clarify a description, statement, or event. In this case, Zechariah mentioned a male donkey (Gk. *hamor,* **ha-MORE**) and a young male donkey or foal (Gk. *ayir,* **AH-year**), noting that it is the offspring of a female donkey (Gk. *atonot,* **ah-toe-NOTE**). The point of the repetition was to intensify and clarify by referring to

the same animal with synonymous words. In Zechariah 9:9, it was not just any donkey, but a young one, the offspring of a female donkey. This intensifies the humility of the royal Messiah, who will not appear on a horse or chariot but a donkey, a regular work animal, even on a donkey's foal, which would not be as strong as a fully mature donkey. This messianic figure, though royal, will stand out from other royal figures in His humility. Although it may seem that Matthew was misinterpreting Zechariah, he in fact was following the prophet's words to the letter in order to show that everything prophesied about the royal Messiah comes about in Jesus.

8 And a very great multitude spread their garments in the way; others cut down branches from the trees, and strawed them in the way. 9 And the multitudes that went before, and that followed, cried, saying, Hosanna to the Son of David: Blessed is he that cometh in the name of the Lord; Hosanna in the highest.

Zechariah did not mention the crowd's response to God's King entering Jerusalem, but for Matthew, the crowds were important. In 15:39, the crowds were sent away and had not been very active, but now in 21:8–11 they became active again, honoring Jesus as they spread their garments and branches in His path and blessing Him as the Son of David (*The New Interpreter's Bible,* 403). A similar response to a king happened in 2 Kings 9:13, when Jehu was anointed king of Israel. The crowds echoed Psalm 118:26 in their shout. This psalm is part of the Passover liturgy, an association with particular relevance since Jesus and His disciples celebrated the Passover together in Matthew 26:17–30 just before He was arrested. "Hosanna" is a Greek transliteration of the Hebrew *hoshiah-na* (**hoe-shee-AH-nah**), which means "Please save!" It is a regular part of the liturgy in the praise psalms (Hallel) and became a common way of expressing joy by Jesus' time (403). The crowds responded with exultation as they recognized that Jesus was the Son of David and chosen by God, despite the fact that Jesus did not behave in particularly royal ways.

10 And when he was come into Jerusalem, all the city was moved, saying, Who is this? 11 And the multitude said, This is Jesus the prophet of Nazareth of Galilee.

Now that Jesus had entered Jerusalem, the response was quite different. Instead of showing honor, the crowd was shaken and asked who He was. Because some of Jerusalem's inhabitants had not encountered Jesus before, His entry caused them great fear. Matthew used the Greek word *seio* (**SAY-oh**), which can refer to both physical trembling (even an earthquake) and emotional disturbance. Douglas Hare notes that in Matthew, *seio* refers to supernatural events, as in 8:24, 24:7, 27:54 and 28:2 (*Matthew*, 239). Then when the people of the city asked whom Jesus was, the crowds proclaimed that He was a prophet. This identification was not incorrect (see 13:57, 23:37). Nevertheless, the response to Jesus in Jerusalem was not fitting for one of God's prophets, for the city responded to His teachings by arresting and crucifying Him. Jesus is not a human King with an earthly throne, despite being the Son of David. In this passage, He fulfilled the prophetic vision of Zechariah, which promised that God would provide a King from David's descendants who would do away with violence and oppression. This King will be victorious but also meek and will provide salvation to Israel and the nations. Despite Jesus' promise of salvation, the people misunderstood. Even Jesus' own disciples did not understand who He was, so it should not be surprising that the crowds were shaken and confused.

Sources:
Bauer, Walter and Frederick William Danker, eds. *A Greek-English Lexicon of the New Testament and Other Early Christian Literature.* 3rd ed. Chicago: University of Chicago Press, 2001.
Boring, M. Eugene. "The Gospel of Matthew." *The New Interpreter's Bible, vol. VIII.* Leander E. Keck, et al, eds. Nashville: Abingdon Press, 1995. 87–105.
Draper, Charles W., Chad Brand, and Archie England, eds. *Holman Illustrated Bible Dictionary.* Grand Rapids, MI: Holman Bible Publishers, 2003.
Hare, Douglas R.A. *Matthew. Interpretation: A Bible Commentary for Teaching and Preaching.* Louisville: Westminster John Knox Press, 1993.
Köhler, Ludwig, L. Koehler, and Walter Baumgartner. *The Hebrew and Aramaic Lexicon of the Old Testament.* 5 vols. Revised by Walter Baumgartner and Johann Jakob Stamm. Translated and edited by M. E. J. Richardson, et al. Leiden: Brill Academic Publishers, 2002.
Orr, James, ed. *The International Standard Bible Encyclopedia.* Chicago, IL: Howard-Severance Co., 1915.
Renn, Stephen D. *Expository Dictionary of Bible Words: Word Studies for Key English Bible Words Based on the Hebrew and Greek Texts.* Peabody, MA: Hendrickson Publishers, 2005.
Schein, Bruce E. "Olives, Mount of." *HarperCollins Bible Dictionary.* Paul J. Achtemeier, et al., eds. San Francisco: HarperCollins, 1996. 782–83.
VanGemeren, Willem A. ed., *New International Dictionary of Old Testament Theology and Exegesis, Vol. 2.* Grand Rapids, MI: Zondervan, 1997. 956.

Say It Correctly

Zechariah. zek-uh-**RYE**-ah.
Bethphage. **BETH**-fayge.

Daily Bible Readings

MONDAY
The Lord Enthroned as King
(Psalm 29)

TUESDAY
The Lord Protects
(Zechariah 9:10–15)

WEDNESDAY
The Lord Gives Victory
(Psalm 20)

THURSDAY
Loud Songs of Joy
(Psalm 47)

FRIDAY
Your Salvation Comes!
(Isaiah 62:8–12)

SATURDAY
Coming in the Lord's Name
(Psalm 118:21–29)

SUNDAY
The Triumphal Entry
(Zechariah 9:9; Matthew 21:1–11)

Notes

_____

_____

_____

_____

Teaching Tips

Words You Should Know

A. Stranger (Isaiah 56:6) *nekar* (Heb.)—A foreigner.

B. Abominations (Jeremiah 7:10) *tobah* (Heb.)—Implies things, acts, or practices that are loathsome and detestable to God or His people.

C. Astonished (Mark 11:18) *ekplesso* (Gk.)—To be amazed, astounded, or thunderstruck.

Teacher Preparation

Unifying Principle—Preserving the Places of Heritage. When an activity becomes rote, the original, helpful intent and purpose may be lost and replaced by new, harmful ones. How can a good activity be prevented from evolving into something with an unintended, harmful result? Jesus' angry action in the Temple called attention to the ways in which the priests and worshipers had lost sight of the tradition of God's dwelling place as being a house of prayer for all peoples.

A. Pray and ask God to help you present this lesson to your students with clarity.

B. Read the Bible Background and Devotional Readings.

O—Open the Lesson

A. Open with prayer.

B. Ask another volunteer to read the In Focus story.

C. Have the students discuss a time when they made plans, but events intervened and forced them to change those plans.

P—Present the Scriptures

A. Ask for a volunteer to read The People, Places, and Times.

B. Now use Search the Scriptures; At-A-Glance outline; In Depth; and More Light on the Text to clarify the verses.

E—Explore the Meaning

A. Review and have students answer the Discuss the Meaning question.

B. Ask several volunteers to share what they thought was the most significant point and how they will use that point this week.

N—Next Steps for Application

A. Complete the Follow the Spirit and Remember Your Thoughts sections.

B. Ask for a volunteer to close the class in prayer.

APR 6th

Worship Guide

For the Superintendent or Teacher
Theme: Jesus Cleanses the Temple
Song: "Silver and Gold"
Devotional Reading: Psalm 27:1–5
Prayer

Jesus Cleanses the Temple

Bible Background • ISAIAH 56:6–7; JEREMIAH 7:9–11; MARK 11:15–19
Printed Text • ISAIAH 56:6–7; JEREMIAH 7:9–11; MARK 11:15–19
Devotional Reading • PSALM 27:1–5

Aim for Change

By the end of the lesson, we will: EXPLORE the importance of keeping worship from becoming a mindless activity; UNDERSTAND the danger of losing our passion for things we habitually do for God; and EMPLOY ways to remember that God's house is first and foremost a house of prayer.

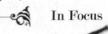 In Focus

Lauren was nervous as she sat across from the pastor's desk. Pastor Woodson smiled at her and tried to make her more comfortable. "Lauren, you're a great usher. In fact, you're one of the best young adult ushers we've ever had. You're always on time, and you really seem to know what you're doing. All of the other ushers seem to enjoy working with you."

Lauren interrupted, "Then what exactly do you need to talk about with me? When you called me, you said that there was a problem."

The pastor leaned back in his chair and said, "Lauren, you're doing a great job ushering, but you don't seem to care very much about the members. What I mean is, you seem a bit mechanical." Before Lauren could interrupt again, Pastor Woodson continued, "Let me give you an example. Last Sunday, I was watching you when Sister Martin came into the sanctuary. Lauren, were you aware that she had buried her husband that previous Wednesday?"

Far too often, our service in the church becomes routine and mundane. In today's lesson, we will see that God intends for His house to be one of prayer, worship, and genuine service.

Keep in Mind

"Is this house, which is called by my name, become a den of robbers in your eyes? Behold, even I have seen it, saith the LORD" (Jeremiah 7:11).

"Is this house, which is called by my name, become a den of robbers in your eyes? Behold, even I have seen it, saith the LORD" (Jeremiah 7:11).

Focal Verses

KJV **Isaiah 56:6** Also the sons of the stranger, that join themselves to the LORD, to serve him, and to love the name of the LORD, to be his servants, every one that keepeth the sabbath from polluting it, and taketh hold of my covenant;

7 Even them will I bring to my holy mountain, and make them joyful in my house of prayer: their burnt offerings and their sacrifices shall be accepted upon mine altar; for mine house shall be called an house of prayer for all people.

Jeremiah 7:9 Will ye steal, murder, and commit adultery, and swear falsely, and burn incense unto Baal, and walk after other gods whom ye know not;

10 And come and stand before me in this house, which is called by my name, and say, We are delivered to do all these abominations?

11 Is this house, which is called by my name, become a den of robbers in your eyes? Behold, even I have seen it, saith the LORD.

Mark 11:15 And they come to Jerusalem: and Jesus went into the temple, and began to cast out them that sold and bought in the temple, and overthrew the tables of the moneychangers, and the seats of them that sold doves;

16 And would not suffer that any man should carry any vessel through the temple.

17 And he taught, saying unto them, Is it not written, My house shall be called of all nations the house of prayer? but ye have made it a den of thieves.

18 And the scribes and chief priests heard it, and sought how they might destroy him: for they feared him, because all the people was astonished at his doctrine.

19 And when even was come, he went out of the city.

NLT **Isaiah 56:6** "I will also bless the foreigners who commit themselves to the LORD, who serve him and love his name, who worship him and do not desecrate the Sabbath day of rest, and who hold fast to my covenant.

7 I will bring them to my holy mountain of Jerusalem and will fill them with joy in my house of prayer. I will accept their burnt offerings and sacrifices, because my Temple will be called a house of prayer for all nations.

Jeremiah 7:9 Do you really think you can steal, murder, commit adultery, lie, and burn incense to Baal and all those other new gods of yours,

10 and then come here and stand before me in my Temple and chant, "We are safe!"— only to go right back to all those evils again?

11 Don't you yourselves admit that this Temple, which bears my name, has become a den of thieves? Surely I see all the evil going on there. I, the LORD, have spoken!

Mark 11:15 When they arrived back in Jerusalem, Jesus entered the Temple and began to drive out the people buying and selling animals for sacrifices. He knocked over the tables of the money changers and the chairs of those selling doves,

16 and he stopped everyone from using the Temple as a marketplace.

17 He said to them, "The Scriptures declare, 'My Temple will be called a house of prayer for all nations,' but you have turned it into a den of thieves."

18 When the leading priests and teachers of religious law heard what Jesus had done, they began planning how to kill him. But they were afraid of him because the people were so amazed at his teaching.

19 That evening Jesus and the disciples left the city.

The People, Places, and Times

The Second Temple. In 586 B.C., the Babylonians destroyed the original temple in Jerusalem that had been built by King Solomon. Following years of exile, a contingent of about 42,360 Jews was given permission by King Cyrus to return and rebuild the temple, which lay in ruins (Ezra 2:64). Renovation of the temple was begun under the direction of the governor Zerubbabel. These renovation attempts were slow, and they focused on the rebuilding of the altar. Not surprisingly, this second temple was not as splendid as the original.

Many years later, in the seventeenth year of his reign, Herod the Great announced his plans to again renovate the temple. He began in 20 or 19 B.C. by enlarging the Temple Mount (also known as Mount Moriah) area to accommodate larger crowds of pilgrims who regularly attended Passover and other religious festivals.

Herod provided a thousand wagons to transport stones from the limestone quarry. Additionally, Herod hired ten thousand skilled craftsmen to work on the building of the temple. Because the law required that only priests could work on the holiest parts of the temple, including the sanctuary and the Court of Priests, more than a thousand priests were trained as carpenters and masons.

According to records by the historian Josephus, the inner courts were completed after a year and a half. He also recorded that during the construction of the inner courts, no rain fell during the day. While Herod had the original foundations of the temple removed, the eastern wall was kept intact. Construction on this temple continued for twenty years; however, it was sufficiently ready for use and was dedicated within three and a half years of its commencement, thus fulfilling Isaiah's prophecy that another temple would be constructed when the people had been restored to the land (Isaiah 2:2–3, 44:28, 56:7, 66:20–21).

Background

Even when they were captives in Babylon, the Jews were required to follow the laws of God. Writings from prophets like Isaiah continued to remind the people that the salvation of the Lord was "close at hand" (Isaiah 56:1, NIV), thus affirming their hope that they would be restored to their land. God's commandment to "remember the sabbath day, to keep it holy" (Exodus 20:8) was especially difficult for Jews living in captivity. They were enslaved in pagan lands and this prohibition against working on the Sabbath was often impractical. Similarly, other pagan customs were imposed on the Jews that made it difficult for them to follow God's laws and commandments. Isaiah had prophesied to King Hezekiah that some of his heirs would one day serve as eunuchs in the palace of Babylon (2 Kings 20:18). While the Bible does not say that this is what happened to Daniel, Shadrach, Meshach, and Abednego, most biblical scholars recognize that this is what happened to foreign men serving in the royal palace of Babylon. Such conditions would have meant that these men would have been prohibited from temple service when they returned to Jerusalem. Moreover, the eunuchs would be unable to father children and ensure the continuity of their family name. However, we read that this law would be overruled if the eunuch kept the Sabbath holy and obeyed God to the best of his ability (Isaiah 56:4–5).

This is a clear indication that God, then as now, is far more concerned about the hearts of His people rather than their physical condition. Similarly, a special place of honor would be established in the temple for the eunuchs (v. 5). Here we see that God would publicly honor the faithfulness of these men who had been physically altered against their will, yet who continued to honor and serve Him and follow His laws. More importantly, this is further confirmation that God has no intention of allowing His beloved to remain as outcasts.

At-A-Glance

1. Isaiah Reminds the People that the Temple is a Symbol of Hope (Isaiah 56:6–7)
2. Jeremiah Warns Against Temple Abuse (Jeremiah 7:9–11)
3. Jesus Expresses Outrage (Mark 11:15–19)

In Depth

1. Isaiah Reminds the People that the Temple is a Symbol of Hope (Isaiah 56:6–7)

God's promise to redeem His people and return them to Israel was not restricted to Jews. These verses offered assurance to the foreigners that they too would be welcomed to the "holy mountain," and even able to participate in temple service, including making sacrifices and offerings. God's love is all-inclusive. Here we see it being extended to those who were previously excluded (foreigners).

The purpose of the temple as a "house of prayer" is further clarified here. This crucial aspect of temple usage was apparent from the beginning. When Solomon, the builder of the first temple, prayed at its dedication, he asked God to "hear the supplication of your servant and of your people Israel when they pray toward this place. Hear from heaven, your dwelling place, and when you hear, forgive" (1 Kings 8:30, NIV). This means that

the temple would be the appointed place where God's people would talk with Him.

In the New Testament account of Philip's encounter with the Ethiopian eunuch (Acts 8:26–39), we get a full picture of God's inclusive grace in action. The Ethiopian was willing to travel all the way to Jerusalem. He was, no doubt, aware that he would be excluded from temple worship because he was both a foreigner (Ethiopian) and a eunuch. Yet, his devotion to God was so complete that he obeyed Him by doing what he knew He required (worship and study), in spite of the consequences. The faith of the Ethiopian overrode his fear of exclusion. God honored his faithfulness by sending Philip to lead him to the truth of Jesus, the Christ.

2. Jeremiah Warns Against Temple Abuse (Jeremiah 7:9–11)

Although he lived in the 6th and 7th centuries B.C., the political and moral climate of the prophet Jeremiah's time was surprisingly similar to our own. The nation of Judah was under constant threat by Egypt and Babylon. Their sister nation, Israel, had already fallen victim to Assyria. The cities belonging to the ten tribes that comprised Israel had been ransacked and the people taken into captivity. God commissioned Jeremiah to minister in the face of Judah's imminent demise and captivity. Over the course of forty years (626 to 587 B.C.), and the reigns of five kings, Jeremiah was tasked with preaching an unpopular truth.

At one point, Jeremiah was instructed to "stand in the gate of the LORD's house" (Jeremiah 7:2) and speak to His people. This is a powerful reminder for present-day Christians that during every age, judgment has always begun at God's house. This is because God's people then, as now, struggle under the false assumption that God will not judge and punish the "religious." The people of Judah wrongly believed that because God had selected the temple as His dwelling, He would not allow it to be destroyed. Jeremiah continually warned the people of Judah, "Do not trust in deceptive words" (from v. 4, NIV) and to change their wicked ways and practices. Jeremiah was calling for national revival, urging the people of God to return to His Word and obey His commandments.

While the people of Judah came to the temple and participated in the ceremonies and rituals, their lives outside of the temple clearly demonstrated that the Word of God was not in their hearts. The Judeans were guilty of acts of injustice and oppression or shedding "innocent blood" (from v. 6). Additionally, the prophet warned that God was aware of their stealing, murder, adultery, and bearing false witness against one another. Perhaps the most serious crime was that the people of Judah walked "after other gods" (from v. 6). This reference to Baal worship is repeated in verse 9. It is interesting to note that "Baal" is the Hebrew word for "husband" and "master." This allows us to see Judah's unfaithfulness to God in a whole new light. Like an unfaithful wife, Judah had turned her back on her true husband (God).

Although Judah had witnessed Israel's destruction for her unfaithfulness, they foolishly continued in their sinful ways. Judah believed that they could live outside of the Word and will of God, but because they kept the outward temple rituals, they would be saved. Jeremiah warned them that they were wrong. In verse 11, we see the ultimate perversion of what God intended—the use of His house as a "den of robbers."

3. Jesus Expresses Outrage (Mark 11:15–19)
During Passover, adult males from all over the world came to worship at the temple.

Every Jew over the age of twenty was obligated to make a temple offering of half a shekel. Additionally, Jewish law called for the sacrifices of large numbers of goats, sheep, and oxen. As the nation had transitioned from tribes of desert wanderers to living in a large and heavily populated city such as Jerusalem, it was no longer practical to select an animal from a flock or herd close by. Stalls and pens were erected in a large temple area located near the sacrificial altar. The Court of the Gentiles, or its adjoining porch, seemed the most likely location. This area was used for worship by Jewish women and Gentiles, and it was spacious and located farthest from the most holy place.

Here, livestock spaces were rented, and the proceeds were used to pay for the repair and upkeep of the temple. In this way, the devout worshipers—many of them having traveled long distances—could be accommodated, and the glory of the Temple would constantly be maintained by the fees that were collected. This system of collecting rents gave rise to questionable practices that were rooted in greed. The attention to income grew more important than spiritual worship. Another way of making money came when the priests rejected sacrifices that pilgrims brought with them to the temple, forcing them to buy an animal from the temple vendors.

Also present in this area were the moneychangers. These men acted as currency bankers and brokers. Granted, their services were needed because foreign money was not accepted in the temple, so these moneychangers would sell the acceptable temple coinage. The problem was the rate was often extraordinarily high, and these moneychangers also charged for their services. Historically, these moneychangers were set up in areas outside of the temple. However, during the special festivals when the Jews and faithful believers from other lands began arriving in Jerusalem, these merchants were allowed to set up their tables within the temple area. The high priests and other religious officials were no doubt aware of these ungodly practices. This is a powerful reminder to present-day Christians that abuse in the church can always be traced to looking the other way amid the protests of few and the silence of the majority.

The moneychangers made large profits at the expense of the foreign-born pilgrims who, in obedience to the word of God, had come to the temple to worship. This speaks to the disdain many of the Jews felt for non-Israelite worshipers—a sad indictment of the religious leadership. This attitude is in direct opposition to Jesus' teaching. Jesus had quoted Isaiah and declared that the temple was to be a "house of prayer for all people" (from Isaiah 56:7). These foreigners, often non-Jews, were restricted to worshiping in the Court of the Gentiles, the outmost court. Upon entering the temple, rather than finding a contemplative and prayerful space, these worshipers encountered a carnival atmosphere. One can imagine how the sounds of clanging coins, the loud yelling of the merchants, and the bleating of animals must have disturbed Jesus. Here, in the most holy place in the world, He encountered dishonest merchants who, with the permission of the religious authorities, were clearly taking advantage of sincere worshipers. Jesus found it so offensive that He likened it to "a den of thieves" (from Mark 11:17).

As we read that Jesus was so outraged that He "cast out them that sold and bought in the temple, and overthrew the tables of the moneychangers, and the seats of them that sold doves" (from Mark 11:15), we must remember that His righteous indignation was an understandable and acceptable response to evil. His action should prompt present-day Christians to question themselves and their personal response to wrongdoing. How outraged are professed Christians when we witness the house of the Lord being desecrated by worldliness, expediency, and self-indulgence?

Search the Scriptures

1. What blessing did God offer to the strangers or foreigners who embraced Him (Isaiah 56:7)?

2. What sins did God accuse the nation of Judah of committing (Jeremiah 7:9)?

3. How did the scribes and the chief priests respond to Jesus exposing the evil being done in the temple (Mark 11:18)?

Discuss the Meaning

In Mark 11:15–17, Jesus was indignant when He saw the temple of God, His Father, being used as a venue for worldly traffic. He overturned the tables and chairs of the moneychangers and chased them from the temple. What do you think should be the appropriate response and action of Christians who witness ungodly behavior and practices in the church?

Lessons in Our Society

Jesus lashed out against a spirit of depravity that had pervaded the temple in the form of monetary greed. This sin is still present today. The Bible teaches that the love of money is "the root of all evil" (from 1 Timothy 6:10). Yet these teachings appear to go unheeded. One need only read the newspaper or watch the news to see the many ways that greed and corruption appear to be imbedded in our society. We witness homes being lost and lifetime savings dissolving when uncaring people floatunsound speculations in the market. Countless catastrophic injuries and deaths result from unjust wars of aggression.

God is calling on His people—the church—to set an example of the opposite of all this through our Christian generosity and self-sacrifice. Attending church is not enough! Our worship and our service to God must be exemplified through our continued and continual care and compassion for others.

Make It Happen

A true believer does more than follow rituals and traditions. Being children of God means that we must not only acknowledge Him, we must make every effort to live according to His Word. When we fail to live committed lives, instead continuing to live according to our own desires, we will eventually begin to cling to fallacies and fall into a life of self-deception and practices that are contrary to the will of God. Pray and ask God to give you a clean heart and hands, so your words of praise to Him will not be empty and void.

Follow the Spirit

What God wants me to do:

_____

_____

_____

_____

Remember Your Thoughts

Special insights I have learned:

_____

_____

_____

_____

More Light on the Text

The passage in Isaiah focuses on the Mosaic Covenant's emphasis on the Sabbath. Isaiah stressed that a life of holiness is not only free of hypocrisy but also embraces people from all nations. The portion of Jeremiah's "temple sermon" (Jeremiah 7:1–15) was delivered during a time of great upheaval, when people were desperately in need of returning—not to religion, but to a right relationship with God. F. B. Huey writes, "In such turbulent times the people grasped at any symbol of security, which for them was the temple" (*Jeremiah, Lamentations*, 104).

The passage in Mark, cleansing the temple, is sandwiched between the story of Jesus not finding fruit on the fig tree and withering it and the teaching on that event. David Garland writes, "Interpreting either in isolation from the other leads one in the wrong direction" (*Mark*, 433).

Isaiah 56:6–7

6 Also the sons of the stranger, that join themselves to the LORD, to serve him, and to love the name of the LORD, to be his servants, every one that keepeth the sabbath from polluting it, and taketh hold of my covenant; 7 Even them will I bring to my holy mountain, and make them joyful in my house of prayer: their burnt offerings and their sacrifices shall be accepted upon mine altar; for mine house shall be called an house of prayer for all people.

Geoffrey Grogan describes this passage as "a beautiful description of true godliness" (*Isaiah, Jeremiah, Lamentations, Ezekiel*, 316). Obedient service is stressed as being inclusive of foreigners, which is God's early introduction to His people of the then-future Gospel's concept of inclusivity of Gentiles, which is made explicit in verse 7 with an emphasis on God's house being open to "all people" (cf. Isaiah 66:23; Malachi 1:11). The trajectory of this inclusive pattern became even more specific in the New Testament (Galatians 3:28).

Jeremiah 7:9–11

9 Will ye steal, murder, and commit adultery, and swear falsely, and burn incense unto Baal, and walk after other gods whom ye know not; 10 And come and stand before me in this house, which is called by my name, and say, We are delivered to do all these abominations? 11 Is this house, which is called by my name, become a den of robbers in your eyes? Behold, even I have seen it, saith the LORD.

Jeremiah listed a total of six of the original Ten Commandments in his indictment of God's people—who, in spite of the extent of their unrighteousness, went to the temple and acted as if its "magical powers" would make them right before God so they could then resume their sinful lifestyles. His message was for them to live "in moral uprightness, faithfulness, and obedience to their God," in Huey's words (*Jeremiah, Lamentations*, 104), and not to have blind trust and faith in the temple as if it were some kind of good-luck charm—a type of "temple talisman," as it were.

Exactly like their predecessors clinging in blind faith to the Ark of the Covenant, these people also forgot that God required obedience in order to bless and protect them (Deuteronomy 7:12–15; Ezekiel 18:5–9). In this matter, the religion that pleased God never changed and has not changed to the present (Micah 6:6–8; James 1:26–27). The Mosaic Covenant had been "if/then" conditional—IF they obeyed, THEN God would keep all His promises (Exodus 19:5). In essence, the people wanted God's promises without His conditions (cf. 2 Peter 1:2–11).

Robbers go out to commit their crimes and then return to the safety of their den. Similarly, God's people lived their unrighteous lives and then returned to temple "den" . . . like thieves retreating to their hideouts.

Mark 11:15–16

15 And they come to Jerusalem: and Jesus went into the temple, and began to cast out them that sold and bought in the temple, and overthrew the tables of the moneychangers, and the seats of them that sold doves; 16 And would not suffer that any man should carry any vessel through the temple.

Understood in the context of the fig tree incident before and after (vv. 12–14, 20–23), this is a story within a story. The fig tree was a symbol of Israel, much like the Star of David today. Essentially, both the tree and Israel seemed to be thriving, that is, they were "leafy," but there was no fruit—and Jesus condemned both. The temple cleansing was "largely symbolic," notes Garland (*Mark*, 434); in other words, Jesus made a scene but did not do anything worthy of calling the Roman police. His immediate point was that the sacred space was for sincere prayer and genuine worship, not commerce, but He made other points in the process.

17 And he taught, saying unto them, Is it not written, My house shall be called of all nations the house of prayer? but ye have made it a den of thieves.

Here Jesus quoted from our other passages (Isaiah 56:7; Jeremiah 7:11), the latter of which, in Lamar Williamson's words, "attacks the use of religious observances to cover up sinful practices" (*Mark*, 207). When Jesus condemned the fig tree, it "withered from the roots up" (Mark 11:20, NLT), just as the temple was being destroyed from the roots up; that is, core corruption. He was making a dramatic statement displaying God's attitude toward the people's fruitless relationship with Him in spite of their faithful temple observance. Here, the fruitlessness of the tree illustrated the need for temple cleansing.

18 And the scribes and chief priests heard it, and sought how they might destroy him: for they feared him, because all the people was astonished at his doctrine. 19 And when even was come, he went out of the city.

The leaders, who were the "roots" of the temple, understood what Jesus was saying, but rather than allowing the truth to humble them, they hardened their hearts. The people, on the other hand, were shocked that Jesus talked this way about their beloved temple. They were astonished (Gk. *ekplesson*, **ek-PLAS-SO**), which meant to be struck with amazement.

R. E. Clements captures the essence of the message of the Old Testament prophets, which Christ vividly brought to life centuries later: "What is at stake is the fundamental principle that God is necessarily greater than any symbol set on earth as a manifestation of his presence" (*Jeremiah*, 46). Such a stern lesson should end on a positive note, which Williamson provides: "The power of God that withered a fig tree and moves mountains can also bring new life to a church and its leaders, though they be dry from their roots up" (210). The people of God had come to see the temple as their perennial good-luck charm against all the evils of life, but God's justice held that a barren tree had a limited lifespan, just like a barren temple. Ultimately, in an even bigger picture, salvation would no longer be secured by sacrifices in the temple but rather through Jesus' sacrifice outside the temple—for all the people, not just for the Jews.

Sources:
Blue Letter Bible. BlueLetterBible.org. http://www.blueletterbible.org/ (accessed August 7, 2012).
Clements, R. E. *Jeremiah. Interpretation: A Bible Commentary for Teaching and Preaching.* Louisville: Westminster John Knox Press, 1989. 103–106.
Cohney, Shelley. "The Second Temple at the Time of Jesus." Jewish Virtual Library. www.jewishvirtuallibrary.org/jsource/History/secondtempletimeofjesus.html (accessed November 12, 2012).
Garland, David E. *Mark. NIV Application Commentary.* Grand Rapids: Zondervan, 1996. 423–449.
Grogan, Geoffrey W. "Isaiah, Jeremiah, Lamentations, Ezekiel." *The Expositor's Bible Commentary, vol. 6.* Edited by Frank E. Gaebelein. Grand Rapids, MI: Zondervan, 1986. 314–316.
Hanson, Paul D. *Isaiah 40–66. Interpretation: A Bible Commentary for Teaching and Preaching.* Louisville: Westminster John Knox Press, 1995. 193–197.
Huey, F. B., Jr. *Jeremiah, Lamentations. New American Commentary, vol. 16.* Louisville: Westminster John Knox Press, 1995. 103–106.
Smith, Barry D. "The Jerusalem Temple and the New Testament." Crandall University Religious Studies. The New Testament and Its Context. www.abu.nb.ca/courses/ntintro/jerusaltempl4.htm (accessed November 13, 2012).
Williamson, Lamar, Jr. *Mark. Interpretation: A Bible Commentary for Teaching and Preaching.* Louisville: Westminster John Knox Press, 2009. 206–210.

Say It Correctly

Baal. **BEYL**.
Zerubbabel. zuh-**RUB**-uh-bul.

Daily Bible Readings

MONDAY
The Holy Temple
(Habakkuk 2:18–20)

TUESDAY
The House of the Lord
(Psalm 27:1–5)

WEDNESDAY
I Cried for Help
(Psalm 18:1–6)

THURSDAY
My Prayer Came to You
(Jonah 2:1–9)

FRIDAY
Something Greater than the Temple
(Matthew 12:1–8)

SATURDAY
A Holy Temple in the Lord
(Ephesians 2:11–22)

SUNDAY
A House of Prayer
(Isaiah 56:6–7; Jeremiah 7:9–11;
Mark 11:15–19)

Notes

Teaching Tips

Words You Should Know

A. Scourged (John 19:1) *mastigoo* (Gk.)—To whip.

B. Fault (vv. 4, 6) *aitia* (Gk.)—Cause for which one is worthy of punishment; crime or accusation.

Teacher Preparation

Unifying Principle—A Perceived Threat. People tend to lash out at perceived threats to established power. How do people form a perception of threat? The perception of Jesus as a king, who would exercise political rule and power, seemingly made Him a threat to the existing Roman and Jewish powers.

A. Read the Bible Background and Devotional Readings.

B. Reread the Focal Verses in a modern translation.

O—Open the Lesson

A. Open with prayer.

B. Ask for a volunteer to read the In Focus story.

C. Discuss how to have humility and endure suffering on the road to our destiny.

P—Present the Scriptures

A. Ask for volunteers to read the Focal Verses and The People, Places, and Times. Discuss.

B. Read and discuss the Background section.

E—Explore the Meaning

A. Review and discuss the Search the Scriptures and Discuss the Meaning questions and the Lesson in Our Society section.

B. Ask students to share the most significant point they learned and how to use that point this week.

N—Next Steps for Application

A. Complete the Follow the Spirit and Remember Your Thoughts sections.

B. Ask the class to think about things that have occurred in their life that don't appear to have worked out the way they wished. Have them reflect on those experiences, having the benefit of time and perspective.

C. Close in prayer, thanking God for His presence in our lives.

APR
13th

Worship Guide

For the Superintendent or Teacher
Theme: A Messianic Priest-King
Song: "Wounded for Me"
Devotional Reading: Hebrews 7:11–19
Prayer

A Messianic Priest-King

Bible Background • JEREMIAH 23:5–6; ZECHARIAH 6:9–14; JOHN 19:1–5
Printed Text • JEREMIAH 23:5–6; ZECHARIAH 6:9–14; JOHN 19:1–5
Devotional Reading • HEBREWS 7:11–19

Aim for Change

By the end of the lesson, we will: OBSERVE how Jesus' humility amid suffering fulfilled prophecies made about Him; TRUST that we will become all that God has ordained us to be, even if the road to our destiny is a humble one; and PRAY for strength to endure when things don't appear as God has promised.

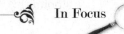 **In Focus**

James continued to rub his eyes as he studied his textbook. He had a big final exam tomorrow, and he wanted to make sure he passed with a "B" or better. Just then, his roommate, Jamal, walked in.

"Hey, James," he said. "Why don't you get your head out of that book and come on to this party?"

James looked up. "Nah, that's alright, man."

"Come on, James! Every time there's a party or something fun, you always have your nose up in a book."

James turned to him and said, "Man, I am the first one in my family to go to college. I believe God has called me to be a doctor, and I won't let anything sidetrack me."

Jamal stood there and paused. "Even doctors have fun. You know, Tameka will be at the party." Jamal knew that James had feelings for Tameka. James was torn. He wanted to go to the party, but he also knew that he needed to study for this test.

We can trust that we will become all that God has ordained us to be. In today's lesson, we will learn how to endure when things don't appear as God promised.

Keep in Mind

"And said, Hail, King of the Jews! and they smote him with their hands"
(John 19:3).

"And said, Hail, King of the Jews! and they smote him with their hands" (John 19:3).

Focal Verses

KJV **Jeremiah 23:5** Behold, the days come, saith the LORD, that I will raise unto David a righteous Branch, and a King shall reign and prosper, and shall execute judgment and justice in the earth.

6 In his days Judah shall be saved, and Israel shall dwell safely: and this is his name whereby he shall be called, THE LORD OUR RIGHTEOUSNESS.

Zechariah 6:9 And the word of the LORD came unto me, saying,

10 Take of them of the captivity, even of Heldai, of Tobijah, and of Jedaiah, which are come from Babylon, and come thou the same day, and go into the house of Josiah the son of Zephaniah;

11 Then take silver and gold, and make crowns, and set them upon the head of Joshua the son of Josedech, the high priest;

12 And speak unto him, saying, Thus speaketh the LORD of hosts, saying, Behold the man whose name is The BRANCH; and he shall grow up out of his place, and he shall build the temple of the LORD:

13 Even he shall build the temple of the LORD; and he shall bear the glory, and shall sit and rule upon his throne; and he shall be a priest upon his throne: and the counsel of peace shall be between them both.

14 And the crowns shall be to Helem, and to Tobijah, and to Jedaiah, and to Hen the son of Zephaniah, for a memorial in the temple of the LORD.

John 19:1 Then Pilate therefore took Jesus, and scourged him.

2 And the soldiers platted a crown of thorns, and put it on his head, and they put on him a purple robe,

3 And said, Hail, King of the Jews! and they smote him with their hands.

NLT **Jeremiah 23:5** "For the time is coming," says the LORD, "when I will raise up a righteous descendant from King David's line. He will be a King who rules with wisdom. He will do what is just and right throughout the land.

6 And this will be his name: 'The LORD Is Our Righteousness.' In that day Judah will be saved, and Israel will live in safety."

Zechariah 6:9 Then I received another message from the LORD:

10 "Heldai, Tobijah, and Jedaiah will bring gifts of silver and gold from the Jews exiled in Babylon. As soon as they arrive, meet them at the home of Josiah son of Zephaniah.

11 Accept their gifts, and make a crown from the silver and gold. Then put the crown on the head of Jeshua son of Jehozadak, the high priest.

12 Tell him, 'This is what the LORD of Heaven's Armies says: Here is the man called the Branch. He will branch out from where he is and build the Temple of the LORD.

13 Yes, he will build the Temple of the LORD. Then he will receive royal honor and will rule as king from his throne. He will also serve as priest from his throne, and there will be perfect harmony between his two roles.'

14 "The crown will be a memorial in the Temple of the LORD to honor those who gave it—Heldai, Tobijah, Jedaiah, and Josiah son of Zephaniah."

John 19:1 Then Pilate had Jesus flogged with a lead-tipped whip.

2 The soldiers wove a crown of thorns and put it on his head, and they put a purple robe on him.

3 "Hail! King of the Jews!" they mocked, as they slapped him across the face.

4 Pilate went outside again and said to the people, "I am going to bring him out to you

4 Pilate therefore went forth again, and saith unto them, Behold, I bring him forth to you, that ye may know that I find no fault in him.

5 Then came Jesus forth, wearing the crown of thorns, and the purple robe. And Pilate saith unto them, Behold the man!

now, but understand clearly that I find him not guilty."

5 Then Jesus came out wearing the crown of thorns and the purple robe. And Pilate said, "Look, here is the man!"

The People, Places, and Times

Pilate. Pilate was the sixth Roman procurator of Judea and Samaria. He held office for twelve years. By the end of that time, because of his insensitivity to Jewish religious concerns and thirst for power, he was hated by both Jews and Samaritans. He was recalled by Tiberius and banished to Vienna, where he committed suicide.

The Crowd. This is the Jewish crowd that decided Jesus was a blasphemer and worthy of death. A few days before, a similar crowd had followed Him through the streets and adored Him with praise as the coming Messiah.

Background

The Jewish people looked forward to a coming Messiah who would bring their nation back to its former glory. This was supported by prophecies from the Old Testament dating back to the book of Genesis. Many of these prophecies describe a coming righteous King who will rule justly and fairly. Jeremiah 23:5–6 and Zechariah 6:9–14 are two prophecies that describe the coming Messiah as a King who will right the wrongs of Israel and restore the nation to its former glory. This Messiah would come from the line of David, and He would not only be a King, but also a Priest. This was unprecedented.

At first glance, Jesus did not fit the descriptions in any of these prophecies. He was lowly and rejected. He suffered humiliation through being flogged with thirty-nine lashes. Ultimately, He was led to death by crucifixion. The soldiers of Pilate capitalized on this and mocked Jesus. They gave Him a crown of thorns and a purple robe. After they slapped Him in the face multiple times and spit on Him, they shouted, "Hail, King of the Jews!" as a bitter way to humiliate Him further.

Although these were acts of humiliation and suffering, they also brought Him further to His destiny as Messiah. The coming Messiah was a King, but He was also described as a Branch, which symbolized lowliness and humility. He was also supposed to be a Priest and a King and, through His death on the cross, He became a Priest for us by offering up His own body as the final and ultimate sacrifice.

At-A-Glance

1. The Messianic Priest-King is Humble and Lowly (John 19:1–3; Jeremiah 23:5; Zechariah 6:12)
2. The Messianic Priest-King is Righteous in His Suffering (John 19:4; Jeremiah 23:6)
3. The Messianic Priest-King Will Be Vindicated (John 19:1–3; Jeremiah 23:5–6; Zechariah 6:12–14)

In Depth

1. The Messianic Priest-King is Humble and Lowly (John 19:1–3; Jeremiah 23:5; Zechariah 6:12)

As the Messianic Priest-King, Jesus is humble and lowly. These are unusual attributes for a king. It is also unusual for a king to be scourged (John 19:1). The traditional Roman scourging consisted of being beaten with a whip. This whip had multiple leather thongs with metal balls or sheep bone tied on the ends. This type of practice was used to beat the victim as a form of punishment, extract a confession, or weaken him before crucifixion in order for him to die more quickly.

After the scourging, soldiers were expected to taunt the victim, and the soldiers who beat Jesus were no exception. They put a crown of thorns and purple robe on Him as mock royal garments. They slapped Him in the face to show that He was not a king and deserved no respect from them.

Jesus endured this humiliation in order to be the Messianic Priest-King, the Branch, who was foretold by Jeremiah, Zechariah, and Isaiah.

2. The Messianic Priest-King is Righteous in His Suffering (John 19:4; Jeremiah 23:6)

After undergoing humiliation and suffering, Jesus was brought back to Pilate. Pilate stood Jesus before the crowd and said that he could find no fault in Him. This shows how righteously Jesus acted in His suffering. He suffered unfairly and was innocent of any charges; no one could bring anything against Him. Pilate had no basis for accusing Him under Roman law.

His crime was being Himself: the Lord our righteousness. Jesus' righteousness is very crucial to Him being a Priest-King. In order to perform the duty of giving the sacrifice of His life for the whole world once and for all,

Jesus had to be spotless and blameless. He was an innocent man who was about to die on the cross. It seems unfair, but this is the road that He had to take as our Messianic Priest-King.

3. The Messianic Priest-King Will Be Vindicated (John 19:1–3; Jeremiah 23:5–6; Zechariah 6:12–14)

The soldiers mocked Jesus and taunted Him by calling Him the King of the Jews, yet there was truth in that title. Jesus could endure the suffering and humiliation because He knew the final outcome. He would fulfill the prophecies about Him as the Messianic Priest-King who would deliver Israel. The purple robe and the crown of thorns were just precursors to the truth that Jesus would be the King who would execute justice and righteousness. He was beaten and slapped in the face by Gentile Roman soldiers, but since one day He would be worshiped by Gentiles who were "far off" from the people of God (Zechariah 6:15). The suffering and mistreatment Jesus endured were offset with the promise that He would be King.

Search the Scriptures

1. What was the purpose of placing the crown on Joshua the high priest's head (Zechariah 6:11–13)?

2. What was the purpose of scourging Jesus if Pilate found "no fault in him" (John 19:1, 4)?

Discuss the Meaning

1. How can Jesus be both Priest and King? What does this mean for us as His followers?

2. What can we do when we endure suffering and humiliation on the road to our destiny?

Lesson in Our Society

Jesus endured mistreatment and suffering in order to see God's promises come to pass. As His followers, sometimes we must go through mistreatment and suffering in order to see God's promises come to pass in our lives as well. There will be times where it feels like God is not there and what He promised will not come to pass. These are the times when we need to trust Him the most. It is then we find God working behind the scenes, doing something far greater than we can understand.

Many times, it seems like the way of humility and suffering is the way of weakness. It is the opposite of the world's way of dominating and forcing people to give us what we want and what is "rightfully ours." This is not the way to go about things if we believe and trust that God is fighting our battles and has our best interest in mind. Jesus knew this, and He suffered for a short time in order to reap greater blessings in the end. This is the way of Christ that we as His followers are called to imitate.

Make It Happen

God's way is different than man's way. In order to get ahead and obtain what we believe is ours, the world says we must do it ourselves and let no one stand in our way. God says to trust Him and endure hardship. It is hard to choose God's way, because it involves pain and suffering, but it is definitely more rewarding in the end. We must remember to choose the way of humility and pray for patience to see God's promises come to pass.

Take time to recall God's promises that you find in the Bible. Serve others who are less fortunate by volunteering at a soup kitchen or homeless shelter. Thank God for the things you do have instead of focusing on what you don't. Finally, pray that God gives you strength to withstand suffering and mistreatment on the way to obtaining His promises.

Follow the Spirit

What God wants me to do:

_____

_____

_____

_____

Remember Your Thoughts

Special insights I have learned:

_____

_____

_____

_____

More Light on the Text
Jeremiah 23:5–6

On the heels of a prediction of woe (vv. 1–4) invoking God's judgment on bad shepherds comes this Messianic prediction regarding the true Shepherd-King (cf. 3:15–18, 31:31–34). People being described as flocks of sheep and kings and leaders as shepherds were clearly understood and widely used metaphors in the ancient Near East (cf. 10:21; Isaiah 63:11; Ezekiel 34:8, 31).

5 Behold, the days come, saith the LORD, that I will raise unto David a righteous Branch, and a King shall reign and prosper, and shall execute judgment and justice in the earth. 6 In his days Judah shall be saved, and Israel shall dwell safely: and this

is his name whereby he shall be called, **THE LORD OUR RIGHTEOUSNESS.**

The late Charles Feinberg affirms the Messianic message: "The formula 'days are coming' is a messianic formula . . . used fifteen times in the book" (*Isaiah, Jeremiah, Lamentations, Ezekiel,* 618) (e.g. 7:32, 9:25; cf. Hebrews 8:8). Most scholars agree with this, and also that the Messiah would come from David's royal line and would reign forever (cf. 2 Samuel 7:8–16). F. B. Huey asserts, "These verses contributed to the developing messianic belief in Israel" (*Jeremiah, Lamentations,* 211) (cf. 30:8–9, 21, 33:15–16).

Notice the similarities of all the following Hebrew words: the righteous Branch (Heb. *tsehmach,* **TSEH-mach**) (see also 33:15; Isaiah 4:2; Zechariah 3:8) or King's name, which means "The Lord our Righteousness" (Heb. *tsedeq,* **TSEH-dek**, meaning justice, justness, rightness) and King Zedekiah's name (Heb. *tsidqiyah,* **tsid-KE-ya**), which means "Jehovah is righteous" or "justice of Jehovah." R. E. Clements observes that in the Hebrew, the word makes a play on the name of Zedekiah, a puppet king whom the Babylonians put on the throne (*Jeremiah,* 138); by comparison, the righteous Branch would "branch out." Also in contrast, the new messianic King would rule right, He would be wise, and He would bring justice and righteousness, a core Old Testament theme (1 Kings 10:9; Psalm 99:4; Isaiah 9:7). Paul applied the same term to Jesus in 1 Corinthians 1:30.

Zechariah 6:9–11

9 And the word of the LORD came unto me, saying, 10 Take of them of the captivity, even of Heldai, of Tobijah, and of Jedaiah, which are come from Babylon, and come thou the same day, and go into the house of Josiah the son of Zephaniah; 11 Then take silver and gold, and make crowns, and set them upon the head of Joshua the son of Josedech, the high priest.

This symbolic crowning ceremony of Joshua the high priest comes after Zechariah's famous series of eight visions. In visions four (chapter 3) and five (chapter 4), he refers to the high priest and ruler. This special type of crown in Hebrew is *atarah* (**at-ta-RAH**) and literally means an ornate crown (see 2 Samuel 12:30; Isaiah 62:3; cf. Revelation 19:12). Scholars agree that Joshua (Heb. *Yehowshuwa,* **yeh-ho-SHU-ah**), whose name means "Jehovah is salvation," was similar to Jesus, whose name means "The Lord saves" (Matthew 1:21). Jesus is the true Branch and Messiah, and here He is symbolically and prophetically, via His prototype Joshua, being crowned both Priest and King.

12 And speak unto him, saying, Thus speaketh the LORD of hosts, saying, Behold the man whose name is The BRANCH; and he shall grow up out of his place, and he shall build the temple of the LORD: 13 Even he shall build the temple of the LORD; and he shall bear the glory, and shall sit and rule upon his throne; and he shall be a priest upon his throne: and the counsel of peace shall be between them both. 14 And the crowns shall be to Helem, and to Tobijah, and to Jedaiah, and to Hen the son of Zephaniah, for a memorial in the temple of the LORD.

In Zechariah's visions, Joshua was priest while Zerubbabel ruled and built the temple—here the Branch will be both Priest and Ruler, and He will build the temple. Kenneth Barker writes, "In 4:14, Joshua and Zerubbabel represent separate offices; here [v. 13] the Branch was to hold both offices" (*Daniel–Minor Prophets,* 518). A key part of our lesson involves the words, "Behold the man whose name is The BRANCH," which is unmistakably similar to the language in the next section, "Behold the man!" (John 19:5). Since Zerubbabel would complete the restoration of the temple, an overly literal interpretation does not work. According to Barker, "It is difficult to see how this could refer to that temple . . . it must have in view the temple of the Messianic Age" (519). Not only will the Branch, the Messiah, build the Messianic temple, but also as Priest and King He will sit on the throne of David and rule with justice and righteousness. Barker quotes Baldwin as saying, "Nowhere else in the Old Testament is it made so plain that the coming Davidic king will also be a priest" (519). All of these prophecies refer to "a future reality . . . the true temple in which God will abide in the midst of his people for all time," in the words of Elizabeth Achtemeier (*Nahum–Malachi*, 130).

John 19:1–5

1 Then Pilate therefore took Jesus, and scourged him. 2 And the soldiers platted a crown of thorns, and put it on his head, and they put on him a purple robe, 3 And said, Hail, King of the Jews! and they smote him with their hands.

The "purple" here was actually a dark red or "scarlet" (see Matthew 27:28), which probably refers to the closest the soldiers could find for a mock royal purple robe. Their mock reverence for Jesus would have been a takeoff of their sincere address to the emperor, "Hail, Caesar!" As Gerald Borchart notes, instead of a kiss of fealty, they delivered a cruel slap; instead of bending their knee, they drove Jesus to His (*John 12–21*, 249).

4 Pilate therefore went forth again, and saith unto them, Behold, I bring him forth to you, that ye may know that I find no fault in him. 5 Then came Jesus forth, wearing the crown of thorns, and the purple robe. And Pilate saith unto them, Behold the man!

Borchart captures the essence of "Jesus the man" along with His other titles: "It is also a theological affirmation that Jesus was indeed 'the man,' the second Adam, God's Son, who dealt with the sin of the world introduced through the first Adam" (*John 12–21*, 250) (cf. Romans 5:12–21; 1 Corinthians 15:22). Indeed, *behold the man* who was the fulfillment of every Old Testament prophecy; *behold the man* who was God's plan for mankind; *behold the man* who was the face and heart of God; *behold the man*—humbled, broken, bleeding, dying; *behold the man*—resurrected and triumphant, the eternal King of kings!

Israel had long been aware of the prophets' predictions of a Messiah, but they envisioned a conquering king who would deliver them from the oppressive Roman rule. When Jesus came instead as a Suffering Servant, the Jewish leaders could not reconcile such a humble man with the grand military victory and liberation they had long entertained in their minds. They had not examined the Scriptures closely enough to realize that the prophesied kingdom and new covenant would not be of this world, but the next. This should give us pause when we envision God answering our prayers one way, only to discover that the reality does not match our imagination. We should consider that perhaps God actually *has* answered our prayers, but in ways we have not considered—sometimes, in fact, in ways opposite what we think we want and need.

Sources:

Achtemeier, Elizabeth. *Nahum–Malachi. Interpretation: A Bible Commentary for Teaching and Preaching.* Louisville: Westminster John Knox Press, 1986. 130–132.

Barker, Kenneth L. *Daniel–Minor Prophets. The Expositor's Bible Commentary*, vol. 7. Frank E. Gaebelein, ed. Grand Rapids, MI: Zondervan, 1986. 517–519.

Blue Letter Bible. BlueLetterBible.org. http://www.blueletterbible.org/ (accessed August 7, 2012).

Borchart, Gerald L. *John 12–21. New American Commentary, vol. 25B.* Louisville: Westminster John Knox Press, 2002. 245–250.

Clements, R. E. *Jeremiah. Interpretation: A Bible Commentary for Teaching and Preaching*. Louisville: Westminster John Knox Press, 1993. 137–140.

Feinberg, Charles L. *Isaiah, Jeremiah, Lamentations, Ezekiel. The Expositor's Bible Commentary, vol. 6*. Frank E. Gaebelein, ed. Grand Rapids, MI: Zondervan, 1985. 638–641.

Harrison, Everett F. and Charles P. Pfeiffer, *Wycliffe Bible Commentary*. Chicago: Moody Publishers. Reprint, 1962.

Huey, F. B., Jr. *Jeremiah, Lamentations. New American Commentary, vol. 16*. Louisville: Westminster John Knox Press, 1995. 210–212.

International Standard Bible Encyclopedia. http://www.blueletterbible.org/search/Dictionary/viewEntries.cfm?Letter=b&DictID=4 (accessed January 6, 2013).

Vine's Expository Dictionary of New Testament Words. http://www.blueletterbible.org/search/Dictionary/viewEntries.cfm?Letter=b&TwoLetter=ba&DictID=9&x=47&y=11 (accessed January 6, 2013)

Say It Correctly

Jedaiah. juh-**DAY**-uh.
Josedech (Jehozadak). yeh-**HO**-tsa-dak.
Heldai. hel-**DYE.**
Tobijah. tohb-**EYE**-yah.
Jeshua. **JESH**-u-ah.

Daily Bible Readings

MONDAY
An Established Throne Forever
(1 Chronicles 17:7–14)

TUESDAY
Light has Dawned
(Matthew 4:12–17)

WEDNESDAY
Seated on the Throne of Glory
(Matthew 19:23–30)

THURSDAY
The Kingdom of God's Beloved Son
(Colossians 1:9–14)

FRIDAY
A Better Hope
(Hebrews 7:11–19)

SATURDAY
King of Kings, Lord of Lords
(Revelation 19:11–16)

SUNDAY
Here is the Man!
(Jeremiah 23:5–6; Zechariah 6:9–14; John 19:1–5)

Notes

Teaching Tips

Words You Should Know

A. Revive. (Hosea 6:2) *chayah* (Heb.)—To be quickened from sickness, discouragement, faintness, or death.

B. Sepulchre (Luke 24:1) *mnemeion* (Gk.)—Any visible object for preserving or recalling the memory of any person or thing; a tomb.

Teacher Preparation

Unifying Principle—Deliverance! Sometimes people do not recognize the accomplishment of long-held goals because they are achieved differently than expected. What sustains the motivation of people to keep going when victory looks improbable? Jesus' forecast of His resurrection on the third day alluded to the Hebrew Scripture theme (tradition) of deliverance in defiance of the horror of the Crucifixion.

A. Begin preparation time with prayer.

B. Review the Scriptural texts related to the Bible Background, Focal Verses, and Devotional Reading.

O—Open the Lesson

A. Open with prayer.

B. Have a volunteer read the In Focus story. Discuss.

P—Present the Scriptures

A. Have volunteers read the Focal Verses, emphasizing the Keep In Mind verses.

B. Present information from In Depth and More Light on the Text.

E—Explore the Meaning

A. Have students respond to the questions found in the Discuss the Meaning section.

B. Direct students to the Lesson in Our Society section. Read aloud or summarize.

N—Next Steps for Application

A. Direct students to the Make It Happen section. Read aloud or summarize.

B. Give students up to five minutes to write their responses in Follow the Spirit and Remember Your Thoughts. Have them share their responses with a partner.

C. The facilitator or a volunteer should close the time together with prayer.

APR
20th

Worship Guide

For the Superintendent or Teacher
Theme: The Third Day
Song: "He Arose"
Devotional Reading:
1 Corinthians 15:12–20

The Third Day

Bible Background • HOSEA 6:1–3; LUKE 24:1–12
Printed Text • HOSEA 6:1–3; LUKE 24:1–12
Devotional Reading • 1 CORINTHIANS 15:12–20

Aim for Change

By the end of the lesson, we will: REVIEW the miraculous story of the Resurrection; EXPLORE the possible feelings and emotions of those who discovered the empty tomb; and LIST ways to share the glorious Gospel message in our everyday lives.

 In Focus

Jason was wrongly convicted of a serious crime. He began serving time in prison as a young man. He was given a life sentence and was incarcerated for more than fifteen years before things changed for him. After years of prayer and a series of legal disappointments, a local Innocence Project investigated his case and provided him free legal representation.

Today a free man, he stands on the stairs of the courthouse with his family. The press asks what sustained him when victory looked improbable and whether he ever believed this day would arrive. Jason then begins to recount God's faithfulness during this trying and difficult time in his life. Jason recalled his unflappable faith and referenced stories of great men who were wrongly jailed, including St. Paul and Dr. Martin Luther King, Jr. He let the news crews know that God is faithful, even when it seems like He's abandoned a cause. That day, Jason became a living example of this truth.

We can trust God's Word as it relates to promises of deliverance, even when victory looks improbable. In today's lesson, we will review the resurrection of Jesus on the third day as the fulfillment of long-awaited prophecies.

Keep in Mind

"He is not here, but is risen: remember how he spake unto you when he was yet in Galilee, Saying, The Son of man must be delivered into the hands of sinful men, and be crucified, and the third day rise again" (Luke 24:6–7).

"He is not here, but is risen: remember how he spake unto you when he was yet in Galilee, Saying, The Son of man must be delivered into the hands of sinful men, and be crucified, and the third day rise again" (Luke 24:6–7).

Focal Verses

KJV **Hosea 6:1** Come, and let us return unto the LORD: for he hath torn, and he will heal us; he hath smitten, and he will bind us up.

2 After two days will he revive us: in the third day he will raise us up, and we shall live in his sight.

3 Then shall we know, if we follow on to know the LORD: his going forth is prepared as the morning; and he shall come unto us as the rain, as the latter and former rain unto the earth.

Luke 24:1 Now upon the first day of the week, very early in the morning, they came unto the sepulchre, bringing the spices which they had prepared, and certain others with them.

2 And they found the stone rolled away from the sepulchre.

3 And they entered in, and found not the body of the Lord Jesus.

4 And it came to pass, as they were much perplexed thereabout, behold, two men stood by them in shining garments:

5 And as they were afraid, and bowed down their faces to the earth, they said unto them, Why seek ye the living among the dead?

6 He is not here, but is risen: remember how he spake unto you when he was yet in Galilee,

7 Saying, The Son of man must be delivered into the hands of sinful men, and be crucified, and the third day rise again.

8 And they remembered his words,

9 And returned from the sepulchre, and told all these things unto the eleven, and to all the rest.

10 It was Mary Magdalene and Joanna, and Mary the mother of James, and other women that were with them, which told these things unto the apostles.

NLT **Hosea 6:1** "Come, let us return to the LORD. He has torn us to pieces; now he will heal us. He has injured us; now he will bandage our wounds.

2 In just a short time he will restore us, so that we may live in his presence.

3 Oh, that we might know the LORD! Let us press on to know him. He will respond to us as surely as the arrival of dawn or the coming of rains in early spring."

Luke 24:1 But very early on Sunday morning the women went to the tomb, taking the spices they had prepared.

2 They found that the stone had been rolled away from the entrance.

3 So they went in, but they didn't find the body of the Lord Jesus.

4 As they stood there puzzled, two men suddenly appeared to them, clothed in dazzling robes.

5 The women were terrified and bowed with their faces to the ground. Then the men asked, "Why are you looking among the dead for someone who is alive?

6 He isn't here! He is risen from the dead! Remember what he told you back in Galilee,

7 that the Son of Man must be betrayed into the hands of sinful men and be crucified, and that he would rise again on the third day."

8 Then they remembered that he had said this.

9 So they rushed back from the tomb to tell his eleven disciples—and everyone else—what had happened.

10 It was Mary Magdalene, Joanna, Mary the mother of James, and several other women who told the apostles what had happened.

11 But the story sounded like nonsense to the men, so they didn't believe it.

11 And their words seemed to them as idle tales, and they believed them not.

12 Then arose Peter, and ran unto the sepulchre; and stooping down, he beheld the linen clothes laid by themselves, and departed, wondering in himself at that which was come to pass.

11 However, Peter jumped up and ran to the tomb to look. Stooping, he peered in and saw the empty linen wrappings; then he went home again, wondering what had happened.

The People, Places, and Times

Luke. The author of the Gospel that bears his name. Luke wrote an orderly account documenting a careful investigation of the things that had been fulfilled to present to Theophilus. Some scholars believe Theophilus to be a Roman official who wanted to know what Christianity was all about. This book was written between the years of 50 and 70 A.D. (see Luke 1:1–4). Luke was an educated Gentile, a doctor, and a traveling companion of the Apostle Paul (Colossians 4:14) (*Encountering the New Testament*, 62).

Hosea. The author of the book that bears his name. Hosea, son of Beeri, was a prophet who addressed the Northern Kingdom of Israel. His book/prophecy is a love story where his marriage to a prostitute named Gomer served as an object lesson for the relationship between God and His covenant people.

Jerusalem. The city captured by David and made the capital of his kingdom where he built his palace and where his son Solomon built the temple. It later became the capital of the Southern Kingdom of Judah. The name means "possession of peace." Ironically, the site of Jesus' crucifixion was a hill called Golgotha just outside the walls of ancient Jerusalem.

Background

The book of Hosea was written and recorded events between 800 and 700 B.C.

It presents dual themes of God's love and wrath. It tells of God's love for a sinful people. Hosea shows that although Israel has rejected God's covenantal love and merits judgment, God still chooses to restore them.

Jesus prepared His disciples for His departure with prophecy and teaching. He foretold His death and resurrection on their way to Jerusalem, but they did not understand. Passing through Jericho, He healed a blind beggar and converted Zacchaeus. Right before the Passover, Jesus presented Himself in Jerusalem as the long-awaited Messiah and then wept over the city. Conflict ensued as He denounced the moneychangers in the temple and challenged scribes, lawyers, and religious leaders who sought to trap and discredit Him. Jesus wanted to observe the Feast of Unleavened Bread by partaking in a Passover meal, often called the Last Supper, with the twelve disciples before He suffered. There He predicted betrayal from among them. He also compared the bread and wine they consumed to His body and blood that would be broken for them. He instructed the disciples to be great through service. Jesus was betrayed by Judas after praying on the Mount of Olives and denied by Peter after being arrested. He appeared before the religious council and Herod before being sentenced to death by Pilate. He was crucified at a place called Calvary (Golgotha) with two others, buried in a tomb, and then resurrected three days later.

At-A-Glance

1. Empty Tomb Discovered
(Luke 24:1–3)
2. Declaration of Prophecy Fulfilled
(vv. 4–9)
3. The Resurrection Proclaimed
(vv. 10–12)

In Depth

1. Empty Tomb Discovered (Luke 24:1–3)

Early in the morning on the first day of the week, while it was still dark, the women brought spices and ointments to the tomb to anoint Jesus (John 20:1). Two evenings before, just as the Sabbath was beginning, they had witnessed Jesus being wrapped in fine linen and laid in the tomb according to Jewish burial customs (19:40). The start of the Sabbath forced them to leave before the burial preparation was completed, so they may have been eager to finish. It must've been painful for the women to return, because since the tomb was located near the place of Jesus' crucifixion (v. 41). They also voiced concern about moving the heavy stone at the tomb's entrance (Mark 16:3). Anxiety was replaced by surprise and then confusion as the women realized the tomb was not only open, but also empty. They likely expected to arrive at a secure tomb holding Jesus' remains (15:46).

2. Declaration of Prophecy Fulfilled (vv. 4–9)

While they wondered about the disappearance of Jesus' remains, two men in clothes that gleamed like lightning stood beside them. The women's confusion turned to fear! They bowed down before the men.

Jesus said before the Crucifixion, "The Son of man must suffer many things, and be rejected of the elders and chief priests and scribes, and be slain, and be raised the third day" (Luke 9:21–22; cf. Matthew 16:20–28; Mark 8:30–31). He also is recorded as saying to the twelve disciples, "Behold, we go up to Jerusalem, and all things that are written by the prophets concerning the Son of man shall be accomplished. For he shall be delivered unto the Gentiles, and shall be mocked, and spitefully entreated, and spitted on: and they shall scourge him, and put him to death: and the third day he shall rise again" (from Luke 18:31–33; c.f. Matthew 20:17–19; Mark 10:32–34).

3. The Resurrection Proclaimed (vv. 10–12)

The disciples failed to believe the proclamation of the women that Jesus was resurrected. It seemed like nonsense to them. Although Jesus had foretold His resurrection to them three different times (Luke 9:21–27, 44–45; 18:31–34), they did not understand any of it. The disciples, like others, had to be convinced that Jesus had risen from the dead.

Search the Scriptures

1. What emotion did the women experience during this event (Luke 24:4)?
2. How did the eleven disciples respond when they heard Jesus had risen (vv. 11–12)?

Discuss the Meaning

The Resurrection is so important to the Gospel message that Paul says without it our faith is in vain (1 Corinthians 15:14). What do you believe about the Resurrection? Why is it essential to the Gospel? Why is it important to share?

Lesson in Our Society

You never know how people will respond when you share the Gospel of Jesus Christ with them. The disciples responded with disbelief to the news of the Resurrection. We can expect that others will react similarly. A sense of anxiety and fear of rejection may hinder believers from sharing the Good News of the Resurrection with others. Be encouraged that, like the disciples, some people simply require time to investigate and view the evidence for themselves.

Make It Happen

List ways you can share the glorious Gospel message in your everyday life. Evaluate what opportunities exist in your daily life that you rarely take advantage of. People communicate in a variety of ways. Consider how technology can assist you.

Follow the Spirit

What God wants me to do:

_____

_____

_____

_____

Remember Your Thoughts

Special insights I have learned:

_____

_____

_____

_____

More Light on the Text

Hosea 6:1–3

1 Come, and let us return unto the LORD: for he hath torn, and he will heal us; he hath smitten, and he will bind us up. 2 After two days will he revive us: in the third day he will raise us up, and we shall live in his sight. 3 Then shall we know, if we follow on to know the LORD: his going forth is prepared as the morning; and he shall come unto us as the rain, as the latter and former rain unto the earth.

There is significance to the third-day motif. In addition to Israel's restoration on the third day (Hosea 6:1–3), Jonah spent three days in the belly of the large fish (commonly referred to as a whale) before being released (Jonah 2:1–9); Esther entered the presence of the king after she and the Jewish people fasted for three days (Esther 5:1); and before Moses presented the Ten Commandments, the Lord appeared to the people of Israel on the third day (Exodus 19:11).

The significance of the third day is debated among scholars as indicating a completion of a journey, the climax of an event, or a day associated with special divine activity. As the principal Old Testament passage cited in the Gospels with respect to resurrection (Jonah 2), Jesus said: "For as Jonah was three days and three nights in the belly of a huge fish, so the Son of Man will be three days and three nights in the heart of the earth" (Matthew 12:40, NIV). "These insights, coupled with some key verses about restoration, salvation, or rescue from death on the third day, give Paul the right to say that the Messiah rose from the dead on the third day according to the Scriptures," writes Michael L. Brown (*Answering Jewish Objections to Jesus*, 98).

Luke 24:1–12

1 Now upon the first day of the week, very early in the morning, they came unto the sepulchre, bringing the spices which they had prepared, and certain others with them.

2 And they found the stone rolled away from the sepulchre. 3 And they entered in, and found not the body of the Lord Jesus.

The Gospels record that Jesus was buried in a tomb owned by a rich man named Joseph of Arimathea, who had followed Jesus secretly out of fear (Matthew 27:57–60; John 19:38). It was customary for wealthier people to have more elaborate rock-cut graves for family burials. In such tombs, there might be room for several bodies, benches cut from the walls where the bodies would be laid, and possibly even chambers with a flat ceiling extending over the cave-like area. The entrance of the tomb would be covered by a large stone that served as protection but also allowed access. Today, the aforementioned tomb attributed to Joseph of Arimathea is said to be located at the western end of the Church of the Holy Sepulchre.

4 And it came to pass, as they were much perplexed thereabout, behold, two men stood by them in shining garments: 5 And as they were afraid, and bowed down their faces to the earth, they said unto them, Why seek ye the living among the dead? 6 He is not here, but is risen: remember how he spake unto you when he was yet in Galilee, 7 Saying, The Son of man must be delivered into the hands of sinful men, and be crucified, and the third day rise again. 8 And they remembered his words,

Other Gospel accounts identify the men as angels who descended from heaven, rolled the stone away from the tomb, and sat during a dramatic, natural "act of God" described as an earthquake (Matthew 28:1–2). Jesus' forecast of His resurrection on the third day alluded to the critical Hebrew Scriptural theme of deliverance. The Hebrew Scriptures record a tradition of deliverance in the face of horror. Some well-known deliverance narratives in the Old Testament include the Exodus of the Israelites from Pharaoh's pursuing army (Exodus 14), Daniel's rescue from the lions' den (Daniel 6), and the preservation of the three Hebrew boys in the fiery furnace (chapter 3), to name a few. There are a number of other Hebrew Scriptures that make reference to restoration or rescue from death on the day of completion—which is the third day.

9 And returned from the sepulchre, and told all these things unto the eleven, and to all the rest. 10 It was Mary Magdalene and Joanna, and Mary the mother of James, and other women that were with them, which told these things unto the apostles. 11 And their words seemed to them as idle tales, and they believed them not. 12 Then arose Peter, and ran unto the sepulchre; and stooping down, he beheld the linen clothes laid by themselves, and departed, wondering in himself at that which was come to pass.

Jesus had healed Mary Magdalene of many evils and illnesses (Luke 8:2). Joanna was the wife of Chuza, who managed Herod's household (v. 3). Mary, the mother of James and Joses, was present. Sometimes called the "other Mary," this woman is possibly the wife of Cleophas (John 19:25). In addition to the women listed above, Susanna (Luke 8:3) and Salome (Mark 15:40, 16:1) were also present. These women had been with Jesus in Galilee. They followed and ministered to Him. These and many other women came up with Him to Jerusalem.

When they came back from the tomb, the women approached the eleven disciples and others as they were weeping and mourning, and told them everything (Mark 16:10). The failure of the disciples to grasp what was being said to them can be attributed to any number of reasonable explanations. First, the Hebrew Scriptures in the book of Isaiah alluded to an anointed king from the line of David who would restore Israel, usher in peace, and rebuild the temple as victorious ruler during a messianic period. So anticipating that Jesus would suffer and die before any of this took place was not likely to be a familiar or comfortable paradigm (even though there is mention of a Suffering Servant in Isaiah 53). Also, resurrection was a traditional Hebrew eschatological theme in the Scriptures, generally applied to all believers during the end times (Isaiah 26:19).

Like the disciples, many among us do not understand the significance of the resurrection of Jesus. There are those who reject the Resurrection because they choose to dismiss all miracles in Scripture. Some in this group may choose to affirm that Jesus is the Messiah, but the salvation He offers to the world has nothing to do with the Crucifixion and Resurrection. Belief in the Resurrection for them is foolish or has no relevance. Then there are those who are not against it, but neither are they convinced. It's an element of the Christian faith that can be adopted or denied. Belief in the Resurrection for them is nonessential.

Sources:
Brown, Michael L. *Answering Jewish Objections to Jesus: Messianic Prophecy Objections.* Grand Rapids, MI: Baker Books, 2003.
Craig, William Lane. The Guard at the Tomb. *New Testament Studies 30* (1984): 273–281.
Elwell, Walter A. and Robert W. Yarbrough. *Encountering the New Testament: A Historical and Theological Survey.* Baker Books: Grand Rapids, MI: Baker Academic, 1998.
Life Application Study Bible (NIV). Wheaton, IL: Tyndale House, 1991.
Morris, Colin. *The Sepulchre of Christ and the Medieval West: From the Beginning to 1600.* New York: Oxford University Press, 2008.
Packer, J. I., Merrill C. Tenney, and William White Jr., eds. *Nelson's Illustrated Encyclopedia of Bible Facts.* Nashville: Thomas Nelson Publishers, 1998.

Say It Correctly

Sepulchre. **SE**-pul-ker.
Gomer. **GO**-mer.

Daily Bible Readings

MONDAY
Death and Despair
(Job 30:20–31)

TUESDAY
Ransomed from the Power of Death
(Psalm 49:5–15)

WEDNESDAY
Received by God with Honor
(Psalm 73:16–28)

THURSDAY
You Shall Live!
(Ezekiel 37:1–14)

FRIDAY
God of the Living
(Mark 12:18–27)

SATURDAY
Christ Has Been Raised
(1 Corinthians 15:12–20)

SUNDAY
Raised on the Third Day
(Hosea 6:1–3; Luke 24:1–12)

Teaching Tips

Words You Should Know

A. Expounded (Luke 24:27) *diermeneuo* (Gk.)—To unfold the meaning of what is said, to explain.

B. Opened (v. 45) *dianoigo* (Gk.)—To open the mind of one, to cause to understand.

C. Understand (v. 45) *syniemi* (Gk.)—To set or join together in the mind, to put (as it were) the perception with the thing perceived.

Teacher Preparation

Unifying Principle—Greater Understanding. Confusion, disappointment, and sorrow in life often result from not understanding fully what has happened. How can the true meaning be discovered and understood? After Jesus explained His life, death, and resurrection within the context of Hebrew Scriptures, the two travelers on the road to Emmaus understood better what had occurred.

A. Read the Bible Background and Devotional Readings.

B. Complete Lesson 9 in the *Precepts For Living Personal Study Guide®*.

O—Open the Lesson

A. Open with prayer.

B. Have students read Aim for Change in unison.

C. Ask for a volunteer to read the In Focus story.

P—Present the Scriptures

A. Have volunteers read the Focal Verses and The People, Places, and Times. Discuss.

B. Read and discuss the Background section.

E—Explore the Meaning

A. Review and discuss the Search the Scriptures and Discuss the Meaning questions and the Lesson in Our Society section.

B. Ask students to share the most significant point they learned and how to use that point this week.

N—Next Steps for Application

A. Complete the Follow the Spirit and Remember Your Thoughts sections.

B. Close in prayer, thanking God for the meaning He brings to life through the Resurrection.

Worship Guide

For the Superintendent or Teacher
Theme: From Suffering to Glory
Song: "Glory to Glory"
Devotional Reading: John 1:10–18

From Suffering to Glory

Bible Background • ISAIAH 53:5–8; LUKE 24:25–27, 44–47
Printed Text • ISAIAH 53:5–8; LUKE 24:25–27, 44–47
Devotional Reading • JOHN 1:10–18

Aim for Change

By the end of the lesson, we will: EXPLORE the story of Jesus' meeting the two travelers after His Resurrection; TRUST that we can find meaning in things we don't understand through Christ; and DEVELOP creative new ways to explain the meaning of Jesus' resurrection to others.

 In Focus

Demetrius could not understand why his life was going down the tubes the way it was. "How long, Lord?" he said as he began to get dressed to look for another job.

Just then, his wife, Andrea, came in. "Demetrius, you're going to do fine today," she said with a calm assurance.

"I don't know, honey. I can't understand why all of this is happening right now," Demetrius replied. "In the last two weeks, I lost my job, found out my mom is sick with cancer, and our car is on its last leg."

Andrea put her hands on his shoulders. "Demetrius, we have to trust that God has a plan for our family and that He will help us to understand. He has a way of burying our hopes and dreams in order for them to come back to life again."

APR 27th

Demetrius stood in front of the mirror straightening his tie and contemplating what Andrea said. Maybe this was for the better. He prayed for God to help him understand it all.

Through Jesus, we can find meaning in the things that we don't understand. In today's lesson, we can learn to trust that Jesus will give us understanding in the difficult times.

Keep in Mind

"And beginning at Moses and all the prophets, he expounded unto them in all the scriptures the things concerning himself" (Luke 24:27).

"And beginning at Moses and all the prophets, he expounded unto them in all the scriptures the things concerning himself" (Luke 24:27).

Focal Verses

KJV Isaiah 53:5 But he was wounded for our transgressions, he was bruised for our iniquities: the chastisement of our peace was upon him; and with his stripes we are healed.

6 All we like sheep have gone astray; we have turned every one to his own way; and the LORD hath laid on him the iniquity of us all.

7 He was oppressed, and he was afflicted, yet he opened not his mouth: he is brought as a lamb to the slaughter, and as a sheep before her shearers is dumb, so he openeth not his mouth.

8 He was taken from prison and from judgment: and who shall declare his generation? for he was cut off out of the land of the living: for the transgression of my people was he stricken.

Luke 24:25 Then he said unto them, O fools, and slow of heart to believe all that the prophets have spoken:

26 Ought not Christ to have suffered these things, and to enter into his glory?

27 And beginning at Moses and all the prophets, he expounded unto them in all the scriptures the things concerning himself.

24:44 And he said unto them, These are the words which I spake unto you, while I was yet with you, that all things must be fulfilled, which were written in the law of Moses, and in the prophets, and in the psalms, concerning me.

45 Then opened he their understanding, that they might understand the scriptures,

46 And said unto them, Thus it is written, and thus it behooved Christ to suffer, and to rise from the dead the third day:

47 And that repentance and remission of sins should be preached in his name among all nations, beginning at Jerusalem.

NLT Isaiah 53:5 But he was pierced for our rebellion, crushed for our sins. He was beaten so we could be whole. He was whipped so we could be healed.

6 All of us, like sheep, have strayed away. We have left God's paths to follow our own. Yet the LORD laid on him the sins of us all.

7 He was oppressed and treated harshly, yet he never said a word. He was led like a lamb to the slaughter. And as a sheep is silent before the shearers, he did not open his mouth.

8 Unjustly condemned, he was led away. No one cared that he died without descendants, that his life was cut short in midstream. But he was struck down for the rebellion of my people.

Luke 24:25 Then Jesus said to them, "You foolish people! You find it so hard to believe all that the prophets wrote in the Scriptures.

26 Wasn't it clearly predicted that the Messiah would have to suffer all these things before entering his glory?"

27 Then Jesus took them through the writings of Moses and all the prophets, explaining from all the Scriptures the things concerning himself.

24:44 Then he said, "When I was with you before, I told you that everything written about me in the law of Moses and the prophets and in the Psalms must be fulfilled."

45 Then he opened their minds to understand the Scriptures.

46 And he said, "Yes, it was written long ago that the Messiah would suffer and die and rise from the dead on the third day.

47 It was also written that this message would be proclaimed in the authority of his name to all the nations, beginning in Jerusalem: 'There is forgiveness of sins for all who repent.'"

The People, Places, and Times

The Suffering Servant. The book of Isaiah contains four songs or poems describing the servant of Yahweh. The most famous of these songs is found within Isaiah 52:14 through 53:12. These songs describe a servant of Yahweh who has been called to lead the nations to worship God. The servant is persecuted and oppressed but ultimately rewarded. Jewish scholars usually identify this servant as the nation of Israel, which had suffered injustice under Assyria and Babylon. In the New Testament, this Servant came to be identified as Jesus, who is the embodiment of Israel.

Emmaus. A village about seven and a half miles from Jerusalem. This was one of the first places where Jesus made a post-resurrection appearance. The name Emmaus probably meant "hot spring." Josephus wrote of a village called Emmaus, but the actual site of the village remains widely disputed.

The Two Disciples. The identity of the two disciples on the road to Emmaus remains unknown. Some scholars believe that these two disciples were Cleophas and Mary.

Background

During the time after Jesus' crucifixion, the disciples experienced confusion and despair. They had watched their hoped-for Messiah ruthlessly murdered at the hands of the Roman establishment. They had trusted that He would be the one who would overthrow foreign oppression and restore Israel to its former glory. Now their leader was dead in a grave, and they had all scattered back to their homes wondering what had happened. If Jesus really was the promised Messiah, they could not understand anything that had transpired within the last few days.

Isaiah 53 gives some insight into what happened when Jesus endured the betrayal of the Jewish leaders and death from the Roman government. His suffering and pain were all a part of God's plan to redeem Israel and the whole world. It was this aspect of Jesus' life that was difficult for the disciples to see; not only would He be a glorious King who would lead Israel to peace and prosperity, but He would also be a Suffering Servant and die at the hands of foreign powers.

It took Jesus Himself to show the disciples that His death was not the end. He had to interpret the Scriptures in order for them to understand the full scope of what God was up to during the Crucifixion and how this played a part in His larger purpose. Jesus showed how, in passages like Isaiah 53, God had already spoken about His death and resurrection. He talked with His disciples about how God's plan could be found throughout the Hebrew Scriptures and how now they were to go out and proclaim the message of forgiveness and love to the entire world.

At-A-Glance

1. Understanding Comes Through Having a Heart of Faith (Luke 24:25, 44)
2. Understanding Comes Through a Relationship with Jesus (vv. 27, 44–45)
3. Understanding Comes Through the Scriptures (vv. 27, 44–46)
4. Understanding Comes Through Being Aligned with God's Purpose (vv. 46–47)

In Depth

1. Understanding Comes Through Having a Heart of Faith (Luke 24:25, 44)

Jesus rebuked the disciples on the road to Emmaus for having a slow heart to believe. They were confused and disappointed. The phrase "slow of heart" means that their hearts were inactive and dull to believe what the Scriptures said concerning the Messiah. He ended His rebuke with a question: "Ought not Christ to have suffered these things, and to enter into his glory?" (v. 26). In asking this question, Jesus made it clear that His dying and rising were plain to understand—unless one did not have a heart to believe.

Jesus also rebuked the disciples for not having hearts of faith. After He appeared to them, they still did not believe. He told them that everything He had experienced in the last few days had been written about in the Scriptures, and that He had told this to them before it even happened. In questioning them, Jesus challenged whether they believed the words that He already spoke to them, as well as whether they truly believed the Scriptures.

2. Understanding Comes Through a Relationship with Jesus (vv. 27, 44–45)

The two disciples who walked on the road to Emmaus were upset and distraught because Jesus had been crucified and was no longer with them. Actually, He was right there—accompanying them on their walk, but unrecognized by them. Jesus used this time to explain the necessity of His death and resurrection. It was during their time spent with Him that they came to understand recent events. It took Jesus to expound on the Scriptures in order for them to understand those passages.

Jesus emphasized His relationship with His disciples when He explained His resurrection to the Twelve. He stated that He had spoken concerning His death and resurrection while He was still with them (v. 44). During His time with them, Jesus had let them know that He was going to suffer, die, and rise on the third day. They had inside

information, and now the things that Jesus told them had been fulfilled right before their very eyes.

Without Jesus, the disciples were confused and disappointed. With Jesus' help, the Scriptures were opened up to them and made sense. Because they had a relationship with Jesus, they could line up His suffering and death with what was written in the Scriptures. This is the case for everyone who wants to understand the Scriptures and the events of their life.

3. Understanding Comes Through the Scriptures (vv. 27, 44–46)

The Scriptures are central for our understanding when life brings sorrow and disappointment. It is important that we go to the Scriptures and remind ourselves of what God has said. The Scriptures provide insight into our situations and give us the hope we need in troubling times.

Jesus rebuked the two disciples on the road to Emmaus, not just for a lack of faith but for a lack of faith in the Scriptures. Their lack of faith in believing what had already been prophesied concerning the Messiah upset Jesus. Being thoroughly acquainted with the Scriptures gives us a firm foundation when our faith is tested. The Scriptures help us understand the broader picture of God's purpose and remind us of His faithfulness.

Jesus also let the disciples know that what He told them concerning His death and resurrection was already written in the Hebrew Scriptures. He enlisted the law of Moses, the psalms, and the prophets as witnesses to His crucifixion and resurrection on the third day (vv. 44–45). By doing this, He showed that His crucifixion and resurrection were not an afterthought—they were the primary purpose of God. It is in the Scriptures where we also can discover a faint glimpse of what God is up to during troubling times.

4. Understanding Comes Through Being Aligned with God's Purpose (vv. 46–47)

The disciples had one idea about Jesus as the Messiah and how He would liberate and rule over the nation of Israel, but God planned differently. Jesus was called to be the Suffering Servant who would be wounded for our transgressions and bruised for our iniquities (Isaiah 53:5). This would result in repentance and forgiveness being available to all nations (Luke 24:47). This turned the idea of Jesus as the Messiah on its head in the minds of the disciples. Their ideas about Jewish liberation focused on them as a people and on the world's definition of power, but God's liberation plan involves all people and the power of love to remove the guilt and shame of sin.

The disciples faced a choice when Jesus appeared to them. They could hold on to their idea of what they expected the Messiah to be and do, or they could align themselves with God's purpose for the Messiah. Their understanding needed to be expanded to go beyond their selfish desires, to the loving purpose of God. Now was the time for them to align with God's purpose by preaching "repentance and remission of sins . . . among all nations" (v. 47). This would be a sure sign that they understood the true purpose of the Messiah's coming.

Search the Scriptures

1. What does it mean for the Suffering Servant to be "wounded for our transgressions . . . bruised for our iniquities" (Isaiah 53:5)?

2. Where in the Scriptures does it say that Jesus was to "rise from the dead the third day" (Luke 24:46)?

3. What is the difference between expounding and opening up the Scriptures (Luke 24:27, 45)?

Discuss the Meaning

1. How does aligning ourselves with God's purpose help us to understand our sorrows and disappointments?

2. How can we use Scripture as our guide through difficult times?

Lesson in Our Society

We all go through difficult times when it is hard to understand what God is doing. We can be tempted to give up and to lose our faith in Him. In these times, we must continue to draw strength from our relationship with Jesus. We must ask the hard questions and continue to seek Him, even when it feels like He is not there. We must use Scripture to increase our faith as we rely on the promises of God. These times are when our faith is made stronger and more mature. In the midst of it all, Jesus' death and resurrection give us hope that God has not forgotten us and that His plan is much bigger than we could even imagine. Many times, it may seem as though our dreams and plans are dead and buried. We do not understand the purpose of what we are going through and why God would allow us to experience the sorrow and disappointment. When we look at Jesus and His resurrection, we discover God working behind the scenes and turning sadness into joy.

Make It Happen

The Resurrection helps us to find meaning in the troubles that come our way. In Christ, we can find meaning in good or difficult times. By doing this, we will be able to share with others the power of Jesus' resurrection. We can share our testimony of how God helps us during our times of doubt when we're wrestling with things we don't understand. We can also share our testimony of how God has performed a "resurrection" in our own lives.

Follow the Spirit

What God wants me to do:

_____

_____

_____

_____

Remember Your Thoughts

Special insights I have learned:

_____

_____

_____

_____

More Light on the Text

Isaiah 53:5–8

5 But he was wounded for our transgressions, he was bruised for our iniquities: the chastisement of our peace was upon him; and with his stripes we are healed. 6 All we like sheep have gone astray; we have turned every one to his own way; and the LORD hath laid on him the iniquity of us all.

This passage is one of several in Isaiah that speaks of the Suffering Servant, a figure who takes on different roles but in every case suffers in a sinful world (see Isaiah 41–45, 49, 52–53, 61). Here the Servant is innocent and suffers on behalf of Israel so they may be healed. The KJV translates the Hebrew word *habburah* (**hab-bore-AH**) as "stripes," but "wounds" or "scars" is probably a better translation here. The idea is that the Servant has been physically wounded on account of Israel's sins, and His wounds will heal them.

7 He was oppressed, and he was afflicted, yet he opened not his mouth: he is brought as a lamb to the slaughter, and as a sheep before her shearers is dumb, so he openeth not his mouth.

Unlike Israel in verse 6, who are sheep who have gone astray and caused problems, the Servant is a lamb that allows itself to be taken to the slaughter, never protesting. "Afflicted" is from the Hebrew word *anah* (**ah-NAH**), which indicates a low position or status, sometimes from oppression or physical violence. *Anah* is probably best understood as "He submitted Himself" so that the first part of the verse should read, "He was oppressed, but He submitted Himself and did not open His mouth." The second part of the verse then provides a metaphoric image that parallels the description in the first part of the verse.

8 He was taken from prison and from judgment: and who shall declare his generation? for he was cut off out of the land of the living: for the transgression of my people was he stricken.

Prison and judgment should be understood in tandem because Isaiah was using a device called *hendiadys*, the expression of one idea with two words connected with "and." A better translation is probably, "He

396

was taken by oppressive judgment." "Prison" is one literal meaning of the Hebrew word *otser* (**OHT-ser**), but it can also refer to any kind of physical restraint or, more generally, oppression or captivity. The idea is that it was injustice and oppression that brought about His calamities. The interrogative portion is ambiguous in Hebrew because the verb *siah* (**SEE-yah**) could mean speak, meditate, or complain, and the noun *dor* (**door**) could mean a dwelling place, a generation, or the future. "Who can speak of His future?" seems suitable here in the sense that His fate is so horrific that everyone would be left speechless.

Luke 24:25–27, 44–47

25 Then he said unto them, O fools, and slow of heart to believe all that the prophets have spoken: 26 Ought not Christ to have suffered these things, and to enter into his glory? 27 And beginning at Moses and all the prophets, he expounded unto them in all the scriptures the things concerning himself.

In two separate scenes, Jesus appeared to His disciples after His resurrection, but they did not immediately recognize Him. Prior to this, two men appeared at the tomb and asked the women why they were seeking the living among the dead, reminding them that Jesus Himself had said that the Son of Man would be arrested, crucified, and resurrected.

Here, after the discovery of the empty tomb, two disciples were on the road to Emmaus (**Em-mah-OOS**), a village in Judea approximately seven and a half miles from Jerusalem. Jesus appeared to them and rebuked them for not understanding that everything that happened to Him was necessary for fulfilling Scripture. However, it was not until He broke bread with them that they realized who He was, but as soon as

they did, He disappeared (vv. 30–31). Jesus' fleeting presence parallels the disciples' fleeting understanding of Him and His death and resurrection; even when He appeared again, they still thought He was a ghost. Luke reminds us once again that human capacity to understand Jesus' purpose, especially in His death and resurrection, is fragile, and we require constant reminders of the true significance of His life.

"O fools, and slow of heart to believe all that the prophets have spoken" (v. 25)—Jesus called them fools (Greek. *anoetoi*, **ah-NOH-ey-toy**), which indicates that they lacked the human capacity of understanding. "Slow of heart" has a similar meaning. In ancient times, the heart was considered to be the seat of both emotions and cognition, so it was central to a person's whole being. To call the disciples slow of heart indicates that both their intellectual and emotional response to the prophets was not what it should be.

"To enter into his glory" (v. 26)—Jesus' reference to His glory—may refer to His resurrection, His ascension, or both. The two are separate events in the Gospels and Acts, but they are not mutually exclusive (*The New Interpreter's Bible*, 478). In the Transfiguration scene, Peter and the other disciples awakened and saw Jesus' glory, and Moses and Elijah standing with Him (Luke 9:32–33). The Greek word for "glory" in both passages is *doxa* (**DOHK-sah**), which refers to light and radiance. The Transfiguration scene on the mountain echoed the scene of Moses on the mountain with God where the appearance of God's glory was like fire (Exodus 24:17), after which his face shone (34:29). There is a sense of brightness or radiance in divine glory, both in Exodus and Luke 9. Furthermore, the Transfiguration contains literary parallels to both the Resurrection and the Ascension. Luke's claim that it was necessary for the Messiah to suffer all these things to enter into His glory is a complex statement, but in Christ's case one thing is for sure—suffering, arrest, crucifixion, and burial preceded glory.

"Beginning at Moses and all the prophets" (Luke 24:27)—The term "Moses and all the prophets" refers to all of the Old Testament Scripture because, in Jesus' time, the phrase "the law and the prophets" was an inclusive way of talking about Scripture broadly (see Luke 16:16). When Luke says that Jesus began with the law and the prophets, he means that Jesus interpreted the law of Moses first, followed by the rest of Scripture.

44 And he said unto them, These are the words which I spake unto you, while I was yet with you, that all things must be fulfilled, which were written in the law of Moses, and in the prophets, and in the psalms, concerning me.

This is the second appearance Jesus made to His disciples after His resurrection. Despite the fact that the two disciples who met Him on the road to Emmaus informed the group of Jesus' resurrection, they still did not fully understand, thinking they had seen a ghost. Then Jesus appeared, showed them His hands and feet, and even ate in front of them to prove that He had a physical body. Then He explained everything to them. Luke reiterates the fact that all of Scripture speaks of the things that happened to Jesus, using what became the tripartite division of the canon in Judaism: "the law of Moses" refers to the five books of the Pentateuch, "the prophets" refers to the historical books as well as the major and minor prophets, and the "psalms" are the first book of the third part of the Jewish canon known as the Writings or *ketuvim* (**ke-too-VEEM**). Jesus told them before His death that all that was written of Him in

Scripture must be fulfilled, but they still did not understand.

45 Then opened he their understanding, that they might understand the scriptures.

The Greek word Luke used here for "opened" is *dianoigo* (**dee-ah-NOY-goh**), which can be used figuratively with eyes or ears as an object to mean "explain" or "make understand." In verse 31, Luke wrote that the disciples' eyes were "opened," using the same verb. As Craddock points out, the disciples needed repeated revelations to understand (*Luke*, 291). Although Luke does not use *apokalupsis* (**ah-poh-KAH-loop-sis**), the Greek word that is usually translated as "revelation," there is a similar idea here because something very difficult to see or understand must be explained. The disciples had been slow of heart to believe the prophets (v. 25), and they needed help comprehending Jesus' physical resurrection.

46 And said unto them, Thus it is written, and thus it behoved Christ to suffer, and to rise from the dead the third day: 47 And that repentance and remission of sins should be preached in his name among all nations, beginning at Jerusalem.

Jesus did not cite any particular Scripture here, but Isaiah wrote of a Suffering Servant who was wounded by the guilt of humans and who submitted to oppression (Isaiah 53:5–7). In addition, Isaiah 49:6 indicates that the prophet must speak not only to Judah but all nations (*The New Interpreter's Bible*, 486). Despite the fact that Jesus did not quote any known verses from Scripture directly, He alluded to motifs and ideas that appear in Scripture, especially Isaiah, a practice that occurs often in the New Testament as a way of showing the connection of Jesus, His disciples, and the early church to God's salvation history with Israel.

"Beginning at Jerusalem" (v. 47)—In Luke and Acts, both of which were written by Luke as a continuous narrative, journeying to Jerusalem and away again is a pattern that plays an important role in Jesus' and the disciples' mission (*Luke*, 284). Jesus journeyed to Jerusalem beginning in 9:51 and ending at 19:28 when He reached Jerusalem for the Triumphal Entry. No other Gospel devotes so much time to Jesus' journey to Jerusalem. Now at the end of Luke's Gospel, Jesus informed the disciples that repentance for forgiveness of sin is to be preached to all nations, beginning in Jerusalem. They had reached Jerusalem, but they would need to leave again so God's message could reach everyone. In Acts, the disciples began in Jerusalem, but later they began to preach to all the nations, with the narrative ending in Rome with Paul's arrest where he continued to preach (Acts 28). Jerusalem is the holy city, and it is the place where Jesus was arrested, crucified, and resurrected, but the message of God in Jesus' death and resurrection are not contained within the holy city. Instead, it must spread to all nations, emanating from Jerusalem.

Sources:

Bauer, Walter and Frederick William Danker, eds. *A Greek-English Lexicon of the New Testament and Other Early Christian Literature, Third Edition.* Chicago: University of Chicago Press, 2001.

Craddock, Fred B. Luke. *Interpretation: A Commentary for Teaching and Preaching.* Louisville: Westminster John Knox, 1990.

Culpepper, R. Alan. "The Gospel of Luke." *The New Interpreter's Study Bible*, vol. *IX.* Leander E. Keck, et al. Nashville: Abingdon Press, 1995.

Harrison, Everett F. and Charles P. Pfeiffer. *Wycliffe Bible Commentary.* Chicago: Moody Publishers. Reprint, 1962.

International Standard Bible Encyclopedia. http://www.blueletterbible.org/search/Dictionary/viewEntries.cfm?Letter=b&DictID=4 (accessed January 6, 2013).

Vine's Expository Dictionary of New Testament Words. http://www.blueletterbible.org/search/Dictionary/viewEntries.cfm?Letter=b&TwoLetter=ba&DictID=9&x=47&y=11 (accessed January 6, 2013)

Wright, N.T. *Luke. N.T. Wright for Everyone Study Guides.* London: Society of Promoting Scripture Knowledge, 2001.

Say It Correctly

Chastisement. **CHAS**-tiz-muhnt.
Emmaus. uh-**MEY**-uhs.

Daily Bible Readings

MONDAY
Seeking the Answer to Suffering
(Job 23:1–7)

TUESDAY
The Completion of God's Plans
(Job 23:8–14)

WEDNESDAY
A Man of Suffering
(Isaiah 52:13–53:4)

THURSDAY
Undergoing Great Suffering
(Matthew 16:21–28)

FRIDAY
Servant of All
(Mark 9:30–37)

SATURDAY
We Have Seen His Glory
(John 1:10–18)

SUNDAY
The Messiah's Necessary Suffering
(Luke 24:25–27, 44–47; Isaiah 53:5–8)

Teaching Tips

Words You Should Know

A. Satan (Luke 4:10) (*Satanas*) (Gk.)—The chief of fallen spirits. Also called the devil, the dragon, and the evil one.

B. Worship (vv. 9, 10) (*proskuneo*) (Gk.)—The act of paying honor to a deity; religious reverence and homage.

Teacher Preparation

Unifying Principle—Just Say No! In a world that offers people countless ways to satisfy their lusts and appetites, it takes discipline to maintain high ethical and moral standards. What helps people stick to their principles when other options tempt them? Jesus' thorough knowledge of Scripture gave Him strength to withstand difficult temptations.

A. Pray for your students.

B. Read and meditate on all the Scriptures from the Bible Background and the Devotional Reading sections.

C. Reread the Focal Verses in two or more translations.

O—Open the Lesson

A. Open with prayer, including the Aim for Change.

B. After prayer, have a volunteer read the In Focus lesson.

C. Have your students read the Aim for Change and Keep in Mind verse in unison.

D. Discuss and allow time to hear student testimonies.

P—Present the Scriptures

A. Have volunteers read the Focal Verses.

B. Now use The People, Places, and Times; Background; and Search the Scriptures to clarify the verses.

E—Explore the Meaning

A. Have volunteers summarize the Discuss the Meaning, Lesson in Our Society, and Make It Happen sections.

B. Connect these sections to the Aim for Change and the Keep in Mind verse with the Lesson in Our Society and Make It Happen sections.

N—Next Steps for Application

A. Summarize the lesson.

B. Allow students to share how the lesson impacted them.

C. Close with prayer and praise God for keeping His promises.

MAY
4th

Worship Guide

For the Superintendent or Teacher
Theme: Jesus Resists Temptation
Song: "Higher Ground"
Devotional Reading: Psalm 91:1–12

Jesus Resists Temptation

Bible Background • DEUTERONOMY 6:13–16; 8:3; PSALM 91:11–12; MATTHEW 4:1–11
Printed Text • DEUTERONOMY 6:13–16, MATTHEW 4:4–11
Devotional Reading • PSALM 91:1–12

Aim for Change

By the end of the lesson, we will: UNDERSTAND the significance of using Scripture to fight and overcome temptation; REFLECT on the awesome power of the written Word of God; and DEVELOP a workable, realistic, desirable, and systematic plan for studying the Bible.

 In Focus

The computer lab was recently given brand new laptops. The students, teachers, and parents were very excited to receive up-to-date technology like other schools in the city. Early in the morning before the other students arrived, Derrick and Candy came to school with their mom. They decided to sneak into the computer lab.

Candy tried to convince Derrick she knew how to log-on to the Internet on the new laptops. Although they knew not to go into the lab without permission, Candy was sure they could go in without being caught. Derrick kept repeating to his sister what their mom said: "Do not go in the computer lab without permission."

Candy became upset with Derrick for repeating what their mom said. "I get it! Stop saying the same thing over and over! You sound just like Mom!" Candy could hear her mother's words even after Derrick stopped repeating them. This made her rethink her decision to disobey her mother.

Today's lesson shows us how we should take delight in God's Word and meditate on it day and night.

Keep in Mind

"Then saith Jesus unto him, Get thee hence, Satan: for it is written, Thou shalt worship the Lord thy God, and him only shalt thou serve" (Matthew 4:10).

"Then saith Jesus unto him, Get thee hence, Satan: for it is written, Thou shalt worship the Lord thy God, and him only shalt thou serve" (Matthew 4:10).

Focal Verses

KJV **Deuteronomy 6:13** Thou shalt fear the LORD thy God, and serve him, and shalt swear by his name.

14 Ye shall not go after other gods, of the gods of the people which are round about you;

15 (For the LORD thy God is a jealous God among you) lest the anger of the LORD thy God be kindled against thee, and destroy thee from off the face of the earth.

16 Ye shall not tempt the LORD your God, as ye tempted him in Massah.

Matthew 4:4 But he answered and said, It is written, Man shall not live by bread alone, but by every word that proceedeth out of the mouth of God.

5 Then the devil taketh him up into the holy city, and setteth him on a pinnacle of the temple,

6 And saith unto him, If thou be the Son of God, cast thyself down: for it is written, He shall give his angels charge concerning thee: and in their hands they shall bear thee up, lest at any time thou dash thy foot against a stone.

7 Jesus said unto him, It is written again, Thou shalt not tempt the Lord thy God.

8 Again, the devil taketh him up into an exceeding high mountain, and sheweth him all the kingdoms of the world, and the glory of them;

9 And saith unto him, All these things will I give thee, if thou wilt fall down and worship me.

10 Then saith Jesus unto him, Get thee hence, Satan: for it is written, Thou shalt worship the Lord thy God, and him only shalt thou serve.

11 Then the devil leaveth him, and, behold, angels came and ministered unto him.

NLT **Deuteronomy 6:13** You must fear the LORD your God and serve him. When you take an oath, you must use only his name.

14 You must not worship any of the gods of neighboring nations,

15 for the LORD your God, who lives among you, is a jealous God. His anger will flare up against you, and he will wipe you from the face of the earth.

16 You must not test the LORD your God as you did when you complained at Massah.

Matthew 4:4 But Jesus told him, "No! The Scriptures say, 'People do not live by bread alone, but by every word that comes from the mouth of God.'"

5 Then the devil took him to the holy city, Jerusalem, to the highest point of the Temple,

6 and said, "If you are the Son of God, jump off! For the Scriptures say, 'He will order his angels to protect you. And they will hold you up with their hands so you won't even hurt your foot on a stone.'"

7 Jesus responded, "The Scriptures also say, 'You must not test the LORD your God.'"

8 Next the devil took him to the peak of a very high mountain and showed him all the kingdoms of the world and their glory.

9 "I will give it all to you," he said, "if you will kneel down and worship me."

10 "Get out of here, Satan," Jesus told him. "For the Scriptures say, 'You must worship the LORD your God and serve only him.'"

11 Then the devil went away, and angels came and took care of Jesus.

The People, Places, and Times

Oaths. Yahweh's name was considered powerful and effective; the utterance of oaths would demonstrate which deity was truly considered powerful. Though inheriting the cities, homes, and farms of the Canaanites, the Israelites were not to inherit the gods that had been associated with protecting those cities and providing fertility to the land. One of the ways to demonstrate their rejection of those gods was to refuse to attribute power to them through oaths.

Massah. The name given to the place at Rephidim near Sinai where water came out of the rock. As the Israelites traveled in the wilderness after their liberation from slavery in Egypt, they complained to Moses about a lack of drinking water (Exodus 17:1–7). Moses accused them of putting the Lord to the test. The Lord told him that he would smite a rock in that place, and water would emerge for the Israelites to drink.

Pinnacle. The NLT and NIV translate "pinnacle" as "highest point." It is impossible to decide definitely what portion of the temple was referred to as the pinnacle. The use of the definite article makes plain that it was not *a* pinnacle but *the* pinnacle. Much difference of opinion exists respecting it, but it may be that it was the battlement ordered by law to be added to every roof.

Background

The Lord was about to give the Israelites "instant prosperity" in their new land. But there is an inherent danger in prosperity, because when a person prospers, he could forget God. It was at the height of David's own prosperity that he committed his greatest acts of unfaithfulness. When the Israelites would come into this prosperity, they were to be all the more careful to fear God and serve Him. The command to "swear" (take oaths) by the name of the Lord reinforces the instruction to fear Him, because one swears by the God he fears, and under whom he is responsible to fulfill his oaths. If they would forget God, they would almost certainly follow other gods, for God created people not only with the capacity but the need to worship. And this act of unfaithfulness would result in judgment, since the Lord "is a jealous God." This means He zealously protects what belongs to Him alone. Jealousy in this sense is ethically right; jealousy in the sense of envy for another's possessions or privileges is, of course, wrong.

Moses envisioned another sin the Israelites might be tempted to in the new land—that of testing the Lord. This implies that at times the people would face hardship as they did at Massah, where they lacked water and thought they would die of thirst. Rather than trusting God in this trial, they tested Him by complaining and quarreling. In the future, the Israelites would remember this embarrassing incident. They were to know that if they obeyed His commands, doing what is right and good, then no matter what hardship they might encounter, God would take care of them.

At-A-Glance

1. General Precepts
(Deuteronomy 6:13–16)
2. The Temptation (Matthew 4:4–11)

In Depth

1. General Precepts (Deuteronomy 6:13–16)

God is our Master and we as His people must learn to revere Him and do His work. We have to honor our God in our words, service, and lives. He tells us to fear Him with a reverence for who He is. In addition, we must serve Him because we have an understanding of who He is and know to give Him honor. We should petition no one else. God is God! He alone is worthy to be praised! God is a jealous God, and His jealousy is stirred when the honor due to Him is given to idols. You shall not distrust the power, presence, and providence of God, nor quarrel with Him.

2. The Temptation (Matthew 4:4–11)

Right after Jesus was declared to be the Son of God and the Savior of the world, He was tempted. He responded to all of Satan's temptations with the reply "It is written," giving us an example to stand on God's Word when we face temptation. Then Satan attacks in a holy place, teaching us to never let our guards down.

Satan tempted Christ to idolatry with the offer of the kingdoms of the world. Christ was also tempted to worship Satan. Christ rejected the temptation with great passion, remembering that God is a jealous God and He alone should be worshiped and served. As with us, some temptations will be an easy turnoff, but others will be harder. The Word of God is the key to resisting any temptation and causing the enemy to flee.

Christ was aided after the temptation; therefore, we may expect, not only that He will feel for His tempted people, but also that He will come to them with relief.

Search the Scriptures

1. Who should you fear, serve, and by His name swear (Deuteronomy 6:13)?

2. Who ministered to Jesus after the devil left Him (Matthew 4:11)?

Discuss the Meaning

Christ is Himself God, yet He was tempted by Satan. How much more will Satan tempt us who struggle in our own sinful lusts? It is profitable to know God's Word, but even more important to serve and worship Him.

Lesson in Our Society

It seems so much easier to do wrong than right, especially when it looks like you can get away with it. Sin has become so common. God has laid out very specific guidelines for those of us who trust Him. It is our responsibility because of who we are and *whose* we are to resist the temptation of the enemy and worship and serve our God.

Make It Happen

We don't have a choice in the matter, but it is our job: do what is right! Resist the devil and he will flee! Don't take chances on what you can get away with. Honor God in your actions and serve Him in obedience. Then watch the Lord help you and send His angels to minister to you.

Follow the Spirit

What God wants me to do:

_____

_____

_____

_____

Remember Your Thoughts

Special insights I have learned:

_____

_____

_____

_____

405

More Light on the Text
Deuteronomy 6:13–16

13 Thou shalt fear the LORD thy God, and serve him, and shalt swear by his name. 14 Ye shall not go after other gods, of the gods of the people which are round about you.

To understand the meaning of fearing the Lord, we turn to Deuteronomy 10:12–13, where we read that to *fear* the Lord is to walk in all His ways and to *serve* Him is to love Him with our whole being. The Hebrew word for "serve" is *abad* (**aw-BAD**), meaning to be in bondage. The Israelites knew what slavery was—their masters in Egypt had been brutal and merciless. But to be in bondage to the Lord is entirely different. It was the Lord who liberated them, and He is a loving, caring Master for them as well as us. The command to "swear by his name" does not mean to insert oaths into our conversations; instead, it means that God's people are called to pledge themselves to love and obey Him only.

As we read this passage, the Lord was preparing His people for their entrance into the Promised Land. The people were acquainted with the many gods of Egypt, which had already tripped them up (remember from Exodus 32 how Aaron led them to worship the golden calf—an Egyptian god). But now they would also be confronted with the gods of Canaan.

We can look down our noses at people who would be so foolish as to worship gods made of wood, stone, or metal, but we should be equally careful not to worship the material gods of our age. To do so is the same as worshiping creations rather than the Creator.

15 (For the LORD thy God is a jealous God among you) lest the anger of the LORD thy God be kindled against thee, and destroy thee from off the face of the earth.

The Hebrew word for jealous is *qanna* (**kan-NAW**). Jealousy describes how intensely God desires to have a love relationship with His people. He cannot tolerate divided loyalties, and when His people forget to worship Him alone, they experience great misery. The Lord God alone has an exclusive right to our worship. Jealousy in a human being can be good or bad, but in our holy God, His jealousy toward us is always good.

16 Ye shall not tempt the LORD your God, as ye tempted him in Massah.

As the Israelites traveled in the wilderness, they experienced a lack of drinking water on three different occasions. In the first situation (Exodus 15:22–27), there was water, but it was not drinkable. In Exodus 17:1–7, the incident referred to in this verse, the Israelites complained to Moses, and he accused them of putting the Lord to the test. The Hebrew for Massah is *maccah* (**mas-SAW**) and the word for tempt is *nacah* (**naw-SAW**). The location name in addition to the words *tempt* and *tempted* all come from the same root, which means to prove, tempt, or try. This brings to mind a picture of a puny child on the playground daring the biggest child to hit him. In the same way, when we brazenly disobey God, we are daring Him to come after us. With one small bolt of lightning, He could vaporize us, so why are we acting so foolishly?

Matthew 4:4–11

Now we switch to Matthew, where Satan is in the midst of tempting Jesus. Some of the very same words we have just looked at are used by Jesus to resist temptation.

4 But he answered and said, It is written, Man shall not live by bread alone, but by every word that proceedeth out of the mouth of God.

Jesus had just submitted to a forty-day fast when Satan suggested that, because Jesus was hungry, He should simply turn some stones into bread. Jesus was weak from hunger at this point, and the wilderness was scattered with stones resembling the round loaves of bread of Jesus' day. Jesus, being the Son of God, certainly had the power to do this. But Satan was tempting Jesus in how He would carry out His task as Savior of the world. Jesus quoted Deuteronomy 8:3 in which God told His people that although He was feeding them with manna, bread which filled their bellies, *real* sustenance comes from committing one's life to God.

The root word of "it is written" is the Greek word *grapho* (**GRAF-o**). Although the tense is translated as *is*, it is the perfect tense and has the meaning of *has been* written or *stands* written, which serves to underline that God's Word stands eternal. Thus, these first words of Jesus immediately after He was baptized are an assertion of the authority of God's Word. Usually Jesus began speaking based upon His own authority, such as, "I say unto you." But in this case, He was emphasizing that He was quoting from the Bible. Jesus was not introducing something new; He was appealing to the Old Testament. In each of the three temptations, Jesus used Scripture to fight against the devil.

5 Then the devil taketh him up into the holy city, and setteth him on a pinnacle of the temple.

Only Matthew refers to Jerusalem as the holy city, which highlights the connection between the old covenant of the Old Testament with the new covenant of the New Testament. "Pinnacle" is a literal translation

of *pterugion* (Gk. **pter-OOG-ee-on**), which can also be translated as a winglet or top corner. This temptation is often pictured with Christ placed on top of a tower or spire, but instead, this probably refers to one of the wings of Herod's temple. The southern wing was a magnificent colonnade that looked out over the valley, a dizzying 450 feet down below. The word "temple" as used here (Gk. *hieron* **hee-er-ON**) refers to the entire temple—the walls around the temple, the courts, and other buildings included as part of the temple. This word is different from the Greek *naos* (**nah-OS**), which refers to the central sanctuary itself.

6 And saith unto him, If thou be the Son of God, cast thyself down: for it is written, He shall give his angels charge concerning thee: and in their hands they shall bear thee up, lest at any time thou dash thy foot against a stone. 7 Jesus said unto him, It is written again, Thou shalt not tempt the Lord thy God.

Satan had already noticed that Jesus was defending Himself against his attacks through Scripture, and so he tried to twist the Word of God to his own purposes. He quoted Psalm 91:11–12, verses not included in today's Scripture passages. These verses give us a promise that God will send His angels to protect us wherever we go. The Greek word for *in*, as "in their hands" (*epi*, **ep-EE**), gives us the picture of the angels holding us up *on* their hands, as on a platform.

While this is a great comfort to us, Jesus gives us great insight into the meaning of this promise. This promise is true, but not in the context which Satan was talking about. Jesus countered Satan's Bible verse attack by quoting Deuteronomy 6:16. If we take our lives into our hands needlessly, such as jumping off a building or driving above the speed limit, we cannot expect God to protect us.

And so in this passage, Jesus was explaining the true meaning of this precious promise. It is extremely important for us as Christians to know the Word of God so well that we are able to use it to defend ourselves against the attacks of the devil. Even well-meaning friends may try to use Scripture to talk us into doing things that we shouldn't, so we need to know the context of His promises in order to interpret them correctly.

8 Again, the devil taketh him up into an exceeding high mountain, and sheweth him all the kingdoms of the world, and the glory of them; 9 And saith unto him, All these things will I give thee, if thou wilt fall down and worship me.

This mountain may have been metaphorical, because there is no mountain from which one may see all the kingdoms of the world. But it may also be one of the abrupt cliffs near Jericho, which present a vast panorama. The devil was here offering Jesus a short-cut—no pain, no sorrow, no cross. This would be a compromise in the worst sense of the word. The NLT has the word *took* (Gk. *anago,* **an-AG-o**), meaning that the devil took Jesus up the mountain, and from there pointed out his kingdom. Even today Satan is the ruler of this world (John 12:31; Ephesians 2:2), but John 16:11 tells us that Satan has already been judged and will not remain ruler. When we think of the shape of our world today, it's pretty evident that God is not responsible for the mayhem we see all around us. When Jesus died on the cross, Satan's kingdom was judged; we are just waiting for God to declare the victory.

10 Then saith Jesus unto him, Get thee hence, Satan: for it is written, Thou shalt worship the Lord thy God, and him only shalt thou serve.

At various times throughout Jesus' life here on earth, Satan tempted Him, even through His disciple Peter (Matthew 16:23). The temptations were very real, but as the Son of God, Jesus could never—would never—sin. Hebrews 4:15 tells us that Jesus was tempted in every way that we are, but He never gave in. But because of His experience with temptation, He understands us when we are tempted and knows how to help us in our time of need (v. 16). So in addition to fighting temptation with Scripture, we have the Lord Jesus Himself to help us avoid sinning.

This last temptation is perhaps the boldest of all. We are amazed that Satan would think he could tempt Jesus to worship him. Here Jesus quoted our beginning verse from Deuteronomy in words that are perhaps easier for us to understand than the Old Testament version. Instead of "Fear the Lord," we read, "Worship the Lord thy God." So that's what fearing the Lord means—worshiping Him. And we see the point of this command—that we are to worship God exclusively.

11 Then the devil leaveth him, and, behold, angels came and ministered unto him.

God the Father watched every second as His Son battled against the devil. Jesus came through victorious but hungry and exhausted. It was at that moment some angels, servants of God, came to minister to Jesus—to the one who always ministers to our needs. We can only imagine this scene of celebration—was there heavenly food to eat? A cool, refreshing drink of water in the wilderness? An opportunity for much-needed rest and sleep? We don't know, but just as the angels cared for Jesus, He knows how to take care of us in our needs.

Sources:

Barclay, William. *The Gospel of Matthew, Vol. 1. The Daily Study Bible Series.* Philadelphia: The Westminster Press, 1958. 57–68.

Keener, Craig S. *The IVP Bible Background Commentary: New Testament.* Downers Grove, IL: IVP Academic, 1994.

Life Application Study Bible (NLT). Wheaton, IL: Tyndale House, 2004. 276.

Unger, Merrill F., R. K. Harrison, Howard Vos, and Cyril Barber. *The New Unger's Bible Dictionary.* Chicago: Moody Publishers, 1988.

Vincent, Marvin R. *Word Studies in the New Testament, Vol. I.* Grand Rapids, MI: Wm. B. Eerdmans Publishing Co., 1957. 28–30.

Walvoord, John F. and Roy B. Zuck. *The Bible Knowledge Commentary.* Wheaton, IL: Chariot Victor Publishing, 1983. 26–27.

Word Biblical Commentary, Vol. 6A. Dallas, TX: Word Books, Publisher, 1991. 147-152.

Say It Correctly

Abihu. uh-**BAHY**-hyoo.
Nadab. **NAY**-dab.

Daily Bible Readings

MONDAY
Testing What is in Your Heart
(Deuteronomy 8:1–11)

TUESDAY
Keep Watching and Praying
(Matthew 26:36–41)

WEDNESDAY
Take Care Against Being Tempted
(Galatians 6:1–5)

THURSDAY
Do Not Lead Us into Temptation
(Matthew 6:9–13)

FRIDAY
Kept from Trial and Testing
(Revelation 3:8–13)

SATURDAY
Guarded in All Your Ways
(Psalm 91:1–12)

SUNDAY
Serve Only God
(Deuteronomy 6:13–16;
Matthew 4:4–11)

Notes

_____

_____

_____

_____

Teaching Tips

Words You Should Know

A. Poor (Luke 4:18) *ptochos* (Gk.)— Destitute of wealth, influence, position, honor.

B. Fulfilled (v. 21) *pleroo* (Gk.)—To carry out or bring to realization, as a prophecy or promise.

Teacher Preparation

Unifying Principle—A Fulfilling Vocation. Many people wrestle with issues in finding, choosing, or accepting a job. What considerations should drive their decision-making process when it comes to vocation? Jesus' identity and mission were informed by the prophetic tradition of the Hebrew Scriptures.

A. Read the Bible Background and Devotional Readings.

B. Complete Lesson 11 in the *Precepts For Living Personal Study Guide*®.

O—Open the Lesson

A. Open with prayer.

B. Discuss the rules of the temple regarding people who could read the Scriptures.

C. Have students read Aim for Change in unison.

P—Present the Scriptures

A. Ask for volunteers to read the Focal Verses and The People, Places, and Times. Discuss.

B. Read and discuss the Background section.

E—Explore the Meaning

A. Have students discuss any jobs that may have been presented to them in the church that they did not accept. Why not?

B. Discuss the call to certain vocations and the gifts we are given to help us in those vocations.

C. Discuss the Lesson in Our Society.

D. Ask students to share the most significant point they learned and how to put it into practice.

N—Next Steps for Application

A. Find a sample spiritual gifts test online and have students complete it.

B. Have students pray about what God may be assigning them to do in the world.

C. Close in prayer, thanking God for His divine purpose for our lives.

MAY 11th

Worship Guide

For the Superintendent or Teacher
Theme: Jesus' Mission on Earth
Song: "My Liberty"
Devotional Reading: John 10:1–10
Prayer

Jesus' Mission on Earth

Bible Background • LUKE 4:14–21
Printed Text • LUKE 4:14–21 | Devotional Reading • JOHN 10:1–10

—————— Aim for Change ——————

By the end of the lesson, we will: UNDERSTAND the particular significance of what Jesus read in the synagogue at Nazareth; BE MOTIVATED to explore our spiritual gifts and consider what God may want us to do with our lives; and CREATE a list of our spiritual gifts with ways that God can use each of these gifts.

 In Focus

Sam showed up for church a few hours early. It was Youth Sunday, and as the youth pastor, he was charged with delivering the sermon this week. He had the usual pre-sermon butterflies. He knew some in the church were more qualified than him; the church was full of people with doctorates and master's degrees. A late bloomer, Sam was still working on his bachelor's degree.

He prayed deeply this morning, asking that the Lord speak through him. An hour later, he delivered one of the most powerful sermons ever preached at this large, Baptist church. Several of those intimidating Ph.D.'s came up to him afterwards to confirm as much. *Wow*, Sam thought to himself. *After I opened myself to God's Word, the words just started to flow.* That day, Sam realized the power of the Word of God apart from his human efforts.

Sometimes the Word of God is powerful all by itself. In today's lesson, we learn of that power as Jesus reads a passage from Isaiah and, without preaching, sits down, letting the Word of God speak to His listeners.

—————— Keep in Mind ——————

"And he began to say unto them, This day is this scripture fulfilled in your ears" (Luke 4:21).

"And he began to say unto them, This day is this scripture fulfilled in your ears" (Luke 4:21).

Focal Verses

KJV **Luke 4:14** And Jesus returned in the power of the Spirit into Galilee: and there went out a fame of him through all the region round about.

15 And he taught in their synagogues, being glorified of all.

16 And he came to Nazareth, where he had been brought up: and, as his custom was, he went into the synagogue on the sabbath day, and stood up for to read.

17 And there was delivered unto him the book of the prophet Esaias. And when he had opened the book, he found the place where it was written,

18 The Spirit of the Lord is upon me, because he hath anointed me to preach the gospel to the poor; he hath sent me to heal the brokenhearted, to preach deliverance to the captives, and recovering of sight to the blind, to set at liberty them that are bruised,

19 To preach the acceptable year of the Lord.

20 And he closed the book, and he gave it again to the minister, and sat down. And the eyes of all them that were in the synagogue were fastened on him.

21 And he began to say unto them, This day is this scripture fulfilled in your ears.

NLT **Luke 4:14** Then Jesus returned to Galilee, filled with the Holy Spirit's power. Reports about him spread quickly through the whole region.

15 He taught regularly in their synagogues and was praised by everyone.

16 When he came to the village of Nazareth, his boyhood home, he went as usual to the synagogue on the Sabbath and stood up to read the Scriptures.

17 The scroll of Isaiah the prophet was handed to him. He unrolled the scroll and found the place where this was written:

18 "The Spirit of the LORD is upon me, for he has anointed me to bring Good News to the poor. He has sent me to proclaim that captives will be released, that the blind will see, that the oppressed will be set free,

19 and that the time of the LORD's favor has come."

20 He rolled up the scroll, handed it back to the attendant, and sat down. All eyes in the synagogue looked at him intently.

21 Then he began to speak to them. "The Scripture you've just heard has been fulfilled this very day!"

The People, Places, and Times

Nazarenes. The people in the town of Nazareth did not have a good reputation in the region of Galilee. Their unpolished dialect and lack of culture, religious devotion, and morals could have been the cause. The residents of Nazareth were considered to be aggressive people, scathing and fiery. Indeed, when Nathanael first heard that Jesus was from Nazareth, he asked, "Can anything good come from Nazareth?" (from John 1:46, NLT).

Nazareth. Jesus spent His childhood and youth in this small town, from which He set out to visit the towns and villages of Galilee. After the destruction of the second temple, some Jews lived at Nazareth and it was the seat of the priestly family of Pises. After His death, Nazareth, in its association with Jesus, began to enjoy a place of prominence.

Background

Luke, a doctor, was not among the twelve apostles. On one of Paul's missionary journeys, it is assumed that Luke possibly came to faith in Jesus Christ. Luke began to accompany the Apostle Paul, and some portions of the book of Acts include "we" sections, denoting Luke's presence (Acts 16:10; 20:5, et al.). Luke 4 begins with the temptation of Jesus. Jesus went on a forty-day fast after His water baptism. Satan came to tempt Him at the end of His fasting period. The temptations reveal the deceit of Satan and what he will do for power. This all occurred before Jesus went into the synagogue at Galilee.

At-A-Glance

1. Return From the Wilderness
   (Luke 4:14–15)
2. Preaching in Nazareth (vv. 16–17)
3. Outlining His Mission (vv. 18–19)
4. The Shortest Sermon Ever (vv. 20–21)

In Depth

1. Return From the Wilderness (Luke 4:14–15)

Here we find the opening scene of Jesus' ministry—in Galilee. He didn't immediately head to Jerusalem, which, for ministry purposes, would have been the most logical thing to do. If you want to impact the religious community, you go to the religious center. In this society, that place was Jerusalem. But Jesus decided to begin His ministry in a region known more for its fishing and strange dialect. Those who aspire to ministry should take note here. Everyone can't pastor a megachurch. Starting in "Galilee" isn't too bad an idea—especially if this is where Jesus began.

2. Preaching in Nazareth (vv. 16–17)

Jesus makes His way to His hometown to preach. Luke goes to great lengths to let us know that it was Jesus' custom to go into the synagogue on the Sabbath day. We tend to forget that Jesus was observant of Jewish customs. Jesus even clarified His position when He stated that He didn't come to abolish the law, but fulfill it. The early Church followed suit, regularly attending and teaching in synagogues throughout the book of Acts (cf. Acts 2:46; 3:1; 4:1). A scroll was brought Jesus' way for Him to read. This moment demonstrates God's sovereignty. In most synagogues, the scrolls were read in a cycle (sort of like a lectionary today). The passage Jesus read specifically referred to His mission on earth.

3. Outlining His Mission (vv. 18–19)

What better place and time to outline His mission than in His hometown at the beginning of His ministry? Jesus had already been anointed (Luke 3:22). Note the relationship between the anointing and God's Spirit. It was now time for a brief outline of His mission. There's a Jubilee theme present here (cf. Leviticus 25:8–55), a time in the Old Testament where prisoners and slaves are released and debts are discharged. Jesus is the true Jubilee in our lives! He sets us free from the spiritual prisons in our lives. Having been locked up in sin, He figuratively breaks chains in our lives. Jesus also makes reference to His preaching ministry and the healings that would take place as He journeys throughout the province.

4. The Shortest Sermon Ever (vv. 20–21)

After reading from the scroll, Jesus sits down. He doesn't wax eloquent about its meaning, nor does He have a three-point sermon for the attendees. He simply states,

"This day is this scripture fulfilled in your ears." Brief, succinct, yet powerful words that left the gathered community speechless. In disbelief, they'd later ask, "Is not this Joseph's son?" (Luke 4:22).

Search the Scriptures

1. What does Luke point out about Nazareth as Jesus enters the city (Luke 4:14)?

2. What does the passage from Isaiah mention was a result of being empowered by the Spirit (v. 18)?

3. What was Jesus sent to proclaim (v. 19)?

Discuss the Meaning

How many times have you heard pastors preach sermons that had little or nothing to do with the text? What does it look like for a preacher to be faithful to the meaning of a Scripture passage? An effective way to minister to people is to stick to what the Word of God says. This is precisely what Jesus does here, and we would do well to follow suit.

Lesson in Our Society

We tend to forget that the same Spirit that Jesus was anointed with resides in us. So that means that the same Spirit gives us the ability to preach the Good News to the poor and proclaim freedom to those imprisoned in sin. We tend to leave that to others—those who are called to evangelism. But this is part of what Jesus commissioned all of His followers to do: go and make disciples. Fear prevents us from doing so, but that fear is unwarranted. We fear because we think about our physical and natural inability, but Jesus wants us to consider the Spirit's supernatural ability.

Make It Happen

Find ways in which you can position yourself to preach the Gospel to those who are disenfranchised. Spend some time outside of your comfort zone and visit a homeless shelter. Allow God's Spirit to empower you to proclaim good news in situations that scream bad news. Ask others to join you in this endeavor.

Follow the Spirit

What God wants me to do:

_____

_____

_____

Remember Your Thoughts

Special insights I have learned:

_____

_____

_____

More Light on the Text

Luke 4:14–21

14 And Jesus returned in the power of the Spirit into Galilee: and there went out a fame of him through all the region round about.

Jesus' ministry was filled with the power of the Holy Spirit and His leading. We first hear of the Holy Spirit descending upon Jesus at His baptism. Next, the Spirit led Him into the wilderness to be tempted. Now, we read that He returned in the power of the Holy Spirit. The fact that He became famous at this time might indicate that the Holy Spirit empowered Him to begin doing miracles.

"Galilee" comes from the Hebrew word *Galiyl* (**gaw-LEEL**), which means a circle and refers to the fact that the region was surrounded by Gentile (non-Jewish) nations.

Because of this, the people were exposed to a variety of ideas, which made them very open in their attitudes. According to the Jewish historian Josephus, they were a very courageous people, many of whom became leaders of rebellions. It was also a very fertile region, so it was able to support many people, probably as many as three million. This was the region where Jesus grew up. God planted His Son in an area in which people would at least be open to hearing Him.

15 And he taught in their synagogues, being glorified of all.

During the exile, when the temple had been destroyed and people lived far from their home in Israel, the Jews began meeting for worship in synagogues—a town could have a synagogue if there were at least ten adult Jewish men. There were no sacrifices in the synagogues, but the worship services on the Sabbath days had a fairly consistent routine. Worship began with prayer, which was followed by the reading of Scripture. Seven people from the congregation read from different parts of the Old Testament. Since few were able to understand the original Hebrew, the reading was followed by translation into either Greek or Aramaic. After Scripture reading, there was teaching. There was no professional minister, but each synagogue had an administrator. This administrator might invite a distinguished person to speak on the Scripture. This would be followed by discussion and questions.

In this context, Jesus may have begun by asking the synagogue administrator for the opportunity to read the Scripture and comment on it. This was not the first time Jesus had spoken in a synagogue, but it was at the beginning of His ministry and His clear, authoritative messages were like a breath of fresh air to the people. The Greek for "glorified" is *doxazo* (**dox-AD-zo**), and it means

to give full honor. The people praised Jesus and His sermons; no opposition had yet begun.

16 And he came to Nazareth, where he had been brought up: and, as his custom was, he went into the synagogue on the sabbath day, and stood up for to read. 17 And there was delivered unto him the book of the prophet Esaias. And when he had opened the book, he found the place where it was written,

It was the custom to stand for the reading of Scripture. The Greek for "read" is *anaginosko* (**an-ag-in-OCE-ko**). The synagogue administrator (also called the president) would take the chosen scroll, remove its case and wrappings, and then hand it to the person who was going to read it. Sections from the Law (the first five books of the Bible) were read first, and then from the prophets. At this time, Jesus was handed the Isaiah (Gk. *Esaias*, **hay-sah-EE-as**) scroll. So Jesus opened the scroll to Isaiah 61:1–2. Although we see the word "book," the Greek (*biblion*, **bib-LEE-on**) does not refer to what we would call a book. It was literally a roll, or more precisely a scroll written on papyrus, which was used before the invention of paper. When Jesus opened the scroll, He literally unrolled it (Gk. *anaptusso*, **an-ap-TOOS-o**).

18 The Spirit of the Lord is upon me, because he hath anointed me to preach the gospel to the poor; he hath sent me to heal the brokenhearted, to preach deliverance to the captives, and recovering of sight to the blind, to set at liberty them that are bruised, 19 To preach the acceptable year of the Lord.

"Anointed" in Greek is *chrio* (**KHREE-o**), and it means consecrated to office. Jesus' anointing is by "the Spirit of the Lord." *Chrio* is a verb, while *Christos* (Greek for Christ) is the noun, so Jesus was claiming the title of

Christ, the Anointed One. The Hebrew form of *Christos* is *mashach*, which we pronounce Messiah—so in Greek and Hebrew, Jesus claimed to be the Messiah.

The Isaiah passage describes the work of the Messiah, how He will be recognized, and how Scripture will be fulfilled in Him. To "preach the gospel" (Gk. *euaggelizo*, **yoo-ang-ghel-ID-zo**) is to announce good news, to declare or bring good tidings. The Messiah comes first to the poor, the vulnerable, and to all those most in need. The "poor" (Gk. *ptochos*, **pto-KHOS**) are those who are most poverty-stricken—the beggars, the paupers, those needing public aid.

He came to "heal the brokenhearted." While this phrase is not in the earliest Greek manuscripts, it is definitely from the passage in Isaiah 61:1–2 that Jesus quoted. And we know from experience that when our hearts are broken, our Savior offers the precious gift of healing.

He came to "preach deliverance to the captives." The "captives" (Gk. *aichmalotos*, **aheekh-mal-o-TOS**) would not be interpreted by the listening Israelites as describing those who committed felonies but instead to their situation as captives to the Roman Empire, the occupying force. The Jews were expecting their Messiah to deliver them from Rome, but Jesus was revealing Himself as the liberator from sin, setting free those imprisoned by Satan. Jesus came to do more than political liberation: He would free us from slavery to sin.

He came to bring "sight to the blind." This phrase calls to mind the many instances in which Jesus healed the sick, the physically challenged, and those afflicted by demons and other causes of mental anguish.

And lastly, we see Jesus as the Messiah who sets "at liberty them that are bruised." "To set at liberty" in Greek is *aphesis* (**AF-es-is**) and also means to release. "Them that are bruised" (Gk. *thrauo*, **THROW-o**) is a verb, which also means crushed or oppressed. When we read the King James Version, we remember that King James did not want a translation that would threaten his rule as king, so the safer translation was to "set at liberty those who are *bruised*," rather than say those who are *oppressed*.

Jesus completes His reading with verse 19, which proclaims "the acceptable year of the Lord," but in the Isaiah passage, the verse goes on to include the proclamation of the day of vengeance of our God. The portion Jesus quoted introduced the day of salvation, the period in which salvation was being proclaimed. We are still in that era; the day of God's final judgment has not yet come.

20 And he closed the book, and he gave it again to the minister, and sat down. And the eyes of all them that were in the synagogue were fastened on him.

So Jesus rolled up the scroll and gave it to the "minister." This would not be a minister as we understand the word; it would have been the attendant in charge of the scrolls, a salaried clerk, not one who would be teaching or preaching (Gk. *huperetes*, **hoop-ay-RET-ace**). He sat down, which was the posture for teaching. All eyes "were fastened" (Gk. *atenizo*, **at-en-ID-zo**) on Him, gazing intently, earnestly, steadfastly.

21 And he began to say unto them, This day is this scripture fulfilled in your ears.

Then Jesus began His sermon with a statement sure to grab the interest of His listeners. The wonderful prophecies from the beginning of Isaiah 61 were being fulfilled in Jesus right before their very eyes. In reading the rest of the Isaiah passage, we also realize that there's also work left for us to do. Empowered by God's Spirit, we're called to continue pro-claiming the Kingdom of God to those who are hurting and alienated from Him.

Sources:

Barclay, William. *The Gospel of Luke. Vol. 2 The Daily Study Bible Series*. Philadelphia: The Westminster Press, 1956. 40–42.

Draper, Charles W., Chad Brand, and Archie England, eds. *Holman Illustrated Bible Dictionary*. Grand Rapids, MI: Holman Bible Publishers, 2003.

Childress, Gavin, *Opening Up Luke's Gospel*. Leominster, UK: Day One Publications: 2006.

Negev, Avraham and Shimon Gibson. *Archaeological Encyclopedia of the Holy Land*. New York: Continuum, 2005.

Vincent, Marvin R. *Word Studies in the New Testament, Vol. I*. Grand Rapids, MI: Wm. B. Eerdmans Publishing Co., 1957. 289–292.

Say It Correctly

Synagogue. **SI**-na-gog.
Nazarenes. na-za-**REENS**.

Daily Bible Readings

MONDAY
I Came from the Father
(John 16:25–33)

TUESDAY
I Came to Do God's Will
(John 6:35–40)

WEDNESDAY
I Came to Bring Light
(John 12:44–50)

THURSDAY
I Came to Testify to Truth
(John 18:33–38)

FRIDAY
I Came to Draw All People
(John 12:27–32)

SATURDAY
I Came to Give Abundant Life
(John 10:1–10)

SUNDAY
The Lord's Spirit is Upon Me
(Luke 4:14–21)

Teaching Tips

Words You Should Know

A. Scribes (Matthew 15:1) *grammateus* (Gk.)—Interpreters and teachers of the Mosaic Law.

B. Pharisees (v. 1) *faresios* (Gk.)—One of the largest groups of Jewish religious leaders in the New Testament. Fierce opponents of Jesus because He refuted their interpretation of the Law.

C. Hypocrites (v. 7) *hypokrites* (Gk.)—People who are pretentious, pretending to be better than they really are.

Teacher Preparation

Unifying Principle—Get it Right. Traditions are powerful guideliness for determining actions and behavior. How can Christians avoid using traditions to pit the word of the Law against the spirit of the Law? While Jesus was a firm believer in tradition, He warned against a misuse of tradition that makes "void the word of God" (Matthew 15:6, NRSV).

A. Read the Bible Background and Devotional Readings.

B. Complete Lesson 12 in the *Precepts for Living Personal Study Guide®*.

C. Reread the Focal Verses in a modern translation.

O—Open the Lesson

A. Ask a volunteer to open the class with prayer.

B. Ask a volunteer to read the In Focus story and the Aim for Change.

P—Present the Scriptures

A. Ask for volunteers to read the Focal Verses.

B. Unpack the lesson using The People, Places, and Times; Background; At-A-Glance; and More Light on the Text.

E—Explore the Meaning

A. Discuss the Search the Scripture questions.

B. Work through the Discuss the Meaning, Lesson in Our Society, and Make It Happen sections. Examine the salient points.

N—Next Steps for Application

A. Complete the Follow the Spirit and Remember Your Thoughts sections.

B. Close in prayer.

Worship Guide

For the Superintendent or Teacher
Theme: Jesus' Teaching on the Law
Song: "Give Me a Clean Heart"
Devotional Reading: Matthew 5:14–20
Prayer

Jesus' Teaching on the Law

Bible Background • MATTHEW 15:1–11, 15–20
Printed Text • MATTHEW 15:1–11, 15–20 | Devotional Reading • MATTHEW 5:14–20

———— Aim for Change ————

By the end of the lesson, we will: UNDERSTAND the significance of the letter of the law versus the spirit of the law; REFLECT on the spirit of some of the traditions we keep; and REPENT for when we have kept physical traditions but lost the spirit behind them.

In Focus

Carla always thought part of being a good Christian was the ability to pay tithes. When she lost her job, she found herself in an awkward situation, having to choose between paying her tithes or using her unemployment checks to pay for basic necessities. She began to feel bad about her inability to tithe.

One day she decided to talk to her mentor about how guilty she felt. "Dr. Green, as you know, I'm unemployed. I haven't paid my tithes in three weeks and I feel horrible about it. I know I'm required to do this and that it's an obligation, but I feel like God won't forgive me for not being able to do so."

Dr. Green looked at her and said, "Sweetheart, that guilty feeling isn't some kind of conviction from God. It seems like it's a personal guilt for not being able to fulfill what you think is an obligation. I think God is more concerned with your heart when you give."

When did the payment of one's tithes become a ritual instead of a sacrifice to God? In this lesson, we'll learn about the Pharisees' hypocrisy when it came to obedience and discover how to avoid a similar fate.

———— Keep in Mind ————

MAY
18th

"This people draweth nigh unto me with their mouth, and honoureth me with their lips; but their heart is far from me. But in vain they do worship me, teaching for doctrines the commandments of men" (Matthew 15:8–9).

"This people draweth nigh unto me with their mouth, and honoureth me with their lips; but their heart is far from me. But in vain they do worship me, teaching for doctrines the commandments of men" (Matthew 15:8–9).

Focal Verses

KJV **Matthew 15:1** Then came to Jesus scribes and Pharisees, which were of Jerusalem, saying,

2 Why do thy disciples transgress the tradition of the elders? for they wash not their hands when they eat bread.

3 But he answered and said unto them, Why do ye also transgress the commandment of God by your tradition?

4 For God commanded, saying, Honour thy father and mother: and, He that curseth father or mother, let him die the death.

5 But ye say, Whosoever shall say to his father or his mother, It is a gift, by whatsoever thou mightest be profited by me;

6 and honour not his father or his mother, he shall be free. Thus have ye made the commandment of God of none effect by your tradition.

7 Ye hypocrites, well did Esaias prophesy of you, saying,

8 This people draweth nigh unto me with their mouth, and honoureth me with their lips, but their heart is far from me.

9 But in vain they do worship me, teaching for doctrines the commandments of men.

10 And he called the multitude, and said unto them, Hear, and understand:

11 Not that which goeth into the mouth defileth a man; but that which cometh out of the mouth, this defileth a man.

15:15 Then answered Peter and said unto him, Declare unto us this parable.

16 And Jesus said, Are ye also yet without understanding?

17 Do not ye yet understand, that whatsoever entereth in at the mouth goeth into the belly, and is cast out into the draught?

18 But those things which proceed out of the mouth come forth from the heart; and they defile the man.

NLT **Matthew 15:1** Some Pharisees and teachers of religious law now arrived from Jerusalem to interview Jesus. They asked him,

2 "Why do your disciples disobey our age-old tradition? For they ignore our tradition of ceremonial hand washing before they eat."

3 Jesus replied, "And why do you, by your traditions, violate the direct commandments of God?

4 For instance, God says, 'Honor your father and mother,' and 'Anyone who speaks disrespectfully of father or mother must be put to death.'

5 But you say, it is all right for people to say to their parents, 'Sorry, I can't help you. For I have vowed to give to God what I would have given to you.'

6 In this way, you say they don't need to honor their parents. And so you cancel the word of God for the sake of your own tradition.

7 You hypocrites! Isaiah was right when he prophesied about you, for he wrote,

8 'These people honor me with their lips, but their hearts are far from me.

9 Their worship is a farce, for they replace teach man-made ideas as commands from God.'"

10 Then Jesus called to the crowd to come and hear. "Listen," he said, "and try to understand.

11 It's not what goes into your mouth that defiles you; you are defiled by the words that come out of your mouth."

15:15 Then Peter said to Jesus, "Explain to us the parable that says people aren't defiled by what they eat."

16 "Don't you understand yet?" Jesus asked.

19 For out of the heart proceed evil thoughts, murders, adulteries, fornications, thefts, false witness, blasphemies:

20 These are the things which defile a man: but to eat with unwashen hands defileth not a man.

17 "Anything you eat passes through the stomach and then goes into the sewer.

18 But the words you speak come from the heart—that's what defiles you.

19 For from the heart come evil thoughts, murder, adultery, all other sexual immorality, theft, lying, and slander.

20 These are what defile you. Eating with unwashed hands will never defile you."

The People, Places, and Times

Pharisees. As one of the largest groups of Jewish religious leaders in the New Testament, they transformed the focus of Judaism from sacrifice to law. They accepted the Scripture (our Old Testament) as the authority because they believed the way to God was obedience to the law. Problems arose, however, because over the years they added hundreds of religious traditions to the law and then made those traditions as important as the law. They were fierce opponents of Jesus because He refuted their interpretation of the law and many of their traditions.

Hypocrite. A Greek word, the original meaning was to give an answer. The meaning later shifted to describe one who is pretentious or believes he is a better person than he really is. The Synoptic Gospels describe Jesus' opposition to the religious leaders who acted like hypocrites (see Matthew 6, 15, 22–24; Mark 7; Luke 11–12).

Background

As the first book of the New Testament, Matthew introduced Jesus Christ: "The book of the genealogy of Jesus Christ, the Son of David, the Son of Abraham" (Matthew 1:1, NKJV). Presented as a proclamation of Good News, the Gospel of Matthew establishes Jesus Christ as the Son of God, the long-awaited Messiah of Israel, and the world's Savior.

The Gospel of Matthew records the birth of Jesus to Mary, who was a virgin; her subsequent marriage to Joseph; the wise men who came to visit the infant Jesus; and the fleeing of Joseph and Mary to Egypt after an angel of the Lord warned Joseph to take his family there for protection. The Gospel of Matthew describes the birth of Jesus as fulfilling prophecy. "So all this was done that it might be fulfilled which was spoken by the Lord through the prophet, saying: 'Behold, the virgin shall be with child, and bear a Son, and they shall call His name Immanuel'" (from vv. 22–23, NKJV).

Jesus taught His disciples and, through the Word of God, teaches us how to live and then how to share with others the way to become His followers. "Go therefore and make disciples of all the nations, baptizing them in the name of the Father and of the Son and of the Holy Spirit, teaching them to observe all things that I have commanded you" (from 28:19–20, NKJV).

At-A-Glance

1. The Scribes and Pharisees (Matthew 15:1–9)
2. The Crowds (vv. 10–11)
3. The Disciples (vv. 15–20)

In Depth

1. The Scribes and Pharisees (Matthew 15:1–9)

In verses 1 and 2, the scribes and Pharisees questioned Jesus' authority because His statements and teachings contrasted with their interpretation of the law. They asked Him why His disciples did not wash their hands prior to eating bread. Jesus did not immediately respond, but instead asked them how they could justify not taking care of their parents, which is a commandment of the law. "Why do you also transgress the commandment of God because of your tradition? For God commanded, saying, 'Honor your father and your mother'; and, 'He who curses father or mother, let him be put to death.' But you say, 'Whoever says to his father or mother, "Whatever profit you might have received from me is a gift to God"—then he need not honor his father or mother.' Thus you have made the commandment of God of no effect by your tradition" (from 15:3–6, NKJV).

The "tradition" to which Jesus referred was called Corban. A person who made a Corban vow was dedicating money to God's temple. Unfortunately, some would make a Corban vow and then hold the money and continue to use it as they saw fit. But they could refuse to help their parents, ostensibly because the money was "spoken for." Jesus pointed out that this was putting tradition above the law to help one's parents.

2. The Crowds (vv. 10–11)

Jesus then explained that too many people were honoring God with their lips, but keeping their hearts far away from Him. Jesus explained what the people should have already known from the Scriptures—that God is honored by obedience. It is not what one eats but rather one's commitment in the heart. The law referred to the consumption of certain foods as a symbol of defilement or uncleanness. Jesus illustrated that it is not food but speech and behavior that matter before God.

3. The Disciples (vv. 15–20)

The disciples were confused by Jesus' explanation of clean and unclean foods and asked Him for clarity. Jesus reminded them that defilement is a moral, not physical, issue. Clean or unclean food has nothing to do with defilement. Edible foods are for enjoyment and nourishment; the body eliminates what it does not use. One's heart is defiled by what comes out of it. Defilement of the heart is a result of disobedience to God.

Search the Scriptures

1. How were the religious leaders using a tradition, Corban, to excuse breaking God's law (Matthew 15:3–6)?

2. Describe how the sins Jesus described come "from the heart" (v. 19).

Discuss the Meaning

1. By not responding to the question on ceremonial hand-washing, the door was opened for Jesus to teach on the defilement of one's heart. What questions today does the church need to respond to?

2. Does today's church have traditions that have a negative impact on God's Word?

Lesson in Our Society

We should periodically review traditions practiced within the church. We need to make sure traditions aren't being practiced just because of ritual behavior without people remembering the meaning or significance behind them. While traditions have their place, they should not take over the mission statement of the church. The church itself must remain a safe, loving, and inviting place where people want to come. Thus, it is essential for the body of Christ to introduce and present Jesus in an inviting and relevant way.

Make It Happen

Review the traditions of the church that might be a hindrance to one's salvation. Examine when the tradition transitioned from being a meaningful remembrance or celebration to an event without meaning. Once that transition has been identified, examine steps to return the tradition to its historical point of reference.

Follow the Spirit

What God wants me to do:

_____

_____

_____

_____

Remember Your Thoughts

Special insights I have learned:

_____

_____

_____

_____

More Light on the Text

Matthew 15:1–11, 15–20

1 Then came to Jesus scribes and Pharisees, which were of Jerusalem, saying, 2 Why do thy disciples transgress the tradition of the elders? for they wash not their hands when they eat bread.

The Pharisees in Jerusalem felt that it was their responsibility to see that the Israelites obeyed the law as they thought it should be done. Generation after generation, the Pharisees and various rabbis had interpreted the law with very detailed explanations about how to obey the smallest phrase. In Exodus 30:18–21, the priests were commanded to wash before they offered sacrifices to the Lord, but somehow this got magnified to having everyone wash before, during, and after eating. Even the individual washing routines were spelled out differently. The Pharisees took baths after they went to market, because they thought that maybe the dust from a Gentile or some other unclean person or thing might contaminate them. In many religions, there are things people avoid doing or touching because they think it will make them impure or even unlucky. To disobey the hand-washing regulations devised by the Pharisees was considered a transgression (Gk. *parabaino*, **par-ab-AH-ee-no**), a violation of a command.

So the Pharisees sent the equivalent of the religious police to check out this new rabbi called Jesus. One of the first things they noticed was that His disciples were not washing their hands with the specific directions passed down by the traditions of the Pharisees. The traditions (Gk. *paradosis*, **par-AD-os-is**) had come to have the same weight as the precepts written in the Old Testament.

3 But he answered and said unto them, Why do ye also transgress the commandment of God by your tradition?

The word *also* (Gk. *kai*, **ki**) should not be overlooked here. When Jesus used this word, He was admitting that His disciples were not obeying the hand-washing customs—but He accused the Pharisees of far worse. They were disobeying the commandments of God plainly written in the Old Testament. Jesus was really putting the Pharisees on the spot. They thought they were politely (although with their noses in the air) correcting this upstart rabbi, but Jesus was boldly accusing them—the moral police of Judaism—of sinning against God's law.

4 For God commanded, saying, Honour thy father and mother: and, He that curseth father or mother, let him die the death. 5 But ye say, Whosoever shall say to his father or his mother, It is a gift, by whatsoever thou mightest be profited by me; 6 And honour not his father or his mother, he shall be free. Thus have ye made the commandment of God of none effect by your tradition.

The King James Version translates the Greek phrase *teleutao thanatos* (**tel-yoo-TAH-o THAN-at-os**) as "to die the death," reversing the order of the words for English readers. This comes from the Hebrew idiom, "he shall certainly be executed," which shows the seriousness with which God's Word treats disrespecting one's parents. The command to honor one's parents was the fifth commandment (Exodus 20:12). As Ephesians 6:2 reminds us, this is the first and only commandment with a promise for obedience attached to it. After the commandments were stated, Exodus elaborated upon them with punishments for disobedience. In Exodus 21:17, we read that the punishment for cursing one's parents is execution. And in verse 15, death is also the punishment for attacking one's parents.

There is no record in Scripture of this ever being carried out, but it does emphasize that God holds obedience and respect within the family as an absolute value. The family is meant to be a picture of the relationship that God desires to have with us—He as our Father and we as His children. Disobedience or disrespect of our heavenly Father deserves eternal punishment. Perhaps the grandest story of the son who disrespected his father was the prodigal son (Luke 15:11–32), but in the end, the father graciously forgave his prodigal son, just as our loving heavenly Father desires to forgive our sins and restore the relationship with Him that has been broken by our sin.

The command to honor one's parents was not meant just for children still living at home with their mother and father; it extended to adult children as well. Understand that this is not about "obedience" to parents, but "honoring" them—something children should do their entire lives. The Jews clearly understood that grown children were responsible for the financial welfare of the parents who raised them, and that is what Jesus was pointing out. The Pharisees had a tradition that allowed adult children to get out of their financial responsibilities to their elderly parents. The Greek word for gift is *doron* (**DO-ron**), referring specifically to an offering or sacrifice. This was just a tricky bit of semantics, because the one making this oath was not promising to give it to the temple, but because it was an oath, his wealth was placed out of reach of his financially needy parents. Thus, he did not have to do anything with his money except keep it for himself.

When an adult son or daughter uttered the phrase, "Corban, it is a gift," it was an oath. In Numbers 30:2, God's people are commanded to keep any oaths they made. See the parallel passage of today's Scripture, Mark 7:1–23, in which the word "Corban" is used. *Corban* is the actual Greek word (**kor-BAN**). This referred to a gift that was designated as an offering for the Lord. In the situation that Jesus was referring to, however, it was not actually given to the Lord. An oath should be kept, but Jesus was teaching that it is more important to obey the direct commands of the Lord.

7 Ye hypocrites, well did Esaias prophesy of you, saying, 8 This people draweth nigh unto me with their mouth, and honoureth me with their lips; but their heart is far from me. 9 But in vain they do worship me, teaching for doctrines the commandments of men.

"Well" conveys the meaning of "honestly" (Gk. *kalos,* **kal-OCE**), so Jesus was telling the Pharisees that Isaiah (Esaias) was correct in what he said in Isaiah 29:13: "These people come near to me with their mouth and honor me with their lips, but their hearts are far from me. Their worship of me is based on merely human rules they have been taught" (NIV).

"Far from me" is "afar off" (Gk. *porrho,* **POR-rho**) and the phrase "their heart is far from me" means to hold off from, to deliberately hold oneself far from God. So the picture Isaiah presented is of a hypocritical religion in which people say they are close to God, but inwardly their hearts are far from Him. The clincher is that instead of teaching people to obey God's Word, the religious leaders raised their own picky interpretations above the biblical text—and then taught the people to do the same!

It's far easier to do the external things. William Barclay gave the example of avoiding pork or avoiding adultery—which one is easier? The dietary rule is much easier. "Religion had got itself mixed up with all kinds of external rules and regulations; and, since, it is much easier both to observe rules and regulations, and to check up on those who do not, these rules and regulations had *become* religion to the orthodox Jews" (*The Gospel of Matthew,* 125). God is far more concerned with our relationships and attitudes with one another and with Him than displays of religiosity.

10 And he called the multitude, and said unto them, Hear, and understand: 11 Not that which goeth into the mouth defileth a man; but that which cometh out of the mouth, this defileth a man.

Here Jesus turned aside from talking with the Pharisees to explain things to the crowd—and what He said was revolutionary. Instead of kosher food going into the mouth and creating holiness (and, by extension, non-kosher food causing defilement), the attitudes of the heart and words of the mouth are important to God, because these show true obedience. We skip over verses 12 through 14 in this lesson, but in these verses the disciples told Jesus that He had offended the Pharisees (as if Jesus did not know!). On top of what the disciples perceived as rudeness toward these religious authorities, Jesus very bluntly called them blind leaders of the blind. The Pharisees thought that rules for eating and washing would make them clean in the sight of the Lord, but God looks at the heart. If people followed the guidance of the Pharisees, they would completely miss out on how to please God.

15 Then answered Peter and said unto him, Declare unto us this parable. 16 And Jesus said, Are ye also yet without understanding?

Peter and the rest of the disciples just did not understand. Jesus was speaking in ways that ought to have made things perfectly clear to the disciples, who were with Him almost 24/7. It took Peter a long time to realize that eating kosher food is not what makes a person holy. In Acts 10, God had to give Peter a vision to finally show him that rules concerning kosher food had been done away with. Although these rules had significance to Israel when they were given, they no longer applied. But Jesus' main point was that God is primarily concerned about what is in our hearts.

17 Do not ye yet understand, that whatsoever entereth in at the mouth goeth into the belly, and is cast out into the draught? 18 But those things which proceed out of the mouth come forth from the heart; and they defile the man.

Jesus gave a very down-to-earth illustration here. The "draught" (Gk. *aphedron*, **af-ed-RONE**) was the outhouse, the toilet. That's what happens to so-called clean food—it goes into the mouth, through the body, and out into the toilet. Viewed from this perspective, kosher food ends up just the same as pork and shrimp—as excrement. So nothing about food can make us clean within. Then Jesus proceeded to talk about what really makes us filthy: what comes from deep down in our hearts and emerges from our mouths.

The Pharisees were concerned about ritual defilement; the Greek for "defile" is *koinoo* (**koy-NO-o**) and applies to spiritual pollution, the very thing that the Jews were worried about. But Jesus said that food isn't the problem. Again He expressed that it is defilement of the heart (Gk. *kardia*, **kar-DEE-ah**)—the thoughts, the mind, the feelings—that God is concerned about.

19 For out of the heart proceed evil thoughts, murders, adulteries, fornications, thefts, false witness, blasphemies: 20 These are the things which defile a man: but to eat with unwashen hands defileth not a man.

The things that concern God are what comes from our hearts. Thoughts (Gk. *dialogismos*, **dee-al-og-is-MOS**) are what we imagine deep within, whether we want to or not. Behavior that violates the Ten Commandments begins in the thoughts:

murder (sixth commandment); adultery, which is sex between two people who are not married to each other, and fornication, which is sex between two unmarried individuals (seventh commandment); theft (eighth commandment); false witness (ninth commandment); and blasphemy (third commandment). So external rules and regulations are not what make us clean. The problem is far deeper; our sinful behavior emanates from the sinful thoughts that come from our hearts. And we thank God that Jesus provided a solution to our sin problem when He died upon the cross to take the penalty for our sins.

Sources:

Barclay, William. *The Gospel of Matthew, Vol. 2. The Daily Study Bible Series.* Philadelphia: The Westminster Press, 1958. 125–131.

Bible Study Tools. www.BibleStudyTools.com. "New Testament Greek Lexicon—King James Version." http://www.biblestudytools.com/lexicons/greek/kjv/hupsoo.html (accessed September 6, 2012.

Bruce, F. F. *The Epistle to the Hebrews.* Grand Rapids, MI: Wm. B. Eerdmans Publishing Co., 1988.

Dictionary.com. http://dictionary.reference.com/ (accessed September 6, 2012.

Draper, Charles W., Chad Brand, and Archie England, eds. *Holman Illustrated Bible Dictionary.* Grand Rapids, MI: Holman Bible Publishers, 2003.

Freedman, David Noel, Allen C. Myers, and Astrid B. Beck, eds. *Eerdman's Dictionary of the Bible.* Grand Rapids, MI: Eerdmans Publishing Co., 2000.

Life Application Study Bible (KJV). Wheaton, IL: Tyndale House, 1997. 2154–55, 2170–72.

The Nelson Study Bible (NKJV). Nashville: Thomas Nelson Publishers, 1997.

The New Interpreter's Bible, Volume Three. Nashville: Abingdon Press, 1999.

Radmacher, Earl D., Ronald B. Allen, and H. W. House, eds. *Nelson's New Illustrated Bible Commentary: Spreading the Light of God's Word into Your Life.* Nashville: Thomas Nelson Publishers, 1999. 1648–53.

Today's Parallel Bible (KJV/NIV/NASB/NLT). Grand Rapids, MI: Zondervan, 2000.

Vincent, Marvin R. *Word Studies in the New Testament, Vol. I.* Grand Rapids, MI: Wm. B. Eerdmans Publishing Co., 1957. 86–88.

Witherington, Ben III. *Smyth & Helwys Bible Commentary: Matthew.* Macon, GA: Smyth & Helwys Publishing, Inc., 2006.

Say It Correctly

Corban. kor-**BAN**.

Daily Bible Readings

MONDAY
Commandments Learned by Rote
(Isaiah 29:13–19)

TUESDAY
Testing and Fear
(Exodus 20:12–21)

WEDNESDAY
We Uphold the Law
(Romans 3:21–31)

THURSDAY
Fulfilling the Law
(Matthew 5:14–20)

FRIDAY
But I Say to You
(Matthew 5:27–37)

SATURDAY
Be Perfect
(Matthew 5:38–48)

SUNDAY
What Proceeds from the Heart
(Matthew 15:1–11,15–20)

Notes

_____

_____

_____

_____

Teaching Tips

Words You Should Know

A. Love (Mark 12:30–31, 33) *agapao* (Gk.)—The inner desire to be loyal or to sacrifice for the good of others.

B. Understanding (v. 33) *synesis* (Gk.)—A running together, a flowing together with, knowledge.

Teacher Preparation

Unifying Principle—First Things First. In societies that traditionally value individual achievement, it is assumed that people will look out for their best interests before those of others. What safeguards exist to counter such narcissistic inclinations? When Jesus quoted Deuteronomy 6:4–5, He reminded the disputants that tradition had already determined which commandment was greatest. In addition, He said Christians are not far from the kingdom of God when the highest priority in their lives is to love God and neighbor.

A. Read the Bible Background and Devotional Readings.

B. Complete Lesson 13 in the *Precepts For Living Personal Study Guide*®.

O—Open the Lesson

A. Open with prayer.

B. Have students read Aim for Change in unison.

C. Ask for a volunteer to read the In Focus story.

D. Discuss how to love God and love your neighbor as yourself.

P—Present the Scriptures

B. Ask for volunteers to read the Focal Verses and The People, Places, and Times. Discuss.

B. Encourage students to give thanks for the opportunity today to love God and to love their neighbor as themselves.

E—Explore the Meaning

A. Review and discuss the Search the Scriptures section.

B. Ask students to share the most significant point they learned.

N—Next Steps for Application

A. Complete the Follow the Spirit and Remember Your Thoughts sections.

B. Close in prayer, thanking God for His presence in our lives.

Worship Guide

For the Superintendent or Teacher
Theme: The Greatest Commandment
Song: "My Worship is For Real"
Devotional Reading: Psalm 15
Prayer

The Greatest Commandment

Bible Background • LEVITICUS 19:18; DEUTERONOMY 4:35; 6:1–9; MARK 12:28–34
Printed Text • LEVITICUS 19:18; DEUTERONOMY 6:4–9; MARK 12:28–34
Devotional Reading • PSALM 15

Aim for Change

By the end of the lesson, we will: EXPLORE the roots of the ancient Hebrew tradition of loving our neighbors; UNDERSTAND how to express genuine kindness to everyone even when it isn't easy; and PRAY for forgiveness for when we haven't universally applied God's love to those around us.

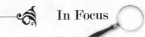

In Focus

"Baby, where are my blue socks?" Darrin asked.

"I don't know. Do I look like the sock keeper?" Shameka snapped back.

"Well, you are the one who does the laundry," Darrin said with irritation in his voice.

"Darrin, I can't keep tabs on everything. I have to work and do all of the chores around the house," she argued. "Plus I am doing my best to take care of the kids."

Darrin walked off in silence. Fifteen minutes later, he returned. "You know what, Shameka?" he said calmly. "I apologize for being so demanding. I want to help out more around here."

"I appreciate that, Darrin," she said, "and I apologize for snapping at you."

"I know, honey. I've been so busy getting ready for church that I was distracted from loving you," Darrin concluded. "Wearing the right socks means nothing if I don't love the people around me."

Loving God is more important than religious ceremony. In today's lesson, we can discover what it means to love God with all of our being and to love our neighbor as ourselves.

Keep in Mind

"And thou shalt love the Lord thy God with all thy heart, and with all thy soul, and with all thy mind, and with all thy strength: this is the first commandment. And the second is like, namely this, Thou shalt love thy neighbour as thyself. There is none other commandment greater than these" (Mark 12:30–31).

"And thou shalt love the Lord thy God with all thy heart, and with all thy soul, and with all thy mind, and with all thy strength: this is the first commandment. And the second is like, namely this, Thou shalt love thy neighbour as thyself. There is none other commandment greater than these" (Mark 12:30–31).

Focal Verses

KJV **Leviticus 19:18** Thou shalt not avenge, nor bear any grudge against the children of thy people, but thou shalt love thy neighbour as thyself: I am the LORD.

Deuteronomy 6:4 Hear, O Israel: The LORD our God is one LORD:

5 And thou shalt love the LORD thy God with all thine heart, and with all thy soul, and with all thy might.

6 And these words, which I command thee this day, shall be in thine heart:

7 And thou shalt teach them diligently unto thy children, and shalt talk of them when thou sittest in thine house, and when thou walkest by the way, and when thou liest down, and when thou risest up.

8 And thou shalt bind them for a sign upon thine hand, and they shall be as frontlets between thine eyes.

9 And thou shalt write them upon the posts of thy house, and on thy gates.

Mark 12:28 And one of the scribes came, and having heard them reasoning together, and perceiving that he had answered them well, asked him, Which is the first commandment of all?

29 And Jesus answered him, The first of all the commandments is, Hear, O Israel; The Lord our God is one Lord:

30 And thou shalt love the Lord thy God with all thy heart, and with all thy soul, and with all thy mind, and with all thy strength: this is the first commandment.

31 And the second is like, namely this, Thou shalt love thy neighbour as thyself. There is none other commandment greater than these.

32 And the scribe said unto him, Well, Master, thou hast said the truth: for there is one God; and there is none other but he:

NLT **Leviticus 19:18** Do not seek revenge or bear a grudge against a fellow Israelite, but love your neighbor as yourself. I am the LORD.

Deuteronomy 6:4 Listen, O Israel! The LORD is our God, the LORD alone.

5 And you must love the LORD your God with all your heart, all your soul, and all your strength.

6 And you must commit yourselves wholeheartedly to these commands that I am giving you today.

7 Repeat them again and again to your children. Talk about them when you are at home and when you are on the road, when you are going to bed and when you are getting up.

8 Tie them to your hands and wear them on your forehead as reminders.

9 Write them on the doorposts of your house and on your gates

Mark 12:28 One of the teachers of religious law was standing there listening to the debate. He realized that Jesus had answered well, so he asked, "Of all the commandments, which is the most important?"

29 Jesus replied, "The most important commandment is this: 'Listen, O Israel! The LORD our God is the one and only LORD.

30 And you must love the LORD your God with all your heart, all your soul, all your mind, and all your strength.'

31 The second is equally important: 'Love your neighbor as yourself.' No other commandment is greater than these."

32 The teacher of religious law replied, "Well said, Teacher. You have spoken the truth by saying that there is only one God and no other.

33 And I know it is important to love him with all my heart and all my understanding

33 And to love him with all the heart, and with all the understanding, and with all the soul, and with all the strength, and to love his neighbour as himself, is more than all whole burnt offerings and sacrifices.

34 And when Jesus saw that he answered discreetly, he said unto him, Thou art not far from the kingdom of God. And no man after that durst ask him any question.

and all my strength, and to love my neighbor as myself. This is more important than to offer all of the burnt offerings and sacrifices required in the law."

34 Realizing how much the man understood, Jesus said to him, "You are not far from the Kingdom of God." And after that, no one dared to ask him any more questions.

The People, Places, and Times

Scribes. The scribes were more than just copiers. During the time that Israel was captive in Babylon, they became interpreters and preservers of the Scriptures. They knew ancient and contemporary law in depth and functioned in society as judges and lawyers. Although they were often associated with the Pharisees, they were a separate group. In the Gospels, they were usually arguing with Jesus over legal matters.

Whole Burnt Offerings and Sacrifices. A whole burnt offering was the whole of an animal, usually a lamb or a bull. The whole animal carcass was placed on the altar, burned, and consumed with fire. The offerings were placed on the altar daily in the temple courts, and their smoke could be seen on a daily basis. This offering symbolized complete and total dedication to God and His will. Those who offered it saw the giving of this offering and other sacrifices as an act of religious devotion to God.

Kingdom of God. The kingdom of God was understood to be the rule and reign of God over His people and the whole earth. This was to be accomplished through the Messiah, who would defeat the enemies of God's people and establish a kingdom of peace and justice. It became the hope and dream of the Jews, and the expectation was that God would expel the Romans and

establish a Jewish king. This was the desire of the Jewish population living in Palestine. Jesus infused this term with spiritual meaning as well, and it became synonymous with the working of the Holy Spirit and righteousness in the life of God's people.

Background

The scribes often argued with Jesus about the correct way to interpret the law. Jesus was questioned on a topic that was currently debated by many rabbis and priests in Israel—which commandment was the greatest. At the time, rabbis, such as Hillel, did not think that all the commandments held equal importance. The idea was to find the "parent" commandment from which all the other commands could be reduced. Jesus responded with two passages familiar to His audience, defining His understanding of the law and what it means to truly follow God's commands.

The command to love was prominent in the Jewish Scriptures and in the religious life of Israel. Love was given first to God. Deuteronomy 6:4–9 states the loyalty that the Israelites were to give to God and God alone by loving or desiring Him with all of their hearts, minds, and strength. This passage is called the *Shema*. The words of the *Shema* were to be worn on the hands and head and placed on the doorpost in order to remind faithful Jews of its obligations. Jesus stated that the greatest commandment is to love the Lord with all of our being.

The next passage that Jesus cited has to do with love on a social and relational level. This command first appears in Leviticus 19:18. In this verse, the Israelites were commanded against holding grudges or taking revenge on each other, but instead to love their neighbors as themselves. This command was given in the context of fostering love between fellow Israelites. Later on, it was widened to include others outside of the nation of Israel. Jesus made this command the second greatest command in the whole Bible. Together, both of these commands constitute what it means to express and experience the kingdom of God.

At-A-Glance

1. Loving God is the Greatest Commandment (Deuteronomy 6:4–9; Mark 12:28–30)
2. Loving Others is the Second Greatest Commandment (Leviticus 19:18; Mark 12:31)
3. Loving God and Loving Others is Greater than Any Religious Ceremony (vv. 32–33)
4. Loving God and Loving Others is a Sign of the Kingdom of God (v. 34)

In Depth

1. Loving God is the Greatest Commandment (Deuteronomy 6:4–9; Mark 12:28–30)

The scribe in this passage presented Jesus with a very significant question: "Of all the commandments, which is the most important?" (v. 28, NLT). This was already on the minds of the religious leaders at the time, and it was expected that Jesus would have an opinion on such a popular question. Jesus said that the first and greatest commandment is to love God, and quoted the *Shema* of Deuteronomy 6:4–9. This means that loving God has to do with acknowledging God above all other allegiances. He then fleshed this out, explaining it as a command to love God with all the heart, soul, mind, and strength. Loving God encompasses the whole of our existence.

The command to love God with all of our heart, mind, and strength is the commandment that holds up all others. It is loyalty to God that causes us to follow His other commands. Without this loyalty, we can rationalize and avoid certain commands because our loyalty would then be only to our selfish desires. In contrast, the *Shema* says that our desire for God must surpass all others. This desire includes our heart, which is the seat of our will and emotions. It also includes our soul, or our entire life. It includes our mind, the center of our intellect and intelligence. Finally, it includes our strength, or all of our physical and material resources and effort.

2. Loving Others is the Second Greatest Commandment (Leviticus 19:18; Mark 12:31)

The second commandment in order of priority and importance is to "love your neighbor as yourself" (v. 31, NLT; see also Leviticus 19:18). This love is the same that Jesus mentioned in Mark 12:30. The same desire for God and His interests must be shown on a social and relational level. First, we desire God and His interests—and He is interested in the well-being of His creation, especially humankind. In the context of Leviticus 19:18, love is defined as the avoidance of keeping a grudge or seeking revenge. Not only was it directed at outward actions but also at inward attitudes and thoughts of the heart. Love is to result in practical actions and generous thoughts toward our neighbor; it's not a mushy, sentimental idea.

The object of our love should be our neighbor. In the Jewish context, the neighbor was the fellow Israelite or foreigner living in Israel, the other person who was near you. Love is not to be directed toward only some; it should be given to all who are in our sight. This leaves out exclusion and favoritism. It makes love a normal part of our daily existence, not just reserved for a few people or a special time.

The measure of our love is to be the love we have for ourselves. The same thoughts and actions we have for ourselves are now to be directed toward our neighbor. This sets the bar high. We do not hold a grudge against ourselves or take revenge on ourselves, so this must not be the way we treat others. We look out for and seek the best for ourselves; now we are called to look out for others and seek the best for them.

3. Loving God and Loving Others is Greater than Any Religious Ceremony (vv. 32–33)

The scribe agreed with Jesus and showed the greatness of these two commands in his reply. He affirmed that God is one and there is no other (v. 32), and he also affirmed that loving God with all of one's heart, understanding, soul, and strength is the first sign of loyalty to God. The word "understanding" (v. 33) is added and speaks of the reasonableness of worshiping and loving God once you know His greatness. The scribe also included loving your neighbor as yourself as the second sign of loyalty to Him.

The next thing the scribe says is that doing these things is greater than all whole burnt offerings and sacrifices (v. 33). This echoes the words of the prophet Samuel, who told a disobedient King Saul, "Hath the LORD as great delight in burnt offerings

and sacrifices, as in obeying the voice of the LORD? Behold, to obey is better than sacrifice, and to hearken than the fat of rams" (from 1 Samuel 15:22). The prophet Amos said that the Lord would not accept the burnt offerings and sacrifices of Israel and instead wanted to see "justice roll down like waters, and righteousness like an everflowing stream" (Amos 5:24, NRSV). This is an amazing statement by the scribe because burnt offerings and sacrifices historically symbolized religious devotion in Israel, and were given at a huge cost to the worshiper. The scribe understood that these religious ceremonies only symbolized the posture of one's heart toward God and the lifestyle of love that should be practiced in real life. This shows that to love God with all of our heart, soul, mind, and strength and to love our neighbors as ourselves is what God really cares about—not just religious ceremony.

4. Loving God and Loving Others is a Sign of the Kingdom of God (v. 34)

Jesus commended the scribe for answering "discreetly" (v. 34), or with wisdom and understanding. He said that the scribe was not far from the kingdom of God. In first-century Palestine, the phrase "kingdom of God" brought up images of conquering and banishing the Gentiles from the land. It stirred up the Jewish desire for freedom and political and military might. Jesus turned this concept upside down and said that loving God and loving others is the true sign of the kingdom.

The kingdom of God is founded on and grounded in love because God is love. It is a kingdom that exhibits and displays the nature and qualities of its King. Jesus knew that allegiance to the kingdom of God is not shown in religious ceremony but in loving God and others. The scribe's answer showed that he understood what it really meant to be someone who lived in the kingdom of God.

Search the Scriptures

1. Why did the scribe ask Jesus which commandment was greatest (Mark 12:28)?

2. Explain why we must love God with all of our heart, soul, mind, and strength (v. 30).

3. What does it mean to be "not far from the kingdom of God" (v. 34)?

Discuss the Meaning

1. How can we make loving God and others a priority in our lives?

2. Do we need to be academic scholars to love God with all of our mind? Why or why not?

Lesson in Our Society

For those who read the Bible, following all the commandments can be overwhelming. It is good to know that loving God and loving our neighbor as ourselves are the greatest commandments. By obeying these commandments, we can obey all the others. This is what it means to live in the kingdom of God. It is simple but difficult. Our challenge is to truly love God with all of our being and everything that we have. This can only be done with a deep understanding of the love that God has for us. When we know that God gave His life for us, then loving Him and others is less of a chore and more a privilege. In our everyday life, we have the opportunity to love God and show that He is the highest priority, as well as love our neighbor as ourselves. This is the test of loyalty to God and displays whether we truly love Him. To love our neighbor as ourselves is a sign that God is truly working in us.

Make It Happen

Loving God and loving our neighbor as ourselves are the most important commandments. When we practice this in our daily lives, people can experience the love Jesus has for them. In order for us to truly obey these commandments, we need to make them practical. In order to love God with all of our being, we can commit to setting aside a time of the day for prayer. We can also choose to memorize and meditate on His Word. Another way to love God is to think of Him all the time while we do the everyday tasks of life. In order to love our neighbor as ourselves, we can call a friend and listen to his or her problems and offer encouragement. We can do chores or babysit for single mothers. We can volunteer to tutor children who need help with homework.

Follow the Spirit

What God wants me to do:

_____

_____

_____

_____

Remember Your Thoughts

Special insights I have learned:

_____

_____

_____

_____

More Light on the Text

Leviticus 19:18

18 Thou shalt not avenge, nor bear any grudge against the children of thy people, but thou shalt love thy neighbour as thyself: I am the LORD.

Let's look at this verse as it would have been understood by the Jews from the time of its original writing in the Torah up to Jesus' day. To "avenge" (Heb. *naqam,* **naw-KAM**) is to punish, take revenge, or take vengeance; to bear any "grudge" (Heb. *natar,* **naw-TAR**) is to hang onto or store up anger. This is the situation in which one is just waiting for the time to vent one's anger against one's own fellow citizens, the "children" (Heb. *ben,* **bane**, i.e., the sons, daughters, servants, or youth) of one's own people (Heb. `*am,* **am**). Elsewhere in Scripture, God's people are told that when harmed by others, they can commit this wrong to God and He will take vengeance for them (Deuteronomy 32:35; Psalm 94:1).

In the second half of this verse, we see the reverse of the first attitude. Instead of just waiting to get even, God's people should be treating others as they would want to be treated. "Thy neighbor" (Heb. *rea`,* **RAY-ah**) may be just an acquaintance, a friend, or a companion, but when used as a counterpoint to "thy people" in the first part of the verse, it is understood to mean any of one's own people. When Jesus quoted the latter half of this verse, He expanded the circle of neighbors to all humankind, especially to those in need.

Deuteronomy 6:4–9

4 Hear, O Israel: The LORD our God is one LORD: 5 And thou shalt love the LORD thy God with all thine heart, and with all thy soul, and with all thy might.

Deuteronomy 6:4–9 is known to Jews as the *Shema,* the Hebrew word for "hear" (**shaw-MAH**), taken from the first word of verse 4. Observant Jews recite these verses daily.

God revealed Himself to Israel as Lord (Heb. *Yahweh*), His personal name, and He gave His people the name Israel (Heb. *Yisrael*), which means "he struggles with God," the name given to Jacob (Genesis 32:28) because he struggled with God and overcame. Knowing that there is only one God should have brought a great sense of security to the Lord's people. They did not have to worry about pleasing competing gods with their competing demands. There is only one God, and He alone deserves our worship, love, and obedience.

God is one, and He is unique. The Hebrew word for "heart" is *lebab* (**lay-BAWB**) and might be better translated as "the mind." The Hebrew for "soul" is *nephesh* (**NEH-fesh**) and may be translated as soul-life. These two words together may be understood as the inner being. "Might" (Heb. *me-od,* **meh-ODE**) refers to consciously disciplining oneself. The Jewish mind would never see these three words as indicating that our beings are split into three parts; rather, we are to love God with our entire beings.

6 And these words, which I command thee this day, shall be in thine heart.

Jeremiah 31:33 prophesied of the day when God would write His Word on the hearts of His people. This is what God desired of His people from the very beginning, that they would know His Word so well that it would be internalized. The Old Testament was not meant only as a legalistic series of rules; God's people were to see in His Word His love demonstrated for them and calling on them to reciprocate. Just as loving parents have strict rules for their children because they love them and want what is best for them, so God's rules are to help us live in the most fulfilling ways—ways in which we discover the great love and care that God has for us.

7 And thou shalt teach them diligently unto thy children, and shalt talk of them when thou sittest in thine house, and when thou walkest by the way, and when thou liest down, and when thou risest up.

Godly parents are to diligently (Heb. *shaman*, **shaw-NAN**) teach their children to obey God's Word—teach them with an intensity that plants God's Word into their lives. The commands of God were to be discussed and lived as examples inside the home and out, permeating every sphere of life.

8 And thou shalt bind them for a sign upon thine hand, and they shall be as frontlets between thine eyes. 9 And thou shalt write them upon the posts of thy house, and on thy gates.

These words were, and still are, taken very literally by many Jews, particularly by Orthodox Jews today. Instead of emphasizing the internalization of God's Word, phylacteries and mezuzahs were created. The frontlet is a small container for a parchment containing Bible verses. One type is attached to the head or forehead, the other to the left arm. These verses from Deuteronomy were among those placed inside the phylacteries. The phylactery is based on a very literal interpretation of verse 8. The mezuzah is based on verse 9. An elongated case is attached to the doorpost at an angle because rabbis could not decide if it should be placed horizontally or vertically. A tiny scroll with verses meticulously handwritten is placed inside. When an Orthodox Jew enters his home, he stops and touches the mezuzah, then kisses the fingers that touched it.

Mark 12:28–34

28 And one of the scribes came, and having heard them reasoning together, and perceiving that he had answered them well, asked him, Which is the first commandment of all?

Now we move to the New Testament and listen in on Jesus' commentary on the previous Old Testament passages. The Pharisees, Herodians, and Sadducees had just finished asking Jesus questions meant to trip Him up, but Jesus displayed the wisdom of God in all His answers. One of the scribes who was listening was impressed. He saw that Jesus answered the questions "well" (Gk. *kalos*, **kal-OCE**); in other words, in his estimation, Jesus had answered their questions admirably. While it was obvious that the motivation of the three groups who were questioning Jesus was to trip Him up (vv. 13, 18), Jesus intimated that this lone scribe was sincere in his question (v. 34).

Devout Jewish men delighted in spending their time discussing Scripture. The Pharisees had verbally added many regulations on how to obey the law. Some scholars discussed which laws were major or minor, while other scholars insisted that every law was equal to all others. So the scholar was asking something that was often discussed.

29 And Jesus answered him, The first of all the commandments is, Hear, O Israel; The Lord our God is one Lord: 30 And thou shalt love the Lord thy God with all thy heart, and with all thy soul, and with all thy mind, and with all thy strength: this is the first commandment.

In these two verses, Jesus recited the *Shema*, words that every devout Jew recited often, if not daily. (See the previous passage from Deuteronomy.) First the *Shema* states that God is one; Judaism is a monotheistic religion. So is Christianity (one God in three persons—Father, Son, and Holy Spirit).

If we look at the first four commandments (Exodus 20:1–11), we see that if we truly love God, we will obey each one of these commands. Each culture and context will give us greater insight into the meaning of Scripture, so we will look at what was originally in Hebrew but is stated in Greek in Mark's Gospel.

The "heart" (Gk. *kardia,* **kar-DEE-ah**) is not only the seat of the affections, but the center of our beings—physical, moral, and intellectual. The "soul" (Gk. *psuche,* **psoo-KHAY**) means the individual person. The "mind" (Gk. *dianoia,* **dee-AN-oy-ah**) is the understanding, but especially the *moral* understanding; this is the aspect of the person not named in the Deuteronomy passage. "Strength" (Gk. *ischus,* **is-KHOOS**) can be translated as power or strength. The addition of "the mind" is not meant to contradict the Hebrew, but was probably added because it's impossible to translate anything word for word and get the exact same meaning. Whether the three aspects of the Hebrew Old Testament version or the four aspects of the Greek New Testament version, the words together are an expression of the totality of one's being. To paraphrase Jesus, God wants us to love Him with all that we have and all that we are.

31 And the second is like, namely this, Thou shalt love thy neighbour as thyself. There is none other commandment greater than these.

The Greek word for "neighbor" is *plesion* (**play-SEE-on**) and means someone nearby or from one's own country, own people, or a friend. But when we look at the parable of the Good Samaritan in Luke 10:29–37, we see that Jesus expanded the meaning of the word to include even someone from another country, or someone who might be considered an enemy. When we look at the last six of the Ten Commandments (Exodus 20:12–17), we see that by loving one's neighbor, every one of these commands would be obeyed. In summarizing the most important commandment and adding the second most important, Jesus was showing that obedience to God's Word is more than just outward behavior; it involves what comes from our hearts.

32 And the scribe said unto him, Well, Master, thou hast said the truth: for there is one God; and there is none other but he.

Again the scribe showed his approval as he called Jesus' answer "well" (see v. 28), and he respectfully called Jesus "Master" (Gk. *didaskalos,* **did-AS-kal-os**), which can mean doctor, master, or teacher. The "truth" (Gk. *aletheia,* **al-AY-thi-a**) would be better translated as "truthfully," since it is an adverb, not a noun.

33 And to love him with all the heart, and with all the understanding, and with all the soul, and with all the strength, and to love his neighbour as himself, is more than all whole burnt offerings and sacrifices.

To show that he understood, the scribe reiterated what Jesus said and added the phrase "is more than all whole burnt offerings and sacrifices," which is a paraphrase of 1 Samuel 15:22. This comes from the incident in which a jittery King Saul began sacrificing animals instead of waiting for Samuel the prophet. The scribe showed that he understood that Jesus was saying that the heart attitude is more important than obeying outward regulations, because it is love for God and love for our neighbors that motivates our actions.

34 And when Jesus saw that he answered discreetly, he said unto him, Thou art not far from the kingdom of God. And no man after that durst ask him any question.

The word "discreetly" (Gk. *nounechos*, **noon-ekh-OCE**) only appears this one time in the entire New Testament, but it means that the scribe answered wisely. Jesus said he was close to the kingdom of God (the rule of God over one's heart). We do not know if he accepted Jesus by faith at this time. Unfortunately, close is not good enough; we must wholeheartedly receive Jesus as Savior and Lord.

Sources:

Barclay, William. *The Gospel of Mark. The Daily Study Bible Series.* Philadelphia: The Westminster Press, 1956. 305–310.

Blue Letter Bible. BlueLetterBible.org. http://www.blueletterbible.org/ (accessed Jan 6, 2013).

Christensen, Duane L. *Deuteronomy 1–11, Vol. 6A. Word Biblical Commentary.* Dallas, TX: Word Books, 1991. 142–145.

Evans, Craig A. *Mark 8:27–16:20, Vol. 34B. Word Biblical Commentary.* Nashville: Thomas Nelson Publishers, 2001. 260–267.

Hartley, John E. *Leviticus, Vol. 4. Word Biblical Commentary.* Dallas, TX: Word Books, 1992. 317–318.

International Standard Bible Encyclopedia. http://www.blueletterbible.org/ (accessed Jan 6, 2013).

Metzger, Bruce M. and Michael D. Coogan. *The Oxford Guide to People & Places of the Bible.* New York: Oxford University Press. 2001.

Pfeiffer, Charles P. and Everett F. Harrison. *The Wycliffe Bible Commentary.* Chicago: Moody Publishers, 1962.

Vincent, Marvin R. *Word Studies in the New Testament, Vol. I.* Grand Rapids, MI: Wm. B. Eerdmans Publishing Co., 1957. 86–88.

Vine's Expository Dictionary of New Testament Words. http://www.blueletterbible.org/ (accessed Jan 6, 2013).

Wright, N.T. *Luke for Everyone.* London: Society of Promoting Scripture Knowledge. 2001.

Daily Bible Readings

MONDAY
Love and Commandment Keeping
(Deuteronomy 7:7–16)

TUESDAY
Serving God with Heart and Soul
(Deuteronomy 10:12–21)

WEDNESDAY
Keeping God's Commandments Always
(Deuteronomy 11:1–7)

THURSDAY
Relating to Your Neighbor
(Leviticus 19:11–17)

FRIDAY
Sin Against a Neighbor or God
(1 Kings 8:31–36)

SATURDAY
They Shall Not be Moved
(Psalm 15)

SUNDAY
Loving God and Neighbor
(Leviticus 19:18; Deuteronomy 6:4–9;
Mark 12:28–34)

Say It Correctly

Phylactery. Fi-**LAK**-ter-e.
Mezuzah. Ma-**ZOO**-za.

Notes

The People of God Set Priorities

This quarter has three units. The first unit is from the book of Haggai in the Hebrew Scriptures and involves a call to community through the rebuilding of the temple. The second and third units are from the letters of 1 and 2 Corinthians in the Christian Scriptures and reflect a call to community through the believers.

UNIT 1 • HOPE AND CONFIDENCE COME FROM GOD

This is a four-lesson study. Each lesson attempts to convey a message on the importance of community in obtaining the goal of rebuilding the temple. The lessons identify the key aspects to living in a community as obedience and trust in God, living in a right relationship with Him, and maintaining hope in Him.

Lesson 1: June 1, 2014
Obey the Lord
Haggai 1:1–11

Sometimes personal needs and desires prevent Christians from giving priority to what's most important in their lives. God spoke through Haggai, saying that the people's first priority should be rebuilding God's house and not their own houses.

Lesson 2: June 8, 2014
Trust God's Promises
Haggai 1:12, 2:1–9

Some communities find it difficult to begin a project that will benefit them. God promised to be with the people as they completed the task of rebuilding His temple.

Lesson 3: June 15, 2014
Live Pure Lives
Haggai 2:10–19

Almost everyone wants to belong to something that will make a difference in the world. God rewards and blesses the community of believers that lives in righteousness and fear of Him.

Lesson 4: June 22, 2014
Hope for a New Day
Haggai 2:23; Zechariah 4:1–3, 6–14

Communities need capable leadership to stay motivated through a project's completion. God speaks through the prophets to affirm that the temple will be completed under Zerubbabel—not by human might or power, but by the Spirit of the Lord.

UNIT 2 • LIVING AS A COMMUNITY OF BELIEVERS

This is a five-lesson unit. The unit looks at the church at Corinth in order to learn how to build and maintain community among believers. The unit lifts up the importance of unity, glorifying God, building up colleagues in ministry, dealing with situations that threaten community, and seeking the good of others.

Lesson 5: June 29, 2014
A Call to Unity
1 Corinthians 1:10–17

Disagreements in a community may cause division. Paul called the disputing people to find common ground by taking on the mind of Christ.

Lesson 6: July 6, 2014
Glorify God with Your Body
1 Corinthians 6:12–20

Personal, moral, and physical purity are beneficial to the community. Paul said that because Christians are all one within the body of Christ, what harms one will harm other members, and what benefits one will benefit all.

Lesson 7: July 13, 2014
Watch What You Eat
1 Corinthians 8:1–13

Believers can have a strong influence on each other. Paul uses the issue of whether to eat food offered to idols to speak about unity and connection among Christians.

Lesson 8: July 20, 2014
Overcoming Temptation
1 Corinthians 10:9–22

The pride of people and communities can lead them to act in harmful ways. Paul reminded the Corinthians that all believers are tempted, but God will not let them be tested beyond their strength—He will provide the way out.

Lesson 9: July 27, 2014
Seek the Good of Others
1 Corinthians 14:13–26

Communities function best when the members can articulate shared values. Paul exhorted the Corinthians to speak plainly so that both believers and unbelievers could benefit from the leading of the Holy Spirit.

UNIT 3 • BEARING ONE ANOTHER'S BURDENS

This five-lesson unit outlines from 2 Corinthians ways to sustain community among believers. The lessons give specific emphasis to prayer, forgiveness, love, cooperation, and sharing.

Lesson 10: August 3, 2014
Consolation Granted Through Prayer
2 Corinthians 1:3–11

In times of trouble, communities may seek consolation and protection from some power or force beyond themselves. Paul gave testimony of God's consolation in times of hardship and gave thanks for the mutual consolation that comes from praying for one another.

Lesson 11: August 10, 2014
A Community Forgives
2 Corinthians 1:23–2:11

When a person violates the code of conduct of a community, he or she may be ostracized or rejected. Paul told the Corinthians to forgive the one who had caused them grief so the entire community might be made well again.

Lesson 12: August 17, 2014
Treasure in Clay Jars
2 Corinthians 4:2–15

Communities rely on one another for protection and continuity of life. Paul reminded the Corinthians that the extraordinary power to proclaim Jesus in the face of adversity is a treasure that comes from God through Jesus Christ.

Lesson 13: August 24, 2014
An Appeal For Reconciliation
2 Corinthians 6:1–13; 7:2–4

Sometimes the community may ignore the good done by a great leader and may become estranged from the leader. Paul reminded the Corinthians of all he had done for the sake of Jesus Christ, and based on that testimony, he asks that they be reconciled to Him.

Lesson 14: August 31, 2014
A Community Shares Its Resources
2 Corinthians 8:1–14

A small community that possesses much may be part of a larger community that has little and needs the smaller community's assistance. Paul reminds the Corinthians that they are part of a larger faith community and that as others have been generous to them, they should repay with equal generosity.

God Restores a Remnant

by Dr. A. O. Ogbonnaya, Ph.D.

The plight of Israel prior to and after the exile is a portrait of the ability of God to salvage and restore even in the midst of the most problematic situations. It is an archetypal manifestation of the life cycle of an institution's demise, renewal, disrepair, and reestablishment. It also typifies a pattern of our own life cycle: our ups and downs, our sickness and health, our sins and forgiveness, our death and resurrection. Scripturally, the evidence for Israel is found in the major prophets as well as the so-called minor prophets: Ezra, Nehemiah, Daniel, Joel, Obadiah, Haggai, Zechariah, and Malachi. Here we see that when we return from our negative situation to a positive one, we may not return with all we once possessed.

The restoration of the remnant of Israel presents us with several lessons. In order to restore the remnant, God raised up leadership in the persons of Joshua and Zerubbabel. They themselves were exiles who began to return to the land. The word "remnant" is instructive also because of an implication for those named in the interweaving of struggles and hopes, the mixture of the old and the new, the commingling of acceptance and resistance, the juxtaposition of new friends and old enemies. We see little setbacks in the broad canvas of divine victories. Also, in restoration, we see that the returning exiles were not left without guidance from God; the voice of the Lord continued to be heard through the prophets.

The restoration of the remnant also entailed "the renewal of the nation." God does not restore us, or these exiles, to the same old thing; rather, with restoration, God offers the opportunity to ponder, rethink, and give new effort to a new vision. Using our experiences of failure and pain from spiritual entanglement, God deals with some of our troubles and moves us to the changes necessary for re-creation and newness. The message of the restored remnant is that we can be helped, that there is renewal. We must then believe that a new era is possible and that this hope is not just imagination. The prophets Obadiah, Joel, Malachi, and Daniel remind us in their texts that in the past God had done great things; therefore, the difficulties we may encounter as we seek renewal can also be overcome.

Restoration calls for courageous action. The statement made by King Cyrus underscores the need for courage by the remnant: "Anyone of his people among you may his God be with him, and let him go up to Jerusalem in Judah and build the temple of the LORD, the God of Israel, the God who is in Jerusalem" (Ezra 1:3, NIV). For the remnants who are weak and overlooked, restoration does not come because they will it to be so, instead because the Lord stirs up the spirit of His people, charging them to build a highway of the Lord for freedom.

Restoration means that we are faced with a God-given opportunity. We are presented with the divine opportunity to move from captivity, pressure, and the stress of exile to the land of liberated joy. It is a call to place our losses because of possessions or honor in the light of God's great power and promise. It is a time to reconsider our disappointment in light of divine appointments. It is a move to balance our nostalgia, or even nausea, for the past with a new vision of the future. It contains within it a message that says being cast aside by society is not the last word; rather, divine restoration and renewal is the persistent word.

So now, because God has promised restoration, we are in a place to begin to rebuild. What was Israel called to rebuild? Was it not their religious and spiritual foundation? For us to be restored completely, we need to begin with the rebuilding of our personal, family, and communal altar. Could it not be said that like Jerusalem before the restoration, our altars and places of worship lie in waste? As the altar remains desolate, our return from exile and our gathering church will be ineffective, and joy will remain half-empty. But the fullness of our joy comes when we rebuild the altar and offer ourselves completely to God. When many people speak of restoration, they seem to think that it means continuing with stale music and unemotional worship. For some, it is the continuation of their racist hegemony and ethnocentric control of the welfare of others. But this restoration is the act of the Lord and must place Him at the center. As Haggai 1:2-14 insists, the act of restoration must make God our priority or it is not genuine. One who is truly restored to the Lord will answer the question, "Is it a time for you yourselves to be living in your paneled houses, while this house remains a ruin?" (Haggai 1:4, NIV) with an unequivocal "no."

Dr. Ogbonnaya holds a B.A. from Hillcrest Christian College in Alberta, Canada and a Ph.D. from Claremont School of Theology. He is a leading lecturer on African world views and their contributions to Christian thought and practices.

Religious Education: From Membership to Discipleship

by Dr. Robert Smith

There are those who would agree that within the context and framework of the African American church, preaching is central. It has the tendency to be the focal point of the worship experience and the propensity to perpetuate and promote numerical growth. While preaching is central, if the African American church is going to be a relevant institution in the new millennium, there must be a greater emphasis on teaching in our churches with an Afro-focal insight and a Christocentric perspective. There must be an intentional critique of and challenge to those who pass the portals of our hallowed doors to do more and be more for Christ.

The problem in many churches is they are filled with more

members than disciples. I define a member as a person who really does not make much of a commitment. However, a disciple is a learner/follower who pursues emulation and excellence. If we are going to transform the landscape of our communities and provide a balance to preaching and teaching, perhaps we need to change the way that we in the church refer to ourselves. It is my contention that we need to intentionally refer to ourselves as disciples and make a move from membership to discipleship. Language is important because it can make the abstract concrete and help us to see (both understand and envision) what we hear.

Sunday after Sunday, congregants gather in sanctuaries across the land in droves to worship God. However, they trickle into Sunday School, Bible Study, or any other teaching ministry. Dr. John Kinney, dean of the Samuel D. Proctor School of Theology (Richmond, VA), once said, "People who are shouting ought to get some learning and people who have learning ought to be shouting."

The lack of knowledge and religious understanding is pervasive in many churches, especially in Black church culture. It is a sad testimony and a terrible indicator for the future of our churches in a highly technological age in which information is the new currency. From a religious perspective, our churches should serve as repositories for the tools needed to make it in this postmodern, semi-agnostic culture. The majority of people who attend worship do not attend teaching ministries, and it is rather difficult to engage in authentic worship without understanding who is being worshiped and why.

If the African American church is going to be relevant in the new millennium, there must be a commitment to making religious education a high priority. This education must be undergirded by a liberation motif and not just a certification mantra. Dr. Mack King Carter states in his book, *A Quest for Freedom: An African American Odyssey*: "However, in the midst of oppression, learning to read can be a path to liberation, or further enslavement by the oppressor's Eurocentricity, which casts aspersions on anything having to do with Africa." In various teaching ministries, we must empower, enhance, and enrich the attendees with the tools and resources to love God, appreciate self, and serve humanity.

Dr. Carlyle Stewart asserts in his book *African American Church Growth: Twelve Principles for Prophetic Ministry* that "the basic tasks of the educational ministry in the growing prophetic church are to raise critical consciousness, help people develop a pragmatic and viable faith, and assist them in the acquisition of spiritual principles, through the development and implementation of meaningful programs." Our churches must be on the cutting edge because we must instill within the disciples inspiration and education. Thus, in all preaching there should be some teaching, and in teaching there must be some preaching.

Nevertheless, it is important for the pastor to be at the forefront of this charge. As the key leader in most churches, the pastor must rise to the challenge and push the educational component of ministry. Religious education must be the heart of the church's ministry. Jesus declared in the Great Commission, "Go ye therefore, and teach all nations, baptizing them in the name of the Father, and of the Son, and of the Holy Ghost: teaching them to observe all things whatsoever I have commanded you: and, lo, I am with you always, even unto the end of the world" (Matthew 28:19–20, KJV). The Master emphasized that disciples are made through teaching. The church cannot neglect or negate the necessity of religious education that goes beyond memorizing Bible verses and telling Bible stories. Disciples must be taught life application components that will empower them to become agents of transformation and bring God's kingdom here on earth. In *The Prophethood of Black Believers*, the idea that theologian J. Deotis Roberts affirms "the goal of the Christian life includes concern from the liberation of an oppressed people." Thus, Christian education goes beyond the Eurocentric motif of spiritual salvation and stresses the importance of holistically addressing the concerns of humanity.

The education of disciples cannot be stressed enough. In the world and in our churches, there are too many people not cognizant of the full Gospel message for living, and they suffer for a lack of knowledge because the church does not take religious education seriously. This is why there is a shift from the mainline Protestant churches to "Word churches," where there seems to be a greater emphasis on teaching than preaching. There is a thirst for knowledge, but some material fed to congregations is somewhat antithetical to the Scriptures and perverts the teachings of Christ. While our preaching is rousing and elevating, without adequate and proper teaching, it becomes like "clanging brass and tinkling cymbals." Pastors must stress the synergism between teaching and preaching in order to move our churches from membership to discipleship.

Therefore, if the Black church wants to impact this postmodern generation, we must pursue the application of information that comes through religious education and nurturing. If our churches are going to have an impact on our homes, our communities, our cities, and this world, we must share information that has the ability to transform individuals into disciples and empower them to live in this present age. The Bible says, "My people are destroyed for lack of knowledge" (Hosea 4:6a, KJV). Let's stop the destruction.

Reverend Dr. Robert Charles Scott is pastor of the historic Central Baptist Church in St. Louis, Missouri. He has earned a B.A. in political science, a masters of divinity, and a doctoral degree from the United Theological Seminary in Dayton, Ohio.

Sources:
Carter, Mack King, *A Quest for Freedom: An African American Odyssey* (Winter Park, FL: Four-G Publishers, 1993), p. 118.
Kinney, John; lecture at Hampton University Minister's Conference (Hampton, VA, 1999).
Roberst, J. Deotis, *The Prophethood of Black Believers* (Louisville, KY: Westminster/John Knox Press, 1994), p. 42.

Why Do We Attend Church?

by Aja Carr

For hundreds of years, millions of people all over the world have attended some form of church service. It seems that in general, people and Christians, in particular, believe that Sunday mornings mark a time of reflection and acknowledgment of Jesus Christ as Lord. Among African Americans and in the inner-city, it appears that it is good to "remember the sabbath day, to keep it holy" (Exodus 20:8). However, our philosophies about church should consider this cliché: Anything worth practicing, and anything valued enough to perform repetitively is worth understanding. We must become comfortable enough in our relationship with God and in our endeavor to practice good Christian values to question our practices and beliefs. Thus, we become comfortable enough to seek the answer to one pressing question in particular: Why do we attend church? Many would argue that the Bible commands it. Hebrews 10:25 admonishes us to "not [forsake] the assembling of ourselves together," meaning that we should often afford ourselves the opportunity to join with other Christians. Some

Christians agree with that notion and some do not; however, it is relatively easy to conclude that many of us attend church because it is a part of our familial upbringing, or because of what the church represents to our society and communities.

I believe the truth about our theology as churchgoers is deeply rooted in our upbringing. It is a part of our familial matrix: We attend church because our parents attended or because our families have been members of a particular church for years. It represents a place where we all come together in fellowship and worship. One could survey any given church and interview countless parishioners capable of testifying about the positive experiences for their families because of their commitment to attending service. Throughout history, we can point to the church as a place that has allowed all of God's children to be a family. Even during slavery, the church represented the one place where the slave family might be allowed to go together. Slaves attended the church of their master, and as long as the family worked on the same plantation, they could almost be assured that Sundays represented a small space in time where they could be with their families and be encouraged through some scriptural interpretation.

What better way is there to view the ministry of churches in inner-city areas than as agents that both prolong life and help avoid decay in communities abandoned by almost every other business and institution? In some respects, churches are among the very few institutions that have remained in the inner-city. A drive through any of America's inner-city communities will reveal that barbershops, beauty salons, bars (and liquor stores), and a wide assortment of small businesses and churches of various sizes occupy almost every corner, amid a sea of vacant lots

and abandoned buildings. This flight from the inner-cities has resulted in the loss of a tax base and rapid decline in the size of the middle class remaining in the cities. Almost everything that inner-city residents need in order to have a meaningful life is located outside of their community, ranging from medical care to adequate shopping facilities to employment beyond minimum wage jobs at fast-food restaurants.

The city of Chicago, for instance, is home to several megachurches. These churches are primarily located in the inner-city in predominantly African American neighborhoods. For example, Salem Baptist Church of Chicago, which boasts some 15,000 members, sits in the heart of the Roseland community (largely African American and partially Latino). The Apostolic Church of God, pastored by Dr. Arthur M. Brazier, and Trinity United Church of Christ, pastored by Rev. Otis Moss, III, are both situated on the South Side of the inner-city and are predominantly African American. The African American church is the only inner-city community presence that has not uprooted itself from the community. While the quality of life for many parishioners has improved—allowing them to relocate to suburban areas—the church has not relocated. I believe many African Americans continue to attend churches in our community for that reason. The church has always been there in the community and is viewed as an entity that will remain. It is a prototype of the nature of Christ in the community; its presence will remain steadfast and unmovable.

As we have changed and grown, so have our churches. The emergence of the African American middle class brought with it the emergence of the African American megachurch. Many scholars committed to the study of church growth and trends would argue that the birth of the megamall brought with it an influx of megachurches. However, I would argue that the expansion of the African American middle class and their ability to participate as valuable consumers in society (meaning that they could now shop at the megamalls) also gave them the affluence to support and become a part of larger church ministries. Thus, this supports the claim that some of us continue to attend church because its complexion has changed to represent the color of society as a whole. Further, every time society "upgrades," we have watched the church "upgrade," creating social constructs in the church. We subscribed to cable television because it was new and exciting; it offered us more channels and programs. Likewise, the church began to embrace the surge of cable markets. Now, we see church services broadcasted on cable television. The African American church has aligned itself with our society's culture, and we continue to attend because we can relate to that.

The dichotomy in the theology of churchgoers exists that we attend church because it has conformed itself to a changing society, but we also attend church to be rescued (emotionally) from that very same society. Moreover, the argument exists regarding the role of the church. The church has been a steadfast part of our community, but the economic incline of the parishioners and the rise of mega-entities have caused the church to change (and we can relate to the fluctuation). These arguments do not carry as much weight as the proceeding argument: We attend church because of our love for Jesus Christ. Countless theologians have harvested mounds of information regarding church membership, trends in church growth, and the theology of churchgoers, but none can easily refute that many Christians simply love the Lord, and that is why they attend church services. Church represents the one place in society where we can worship and praise God in our own way and with few inhibitions. While we might acknowledge the role of our families in our relationship with God and might identify with the conversely consistent and changing roles of the church, it is beyond debate that Jesus is the number-one reason why Christians attend church.

Aja M. Carr is a graduate of the University of Illinois at Urbana-Champaign and Garrett-Evangelical Theological Seminary. She is currently pursuing a law degree and Ph.D., and has more than 13 years experience in educational and Christian publishing.

Source:
McMickle, Marvin, and Gardner C. Taylor. *Preaching to the Black Middle Class: Words of Challenge, Words of Hope* (Valley Forge, Pa. Judson Press, 2000). 57-58.

GEORGE WASHINGTON CARVER
(1864?-1943)

"Lord, tell me the secrets of the universe."

"No. It's too much for you."

"Then tell me the secrets of the peanut."

An African American educator and agricultural scientist, George Washington Carver was born around 1864 on the Moses Carver plantation in Diamond Grove, Missouri. Carver's father died shortly before he was born. Slave raiders kidnapped both Carver and his mother; Carver was returned, but his mother was never found. A sickly child, he did chores around the house and explored the surrounding woods. He helped the neighbors with their plants, earning the name "plant doctor." He attended church with his "owner" and accepted God at an early age. He left the farm at ten years old, making his homes in Minneapolis and Kansas, and working his way through high school.

In 1890, he enrolled in Simpson College to study art and music. A gifted artist, poet, and musician, Carver's paintings were on display at the 1893 Chicago World's Fair. His art instructor, Etta Budd, knew about Carver's gift with plants and arranged for him to enroll at Iowa State College of Agriculture and Mechanic Arts (now Iowa State College). In spite of his poor health, Carver became extremely involved in many areas during his college years. He was convinced by Budd's father, who saw Carver's gift in horticulture, to remain for graduate work at the college, after which Carver joined the faculty as its first African American member.

As a graduate student, he specialized in bacteriological botany. He later became director of the Department of Agricultural Research at Tuskegee Normal and Industrial Institute (now Tuskegee University) at the invitation of Booker T. Washington.

In 1896, he began intensive research and experiments with peanuts. Carver developed hundreds of uses for peanuts, sweet potatoes, and soybeans and developed a new type of cotton—Carver's hybrid. His work inspired farmers in the South to raise other crops in addition to cotton, and also showed farmers how to improve the quality of their soil. Carver wrote in *The Need of Scientific Agriculture in the South*: "The virgin fertility of our soils and the vast amount of unskilled labor have been more of a curse than a blessing to agriculture. This exhaustive system for cultivation, the destruction of forest, the rapid and almost constant decomposition of organic matter, have made our agricultural problem one requiring more brains than of the North, East, or West."

Carver was awarded the Spingarn Medal in 1923 by the NAACP. In 1935, he went to work for the Department of Agriculture. In 1940, all his savings were donated to the establishment of the George Washington Carver Foundation at Tuskegee for natural science research.

What is not commonly known about Carver is that around 1933, he funded the overseas travel expenses for a group of African Americans and their families, who had been denied work in the United States after getting degrees in their fields (civil engineering, architecture, etc.). Overseas, the engineers found work and freedom from racism.

Carver died at Tuskegee on January 5, 1943. That same year, his birth home was established as the George Washington Carver National Monument.

Carver's relationship with God was probably enhanced by his work with nature. He once said, "We get closer to God as we get more intimately understandingly acquainted with the things He has created." Carver shared his faith with others, especially during a weekly Bible class that he organized and led at Tuskegee.

God truly used this outstanding son of faith to bless the world.

Teaching Tips

June 1
Bible Study Guide 1

Words You Should Know

A. Ways (Haggai 1:5) *derek* (Heb.)—Walk, manner, course, or lot in life, worship; actions and behavior of men.

B. Called for (v. 11) *qara* (Heb.)—To summon, proclaim, pronounce.

Teacher Preparation

Unifying Principle—Do What is Required. Sometimes personal needs and desires prevent Christians from giving priority to what's most important in their lives. How can Christians identify and give priority to what is important? God spoke through Haggai, saying that the people's first priority should be rebuilding the Lord's house and not their own homes.

A. Read the Background and Devotional Readings.

B. Review More Light on the Text and make note of pertinent details.

O—Open the Lesson

A. Have students consider and make a list of their life priorities (e.g., family, work, money, goals, and dreams). Have them keep their lists for later in the lesson discussion.

B. Ask for a volunteer to read the In Focus story and briefly discuss.

P—Present the Scriptures

A. Ask for volunteers to read the Focal Verses and The People, Places, and Times. Discuss.

B. Read and discuss the implications of the Background section and the parallels in today's context.

E—Explore the Meaning

A. Review and discuss the Search the Scriptures and Discuss the Meaning questions and the Lesson in Our Society section.

B. Ask students to revisit their life priorities listed earlier. Based on the lesson, have them consider how they fare on esteeming the things of God versus their own pursuits.

N—Next Steps for Application

A. Complete the Follow the Spirit and Remember Your Thoughts sections.

B. Have students silently reflect on the lesson and journal about priorities in their life. Pray for God to reveal areas for improvement.

C. Close in prayer.

Worship Guide

For the Superintendent or Teacher
Theme: Obey the Lord
Song: "Only What You Do For Christ Will Last"
Devotional Reading: Luke 19:41–48
Prayer

Obey the Lord

Bible Background • HAGGAI 1
Printed Text • HAGGAI 1:1–11 | Devotional Reading • LUKE 19:41–48

Aim for Change

By the end of the lesson, we will: UNDERSTAND why God commanded Haggai's encouragement to the Israelites to rebuild the Temple; INTERNALIZE the connection between the neglect of God's house and the poor results of the Israelites' selfish efforts; and LIST ways to carry out God's desires before attempts to satisfy our personal agendas.

In Focus

Brian and Carmen were second-generation members of their church, but over time things started to change. They noticed that the church was not an active part of the community anymore, and grew especially concerned about the church's commitment to social justice. The pastor admitted he lacked the support of the congregation on important issues impacting the city. As the members grew more successful in their personal lives, they began to focus more on their own prosperity rather than helping others.

Brian and Carmen were discouraged because it was not the church they had known growing up. They began visiting other churches and prayed about whether they should consider changing churches. Ultimately, they agreed not to move until they received clear direction from the Lord.

There is nothing wrong with personal pursuits of success. When they interfere with following through with God's assignments, however, we ought not to be surprised if He corrects or disciplines us. In today's lesson, the prophet Haggai is sent to call the people back to God's business.

Keep in Mind

"Then came the word of the LORD by Haggai the prophet, saying, Is it time for you, O ye, to dwell in your cieled houses, and this house lie waste?" (Haggai 1:3–4).

"Then came the word of the LORD by Haggai the prophet, saying, Is it time for you, O ye, to dwell in your cieled houses, and this house lie waste?" (Haggai 1:3–4).

Focal Verses

KJV **Haggai 1:1** In the second year of Darius the king, in the sixth month, in the first day of the month, came the word of the LORD by Haggai the prophet unto Zerubbabel the son of Shealtiel, governor of Judah, and to Joshua the son of Josedech, the high priest, saying,

2 Thus speaketh the LORD of hosts, saying, This people say, The time is not come, the time that the LORD's house should be built.

3 Then came the word of the LORD by Haggai the prophet, saying,

4 Is it time for you, O ye, to dwell in your cieled houses, and this house lie waste?

5 Now therefore thus saith the LORD of hosts; Consider your ways.

6 Ye have sown much, and bring in little; ye eat, but ye have not enough; ye drink, but ye are not filled with drink; ye clothe you, but there is none warm; and he that earneth wages earneth wages to put it into a bag with holes.

7 Thus saith the LORD of hosts; Consider your ways.

8 Go up to the mountain, and bring wood, and build the house; and I will take pleasure in it, and I will be glorified, saith the LORD.

9 Ye looked for much, and, lo it came to little; and when ye brought it home, I did blow upon it. Why? saith the LORD of hosts. Because of mine house that is waste, and ye run every man unto his own house.

10 Therefore the heaven over you is stayed from dew, and the earth is stayed from her fruit.

11 And I called for a drought upon the land, and upon the mountains, and upon the corn, and upon the new wine, and upon the oil, and upon that which the ground

NLT **Haggai 1:1** On August 29 of the second year of King Darius's reign, the LORD gave a message through the prophet Haggai to Zerubbabel son of Shealtiel, governor of Judah, and to Jeshua son of Jehozadak, the high priest.

2 "This is what the LORD of Heaven's Armies says: The people are saying, 'The time has not yet come to rebuild the house of the LORD.'"

3 Then the LORD sent this message through the prophet Haggai:

4 "Why are you living in luxurious houses while my house lies in ruins?

5 This is what the LORD of Heaven's Armies says: Look at what's happening to you!

6 You have planted much but harvest little. You eat but are not satisfied. You drink but are still thirsty. You put on clothes but cannot keep warm. Your wages disappear as though you were putting them in pockets filled with holes!

7 This is what the LORD of Heaven's Armies says: Look at what's happening to you!

8 Now go up into the hills, bring down timber, and rebuild my house. Then I will take pleasure in it and be honored, says the LORD.

9 You hoped for rich harvests, but they were poor. And when you brought your harvest home, I blew it away. Why? Because my house lies in ruins, says the LORD of Heaven's Armies, while all of you are busy building your own fine houses.

10 It's because of you that the heavens withhold the dew and the earth produces no crops.

11 I have called for a drought on your fields and hills—a drought to wither the bringeth forth, and upon men, and upon cattle, and upon all the labour of the hands.

grain and grapes and olive trees and all your other crops, a drought to starve you and your livestock and to ruin everything you have worked so hard to get."

The People, Places, and Times

Prophet. As God's messenger, a prophet's responsibility was to represent, declare, and announce God's will to the people. A prophet was not primarily a "fore" teller but a "forth" teller. The prophets spoke about social, cultural, and political situations and gave moral and spiritual guidance to God's people. In particular, the prophets carried oracles from God directed at Israel, Judah, and surrounding foreign nations. The purpose of such oracles was to reiterate God's promises to their ancestors, give assurance of His presence, correct the people by expressing His displeasure, or give warning before judgment for wrongdoing. Interwoven in Israel's prophetic messages before, during, and after the exile were foreshadows of the coming Messiah.

Temple. Building erected and sanctified for the worship of God. King Solomon completed the first structure in the 11th year of his reign in 949 B.C., which mirrored the composition of the tabernacle—containing the outer court, inner court, and most holy place. The temple has great significance in Jewish history, as it housed the Ark of the Covenant, which represented the presence of God. The Levites (descendants of Levi) were the designated caretakers of the temple, and only the high priest was allowed to enter into the most holy place once a year, as he represented God to the people and the people before God. The Babylonians destroyed the first temple in 586 B.C. when the southern kingdom was led into captivity (2 Kings 25:9).

Background

After seventy years in captivity in Babylon, the Israelites were allowed to return to their native land. King Cyrus of Persia defeated the Babylonians in 538/9 B.C., and he then decreed that the exiled people could return to their land, reestablish worship of their God, and rebuild the temple (Ezra 1:1–8; cf. Isaiah 44:28). The first order of business was to record an account of the first wave of people returning from captivity. Their first goal was building an altar on the temple site and the reinstitution of the sacrificial system (Ezra 2–3). In 535 B.C., plans were underway to rebuild the temple as the foundation was laid, but work stopped in 520 B.C. due to political and economic struggles with neighboring nations who were "adversaries of Judah and Benjamin" (Ezra 4:1). Sixteen years passed. It wasn't until the second year of King Darius' reign that the release was given to resume work in 520/1 B.C. God called both Haggai and Zechariah to usher in revival by imploring His people to honor Him by finishing what they started.

At-A-Glance

1. Call to Rebuild (Haggai 1:1–2)
2. Call to Reflect (vv. 3–9)
3. Call to Reap (vv. 10–11)

In Depth

1. Call to Rebuild (Haggai 1:1–2)

Haggai the prophet was commissioned by God to speak directly to political power;

Zerubbabel, son of Shealtiel, was governor of Judah and spiritual authority; Joshua, son of Jehozadak, was the high priest. Both Zerubbabel and Joshua were from families of influence among the exiles. Because they were considered leaders, the "word of the Lord" came to them through the prophet Haggai. God now required that His temple be complete as a sign of His restoration and abiding presence.

Haggai was God's mouthpiece; he did not speak of his own accord. To say that "the word of the LORD [came by] Haggai the prophet" (Haggai 1:1) was not said lightly. When the prophet spoke, the people would do well to pay attention. A prophet was considered credible in speaking the oracles of God when every word he spoke proved true (1 Samuel 3:19, 9:6). Haggai, along with the prophet Zechariah (believed to be considerably younger), worked in tandem to promote revival among the returning exiles. They began with the first wave under Zerubbabel's leadership, then continued with subsequent exiles in the second and third waves who returned under Ezra and Nehemiah.

Even after receiving clearance to rebuild, however, the people decided that the time was not right and neglected their charge to rebuild. Haggai called this decision into question; his proclamation was a strong rebuke to hold God's people accountable. When God clears the way for us to accomplish His work, we should promptly obey and follow through to accomplish His plans in the earth.

2. Call to Reflect (vv. 3–9)

Continuing "the word of the LORD" (Haggai 1:1), Haggai addressed the people, telling them to look within and "consider [their] ways" (v. 5). Why were they disobeying the Lord? God's house remained unfinished while the exiles focused on restoring their own lives and homes. The temple

was a symbol of God's presence and holiness among His people; for it to remain incomplete was a sign of ingratitude for His deliverance from captivity. Through Haggai, God inquired about their ungrateful behavior. Humility should have followed their deliverance—completing God's temple an eagerly anticipated undertaking. Such thankfulness and obedience would have brought them prosperity and security; instead, the exiles did just the opposite. They refused to obey God's command. They had sown but not harvested. As a result, their earnings disappeared as quickly as if they had "put it into a bag with holes" (v. 6).

God expressed displeasure with the hearts of His people. As Haggai continued to preach for them to "consider [their] ways," the Lord commanded immediate action by holding the leaders accountable first. The directive was for the men to take action and build His house. Only when they made this a reality would He be pleased. As much as God appreciates our praise, true worship (surrender) requires action. God declared to the exiles that it was He who rewarded them, and it was He who punished when His word was not obeyed. His word should be their first priority. Their decision to focus on themselves resulted in God's house remaining in ruins. We would do well to also consider our ways. Where do we place our priorities? Do we promptly obey God? Do we start but leave things unfinished?

3. Call to Reap (vv. 10–11)

The exiles were held accountable for their collective negligence in rebuilding the temple. They were experiencing economic stress from a drought, the land would not produce, and wages were lost. Today, we might equate their situation to rampant unemployment and recession. In other words, there seemed to be a direct connection between their obedience and their prosperity. Though there are many who have abused the idea of prosperity as it pertains to the people of God, there is scriptural evidence that connects God-honoring obedience with blessings and favor. "So be careful to do what the LORD your God has commanded you; do not turn aside to the right or to the left. Walk in obedience to all that the LORD your God has commanded you, so that you may live and prosper and prolong your days in the land that you will possess" (Deuteronomy 5:32–33, NIV). It is not to say that we won't experience hardship while walking in obedience, but it does say that there is great blessing in our obedience.

Because the exiles did not honor God by finishing the restoration of His temple, He called their irreverence to their attention. God was giving them an opportunity to make corrections. The Lord has not changed. He does the same for us today when He makes us aware of our sin—He gives us an opportunity to make corrections. Sometimes the consequences are averted and sometimes, in order to learn the lesson, we must endure the consequences. In either case, God is always just and His judgments are righteous.

Search the Scriptures

1. What were the people doing that displeased God (Haggai 1:3)?

2. What does God direct the people to do in order to please Him (v. 8)?

Discuss the Meaning

1. Why do you think God specifically called out Zerubbabel and Joshua? What's the significance? How can we as the people of God hold our political and spiritual leaders respectfully accountable?

2. What does it mean for us to "consider our ways"? How might our socio-economic conditions answer that question?

Lesson in Our Society

It is easy for us to get caught up in our own world and not consider what is happening around us. When personal or corporate tragedy hits a community, it makes us more cognizant of our need to completely depend on God. Our love for God and others demonstrates ways in which we may honor God in our daily lives. In fact, Jesus stated that all the commandments and prophetic passages of the Old Testament hang on those two concepts—loving God and loving our neighbor (Matthew 22:37–40). God's heart for justice and righteousness has not changed; He desires that His people always "consider their ways" by being reflective of how they are representing His kingdom in this world. The world would be a better place if we would put God first and others before ourselves.

Make It Happen

This week, take to heart Haggai's message to "consider your ways." Consider the purity of your motives; is God truly the head of your life and at the center of it all? Do you hold the things of God in high esteem? Ask the Holy Spirit to show you what is right in your relationship with God and praise Him for the progress. What are areas of improvement—those things you know the Lord has tugged on your heart to start or complete? Seek to promptly obey the Lord when He gives you instruction to move, not so you can receive but so He can have an opportunity to bless with His goodness.

Follow the Spirit

What God wants me to do:

_____

_____

_____

_____

Remember Your Thoughts

Special insights I have learned:

_____

_____

_____

_____

More Light on the Text

Haggai 1:1–11

1 In the second year of Darius the king, in the sixth month, in the first day of the month, came the word of the LORD by Haggai the prophet unto Zerubbabel the son of Shealtiel, governor of Judah, and to Joshua the son of Josedech, the high priest, saying, 2 Thus speaketh the LORD of hosts, saying, This people say, The time is not come, the time that the LORD's house should be built.

Experts date the writing of Haggai to Elul 1 according to the Jewish calendar (which corresponds to August 29 on a contemporary calendar) in the year 520 B.C. A contemporary of Zechariah, little else is known of the prophet Haggai. However, his important message to the nation of Israel is mentioned again in Ezra 5:1–2. In a plain and simple voice, Haggai began by pricking the conscience of the returned Jewish exiles from

Babylon by reminding them of their historical lineage—Zerubbabel was the great-grandson of King Jehoiakim (see 1 Chronicles 3:16–19) and the nephew of Shealtiel; Joshua was of the Aaronic priestly line (see 1 Chronicles 6:1–15). Both men had returned with the first group of Jewish exiles around 532 B.C. (see Ezra 2:2, 3:2). Haggai also confronted them with the fact that God heard what they were saying: "This people say" (Heb. *amar*, **aw-MAR**, meaning spoke or kept saying) that the time was not right for rebuilding the Lord's house, even though they had been in the land for nearly twenty years.

3 Then came the word of the LORD by Haggai the prophet, saying, 4 Is it time for you, O ye, to dwell in your cieled houses, and this house lie waste?

Repeated from verse 1, the "LORD" (Heb. *Yehovah*, **yeh-ho-VAW**, meaning the self-existent or eternal) spoke through Haggai with a probing question: Is this the time for you to be so taken with the state of your own living condition? The people who had returned from the Babylonian exile had become concerned solely with their physical living conditions and had forgotten the God who delivered them. They built "cieled" (Heb. *caphan*, **saw-FAN**) homes (NLT translates "luxurious") but were neglecting God's house. Upon entering the land two decades earlier, Cyrus had given the returning exiles an edict to rebuild Solomon's temple. They had begun the work but abandoned it when some of the nearby inhabitants began to complain (see Ezra 4:1–4). After abandoning the rebuilding of God's house, the Jewish exiles turned their attention away from God and His temple and focused on building their own homes. God's temple, which lay in "waste" (Heb. *chareb*, **khaw-RABE**), would have been a constant and visible reminder to the people of their place within the empire in which they now found themselves. They were still subjects under the rule of the conquering King Darius and were suffering economically with resources sufficient only for the building of their own homes. One scholar suggests that in the face of the native inhabitants' overwhelming opposition, the returning exiles had grown to accept their subject status and withdrawn into themselves. They then sought to make themselves as comfortable and unnoticeable as possible (*The New Layman's Bible Commentary*, 1020).

5 Now therefore thus saith the LORD of hosts; Consider your ways.

Speaking through the prophet Haggai, God sought to awaken the people from their state of despondency by calling for them to look at how they were living and "consider" (Heb. *suwm*, **soom**, meaning to think about or regard) their "ways" (Heb. *derek*, **DEH-rek**, meaning a course of life or mode of action) as they lived in luxury while God's house lay in ruins.

6 Ye have sown much, and bring in little; ye eat, but ye have not enough; ye drink, but ye are not filled with drink; ye clothe you, but there is none warm; and he that earneth wages earneth wages to put it into a bag with holes.

God then helped the people to see their condition through His eyes. Upon returning to the land two decades earlier, the returning exiles found the land desolate and idle, awaiting its restoration as prophesied by Jeremiah (see Jeremiah 25–26). The returned exiles immediately began work on two fronts—first to rebuild Solomon's temple as Cyrus had ordered; second, to plant crops and make the land fruitful. However, King Cyrus died in battle a year after their return. As the invading armies of his son,

Cambyses, made their way across the land to subdue Egypt, they demanded tribute from the people, probably paid in the form of produce, which impoverished the land and its inhabitants further. As a result, work on the temple halted as the Jewish exiles became depressed and settled into passivity. The people tried unsuccessfully to eke out a living, but their efforts proved unfruitful. Planted crops produced little in the way of food, water did not satisfy their thirst, and the clothing they made did not keep them warm. Even the few dollars they were able to earn didn't do much to alter their living conditions.

7 Thus saith the LORD of hosts; Consider your ways. 8 Go up to the mountain, and bring wood, and build the house; and I will take pleasure in it, and I will be glorified, saith the LORD.

God once more spoke to the people through Haggai and offered them instruction on how to go about correcting their situation. Haggai instructed the people to go to the mountains and gather wood to rebuild God's house. Wood, though sparse in the fields, would have been plentiful in the mountains. In calling for the people to unite around the task of gathering wood, Haggai reasoned that the people would be stirred from their passive state. As a result, they would experience a revival of their religious commitment and spiritual zeal. The people were to ascend up to gain a different perspective. It is likely that the people only needed to gather wood because the stones of the original foundation and earlier aborted reconstruction of the temple were still in place.

Haggai tried to communicate to the people that their depression and passivity were not a result of their condition as subjects of a foreign king, which they probably offered as an excuse, but rather the result of not obeying God. Only as they actively altered the course of their daily activities and redirected their energies into the completion of God's house, would God "take pleasure" (Heb. *ratsah*, **raw-TSAW**, meaning to be pleased with) in them and be "glorified" (Heb. *kabad*, **kaw-BADE**, meaning to enjoy honor). Haggai realized that the people had placed their own living in front of a concern for God and, as a result, He withheld His blessings. Haggai called the people to remember God and place Him first. Jesus may have had this prophecy in mind when He admonished the populace of His day to "seek ye first the kingdom of God" (from Matthew 6:33) in order to receive God's blessing.

9 Ye looked for much, and, lo it came to little; and when ye brought it home, I did blow upon it. Why? saith the LORD of hosts. Because of mine house that is waste, and ye run every man unto his own house. 10 Therefore the heaven over you is stayed from dew, and the earth is stayed from her fruit. 11 And I called for a drought upon the land, and upon the mountains, and upon the corn, and upon the new wine, and upon the oil, and upon that which the ground bringeth forth, and upon men, and upon cattle, and upon all the labor of the hands.

It is noteworthy that Haggai did not mention the earlier decree from Cyrus to encourage the people to continue rebuilding God's house. Rather, he directed their attention to the drought, which now gripped the land, and the lack of harvest from their labor. Nothing was spared from God's displeasure. The people, land, crops, and animals were all suffering. The sight of Solomon's temple still in ruins coupled with the lack of success on the part of the people to produce from the land provided ample evidence of the truthfulness of Haggai's words.

Sources:
Burton, James. *Coffman Commentaries on the Old Testament and New Testament.* Abilene, TX: Abilene Christian University Press, 2000.
Dunn, James D. G. and John W. Rogerson. *Commentary on the Bible.* Grand Rapids, MI: Wm. B. Eerdmans Publishing Company, 2003.
HarperCollins Study Bible (NRSV). New York: Harper Collins Publishers, 2006. 1265–66.
Hebrew Greek Key Word Study Bible (KJV) 2nd ed. Chattanooga, TN: AMG Publishers, 1991. 1152, 1607–08.
Howley, Bruce and Ellison Howley. *The New Layman's Bible Commentary.* Grand Rapids, MI: Zondervan, 1979.
Unger, Merrill, and Robert F. Ramey. *Unger's Bible Dictionary.* Chicago: Moody Press, 1981. 439, 890–92,1076–78.
Unger, Merrill. *Unger's Bible Handbook.* Chicago: Moody Press, 1967. 255–56, 432.

Say It Correctly

Shealtiel. shee-**AL**-tih-ehl.
Josedech. jo-tsaw-**DAWK**.

Daily Bible Readings

MONDAY
A House of Prayer
(Luke 19:41–48)

TUESDAY
The Fall of Jerusalem
(Jeremiah 52:1–9)

WEDNESDAY
The Temple Destroyed
(Jeremiah 52:10–14)

THURSDAY
Given into Enemy Hands
(2 Chronicles 36:15–21)

FRIDAY
Carried Away into Captivity
(2 Kings 24:8–17)

SATURDAY
Rebuild God's House
(Ezra 1:1–8)

SUNDAY
God's House Lies in Ruins
(Haggai 1:1–11)

Notes

_____

_____

_____

_____

Teaching Tips

Words You Should Know

A. Prophet (Haggai 2:1) *navi* (Heb.)—Speaker of oracles, an authorized spokesman for God.

B. Glory (vv. 3, 7, 9) *kavod* (Heb.) Weight, honor esteem, majesty, abundance, wealth.

Teacher Preparation

Unifying Principle—Build for the Future. Some communities find it difficult to begin projects. What motivates communities to get started on a new project? God promised to be with the people as they completed the rebuilding of His temple.

A. Read the Background and Devotional Readings.

B. Review More Light on the Text and make note of pertinent details.

O—Open the Lesson

A. Open with prayer.

B. Ask for a volunteer to read the In Focus story.

P—Present the Scriptures

A. Ask for volunteers to read the Focal Verses and The People, Places, and Times. Discuss.

B. Read and discuss the Background section and insights from last week's lesson.

C. Look at each section of the lesson and have students break into groups to discuss Haggai's message strategy.

E—Explore the Meaning

A. Ask student groups to report back to the larger group their findings as they reviewed Haggai's message.

B. Review and discuss the Search the Scriptures and Discuss the Meaning questions and the Lesson in Our Society section.

N—Next Steps for Application

A. Complete the Follow the Spirit and Remember Your Thoughts sections.

B. Remind students to read the Daily Bible Readings in preparation for next week's lesson.

C. Ask students to make a commitment to complete the Make It Happen exercise and report their experience next week.

D. Close in prayer, thanking God for His presence in our lives.

Worship Guide

For the Superintendent or Teacher
Theme: Trust God's Promises
Song: "May the Work I've Done Speak For Me"
Devotional Reading: Psalm 27:7–14

Trust God's Promises

Bible Background • HAGGAI 1:12–15, 2:1–9
Printed Text • HAGGAI 1:12, 2:1–9 | Devotional Reading • PSALM 27:7–14

Aim for Change

By the end of the lesson, we will: KNOW God's promises to the Israelites linked to His command to rebuild the Temple; TRUST that God pledges assistance and prosperity in response to obedience to Him; and IDENTIFY ways that God seeks our obedience and how we can demonstrate it.

In Focus

James was a high school all-American athlete. He was aggressively recruited by some of the top collegiate teams in the country. James always dreamed of going pro so he could come back and help his family and community.

A few years later, James reached his goal. He applied to, and was accepted by, one of the top-ranked programs, and worked hard enough to get drafted his junior year. He signed a multimillion-dollar deal, and guest appearances and endorsements soon followed. James started a foundation in his mother's honor because she had wanted him to get a good education. James' mom was very proud of her son, and she managed the day-to-day operations of the foundation. James and his mother built a community center that provided programming for youth and adults. The community center was a fulfillment of a dream and a promise to God to give Him glory by giving back to others.

God blesses our obedience in many ways: health, protection, and even prosperity. In today's lesson, we will see how God proclaimed His promise of restored glory to the returning exiles as they obeyed His command to rebuild His temple.

Keep in Mind

"The glory of this latter house shall be greater than of the former, saith the LORD of hosts: and in this place will I give peace, saith the LORD of hosts" (Haggai 2:9).

"The glory of this latter house shall be greater than of the former, saith the LORD of hosts: and in this place will I give peace, saith the LORD of hosts" (Haggai 2:9).

Focal Verses

KJV **Haggai 1:12** Then Zerubbabel the son of Shealtiel, and Joshua the son of Josedech, the high priest, with all the remnant of the people, obeyed the voice of the LORD their God, and the words of Haggai the prophet, as the LORD their God had sent him, and the people did fear before the LORD.

2:1 In the seventh month, in the one and twentieth day of the month, came the word of the LORD by the prophet Haggai, saying,

2 Speak now to Zerubbabel the son of Shealtiel, governor of Judah, and to Joshua the son of Josedech, the high priest, and to the residue of the people, saying,

3 Who is left among you that saw this house in her first glory? and how do ye see it now? is it not in your eyes in comparison of it as nothing?

4 Yet now be strong, O Zerubbabel, saith the LORD; and be strong, O Joshua, son of Josedech, the high priest; and be strong, all ye people of the land, saith the LORD, and work: for I am with you, saith the LORD of hosts:

5 According to the word that I covenanted with you when ye came out of Egypt, so my spirit remaineth among you: fear ye not.

6 For thus saith the LORD of hosts; Yet once, it is a little while, and I will shake the heavens, and the earth, and the sea, and the dry land;

7 And I will shake all nations, and the desire of all nations shall come: and I will fill this house with glory, saith the LORD of hosts.

8 The silver is mine, and the gold is mine, saith the LORD of hosts.

9 The glory of this latter house shall be greater than of the former, saith the LORD

NLT **Haggai 1:12** Then Zerubbabel son of Shealtiel, and Jeshua son of Jehozadak, the high priest, and the whole remnant of God's people began to obey the message from the LORD their God. When they heard the words of the prophet Haggai, whom the LORD their God had sent, the people feared the LORD.

2:1 Then on October 17 of that same year, the LORD sent another message through the prophet Haggai.

2 "Say this to Zerubbabel son of Shealtiel, governor of Judah, and to Jeshua son of Jehozadak, the high priest, and to the remnant of God's people there in the land:

3 'Does anyone remember this house—this Temple—in its former splendor? How, in comparison, does it look to you now? It must seem like nothing at all!

4 But now the LORD says: Be strong, Zerubbabel. Be strong, Jeshua son of Jehozadak, the high priest. Be strong, all you people still left in the land. And now get to work, for I am with you, says the LORD of Heaven's Armies.

5 My Spirit remains among you, just as I promised when you came out of Egypt. So do not be afraid.'

6 For this is what the LORD of Heaven's Armies says: In just a little while I will again shake the heavens and the earth, the oceans and the dry land.

7 I will shake all the nations, and the treasures of all the nations will be brought to this Temple. I will fill this place with glory, says the LORD of Heaven's Armies.

8 The silver is mine, and the gold is mine, says the LORD of Heaven's Armies.

9 The future glory of this Temple will be greater than its past glory, says the LORD of Heaven's Armies. And in this place I will of hosts: and in this place will I give peace, saith the LORD of hosts.

bring peace. I, the LORD of Heaven's Armies, have spoken!"

The People, Places, and Times

Zerubbabel. The son of Shealtiel from the line of Judah; his name means "seed or offspring of Babylon." His Babylonian name was Sheshbazzar, and he was recognized as a prince while in captivity. He was believed to be a man of great influence in direct service to King Cyrus. He led the first wave of exiles from Babylonian captivity. Zerubbabel was given favor with the king to rebuild the second temple and reestablish worship in Jerusalem.

Joshua. A common name among the Hebrews, he is distinguished as son of Jehozadak. The name means "Jehovah is his help" or "Jehovah the Savior." His father, who was also a priest, served while in exile, which means Joshua was probably born in exile. Appointed by King Cyrus in 535 B.C. after the captivity in Babylon, he and Zerubbabel led the first wave of exiles in returning to their homeland and rebuilding the temple.

Background

In the previous lesson, we saw how the exiles were released from captivity and returned with great energy to rebuild their land and worship. However, a series of setbacks led them to stop rebuilding God's temple. Through Haggai, God rebuked them for leaving the rebuilding of the temple unfinished when faced with opposition. The Lord called on them to "consider [their] ways" (Haggai 1:5, 7) and realize the results of their irreverence when His commands were selfishly ignored—economic downturn, lost wages, and unfruitfulness (vv. 7–11). God called the political and spiritual leaders to direct the people away from their folly. With God on their side and the

favor King Cyrus had given Zerubbabel and Joshua for rebuilding the temple, they had no excuse (v. 1).

The temple was symbolic of God's presence and power; it was their place of worship. Leaving the temple undone was not an option. God extended mercy by sending His prophet to show the people their sin and to help them return to God.

At-A-Glance

1. The Fear of the Lord Restored (Haggai 1:12)
2. The Former Glory Revisited(2:1–3)
3. The Promise Reaffirmed (vv. 4–5)
4. The New Prophecy Revealed (vv. 6–9)

In Depth

1. The Fear of the Lord Restored (Haggai 1:12)

Zerubbabel, the governor of Judah, represented political power while Joshua, the high priest, represented spiritual authority. These two led the first of the exiles from captivity and back to their land. As the people were summoned to obey the voice of the Lord through the prophet, they once again feared God. Haggai's words must have pierced their hearts as they reflected on the current state of affairs. A word from the Lord is not always good news; often the prophets brought bad news, telling the people of their sins against God. In this case, the incomplete temple reflected the spiritual state of the returning exiles, who should have shown their gratitude to God by reinstituting worship in a rebuilt temple. Zerubbabel and Joshua set the tone in leading the people in demonstrating what it meant to hear the word of the Lord and promptly obey.

2. The Former Glory Revisited (2:1–3)

In the second year of King Darius' reign, Haggai was sent as God's mouthpiece. His mission was to hold the political and spiritual leadership accountable to complete the temple, but he used a different message strategy. To motivate completion, Haggai spoke to those who would have been old enough to remember the brilliance of the former temple. He called on them to recall the glory of Solomon's temple as they continued work. God had always been faithful to His people. Solomon's temple had been a beacon of hope and source of pride for the people; it represented God's presence with them. Solomon's father, the great King David, had gathered the materials, but it was Solomon who completed the first temple in 949 B.C. The temple's beauty was unsurpassed. Unfortunately, due to the nation's sinful actions, the nation was destroyed, the temple burned, and the people taken captive in Babylon for seventy years.

Those old enough to recall the first temple would have been very young; now they were the elders who lived to describe its former glory. Ezra recorded that when the foundation was laid for the second temple, some rejoiced because restoration of the temple represented their return from captivity. However, the older people who remembered the first temple wept because they knew it would be a far cry from its former glory (Ezra 3:8–13).

3. The Promise Reaffirmed (vv. 4–5)

Scripture bears out that God always assures His people of His faithfulness to His promises. Haggai now moves from rebuking the people to encouraging them. He proclaims that they should not despair over the former temple; it was more important for them to know that the Lord of Hosts was with them. Through use of His name as the "Lord of hosts," or Lord of armies, God reassured His people of His divine protection. He promised that He would watch over them as they completed the restoration of the temple. He reminded them of the covenant He made to their ancestors in the exodus from captivity out of Egypt. God's promises are timeless and He is faithful; therefore, Haggai encouraged the people to move forward without fear. Just as He had been with them and their ancestors in Egypt, and with them through their captivity in Babylon, God continued to be with them in the land. His abiding presence remained (v. 5).

God's promises are always with us (Isaiah 30:21, 43:1–7; Matthew 28:20; John 15:4–5). In the Exodus, the Israelites experienced this reality in the form of a cloud by day and a pillar of fire by night to guide them (Exodus 13:21–22). In addition, an angel went before them as they sought to go into the Promised Land to overtake their enemies (23:20). Just as God had been with His people to help them conquer the powerful nations when they entered the land the first time, He was still with them and would keep His covenant. Today, we have God's abiding presence through a personal relationship with His Son Jesus Christ and the indwelling of the Holy Spirit.

4. The New Prophecy Revealed (vv. 6–9)

In this phase of Haggai's message, his pronouncement moves to judgment against the other nations. Jehovah Sabaoth, Lord of hosts, is the mighty Warrior who "will shake the heavens, and the earth, and the sea, and the dry land" (v. 6). God here says that He will literally agitate the heavens and the earth, sending forth a wave to upset the status quo.

Babylon, Persia, and later Rome would exert great power over Israel as a nation and all would seem lost. However, this message was one of hope—not only for immediate restoration but also a projection of what was to come in the future.

At God's appointed time, Christ will shake the status quo to bring God's will to pass on earth as in heaven. Upon His return, Christ will enforce worldwide judgment upon the nations for their obedience or disobedience to God's commands. God promises He will fill this temple with glory: "The earth is the LORD's and all that is in it, the world, and those who live in it" (Psalm 24:1, NRSV). God declared that the silver and gold belonged to Him, so in building the temple, they were using what belonged to Him anyway. He encouraged His people that those who oppressed them and plundered their treasured possessions would meet a worse fate, and they would one day bring their offerings and treasure into the Lord's temple.

God promised to fill the new temple with glory and splendor greater than that of Solomon's temple. God's peace (some translations use the word "prosperity") will rest in this temple. In the book of Revelation, John recorded his vision: "And I saw a new heaven and a new earth: for the first heaven and the first earth were passed away; and there was no more sea. And I John saw the holy city, new Jerusalem, coming down from God out of heaven, prepared as a bride adorned for her husband" (Revelation 21:1–2). As a glimpse of what is to come, Jesus Christ is the fulfillment of this promise of "latter glory" because it is through Him that all the nations of the world are blessed.

We too have the assurance that God will do what He promised. God promises a new city where the Lamb will dwell with humanity and wipe away every tear. There will be no more death, crying, mourning, or pain;

nothing unclean will enter and the Lord God will be our light forever and ever (Revelation 21:2–4, 22–23, 27, 22:3–5).

Search the Scriptures

1. What did the people do in response to Haggai's message (Haggai 1:12)?

2. What did Haggai ask the elders to compare (2:3)?

3. How did Haggai encourage the people (vv. 4–5)?

4. What did God promise would happen to the nations (vv. 6–7)?

Discuss the Meaning

1. What does it mean to rest on the promises of God in tough times? How can we apply holding on to God's promises in today's context?

2. What is the impact of corporate obedience on communities? Do we see evidence of humanity's obedience to God in recent history?

Lesson in Our Society

God demonstrated His love toward us when He sent His Son Jesus Christ to die for us. We can demonstrate our love in return by how we obey His Word and live out His commands. After the prophet reminded them of God's covenant, the exiles were motivated to not only rebuild the temple but reestablish their relationship with Him. We too can take God at His word; if we have fallen into sin or wandered from God, He invites us to recommit our lives to Him. We were created to bring God glory and be His "treasured possession." As we commit or recommit our way to Him, the Lord promises that our plans will succeed and we shall be established (Proverbs 16:3). As Christians, we can take a leadership role in helping our nation turn back to God so we can dwell in peace—and it starts one neighborhood at a time. We can start by being a light in dark places and showing a better way of doing and being. When opportunities arise, we can seek the Holy Spirit's guidance in how to live, act, and behave to reflect our Savior. Everything we do should be done as if we're doing it for the Lord (Colossians 3:23). Take the time to pray and think of how you can glorify the Lord every day.

Make It Happen

This week, pray and determine how you may glorify God in your sphere of influence. Take advantage of daily opportunities to consciously obey God and reflect His character. As you pray about a particular situation you sense God calling to your attention, find Scripture(s) that helps you understand God's desires and promises. Write in a journal what the Lord speaks to you and record answered prayers. Share your experience next week with your classmates.

Follow the Spirit

What God wants me to do:

_____

_____

_____

_____

Remember Your Thoughts

Special insights I have learned:

_____

_____

_____

_____

More Light on the Text

Haggai 1:12, 2:1–9

12 Then Zerubbabel the son of Shealtiel, and Joshua the son of Josedech, the high priest, with all the remnant of the people, obeyed the voice of the LORD their God, and the words of Haggai the prophet, as the LORD their God had sent him, and the people did fear before the LORD.

Probably nothing pleases the Lord more than an obedient, positive response from those He speaks to. Such was the response from "all the remnant" (Heb. *sheeriyth*, **sheh-ay-REETH**, meaning those who remained alive) of the returned exiles and their leadership. Haggai could only have been pleased that the people did not protest at his words but set about at once to do as he instructed. Not only had the work of rebuilding the house of God begun anew, but the chosen people found a renewed spiritual zeal and "did fear" (Heb. *yare*, **yaw-RAY**, meaning to revere, respect, or worship) the Lord who had delivered them from Babylonian captivity.

2:1 In the seventh month, in the one and twentieth day of the month, came the word of the LORD by the prophet Haggai, saying, 2 Speak now to Zerubbabel the son of Shealtiel, governor of Judah, and to Joshua the son of Josedech, the high priest, and to the residue of the people, saying,

The twenty-first day of the seventh month (Tishri on the Jewish calendar) would have been October 17, 520 B.C. on our contemporary calendars and would have been the seventh or last day of the celebration of the Feast of Tabernacles (see Numbers 29:32–34). On the same date, 440 years earlier (960 B.C.), Solomon finished the original construction of the temple (see 1 Kings 6:38, 8:2). It is fitting then that God chose this date to once more speak to the Jewish leadership and

His chosen people. Just under a month had passed since they began to rebuild the house of God. It is conceivable that the people had become discouraged by the way the structure was looking and had slowed or halted their work in response.

3 Who is left among you that saw this house in her first glory? And how do ye see it now? is it not in your eyes in comparison of it as nothing?

Haggai here spoke pointedly to the people's discouragement. In 587 B.C., Solomon's temple had been destroyed by the Babylonians. Coupled with the fact that the Jewish captivity by the Babylonians had lasted 70 years, it was likely that some of the oldest of the returned exiles would have remembered seeing the splendor and glory of God's house with their own "eyes" (Heb. *ayin*, **AH-yin**, meaning sight or of mental and spiritual faculties). Then, remembering that house "in her first" (Heb. *rishown*, **ree-SHONE**, meaning former or most prominent) glory and viewing the reconstruction in progress, they would have grown discouraged. The reconstruction was pitiful or "as nothing" in comparison. Such discouragement is not easily hidden and, by this point, had infected the whole community.

4 Yet now be strong, O Zerubbabel, saith the LORD; and be strong, O Joshua, son of Josedech, the high priest; and be strong, all ye people of the land, saith the LORD, and work: for I am with you, saith the LORD of hosts: 5 According to the word that I covenanted with you when ye came out of Egypt, so my spirit remaineth among you: fear ye not.

Part of the function of leadership is to guide a group into accomplishing what it might not think possible. So Haggai addressed his remarks to the political (Zerubbabel) and spiritual (Joshua) leadership of the people as well as to the people themselves. He encouraged them to "yet now be strong" (Heb. *chazaq*, **khaw-ZAK**, meaning take heart or hold firmly) in the resolve to which they had committed themselves and continue the "work" (Heb. *asah*, **aw-SAW**, meaning doing or practice) of rebuilding the temple. Through Haggai, the Lord was communicating to the people that the work they were doing was not to be despised. "I am with you" (Heb. *neum*, **neh-OOM**, meaning utterance or declaration preceding the diving name) said "the LORD of hosts" (Heb. *Yehovah*, **yeh-ho-VAW**, meaning the existing One and the proper name of the one true God). Haggai wanted the people to understand that though they were the instruments through which God was working to rebuild His house, He was, in fact, in their midst. The very same God that "covenanted" (Heb. *karath*, **kaw-RATH**, meaning to establish or promise) with the people to lead them from captivity out of Egypt across the Red Sea was at work with them in rebuilding the temple. That knowledge was intended to give a sense of relief and joy to the people; they were not laboring in vain, no matter how the physical appearance of the structure might look. God's Spirit remained with them; therefore, the people only needed to be faithful to complete the work He had called them to do. Because God was with them, they did not need to "fear" disappointing Him and should not be discouraged themselves.

6 For thus saith the LORD of hosts; Yet once, it is a little while, and I will shake the heavens, and the earth, and the sea, and the dry land; 7 And I will shake all nations, and the desire of all nations shall come: and I will fill this house with glory, saith the LORD of hosts.

Haggai then encouraged the people even more by reminding them of just exactly who the God was who had commanded the rebuilding of His house. He is the self-existent One who established the heavens, earth, sea, and dry land. Though it has not yet happened, "yet once, it is a little while" (better understood as one moment yet, a little while), the day will come when He will "shake" (Heb. *raash*, **raw-ASH**, meaning to be made to quake) the nations whose desire will then become to come to His house. Though there have been many "shakings" of different countries across the centuries, there has not been a final "shaking" that has involved both earth and sky (see Hebrews 12:26). Looking through prophetic eyes, Haggai here spoke of a future time when the Messiah will occupy the temple they are restoring. It will be then that the temple will be filled with God's glory.

8 The silver is mine, and the gold is mine, saith the LORD of hosts. 9 The glory of this latter house shall be greater than of the former, saith the LORD of hosts: and in this place will I give peace, saith the LORD of hosts.

Haggai then reminded the people that both silver and gold belong to God and He had the ability to lavish upon the temple so much of it that the "latter house" (not the one of their efforts, but the one that Christ will build when He returns to the earth to set up His kingdom and rule) will be greater than the original temple Solomon built. While the inhabitants of Haggai's Palestine would not live to see how God would fulfill His promise, they could take heart that the labor of their hands, no matter how pitiful it seemed in their eyes, would serve God's greater purpose. God was using the rebuilding of Solomon's temple to prepare the hearts of His people for the indwelling of His Spirit. The Apostle John pointed to this time when he told us that in the New Jerusalem, there will be no temple because the temple is the Lord God the Almighty (see Revelation 21:22). It will be then that God will give peace. This will not be a peace that the world understands (see Philippians 4:7), but God's peace, which promises ultimate contentment and satisfaction. This is the wonderful hope for which we all wait.

Sources:

Burton, James. *Coffman Commentaries on the Old Testament and New Testament.* Abilene, TX: Abilene Christian University Press, 2000.

Dunn, James D. G. and John W. Rogerson. *Commentary on the Bible.* Grand Rapids, MI: Wm. B. Eerdmans Publishing Company, 2003.

HarperCollins Study Bible (NRSV). New York: Harper Collins Publishers, 2006. 752, 1266–67.

Hebrew Greek Key Word Study Bible (KJV) 2nd ed. Chattanooga, TN: AMG Publishers, 1991. 1153, 1621, 1633.

Howley, Bruce and Ellison Howley. *The New Layman's Bible Commentary.* Grand Rapids, MI: Zondervan, 1979.

Unger, Merrill, and Robert F. Ramey. *Unger's Bible Dictionary.* Chicago: Moody Press, 1981. 580, 1076–78, 1187.

Unger, Merrill. *Unger's Bible Handbook.* Chicago: Moody Press, 1967. 433.

Say It Correctly

Sheshbazzar. shesh-**BAZ**-sr.

Daily Bible Readings

MONDAY
My Spirit Seeks You
(Isaiah 26:1–13)

TUESDAY
The Blessings of Obedience
(Leviticus 26:3–13)

WEDNESDAY
The Consequences of Disobedience
(Leviticus 26:14–26)

THURSDAY
The Fear of the Lord
(Deuteronomy 6:17–25)

FRIDAY
I Am with You
(Isaiah 41:1–10)

SATURDAY
Take Courage!
(Psalm 27:7–14)

SUNDAY
Obeying the Voice of God
(Haggai 1:12–2:9)

Notes

_____

_____

_____

_____

Teaching Tips

Words You Should Know

A. Holy (Haggai 2:12) *kodesh* (Heb.)—A sacred place or thing; rarely abstract sanctity.

B. Unclean (v. 13) *tame* (Heb.)—Foul in a religious sense.

Teacher Preparation

Unifying Principle—Live Honorably. Almost everyone wants to belong to something that will make a difference in the world. What or who could help Christians feel that sense of belonging? God rewards and blesses the community of believers that lives in righteousness and fear of God.

A. Pray for your students.

B. Read and meditate on all the Scriptures from the Background and the Devotional Reading sections.

C. Reread the Focal Verses in three or more translations (NLT, ESV, NIV, etc.).

O—Open the Lesson

A. Open with prayer, including the Aim for Change.

B. After prayer, have a volunteer to read the In Focus story.

C. Have a volunteer read the Aim for Change and Keep in Mind verse.

D. Discuss and allow time to hear student testimonies.

P—Present the Scriptures

A. Have volunteers read the Focal Verses.

B. Now use The People, Places, and Times; Background; and Search the Scriptures to bring clarity to the verses.

E—Explore the Meaning

A. Have volunteers summarize the Discuss the Meaning, Lesson in Our Society, and Make It Happen sections.

B. Connect these sections to the Aim for Change and the Keep in Mind verse with the Lesson in Our Society and Make It Happen sections.

N—Next Steps for Application

A. Summarize the lesson.

B. Allow for students to share how the lesson impacted them.

C. Close with prayer and praise God for keeping His promises.

Worship Guide

For the Superintendent or Teacher
Theme: Live Pure Lives
Song: "Trust and Obey"
Devotional Reading: 1 Peter 1:13–21

Live Pure Lives

Bible Background • HAGGAI 1:15–2:1
Printed Text • HAGGAI 2:10–19 | Devotional Reading • 1 PETER 1:13–21

—————————— Aim for Change ——————————

By the end of this lesson, we will: GRASP Haggai's message of encouragement to press forward in rebuilding the Temple; REALIZE that reneging on promises to God yields catastrophic results; and DEVELOP ways to commit to doing God's work on behalf of the community.

————————— 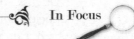 **In Focus** —————————

The church was finally complete and the first service was scheduled for the next day. As Deanna and Anita jumped rope in front of the new church, they laughed about what they had done. While helping clean the new building and prepare for the exuberant service, the girls made a mess in the kitchen and did not clean it up. They thought no one would notice, so they left the disaster they created.

The girls were excited because they had been chosen to escort the pastor down the aisle for the service. However, their parents found out what they had done in the kitchen and refused to allow them to participate. At the service, the committee thanked the people who helped make the event successful, but omitted Deanna and Anita's names. The girls were very disappointed, and hoped helping clean the building would excuse what they had done.

In today's lesson, we learn that God will bless His people for their obedience, while there are times He will not erase the consequences that previous sins cause. Sin always brings death. Sometimes that punishment must run its course before blessing can begin.

—————————— Keep in Mind ——————————

"Is the seed yet in the barn? yea, as yet the vine, and the fig tree, and the pomegranate, and the olive tree, hath not brought forth: from this day will I bless you"
(Haggai 2:19).

"Is the seed yet in the barn? yea, as yet the vine, and the fig tree, and the pomegranate, and the olive tree, hath not brought forth: from this day will I bless you"
(Haggai 2:19).

Focal Verses

KJV **Haggai 2:10** In the four and twentieth day of the ninth month, in the second year of Darius, came the word of the LORD by Haggai the prophet, saying,

11 Thus saith the LORD of hosts; Ask now the priests concerning the law, saying,

12 If one bear holy flesh in the skirt of his garment, and with his skirt do touch bread, or pottage, or wine, or oil, or any meat, shall it be holy? And the priests answered and said, No.

13 Then said Haggai, If one that is unclean by a dead body touch any of these, shall it be unclean? And the priests answered and said, It shall be unclean.

14 Then answered Haggai, and said, So is this people, and so is this nation before me, saith the LORD; and so is every work of their hands; and that which they offer there is unclean.

15 And now, I pray you, consider from this day and upward, from before a stone was laid upon a stone in the temple of the LORD:

16 Since those days were, when one came to an heap of twenty measures, there were but ten: when one came to the pressfat for to draw out fifty vessels out of the press, there were but twenty.

17 I smote you with blasting and with mildew and with hail in all the labours of your hands; yet ye turned not to me, saith the LORD.

18 Consider now from this day and upward, from the four and twentieth day of the ninth month, even from the day that the foundation of the LORD's temple was laid, consider it.

19 Is the seed yet in the barn? yea, as yet the vine, and the fig tree, and the pomegranate, and the olive tree, hath not brought forth: from this day will I bless you.

NLT **Haggai 2:10** On December 18 of the second year of King Darius's reign, the LORD sent this message to the prophet Haggai:

11 "This is what the LORD of Heaven's Armies says. Ask the priests this question about the law:

12 'If one of you is carrying some meat from a holy sacrifice in his robes and his robe happens to brush against some bread or stew, wine or olive oil, or any other kind of food, will it also become holy?'" The priests replied, "No."

13 Then Haggai asked, "If someone becomes ceremonially unclean by touching a dead person and then touches any of these foods, will the food be defiled?" And the priests answered, "Yes."

14 Then Haggai responded, "That is how it is with this people and this nation, says the LORD. Everything they do and everything they offer is defiled by their sin.

15 Look at what was happening to you before you began to lay the foundation of the LORD's Temple.

16 When you hoped for a twenty-bushel crop, you harvested only ten. When you expected to draw fifty gallons from the winepress, you found only twenty.

17 I sent blight and mildew and hail to destroy everything you worked so hard to produce. Even so, you refused to return to me, says the LORD.

18 Think about this eighteenth day of December, the day when the rebuilding of the LORD's Temple began. Think carefully.

19 I am giving you a promise now while the seed is still in the barn. You have not yet harvested your grain, and your grapevines, fig trees, pomegranates, and olive trees have not yet produced their crops. But from this day onward I will bless you."

The People, Places, and Times

Cyrus. The most celebrated of the Achaemenid (a name for the first Persian empire) leaders was Cyrus the Great, who ruled Persia from 559–530 B.C. Coming to the throne at about the age of forty, Cyrus ruled Persia for about three decades. He is remembered as an effective leader and innovative administrator of the vast Persian empire, a leader who for the most part succeeded in gaining the trust and goodwill of his subjects. Persia's dominance in the ancient Near East was secured when Cyrus's forces captured the Babylonian empire. Cyrus sought to encourage and befriend his subjects by granting them considerable religious freedom.

Darius. Darius I Hystapes came to power in Persia in 522 B.C. after first disposing of a perceived imposter, Gaumata. He was 28 years old at the time. Darius settled into what would be a long and effective reign (522–486 B.C.). In addition to his military exploits, Darius is remembered for his contributions to the organization for the empire, the development of roads and postal service within the empire, the organizational structure of the Persian military, the revision of legal and tax systems, the expansion of building infrastructure, and innovation with regard to coinage.

Background

Haggai's previous sermon had been given in the second year of King Darius, or 520 B.C. In the Jewish calendar, the twenty-first day of the seventh month was the seventh day of the Feast of Tabernacles, when work was suspended to celebrate the time of the harvest (Haggai 2:1). The timing of that message was opportune because his audience had reason to be in Jerusalem and were available to gather.

In addition to commemorating the experiences of the Israelites wandering the wilderness, the Feast of Tabernacles was also a time for celebrating God's provision through the harvest. But on this occasion, a dark cloud hung over what should have been joyous remembrance. A drought had reduced agricultural production to a fraction of what it should have been. Because of these recent crop failures, the people were probably less inclined to celebrate than they might have been in good times.

Since the presentation of Haggai's first sermon, less than two months had passed. In that small amount of time, however, the people's outlook had changed significantly. Discouragement over the enormity of their task now threatened the success of the mission. Haggai's challenge was to address these issues and instill a vision of what the future held for the temple structure and for the nation.

At-A-Glance

1. Object Lesson (Haggai 2:10–13)
2. Indictment (vv. 14–17)
3. Pressing Forward (vv. 18–19)

In Depth

1. Object Lesson (Haggai 2:10–13)

The messenger is identified as the prophet Haggai. Here he instructed the people to ask the priests about purity and defilement according to religious standards. This sermon is didactic, designed to teach about religious impurity.

The first question asked concerned holiness. The people learned that meat carried in the garment would make the garment holy, but the holiness would not be communicated beyond the garment to anything else. The people thought that since they were working on the holy temple, all that they contacted and did became holy. A second question was asked concerning holiness touching dead bodies. The people were informed that touching a dead body would make them unclean. The Mosaic Law taught that moral uncleanness could be transmitted, but moral cleanness could not.

2. Indictment (vv. 14–17)

Haggai told the people their sacrifices and offerings were unacceptable to God because they were "unclean." They should not think that contact with something holy made them acceptable to God. They had previously been unclean, so their present sacrifices were unacceptable to Him.

The people needed to remember that before they began to obey the Lord by rebuilding the temple, they had been disobedient to the Mosaic Covenant. The Lord's punishment for their covenant unfaithfulness was a greatly reduced harvest. Their grains and grapes had decreased significantly. The Lord used hot winds and dry heat to reduce their grains and grapes. The excessive moisture created by mildew created other problems, and hail caused severe damage to unprotected crops.

3. Pressing Forward (vv. 18–19)

The people were to notice that from the day they started to rebuild the temple, their hardships had continued. They still suffered shortages of staples such as seed, grapes,

olives, as well as other luxuries such as figs and pomegranates. However, the Lord revealed that He would now "bless" them, beginning "from this day," the twenty-fourth of the ninth month.

This blessing would have temporal and tangible dimensions, since it referred primarily to renewed productivity of the land as a result of the Lord's lifting the agricultural and economic curses. The Israelites' future was brighter than their past. As surely as the curses for disobedience (as recorded in the book of Deuteronomy) had dogged the heels of their half-hearted commitment to covenant responsibilities, the Lord's blessings would reward their renewed faithfulness to those obligations. His blessings would accompany the obedience of His people.

Search the Scriptures

1. Who told Haggai to ask the priests about the law (Haggai 2:11)?

2. Where did the blasting heat, mildew, and hail come from (v. 17)?

Discuss the Meaning

How might past disobedience in our lives play itself out in our current situations? Failed businesses, unmet financial goals, and other hardships may be a result of our disobedience. The Israelites understood this. Their current obedience did not wipe out their past sin and its punishments. That punishment had to run its course, but eventually God began to bless the people with better harvests. How might this inform our understanding of hardships?

Lesson in Our Society

Have you ever noticed that some people seem to participate in every program or service at church? Can you think of people who might do things for the purpose of hearing or seeing their names mentioned? Could these people think that their constant service exemplifies holy living? We have learned this is not the case; outward deeds do not represent the condition of the soul.

Make It Happen

As we render our service to the Lord this week, let us remember that we serve God because we have been changed and not because we are working to earn status. Works, good deeds, or outstanding accomplishments will not save our souls, but our salvation causes us to work for the glory of our Lord.

Follow the Spirit

What God wants me to do:

_____

_____

_____

_____

Remember Your Thoughts

Special insights I have learned:

_____

_____

_____

_____

More Light on the Text

Haggai 2:10–19

10 In the four and twentieth day of the ninth month, in the second year of Darius, came the word of the LORD by Haggai the prophet, saying:

The prophet Haggai had been conveying messages from the Lord to Zerubbabel, the appointed governor of Judah, and to Joshua, the high priest, to deliver to the people concerning rebuilding the temple that the Babylonians destroyed in 587 B.C. King Cyrus allowed the Hebrews taken into Babylonian captivity to return to Judah in 539 B.C., although they were still under Persian rule. A new Persian ruler, Darius, was on the throne in 520 B.C. The specific date of Haggai's message is December 18, 520 B.C. Nearly twenty years had passed, and the returnees had finally rebuilt the Lord's temple. This is the third message to Haggai in three months concerning the temple.

11 Thus saith the LORD of hosts; Ask now the priests concerning the law, saying,

"LORD of hosts" (Heb. *Yahveh*, **yaw-VEH**; *tsaba*, **tsaw-BAW**; pl. *tsebaoth*, **tsay-baw-OTH**) or "Lord of armies" is a frequently used title for the Lord in prophetic literature. Haggai's use of the phrase suggests an enlisting of the troops for service (1 Samuel 8:11–12). The Lord had been trying to enlist the returning Hebrews to rebuild the temple so that they could resume the sacred rituals and sacrifices. Eventually, they put aside their self-interests and attended to the reconstruction project.

Haggai commanded the people to ask the priests about the law. The Jews consider the first five books of our Old Testament as the Torah, which is usually translated as "law," but also means "instruction" or "direction." In this instance, it should be understood as the latter. Haggai was seeking a ruling from the priests on the people's behalf. The inquiry took the form of a question-and-answer between Haggai and the priests.

12 If one bear holy flesh in the skirt of his garment, and with his skirt do touch bread, or pottage, or wine, or oil, or any meat, shall it be holy? And the priests answered and said, "No."

Haggai's first question concerned the holy and unholy. The Hebrew word for "holy" is *qadosh* (**kaw-DOSHE**) and means to "sanctify," "consecrate," or "set apart." In the Old Testament, God is inherently holy, but people and things are not. People and things can be made holy by being set apart by God, such as the Sabbath (Genesis 2:3; Exodus 20:11) and the Israelites (Exodus 29:44), or through rituals performed by the priests. The priests responded that profane food and drink could not be made holy, even if they came in contact with a garment set apart for holy purposes.

13 Then said Haggai, "If one that is unclean by a dead body touch any of these, shall it be unclean?" And the priests answered and said, "It shall be unclean."

The next question concerned matters of purity and impurity or clean and unclean, which are closely related to issues of holiness. Certain people and things were prohibited from mixing, for fear of contamination or uncleanness (for example, the prohibition against mixing dissimilar things such as animals, plant seeds, or fabrics; see Leviticus 19:19). Priests were responsible for seeing that purity requirements were maintained in ancient Israel. The priestly instructions on purification in Numbers 19:11–13 declared that a person who came in contact with a corpse was defiled or unclean for seven days and needed to purify himself with water to return to a state of purity. Therefore, the priests instructed Haggai that the individual in a state of uncleanness could indeed make the food and drink unclean by touching it.

14 Then answered Haggai, and said, So is this people, and so is this nation before me, saith the LORD; and so is every work of their hands; and that which they offer there is unclean.

Haggai obviously already knew the answers, but wanted the people to hear the priests' ruling on the inquiries. However, the answer had to come as a shock to the people—that they were being compared to an unclean corpse. Their state of ritual impurity, as a result of a lapse in ritual performances in the temple's absence, made the harvest they reaped impure. Therefore, they could not present it as offerings in the temple. They would have been as concerned with *why* the prophet compared them to something as unclean as a dead person as the fact that he did.

15 And now, I pray you, consider from this day and upward, from before a stone was laid upon a stone in the temple of the LORD.

"From this day" refers back to the December date in verse 10. The phrase "to consider" literally means in Hebrew to "set your heart" (Heb. *leb*, **LABE**). Another possible translation is "search your soul." This was a very serious message that Haggai was bringing for them to reflect upon. He was telling them to think back to before they set about rebuilding the temple as he made plain what would be their situation from that day forward.

16 Since those days were, when one came to an heap of twenty measures, there were but ten: When one came to the pressfat for to draw out fifty vessels out of the press, there were but twenty.

Haggai described the dire situation before they rebuilt the temple. The Lord caused a drought in the land because of their lack of interest in continuing the reconstruction (1:10–11). He recounted that when they went out to reap the harvest they had sowed earlier, they found only half the return in produce; when they went to press the grapes for wine, there was less than half what they expected. This created an economic hardship since the people produced food not only for their families' use, but also to sell for profit.

17 I smote you with blasting and with mildew and with hail in all the labours of your hands; yet ye turned not to me, saith the LORD.

With the extreme weather conditions taking place across the United States, there is much discussion about climate change, but the Lord takes the concept to another level by using polar opposites to take place in Judah as a result of the people's unresponsiveness. The Lord smote their crops with blight (Heb. *shadaph*, **shaw-DAF**, a scorching heat that caused the crops to wither) and mildew (Heb. *yeraqon*, yay-**raw-KONE**, a grain disease that discolors the plant). Then, as if that were not enough, the Lord caused hail (Heb. *barad*, **baw-RAD**) to fall, causing total crop failure. Yet the Hebrews were not moved to turn to the Lord in repentance.

18 Consider now from this day and upward, from the four and twentieth day of the ninth month, even from the day that the foundation of the LORD's temple was laid, consider it.

Twice more, at the beginning and end of the verse, Haggai pled with the people to remember the day that they finally laid the foundation for the Lord's temple. The solemnity of the occasion called the people to reflect on how their lives might change with the resumption of the temple sacrifices and rituals. For contemporary Jews and Christians, ritual purity is not a daily concern for us. However, for the ancient Israelites, covenant faithfulness included observing certain holiness codes and ritual purity. A return to these observances implied an agreement to keep the covenant.

19 Is the seed yet in the barn? Yea, as yet the vine, and the fig tree, and the pomegranate, and the olive tree, hath not brought forth: From this day will I bless you.

Haggai's question concerning whether there was seed in the barn hearkened back to verse 16 and the dire circumstances of the people due to the crop failure, yet it is ambiguous. On the one hand, the lack of seed suggests that there was nothing with which to plant and produce new crops. This would exacerbate an already disastrous situation. Not only had the Hebrews' crops been destroyed and no seed remained, but the trees also would no longer bear any fruit. On the other hand, it implies that there would soon be seed in the barn and the trees would soon bear fruit again. The next line appears to support the latter interpretation. The Lord promised to bless the people. Their misfortunes were about to be reversed.

Sources:

Brown, Francis, Samuel R. Driver, and Charles Briggs, et. al. *A Hebrew and English Lexicon of the Old Testament.* Peabody, MA: Hendrickson Publishers, 1906.

Constable, Thomas. "Dr. Constable's Expository (Bible Study) Notes." Sonic Light. (http://www.soniclight.com, accessed January, 20, 2013).

Rose, Martin. "Names of God in the OT" Vol. 4. *In Anchor Bible Dictionary.* New York: Doubleday, 1992, 1001–1011.

Taylor, R. A., and Clendenen, E. R. *Haggai, Malachi. The New American* Commentary, Vol. 21A. Nashville: Holman Reference, 2004. 190.

Say It Correctly

Achaemenid. ah-**KEY**-mon-id.
Gaumata. **GAW**-muh-tuh.

Daily Bible Readings

MONDAY
A Highway Called the Holy Way
(Isaiah 35)

TUESDAY
Established as God's Holy People
(Deuteronomy 28:1–9)

WEDNESDAY
You Shall Be Holy
(1 Peter 1:13–21)

THURSDAY
You Have Been Born Anew
(1 Peter 1:22–2:3)

FRIDAY
You are God's People
(1 Peter 2:4–10)

SATURDAY
You are the Temple of God
(2 Corinthians 6:14–7:1)

SUNDAY
The Hope for God's Blessing
(Haggai 2:10–19)

Notes

_____

_____

_____

_____

Teaching Tips

June 22
Bible Study Guide 4

Words You Should Know

A. Might (Zechariah 4:6) *chayil* (Heb.)—Strength, ability, efficiency, valor, wealth, or might (especially warlike).

B. Despised (v. 10) *buwz* (Heb.)—To hold in contempt, hold as insignificant; to trample with the feet.

Teacher Preparation

Unifying Principle—Expect Success. Communities need capable leadership to stay motivated through a project's completion. Where can Christian communities find this kind of leadership? God speaks through the prophets to affirm that the temple will be completed under Zerubbabel—not by human might or power, but by the Spirit of the Lord.

A. Pray that God will give you insight into His Word as you study.

B. Read the entire lesson, then complete the companion lesson in the *Precepts For Living Personal Study Guide®*.

C. Pray for your students, that they will be receptive to learning God's Word.

O—Open the Lesson

A. Open with prayer.

B. Introduce today's lesson title, including the Aim for Change.

C. Have your students read the In Focus Story and Keep in Mind verse together. Discuss.

D. Ask a volunteer to share a time when God blessed him or her for their obedience.

P—Present the Scriptures

A. Have volunteers read the Focal Verses.

B. Use The People, Places and Times; Background; Search the Scriptures; At-A-Glance outline; In Depth; and More Light on the Text to clarify the verses.

E—Explore the Meaning

A. Divide the class into groups to discuss the Discuss the Meaning, Lesson in Our Society, and Make It Happen sections. Tell the students to select a representative to report their responses.

B. Connect these sections to the Aim for Change and the Keep in Mind verse.

N—Next Steps for Application

A. Summarize the lesson.

B. Close with prayer.

Worship Guide

For the Superintendent or Teacher
Theme: Hope for a New Day
Song: "New Season"
Devotional Reading: Psalm 43
Prayer

Hope for a New Day

Bible Background • HAGGAI 2:23, ZECHARIAH 4:1–3, 6–14
Printed Text • HAGGAI 2:23; ZECHARIAH 4:1–3, 6–14
Devotional Reading • PSALM 43

Aim for Change

By the end of the lesson, we will: ACKNOWLEDGE the connection between God's promises to Israel for rebuilding the Temple and the Israelites' obedience to Him; APPRECIATE the community's restoration of the Temple and God's restoration of the people; and ARTICULATE our thankfulness to God for the blessings bestowed upon us for our obedience.

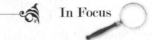 In Focus

Myla had just moved to a new town. She had a great job, but hadn't made any friends yet. Every day as she drove to work, she passed the county jail. After a few weeks, she knew God wanted her to go to the jail to visit the inmates. This was way out of her comfort zone, but she wanted to obey God. Finally, she got up the courage to fill out the application to volunteer.

Shortly after, she nervously arrived at the jail, Bible in hand, for her first visit with the female inmates. As she prayed to God for courage, she noticed another group of women enter with their Bibles. She introduced herself and found that the other women had been coming to the jail for months to conduct Bible study sessions. The women welcomed Myla. As they ministered together over the next couple of weeks, Myla not only made new friends, but discovered an unexpected joy in serving others.

Obedience to God brings blessing. In today's lesson, we will learn how God enables us and works on our behalf to help us accomplish what He wants us to do.

Keep in Mind

"Then he answered and spake unto me, saying, This is the word of the LORD unto Zerubbabel, saying, Not by might, nor by power, but by my spirit, saith the LORD of hosts" (Zechariah 4:6).

"Then he answered and spake unto me, saying, This is the word of the LORD unto Zerubbabel, saying, Not by might, nor by power, but by my spirit, saith the LORD of hosts" (Zechariah 4:6).

Focal Verses

KJV **Haggai 2:23** In that day, saith the LORD of hosts, will I take thee, O Zerubbabel, my servant, the son of Shealtiel, saith the LORD, and will make thee as a signet: for I have chosen thee, saith the LORD of hosts.

Zechariah 4:1 And the angel that talked with me came again, and waked me, as a man that is wakened out of his sleep.

2 And said unto me, What seest thou? And I said, I have looked, and behold a candlestick all of gold, with a bowl upon the top of it, and his seven lamps thereon, and seven pipes to the seven lamps, which are upon the top thereof:

3 And two olive trees by it, one upon the right side of the bowl, and the other upon the left side thereof.

4:6 Then he answered and spake unto me, saying, This is the word of the LORD unto Zerubbabel, saying, Not by might, nor by power, but by my spirit, saith the LORD of hosts.

7 Who art thou, O great mountain? before Zerubbabel thou shalt become a plain: and he shall bring forth the headstone thereof with shoutings, crying, Grace, grace unto it.

8 Moreover the word of the LORD came unto me, saying,

9 The hands of Zerubbabel have laid the foundation of this house; his hands shall also finish it; and thou shalt know that the LORD of hosts hath sent me unto you.

10 For who hath despised the day of small things? for they shall rejoice, and shall see the plummet in the hand of Zerubbabel with those seven; they are the eyes of the LORD, which run to and fro through the whole earth.

11 Then answered I, and said unto him, What are these two olive trees upon the right

NLT **Haggai 2:23** "But when this happens, says the LORD of Heaven's Armies, I will honor you, Zerubbabel son of Shealtiel, my servant. I will make you like a signet ring on my finger, says the LORD, for I have chosen you. I, the LORD of Heaven's Armies, have spoken!"

Zechariah 4:1 Then the angel who had been talking with me returned and woke me, as though I had been asleep.

2 "What do you see now?" he asked. I answered, "I see a solid gold lampstand with a bowl of oil on top of it. Around the bowl are seven lamps, each having seven spouts with wicks.

3 And I see two olive trees, one on each side of the bowl."

4:6 Then he said to me, "This is what the LORD says to Zerubbabel: It is not by force nor by strength, but by my Spirit, says the LORD of Heaven's Armies.

7 Nothing, not even a mighty mountain, will stand in Zerubbabel's way; it will become a level plain before him! And when Zerubbabel sets the final stone of the Temple in place, the people will shout: 'May God bless it! May God bless it!'"

8 Then another message came to me from the LORD:

9 "Zerubbabel is the one who laid the foundation of this Temple, and he will complete it. Then you will know that the LORD of Heaven's Armies has sent me.

10 Do not despise these small beginnings, for the LORD rejoices to see the work begin, to see the plumb line in Zerubbabel's hand." (The seven lamps represent the eyes of the LORD that search all around the world.)

11 Then I asked the angel, "What are these two olive trees on each side of the lampstand, side of the candlestick and upon the left side thereof?

12 And I answered again, and said unto him, What be these two olive branches which through the two golden pipes empty the golden oil out of themselves?

13 And he answered me and said, Knowest thou not what these be? And I said, No, my lord.

14 Then said he, These are the two anointed ones, that stand by the LORD of the whole earth.

12 and what are the two olive branches that pour out golden oil through two gold tubes?"

13 "Don't you know?" he asked. "No, my lord," I replied.

14 Then he said to me, "They represent the two heavenly beings who stand in the court of the LORD of all the earth."

The People, Places, and Times

Zechariah. A prophet (Zechariah 1:1) and a priest (Nehemiah 12:10–16) who was a contemporary of the prophet Haggai. Zechariah was born in Babylonia during the exilic period and was one of the estimated fifty thousand exiles who returned to Judah under the leadership of Zerubbabel and Joshua in 538 B.C. During the long span of his ministry to God's people, Zechariah's main purpose was to encourage the people in their work to rebuild the temple and continually remind them of God's promise that He would take care of them and bless them if they would return to Him.

Background

Apparently, some of the Israelites chose not to leave Babylon at the end of the seventy-year exile. But "everyone whose heart God had moved—prepared to go up and build the house of the LORD in Jerusalem" (from Ezra 1:5, NIV). They returned with joy and purpose, bringing with them gifts of livestock, gold, and silver bestowed upon them by the people of Babylon.

After settling themselves in their towns, the people came together to begin the joyful but daunting project of rebuilding the temple that had been destroyed seventy years

earlier. Their first step was to rebuild the altar so they could reestablish the offering of sacrifices as required of God's people (3:1–6). The people then began to give offerings to pay for the materials and labor needed to build the temple's foundation.

Approximately two years after arriving back in Judah, God's people finally finished building the foundation of the temple. The people sang and praised God, accompanied by the priests and Levites. They shouted and wept with joy, and the celebration was so loud it could be heard from far away (vv. 10–13).

Unfortunately, Zerubbabel and his builders soon faced opposition from their enemies, mostly inhabitants of nearby Samaria. These enemies purposely set out to discourage God's people from rebuilding the temple, even going so far as to hire people to work against them (4:4–5). Sadly, the rebuilding of the temple was halted for seventeen years.

At-A-Glance

1. God's Promise (Haggai 2:23)
2. God's Servants
(Zechariah 4:1–3, 6–7)
3. God's Sovereignty (vv. 8–14)

In Depth

1. God's Promise (Haggai 2:23)

All work on rebuilding the temple had been halted for seventeen years, and God's people had lost hope of ever finishing what they had started. But then the Word of the Lord came to the prophet Haggai. God instructed him to tell Zerubbabel that He would literally move heaven and earth (Haggai 2:21–22) to accomplish His plan. God's plan was not only that the temple would be rebuilt, but that Zerubbabel would be honored. God says that He would make Zerubbabel like a signet ring on His finger. In biblical times, a signet ring was used as one's signature and symbolized a pledge, a guarantee of payment or fulfilling one's promise. God was promising to not only honor Zerubbabel, but He was also telling His people that He would fulfill His promises to them. It was time for His people to once again return to Him and the work He had called them to.

2. God's Servants (Zechariah 4:1–3, 6–7)

Along with the promise given to Zerubbabel through the prophet Haggai, God also gave Zechariah a vision concerning the completion of the temple. In 4:1–3, Zechariah saw an angel who showed him a golden lampstand with two olive trees, one on either side. The trees represented the offices of priest and king. Joshua, the high priest, and Zerubbabel, as the leader of God's people and a descendant of the royal house of David, were to lead God's people forward to completion of the temple. However, neither the people nor their leaders were going to be able to accomplish anything on their own. In verse 6, the Lord says, "It is not by force nor by strength, but by my Spirit, says the LORD of Heaven's Armies" (NLT).

Only by the power of the Spirit would Zerubbabel be enabled to finish the rebuilding. The angel assured and encouraged him through Zechariah that even though there was a "mountain" of opposition and discouragement in his way, nothing would be able to stand before God's power working through His servant. Zerubbabel would see God's plan accomplished amidst much rejoicing.

3. God's Sovereignty (vv. 8–14)

God then reminded His people that Zerubbabel had already laid the foundation for the temple. He promised that He would use Zerubbabel to finally complete the rebuilding and, when this was done, everyone would know that it was God who had accomplished this great deed.

Some people apparently thought that rebuilding the temple wasn't worth it, or that what had already been accomplished was insignificant. However, God said that no one should discount what had already been done. Even though it seemed to be a small beginning, God was going to bring it to a glorious conclusion. And when God accomplished His plan, everyone would rejoice.

Finally, Zechariah asked for clarification about the olive trees and branches he saw in the vision. The angel clarified that Joshua the high priest and Zerubbabel the descendant of David were the ones chosen for God's purpose in His plan to rebuild the temple. The oil that was poured out of the olive branches and used to anoint the leaders signified the Holy Spirit. The symbolism of both the king and priest point to the Messianic fulfillment in Jesus, who also descended from the royal line of David and is now our King and Priest, the "LORD of all the earth" (v. 14, NLT). Zerubbabel and the exiles, as well as believers down through the ages, are governed by God's sovereign plan. He will do what needs to be done to accomplish His purposes and give us what we need to obey Him.

Search the Scriptures

1. Why is it significant that God calls Himself the "LORD of Heaven's Armies" when speaking to both Haggai and Zechariah (Haggai 2:23; Zechariah 4:6, 9, NLT)?

2. What do the seven golden lamps represent? Why would this be important for Zechariah to know (Zechariah 4:2, 10)?

Discuss the Meaning

After God delivered His people from exile, He had a specific task for them to complete—the rebuilding of the temple.

1. Why did the people stop building the temple?

2. How was the Israelites' obedience to build the temple tied to their restoration to God?

Lesson in Our Society

God promised the people of Israel that He would restore them to their land, but He also instructed them to rebuild His temple. He did not leave them to their own devices; He provided favor, materials, and the power of the Spirit to enable them to obey what He asked. We often resist obeying God because what He is asking seems too difficult or demanding, yet when we choose to obey, He will bless us.

Make It Happen

Obedience to God brings great reward. One way to learn to be obedient is to read His Word on a regular basis. God's Word contains everything we need to know about how to treat others, how to handle our money, and how to be a good employee, parent, or spouse. When we read God's Word to apply it to our lives, we please Him.

Follow the Spirit

What God wants me to do:

_____

_____

_____

_____

Remember Your Thoughts

Special insights I have learned:

_____

_____

_____

_____

More Light on the Text

Haggai 2:23; Zechariah 4:1–3, 6–14

2:23 In that day, saith the LORD of hosts, will I take thee, O Zerubbabel, my servant, the son of Shealtiel, saith the LORD, and will make thee as a signet: for I have chosen thee, saith the LORD of hosts.

"We must remember that Haggai was speaking eschatologically to a definite circumstance" (*Word Biblical Commentary,* 163). The temple was being restored, but at a very slow rate, and wouldn't be finished until 516 B.C. (see Ezra 6:14–15). However, in this eschatological promise was hope for what would be. This made clear what Zerubbabel represented for the nation. This verse confirmed that Zerubbabel was God's chosen servant, and this also speaks to God's people. Not only was Zerubbabel chosen, he represented God's signet. "The significance of comparing Zerubbabel to a 'signet ring' (a seal of royal authority or personal ownership) is clarified by the imagery in Jeremiah 22:24–25. God said that if Jehoiachin (Zerubbabel's grandfather) were His signet ring, he would pull him off His hand and give him over to Nebuchadenezzar. Possibly Haggai was saying that in Zerubbabel God was reversing the curse pronounced by Jehoiachin" (*The Bible Knowledge Commentary*, 1544). With that knowledge, it is interesting that the author would use the signet ring imagery here. Reversing the curse is God's modus operandi (His mode of operation). That's precisely what He's done for us through the redemptive work of Christ on the Cross.

Zechariah 4:1 And the angel that talked with me came again, and waked me, as a man that is wakened out of his sleep. 2 And said unto me, What seest thou? And I said, I have looked, and behold a candlestick all of gold, with a bowl upon the top of it, and his seven lamps thereon, and seven pipes to the seven lamps, which are upon the top thereof: 3 And two olive trees by it, one upon the right side of the bowl, and the other upon the left side thereof.

The form of this chapter is a vision that is sandwiched between two oracles addressed to Zerubbabel, thus connecting the book of Zechariah with the closing of Haggai. It was typical for God to speak to His prophets via dreams and visions; therefore, this form fits God's pattern. The dreamer is also expected to make sense of the signs and symbols in the dream; in this case, the questions asked in the dream. "What seest thou?" (v. 2) is not a literal question. It is a metaphorical question that moved to the interpretive eschatological for the dreamer, who had now been awakened.

The dream included a candlestick, a bowl, seven lamps, seven pipes, and seven lamps. There were also the two olive trees beside the bowl on either side. "What do you see and

what does this mean?" becomes the central question in the opening of this chapter.

6 Then he answered and spake unto me, saying, This is the word of the LORD unto Zerubbabel, saying, Not by might, nor by power, but by my spirit, saith the LORD of hosts. 7 Who art thou, O great mountain? before Zerubbabel thou shalt become a plain: and he shall bring forth the head-stone thereof with shoutings, crying, Grace, grace unto it.

While Zerubbabel was a literal person and this prophecy spoke to a contemporary situation, this is also about God and His plan. The temple was going to be rebuilt. Even though Zerubbabel was in the picture, the job was not only for him. In reality, the job wasn't complete until much later in history, but God was making clear that this will be done by His power and might. While the Lord never directly answered what each figure in the vision represented, He gave the prophet a broader understanding of what was going on. God was with Zerubbabel literally, figuratively, symbolically, and eschatologically. God's Spirit would ultimately be the driving force behind the task at hand. Human effort is never enough, and though there were mountains Zerubbabel faced, God, by His spirit, was going to symbolically turn them into plains. We can expect the same thing with the mountains in our lives.

8 Moreover the word of the LORD came unto me, saying, 9 The hands of Zerubbabel have laid the foundation of this house; his hands shall also finish it; and thou shalt know that the LORD of hosts hath sent me unto you.

The Lord explained to Zechariah (vv. 8–10) that Zerubbabel's finishing the restoration of the temple would drive the critics to silence, for they would know God had sent the prophet and the reconstructionists. The mere beginning of this project and prophecy would serve as a sign of God being with Zerubbabel. As the passage continues, we see that it was the work of Zerubbabel to the lay the foundation. God's Word, as spoken in prophecy, is a type of foundation that has been laid. Embarking on the restoration project was as important as finishing it.

10 For who hath despised the day of small things? for they shall rejoice, and shall see the plummet in the hand of Zerubbabel with those seven; they are the eyes of the LORD, which run to and fro through the whole earth. 11 Then answered I, and said unto him, What are these two olive trees upon the right side of the candlestick and upon the left side thereof? 12 And I answered again, and said unto him, What be these two olive branches which through the two golden pipes empty the golden oil out of themselves?

The Lord now began to answer Zechariah's questions about what the symbols in the vision represented. While the text provides answers to Zechariah's questions, scholars debate about the meaning of these symbols. For example, it is said that the phrase "eyes of the LORD" symbolizes God's worldwide scrutiny and the fact that nothing is hidden from Him. In any event, the practical application here is that Zerubbabel will be given the power to finish the temple.

13 And he answered me and said, Knowest thou not what these be? And I said, No, my lord. 14 Then said he, These are the two anointed ones, that stand by the LORD of the whole earth.

Here we find more symbolism. The olives and accompanying olive oil represented God's anointing or blessing of the project and His chosen vessel to do the work. "The two oil-supplying branches represent the two who are anointed to serve the Lord of all the earth" (*The Bible Knowledge Commentary*, 1556)—in this passage, Joshua and Zerubbabel. "The candlestick [from the previous section], then, seems to represent Israel as a light to the nations (see Isaiah 42:6; 49:6), potentially in Zechariah's time . . ." (1556).

Sources:
"*Chayil.*" Blue Letter Bible. BlueLetterBible.org. http://www.blueletterbible.org/ (accessed January 4, 2013).
"Despised." Blue Letter Bible. BlueLetterBible.org. http://www.blueletterbible.org/ (accessed January 4, 2013).
Matthew Henry Bible Commentary. http://www.biblestudytools.com/commentaries/matthew-henry-complete/zechariah/4.htm (accessed January 4, 2013).
NIV Study Bible (NIV). Grand Rapids, MI: Zondervan Publishing House, 1995. 665, 1393, 1397–99, 1403–04.
Smith, Ralph L. *Micah—Malachi. Word Biblical Commentary. Volume 32.* Waco, TX: Word Books, 1984. 163.
Walvoord, John F. and Roy B. Zuck, eds. *The Bible Knowledge Commentary: Old Testament.* Wheaton, IL: Chariot Victor Publishing, 1985. 1544, 1555–56.
"Zerubbabel." AboutBibleProphecy.com http://www.aboutbibleprophecy.com/p185.htm (accessed January 4, 2013).

Say It Correctly

Nebuchadnezzar.
NEH-buh-kuhd-**NEH**-zer.

Daily Bible Readings

MONDAY
What Hope for the Godless?
(Job 27:8–12)

TUESDAY
Hope in God
(Psalm 43)

WEDNESDAY
Hope in God's Steadfast Love
(Psalm 33:13–22)

THURSDAY
In Hope We Were Saved
(Romans 8:18–25)

FRIDAY
Accounting for the Hope in You
(1 Peter 3:13–17)

SATURDAY
The Confession of Our Hope
(Hebrews 10:19–24)

SUNDAY
I Have Chosen You
(Haggai 2:23; Zechariah 4:1–3, 6–14)

Notes

_____

_____

_____

_____

Teaching Tips

Words You Should Know

A. Perfectly joined together (1 Corinthians 1:10) *katartizo* (Gk.)—To fit, mend, arrange, adjust; to set in order; to put a thing in its appropriate condition; to perfect; to make deficient in no part.

B. Contentions (v. 11) *schisma* (Gk.)—To split or tear into factions.

Teacher Preparation

Unifying Principle—A Call To Unity. Disagreements in a community may cause division. How can community disagreements be resolved? Paul called the disputing people to find common ground by taking on the mind of Christ.

A. Read the Background and Devotional Readings.

B. Complete the companion lesson in the *Precepts For Living Personal Study Guide®*.

O—Open the Lesson

A. Open with prayer.

B. Have students read Aim for Change in unison.

C. Ask for a volunteer to read the In Focus story.

D. Discuss how to live by faith and experience God's presence.

P—Present the Scriptures

A. Ask for volunteers to read the Focal Verses and The People, Places, and Times. Discuss.

B. Read and discuss the Background section.

C. Encourage students to understand the importance of settling disputes amicably.

E—Explore the Meaning

A. Review and discuss the Search the Scriptures and Discuss the Meaning questions and the Lesson in Our Society section.

B. Ask students to share the most significant point they learned and how to use that point this week.

N—Next Steps for Application

A. Complete the Follow the Spirit and Remember Your Thoughts sections.

B. Remind students to read the Daily Bible Readings in preparation for next week's lesson.

C. Close in prayer, thanking God for His presence in our lives.

Worship Guide

For the Superintendent or Teacher
Theme: A Call To Unity
Song: "Sing Praises to Thee"
Devotional Reading:
1 Corinthians 12:12–20

A Call to Unity

Bible Background • 1 CORINTHIANS 1:10–17
Printed Text • 1 CORINTHIANS 1:10–17
Devotional Reading • 1 CORINTHIANS 12:12–20

—————————— Aim for Change ——————————

By the end of the lesson, we will: INVESTIGATE the divisions within the Corinthian community; IDENTIFY past hurts caused by divisions experienced within a faith community; and INTRODUCE methods of achieving unity within the body of Christ.

———————  In Focus ———————

Tina dreaded going to her next committee meeting. She worked on the planning committee for the church's anniversary celebration. This was their first anniversary since the founding pastor retired and their new pastor was installed.

At first it was fun, but slowly the committee meetings became more and more uncomfortable. The members were divided. Some of them wanted to maintain the anniversary traditions that the founding pastor started. Others believed that the installation of a new pastor created an opportunity for new traditions to be established.

Planning began to take a back seat to arguing, and the meetings became more and more stressful. Hard feelings and frustration started to create tension that could be felt during worship services and Bible study. Tina wondered how anyone could see God's glory in all of this chaos.

This lesson discusses the importance of unity in the body of Christ. Let's encourage one another not to allow disagreements to hinder our fellowship and distract us from the work that we are called to do for Christ.

—————————— Keep in Mind ——————————

"Now I beseech you, brethren, by the name of our Lord Jesus Christ, that ye all speak the same thing, and that there be no divisions among you; but that ye be perfectly joined together in the same mind and in the same judgment" (1 Corinthians 1:10).

"Now I beseech you, brethren, by the name of our Lord Jesus Christ, that ye all speak the same thing, and that there be no divisions among you; but that ye be perfectly joined together in the same mind and in the same judgment" (1 Corinthians 1:10),

Focal Verses

KJV 1 **Corinthians 1:10** Now I beseech you, brethren, by the name of our Lord Jesus Christ, that ye all speak the same thing, and that there be no divisions among you; but that ye be perfectly joined together in the same mind and in the same judgment.

11 For it hath been declared unto me of you, my brethren, by them which are of the house of Chloe, that there are contentions among you.

12 Now this I say, that every one of you saith, I am of Paul; and I of Apollos; and I of Cephas; and I of Christ.

13 Is Christ divided? was Paul crucified for you? or were ye baptized in the name of Paul?

14 I thank God that I baptized none of you, but Crispus and Gaius;

15 Lest any should say that I had baptized in mine own name.

16 And I baptized also the household of Stephanas: besides, I know not whether I baptized any other.

17 For Christ sent me not to baptize, but to preach the gospel: not with wisdom of words, lest the cross of Christ should be made of none effect.

NLT 1 **Corinthians 1:10** I appeal to you, dear brothers and sisters, by the authority of our Lord Jesus Christ, to live in harmony with each other. Let there be no divisions in the church. Rather, be of one mind, united in thought and purpose.

11 For some members of Chloe's household have told me about your quarrels, my dear brothers and sisters.

12 Some of you are saying, "I am a follower of Paul." Others are saying, "I follow Apollos," or "I follow Peter," or "I follow only Christ."

13 Has Christ been divided into factions? Was I, Paul, crucified for you? Were any of you baptized in the name of Paul? Of course not!

14 I thank God that I did not baptize any of you except Crispus and Gaius,

15 for now no one can say they were baptized in my name.

16 (Oh yes, I also baptized the household of Stephanas, but I don't remember baptizing anyone else.)

17 For Christ didn't send me to baptize, but to preach the Good News—and not with clever speech, for fear that the cross of Christ would lose its power.

The People, Places, and Times

Apostle Paul. A well-educated Jewish scholar and Roman citizen, as well as a skilled tent maker. This extensive knowledge allowed him to be able to identify with and talk to a wide range of people. Paul was a devout Jew who passionately sought to stop this new Jesus movement until he was converted to Christ one day on the road to Damascus. After that, Paul began to spread the Gospel throughout the Roman Empire. He developed small, close-knit Christian groups in different cities. These small groups were linked together to form a large movement.

Corinth. Known for its beauty, diversity, and culture, Corinth was a favored port city during Paul's time. Located on the narrow isthmus that connected the Peloponnese to mainland Greece, it was a center for trade and an administration site for the Roman Empire. Corinth was also known for its relaxed morals and numerous pagan temples. Paul ministered in Corinth for eighteen months during his second missionary journey. During that time, he preached the Gospel and organized new converts into small congregations that usually met in households.

Background

Our Keep in Mind verse, 1 Corinthians 1:10, plays a key role in Paul's letter to the Corinthian church. In order to really appreciate how important this verse is, we need to take a closer look at the structure of the letter. In ancient times, letters were the primary means of communication between people who were far away from each other. Like modern letters, ancient letters were usually addressed to a person, family, or small group and were intended to be read privately.

Paul's letter, however, was written to a large group and intended to be read out loud. With that said, his letter needed to follow the same rhetorical guidelines that were used for public speeches. Speeches and letters are used to persuade an audience on a particular point of view. In modern times, this style of persuasion is most often seen in courts and used by lawyers.

One fundamental element in this style of writing is known in Latin as the *propositio*. The *propositio* serves as the foundation or thesis for Paul's entire letter. Every theme that Paul discusses in 1 Corinthians points back to this verse. Paul passionately appealed to the church to understand that power, prestige, and even spiritual gifts should never take precedence over unity. With this statement, Paul reminded the Corinthians that the most valuable gifts they had were one another and the love that united them as one body in Christ.

In Depth

1. Unity is Essential (1 Corinthians 1:10–11)

Why was Paul so concerned about the arguing in the church? Certainly disagreements among groups of people are not uncommon.

In order to answer this question, we must first understand that this was no petty squabble that Paul was addressing. The word *schisma* means to split or tear apart. The divisions that Paul was addressing had the potential to tear the congregation apart. This brings to mind Jesus' words in Mark 3:25, when He stated that "if a house be divided against itself, that house cannot stand."

This *schisma* was the exact opposite of the *katartizo* (joining) that Paul desired to see in the church. He wanted the congregation to develop harmonious relationships with one another. Just like in music, harmony is not achieved by each voice sounding exactly the same. Harmony is achieved when different voices make an intentional adjustment to produce one sound. Paul was encouraging the church to find a way to work together and adjust to each other despite their differences.

2. Let Christ be the Focus (vv. 12–17)

Part of the problem was that the Corinthians had started following personalities instead of Christ, causing them to break into factions. Some aligned themselves with Paul, the founder of the church. Others, who considered themselves more intellectual, aligned with Apollos. Some believed the Apostle Peter should be followed; this may have been because Peter had been a firsthand witness to Christ's ministry. Then there were those who claimed to follow Christ only. At first glance, the "Christ only" group seems like a good thing, but it most likely made them resistant to leadership, regardless of who was providing it.

But the essence of the problem was not that these groups had differing loyalties, but their attitudes toward one another. The divisions in the church served as evidence that this congregation was failing to let the love of God soften their hearts toward each other. It was the lack of love, not difference of opinion, that was causing the congregation to self-destruct.

Search the Scriptures

1. What are some of the other places in 1 Corinthians where Paul discusses unity?

2. Who notified Paul that there was bickering going on in the church (1 Corinthians 1:11)?

3. Why does Paul say that contentions should not exist in the church (v. 13)?

Discuss the Meaning

1. Why is unity in the church important? How far should we go to maintain it?

2. How do unity and love work together?

Lesson in Our Society

In our society, we are inundated with messages that encourage prideful behavior. We are told that the only things that are important are what *we* think, what *we* want, and how *we* feel. Society would have us to believe that the relentless pursuit of these things will lead to happiness and fulfillment. But God instructs us as believers to choose a different path.

What is it worth to you to be right—is it worth risking someone else's feelings? What is it worth to you to get what you want—is it worth causing someone else pain? As believers, we are encouraged to think about more than ourselves when we make decisions. We are to consider not just what's best for us, but for everyone. This is one way that we set ourselves apart from society and maintain unity, and that our love for one another serves as a beacon that points to God.

Make It Happen

Have you ever had a disagreement with another person that went unresolved? A simple difference of opinion can damage a relationship to a point that seems irreparable. Christ gave us two essential commandments: love God completely and love each other (Matthew 22:37–39). Christ's body was broken so our relationship with God and others could be mended. Each time we take communion, we are reminded of His sacrifice. Don't let communion become a ritual act of worship; instead, let it prompt us to do the work necessary to mend the broken relationships in our lives. Let it prompt us to find new ways to overlook differences, work together, appreciate one another, and accept and love each other.

Follow the Spirit

What God wants me to do:

_____

_____

_____

_____

Remember Your Thoughts
Special insights I have learned:

_____

_____

_____

_____

More Light on the Text
1 Corinthians 1:10–17

10 Now I beseech you, brethren, by the name of our Lord Jesus Christ, that ye all speak the same thing, and that there be no divisions among you; but that ye be perfectly joined together in the same mind and in the same judgment.

Having concluded the introduction to the letter, Paul came to the main point that he was about to address in the first four chapters of the epistle: an exhortation to the Corinthians to put an end to all squabbles. Verse 10 is an appeal for a common mind and the repudiation of cliques. In this verse, which introduces the body of the letter, Paul called the Corinthian believers to perfect Christian unity. The word "beseech" (Gk. *parakaleo*, **par-ak-al-EH-o**) carries with it the connotations of request and exhortation. The basis of Paul's appeal is striking. He did not make his appeal based on his apostolic authority. Instead, first he appealed to them as "brethren," a word that denotes equality. He stood on common ground with those he wrote to. Second, he appealed to them on account of the name of the Lord Jesus Christ, revealing the intensity of his feelings.

Paul's appeal was for the Corinthians to do away with all "schisms" (Gk. *schismata*, **SKHIS-mah-tah**), a metaphor related to clothing. Thus, Paul was saying that there should be no "ripping apart" in the community. Rather, as one piece of cloth, the people of God should be perfectly united. In turn, such unity was to be evidenced in their confession; they were to speak the same thing. To be united in the same mind is to share the same convictions about God and Jesus Christ. Paul told them to speak the same thing and avoid ministry-based factions. It is possible to have different views and not be divisive. The reason for the appeal is provided in 3:3, where Paul states that if Christians are divided, they are no different from other people. In such a case, it is impossible for them to do the special work God has called them to. So deep was Paul's concern for the Corinthians that he reiterated his plea for unity three times in this verse: "speak the same thing, and that there be no divisions among you; but that ye be perfectly joined together in the same mind and in the same judgment."

11 For it hath been declared unto me of you, my brethren, by them which are of the house of Chloe, that there are contentions among you.

Verses 11 and 12 show the reason why Paul considered the plea so urgently necessary. Paul had received a report from Chloe's people. The word translated "declared" (Gk. *deloo*, **day-LO-o**) literally means "make known." The fact that contentions existed among them was made explicitly clear to Paul and was beyond dispute; therefore, he could confidently address the situation. Paul's method was equally instructive. He did not hide the identity of Chloe and just refer to her report as "anonymous." The gravity of the divisions is shown in the use of the word "contentions" (Gk. *eris*, **ER-is**). In its original usage, it always referred to disputes that endangered the church. The word points to quarrels and indicates the hot dispute and emotional flame that ignites whenever rivalry becomes intolerable. Strife is listed as one of the works of the flesh (Galatians 5:20) of which Christians should have no part.

12 Now this I say, that every one of you saith, I am of Paul; and I of Apollos; and I of Cephas; and I of Christ.

Paul became more specific as he wrote about the content of the report that he received. The mistake that the Corinthians were making was to put a human leader in the place of God. What a tragedy—and how true it is even in the twenty-first century. Apparently, members of the Corinthian church were divisively forming allegiances to various leaders within the church. We cannot fully determine the exact nature of the divisions, other than that they were drawn along partisan lines. Each group used the name of its particular favored leader—Paul, Peter, Apollos, and even Jesus—as a "war cry." They gave their loyalties to human leaders instead of to Jesus Christ. Somehow, as they magnified the human instruments, they lost sight of the Savior. It is a mistake that Christians and others have often made and continue to make; there are still many groups and religious organizations that honor one human being, particularly the founder, as if he or she were a sort of second Christ. But Paul would have none of it. A group in the Corinthian church prided itself on belonging to Christ, probably suggesting that they alone followed Christ properly. However, Paul said many times that Jesus is for everyone. Therefore, no Christians have the right to think that Jesus belongs to their group alone.

13 Is Christ divided? was Paul crucified for you? or were ye baptized in the name of Paul?

Paul asked three rhetorical questions that underline the absurdity of the state of affairs in the Corinthian church that he had just sketched. The answer to each question is an emphatic "no!"

"Is Christ divided?" Implicit in this question is the notion of the church as the body of Christ, which Paul would later develop in chapters 10–12. Christ cannot be divided, for He is one (12:12), nor can He be apportioned out so that only one group may claim to follow Him. Rather, all of the Corinthians are supposed to follow Christ.

"Was Paul crucified for you?" Paul was not crucified for them, nor were they baptized into his name. The Corinthians were to follow and imitate Paul only to the extent that he followed and imitated Christ (11:1). The point is that the Corinthians were in danger of giving to mere human leaders the allegiance that belonged to Christ alone as their Savior. As Paul puts it in 4:1, the Corinthians should think of him and his fellow apostles simply as servants of Christ to whom the mysteries of God were committed and who were responsible to Him.

"Were ye baptized in the name of Paul?" Some Corinthians were probably touting the name of the person who baptized them, suggesting that such people were either more spiritual or exhibited greater wisdom. Once again, Paul used his own name to show up the error of the Corinthian partisanship. The Greek phrase *en to onoma* (**en to ON-om-ah**), literally "into the name," when used with baptism, implies that the person baptized is the exclusive property of Christ.

14 I thank God that I baptized none of you, but Crispus and Gaius; 15 Lest any should say that I had baptized in mine own name. 16 And I baptized also the household of Stephanas: besides, I know not whether I baptized any other.

Was Paul saying that baptism was unnecessary? Absolutely not. One should by no means interpret these verses to mean that.

Paul simply placed the emphasis where it belonged: on the preaching of the Gospel (see v. 17). Nevertheless, when Paul was with the Corinthians, as far as he could recall he only baptized a few people. He might have considered this to be fortunate, because if he had indeed baptized many of them, they could potentially have used the fact to support the absurd claims found in verses 12–13. With certainty, Paul could say that he baptized Crispus, the synagogue ruler (Acts 18:8); Gaius, his host (Romans 16:23); and the household of Stephanas (cf. 1 Corinthians 16:15–16).

17 For Christ sent me not to baptize, but to preach the gospel: not with wisdom of words, lest the cross of Christ should be made of none effect.

If baptism was not Paul's primary task, what was? Paul here reiterated his God-given commission: "to preach the gospel." However, baptism was by no means insignificant to Paul (see Romans 6:3–7), although it remained secondary to the proclamation of the Gospel for which Christ sent him. The word "sent" (Gk. *apostello*, **ap-os-TEL-lo**) is the verb form of the noun "apostle," which indicates the special task to which Paul was called as well as the authority that was vested in him by God. Paul's authority lay in being Christ's apostle or "sent one."

As for the manner in which his task was to be carried out, it was imperative that it be consistent with the content of his message, the Good News of God's saving work in Christ. As such, Paul's Gospel proclamation was to be done not with humanistic rhetorical eloquence or worldly wisdom, which would render the Cross of Christ powerless. For Paul, there could be no room for pyrotechnic displays of rhetorical virtuosity, such as were offered by the traveling sophists whose

voices were often heard in the marketplaces of any Mediterranean cities. Such methods of proclamation would only serve to exalt the proclaimer and not the One proclaimed. If Paul had done so, he could have been guilty of promoting the factions spoken of in verses 11–13. On the contrary, Paul promoted true Christian unity through his undiluted proclamation of Christ crucified. The unity of speaking, mind, and judgment that the Corinthian believers were called to have in verse 10 was to have its origin in and be centered on the message of the Cross of Christ, which Paul proclaimed. In this verse, Paul lay the groundwork for what he would immediately say about his evangelizing (1:18–2:5).

Sources:
"Corinth." *NIV Archaeological Study Bible*. Grand Rapids, MI: Zondervan, 2005. 1887.
Furnish, Victor Paul. *The Theology of the First Letter to the Corinthians*. 2nd edition. Edited by James D. G. Dunn. Cambridge: Cambridge University Press, 1999.
Meeks, Wayne A. *The First Urban Christians: The Social World of the Apostle Paul*. 2nd edition. New Haven: Yale University Press, 1983.
Prior, David. *The Message of 1 Corinthians: Life in the Local Church*. *Vol. 18*. Series edited by John R. W. Stott. Downers Grove, IL: InterVarsity Press, 1985.
Witherington, Ben, III. *Conflict & Community in Corinth: A Socio-Rhetorical Commentary on 1 and 2 Corinthians*. Grand Rapids, MI: William B. Eerdmans Publishing Co., 1995.
Zodhiates, Spiros, ed. *The Complete Word Study Dictionary: New Testament*. Chattanooga, TN: AMG Publishing, 1992.

Say It Correctly

Peloponnese. pe-le-po-**NEEZ**.
Corinthian. ka-**RIN**-thee-an.

Daily Bible Readings

MONDAY
Being of the Same Mind
(Philippians 4:1–7)

TUESDAY
Empowered by the Same Spirit
(1 Corinthians 12:4–11)

WEDNESDAY
Maintaining the Unity of the Spirit
(Ephesians 4:1–6)

THURSDAY
Many Members in One Body
(1 Corinthians 12:12–20)

FRIDAY
No Dissension within the Body
(1 Corinthians 12:21–26)

SATURDAY
Members of the Body of Christ
(1 Corinthians 12:27–31)

SUNDAY
Agreement without Divisions
(1 Corinthians 1:10–17)

Notes

Teaching Tips

Words You Should Know

A. Expedient (1 Corinthians 6:12) *symphero* (Gk.)—To contribute in order to help, helpful, profitable.

B. Fornication (v. 18) *porneia* (Gk.)—Sexual sin.

C. Glorify (v. 20) *doxazo* (Gk.)—Honor, magnify, make glorious, to cause the dignity and worth of someone or something to become manifest and acknowledged.

Teacher Preparation

Unifying Principle—Do No Harm. Personal, moral, and physical purity are beneficial to the community. How does the behavior of one person affect the whole community? Paul said that because Christians are all one within the body of Christ, what harms one will harm other members, and what benefits one will benefit all.

A. Read the Background and Devotional Readings.

B. Complete Lesson 6 in the *Precepts For Living Personal Study Guide®*.

O—Open the Lesson

A. Open with prayer.

B. Have students read Aim for Change in unison.

C. Ask for a volunteer to read the In Focus story.

D. Discuss how to live by faith and experience God's presence.

P—Present the Scriptures

A. Ask for volunteers to read the Focal Verses and The People, Places, and Times. Discuss.

B. Encourage students to live their lives in a way that honors the sacredness of our bodies.

E—Explore the Meaning

A. Review and discuss the Search the Scriptures and Discuss the Meaning questions and the Lesson in Our Society section.

B. Ask students to share the most significant point they learned and how they will use that point this week.

N—Next Steps for Application

A. Complete the Follow the Spirit and Remember Your Thoughts sections.

B. Close in prayer, thanking God for His presence in our lives.

JULY
6th

Worship Guide

For the Superintendent or Teacher
Theme: Glorify God with Your Body
Song: "My Everything
(Praise Waiteth)"
Devotional Reading: Ephesians 4:7–16
Prayer

Glorify God with Your Body

Bible Background • 1 CORINTHIANS 6:12–20
Printed Text • 1 CORINTHIANS 6:12–20 | Devotional Reading • EPHESIANS 4:7–16

―――――――――― **Aim for Change** ――――――――――

By the end of the lesson, we will: RECALL the Apostle Paul's comparison of the body to a Temple; RECOGNIZE how as Christians we're called to keep our bodies pure; and RESOLVE to promote and practice personal, moral, and physical purity as part of the body of Christ.

―――――――― **In Focus** 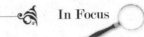 ――――――――

Joy sat in shock and disbelief as she received the news. No one could imagine the despair she felt. She asked herself, "How could I have let this happen? How will I tell my parents?"

Joy's father was a minister and her mother was the choir director at their church. They raised her in a loving Christian home and were making a tremendous financial sacrifice so she could attend a good college.

But while she was away at school, she began seeing a young man. Joy discovered that this young man was dating another girl and she ended their relationship. Now, Joy was sitting in the nurse's office, shocked by the news that she was pregnant by a man that she didn't know as well as she thought she did.

All at once she realized how many people will be affected by the choices she made. As she thought about her parents, her church, and her future, she was overwhelmed and speechless.

In today's lesson, we'll discusses the importance of understanding that our bodies are a wonderful creation and gift and that we should treat them in a way that brings glory to God.

―――――――――― **Keep in Mind** ――――――――――

"What? know ye not that your body is the temple of the Holy Ghost which is in you, which ye have of God, and ye are not your own?" (1 Corinthians 6:19).

"What? know ye not that your body is the temple of the Holy Ghost which is in you, which ye have of God, and ye are not your own?" (1 Corinthians 6:19).

Focal Verses

KJV **1 Corinthians 6:12** All things are lawful unto me, but all things are not expedient: all things are lawful for me, but I will not be brought under the power of any.

13 Meats for the belly, and the belly for meats: but God shall destroy both it and them. Now the body is not for fornication, but for the Lord; and the Lord for the body.

14 And God hath both raised up the Lord, and will also raise up us by his own power.

15 Know ye not that your bodies are the members of Christ? shall I then take the members of Christ, and make them the members of an harlot? God forbid.

16 What? know ye not that he which is joined to an harlot is one body? for two, saith he, shall be one flesh.

17 But he that is joined unto the Lord is one spirit.

18 Flee fornication. Every sin that a man doeth is without the body; but he that committeth fornication sinneth against his own body.

19 What? know ye not that your body is the temple of the Holy Ghost which is in you, which ye have of God, and ye are not your own?

20 For ye are bought with a price: therefore glorify God in your body, and in your spirit, which are God's.

NLT **1 Corinthians 6:12** You say, "I am allowed to do anything"—but not everything is good for you. And even though "I am allowed to do anything," I must not become a slave to anything.

13 You say, "Food was made for the stomach, and the stomach for food." (This is true, though someday God will do away with both of them.) But you can't say that our bodies were made for sexual immorality. They were made for the Lord, and the Lord cares about our bodies.

14 And God will raise us from the dead by his power, just as he raised our Lord from the dead.

15 Don't you realize that your bodies are actually parts of Christ? Should a man take his body, which is part of Christ, and join it to a prostitute? Never!

16 And don't you realize that if a man joins himself to a prostitute, he becomes one body with her? For the Scriptures say, "The two are united into one."

17 But the person who is joined to the Lord is one spirit with him.

18 Run from sexual sin! No other sin so clearly affects the body as this one does. For sexual immorality is a sin against your own body.

19 Don't you realize that your body is the temple of the Holy Spirit, who lives in you and was given to you by God? You do not belong to yourself,

20 for God bought you with a high price. So you must honor God with your body.

The People, Places, and Times

The Temple. King Herod built the temple that existed during Paul's time. Construction began around 20 B.C. and took approximately ten years. However, adornment was lavished on the temple until 63 A.D. It was one of the most beautiful buildings in the Roman Empire. Herod's temple was modeled after Solomon's famous temple, as described in 2 Chronicles.

Background

It is important to point out the Greco-Roman culture prevalent during Paul's time. One of the most popular tourist attractions in Corinth was the temple of Aphrodite. Travelers from near and far indulged in the services of her many temple prostitutes. Pleasure was of great value and many sought after it. They considered their bodies simply a vehicle that could be used to obtain it. The body itself was of little significance; it was considered a simple container for the soul. One could do with it what one wished and their actions had no impact on their moral integrity.

The point Paul was trying to make in this letter is that the body does indeed matter. He countered the casual attitude that society had with the theological understanding of the body as a beautiful creation designed by God to bring glory to Him. He wanted the Corinthians to see their bodies as a wonderful gift and understand that their choices have an eternal impact.

At-A-Glance

1. Building the Temple
(1 Corinthians 6:12–14)
2. Purifying the Temple (vv. 15–17)
3. Glorifying the Temple (vv. 18–20)

In Depth

1. Building the Temple (1 Corinthians 6:12–14)

Our lesson begins with the statement, "All things are lawful unto me, but all things are not expedient." Understanding this statement is essential to understanding the point Paul was trying to convey to the church in Corinth. This statement speaks to the perception that sexual practices are a private matter and one is free to do as one wishes. While this behavior may be legal, Paul questioned if this alone is a valid reason to engage in such activity. This statement encourages the hearer to make additional considerations.

Paul reminded the church that all things are not expedient or suitable for edifying. He wanted the believers to look at their behavior and consider if it was helpful. He encouraged them to make an intentional decision to restrain their personal freedom for the sake of the Gospel. It was a request that they only engage in behaviors that would be genuinely helpful for building their relationship with Christ and with those whom God was trying to reach through them.

2. Purifying the Temple (vv. 15–17)

In this section of Scripture, Paul discussed the special bond that exists between a believer and Christ and alluded to the fact that Christ's redemption of us is complete. We have been redeemed in soul, spirit, and body. It is the acceptance of Christ as our Redeemer that joins us to Him eternally as His church and bride. We now carry in us the same Spirit that Christ has in Him. It is this union that identifies us as Christians and heirs of the promises of God. We cannot have true communion with God without commitment to Him. Our commitment to God provides the basis and balance for human love.

This relationship with Christ is described in very intimate language. The reality is intimacy ignites passion. The intensity of our relationship with Christ is evidenced by what we display in our bodies. When we hold Christ close to our hearts, we pursue the things of Christ. Pursuit of ungodly passions serves as evidence that we have allowed other desires to take the place of Christ in our hearts.

3. Glorifying the Temple (vv. 18–20)

In these verses, Paul began with the command to "flee fornication." This command is justified by the reminder of just how much our redemption costs. As mentioned earlier, Paul alluded to the mystical union that exists between Christ and the church: Christ as the Bridegroom and the church as the bride. In modern times, when a man proposes, it is customary for him to make a sacrifice and purchase an engagement ring. The rationale behind this is to give a token that represents how much he is willing to sacrifice in order to gain a woman's affection. This ring serves as a constant reminder of his love for her and the price he was willing to pay.

What would happen if we looked at the Crucifixion as a marriage proposal? What if we let the Crucifixion serve as a constant reminder of the sacrifice God made in order to gain our affection? Paul reminds us that we were bought with a price. These words compel the church to take seriously what we do with our bodies and where we place our affections. Let our bodies be the place where God's glory can be found.

Search the Scriptures

1. What responsibilities come with being the body of Christ? What are some of our obligations to people inside and outside of the body (1 Corinthians 6:12–17)?

2. Why is it important to flee fornication (v. 18)?

3. Why does what we choose to do with our bodies matter (vv. 19–20)?

Discuss the Meaning

1. How is our willingness to sacrifice some of our freedoms a reflection of Christ's willing sacrifice for us?

2. How might something like fasting bring us to properly understand the priority of our spiritual needs?

Lesson in Our Society

There are many similarities between the casual attitude toward sex that was prevalent during Paul's time and that of our own time. We are daily inundated with images that would cause us to believe that sex is meaningless outside of its ability to give us pleasure. Our bodies are treated like disposable trinkets instead of being honored as priceless treasures. We see the impact that sex without commitment has on our society as a whole. Single parent households have become commonplace. The impact that this lack of commitment has on children is staggering.

During moments like this, God calls the church to stand up and be an example. The first step is to instill within ourselves a healthy respect for the physical bodies God has given to us. Let this inner respect govern how we treat our bodies and allow them to be treated. The next step is to invite others to come along with us as we learn to treat ourselves and others with dignity and respect while honoring God, who so richly blesses us.

Make It Happen

It is time for us to take seriously what we do with our bodies. In our lesson, Paul highlights the problems with fornication, which he describes as a sin against our bodies (v. 18). Times have hardly changed since the

Apostle Paul wrote this letter. Humanity has come up with a number of ways to sin against our bodies with alcohol, drug use, poor eating habits, lack of physical activity, etc. While the primary topic of the lesson is fornication, it also speaks to the overall respect we should have for our physical bodies. Let's take a moment to truly examine ourselves, whether we are married or single, and decide if there is more we can do to take better care of the temple that is our body. Then let us make a commitment to do so.

Follow the Spirit

What God wants me to do:

_____

_____

_____

_____

Remember Your Thoughts

Special insights I have learned:

_____

_____

_____

_____

More Light on the Text

1 Corinthians 6:12–20

12 All things are lawful unto me, but all things are not expedient: all things are lawful for me, but I will not be brought under the power of any.

It was once observed, "that to which you give yourself, is the thing to which you belong." Paul, here, reminds the church in Corinth that as Christians, they had all liberty in Christ. Likewise, we as believers today are free to be or to do anything. All things are "lawful" (Gk. *exesti*, **EX-es-tee,** meaning right or permitted). This teaching was probably well-known to the Corinthians who would have used their liberty to indulge in practices Paul knew to be unhealthy; therefore, he went on to explain that not all things are "expedient" (Gk. *sumphero*, **soom-FER-o,** meaning profitable or beneficial). Paul understood the deceptive power of the type of freedom that Christians enjoy in Christ and agreed with the Corinthians that indeed all things were lawful for him as well; however, he chose not to give himself to any "power" (Gk. *exousiazo*, **ex-oo-see-AD-zo,** meaning to exercise authority over) save Christ and His crucifixion.

13 Meats for the belly, and the belly for meats: but God shall destroy both it and them. Now the body is not for fornication, but for the Lord; and the Lord for the body. 14 And God hath both raised up the Lord, and will also raise up us by his own power.

God, who designed the human body, provided the means for the body's needs to be satisfied. When the stomach informs the body that it desires food, then food should be supplied to it or its need will not be met. However, Paul wanted the Corinthians to understand that God is sovereign over the belly and the meat required to satisfy its wants. This is natural; God has provided, but He also has the power to destroy them both should He choose to do so. The same God who is sovereign over the belly and its wants is sovereign over the sexual appetites of the human body. Paul counseled that the sexual appetites of the body were not to be satisfied by "fornication" (Gk. *porneia*, **por-NI-ah,** meaning illicit sexual intercourse).

Porneia is the Greek root for our contemporary word "pornography," and the original meaning behind the word pornography was "the prostitute's story." Paul's use of the word *porneia* was probably his attempt to warn the Corinthian Christians against having sexual intercourse with prostitutes. Paul wanted the Corinthians to understand that satisfying the stomach's desires for food and satisfying the body's sexual urges are not the same. Both the stomach and food are temporal and natural to this world; there will come a time when they will be no more. But there is a spiritual dimension that attaches to the body because it was created for the Lord and will one day be transformed and glorified (cf. Philippians 3:21). The body, therefore, is not to be disregarded as something that will suffer destruction; rather, just as God raised Christ Jesus from the dead, He will likewise resurrect or "raise up" (Gk. *exegeiro*, **ex-eg-I-ro,** meaning to arouse or stir up) our bodies.

15 Know ye not that your bodies are the members of Christ? shall I then take the members of Christ, and make them the members of an harlot? God forbid.

Paul drove home his point by asking three rhetorical questions of the Corinthian Christians. The first question asked whether or not they understood that their bodies were in fact "members" (Gk. *melos*, **MEL-os,** meaning part of the body) of Christ's body. In Corinthian society, paganism was rampant. Both the Greeks and the Romans were known to frequent the temple of Aphrodite and consecrate themselves to the false god there by having sexual intercourse with the temple "harlots" (Gk. *porne*, **POR-nay,** meaning one who yields herself to defilement for sexual uses). These prostitutes served in the temple acting as priestesses for the goddess. Paul wanted the Christians at Corinth to understand that just as their fingers and toes were parts of their own bodies, they had become the parts of Christ's body. Therefore, "God forbid" (Gk. *me*, **may,** meaning keep from or prevent) that such a thing should occur among any within His church.

16 What? know ye not that he which is joined to an harlot is one body? for two, saith he, shall be one flesh.

Paul's second inquiry of the Corinthian Christians sought to determine whether or not they understood that having sexual intercourse with a person causes the two individuals to become one flesh. Of course, this was probably common knowledge among the Corinthians, but Paul was seeking to move them from the natural and secular thinking of their day to consider what the Scriptures had to say. Paul referred to Genesis 2:24 where Adam was joined to his wife, Eve. By permitting their bodies to be "joined" (Gk. *kollao*, **kol-LAH-o,** meaning to be glued) to a temple prostitute in sexual intercourse, the Corinthians were becoming one flesh with them and consecrating themselves to their false god—Aphrodite.

17 But he that is joined unto the Lord is one spirit.

In the previous verse, Paul intimated that the joining through sexual intercourse was but a physical union. Now he pointed out that the Corinthian Christian who has joined with Christ the Lord shares a union so close with Him that their "spirits" (Gk. *pneuma*, **NOO-mah,** meaning a life-giving essence, possessed of the knowing, desiring, deciding and acting) become one. The choice, therefore, becomes one of being one body with the prostitute or being one spirit with Christ. The two are not compatible.

18 Flee fornication. Every sin that a man doeth is without the body; but he that committeth fornication sinneth against his own body.

One of the strongest human drives is the sex drive. Paul understood this and counseled that because the sin of fornication strikes at the very root of a person's being, it needed to be avoided at all costs. One would be best served by "fleeing" (Gk. *pheugo*, **FYOO-go,** meaning to shun or avoid by flight) from even the possibility of that particular sin. Paul's counsel to the Corinthian church was especially forceful on this point because the sin of fornication differs from other sins. While no sin is more serious than any other, Paul wanted the Christians to understand that other sins impact the body from without. Gluttony, envy, pride, to name but a few, all have their focus "without" (Gk. *ektos*, **ek-TOS,** meaning exterior to or outside of) the human body and are the fruit of a desire to indulge in sinful excesses; the sin of fornication, however, occurs internally for the express purpose of gratifying a sexual desire. Though the "doing" of sin is always outside of the body, Paul's concern was with the result of the sin rather than the actual act. For one to sin the sin of fornication, one sins against his very personality. For anyone who has joined with Christ, that personality has become holy, and anything that seeks to contaminate that holiness must be avoided.

19 What? know ye not that your body is the temple of the Holy Ghost which is in you, which ye have of God, and ye are not your own?

Paul here began the third of his inquiries of the Corinthian Christians. Paul had already referred to the whole church as God's temple; now he narrowed the focus of his argument and pointed out that each person's individual body was also a "temple" (Gk. *naos*, **nah-OS,** meaning a shrine, a sacred place). Paul explained that the Holy Ghost was a divine member of the Godhead who took up residence within a believer when Christ was embraced as Lord and Savior. The fact of the Holy Spirit's residence within a Christian was not the product of the believer's efforts but a gift from God. Further, the presence of the Holy Spirit indwelling a believer makes that believer a constituent part of a whole. The Christian no longer belongs solely to himself but now helps to make up the body of Christ. For this reason, any activity that would pollute the corporate body must be avoided.

20 For ye are bought with a price: therefore glorify God in your body, and in your spirit, which are God's.

Paul now drew upon the imagery of a slave market as he directed the Corinthian believers to the truth that they no longer belonged to themselves because God had "bought" (Gk. *agorazo*, **ag-or-AD-zo,** meaning purchased or redeemed) them. The "price" (Gk. *time*, **tee-MAY,** meaning the sum paid or received for a person bought or sold) that was paid was nothing less than the blood of His Son, Jesus Christ. Because we are now slaves who belong to God, we are bound to Him, not the sin that once enslaved us. Though God could demand anything of us as His possessions, He demands nothing but asks only that we "glorify" (Gk. *doxazo*, **dox-AD-zo,** meaning to praise, extol, magnify, celebrate) Him with our bodies and our spirits. This is a positive injunction from Paul that balances out the earlier negative command from him to flee sexual immorality.

Sources:
Dunn, James D. G. and John W. Rogerson. *Commentary on the Bible.* Grand Rapids, MI: Wm. B. Eerdmans Publishing Co., 2003.
Furnish, Victor Paul. *The Theology of the First Letter to the Corinthians.* 2nd edition. Edited by James D. G. Dunn. Cambridge: Cambridge University Press, 1999.

"Herod's Temple." *NIV Archaeological Study Bible.* Grand Rapids, MI: Zondervan, 2005. 1648.

The Holy Bible: Pilgrim Edition (KJV). New York: Oxford University Press, Inc., 1952.

Howley, Bruce and Ellison Howley. *The New Layman's Bible Commentary.* Grand Rapids, MI: Zondervan, 1979.

Keener, Craig S. *The IVP Bible Background Commentary: New Testament.* Downers Grove, IL: IVP Academic, 1994.

Prior, David. *The Message of 1 Corinthians: Life in the Local Church.* Vol. 18. Series edited by John R. W. Stott. Downers Grove, IL: InterVarsity Press, 1985.

Zodhiates, Spiros, ed. *The Complete Word Study Dictionary: New Testament.* Chattanooga, TN: AMG Publishing, 1992.

Say It Correctly

Aphrodite. af-ruh-**DAHY**-tee.

Daily Bible Readings

MONDAY
Building Up the Body of Christ
(Ephesians 4:7–16)

TUESDAY
Building Up the Beloved
(2 Corinthians 12:14–21)

WEDNESDAY
Sincerity and Truth in the Body
(1 Corinthians 5:1–8)

THURSDAY
Dissociating from Immorality
in the Body
(1 Corinthians 5:9–13)

FRIDAY
Washed, Sanctified, and Justified
(1 Corinthians 6:1–11)

SATURDAY
A Particular Gift from God
(1 Corinthians 7:1–9)

SUNDAY
Glorify God in Your Body
(1 Corinthians 6:12–20)

Notes

Teaching Tips

Words You Should Know

A. Knowledge (1 Corinthians 8:1) *gnosis* (Gk.)—A term denoting the act of knowing something; can also mean science.

B. Liberty (v. 9) *exousia* (Gk.)—Freedom, power, or ability to do something of one's own choosing.

Teacher Preparation

Unifying Principle—Love Builds Up. What may be right for some members of a community may not be right for others. How are community members to hold one another accountable? Paul cautioned the faithful to behave in ways that would not cause others to falter in their faith.

A. Locate a video clip (humorous or serious) from a favorite movie that shows a stereotypical scene of a Christian being insensitive to a non-Christian. Be prepared to share it with the class.

B. Pray for students and their willingness to evaluate their behavior in light of the lesson's admonition to prefer love over knowledge.

O—Open the Lesson

A. Open with prayer.

B. Have a volunteer read the In Focus Story, then discuss.

P—Present the Scriptures

A. Use The People, Places, and Times; Background; Search the Scriptures; At-A-Glance outline; In Depth; and More Light on the Text to clarify the verses.

B. Ask for volunteers to share ways they've been negatively impacted by others, or how they've positively impacted others based on the Scriptures.

E—Explore the Meaning

A. Have volunteers summarize the Lesson in Our Society and Make It Happen sections.

B. Ask for suggestions on how students can "watch what they eat" without becoming legalistic.

N—Next Steps for Application

A. Play the video clip.

B. Ask students to discuss how it relates to the lesson.

C. Have students commit to praying about one or two areas that they need to begin working on to better build up others. Have them write these down.

Worship Guide

For the Superintendent or Teacher
Theme: Watch What You Eat
Song: "More Than Anything"
Devotional Reading: Romans 14:7–12
Prayer

Watch What You Eat

Bible Background • 1 CORINTHIANS 8:1–13
Printed Text • 1 CORINTHIANS 8:1–13 | Devotional Reading • ROMANS 14:7–12

—————————— Aim for Change ——————————

By the end of the lesson, we will: EXPLORE the positive and negative influences that community members have on one another; EMPATHIZE with Christians who may have been negatively affected by others in the community; and EVALUATE our own behavior to rid ourselves of actions that might negatively influence the people around us.

In Focus

Fredrica and her cousin, Beth, drew closer to the Chinese restaurant where they planned to eat lunch. "I can't wait to try this place," Beth said. With Beth having become a new Christian, the two were enjoying a deeper relationship based on their shared faith.

"I can't get enough of it," Fredrica said as they approached the eatery.

Fredrica shoved the door open and stepped inside. Giving their names to the waiting maître d', she turned toward Beth and stopped. "Are you okay?"

"Is that Buddha?" Beth pointed to a statue nestled in a corner near the front door. A waiter walked over. "Your table is ready."

Fredrica started to follow him but stopped when she realized Beth had failed to follow. Smiling at the waiter, Fredrica apologized. "It's a great spot, but we've changed our minds." She hurried toward Beth and pulled her outside.

Fredrica folded her arm into her cousin's. "Hey, how does a hamburger sound?"

Changing one's plans or behavior to build up a new believer's faith is a mark of spiritual maturity. In today's lesson, the church at Corinth is advised to do the same.

—————————— Keep in Mind ——————————

"But take heed lest by any means this liberty of yours become a stumblingblock to them that are weak" (1 Corinthians 8:9)

"But take heed lest by any means this liberty of yours become a stumblingblock to them that are weak" (1 Corinthians 8:9)

Focal Verses

KJV **1 Corinthians 8:1** Now as touching things offered unto idols, we know that we all have knowledge. Knowledge puffeth up, but charity edifieth.

2 And if any man think that he knoweth any thing, he knoweth nothing yet as he ought to know.

3 But if any man love God, the same is known of him.

4 As concerning therefore the eating of those things that are offered in sacrifice unto idols, we know that an idol is nothing in the world, and that there is none other God but one.

5 For though there be that are called gods, whether in heaven or in earth, (as there be gods many, and lords many,)

6 But to us there is but one God, the Father, of whom are all things, and we in him; and one Lord Jesus Christ, by whom are all things, and we by him.

7 Howbeit there is not in every man that knowledge: for some with conscience of the idol unto this hour eat it as a thing offered unto an idol; and their conscience being weak is defiled.

8 But meat commendeth us not to God: for neither, if we eat, are we the better; neither, if we eat not, are we the worse.

9 But take heed lest by any means this liberty of yours become a stumblingblock to them that are weak.

10 For if any man see thee which hast knowledge sit at meat in the idol's temple, shall not the conscience of him which is weak be emboldened to eat those things which are offered to idols;

11 And through thy knowledge shall the weak brother perish, for whom Christ died?

NLT **1 Corinthians 8:1** Now regarding your question about food that has been offered to idols. Yes, we know that "we all have knowledge" about this issue. But while knowledge makes us feel important, it is love that strengthens the church.

2 Anyone who claims to know all the answers doesn't really know very much.

3 But the person who loves God is the one whom God recognizes.

4 So, what about eating meat that has been offered to idols? Well, we all know that an idol is not really a god and that there is only one God.

5 There may be so-called gods both in heaven and on earth, and some people actually worship many gods and many lords.

6 But we know that there is only one God, the Father, who created everything, and we live for him. And there is only one Lord, Jesus Christ, through whom God made everything and through whom we have been given life.

7 However, not all believers know this. Some are accustomed to thinking of idols as being real, so when they eat food that has been offered to idols, they think of it as the worship of real gods, and their weak consciences are violated.

8 It's true that we can't win God's approval by what we eat. We don't lose anything if we don't eat it, and we don't gain anything if we do.

9 But you must be careful so that your freedom does not cause others with a weaker conscience to stumble.

10 For if others see you—with your "superior knowledge"—eating in the temple of an idol, won't they be encouraged to violate their conscience by eating food that has been offered to an idol?

12 But when ye sin so against the brethren, and wound their weak conscience, ye sin against Christ.

13 Wherefore, if meat make my brother to offend, I will eat no flesh while the world standeth, lest I make my brother to offend.

11 So because of your superior knowledge, a weak believer for whom Christ died will be destroyed.

12 And when you sin against other believers by encouraging them to do something they believe is wrong, you are sinning against Christ.

13 So if what I eat causes another believer to sin, I will never eat meat again as long as I live—for I don't want to cause another believer to stumble.

The People, Places, and Times

"Gods" and "Lords." Greek and Roman mythologies included worship of many "gods" such as Apollo, Diana (Acts 19:24), Athena, and Aphrodite. Shrines, altars, and temples were erected for worship, including sacrificial offerings and shrine prostitution. In sharing the Gospel, Paul was emphatic in teaching the concept of a monotheistic religion. For instance, when Paul and Barnabas were in Lystra and mistakenly thought to be the gods Mercurius and Jupiter, Paul set the record straight. He noted, "We also are men of like passions with you, and preach unto you that ye should turn from these vanities unto the living God" (from Acts 14:15).

Idol Feasts. Corinth was a thriving metropolis known for its maritime trade, cultural diversity, and sexual immorality. It was also infamous for its idolatrous worship of Grecian gods. Pagan practices allowed for a share of food sacrificed to idols to be used by worshipers for personal gain—kept for meals or sold at marketplaces frequented by Jews and Gentiles. Thus, it was possible that the Corinthian believers could unknowingly come into contact with such fare if visiting a non-believer or shopping at local venues.

Background

Jewish and Gentile believers comprised the Corinthian church, a body established on one of Paul's missionary journeys during which he spent eighteen months teaching the Word of God in Corinth (Acts 18:1–18). Many members formerly grounded in Jewish tradition or idolatrous behaviors had difficulty reconciling their former conduct with Paul's teachings. Because of this, they were not always successful in dealing with situations that threatened the believing community.

Paul's epistle addressed concerns posed in a letter to him from the church (1 Corinthians 7:1). He responded by: (1) reminding believers of their position in Christ; (2) exposing and refuting sinful practices that threatened community; and (3) offering Christ-centered solutions. In chapter 8, Paul dealt with food sacrificed to idols and offered a deeper revelation of the issue. He inspires us to "watch what we eat"—to evaluate our own behavior and rid ourselves of actions that might negatively influence the people around us.

At-A-Glance

1. Food Fight (1 Corinthians 8:1)
2. Soul-destroying Knowledge (vv. 2–3)
3. Food for Thought (vv. 4–8)
4. Nourishing Love (vv. 9–13)

In Depth

1. Food Fight (1 Corinthians 8:1)

The issue of food sacrificed to idols became a divisive issue in the fledgling Corinthian church. Paul acknowledged that eating such fare was a contentious issue, yet argued that the issue was deeper than where food comes from. He advised that eating food sacrificed to idols was akin to anything that is insignificant to a mature Christian believer but which might be monumental to a less seasoned saint.

Paul's teaching prescribes community unity and reminds us not to allow divisive issues to wreck Christian fellowship, such as what constitutes "real" fasting, whether drinking wine is acceptable, and if tithing is calculated on gross or net income. What other issues can you think of? Whatever the area of concern, Paul encourages mature Christians to avoid "food fights"—spiritual battles that cause others to sin or stumble.

2. Soul-destroying Knowledge (vv. 2–3)

Born into an influential family and educated by renowned Jewish teachers (Acts 22:3, 5; Galatians 1:14; Philippians 3:4–6), Paul had once been a zealous Pharisee who persecuted Christians. After his conversion to Christ, Paul used his knowledge to teach in synagogues and among the Gentiles, but always acknowledged that love trumped knowledge. Having firsthand experience of the potentially soul-destroying impact of knowledge, Paul warned the believers that "knowledge puffs up while love builds up" (1 Corinthians 8:1, NIV).

As in the Corinthian church, there are many Christians sitting in pews who have been hurt by "knowledgeable" Christians who "set them straight" regarding issues of doctrine, faith, or some other area. Paul's epistle compels us to reach out to such wounded saints by building bridges of fellowship that reunite estranged members, and by using our knowledge to protect weaker believers as they strive toward spiritual maturity.

3. Food for Thought (vv. 4–8)

Paul wrote that, despite the idol worship in Corinth, there is only one God who matters! Thus, he refocused attention away from the issue of eating food offered to idols, and wrote that "food does not bring us near to God" (from v. 8, NIV). This was a needed reminder to weaker believers who may have struggled with superstitious or idolatrous thoughts despite having become born again.

This should not have been a novel idea. History proved that food—such as the provision of manna—did not bring the Israelites closer to God (Exodus 16:11–16; Numbers 11:4–34). For Christians today, Paul's teaching reminds us that food-related activities like fasting neither bring us closer to God nor give us spiritual maturity. We are warned not to latch on to popular movements or disciplines that place more focus on fleshly development than spiritual maturity.

4. Nourishing Love (vv. 9–13)

In addressing the food fight at Corinth, Paul argued that loving God is not measured by one's *head* knowledge but one's *heart* knowledge. It is clear that he was not advocating a legalistic faith based on what one eats or how one acts. Rather, the primary goal is a unified community forged by faith in Christ and built on the sacrificial, unconditional love of Jesus. How can community members hold each other accountable in using knowledge to build up others? We can:

- Share strengths.
- Connect in love.
- Respect others' weaknesses.
- Consider others first.
- Turn others to Christ.

Community love is not based on knowledge, but love. A "little taste" may be more than enough for someone to go back to destructive habits, as in the case of drug and food addictions.

Search the Scriptures

1. What did the Apostle Paul remind Christians about "so-called gods" (1 Corinthians 8:4–6, NLT)?

2. How should we handle the issue of what we eat (vv. 9, 13)?

Discuss the Meaning

1. Paul advocated reining in our actions to build others up and not cause them to stumble. How can we balance this without becoming legalistic, forcing ourselves or others to live as if we are under the Law?

2. What kind of prescriptive things in your life may cause you to miss the bigger picture when it comes to being a follower of Christ?

Lesson in Our Society

Many non-Christians and unchurched believers share a common bond: They've been negatively impacted by the actions of "mature" believers who caused them to falter. Sharing our faith with compassion and behaving in ways that build up others can lead others back to God. Have you been a beacon of light in this way in your job,

community, or family? If so, how? If not, how does today's lesson equip you to make such a positive impact?

Make It Happen

What behavior do you exhibit that makes others feel inferior or less spiritually mature (that you may not even realize)? Today's lesson sounds a clarion call for change! Pray for forgiveness, and pray daily this week for ways to promote love over knowledge when dealing with others.

Follow the Spirit

What God wants me to do:

_____

_____

_____

_____

Remember Your Thoughts

Special insights I have learned:

_____

_____

_____

_____

More Light on the Text

1 Corinthians 8:1

1 Now as touching things offered unto idols, we know that we all have knowledge. Knowledge puffeth up, but charity edifieth.

Food offered to idols is the second concern of the Corinthian church to which Paul responded. Many religions offer food to their god(s) for a variety of purposes. It is difficult to pinpoint the precise purpose for the offering without observing the ritual; even within a single ritual, individuals may experience the ritual differently. However, one may find three general purposes for food offerings: sacramental, communion, and celebration. As a sacrament, the participants symbolically consume the flesh and blood of the god to take on the life energy or power of the god. As when we take communion, the participants bring to memory some event or act their faith depends on. As a celebration, the community of believers shares a meal in which they might recognize their common belief or dependency on the god.

When Paul stated, "We know that we all have knowledge," he leveled any hierarchy that might exist in the readers' minds. "I know as well as you do." This knowledge or *gnosis* may be thought of as revealed teachings obtained through secret societies, deep intellectual thought or study, or by some direct revelation from the divine. *Gnosis* was prized in Greek societies and used to elevate one's status above others. The "we" that Paul referred to was probably the leaders or teachers of the Corinthian church who had obtained a greater level of *gnosis* regarding the Christian teachings than the average worshiper.

"Knowledge puffs up while love builds up" (8:1, NIV). *Gnosis*, as personal knowledge, puffs up the individual's ego, when compared to those who do not have this same *gnosis*; it only benefits the individual. By contrast, love builds up the community and is the standard which Christians ought to strive to obtain (see 1 Corinthians 13:6–8).

2 And if any man think that he knoweth any thing, he knoweth nothing yet as he ought to know.

"A little knowledge is a dangerous thing." This popular saying catches the spirit of Paul's challenge to the Corinthian leaders. The one who thinks he or she knows something has yet to realize how much more there is to know; the ego becomes inflated, demonstrating that he or she has not yet arrived at full knowledge. True knowledge humbles.

3 But if any man love God, the same is known of him.

Verse 3 gives Paul's main point in this discussion on *gnosis*. Human knowledge, even if it concerns God, is not as important as love for God. This love for God is demonstrated within the human community, building up the community rather than puffing up the individual. It is more important to be known by God, for therein lies redemption and blessing. In 1 Corinthians 13:8, Paul says that love never ends, but knowledge passes away.

4 As concerning therefore the eating of those things that are offered in sacrifice unto idols, we know that an idol is nothing in the world, and that there is none other God but one.

We might wonder under what circumstances a Christian would have had occasion to eat such food. It is known that the leftover meats from these sacrifices found their way into the public market. The parts not burned or consumed at a feast were sold in the marketplace; thus, anyone who ate any meat was at risk of encountering meat that had been offered to idols. Another concern was if a Christian was invited to the home of a non-Christian and served a hospitality meal, some of that meat might be served. Thus, to avoid being defiled by idol meat, many Christians became vegetarians.

Also, often people of status or particular affiliation would gather for festive occasions in the Greek temples. These might include Christians with social rank or family affiliation, regardless of their religious affiliation.

At such events, one was certain to be served idol meat.

"We all know that an idol is not really a god" (from v. 4, NLT). In Deuteronomy 6:4, Moses pronounced the oneness of God to the Israelites. This affirmation of sole devotion to and acknowledgment of the one God is known as the *Shema*, because the first word in the command is "Hear!" and set the Israelites apart from the surrounding polytheistic (many gods) religions in the region. This fundamental tenet was also incorporated into Christianity from its earliest stages. This monotheistic view meant that one God was responsible for the creation of the cosmos and maintaining its order, rather than many gods battling one another. The God of Jews and Christians was not viewed as the strongest among many, but the only real God. With this knowledge, the Corinthian Christian could eat the idol meat with a clear conscience, because the idol was not real.

5 For though there be that are called gods, whether in heaven or in earth, (as there be gods many, and lords many,)

This statement acknowledges the circumstances of the pluralistic culture the Corinthian church found itself in. The Greek pantheon consisted of many gods and demigods who were believed to exert control over the heavens and human affairs. Even amongst the nobility, who ruled earthly affairs, there were some who claimed divinity.

6 But to us there is but one God, the Father, of whom are all things, and we in him; and one Lord Jesus Christ, by whom are all things, and we by him.

For us, the Christians, trained in the teachings of Jesus, we know that there is only one God, who is the Father of creation. This encapsulates the so-called gods in heaven and earth. It is this Father from whom all things issued and to whom we owe our existence. As for the many lords of the land, the Christian acknowledges Jesus Christ only. The understanding of the Lord as the one through whom creation took place sounds very much like the concept of the *logos* (the pre-existent and co-existent agent through whom the creation occurred) found in the first chapter of the Gospel of John.

7 Howbeit there is not in every man that knowledge: for some with conscience of the idol unto this hour eat it as a thing offered unto an idol; and their conscience being weak is defiled.

This knowledge of God the Father and Jesus Christ the Lord was not fully known or understood equally by all Christians. Those who had been accustomed to eating food offered to idols, because they had formerly worshiped those idol gods, sometimes found it difficult to re-think that experience. They may have heard the words, but the words did not sink deep into their consciences to transform their understanding. Therefore, in their consciences they felt defiled, because they had conflicting thoughts while eating or seeing other Christians eat such meat.

The "weak" are those who do not know, and the counterpart to those who know the teachings. Paul did not condemn them for being weak at all.

8 But meat commendeth us not to God: for neither, if we eat, are we the better; neither, if we eat not, are we the worse.

Those with understanding knew that the Christian would not be affected for better or worse by eating idol meat, because the idol had no real existence. So, the Christians had the liberty to choose for themselves whether to eat.

9 But take heed lest by any means this liberty of yours become a stumblingblock to them that are weak.

Having this knowledge, the Christians gained liberty to eat or abstain without consequence to their salvation. However, Paul warned that this liberty was not to be exercised without consideration of its impact upon the weak. Liberty is not absolute.

10 For if any man see thee which hast knowledge sit at meat in the idol's temple, shall not the conscience of him which is weak be emboldened to eat those things which are offered to idols;

This is the stumbling block: that the weak, seeing those who know more than them eat idol meat, may feel pressured or encouraged to eat as well. But in the mind of the weak, they may be violating their conscience. This may keep them from ever breaking away from their former understanding of eating idol meat.

11 And through thy knowledge shall the weak brother perish, for whom Christ died?

Thus the exercise of liberty may not only be a stumbling block but lead to the destruction of a weak believer; the knowledge which puffs up could destroy one for whom Christ died.

12 But when ye sin so against the brethren, and wound their weak conscience, ye sin against Christ.

Now Paul's argument has come full circle. Yes, knowledge gives liberty, but that liberty should not be exercised if it would wound a weak believer. Destroying the weak is a sin against Christ Himself. While eating idol food may have no consequence against one's soul, behavior that would destroy the Christian community does. Paul firmly stated his position in his concluding statement.

13 Wherefore, if meat make my brother to offend, I will eat no flesh while the world standeth, lest I make my brother to offend.

Because love is greater than knowledge, Paul would gladly give up his liberty of eating idol meat to build up the Christian community. He considered the relinquishing of meat an insignificant loss compared to the loss of a soul.

Sources:
Adeyemo, Tokunboh, ed. *Africa Bible Commentary*. Grand Rapids, MI: Zondervan, 2010. 1412–1413.
Draper, Charles W., Chad Brand, and Archie England, eds. *Holman Illustrated Bible Dictionary*. Grand Rapids, MI: Holman Bible Publishers, 2003. 342–346, 590.
Henry, Matthew. *Concise Commentary of the Whole Bible*. Nashville, TN: Thomas Nelson, 1997, 1104–05.
Strong, James. *Strong's Exhaustive Concordance of the Bible*. Updated ed. Peabody, MA: Hendrickson Publishers, Inc., 2007. 1615, 1626.

Say It Correctly

Emboldened. em-**BOHL**-duhned.
Grecian. **GREE**-shuhn.

Daily Bible Readings

MONDAY
Regulations for the Interim
(Hebrews 9:1–10)

TUESDAY
Human Commands and Teachings
(Colossians 2:16–23)

WEDNESDAY
Faith and Knowledge
(2 Peter 1:2–11)

THURSDAY
Grow in Grace and Knowledge
(2 Peter 3:14–18)

FRIDAY
Honoring and Giving Thanks to God
(Romans 14:1–6)

SATURDAY
Accountable to God
(Romans 14:7–12)

SUNDAY
Liberty or Stumbling Block?
(1 Corinthians 8)

Notes

Teaching Tips

Words You Should Know

A. Tempt (1 Corinthians 10:9) *ekpi-radzo* (Gk.)—To negatively test, prove; used in connection with testing God or His character.

B. Partakers (v. 18) *koinonos* (Gk.)—Denotes someone who shares, partners, or serves as a companion in something—as in a partner in spreading the Gospel.

Teacher Preparation

Unifying Principle—Strength to Endure Temptation. The pride of individual people and communities can lead them to act in destructive or harmful ways. How can communities resist the desire to move in harmful directions? Paul reminded the Corinthians that all believers are tempted, but God will not let them be tested beyond their strength—He will provide the way out.

A. Prepare for the lesson by brainstorming a list of common temptations. Type the words on single pieces of paper for students.

B. Be prepared to discuss the consequences of one of the temptations on your list.

O—Open the Lesson

A. Distribute the sheets of temptation terms to students.

B. Have volunteers read Aim for Change.

C. Ask students to define the temptation terms on the list and provide a real-life example and consequence.

P—Present the Scriptures

A. Invite students to read the Focal Verses.

B. Discuss the current event temptation you've researched and how it relates to the lesson.

E—Explore the Meaning

A. Have students silently read the Lesson in Our Society and Make It Happen sections.

B. Ask for volunteers to share their struggle or success overcoming any of the temptations mentioned in today's lesson.

N—Next Steps for Application

A. Invite students to pray for each other in groups for strength to endure temptations they may face this week.

B. Close in prayer.

Worship Guide

For the Superintendent or Teacher
Theme: Overcoming Temptation
Song: "More Than I Can Bear"
Devotional Reading:
Hebrews 3:7–14
Prayer

Overcoming Temptation

Bible Background • 1 CORINTHIANS 10:9–22
Printed Text • 1 CORINTHIANS 10:9–22 | Devotional Reading • HEBREWS 3:7–14

—— Aim for Change ——

By the end of the lesson, we will: PONDER Paul's warnings about yielding to temptation; SENSE the joy of resisting the temptation of sin; and PRAY over specific needs of one another for God's help in overcoming temptation.

 In Focus

Kim listened intently to the women as they shared their struggles with pornography. Before learning about the group, she had thought that she alone suffered a temptation usually associated with men. Sitting in the circle, tissue clinched in her hands, Kim quickly realized that pornography use was more common among women than she ever imagined.

JULY 20th

One thing became crystal clear to Kim: The consequence of falling into this temptation was great. Stories of failed marriages, lost kids, and financial woes had Kim's heart breaking for her Christian sisters assembled here. Her situation wasn't nearly that bad . . . yet. One thing was also certain: There was hope. If Kim was willing to receive God's strength to endure the temptation pornography posed, she could succeed. As she readied to share her story for the first time, Kim prayed a silent petition of thanksgiving for the co-worker who told her about the group. Maybe someday Kim would also be among those giving praises for deliverance.

God's Word reveals how yielding to temptation harms individuals and communities. Community support enables members to overcome temptation . . . often, one day at a time.

—— Keep in Mind ——

"There hath no temptation taken you but such as is common to man: but God is faithful, who will not suffer you to be tempted above that ye are able; but will with the temptation also make a way to escape, that ye may be able to bear it" (1 Corinthians 10:13).

"There hath no temptation taken you but such as is common to man: but God is faithful, who will not suffer you to be tempted above that ye are able; but will with the temptation also make a way to escape, that ye may be able to bear it" (1 Corinthians 10:13).

Focal Verses

KJV **1 Corinthians 10:9** Neither let us tempt Christ, as some of them also tempted, and were destroyed of serpents.

10 Neither murmur ye, as some of them also murmured, and were destroyed of the destroyer.

11 Now all these things happened unto them for examples: and they are written for our admonition, upon whom the ends of the world are come.

12 Wherefore let him that thinketh he standeth take heed lest he fall.

13 There hath no temptation taken you but such as is common to man: but God is faithful, who will not suffer you to be tempted above that ye are able; but will with the temptation also make a way to escape, that ye may be able to bear it.

14 Wherefore, my dearly beloved, flee from idolatry.

15 I speak as to wise men; judge ye what I say.

16 The cup of blessing which we bless, is it not the communion of the blood of Christ? The bread which we break, is it not the communion of the body of Christ?

17 For we being many are one bread, and one body: for we are all partakers of that one bread. .

18 Behold Israel after the flesh: are not they which eat of the sacrifices partakers of the altar?

19 What say I then? that the idol is any thing, or that which is offered in sacrifice to idols is any thing?

20 But I say, that the things which the Gentiles sacrifice, they sacrifice to devils, and not to God: and I would not that ye should have fellowship with devils.

NLT **1 Corinthians 10:9** Nor should we put Christ to the test, as some of them did and then died from snakebites.

10 And don't grumble as some of them did, and then were destroyed by the angel of death.

11 These things happened to them as examples for us. They were written down to warn us who live at the end of the age.

12 If you think you are standing strong, be careful not to fall.

13 The temptations in your life are no different from what others experience. And God is faithful. He will not allow the temptation to be more than you can stand. When you are tempted, he will show you a way out so that you can endure.

14 So, my dear friends, flee from the worship of idols.

15 You are reasonable people. Decide for yourselves if what I am saying is true.

16 When we bless the cup at the Lord's Table, aren't we sharing in the blood of Christ? And when we break the bread, aren't we sharing in the body of Christ?

17 And though we are many, we all eat from one loaf of bread, showing that we are one body.

18 Think about the people of Israel. Weren't they united by eating the sacrifices at the altar?

19 What am I trying to say? Am I saying that food offered to idols has some significance, or that idols are real gods?

20 No, not at all. I am saying that these sacrifices are offered to demons, not to God. And I don't want you to participate with demons.

21 You cannot drink from the cup of the Lord and from the cup of demons, too. You

21 Ye cannot drink the cup of the Lord, and the cup of devils: ye cannot be partakers of the Lord's table, and of the table of devils.

22 Do we provoke the Lord to jealousy? are we stronger than he?

cannot eat at the Lord's Table and at the table of demons, too.

22 What? Do we dare to rouse the Lord's jealousy? Do you think we are stronger than he is?

The People, Places, and Times

Jewish Forefathers. Paul referred to Moses and Israel's wanderings after leaving Egypt. He used these ancestors as examples of people who did not overcome sin because they did not accept God's way out of the temptations they encountered. Because of their sin, they wandered forty years, enough time for those who murmured, complained, and tempted God to die out. He specifically pointed out that these forefathers had the presence and promise of God with them, but they yielded to temptation. God was not pleased with them, so they did not enter the Promised Land.

Background

Israel's history of falling into temptation by not avoiding the sins of neighboring nations had repeated itself in Corinth. Hundreds of years after being delivered from Egypt and wandering in the wilderness, God's children were once again mirroring the practices of non-believers, reveling in sin and condoning ungodly practices. The Apostle Paul wrote to the believers in Corinth to encourage them to resist such conduct.

Paul challenged the Corinthians to examine behavior that mimicked what their forefathers had done and could fall into the category of tempting God. He also addressed the arrogance and pride that could make believers think they were not in sin, warning, "If you think you are standing strong, be careful not to fall" (1 Corinthians 10:12, NLT). Stirring believers to repentance was one of Paul's aims, but he also wanted

them to sense the joy of resisting the temptation of sin and live in such a joyful state. By doing so, the community would be built on a strong foundation of role models who eschewed sin and received strength from God to endure temptation.

Like the Corinthian church, believers today sometimes fail to look back at the examples provided in Scripture and everyday life that enable us to identify and overcome temptation. Like those early believers, we, too, must ponder Paul's warnings about yielding to temptation. Where needed, we must be willing to repent.

At-A-Glance

1. Temptation Defined
(1 Corinthians 10:9–11; Hebrews 3:7–14)
2. Price of Temptation
(1 Corinthians 10:11–12)
3. Temptation Overcome (vv. 14–21)

In Depth

1. Temptation Defined (1 Corinthians 10:9–11; Hebrews 3:7–14)

Paul made a passionate plea with stories dating back to Moses as the leader charged with bringing Israel into the Promised Land. He explained that these stories of temptations served as warnings. The message? Do not succumb to temptation; overcome it! The Greek word for temptation in verse 13 translates as "provocation" (also used in Hebrews

3:8) and can mean "the enticement to do evil."

According to Paul, no one is exempt from the enemy's enticement to evil. Hence his usage of the word "common" to describe temptation's ability to entrap. Paul's warning comes with an encouraging caveat: While all believers are tempted to sin, God promises a way out (v. 13). Yes, God has a way out of every temptation. We can overcome temptation as we follow Him and resist the desire to move in harmful directions.

2. Price of Temptation (1 Corinthians 10:11–12)

Temptation causes people and entire communities to stumble. Paul contends yielding to sin costs plenty. Thus, he called believers to remember the high price of yielding to temptation. The costliest is to be destroyed by our behaviors. We also pay when, out of pride, we believe we are standing firmly in faith and obedience but have sinned. Such pride obliterates the need for repentance. Finally, Paul warned of the chance that our fellowship with Christ will be broken.

Is sin really worth broken fellowship with our Savior and Lord? Absolutely not! As we rely on God for strength to endure temptation, our fellowship with Christ and others is sweet. We also experience an awesome sense of joy and triumph when we choose to use God-given strength to endure temptation. And we come to better understand how "we are more than conquerors through him that loved us" (from Romans 8:37).

3. Temptation Overcome (vv. 14–21)

Overcoming temptation is easier when we identify it and choose not to pay its high price. Practical ways we can overcome temptation include: (1) examination of oneself; (2) recognition of commonality of temptation;

(3) acceptance of God's way out (be open to repentance or avoidance of sin); and (4) willingness to flee idolatry.

How can one overcome temptations and help encourage accountability to and with others?

Remember common purpose. Our lives are to bring glory to God. As we strive to fulfill that purpose, we will hold ourselves and others more accountable for their actions.

Remember common passions. It is encouraging to know that temptation is not targeted to a few members of a church or community. Openly sharing our temptations and seeking prayer support as we attempt to overcome them can help us bear each other's burdens and spur one another on to Christ-like living.

Remember common courtesy. Enticing another person to sin is wrong. The stories Paul shared warn us not to fall into temptation . . . or drag others with us.

Remember our common Deliverer. Undoubtedly, temptation clouds focus and vision. It causes us to believe we are hopeless and helpless. That is not the case; God is our ever-present help.

Search the Scriptures

1. What was, and is, a consequence of tempting Christ (1 Corinthians 10:9–12)?

2. What advice does Paul give concerning idolatry? Why (10:14, 22)?

Discuss the Meaning

How can Paul's contention in 1 Corinthians 10:13 make it easier for Christians to identify and flee from sin? How can this direct our prayers for our communities today . . . and generations to come?

Lesson in Our Society

The news sometimes includes reports of church leaders who fall into sin and are caught in the act or even die while yielding to temptation. How does this impact churches, communities, and families? What can we do to help strengthen leaders so they can endure temptation?

Make It Happen

An accountability partner can help provide needed strength to endure temptation. Today, make a list of people who can keep you accountable in one or more areas. Ask God to show you who is the right person to assist you, then ask that person to partner with you.

Follow the Spirit

What God wants me to do:

_____

_____

_____

_____

Remember Your Thoughts

Special insights I have learned:

_____

_____

_____

_____

More Light on the Text

1 Corinthians 10:9–22

9 Neither let us tempt Christ, as some of them also tempted, and were destroyed of serpents. 10 Neither murmur ye, as some of them also murmured, and were destroyed of the destroyer.

After being delivered from bondage in Egypt, the Children of Israel wandered in the desert as God began the process of growing them into a holy nation. Numbers 21:5 records one occasion where the congregation grew thirsty and "spake against God" (Gk. *gogguzo*, **gong-GOOD-zo,** meaning to grumble, say anything against in a low tone). The murmuring or grumbling was seen as a persistent ingratitude toward God and disbelief in His ability to provide for their needs. As a consequence of their trying His hand, God sent serpents to "destroy" (Gk. *apollumi*, **ap-OL-loo-mee,** meaning to put out of the way entirely, abolish, put an end to) the people. Paul referred to that incident as he warned the Corinthians not to be guilty of "tempting" (Gk. *ekpeirazo*, **ek-pi-RAD-zo,** meaning to try or put to the test) God in the same manner. The "destroyer" (Gk. *olothreutes*, **ol-oth-ryoo-TACE,** meaning the ruiner) is the one sent by God to punish those who displease Him.

11 Now all these things happened unto them for examples: and they are written for our admonition, upon whom the ends of the world are come.

The "things" Paul referred to are the events related to the history of the nation of Israel. At the beginning of the chapter, Paul offered several positive elaborations that spoke to the Corinthians about God's blessings on the Children of Israel. These blessings included divine guidance of the cloud by day and fire by night; divine protection in the crossing of the Red Sea; and divine provision by the giving of manna from heaven and water from a rock. Even so, though on the receiving end of God's blessings, some of the Israelites became self-indulgent and complacent in their worship of God, and His blessings were replaced with His wrath. Paul explained that the experiences of the

Children of Israel (both successes and failures) were intended by God to teach them that they were not to be ungrateful or complacent in their walk or attitude of reverence toward God and His blessings. The Old Testament record of God's dealings with the nation of Israel was written for our "admonition" (Gk. *nouthesia*, **noo-thes-EE-ah,** meaning instruction or warning) and was to be received as an expression of His love for His people. Hawley, Bruce, and Ellison suggest that when Paul was speaking of those "upon whom the ends of the world are come," he wanted the Corinthians to understand that the end of an age had been completed, the culmination of all past ages has arrived with the inauguration of Christ, and the lessons those ages taught are now to be evident (*The New Layman's Bible Commentary*, 89).

12 Wherefore let him that thinketh he standeth take heed lest he fall.

Most prevalent among the lessons for the Corinthian Christians to learn from the experiences of the Children of Israel was not to be overconfident in the midst of God's blessings. The Jews who had been delivered from Egyptian bondage and whom God poured His blessings on in the desert knew that they were God's special possession. This knowledge caused some of them to begin to take His care and concern for granted and turn to their own evil desires. Scholars generally agree that several million Jews were delivered from bondage in Egypt and wandered in the wilderness with Moses; of those millions, only two lived to enter the Promised Land. Paul's warning was that those Corinthians who "thinketh" (Gk. *dokeo*, **dok-EH-o,** meaning to be of the opinion or suppose) they "standeth" (Gk. *histemi*, **HIS-tay-mee,** meaning to make firm, fix, or establish) should be careful. The Jews delivered from bondage and blessed

by God eventually stumbled and fell. The Corinthians were to be careful as well not to become indifferent to God's blessings for fear that they would ultimately stumble and "fall."

13 There hath no temptation taken you but such as is common to man: but God is faithful, who will not suffer you to be tempted above that ye are able; but will with the temptation also make a way to escape, that ye may be able to bear it. 14 Wherefore, my dearly beloved, flee from idolatry.

Scholars generally agree that there are three sources of our temptations: our environments, Satan, and our own sinful nature. It is easy to think that God must be the source of our temptations and that, at times, those temptations are unique to us, but Paul corrected that assertion. God is not the source of our "temptations" (Gk. *peirasmos*, **pi-ras-MOS,** meaning an enticement to sin, whether arising from desires or outward circumstances) and no temptation is unique to a given individual. They are "common to man." God, however, does use temptations to help us grow. Because He is "faithful" to us in His desire to guide us into His kingdom and presence, He will not "suffer" us to be tempted beyond what we can endure. He provides the means to escape the temptation. Our singular response to God's faithfulness should be to "flee" (Gk. *pheugo*, **FYOO-go,** meaning to shun or avoid by flight) anything that might be considered idolatry. Some scholars believe that some Christians within the Corinthian church attended pagan festivals, bringing their sexual license back to the church, and/or eating meat that had been offered to those pagan deities. Paul understood that threats to the Corinthian church came both from without and within, and he counseled the church members to flee from it all.

15 I speak as to wise men; judge ye what I say.

Remember that what you give yourself to is the thing you belong to. Paul asked those within the Corinthian church who considered themselves "wise men" (Gk. *phronimos*, **FRON-ee-mos,** meaning intelligent or mindful of one's interest) to "judge" (Gk. *krino*, **KREE-no,** meaning to determine or consider) what he was saying as to how sensible their practice of eating meat that had been offered to idols truly was. He then offered three types of meals for their consideration.

16 The cup of blessing which we bless, is it not the communion of the blood of Christ? The bread which we break, is it not the communion of the body of Christ? 17 For we being many are one bread, and one body: for we are all partakers of that one bread.

The first meal that Paul wanted the Corinthian church to reflect upon was the Lord's Supper. The phrase "cup of blessing" is a Hebraism—the name given to the third cup of the Passover feast over which a prayer of thanksgiving was pronounced. Paul helped the Corinthians reflect on the fact that the cup they "blessed" (Gk. *eulogia*, **yoo-log-EE-ah)** was not the actual cup, as in pagan festivals, but was in fact the prayer of praise and laudation of Christ the one true God. This they confirmed with their "communion" (Gk. *koinonia*, **koy-nohn-EE-ah,** meaning fellowship, association, or joint participation) with the blood of Christ. The fact that Paul placed the cup before the breaking of the bread was probably to help emphasize the supremacy of the cup of Christ's blood and the fact that bread did not play a part in pagan festivals.

18 Behold Israel after the flesh: are not they which eat of the sacrifices partakers of the altar?

The second meal that Paul wanted the Corinthian church to reflect upon was "Israel after the flesh." This referred to national Israel, which still observed the sacrificial rituals of the synagogue, as opposed to spiritual Israel that was God's inheritance. Paul wanted the Corinthians to understand that they were God's spiritual possession, and when they partook of the blood and bread of Christ, they affirmed their fellowship with His kingdom.

19 What say I then? that the idol is any thing, or that which is offered in sacrifice to idols is any thing? 20 But I say, that the things which the Gentiles sacrifice, they sacrifice to devils, and not to God: and I would not that ye should have fellowship with devils.

The third meal that Paul wanted the Corinthian church to reflect upon took them back to his original point—namely that you belong to whatever you join yourself in fellowship with. Paul wanted the Corinthians to consider whether or not the idol (Gk. *eidolon*, **I-do-lon,** meaning whatever represents the form of an object, either real or imaginary) was really anything at all. Further, Paul wanted the Corinthians to consider whether the meat offered to those idols had any significance. Paul did not dispute the belief that there was some source of power behind the idols because he understood that some demonic force was at work (see Deuteronomy 32:17). In partaking of the "sacrifice" (Gk. *thuo*, **THOO-o,** meaning slaughter, slay, or kill) offered to idols, Paul was telling the Corinthians that they were joining in fellowship with whatever the sacrifice was dedicated to, and in this case, it was to "devils" (Gk. *daimonion*, **dahee-MON-ee-on,** meaning evil spirits or the messengers and ministers of Satan).

21 Ye cannot drink the cup of the Lord, and the cup of devils: ye cannot be partakers of the Lord's table, and of the table of devils. 22 Do we provoke the Lord to jealousy? are we stronger than he?

Paul concluded this portion of his discourse with the Corinthians by reminding them that it is not possible to have fellowship with the one true Lord and with the devil at the same time. A choice has to be made. To partake of both the Lord's Table and the heathen's feast would only serve to provoke God to jealousy. Israel had not been able to stand before the might of Jehovah, and neither would the Corinthian believers.

Sources:
Adeyemo, Tokunboh, ed. *Africa Bible Commentary*. Grand Rapids, MI: Zondervan, 2010. 1412–13.
Draper, Charles W., Chad Brand, and Archie England, eds. *Holman Illustrated Bible Dictionary*. Grand Rapids, MI: Holman Bible Publishers, 2003. 342–346, 590.
Dunn, James D. G. and John W. Rogerson. *Commentary on the Bible*. Grand Rapids, MI: Wm. B. Eerdmans Publishing Company, 2003.
Henry, Matthew. *Concise Commentary of the Whole Bible*. Nashville, TN: Thomas Nelson, 1997. 1568.
The Holy Bible: Pilgrim Edition (KJV). New York: Oxford University Press, Inc., 1952.
Howley, Bruce and Ellison Howley. *The New Layman's Bible Commentary*. Grand Rapids, MI: Zondervan, 1979.
Keener, Craig S. *The IVP Bible Background Commentary: New Testament*. Downers Grove, IL: IVP Academic, 1994.
Strong, James. *Strong's Exhaustive Concordance of the Bible*. Updated ed. Peabody, MA: Hendrickson Publishers, Inc., 2007. 1623, 1642.

Daily Bible Readings

MONDAY
Turning Aside from God's Commands
(Exodus 32:1–10)

TUESDAY
Turning Away from Following God
(Deuteronomy 7:1–6)

WEDNESDAY
Putting the Lord to the Test
(Acts 5:1–11)

THURSDAY
Search with Heart and Soul
(Deuteronomy 4:25–31)

FRIDAY
Holding Firm to the End
(Hebrews 3:7–14)

SATURDAY
Examples that Deter from Evil
(1 Corinthians 10:1–8)

SUNDAY
God's Faithfulness in Our Testing
(1 Corinthians 10:9–21)

Say It Correctly

Admonition. ad-muh-**NISH**-uhn.
Communion. kuh-**MYOON**-yuhn.

Teaching Tips

Words You Should Know

A. Tongue (1 Corinthians 14:13) *glossa* (Gk.)—Fluid vocalizing of speech-like syllables that lack any readily comprehended meaning.

B. Prophesying (v. 22) *propheteia* (Gk.)—To make inspired declarations of what is to come; also to teach. It does not always refer to telling the future.

Teacher Preparation

Unifying Principle—Build Up Your Neighbor. Communities function best when the members can articulate shared values. How do community members communicate their beliefs to one another? Paul exhorted the Corinthians to speak plainly so both believers *and* unbelievers could benefit from the leading of the Holy Spirit.

A. Read the Background and Devotional Readings.

B. Complete Lesson 9 in the *Precepts For Living Personal Study Guide®*.

C. Reread the Focal Verses in a modern translation.

O—Open the Lesson

A. Open with prayer.

B. Ask how many people have been at a service where someone spoke in tongues. Did they understand them?

C. Have students read Aim for Change and Keep in Mind.

D. Read the In Focus story and discuss.

P—Present the Scriptures

A. Ask for volunteers to read the Focal Verses and The People, Places, and Times. Discuss.

B. Read and discuss the Background section.

C. Encourage students to give thanks for the opportunity today to approach God through faith in Christ.

E—Explore the Meaning

A. Utilize groups of three to discuss the Lesson in Our Society and Make It Happen. Have one person take notes and then another present the notes to the group.

B. Connect these sections to Aim for Change and Keep in Mind verse.

N—Next Steps for Application

A. Summarize the lesson and theme from the Scriptures.

B. Close in prayer.

Worship Guide

For the Superintendent or Teacher
Theme: Seek the Good of Others
Song: "Endow Me"
Devotional Reading: Titus 3:8–14
Prayer

Seek the Good of Others

Bible Background • 1 CORINTHIANS 14:13–26
Printed Text • 1 CORINTHIANS 14:13–26 | Devotional Reading • TITUS 3:8–14

——————— Aim for Change ———————

By the end of the lesson, we will: RECOUNT what Paul says about the value of speaking in tongues; REALIZE the importance of speaking plainly in the company of others; and REAFFIRM strategies for effectively communicating the Gospel to both believers and unbelievers.

 In Focus

In the last two decades, the NBA (National Basketball Association) has recruited players from all over the world. Some of the players couldn't even speak English when they were recruited. However, because of their skill and talent in basketball, coaches were willing to work with them. As the recruits trained on the floor for basketball, they had to have a tutor teach them how to speak English. The players all knew that to stay on the team, they had to put the time in both on and off the court.

Some African players have stated that after a year on the team, they are able to speak English, communicate with their teammates, and read all of the necessary documents that will assist them in their careers as professional basketball players. For these players, in spite of their language barrier, it is a dream come true if they work hard and follow the rules.

When looking at our destiny, it is not always a clear path. Sometimes there are barriers that must be overcome and bridges that must be crossed. But with God's help and with our determination, we can walk in our destiny. In today's lesson, we learn about a barrier that hindered the church at Corinth.

JULY 27th

——————— Keep in Mind ———————

"How is it then, brethren? when ye come together, every one of you hath a psalm, hath a doctrine, hath a tongue, hath a revelation, hath an interpretation. Let all things be done unto edifying" (1 Corinthians 14:26).

"How is it then, brethren? when ye come together, every one of you hath a psalm, hath a doctrine, hath a tongue, hath a revelation, hath an interpretation. Let all things be done unto edifying" (1 Corinthians 14:26).

Focal Verses

KJV 1 **Corinthians 14:13** Wherefore let him that speaketh in an unknown tongue pray that he may interpret.

14 For if I pray in an unknown tongue, my spirit prayeth, but my understanding is unfruitful.

15 What is it then? I will pray with the spirit, and I will pray with the understanding also: I will sing with the spirit, and I will sing with the understanding also.

16 Else when thou shalt bless with the spirit, how shall he that occupieth the room of the unlearned say Amen at thy giving of thanks, seeing he understandeth not what thou sayest?

17 For thou verily givest thanks well, but the other is not edified.

18 I thank my God, I speak with tongues more than ye all:

19 Yet in the church I had rather speak five words with my understanding, that by my voice I might teach others also, than ten thousand words in an unknown tongue.

20 Brethren, be not children in understanding: howbeit in malice be ye children, but in understanding be men.

21 In the law it is written, With men of other tongues and other lips will I speak unto this people; and yet for all that will they not hear me, saith the Lord.

22 Wherefore tongues are for a sign, not to them that believe, but to them that believe not: but prophesying serveth not for them that believe not, but for them which believe.

23 If therefore the whole church be come together into one place, and all speak with tongues, and there come in those that are unlearned, or unbelievers, will they not say that ye are mad?

NLT 1 **Corinthians 14:13** So anyone who speaks in tongues should pray also for the ability to interpret what has been said.

14 For if I pray in tongues, my spirit is praying, but I don't understand what I am saying.

15 Well then, what shall I do? I will pray in the spirit, and I will also pray in words I understand. I will sing in the spirit, and I will also sing in words I understand.

16 For if you praise God only in the spirit, how can those who don't understand you praise God along with you? How can they join you in giving thanks when they don't understand what you are saying?

17 You will be giving thanks very well, but it won't strengthen the people who hear you.

18 I thank God that I speak in tongues more than any of you.

19 But in a church meeting I would rather speak five understandable words to help others than ten thousand words in an unknown language.

20 Dear brothers and sisters, don't be childish in your understanding of these things. Be innocent as babies when it comes to evil, but be mature in understanding matters of this kind.

21 It is written in the Scriptures: "I will speak to my own people through strange languages and through the lips of foreigners. But even then, they will not listen to me," says the LORD.

22 So you see that speaking in tongues is a sign, not for believers, but for unbelievers. Prophecy, however, is for the benefit of believers, not unbelievers.

23 Even so, if unbelievers or people who don't understand these things come into your church meeting and hear everyone

24 But if all prophesy, and there come in one that believeth not, or one unlearned, he is convinced of all, he is judged of all:

25 And thus are the secrets of his heart made manifest; and so falling down on his face he will worship God, and report that God is in you of a truth.

26 How is it then, brethren? when ye come together, every one of you hath a psalm, hath a doctrine, hath a tongue, hath a revelation, hath an interpretation. Let all things be done unto edifying.

speaking in an unknown language, they will think you are crazy.

24 But if all of you are prophesying, and unbelievers or people who don't understand these things come into your meeting, they will be convicted of sin and judged by what you say.

25 As they listen, their secret thoughts will be exposed, and they will fall to their knees and worship God, declaring, "God is truly here among you."

26 Well, my brothers and sisters, let's summarize. When you meet together, one will sing, another will teach, another will tell some special revelation God has given, one will speak in tongues, and another will interpret what is said. But everything that is done must strengthen all of you.

The People, Places, and Times

Corinthian Church. Most of the converts in the Corinthian church were Gentile, but some were Jewish. Many Christians were in the lower socio-economic class; however, there were some people with recognizable economic position and from a higher social class than most. It is believed that some Christians during this time were Gnostic because the attainment of special religious knowledge and wisdom was of great importance to them. This group of Christians also equated spirituality with spectacular kinds of spiritual gifts and the believers' present life was shifted from the hope for resurrection.

Background

This book was specifically written to deal with problems the Apostle Paul learned were endangering the believers' Christian lifestyles. The church's unity was being threatened, and the lack of discipline for a brother's incestuous relationship with his stepmother had caused an uproar among believers. The

church had sent Paul a letter asking about appropriate sexual relationships, marriage and divorce, eating foods sacrificed to idols, various aspects of Christian worship, speaking in tongues, the resurrection of the dead, and collections for the church in Jerusalem. So Paul took time to address the many issues of the growing churches in Corinth.

At-A-Glance

1. Making the Unknown Known
   (1 Corinthians 14:13–16)
2. Time to Grow (vv. 19–20)
3. Is Anybody Getting It? (vv. 22–23)
4. It's About the Masses (v. 26)

In Depth

1. Making the Unknown Known (1 Corinthians 14:13–16)

Paul acknowledged that we can pray in an unknown tongue. He wrote that when we pray that way, the mind doesn't comprehend, but can still give glory to God. A problem arises, however, if such praying is done in public settings. An unbeliever may visit the church and be confused because he doesn't understand what the person praying is saying. Paul here does not preclude the act of speaking in an unknown tongue. Rather, he encourages a balanced approach, exhorting the church to pray with both the Spirit and understanding. It appears that the church at Corinth misunderstood and misapplied this gift from God.

2. Time to Grow (vv. 19–20)

Paul encouraged the Corinthian believers to no longer be children in their thinking; they must mature. Church growth is not about numbers, but change and transforming hearts; it's about discipleship. When our focus turns to spiritual growth instead of attendance, we show signs of growth and maturity as a church. The enemy would have us to continue doing "church" the way we have done it for many years and not reach any more than before. However, when we realize that growth comes on the heels of change, we will direct our focus to reach everyone and not just those who have already heard and responded to the Word of God.

3. Is Anybody Getting It? (vv. 22–23)

When people speak in tongues and unbelievers are present, it can drive them away because of their lack of understanding. We must make our messages straightforward and our actions plain and clear so everyone can understand the Gospel message we want to tell them. We cause people to leave the church and Christ when we publicly present things (such as speaking in tongues) that many don't understand. When tongues are spoken in the gathering, does anybody get it? We have to wonder if even the person

who spoke in tongues understood what was said. Instead, prophesy is more desireable (which does not have to mean foretelling the future—the word also means to proclaim or teach) so all who hear can understand the message and be convicted by God's Word.

4. It's About the Masses (v. 26)

Paul reminded the Christians that when they come together, everyone has a hymn, doctrine, tongue, or revelation that they give, but it was time now to do things that would edify all. In other words, each must stop doing things that would only give them the glory, make them look good, or make them seem as if they were the only ones getting a revelation from the Lord. We must do things in the church that benefit everyone. It's not about us; it's all about the Lord. Every assignment we are given is greater than us. Jesus wants the masses to be able to be blessed by our songs, doctrine, and teachings.

Search the Scriptures

1. What reason does Paul give that the unlearned cannot say "Amen" (1 Corinthians 14:16)?

2. What would Paul rather speak so that his voice might teach others (v. 19)?

3. Tongues are a sign to whom (v. 22)?

Discuss the Meaning

How many times have you heard people speak in tongues? Did you understand what was said? Most likely not, if no interpreter was present, and probably no one else in the gathering understood either. If we are going to speak in a large group, shouldn't it be in a way that listeners can understand? When we speak in ways that they understand, we have a greater opportunity to reach the masses.

Lesson in Our Society

America is known as a cultural melting pot. We have people of all races, cultures, and ethnic backgrounds who comprise many of our communities. In striving for diversity in many companies, different people are brought together under one mission and vision. Over the years, when it's time for training and seminars, we have learned that it is best to have interpreters because everyone may not speak or understand English. It is quite unfair to assume that just because we speak a language, everyone else can. We have to find a way to cross the communication barrier so goals will be accomplished and the message will be understood.

It is the same way in the church. If we want people to receive a message, we must make sure that there is no barrier to their understanding. Speaking in tongues edifies the speaker, but not the group as a whole; it allows a person's spirit to speak, but who understands with no interpreter? When we prophesy and speak so everyone understands, we can reach more people with our message. Let us make sure that the message reaches the masses and proves to be for the good of all who hear it.

Make It Happen

Remember that the goal of the church is to give the message across the world that Jesus lived, died, and rose to save us from our sins. The message must be given where those who have not heard or responded to the Word can hear and understand it. We must always be sure to give the message in a way that listeners can understand, be convinced, and say "Amen."

Follow the Spirit

What God wants me to do:

_____

_____

_____

Remember Your Thoughts

Special insights I have learned:

_____

_____

_____

More Light on the Text

1 Corinthians 14:13–26

13 Wherefore let him that speaketh in an unknown tongue pray that he may interpret.

The Corinthian Christians, like many of us today, gave great sway to the mysteriousness and ecstasy of "speaking" (Gk. *laleo*, **lal-EH-o,** meaning to use words in order to declare one's mind and disclose one's thoughts) in an "unknown" (Gk. *glossa*, **gloce-SAH,** meaning the language or dialect used by a particular people distinct from that of other nations) tongue. Paul counseled those Christians who had the gift of *glossa* to also pray for the gift to interpret what was being said. It is noteworthy that Paul was teaching that spiritual gifts are not given in a package deal or fixed set, but that a believer can, by prayer, seek additional gifts.

14 For if I pray in an unknown tongue, my spirit prayeth, but my understanding is unfruitful. 15 What is it then? I will pray with the spirit, and I will pray with the understanding also: I will sing with the spirit, and I will sing with the understanding also.

Praying in an unknown tongue may enhance the spirit within an individual and produce a sense of zeal as the spirit rejoices, but it may produce no fruit with regard to "understanding" (Gk. *nous*, **nooce,** meaning the power of considering and judging soberly, calmly, and impartially). For Paul, understanding and intelligence went hand in hand, and he questioned the value of having the ability to speak in an unknown tongue if what was being said did not educate the speaker or listener. As an additional note, Paul singled out singing and prayer as activities that can also be coupled with the spirit. When exercised wholeheartedly, both activities greatly add to private and public worship.

16 Else when thou shalt bless with the spirit, how shall he that occupieth the room of the unlearned say Amen at thy giving of thanks, seeing he understandeth not what thou sayest? 17 For thou verily givest thanks well, but the other is not edified.

The ability to speak in tongues may be well and good for the individual as a means of praising God, but what real benefit is the gift if the speaker or listener does not understand what has been said? Paul asked how someone who may be an outsider, inexperienced believer ("occupieth the room of the unlearned"), or "unlearned" (Gk. *idiotes*, **id-ee-O-tace,** meaning uninformed person, or one without the gift) could be edified if they didn't know what was being said. The purpose of our public worship should be to build up the body of believers. Paul counseled that

speaking in tongues was not to be a personal pursuit in public discourse unless someone was also able to interpret.

18 I thank my God, I speak with tongues more than ye all: 19 Yet in the church I had rather speak five words with my understanding, that by my voice I might teach others also, than ten thousand words in an unknown tongue.

What a shock it must have been for the Corinthians to learn that Paul also spoke in tongues and perhaps more than all of them. Without that knowledge, it would have been easy for them to dismiss his counsel as one who was misguided or inexperienced. However, Paul did possess that spiritual gift, and now his counsel, as a premier leader within the Christian church, had to be given serious consideration. Paul's gift of speaking in an unknown tongue was not paraded in public for personal adulation, but was a private matter between himself and God. Paul used the gift as a means to express to God his deep joy of having his soul redeemed. For a public gathering in worship (the article "the" does not exist in the Greek, so Paul was saying "in church," meaning the assembled congregation and not a building), however, he would rather "speak" (Gk. *laleo*, **lal-EH-o,** meaning to utter articulate sounds) just five words that could be understood than ten thousand words that no one listening could know.

20 Brethren, be not children in understanding: howbeit in malice be ye children, but in understanding be men.

The innocence of childhood permits many offenses to be excused by an adult; childhood is a time for growth and development. By speaking to the Corinthians as "brethren" (Gk. *adelphos*, **ad-el-FOS,** meaning fellow believers united by the bond of affection), Paul began to soften his address to them by reminding them of their association as family. As growing believers, the Corinthians were to understand that in their activities there might be occasion to act childlike, but in their understanding, they were to mature and understand as a grown person would.

21 In the law it is written, With men of other tongues and other lips will I speak unto this people; and yet for all that will they not hear me, saith the Lord. 22 Wherefore tongues are for a sign, not to them that believe, but to them that believe not: but prophesying serveth not for them that believe not, but for them which believe.

In an effort to aid in the growth and development of the Corinthian believers and drive home his point, Paul quoted Isaiah 28:11. In that passage, God spoke through the Assyrian invaders (men with other tongues and other lips), who were the enemies of His holy people. The Jews probably did not understand the tongue of their invaders, so communications would have been difficult, if not impossible. In similar fashion, though God was with them, still the Jews would not "hear" (Gk. *eisakouo*, **ice-ak-OO-o,** meaning to give heed to, comply with admonition, to obey) Him. God was punishing the Jews for not heeding the prophet by allowing them to hear words that they did not understand—words of a nation that would conquer them (and obviously be of no benefit). So, too, there would be little benefit for those hearing the words of the Corinthian believers speaking in an unknown tongue if they were unable to understand. Speaking in an unknown tongue would have been a "sign" (Gk. *semeion*, **say-MI-on,** meaning that by which a person or a thing is distinguished from others and is known) to an outsider of God's favor and manifest presence as a

missionary expression, but "prophesying" (Gk. *propheteia*, **prof-ay-TI-ah,** meaning the gifts and utterances of these prophets, especially of their predictions of the works of them set apart to teach the Gospel) would have much more value to the congregation.

23 If therefore the whole church be come together into one place, and all speak with tongues, and there come in those that are unlearned, or unbelievers, will they not say that ye are mad?

Paul painted a picture for the Corinthians: the whole congregation coming together and everyone there speaking in an unknown tongue. Into this situation came the unlearned, immature, or "unbelievers" (Gk. *apistos*, **AP-is-tos**). These groups would look at those "with tongues" and think they had gone mad. Such was the impression given at Pentecost when God first gave the Spirit to the growing church in Jerusalem (see Acts 2), except at that time the apostles were most likely speaking in existing languages so the mixed crowd that had come together at Pentecost each heard the Gospel message in their own language. But a cacophony of unknown tongues would not be edifying to the body of believers or helpful to the unbelievers who might come into their midst.

24 But if all prophesy, and there come in one that believeth not, or one unlearned, he is convinced of all, he is judged of all: 25 And thus are the secrets of his heart made manifest; and so falling down on his face he will worship God, and report that God is in you of a truth.

A church in which the gift of prophecy is bestowed upon all of its members appears to be the type of church preferred by the Apostle Paul. Prophecy is the gift of God to speak forth by divine inspiration and has the power to "convince" (Gk. *elegcho*, **el-ENG-kho,** meaning by conviction to bring to the light) and even aid in the judgment of any who might hear. A purpose of the prophetic word is to help expose the inner man and thus are the "secrets" (Gk. *kruptos*, **kroof-AY-os,** meaning hidden things) of his "heart" (Gk. *kardia*, **kar-DEE-ah,** meaning the soul or mind, as it is the fountain and seat of the thoughts, passions, desires, appetites, affections, purposes, or endeavors) made manifest. One who accepts and believes will respond by surrendering to God's instruction. These verses provide a glimpse into the more intimate workings of the church of Paul's understanding and desire, and help explain his preference for the gift of prophecy over speaking in unknown tongues.

26 How is it then, brethren? when ye come together, every one of you hath a psalm, hath a doctrine, hath a tongue, hath a revelation, hath an interpretation. Let all things be done unto edifying.

Finally, Paul counseled that when the Christian body in Corinth had "come together," probably for the purpose of worship, each member should come prepared to participate in some way, even if simply to agree with the member who had brought a "psalm" (Gk. *psalmos*, **psal-MOS,** meaning a pious song or the striking of chords of a musical instrument), a "doctrine" (Gk. *didache*, **did-akh-AY,** meaning the act of teaching or offering instruction), a tongue, an "interpretation" (Gk. *hermeneia*, **her-may-NI-ah,** meaning an understanding of what has been spoken more or less obscurely by others), or a "revelation" (Gk. *apokalupsis*, **ap-ok-AL-oop-sis,** meaning a disclosure of truth, instruction). In all things, however, their purpose was to be for the "edifying" (Gk. *oikodome*, **oy-kod-om-AY,** meaning the strengthening or building up) of the body of Christ.

Sources:
"Corinthians." *Harper's Bible Dictionary.* Edited by Paul J. Achtemeier. San Francisco: HarperCollins, 1985.
Drane, John. *Introducing the New Testament.* Minneapolis: Fortress Press, 2001.
Dunn, James D. G. and John W. Rogerson. *Commentary on the Bible.* Grand Rapids, MI: Wm. B. Eerdmans Publishing Company, 2003.
The Holy Bible: Pilgrim Edition (KJV). New York: Oxford University Press, Inc., 1952.
Howley, Bruce and Ellison Howley. *The New Layman's Bible Commentary.* Grand Rapids, MI: Zondervan, 1979.
Keener, Craig S. *The IVP Bible Background Commentary: New Testament.* Downers Grove, IL: IVP Academic, 1994.
Myers, Allen C., John W. Simpson, Philip A. Frank, Timothy P. Jenney, and Ralph W. Vunderink, eds. *The Eerdmans Bible Dictionary.* Grand Rapids, MI: Wm. B. Eerdmans Publishing Company, 1996.

Say It Correctly

Incestuous. in-**SES**-choo-uhs.
Edified. **ED**-uh-fide.

Daily Bible Readings

MONDAY
Imitate What is Good
(3 John 2–12)

TUESDAY
Doing the Right Thing
(James 4:13–17)

WEDNESDAY
Complete in Everything Good
(Hebrews 13:16–21)

THURSDAY
Devoted to Good Works
(Titus 3:8–14)

FRIDAY
So All Learn and are Encouraged
(1 Corinthians 14:27–33)

SATURDAY
All Done Decently and in Order
(1 Corinthians 14:37–40)

SUNDAY
Praying with Spirit and Mind
(1 Corinthians 14:13–26)

Notes

_____

_____

_____

_____

Teaching Tips

Words You Should Know

A. Tribulation (2 Corinthians 1:4) *thlipsis* (Gk.)—pressure, oppression, affliction.

B. Delivered (v.10) *rhyomai* (Gk.)—to draw to oneself, to rescue.

Teacher Preparation

Unifying Principle—Knowing Someone Cares. In times of trouble, communities may seek consolation and protection from some power beyond themselves. What consolation do Christians receive when seeking assistance from a higher power? Paul gave testimony of God's consolation in times of hardship and gave thanks for the mutual consolation that comes from praying for one another.

A. Begin preparation time with prayer.

B. Use Bible study aids by reading The People, Places, and Times and Background.

O—Open the Lesson

A. Have a volunteer read the In Focus story. Ask for volunteers to describe consolation they received when seeking assistance from God.

B. Introduce the Aim for Change and Words You Should Know.

P—Present the Scriptures

A. Present information from The People, Places, and Times and Background based on notes taken during teacher preparation time.

B. Have volunteers read the Focal Verses, emphasizing the Keep in Mind text.

C. Follow up with questions from Search the Scriptures.

D. Present information from In Depth based on notes taken during teacher preparation time.

E—Explore the Meaning

A. Have students respond to the questions found in the Discuss the Meaning section. You may ask for volunteers in smaller group settings. For a larger number of students, have the discussion take place in pairs or groups.

B. Direct students to the Lesson in Our Society section. Read aloud or summarize.

N—Next Steps for Application

A. Direct students to the Make It Happen section. Read aloud or summarize.

B. The facilitator or volunteer should close the time together with prayer.

AUG 3rd

Worship Guide

For the Superintendent or Teacher
Theme: Consolation Granted
Through Prayer
Song: "The Prayer"
Devotional Reading: Psalm 46
Prayer

Consolation Granted Through Prayer

Bible Background • 2 CORINTHIANS 1:3–11
Printed Text • 2 CORINTHIANS 1:3–11 | Devotional Reading • PSALM 46

Aim for Change

By the end of the lesson, we will: DISCERN Paul's meaning in explaining reliance on God during affliction; SENSE the joy of resting in God's protection and consolation; and DETERMINE how we can extend the loving concern that God has for us to others.

In Focus

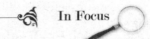

The honeymoon didn't last long for newlyweds Wesley and Nia. They were both unemployed only twelve months after exchanging their marriage vows. Nia had resigned her position two months prior to take care of their newborn. Unexpectedly, Wesley was laid off.

For the next eighteen months, they were only able to find temporary jobs. They felt their financial burdens would overwhelm them. They were sure only their faith in God would get them through this, but they were often too tired to pray.

They studied together, prayed for others, and experienced the joy of abiding in Christ again once they joined a small Bible discussion group at church. It was so life-changing they volunteered to facilitate the next class. Within the next two weeks, Wesley was offered a position that included a title promotion and twice his previous salary. This allowed him to minister to others in the group who may have felt the same burden he felt while unemployed.

In today's lesson, we will explore how believers can rely on God and one another during a time of crisis.

Keep in Mind

"And our hope of you is stedfast, knowing, that as ye are partakers of the sufferings, so shall ye be also of the consolation" (2 Corinthians 1:7).

"And our hope of you is stedfast, knowing, that as ye are partakers of the sufferings, so shall ye be also of the consolation" (2 Corinthians 1:7).

Focal Verses

KJV **2 Corinthians 1:3** Blessed be God, even the Father of our Lord Jesus Christ, the Father of mercies, and the God of all comfort;

4 Who comforteth us in all our tribulation, that we may be able to comfort them which are in any trouble, by the comfort wherewith we ourselves are comforted of God.

5 For as the sufferings of Christ abound in us, so our consolation also aboundeth by Christ.

6 And whether we be afflicted, it is for your consolation and salvation, which is effectual in the enduring of the same sufferings which we also suffer: or whether we be comforted, it is for your consolation and salvation.

7 And our hope of you is stedfast, knowing, that as ye are partakers of the sufferings, so shall ye be also of the consolation.

8 For we would not, brethren, have you ignorant of our trouble which came to us in Asia, that we were pressed out of measure, above strength, insomuch that we despaired even of life:

9 But we had the sentence of death in ourselves, that we should not trust in ourselves, but in God which raiseth the dead:

10 Who delivered us from so great a death, and doth deliver: in whom we trust that he will yet deliver us;

11 Ye also helping together by prayer for us, that for the gift bestowed upon us by the means of many persons thanks may be given by many on our behalf.

NLT **2 Corinthians 1:3** All praise to God, the Father of our Lord Jesus Christ. God is our merciful Father and the source of all comfort.

4 He comforts us in all our troubles so that we can comfort others. When they are troubled, we will be able to give them the same comfort God has given us.

5 For the more we suffer for Christ, the more God will shower us with his comfort through Christ.

6 Even when we are weighed down with troubles, it is for your comfort and salvation! For when we ourselves are comforted, we will certainly comfort you. Then you can patiently endure the same things we suffer.

7 We are confident that as you share in our sufferings, you will also share in the comfort God gives us.

8 We think you ought to know, dear brothers and sisters, about the trouble we went through in the province of Asia. We were crushed and overwhelmed beyond our ability to endure, and we thought we would never live through it.

9 In fact, we expected to die. But as a result, we stopped relying on ourselves and learned to rely only on God, who raises the dead.

10 And he did rescue us from mortal danger, and he will rescue us again. We have placed our confidence in him, and he will continue to rescue us.

11 And you are helping us by praying for us. Then many people will give thanks because God has graciously answered so many prayers for our safety.

The People, Places, and Times

2 Corinthians. The Apostle Paul wrote this letter to the Corinthians around 56 A.D. Paul, who was first called Saul, was a Jew from the city of Tarsus, which served as the capital of Cilicia in the eastern part of Asia Minor (Acts 21:39), and a Roman citizen (22:25). Saul persecuted Jesus' disciples until he was blinded during an encounter with Christ on the road to Damascus. The Lord declared him a "chosen vessel unto me, to bear my name before the Gentiles, and kings, and the children of Israel: For I will shew him how great things he must suffer for my name's sake" (from 9:15–16). Afterward, his sight was restored, and he was filled with the Holy Spirit and baptized.

Background

The Apostle Paul wrote letters to the Corinthian church to provide theological clarity concerning essential church doctrines in an effort to help them mature in their faith. The Corinthian church was one of the churches Paul established on his second missionary journey with Silas and Timothy between 50 and 55 A.D. Consequently, the Apostle Paul's letters to the Corinthian church were written in Ephesus and Macedonia, respectively, during his third missionary journey, which took place before the end of that same decade.

The multicultural Corinthian church was zealous and prosperous but error prone. Struggling with influences from the larger society, the diverse congregation of Jews, Greeks, and other Gentiles faced challenges with bigotry, idle philosophizing, and sexual depravity. While Paul was on his third missionary journey in Ephesus, he received an unfavorable report concerning immorality and division in the Corinthian church. Some members of the church sought advice from the Apostle Paul on how to deal with problems in their congregation. In response, Paul wrote his first letter to the Corinthians to address questions about marriage, idol sacrifices, spiritual gifts, and charitable collections. Paul learned of the church's reaction to his letter in Macedonia from Titus. Although many had adjusted their beliefs and practices to align with Paul's advice, there were still some who refused to yield to Paul's authority and teachings. So within a year of the first, Paul penned another letter defending his credibility and motives.

At-A-Glance

1. Blessings for God's Provision of Comfort (2 Corinthians 1:3–7)
2. Paul's Trials Teach Reliance on God (vv. 8–11)

In Depth

1. Blessings for God's Provision of Comfort (2 Corinthians 1:3–7)

The Apostle Paul began this second letter to the Corinthian church by blessing God's name. Paul stated that God, being compassionate and merciful, provides comfort for His followers in troubled times. This comfort is not only supposed to be focused inward, but also directed outward to encourage others.

Paul then described how his suffering for the Gospel's sake was for their gain. He described an interdependence where he and the Corinthians mutually shared in both the suffering and comfort of Christ. The result was not despair, but a steadfast hope in their ability to be comforted by a secure or guaranteed source—God.

2. Paul's Trials Teach Reliance on God (vv. 8–11)

Paul's theology of suffering was developed here in the form of a theodicy—a defense of divine attributes such as compassion, omnipresence, and omnipotence in the face of moral and physical evil. Here, and in the previous verses, Paul provided a redemptive suffering argument. Redemptive suffering presents honorable reasons for and good outcomes from suffering. Paul said trials in ministry taught him to rely solely on God and allowed him to exhort and preach salvation to the Corinthians and others. These types of arguments have traditionally been widely accepted in the African American church. Paul ended this news about his trials with confidence that he and his traveling companions would continue to be delivered from deadly troubles with the assistance of the prayers of the Corinthian church.

Search the Scriptures

1. What did Paul identify as some of the attributes of God (2 Corinthians 1:3)?

2. What does God provide for those who experience trouble (v. 4)?

Discuss the Meaning

It can be difficult to continue in faith or ministry while facing constant or severe adversity. What did Paul say are the benefits of his suffering? How do you reconcile God's divine attributes, such as compassion, with troubles you've experienced?

Lesson in Our Society

You should make room for a theology of suffering in your life because you will experience trials in life and ministry. Beware: Christians without a sound theology of suffering will eventually find themselves in a danger zone! The shock, disappointment, and disillusionment of a trial can lead to them abandoning their commitments or covenant relationships (i.e., faith, marriage, etc.) and relying on indicators of success instead of God.

Make It Happen

Often when we receive comfort from God, we take it in without ever turning it outward to others. Identify opportunities to turn your suffering into someone else's comfort and encouragement. Decide what vehicle exists within your church or community to support you in this endeavor.

Follow the Spirit

What God wants me to do:

_____

_____

_____

_____

Remember Your Thoughts

Special insights I have learned:

_____

_____

_____

_____

More Light on the Text

2 Corinthians 1:3–11

3 Blessed be God, even the Father of our Lord Jesus Christ, the Father of mercies, and the God of all comfort; 4 Who comforteth us in all our tribulation, that we may be able to comfort them which are in any

trouble, by the comfort wherewith we ourselves are comforted of God.

Paul began this letter to the Corinthians with a eulogy instead of thanksgiving, as was his custom. He used the Greek word *eulogētos* (**yoo-log-ay-TOS**), an adjective meaning praised or blessed. In the New Testament, this word was only applied to God. Paul described God as a parent who takes pity and shows mercy. He also used the Greek word *paraklesis* (**par-AK-lay-sis**), meaning to help, exhort, or console. Trouble, in this context, is grievous affliction or distress from external sources. The Greek word Paul used is *thlipsis* (**thlip-sis**), referring to pressure or burden upon one's spirit.

5 For as the sufferings of Christ abound in us, so our consolation also aboundeth by Christ. 6 And whether we be afflicted, it is for your consolation and salvation, which is effectual in the enduring of the same sufferings which we also suffer: or whether we be comforted, it is for your consolation and salvation. 7 And our hope of you is stedfast, knowing, that as ye are partakers of the sufferings, so shall ye be also of the consolation.

Paul identified the interdependence of the body of Christ that allowed the Corinthian believers to benefit from his suffering and him to benefit from their prayers. He described a situation where he and others were excessively sharing in the sufferings and comforts of Christ. Endurance brought patience. The Greek word *hupomone* (**hoop-om-on-AY**) means to patiently abide under suffering with a steadfast hope that expects to obtain a good result. It refers to the quality of not surrendering to circumstances or succumbing under trial.

8 For we would not, brethren, have you ignorant of our trouble which came to us in Asia, that we were pressed out of measure, above strength, insomuch that we despaired even of life: 9 But we had the sentence of death in ourselves, that we should not trust in ourselves, but in God which raiseth the dead.

Paul's introduction of new information by saying that he did not want the reader to be ignorant was common practice in first-century writings. Paul encountered trouble in the province of Asia he felt powerless to withstand. He despaired because he found himself utterly without direction or resources. He felt condemned. This happened so his confidence could be placed with God only.

Paul's writings demonstrate that his apostleship was characterized by affliction and hardship. Although it sounds foolish in hindsight, many in Paul's audience may have questioned his apostleship and authority because he was experiencing trials instead of success. Theodicy of suffering can be a challenge in wealthy societies where a prosperity theology dominates. Many scholars believe this was the case in Corinth. It is also likely true in contemporary American culture. A dissonance exists because the prevailing mentality is characterized by egocentrism, continual self-betterment, and a success orientation. There is an expectation of a progressive (good, better, best) trajectory in all of our experiences. Believers should make room for a theology of suffering in their lives because they will experience trials in life and ministry.

10 Who delivered us from so great a death, and doth deliver: in whom we trust that he will yet deliver us; 11 Ye also helping together by prayer for us, that for the gift bestowed upon us by the means of many

persons thanks may be given by many on our behalf.

Paul continued to highlight their interdependence and their shared goal of bringing God glory. He testified of God's deliverance. The Greek word Paul used for deliverance is *rumoi* (**RHOO-om-ahee**), which means to draw out of danger or calamity and liberate. He also spoke of his continued confidence in God's intention to rescue him with their help. Here, the power of intercessory prayer is highlighted. He gave yet another example of how they mutually supported one another through the power of intercessory prayer, which brings glory to God.

Sources:

Blue Letter Bible. BlueLetterBible.org. http://www.blueletterbible.org/ (accessed November 24, 2012).

Elwell, Walter A. and Robert W. Yarbrough. *Encountering the New Testament: A Historical and Theological Survey.* Grand Rapids, MI: Baker Books, 1998.

Garland, David E. *The New American Commentary: An Exegetical and Theological Exposition of Holy Scripture, 2 Corinthians, Vol. 29.* Nashville: Holman Reference: 1999.

The Hebrew-Greek Key Study Bible (KJV). Chattanooga: AMG Publishers, 1991.

Packer, J. I., Merrill C. Tenney, and William White, Jr. eds. *Nelson's Illustrated Encyclopedia of Bible Facts.* Nashville: Thomas Nelson Publishers, 1998.

Vine, W. E. *Vine's Expository Dictionary of New Testament Words.* Nashville: Thomas Nelson Publishers, 2003.

Zodhiates, Spiros, ed. *The Complete Word Study Dictionary: New Testament.* Chattanooga, TN: AMG Publishing, 1992.

Say It Correctly

Tribulation. trib-yuh-**LEY**-shuhn.
Bestowed. bih-**STOHED**.

Daily Bible Readings

MONDAY
Our Refuge and Strength
(Psalm 46)

TUESDAY
The Shield of Your Help
(Deuteronomy 33:24–29)

WEDNESDAY
O Lord, We Rely on You
(2 Chronicles 14:1–12)

THURSDAY
Support the Weak
(Acts 20:28–35)

FRIDAY
Admonish, Encourage, Help, and Do Good
(1 Thessalonians 5:12–22)

SATURDAY
A Cause for Giving Thanks
(Philemon 3–7)

SUNDAY
The God Who Consoles Us
(2 Corinthians 1:3–11)

Notes

Teaching Tips

Words You Should Know

A. Overcharge (2 Corinthians 2:5) *epibareo* (Gk.)—To be heavy upon, to be expensive to.

B. Forgive (v. 7) *kharidzomai* (Gk.)—To excuse for a fault or an offense; pardon.

Teacher Preparation

Unifying Principle—Restored Relationships. When a person violates the rules of a community, he or she may be ostracized or rejected. How can the offender be restored to wholeness within the community? Paul told the Corinthians to forgive the one who had caused them grief so the entire community might heal again.

A. Read the Bible Background and Devotional Readings.

B. Complete Lesson 11 in the *Precepts For Living Personal Study Guide*®.

C. Reread the Focal Verses in a modern translation.

O—Open the Lesson

A. Open with prayer.

B. Ask how many people have ever had to forgive someone.

C. Have someone share one of their forgiveness stories.

D. Have students read the Aim for Change, Keep in Mind verse, and In Focus.

P—Present the Scriptures

A. Ask for volunteers to read the Focal Verses and The People, Places, and Times. Discuss.

B. Read and discuss the Background section.

E—Explore the Meaning

A. Discuss the Lesson in Our Society and Make It Happen.

B. Connect these sections to the Aim for Change and the Keep in Mind verse.

N—Next Steps for Application

A. Have students role-play a forgiveness situation/scenario. Partner them and let one person be the forgiver and the other be the forgiven. Then have them switch roles.

B. Summarize the lesson and themes from Scripture.

C. Close with prayer.

Worship Guide

For the Superintendent or Teacher
Theme: A Community Forgives
Song: "Lord I Lift Your Name On High"
Devotional Reading: Luke 17:1–6

AUG
10th

A Community Forgives

Bible Background • 2 CORINTHIANS 1:23–2:11
Printed Text • 2 CORINTHIANS 1:23–2:11 | Devotional Reading • LUKE 17:1–6

Aim for Change

By the end of the lesson, we will: GRASP Paul's message to the Corinthians about the connection among people in a community; GAUGE the influence of harm or benefit to one person in a community on the whole group; and GENERATE a list of people to pray for who may need forgiveness for harming others.

In Focus

John and Jack were best friends growing up. They wore the same style of clothes. They were baptized together in church. They even dated sisters from the cheerleading squad together. There was nothing John wouldn't do for his buddy Jack.

One night after a senior event at the school, John bought some beers and asked Jack to ride with him to meet some other friends. While riding, John and Jack both drank but didn't think it would affect their ability to drive. The unthinkable happened: An 18-wheeler collided with their truck as they turned at a traffic light. John was injured, but Jack died upon arrival to the hospital.

Many in the community blamed John for taking Jack's life, their town's star quarterback. Some pushed for him to be charged with murder. John didn't feel like he could go on. He needed forgiveness and the opportunity to be reconciled with everyone who had loved Jack as much as he did.

We are all instructed to forgive as God has forgiven us. In today's lesson, we will consider Paul's instruction for the community to exercise forgiveness and know when a person has been punished enough.

Keep in Mind

"To whom ye forgive any thing, I forgive also: for if I forgave any thing, to whom I forgave it, for your sakes forgave I it in the person of Christ"
(2 Corinthians 2:10).

"To whom ye forgive any thing, I forgive also: for if I forgave any thing, to whom I forgave it, for your sakes forgave I it in the person of Christ" (2 Corinthians 2:10).

Focal Verses

KJV **2 Corinthians 1:23** Moreover I call God for a record upon my soul, that to spare you I came not as yet unto Corinth.

24 Not for that we have dominion over your faith, but are helpers of your joy: for by faith ye stand.

2:1 But I determined this with myself, that I would not come again to you in heaviness.

2 For if I make you sorry, who is he then that maketh me glad, but the same which is made sorry by me?

3 And I wrote this same unto you, lest, when I came, I should have sorrow from them of whom I ought to rejoice; having confidence in you all, that my joy is the joy of you all.

4 For out of much affliction and anguish of heart I wrote unto you with many tears; not that ye should be grieved, but that ye might know the love which I have more abundantly unto you.

5 But if any have caused grief, he hath not grieved me, but in part: that I may not overcharge you all.

6 Sufficient to such a man is this punishment, which was inflicted of many.

7 So that contrariwise ye ought rather to forgive him, and comfort him, lest perhaps such a one should be swallowed up with overmuch sorrow.

8 Wherefore I beseech you that ye would confirm your love toward him.

9 For to this end also did I write, that I might know the proof of you, whether ye be obedient in all things.

10 To whom ye forgive any thing, I forgive also: for if I forgave any thing, to whom I forgave it, for your sakes forgave I it in the person of Christ;

NLT **2 Corinthians 1:23** Now I call upon God as my witness that I am telling the truth. The reason I didn't return to Corinth was to spare you from a severe rebuke.

24 But that does not mean we want to dominate you by telling you how to put your faith into practice. We want to work together with you so you will be full of joy, for it is by your own faith that you stand firm.

2:1 So I decided that I would not bring you grief with another painful visit.

2 For if I cause you grief, who will make me glad? Certainly not someone I have grieved.

3 That is why I wrote to you as I did, so that when I do come, I won't be grieved by the very ones who ought to give me the greatest joy. Surely you all know that my joy comes from your being joyful.

4 I wrote that letter in great anguish, with a troubled heart and many tears. I didn't want to grieve you, but I wanted to let you know how much love I have for you.

5 I am not overstating it when I say that the man who caused all the trouble hurt all of you more than he hurt me.

6 Most of you opposed him, and that was punishment enough.

7 Now, however, it is time to forgive and comfort him. Otherwise he may be overcome by discouragement.

8 So I urge you now to reaffirm your love for him.

9 I wrote to you as I did to test you and see if you would fully comply with my instructions.

10 When you forgive this man, I forgive him, too. And when I forgive whatever needs to be forgiven, I do so with Christ's authority for your benefit,

11 so that Satan will not outsmart us. For we are familiar with his evil schemes.

11 Lest Satan should get an advantage of us: for we are not ignorant of his devices.

The People, Places, and Times

Pride at Corinth. The believers in the church in Corinth dealt with pride, jealousy, selfishness, and immorality. There was rivalry between people in leadership, and they had formed rival groups. Their concerns for the church were sex and marriage, paying apostles, and living with pagans.

Background

This book is considered the tearful letter from Paul to the people of Corinth. It was written with much anguish to address the immediate concerns of the church. Paul was expected to come to Corinth and deal with the issues in person, but instead he sent this letter to address the people's concerns. This letter to Corinth was to clarify his apostolic commission as well as his continued care for them as the church.

At-A-Glance

1. Respect Where Christians Are
   (2 Corinthians 1:23–24)
2. Challenging Corrections (2:3–4)
3. When Enough is Enough (vv. 6–7)
4. Avoiding Satanic Schemes (vv. 8–11)

In Depth

1. Respect Where Christians Are (2 Corinthians 1:23–24)

Paul clearly explained to the people that it wasn't that he didn't want to come in person and assist with their troubles; he felt it would spare the pain of correction if he sent answers to their concerns by letter. Here Paul made

clear he had a tremendous amount of respect for the growth and faith of the Christians in Corinth. He understood that growing in a relationship with the Lord is a process that takes time. While on the journey, a lot of mistakes are made and many questions must be answered, especially when you have come from another faith tradition or culture and are now a follower of Christ.

Today, the church must meet people where they are on their journey. Every Christian is not at the same point: We have new converts, baby Christians, teenage Christians, mature Christians, and senior Christians. With all the different places people find themselves in their walk with the Lord, the church leadership has to find a way to encourage them where they are, while at the same time bringing correction that will move them to the next level in their walk with the Lord. At all times, the leadership must expect great things for those who are growing in the Lord, just as Paul expected for the people of Corinth.

2. Challenging Corrections (2:1–4)

Paul went into more detail about what he personally experienced in writing this letter to them. He informed the people that he had pain in writing the letter; he shed tears. In no way did he mean to cause them pain; he simply wanted to show his love in addressing the concerns in their letter. Today, many leaders are challenged with bringing correction to the body of Christ. Correction is not easy when you love the people and you understand where they are on their journey. Correction is not easy when people may be offended by what you say instead of seeing the love with which you mean it. In the church today, correction for Christians is a challenge. With all of the "feel good" Gospel that Christians watch on television, hear on the radio, and read in the top-selling books, who wants to be corrected? God would not have His children go uncorrected. Paul told the truth about how they should live and treat one another. Even at the cost of shedding tears, if we know that other Christians are struggling and going astray in their lives, it is our duty to bring correction to them to help them back onto the right path.

3. When Enough is Enough (vv. 5–7)

Paul informed the Christians that the majority was able to decide on the punishment for the offender and he was satisfied with the punishment given. Paul asked that they now forgive and encourage the offender, because if they didn't, he might experience excessive sorrow. Many times in our churches when we institute rules about offenses, we make the Christian do the time for the crime, but then we don't offer love and forgiveness once it is over. As the body of Christ, we must begin to assure Christians that in spite of their wrongdoings, God loves them and so do we. We must be intentional in demonstrating that we are prepared to support, encourage, and even reinstate them back into the church and to the fellowship of believers after they have done their time. God is a forgiving God. We, too, have been forgiven, cleansed, and washed of our sins. Therefore, as God has forgiven us, we should forgive others.

4. Avoiding Satanic Schemes (v. 8–11)

The Corinthians are asked here to reaffirm their love for their forgiven brother. Paul reminded the Christians that they were dealing with an enemy force. He asked them not to allow Satan to get the advantage over them. The enemy still uses small things to separate the body of Christ. He uses unexpected things to keep Christians from being forgiven and reconciled. That's why we must never give the enemy any space in our lives or in the church. We must not allow unforgiveness to enter into our hearts or the church. We must send a clear message that forgiveness is at the forefront of who we are as the church and the body of Christ.

Search the Scriptures

1. Why did Paul encourage the people to forgive the offender who had been earlier recommended for punishment (2 Corinthians 2:7)?

2. What should be reaffirmed to the offender by the people (v. 8)?

3. Why did Paul say that forgiveness is so important among believers (v. 11)?

Discuss the Meaning

Do people forgive one another today? Can we ask God to forgive us when we can't forgive others? If we are going to live happily in community with others, then why aren't we willing to forgive and allow time served to clear people of their sins? If it were our family member who needed forgiveness, wouldn't we want that person to be forgiven? Satan should not get the joy of plaguing our community with unforgiveness; we must forgive as Christ forgives.

Lesson in Our Society

In America we have a penal system that deals with people who have committed crimes. Often after the person is released, society still penalizes him or her for the crime. People with prison records often cannot find jobs, get grants or assistance to further their education, find decent housing, or attain certain licenses for business. In essence, even though they have served their sentence, they will continue to be punished. If that is the case, what is the use of letting them out of prison if they are going to continue to be imprisoned by society? Our churches can be places of refuge for these people. We can forgive their sins and help to reinstate them to citizenship in our communities. It is just by the grace of God that our sins have not been charged to us by society. Surely we have not done everything right or are without any sin in our lives. Once time is served, let us not add additional time to those who ought to be free. Let us open our hearts, community, and church to those who need us the most.

Make It Happen

Remember where you were when you first got saved and received Jesus into your heart? Remember how many mistakes you made even after that? Reflect on how sin still comes into your mind. Understand how you constantly need forgiveness for the wrongs that you do. After understanding your life and seeing how others are just like you, begin to forgive others and advocate for them to be restored in the community and church.

Follow the Spirit

What God wants me to do:

_____

_____

_____

_____

Remember Your Thoughts

Special insights I have learned:

_____

_____

_____

_____

More Light on the Text

2 Corinthians 1:23–2:11

23 Moreover I call God for a record upon my soul, that to spare you I came not as yet unto Corinth.

Scholars believe that this letter was written between six and eighteen months after the writing of the first letter to the Corinthians (and it is possible that this is not the second letter, but actually the third one, with a previous letter now lost). In 1:15, Paul indicated to the Corinthian church that he would visit them (it is not certain how many earlier visits had taken place); however, he had delayed and now explained why. He had not come because he did not want to visit the Corinthian church and punish its members. Rather, he delayed his visit so he could "spare" (Gk. *pheidomai*, **FI-dom-ahee,** meaning to abstain or to treat leniently) the congregation the pain of a harsh reprimand. This letter to the church served to express Paul's sincerity and love for the church. In order to convince the Corinthian believers that he was being truthful, Paul called upon God "for a record" (Gk. *martus*, **MAR-toos,** meaning to be a witness in a legal sense) and pledged this truthfulness upon his very "soul" (Gk. *psuche*, **psoo-KHAY,** meaning that in which there is life, an essence which differs from the body). Paul wanted to convince the Corinthians that there was no self-interest or fickleness in his delay.

24 Not for that we have dominion over your faith, but are helpers of your joy: for by faith ye stand.

As an apostle of Jesus Christ, Paul had the authority to deal with the wrongs he believed existed within the Corinthian church, but that was not his desire. Rather, he assured the believers that the liberty they had found through their faith in Christ placed them on equal standing. Paul had no wish to exercise apostolic "dominion" (Gk. *kurieuo*, **ko-ree-YOO-o,** meaning to exercise influence upon or to have power over) over the congregation or minimize their freedom. Rather, Paul explained that he had come alongside as a partner or "helper" (Gk. *sunergos*, **soon-er-GOS,** meaning companion in labor) in the church's ministry. The tender tone of Paul's words in this verse was meant to assure the Corinthians that he wanted to help increase their "joy" (Gk. *chara*, **khar-AH,** meaning gladness or cheerfulness). This is probably one of the highest privileges a Christian leader can have. When done in love, even a reprimand or rebuke can increase joy in a believer. Paul's gentle tone resulted from the fact that the response from the Corinthian believers to his first letter had been obedience. Nothing had caused their "faith" (Gk. *pistis*, **PIS-tis,** meaning a belief respecting man's relationship to God and divine things, generally with the included idea of trust and holy fervor) to waver and the church continued to "stand" (Gk. *histemi*, **HIS-tay-mee,** meaning to fix or establish) firm in the truth of the Gospel.

2:1 But I determined this with myself, that I would not come again to you in heaviness. 2 For if I make you sorry, who is he then that maketh me glad, but the same which is made sorry by me?

Paul repeated the sentiment that he shared in 1:23. Rather than visit the Corinthian church knowing that his visit would be painful to both, he had decided not to visit at all. Certain disorders had sprung up in the Corinthian church that Paul needed to address, and there is a hint that he had visited the congregation earlier to correct the problem. However, Paul's visit at that time had caused hurt and pain within the church and he did not want that to happen again. For that reason, Paul "determined" (Gk. *krino*, **KREE-no,** meaning to resolve or decree) within himself that he would follow a different course. He wanted his next visit with the Corinthians to be agreeable to both. He truly loved the Corinthians. If he joined them in feeling sorrow for his presence, who would bring any joy or cheer?

3 And I wrote this same unto you, lest, when I came, I should have sorrow from them of whom I ought to rejoice; having confidence in you all, that my joy is the joy of you all.

So instead of a painful personal visit, Paul wrote a letter to the Corinthian church. Scholars generally agree that the two letters to the Corinthians we have in our Bible were probably two of four letters. The first one was lost; the second is our book of 1 Corinthians; the third letter was lost; the fourth letter is our book of 2 Corinthians. In one of the lost letters, Paul probably wrote with regards to an individual in the congregation who was involved in an incestuous relationship. Paul's instruction to the church was to excommunicate the offending member and reform their behavior in general. Apostolic leadership is never easy and Paul knew that a return visit to the believers in Corinth would result in the need for him to severely discipline the church, which would cause great "sorrow" (Gk. *lupe*, **LOO-pay,** meaning grief or affliction) both for himself and them.

Paul wanted the church to discipline itself and the offending member before he came to visit so that all could avoid the pain of his rebuke. "Having confidence in you all" was Paul's way of expressing his belief that the general character of the church and its inhabitants was that they wanted to do the proper thing. Rather than being sorrowful at Paul's visit, they would want to share one another's joy. There is great tenderness in Paul's approach to the Corinthian church.

4 For out of much affliction and anguish of heart I wrote unto you with many tears; not that ye should be grieved, but that ye might know the love which I have more abundantly unto you.

Paul deeply loved all the Christians under his charge, but "more abundantly" (Gk. *perissoteros*, **per-is-sot-ER-oce,** meaning more earnestly, more exceedingly) showed a very special "love" (Gk. *agape*, **ag-AH-pay,** meaning affection or good will) for the Corinthians. It pained him deeply to have to write to the Corinthian church in this manner, but he knew that in order for the believers to continue to grow in Christ and for the church to progress, the sin they had permitted in their midst had to be dealt with. So with deep "anguish" (Gk. *sunoche*, **soon-okh-AY,** meaning a narrowing) of heart and many "tears," Paul wrote his letter to the church knowing it would be difficult for them to read. Paul's objective was not to hurt the church, but he wanted them to know that if pain resulted from the reading of his letter, then he would share it as well.

5 But if any have caused grief, he hath not grieved me, but in part: that I may not overcharge you all.

There was no cowardly fear emanating from Paul. He had enemies within the congregation at Corinth, but that did not deter him from addressing his concerns head-on. The offender, probably the same individual who had been involved in the incestuous marriage (cf. 1 Corinthians 5:1), is not named. Rather, Paul sought not to add further injury and used the phrase "if any have caused grief." Again, Paul's love and tenderness were revealed as he pointed out that the situation in the Corinthian church, though grievous, had not been taken personally. He was only grieved "in part" (Gk. *meros*, **MER-os,** meaning in some respect). Paul did not point fingers or name names because he did not wish his rebuke to be heavier than necessary. To punish the church was not his objective; for that reason, he did not "overcharge" (Gk. *epibareo*, **ep-ee-bar-EH-o,** meaning to put a burden upon) the Corinthian believers with their need to punish, nor did he seek to have the wrongdoer alienated forever from the fellowship of the congregation.

6 Sufficient to such a man is this punishment, which was inflicted of many. 7 So that contrariwise ye ought rather to forgive him, and comfort him, lest perhaps such a one should be swallowed up with overmuch sorrow. 8 Wherefore I beseech you that ye would confirm your love toward him.

The whole congregation had suffered because of the sin of one man, and the man has been punished. The church had obviously heeded Paul's earlier admonition to deal with the sin and excommunicated the wrongdoer. Paul did not wish permanent damage to the reputation of the wrongdoer, and since the wrongdoer had been repentant, Paul counseled the church to forgive him, comfort him, and welcome him back into their fellowship. He wanted to ensure that the offender not be "swallowed up" or consumed with his sorrow. It is probable that the wrongdoer had friends within the fellowship who did not take kindly to the letter's words regarding their friend and rose up against the apostle, but Paul's heartfelt desire had always been that the congregation would correct the offense and continue to abide in their love for one another. Paul's use of "beseech" (Gk. *parakeleo*, **par-ak-al-EH-o,** meaning to exhort or beg) reinforced his desire that both the wrongdoer and the church know how much he was affectionately disposed toward them.

9 For to this end also did I write, that I might know the proof of you, whether ye be obedient in all things. 10 To whom ye forgive any thing, I forgive also: for if I forgave any thing, to whom I forgave it, for your sakes forgave I it in the person of Christ;

Paul expanded his explanation to the Corinthians as to why he wrote instead of visiting. The "proof" (Gk. *dokime*, **dok-ee-MAY,** meaning proving, trial, or test) Paul wanted was to see if the church would act without his having to oversee them. They passed his test, and now he was satisfied that they respected his authority. Now that they had been obedient and done the proper things, he wanted the church to know that the forgiveness they extended, he also extended. Paul did this not for the sake of the offender but for the sake of the unity and purity of the congregation. And the forgiveness Paul extended, he did so in the "person" or presence of Christ to whom he knows he will have to answer.

11 Lest Satan should get an advantage of us: for we are not ignorant of his devices.

No stranger to the wiles of "Satan" (Gk. *Satanas*, **sat-an-AS,** meaning the name given to the prince of evil spirits, the adversary of God and Christ), Paul did not want to offer any opportunity for the great adversary of the Christian church to subvert its growth and development. Paul counseled the congregation at Corinth to not be "ignorant

of his devices" but to forgive and restore in the spirit of sincere love. Paul did not state what he believed Satan's advantage might be, but he did not want to open the door to any possibility.

Sources:

Drane, John. *Introducing The New Testament.* Minneapolis: Fortress Press, 2001.

Dunn, James D. G. and John W. Rogerson. *Commentary on the Bible.* Grand Rapids, MI: Wm. B. Eerdmans Publishing Co., 2003.

The Holy Bible: Pilgrim Edition (KJV). New York: Oxford University Press, Inc., 1952.

Howley, Bruce and Ellison Howley. *The New Layman's Bible Commentary.* Grand Rapids, MI: Zondervan, 1979.

Keener, Craig S. *The IVP Bible Background Commentary: New Testament.* Downers Grove, IL: IVP Academic, 1994.

Knowles, Andrew. *The Bible Guide.* London: Lion Publishing, 2006.

Myers, Allen C., John W. Simpson, Philip A. Frank, Timothy P. Jenney, and Ralph W. Vunderink, eds. *The Eerdmans Bible Dictionary.* Grand Rapids, MI: Wm. B. Eerdmans Publishing Company, 1996.

Say It Correctly

Contrariwise. kon-**TRER**-ee-wise.

Daily Bible Readings

MONDAY
Sin and Forgiveness
(Acts 13:36–41)

TUESDAY
Confession and Forgiveness
(1 John 1:5–10)

WEDNESDAY
Repentance and Forgiveness
(Luke 17:1–6)

THURSDAY
Redemption and Forgiveness
(Ephesians 1:3–10)

FRIDAY
Grace and Justification
(Romans 5:15–21)

SATURDAY
Speaking as People of Sincerity
(2 Corinthians 2:12–17)

SUNDAY
Forgiving and Consoling
(2 Corinthians 1:23–2:11)

Notes

_____

_____

_____

_____

Teaching Tips

Words You Should Know

A. Perplexed (2 Corinthians 4:8) *aporeo* (Gk.)—To be without resources, to be in straits, to be left wanting, to be embarrassed, to be in doubt, to not know which way to turn.

B. Grace (v. 15) *charis* (Gk.)—Good will, loving-kindness, favor; of the merciful kindness by which God, exerting His holy influence upon souls, turns them to Christ; keeps, strengthens, increases them in Christian faith, knowledge, and affection; and kindles them to the exercise of the Christian virtues.

Teacher Preparation

Unifying Principle—Down But Not Out. Communities rely on one another for protection and continuity of life. Where does the ability to protect and continue the community come from? Paul reminded the Corinthians that the extraordinary power to proclaim Jesus in the face of adversity is a treasure that comes from God through Jesus Christ.

A. Pray that God will give you insight into His Word as you study.

B. Read the entire lesson, then complete the companion lesson in the *Precepts For Living Personal Study Guide®*.

O—Open the Lesson

A. Open with prayer, including the Aim for Change.

B. Have your students read the Aim for Change and Keep in Mind verses together. Discuss.

P—Present the Scriptures

A. Have volunteers read the Focal Verses.

B. Use The People, Places and Times; Background; Search the Scriptures; At-A-Glance outline; In Depth; and More Light on the Text to clarify the verses.

E—Explore the Meaning

A. Divide the class into groups to discuss the Discuss the Meaning, Lesson in Our Society, and Make It Happen sections. Tell the students to select a representative to report their responses.

B. Connect these sections to the Aim for Change and the Keep in Mind verses.

N—Next Steps for Application

A. Summarize the lesson.

B. Close with prayer.

Worship Guide

For the Superintendent or Teacher
Theme: Treasure in Clay Jars
Song: "I Need You To Survive"
Devotional Reading: Jude 17–25
Prayer

Treasure in Clay Jars

Bible Background • 2 CORINTHIANS 4:2–15
Printed Text • 2 CORINTHIANS 4:2–15 | Devotional Reading • JUDE 17–25

Aim for Change

By the end of the lesson, we will CONSIDER Paul's position in seeing himself as a slave for Christ's sake; CONTEMPLATE goodness in relation to God and community; and COUNT on God's power to work through us to do His will in ministry to others.

In Focus

The past year had been the worst of Juron's life. He was in a terrible car accident that left him facing months of painful rehabilitation. Juron knew that God would see him through this difficult time, but sometimes he felt alone and desperate. Determined to keep trusting God, Juron began to consciously thank Him for His blessings. As Juron praised God for his home, his wife, his church, and his children, he began to think about others who were worse off than himself.

Juron knew he couldn't physically go out and help other people, but he could let God use him in a different way. Juron asked his pastor for a list of names and addresses of people who were hospitalized, in a nursing home, or in jail. He began to pray for these people on a regular basis and began to write letters of encouragement to each one. Soon, he began to receive letters back from people who were encouraged in their relationship with God or had come to know Christ through Juron's testimony of God's faithfulness.

God calls each believer to spread the Gospel. Today we will learn that we are God's servants, and He will give us the power to serve Him despite our weaknesses or circumstances.

Keep in Mind

AUG 17th

"We are troubled on every side, yet not distressed; we are perplexed, but not in despair; Persecuted, but not forsaken; cast down, but not destroyed" (2 Corinthians 4:8–9).

"We are troubled on every side, yet not distressed; we are perplexed, but not in despair; Persecuted, but not forsaken; cast down, but not destroyed" (2 Corinthians 4:8–9).

Focal Verses

KJV **2 Corinthians 4:2** But have renounced the hidden things of dishonesty, not walking in craftiness, nor handling the word of God deceitfully; but by manifestation of the truth commending ourselves to every man's conscience in the sight of God.

3 But if our gospel be hid, it is hid to them that are lost:

4 In whom the god of this world hath blinded the minds of them which believe not, lest the light of the glorious gospel of Christ, who is the image of God, should shine unto them.

5 For we preach not ourselves, but Christ Jesus the Lord; and ourselves your servants for Jesus' sake.

6 For God, who commanded the light to shine out of darkness, hath shined in our hearts, to give the light of the knowledge of the glory of God in the face of Jesus Christ.

7 But we have this treasure in earthen vessels, that the excellency of the power may be of God, and not of us.

8 We are troubled on every side, yet not distressed; we are perplexed, but not in despair;

9 Persecuted, but not forsaken; cast down, but not destroyed;

10 Always bearing about in the body the dying of the Lord Jesus, that the life also of Jesus might be made manifest in our body.

11 For we which live are always delivered unto death for Jesus' sake, that the life also of Jesus might be made manifest in our mortal flesh.

12 So then death worketh in us, but life in you.

13 We having the same spirit of faith, according as it is written, I believed, and therefore have I spoken; we also believe, and therefore speak;

NLT **2 Corinthians 4:2** We reject all shameful deeds and underhanded methods. We don't try to trick anyone or distort the word of God. We tell the truth before God, and all who are honest know this.

3 If the Good News we preach is hidden behind a veil, it is hidden only from people who are perishing.

4 Satan, who is the god of this world, has blinded the minds of those who don't believe. They are unable to see the glorious light of the Good News. They don't understand this message about the glory of Christ, who is the exact likeness of God.

5 You see, we don't go around preaching about ourselves. We preach that Jesus Christ is Lord, and we ourselves are your servants for Jesus' sake.

6 For God, who said, "Let there be light in the darkness," has made this light shine in our hearts so we could know the glory of God that is seen in the face of Jesus Christ.

7 We now have this light shining in our hearts, but we ourselves are like fragile clay jars containing this great treasure. This makes it clear that our great power is from God, not from ourselves.

8 We are pressed on every side by troubles, but we are not crushed. We are perplexed, but not driven to despair.

9 We are hunted down, but never abandoned by God. We get knocked down, but we are not destroyed.

10 Through suffering, our bodies continue to share in the death of Jesus so that the life of Jesus may also be seen in our bodies.

11 Yes, we live under constant danger of death because we serve Jesus, so that the life of Jesus will be evident in our dying bodies.

14 Knowing that he which raised up the Lord Jesus shall raise up us also by Jesus, and shall present us with you.

15 For all things are for your sakes, that the abundant grace might through the thanksgiving of many redound to the glory of God.

12 So we live in the face of death, but this has resulted in eternal life for you.

13 But we continue to preach because we have the same kind of faith the psalmist had when he said, "I believed in God, so I spoke."

14 We know that God, who raised the Lord Jesus, will also raise us with Jesus and present us to himself together with you.

15 All of this is for your benefit. And as God's grace reaches more and more people, there will be great thanksgiving, and God will receive more and more glory.

The People, Places, and Times

Jars of Clay. Clay was a common commodity in the Mediterranean, and earthen vessels made of clay were strictly utilitarian, considered almost disposable. Clay jars were ordinary, relatively fragile, and of little value compared to the more beautiful and enduring bronze vessels of the day. A clay jar would be thrown away if it was flawed or became ceremonially unclean. In biblical times, people would sometimes hide their treasures in clay jars, thinking that thieves would assume that an ugly earthen jar would hold nothing of value.

Background

Paul's opponents accused him of not acting or preaching like a "true" apostle—that he was weak, unauthoritative, and didn't possess the oratorical skills of some of the false teachers of the day. In addition, these false teachers accused Paul of misusing funds, implying that because he had to change his planned visit to the Corinthian church, he could not be trusted to keep his word.

Paul countered these accusations by reminding the Corinthians that God had miraculously intervened in his life and chose him as an apostle (1:1; Acts 9:15). He also urged the Corinthian believers to remember his demeanor and behavior while he lived and worked among them. He freely admitted that he was not a polished orator, but reminded the church that his knowledge of the Gospel and his personal integrity were more important than masterful delivery of a speech (2 Corinthians 10:10–11, 11:6). Paul also reiterated that his humble demeanor was modeled after Jesus' example and that Christ's power was more clearly seen because of Paul's weakness (11:30, 12:9–10).

At-A-Glance

1. The Gospel (2 Corinthians 4:2–6)
2. The Trials (vv. 7–11)
3. The Hope (vv. 12–15)

In Depth

1. The Gospel (2 Corinthians 4:2–6)

In these verses, Paul continued to refute his opponents, who were apparently accusing him of being underhanded or deceitful. He appealed to the Christians to examine their consciences and to remember that he had always been truthful with them and taught the Gospel plainly. He asserted that if anyone did not understand the truth of the Gospel, it was because they had been blinded by the "god of this world" (v. 4). Only people who have embraced the new covenant of Jesus Christ and have come to salvation can understand spiritual truth. Satan's plan is to prevent people from comprehending and therefore receiving the truth.

Paul reiterated that he did not preach to build his popularity, but because he sought to serve others on behalf of Jesus. He was imitating Jesus, who humbled Himself as a servant in order to secure our redemption (Philippians 2:5–8).

2. The Trials (vv. 7–11)

In verse 7, Paul pointed out that God has chosen to use frail humans to accomplish His will. This is a striking juxtaposition—flawed, fragile, and ugly pots holding the greatest treasure of all, the light and hope of the Gospel. Because Paul had committed himself as a slave to Christ, he shared in His suffering. The various hardships and persecution he endured were a constant reminder of his human frailty and of God's power. Though he was jailed, beaten, and falsely accused, Paul's enemies were not able to destroy him.

Paul said that he always carried around or bore in his physical body the death of Jesus Christ, not forgetting the sacrifice that He made. Paul had learned to die daily to his flesh so Jesus' resurrection power could be revealed in him.

3. The Hope (vv. 12–15)

Paul's willingness to suffer as a servant of Christ brought great benefit to the Christian believers at Corinth. He reminded them that his hardships were part of the cost he paid as a servant to bring the light of the Gospel to them (v. 12). Then, quoting from Psalm 116:10, Paul said along with the psalmist that he was compelled to tell others what God had done for him. His own story of deliverance, suffering, and servanthood had only served

to make him more certain of his position in Christ. He exalted in the promise that one day, every believer will be resurrected to stand in God's presence with all the saints.

Paul was encouraged that his labor and suffering were not in vain. Many Corinthians had come to know Christ, and the kingdom of God was advancing. More and more people were gaining salvation as the Corinthians shared their faith and, as a result, God was receiving glory.

Search the Scriptures

1. How did Paul maintain a clear conscience before his opponents (2 Corinthians 4:2)?

2. Why did Paul remind the Corinthians that God created light out of darkness (v. 6)?

Discuss the Meaning

God gives believers the power they need to carry out His work even in the midst of hardship and trials.

1. What is the main task that God gives to every believer?

2. How do our struggles and trials enable others to more clearly see Jesus' power?

Lesson in Our Society

Self-sacrifice and service to others are not very popular these days. People seek to please themselves and are willing to go to great lengths to satisfy their desires. As believers, we must reject self-absorption and accept our responsibility to put our own fleshly wants aside in order to serve others. When we receive Jesus as Savior and Lord, we accept the amazing gift of salvation, but with that gift comes responsibility to share the Gospel of Christ with others, no matter the cost. The only way we are able to accomplish this is to allow His power to work in us, despite (and even through) our human weaknesses.

Make It Happen

On a sheet of paper, list those things you see as your own personal weaknesses or disadvantages. Perhaps you have a physical disability. Perhaps you are out of work or don't own a vehicle. Maybe you struggle to control your temper.

God wants to show Himself powerful in the things you consider "weak." Make a commitment to yourself and to God for Him to work through you to reach others with the Gospel, no matter your frailties or problems.

Follow the Spirit

What God wants me to do:

_____

_____

_____

_____

Remember Your Thoughts

Special insights I have learned:

_____

_____

_____

_____

More Light on the Text

2 Corinthians 4:2–15

2 But have renounced the hidden things of dishonesty, not walking in craftiness, nor handling the word of God deceitfully; but by manifestation of the truth commending ourselves to every man's conscience in the sight of God.

When proclaiming the Word of God, Paul had been accused of "craftiness" (Gk. *panourgia*, **pan-oorg-EE-ah,** meaning cunning or a specious or false wisdom) and now began his defense. Mays offers the suggestion that the accusations were being made by other "apostles" in Corinth who were challenging Paul's authority. The word used here to accuse Paul is the same word that was used to describe Satan's deception of Eve in the Garden of Eden (cf. 11:3). Paul asserted that unlike Satan, he did not walk in craftiness and had renounced the "hidden things" (Gk. *kryptos*, **kroop-TOS,** meaning concealed or secret). Rather, he sought to speak the truth of God's Word exactly as it is. Paul believed that this Word is powerful and, when presented directly and unadulterated, has the ability to prick the "conscience" (Gk. *suneidesis*, **soon-I-day-sis,** meaning distinguishing between what is morally good and bad, prompting to do the former and shun the latter, commending one, condemning the other). Paul was ever mindful that he preached "in the sight of God" and for that reason alone sought to be above reproach in how he conducted the responsibilities of his ministry.

3 But if our gospel be hid, it is hid to them that are lost: 4 In whom the god of this world hath blinded the minds of them which believe not, lest the light of the glorious gospel of Christ, who is the image of God, should shine unto them.

Paul reminded the Corinthians that Satan had not been absent but continually worked to "blind" (Gk. *tuphloo*, **toof-LO-o,** meaning to blunt the mental discernment) their minds. That is the reason that the truth of the Gospel was hidden from them. Satan, "the god of this world," or the prince of this present age, was not desirous that the light of the Gospel (Gk. *euaggelion*, **yoo-ang-GEL-ee-on,** meaning the proclamation of the grace of God manifest and pledged in Christ) should shine on them. Still, their unbelief did not diminish the truth that Christ is God (cf. Hebrews 1:3). As the "image of God" (Gk. *eikon*, **i-KONE,** meaning likeness seen on account of His divine nature and absolute moral excellence), Paul wanted the Corinthians to understand that the light of Christ's "glorious" (Gk. *doxa*, **DOX-ah,** meaning a thing belonging to God) Gospel, when received, can pierce the veil of Satan's darkness.

5 For we preach not ourselves, but Christ Jesus the Lord; and ourselves your servants for Jesus' sake.

One could be tempted to think that a learned man like Paul, with the type of education and training he had received and his ability to draw a crowd, would get caught up in the fame and say whatever the crowd wanted to hear. But Paul's experience on the Damascus Road (cf. Acts 9:1–9) where he met Christ Jesus (Gk. *Iesous*, **ee-ay-SOOCE,** meaning Jesus, the Son of God, the Savior of mankind, God incarnate) so affected him that he presented himself as a "servant" (Gk. *doulos*, **DOO-los,** meaning one devoted to another to the disregard of one's own interests) to the Corinthians for Christ's sake. Because of Christ and the mission with which Paul was charged, he would not flatter the people with flowery words, wit, or charm. His purpose was to show Christ and not himself.

6 For God, who commanded the light to shine out of darkness, hath shined in our hearts, to give the light of the knowledge of the glory of God in the face of Jesus Christ. 7 But we have this treasure in earthen vessels, that the excellency of the power may be of God, and not of us.

Paul drew the Corinthians' attention back to the beginning of God's creation, when He pierced the darkness that encased the earth and caused light to shine through (cf. Genesis 1:3). In the same fashion, He gave Jesus Christ to the world. For any who would look, the knowledge of God's glory could be seen in Christ's face, which reflected the light of God's glory. Now Christ the light, which pierced Paul's darkness of heart on the Damascus Road, shone forth to pierce the darkness of any who would believe. Paul explained that the "treasure" (Gk. *thesauros*, **thay-sow-ROS,** meaning the place in which good and precious things are collected and laid up) of this knowledge was entrusted to "earthen" (Gk. *ostrakinos*, **os-TRA-kin-os,** meaning clay with a suggestion of frailty) vessels or human bodies made of dirt as another means for displaying the "excellency" (Gk. *huperbole*, **hoop-er-bol-AY,** meaning beyond all measure) of God's great power.

8 We are troubled on every side, yet not distressed; we are perplexed, but not in despair; 9 Persecuted, but not forsaken; cast down, but not destroyed;

Paul had become used to being a hunted man. Because of his witness for Christ, he constantly had to flee from one city to another for his own safety (cf. Matthew 10:23). Even now upon his return to Corinth and within the church he founded, he had accusers who questioned his motives. In the face of such treatment, one would be tempted toward discouragement, but Paul shared in four powerful statements his faith and trust in the supremacy of God's great power. Though "troubled" (Gk. *thlibo*, **THLEE-bo,** meaning to press hard upon), Paul was not distressed. Though "perplexed" (Gk. *aporeo*, **ap-or-EH-o,** meaning to be without resources or to be left wanting), he was not in despair. God had always provided for Paul's sustenance and well-being. His trials only served to reinforce his faith in Christ. Paul knew "persecution" (Gk. *dioko*, **dee-O-ko,** meaning to make to run or flee, to put to flight) firsthand and had even been "cast down" (Gk. *kataballo*, **kat-ab-AL-lo,** meaning to throw to the ground) as though dead, but had been able to raise himself up and continue on (cf. Acts 14:19–20). He knew that God would never "forsake" (Gk. *egkataleipo*, **eng-kat-al-I-po,** meaning to leave in straits or helpless) him.

also experience a constant dying as we are "delivered" (Gk. *paradidomi*, **par-ad-ID-o-mee,** meaning to give over into the hands of) to death. This should not be surprising for the believer, for God the Father sees all those who believe in Christ as having died with Him (cf. 5:14). This He does for our sake so that the life that is through Christ can be made "manifest" (Gk. *phaneroo*, **fan-er-O-o,** meaning has made plain or evident) in our mortal bodies for all the world to see. Such sacrifice is to the service of humanity and the glory of God.

10 Always bearing about in the body the dying of the Lord Jesus, that the life also of Jesus might be made manifest in our body. 11 For we which live are always delivered unto death for Jesus' sake, that the life also of Jesus might be made manifest in our mortal flesh.

Paul tried to help them understand that Christ's purpose on earth—to redeem mankind—involved a constant "dying" (Gk. *nekrosis*, **NEK-ro-sis,** meaning being put to death) on the Lord's part. The Lord Jesus had constantly been the target of Jewish leadership who sought His earthly life. Even so, Christ spent His physical energies and spiritual strength in the service of those He came to save. Christ knew sleepless nights and emotional distress. In a sense, His death upon Calvary's cross was but the culmination of the dying process He had been experiencing until He reached Golgotha. Christ endured this gradual dying so that in His resurrection, His life could show forth in the bodily ministry of those who believed in Him.

Paul understood this gradual dying because he lived daily under the constant threat of death. He explained that like Christ, we who live and belong to Christ

12 So then death worketh in us, but life in you. 13 We having the same spirit of faith, according as it is written, I believed, and therefore have I spoken; we also believe, and therefore speak;

Paul's daily physical suffering and dying was to be seen for the benefit of the Corinthians. As he emulated the life and ministry of Christ, so they too were to emulate this example, daily dying so that it might work to the benefit of life. Paul then reminded the Corinthians of the teaching of Psalm 116:10. The writer of that psalm knew affliction, but that did not deter him from speaking. Paul wanted the Corinthian church to understand that to speak even in the midst of suffering and affliction was true evidence of having "believed" (Gk. *pisteuo*, **pist-YOO-o,** meaning to trust in Jesus or God as able to aid either in obtaining or in doing something) and would serve to strengthen faith. Paul's encouragement to the Corinthians was for them to "speak" (Gk. *laleo*, **lal-EH-o,** meaning to use words in order to declare).

14 Knowing that he which raised up the Lord Jesus shall raise up us also by Jesus, and shall present us with you.

For Paul, everything found its purpose in the Lord Jesus. Like Jesus, Paul could know suffering and rejoice in it. Like Jesus, Paul could give his life in ministry and self-sacrifice. Because of Jesus, Paul believed that God would bring him and all other believers to newness of life. Death would have no hold. Life on earth, no matter how unpleasant, would have found a purpose that served humanity and also brought honor to God. In the end, Paul promised to the Corinthians that they would all be together in the presence of God. This Paul "knew" (Gk. *eido*, **I-do,** meaning to be confident of). It is a confidence we also can share.

15 For all things are for your sakes, that the abundant grace might through the thanksgiving of many redound to the glory of God.

Everything Christ accomplished and everything Paul sought to accomplish had one grand end: to bring glory to God. On the strength of the abundant grace bestowed upon him, even in the midst of his sufferings and trials, Paul gave thanks, believing that as a result, many others would also come to God with "thanksgiving" (Gk. *eucharistia*, **yoo-khar-is-TEE-ah,** meaning gratitude; actively grateful to God as an act of worship). The worship and thanksgiving would then "redound" (Gk. *perisseuo*, **per-is-SYOO-o,** meaning to overflow) to the glory of God.

Sources:
"*aporeo.*" Blue Letter Bible. BlueLetterBible.org. http://www.blueletterbible.org/ (accessed January 12, 2013).
Arrington, French L., Roger Stronstad, and Timothy Jenney, eds. *Life in the Spirit New Testament Commentary*. Grand Rapids, MI: Zondervan, 1999. 921–22, 935–37.
"*charis.*" Blue Letter Bible. BlueLetterBible.org. http://www.blueletterbible.org/ (accessed January 12, 2013).
Dunn, James D. G. and John W. Rogerson. *Commentary on the Bible*. Grand Rapids, MI: Wm. B. Eerdmans Publishing Co., 2003.
The Holy Bible: Pilgrim Edition (KJV). New York: Oxford University Press, Inc., 1952.
Howley, Bruce and Ellison Howley. *The New Layman's Bible Commentary*. Grand Rapids, MI: Zondervan, 1979.
Keener, Craig S. *The IVP Bible Background Commentary: New Testament*. Downers Grove, IL: IVP Academic, 1994. 451–52, 499.
NIV Study Bible (NIV). Grand Rapids, MI: Zondervan Publishing House, 1995. 1762, 1768.

Say It Correctly

Manifestation.
man-uh-fuh-**STEY**-shuhn.
Redound. ri-**DOUND**.

Daily Bible Readings

MONDAY
Enduring Troubles and Calamities
(Psalm 71:17–24)

TUESDAY
Finding Grace in the Wilderness
(Jeremiah 31:1–6)

WEDNESDAY
Sharing Christ's Sufferings and Glory
(1 Peter 4:12–19)

THURSDAY
Standing Fast in God's True Grace
(1 Peter 5:8–14)

FRIDAY
Walking in Truth and Love
(2 John 1–9)

SATURDAY
Waiting for the Lord's Mercy
(Jude 17–25)

SUNDAY
Proclaiming Jesus Christ as Lord
(2 Corinthians 4:2–15)

Teaching Tips

Words You Should Know

A. Bowels (2 Corinthians 6:12) *splangchnon* (Gk.)—Intestines (the heart, liver, lungs, etc.).

B. Enlarged (v. 13) *platyno* (Gk.)—Make broad.

Teacher Preparation

Unifying Principle—Addressing Tensions. Sometimes the community may ignore the good done by a great leader and become estranged. What must be done to end separation of a community from its leaders? Paul reminded the Corinthians of all he had done for the sake of Jesus Christ, and based on that testimony, he asks that they be reconciled to him.

A. Ask God to help you examine your relationships. If there is conflict in a relationship(s), ask God to help you reconcile with the individual(s).

B. Pray for the presence of the Holy Spirit to help you guide the class into a healing posture.

O—Open the Lesson

A. Begin with prayer.

B. Ask for a volunteer to read the In Focus section.

C. Discuss how relationships become distant.

P—Present the Scriptures

A. Ask for volunteers to read the Focal Verses and The People, Places, and Times. Discuss.

B. Discuss the pastor's responsibility to lovingly admonish the church when needed.

E—Explore the Meaning

A. Ask students to share the most insightful point they have learned and how they would use it to reconcile with someone.

B. Ask students to think of ways they could work to heal conflicts in families and personal relationships.

N—Next Steps for Application

A. Summarize the lesson.

B. Close in prayer, thanking God for His ministry of reconciliation.

Worship Guide

For the Superintendent or Teacher
Theme: An Appeal for Reconciliation
Song: "Didn't You Know"
Devotional Reading:
2 Corinthians 5:16–21
Prayer

An Appeal for Reconciliation

Bible Background • 2 CORINTHIANS 6:1–13, 7:2–4
Printed Text • 2 CORINTHIANS 6:1–13, 7:2–4
Devotional Reading • 2 CORINTHIANS 5:16–21

Aim for Change

By the end of the lesson, we will: ACKNOWLEDGE Paul's estrangement he felt from the Corinthians and assess his reaction to it; FEEL the need to heal estrangement within the church fellowship; and ARTICULATE ways to end any misunderstandings and estrangements and list ways to restore health to the community.

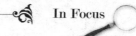 **In Focus**

Murray Bowen (1913–1990), an expert in family relationships, wrote, "An average family situation in our society today is one in which people maintain a distant and formal relationship with the family of origin, returning home for duty visits at infrequent intervals." This quote is what Murray and many experts who study family relationships describe as "cutoff." Experts further explain "cutoff" as the result of unresolved disagreements and conflicts. Instead of coming together to resolve the strained relationship, individuals choose to remain apart from each other.

Not surprisingly, because "cutoff" affects many of our relationships, it also exists in the family of Christ—the church. Unresolved conflicts and disagreements have at times led to denominations splitting within a Christian community. Effective communication is just as important—if not more important—in the body of Christ in order to effect the change necessary in our society.

In today's lesson, we find Paul's attempt at healing the "cutoff" that characterized his relationship with the Corinthian church.

Keep in Mind

"Receive us; we have wronged no man, we have corrupted no man, we have defrauded no man"(2 Corinthians 7:2).

AUG
24th

"Receive us; we have wronged no man, we have corrupted no man, we have defrauded no man" (2 Corinthians 7:2).

Focal Verses

KJV **2 Corinthians 6:1** We then, as workers together with him, beseech you also that ye receive not the grace of God in vain.

2 (For he saith, I have heard thee in a time accepted, and in the day of salvation have I succoured thee: behold, now is the accepted time; behold, now is the day of salvation.)

3 Giving no offence in any thing, that the ministry be not blamed:

4 But in all things approving ourselves as the ministers of God, in much patience, in afflictions, in necessities, in distresses,

5 In stripes, in imprisonments, in tumults, in labours, in watchings, in fastings;

6 By pureness, by knowledge, by long suffering, by kindness, by the Holy Ghost, by love unfeigned,

7 By the word of truth, by the power of God, by the armour of righteousness on the right hand and on the left,

8 By honour and dishonour, by evil report and good report: as deceivers, and yet true;

9 As unknown, and yet well known; as dying, and, behold, we live; as chastened, and not killed;

10 As sorrowful, yet alway rejoicing; as poor, yet making many rich; as having nothing, and yet possessing all things.

11 O ye Corinthians, our mouth is open unto you, our heart is enlarged.

12 Ye are not straitened in us, but ye are straitened in your own bowels.

13 Now for a recompence in the same, (I speak as unto my children,) be ye also enlarged.

7:2 Receive us; we have wronged no man, we have corrupted no man, we have defrauded no man.

NLT **2 Corinthians 6:1** As God's partners, we beg you not to accept this marvelous gift of God's kindness and then ignore it.

2 For God says, "At just the right time, I heard you. On the day of salvation, I helped you." Indeed, the "right time" is now. Today is the day of salvation.

3 We live in such a way that no one will stumble because of us, and no one will find fault with our ministry.

4 In everything we do, we show that we are true ministers of God. We patiently endure troubles and hardships and calamities of every kind.

5 We have been beaten, been put in prison, faced angry mobs, worked to exhaustion, endured sleepless nights, and gone without food.

6 We prove ourselves by our purity, our understanding, our patience, our kindness, by the Holy Spirit within us, and by our sincere love.

7 We faithfully preach the truth. God's power is working in us. We use the weapons of righteousness in the right hand for attack and the left hand for defense.

8 We serve God whether people honor us or despise us, whether they slander us or praise us. We are honest, but they call us impostors.

9 We are ignored, even though we are well known. We live close to death, but we are still alive. We have been beaten, but we have not been killed.

10 Our hearts ache, but we always have joy. We are poor, but we give spiritual riches to others. We own nothing, and yet we have everything.

3 I speak not this to condemn you: for I have said before, that ye are in our hearts to die and live with you.

4 Great is my boldness of speech toward you, great is my glorying of you: I am filled with comfort, I am exceeding joyful in all our tribulation.

11 Oh, dear Corinthian friends! We have spoken honestly with you, and our hearts are open to you.

12 There is no lack of love on our part, but you have withheld your love from us.

13 I am asking you to respond as if you were my own children. Open your hearts to us!

7:2 Please open your hearts to us. We have not done wrong to anyone, nor led anyone astray, nor taken advantage of anyone.

3 I'm not saying this to condemn you. I said before that you are in our hearts, and we live or die together with you.

4 I have the highest confidence in you, and I take great pride in you. You have greatly encouraged me and made me happy despite all our troubles.

The People, Places, and Times

Aquila and Priscilla. In A.D. 49, Emperor Claudius expelled all Jews from Rome. Under the expulsion order, Aquila and his wife, Priscilla, traveled to Corinth. In the same year while in Corinth, Paul met Aquila and Priscilla, who shared his profession of making tents and working with leather (Acts 18:2). Aquila and Priscilla were prominent and affluent members of the Corinthian church. They apparently owned a large house capable of accommodating a church and might have been prosperous enough to have been able to lease a building large enough to serve as both their home and a shop.

Background

The passage brings to light that the relationship between Paul and the believers at Corinth was strained. With deep longing to resolve the conflict, Paul wrote, "Make room for us in your hearts" (from 2 Corinthians 7:2, NIV). In the entire biblical history of God's people, He has had to admonish His chosen ones—sometimes severely. In continuity with the prophets of old, Paul's pastoral ministry sometimes called for admonition of individuals, and other times of an entire congregation. In 7:8, we find clues of what had transpired between Paul and the Corinthians that now required reconciliation. Paul wrote, "For even if I made you sorry with my letter, I do not regret it; though I did regret it. For I perceive that the same epistle made you sorry, though only for a while" (NKJV). Scholars are not clear what "sorrowful letter" Paul was referring to, but the passage makes clear that the content of Paul's letter to the Corinthians caused pain to both parties.

At-A-Glance

1. Integrity of Belief and Action
(2 Corinthians 6:3)
2. Suffering on Behalf of Others
Precedes Reconciliation (vv. 4–10)
3. Appealing to the Heart (vv. 11–13)
4. Joy in Reconciliation (7:2–4)

In Depth

1. Integrity of Belief and Action (2 Corinthians 6:3)

Aware of the conflict in his relationship with the Corinthians, Paul began to work toward reconciliation by making himself vulnerable and inviting the Corinthian believers to examine his ministry. Paul stated that there was harmony of integrity between his personal behavior and his ministry: "We live in such a way that no one will stumble because of us, and no one will find fault with our ministry" (6:3, NLT). Paul understood the importance of maintaining the credibility and integrity of the ministry through irreproachable behavior. To Timothy, Paul wrote, "Watch your life and doctrine closely" (from 1 Timothy 4:16, NIV). When examined by God, the Christian's behavior and professed beliefs should always agree.

2. Suffering on Behalf of Others Precedes Reconciliation (vv. 4–10)

In the next verses, Paul laid out the character of his ministry. For this, he did not commend the numerous churches he had established, nor mention the many leaders he had trained and ordained in the ministry. While Paul could mention the weight of his authority because of his divine appointment and the power of the Holy Spirit that attended his ministry, Paul instead presented the evidence of his suffering as a servant of God on behalf of the Corinthian believers (vv. 4–10). Taking a cue from Jesus, Paul seemed to say to the Corinthians, "Reach here with your finger, and see My hands; and reach here your hand and put it into My side" (from John 20:27, NASB).

With this vivid description of the suffering he had endured to bring the Gospel and God's ministry of reconciliation (cf. 2 Corinthians 5:17–18) to the Corinthians, Paul seemed to say to the believers that enduring such deep personal suffering was proof of his true feelings of love for them. However, Paul's enemies, the "super-apostles" (cf. 2 Corinthians 11:5, NRSV), could not have presented themselves in a similar way.

One cannot ignore the parallels in Paul's suffering with Jesus' own ministry of reconciling fallen humanity to God. Jesus said of Himself, "I am the good shepherd. The good shepherd lays down his life for the sheep" (John 10:11, NIV). A true ministry that works to reconcile humanity to God sometimes requires patient endurance of suffering of those who minister to the body of Christ.

3. Appealing to the Heart (vv. 11–13)

Paul's accounts of personal suffering were well known by believers everywhere, and on that basis the Corinthians would have to judge Paul's words and characterization of his ministry as true. After appealing to their minds by a rational exposition of his love for them proven by his sufferings, Paul knew that the admission of his genuineness could be the only possible conclusion available to the Corinthian believers. Appealing to their hearts next, and with a longing for a normalization of their relationship, he cried out to them, "O Corinthians, our heart is opened wide" (from 2 Corinthians 6:11, NASB). Paul seemed to imitate Christ's lament over the Jews, who desiring that they accept Him as the One sent from heaven cried out, "Jerusalem,

Jerusalem, who kills the prophets and stones those who are sent to her! How often I wanted to gather your children together, the way a hen gathers her chicks under her wings, and you were unwilling" (Matthew 23:37, NASB).

After commending his sufferings, in 2 Corinthians 6:12–13, Paul stated that his love for the Corinthians had been without any restrictions. However, the Corinthian believers had not reciprocated his affections. Paul called on the Corinthians to respond by also making themselves vulnerable and bringing about the reconciliation that he desired. He exclaimed, "Open wide your hearts also" (from v. 13, NRSV).

4. Joy in Reconciliation (7:2–4)

In 7:2–4, Paul's words reveal a distinct change in disposition toward the Corinthian believers. He exuberantly gave witness that his work to reconcile with the Corinthians had been successful. He now exclaimed that both he and the believers could have pride in each other. Moreover, his pride in the Corinthians led him to openly brag about them. He exclaimed that he had joy even in tribulation (v. 4). Paul's previous anguish brought about by his conflict with the church now gave way to exuberant joy. There was now a restoration of friendly relations.

Paul's work to reconcile with the Corinthian believers followed God's example to reconcile himself with every individual and with the world, and it is the model for seeking reconciliation in human relationships.

In seeking reconciliation with the Corinthian church, Paul followed the divine model of reconciliation. In wanting to reestablish the relationship with a fallen world, the Father did not spare any effort. He sent His own Son to put into effect His ministry of reconciliation, with Jesus as the medium. With His own body, Jesus brought God and humanity closer together, and in His own body, Jesus mingled both divine and human nature.

Search the Scriptures

1. What kind of things did Paul feel confirm his ministry (2 Corinthians 6:4–5)?

2. Despite Paul's tribulation, what did he mention he was filled with? (2 Corinthians 7:4)?

Discuss the Meaning

How might we learn from Paul when handling conflict? Rather than high-handedly dealing with the church at Corinth, Paul chose to lovingly rebuke them and call them to action. This approach disarms others when handling matters as sensitive as those Paul addressed at Corinth. How do you handle these types of conflict—loving rebuke or unloving condemnation?

Lesson in Our Society

The In Focus section of this lesson painted the stark reality of "cutoff" present in many families, churches, and government. Some families experience "cutoff" when at the passing of a loved one, family secrets come to light. Others disintegrate even during weddings over perceived snubs. Many marriages are in a state of tension as spouses experience estrangement over finances, discipline of children, or infidelity.

Perhaps the most visible relationship characterized by "cutoff" in society today is that of lawmakers in this country who refuse to reconcile their deep-seated ideological differences. However, as spiritual as Christians would like to portray their churches, the truth is that for various reasons, "cutoff" characterizes many relationships within the church as well.

May the principles in this lesson become a catalyst to heal divisions in our families, churches, communities, government, and society. May we remember that the first step of reconciling with God is reconciliation with one another.

Make It Happen

God's ministry of reconciliation through Christ is a model for all believers to practice whenever there is conflict. Jesus instructed that anyone seeking to reconcile with God must first reconcile with his brother: "Therefore if you bring your gift to the altar, and there remember that your brother has something against you, leave your gift there before the altar, and go your way. First be reconciled to your brother, and then come and offer your gift" (Matthew 5:23–24, NKJV). Below are seven principles of reconciliation from this lesson that will guide you in your quest for reconciliation:

The party who has suffered wrong takes the initiative to reconcile with the other party.

The estranged party makes himself or herself vulnerable.

The party seeking reconciliation makes himself or herself a servant.

The one seeking reconciliation loves the other party unrestrictedly.

True love is willing to suffer.

The evidence of true love—suffering—will speak for itself.

Only an opened, vulnerable heart can win another.

Follow the Spirit

What God wants me to do:

_____

_____

_____

_____

Remember Your Thoughts

Special insights I have learned:

_____

_____

_____

_____

More Light on the Text

2 Corinthians 6:1–13, 7:2–4

1 We then, as workers together with him, beseech you also that ye receive not the grace of God in vain.

Being a Christian is never a private matter. While our faith is absolutely personal, it is also absolutely communal. The phrase "workers together" is the single word *synergeo* (**soon-ER-geo**)—an irony in itself that two words form into one, which refers to multiple sources putting forth power to assist in some great cause. It's also where we get the modern word "synergy."

The purpose of this type of co-laboring is so that no one would squander the life that God offers us. One of the greatest tragedies for a Christian would be to be a spectator who neglects the opportunity to use his or her spiritual gift for the Lord; the greatest tragedy for a non-Christian would be to not hear about or recognize the opportunity to receive the grace of God. In both scenarios, there is a much larger and fully alive life that we always have the opportunity to enter into. Only together in Christian community can we form the type of complementary work that unearths what we have been promised. This is what is called the ministry of reconciliation.

2 (For he saith, I have heard thee in a time accepted, and in the day of salvation have I succoured thee: behold, now is the accepted time; behold, now is the day of salvation.)

The context of this quote refers back to Isaiah 49:8, which in its entirety reads: "In the time of my favor I will answer you, and in the day of salvation I will help you; I will keep you and will make you to be a covenant for the people, to restore the land and to reassign its desolate inheritances" (NIV). Essentially, God reminds us that the Lord is aware of timing better than we are and wants us to respond to His grace by receiving and sharing it right now. We have to live with a sense of urgency so our focus will be on the big picture as we live in the details.

The New Testament is full of these types of reminders, often quoting the Old Testament as foundation. Many of the Jews who received this were just beginning to understand how Jesus Christ came to fulfill the law through grace, while the non-Jews (Gentiles) were starting to see how they were a part of a much larger story that was rooted in the Hebrew Scriptures. As Galatians 3:28 states, in Christ, "there is neither Jew nor Gentile, neither slave nor free, nor is there male and female, for you are all one in Christ Jesus" (NIV).

3 Giving no offence in any thing, that the ministry be not blamed:

Humanity cannot ever invalidate the work of God, but people can affect the Lord's

reputation and soil how ministry is understood. Paul's charge to fellow Christians was that the world should have no reason to question the authenticity of the Good News if we live up to our God-given potential. He took on many personal sacrifices so this could happen, such as giving up his own credentials, enduring harsh persecution, and allowing others to be in the spotlight ahead of himself (1 Corinthians 1:18–25, 9:3–15; Philippians 3:1–11). Although he couldn't stop people from making accusations, his life was filled with such integrity that their claims fell apart.

4 But in all things approving ourselves as the ministers of God, in much patience, in afflictions, in necessities, in distresses, 5 In stripes, in imprisonments, in tumults, in labours, in watchings, in fastings.

In the book of Job, Satan challenged God that Job would curse the Lord if his life was made uncomfortable and he experienced great suffering (Job 1:9–11). God countered back that he would not, and Job endured great loss without becoming rebellious in his faith. Paul stated that our faith may not be fully revealed until it's under pressure. Sometimes when we aren't strong and at our best, all people get to see is what and Who is inside of us.

Paul's list contains both daily struggles and random pressure, as if he were attempting to remind the Corinthian church that they had to reveal Christ whether life was what they expected. Faith is never passive, even when we are resting in the Lord. Our task isn't to try to do good things, as much as to surrender our lives and let Him work through us.

As an example, the word for "patience" in this passage is *hypomone* (**HOO-po-mon-a**). This Greek word references being steadfast, constant, and enduring. Every Christian is to be intentional in following through on even the hardest of trials. Paul not only taught this but lived it out himself through many instances of persecution.

6 By pureness, by knowledge, by long suffering, by kindness, by the Holy Ghost, by love unfeigned, 7 By the word of truth, by the power of God, by the armour of righteousness on the right hand and on the left.

Spiritual disciplines, such as practicing your faith or studying the Bible, open the doorway to a deeper relationship with God. Each one mentioned here is a tool in the Christian's toolbox, whether in a time of prosperity or challenge. Rather than focus on the problem, we can instead focus on Jesus Christ.

Additionally, the Holy Ghost is mentioned. Rather than expecting humanity to be good or productive on its own, the "power of God" gives us a greater measure of boldness and defense against whatever we face. Its Greek word, *dynamis* (**DOO-a-mees**), is where we get the word "dynamite," as if the Lord is reminding us that our lives are meant to be full of explosive purpose and power that comes from God Himself.

8 By honour and dishonour, by evil report and good report: as deceivers, and yet true; 9 As unknown, and yet well known; as dying, and, behold, we live; as chastened, and not killed; 10 As sorrowful, yet alway rejoicing; as poor, yet making many rich; as having nothing, and yet possessing all things.

The Corinthian church had experienced the teaching of many false apostles who spoke against the character and teaching of Paul. In response, Paul left Ephesus and arrived in Corinth, only to experience a painful visit full of insult (2:1–10), and eventually had to regroup to be able to speak truth to these people. He eventually heard that the majority of Christians in Corinth did return back to the Lord, so he spoke directional truth into their lives.

This is why each piece of this passage contrasts tough times and good times. Paul had experienced this firsthand and wanted them to experience the joy of being consistent in their faith. There were things that were seen and unseen, but in every situation the choice remained: honor God or walk away from Him when things became tough. It's the same choice we have today—to let hard times *define* us or *refine* us.

11 O ye Corinthians, our mouth is open unto you, our heart is enlarged. 12 Ye are not straitened in us, but ye are straitened in your own bowels.

Each of the epistles, including 1 and 2 Corinthians, were written to a specific church for a specific purpose. The Corinthian Christians were often influenced by the pagan culture around them. This letter shows the heart of Paul (and ultimately God) even in light of the tense relationship between him and this church community he loved.

The word "O" indicates a cry of Paul's heart as he made his appeal to the people. By citing that his mouth was open, he further indicated that he was holding nothing back in speaking the truth in love. In contrast, the Corinthians were still being reserved about Paul due to his having been firm on them in the past (1 Corinthians 4; 2 Corinthians 1). Still, this was only a secondary matter that revealed the true one—they loved the pursuit of their own happiness too much. Likewise, they were still housing false teachers who were harsh critics of all that God was doing through Paul.

13 Now for a recompence in the same, (I speak as unto my children,) be ye also enlarged.

The book of 2 Corinthians reads like a letter written from one person to others to work out a strained relationship. Paul wasn't just trying to "agree to disagree" with those he had issues with, but wanted to proclaim the truth in an emotional situation. What not everyone realized was that every natural matter was actually a supernatural matter. Such things are not according to human standards but reveal how God reconciles even through tough times.

Similarly, the idea of being known as someone's "children" is a rabbinical idea. Disciples who followed their teacher were so intertwined in his life that they were like his kids. God used this language when describing His relationship with Israel. By emphasizing these ties, Paul created a common ground for everyone to interact.

7:2 Receive us; we have wronged no man, we have corrupted no man, we have defrauded no man.

There is a time that a good offense requires a good defense, especially when one is accused by others of doing something wrong. Paul clarified that no matter what others said of him, he hadn't done anything wrong. Just as he had been honest with them, he wanted them to be honest with him. It's also why he suggested the idea of receiving one another, for culturally that underscored that there would be no ill will toward each other.

3 I speak not this to condemn you: for I have said before, that ye are in our hearts to die and live with you.

Letters like this were typically read in community, and Paul knew that it would be a perfect time to clarify the nature of the relationship he wanted to have with the Corinthians. He had as much opportunity to condemn them for their critical or doubting spirits as to speak more positively. By extending grace, he further modeled what reconciliation looks like.

That isn't to say that he didn't confront them for where they were in error. Rather, it is possible to hold someone accountable without condemning him. Our ministry on earth is never to be the voice of God but to help others hear His voice.

4 Great is my boldness of speech toward you, great is my glorying of you: I am filled with comfort, I am exceeding joyful in all our tribulation.

One troubling experience can derail many things, let alone several hardships. As quickly as Paul was reconciling with the Corinthians, he was also boasting about their potential. The word "comfort" is *paraklesis* (**pa-ra-KLE-sis**) and speaks of the kind of consultation or solace that is refreshing. No matter how many problems Christians may have with each other, we are ultimately bound to bring out the best in one another by revealing Christ in how we regard each other.

Sources:
The Apologetics Study Bible: Real Questions, Straight Answers, Stronger Faith (HCSB). Nashville: Holman Bible Publishers, 2007. 1665.
Blue Letter Bible. BlueLetterBible.org. http://www.blueletterbible.org/ (accessed November 28, 2012).
Blomberg, C. *The New American Commentary: An Exegetical and Theological Exposition of Holy Scripture, Vol. 22.* Nashville: Holman Reference, 1992. 106.
Bowen, Murray (1976). Quoted in Roberta Gilbert, *The Eight Concepts of Bowen Theory: A New Way of Thinking About The Individual and The Group.* Front Royal, VA: Business Manager Leading Systems Press, 2006.
Craig Evans, and Stanley Porter, ed. *Dictionary of New Testament Background.* Downers Grove, IL: IVP Academic, 2000. 228–29.
Elwell, W. A., and B. Beitzel. *Baker Encyclopedia of the Bible.* Grand Rapids: Baker Book House, 1997. 1823.
"Enter the Bible." www.enterthebible.org/resourcelink.
Evans, Craig, and Stanley Porter, ed. *Dictionary of New Testament Background.* Downers Grove: Intervarsity Press, 2000.
The Holy Bible: New Revised Standard Version (NRSV). Nashville: Thomas Nelson Publishers, 1989.

Hubbard, David and Glenn Barker, ed. *World Biblical Commentary, 2 Corinthians. Vol. 40.* Waco, TX: Word Books Publisher, 1986.

New American Standard Bible 1995 Update (NASB). LaHabra, CA: The Lockman Foundation, 1995.

The New King James Version (NKJV). Nashville: Thomas Nelson, 1982.

Richards, Lawrence O. *The Teacher's Commentary.* Wheaton: Victor Books, 1989. 880.

Walvoord, John F. and Roy B. Zuck. *The Bible Knowledge Commentary.* Wheaton, IL: Chariot Victor Publishing, 1983. 2 Corinthians 5:21.

Say It Correctly

Succoured. **SUHK**-ered.
Recompense. **REK**-uhm-pens.

Daily Bible Readings

MONDAY
A Failed Attempt at Reconciliation
(Acts 7:23–28)

TUESDAY
Reconciled to God through Christ
(Romans 5:6–11)

WEDNESDAY
Making Peace through the Cross
(Colossians 1:15–23)

THURSDAY
The Ministry and Message
of Reconciliation
(2 Corinthians 5:16–21)

FRIDAY
A Harvest of Righteousness
(James 3:13–18)

SATURDAY
First Be Reconciled
(Matthew 5:21–26)

SUNDAY
Open Wide Your Hearts
(2 Corinthians 6:1–13, 7:2–4)

Notes

Teaching Tips

Words You Should Know

A. Poor (v. 9) *ptocheuo* (Gk.)—To be destitute.

B. Rich (v. 9) *plouteo* (Gk.)—The spiritual enrichment of believers through Jesus' poverty.

Teacher Preparation

Unifying Principle—Giving to Others. A small community that possesses much may be part of a larger community that has little and needs the smaller community's assistance. How should members support one another? Paul reminds the Corinthians that they are part of a larger community and that as others have been generous to them, they should repay with equal generosity.

A. Read the Bible Background and Devotional Readings.

B. Study carefully the More Light on the Text section.

C. Bring in a copy of a sample bank statement to show the class.

O—Open the Lesson

A. Open with prayer.

B. Ask for a volunteer to read the In Focus story and show the class the bank statement. Discuss how class members feel about giving tithes and offering regularly.

P—Present the Scriptures

A. Ask for volunteers to read the Focal Verses and The People, Places, and Times. Discuss.

B. Read and discuss the Background section.

E—Explore the Meaning

A. Review and discuss the Search the Scriptures and Discuss the Meaning questions and the Lesson in Our Society section.

B. Ask students to share why they think Paul's exhortation was necessary for the church at Corinth.

N—Next Steps for Application

A. Ask the students to think about their personal giving over the past year. Have them compare it with what they have spent on other must-have items. Remind them of Jesus' words in Matthew 6:21: "For where your treasure is, there your heart will be also" (NIV).

B. Close in prayer.

Worship Guide

For the Superintendent or Teacher
Theme: A Community Shares
Its Resources
Song: "Give of Your Best to the Master"
Devotional Reading: 1 Corinthians
13:1–7

A Community Shares Its Resources

Bible Background • 2 CORINTHIANS 8:1–14
Printed Text • 2 CORINTHIANS 8:1–14 | Devotional Reading • 1 CORINTHIANS 13:1–7

—— Aim for Change ——

By the end of the lesson, we will: RECALL Paul's attempt to get Christian communities to help one another when there was a need; SENSE the need to sometimes contribute to a larger cause than ourselves; and DECIDE to respond to a need in the larger faith community.

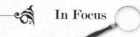

In Focus

David and Melissa have been married for three years. They both consider themselves faithful members of their local church. David serves in the helps ministry and Melissa uses her legal expertise to assist the church. Neither of them was quite sure about giving money to the church. One Sunday, the pastor preached about meeting the needs of a small church in Haiti. After the service, David and Melissa were still uncertain about their giving. They wanted to ensure that the money would be used where they earmarked it.

The next week, David and Melissa visited their accountant. He sat across from them at his desk and asked for the documents necessary to complete their tax return. While asking for documents, the accountant said, "I'll also need a copy of relevant portions of your bank statement. You'd be surprised, but a bank statement can tell me a lot about people." Convicted, the next week David and Melissa decided to start giving to their church's effort in Haiti.

Writing from Macedonia, Paul encouraged the Corinthian believers to give generously and unite with other churches in fellowship. Do you believe God gives so you can give to others?

—— Keep in Mind ——

"Therefore, as ye abound in every thing, in faith, and utterance, and knowledge, and in all diligence, and in your love to us, see that ye abound in this grace also" (2 Corinthians 8:7).

"Therefore, as ye abound in every thing, in faith, and utterance, and knowledge, and in all diligence, and in your love to us, see that ye abound in this grace also" (2 Corinthians 8:7).

Focal Verses

KJV **2 Corinthians 8:1** Moreover, brethren, we do you to wit of the grace of God bestowed on the churches of Macedonia;

2 How that in a great trial of affliction the abundance of their joy and their deep poverty abounded unto the riches of their liberality.

3 For to their power, I bear record, yea, and beyond their power they were willing of themselves;

4 Praying us with much intreaty that we would receive the gift, and take upon us the fellowship of the ministering to the saints.

5 And this they did, not as we hoped, but first gave their own selves to the Lord, and unto us by the will of God.

6 Insomuch that we desired Titus, that as he had begun, so he would also finish in you the same grace also.

7 Therefore, as ye abound in every thing, in faith, and utterance, and knowledge, and in all diligence, and in your love to us, see that ye abound in this grace also.

8 I speak not by commandment, but by occasion of the forwardness of others, and to prove the sincerity of your love.

9 For ye know the grace of our Lord Jesus Christ, that, though he was rich, yet for your sakes he became poor, that ye through his poverty might be rich.

10 And herein I give my advice: for this is expedient for you, who have begun before, not only to do, but also to be forward a year ago.

11 Now therefore perform the doing of it; that as there was a readiness to will, so there may be a performance also out of that which ye have.

NLT **2 Corinthians 8:1** Now I want you to know, dear brothers and sisters, what God in his kindness has done through the churches in Macedonia.

2 They are being tested by many troubles, and they are very poor. But they are also filled with abundant joy, which has overflowed in rich generosity.

3 For I can testify that they gave not only what they could afford, but far more. And they did it of their own free will.

4 They begged us again and again for the privilege of sharing in the gift for the believers in Jerusalem.

5 They even did more than we had hoped, for their first action was to give themselves to the Lord and to us, just as God wanted them to do.

6 So we have urged Titus, who encouraged your giving in the first place, to return to you and encourage you to finish this ministry of giving.

7 Since you excel in so many ways—in your faith, your gifted speakers, your knowledge, your enthusiasm, and your love from us—I want you to excel also in this gracious act of giving.

8 I am not commanding you to do this. But I am testing how genuine your love is by comparing it with the eagerness of the other churches.

9 You know the generous grace of our Lord Jesus Christ. Though he was rich, yet for your sakes he became poor, so that by his poverty he could make you rich.

10 Here is my advice: It would be good for you to finish what you started a year ago. Last year you were the first who wanted to give, and you were the first to begin doing it.

11 Now you should finish what you started. Let the eagerness you showed in the

12 For if there be first a willing mind, it is accepted according to that a man hath, and not according to that he hath not.

13 For I mean not that other men be eased, and ye burdened:

14 But by an equality, that now at this time your abundance may be a supply for their want, that their abundance also may be a supply for your want: that there may be equality.

12 Whatever you give is acceptable if you give it eagerly. And give according to what you have, not what you don't have.

13 Of course, I don't mean your giving should make life easy for others and hard for yourselves. I only mean that there should be some equality.

14 Right now you have plenty and can help those who are in need. Later, they will have plenty and can share with you when you need it. In this way, things will be equal.

The People, Places, and Times

The Jerusalem Church. Jerusalem is considered the political and religious capital for the Jewish people. During the day of Pentecost, the disciple Peter preached and 3,000 people were saved. Day by day the Lord increased the number of believers. The believers in Jerusalem developed into the first church (Acts 2). After Paul's conversion, he visited Jerusalem on many occasions. At one time, he met with the leaders of the Jerusalem Council to get their approval of his preaching to the Gentiles (Galatians 2). Barnabas and Titus were also present during this visit. The leaders gave their approval and requested that Paul remember the poor. The Jerusalem church was suffering from a serious food shortage due to a drought in Palestine (Acts 11:28–30). Many of the other Gentile churches were financially stable and prospering. During Paul's missionary journeys, he took collections for the poor in Jerusalem.

Background

Paul, who had written this letter from Macedonia, was appealing to the Corinthians to participate in the collection for the poor in Jerusalem. This letter tried to build on the success of his harsh letter (an earlier letter that is now lost). It led to forgiveness and reconciliation among the believers in Corinth. He was building upon the foundation that they had realigned themselves with him and obeyed his commands (2 Corinthians 2:9). Since they had been obedient to his directions before, Paul wanted the Corinthians to continue in their allegiance to him. His goal was their full participation in the collection for the saints in Jerusalem.

At-A-Glance

1. Give Like the Macedonians
(2 Corinthians 8:1–5)
2. Give as You Promised (vv. 6–8)
3. Give in Response to God's Grace
(v. 9)
4. Give According to Your Ability
(vv. 10–14)

In Depth

1. Give Like the Macedonians (2 Corinthians 8:1–5)

Paul wanted to call attention to the grace of God given to the Macedonian churches. He acquainted the Corinthians with the gifts of God given through them. The Macedonians were Christians who gave to the collection for the poor in Jerusalem. They were in the midst of affliction and poverty but joyfully responded because of the sense of favor God had bestowed upon them. The Macedonians gave sacrificially on behalf of other saints in need. They wanted to assist other believers and show their commitment as followers of Christ.

When we think about the gift that God gave to the world through Jesus Christ, we should be motivated to respond. We should show our appreciation for the sacrifice He made. The Macedonians not only were appreciative but also proved it by their actions. "As we have therefore opportunity, let us do good unto all men, especially unto them who are of the household of faith" (Galatians 6:10). Paul was challenging the Corinthians to emulate the Macedonians.

2. Give as You Promised (vv. 6–8)

Titus, who was Paul's representative, had previously encouraged the Corinthians to give toward the collection for the poor. But in light of their recent conflict with Paul, they had lost their zeal for collections (7:2–15). When affliction abounds in our lives, we should still be committed to God and to ministering to others. The Macedonians were rejoicing in the midst of their troubles; Paul was encouraging the Corinthians to do the same. He told Titus to complete the gathering of collections from the Macedonians. Paul wanted them to prove their allegiance to him and their love for others.

The Corinthian believers excelled in everything. They had strong faith, good preaching, and much knowledge, enthusiasm, and love. Paul appealed to them to have the same passion and commitment for the collections. For him, the offering was a

remembering (Galatians 2:10), a collection of money (1 Corinthians 16:1–2), a ministry (Romans 15:25), and a gift (2 Corinthians 8:6).

He was not commanding them to give but urging them to prove that their love was sincere. Love manifests itself in action. "Little children, let us love, not in word or speech, but in truth and action" (1 John 3:18, NRSV). Our actions reveal our hearts. Paul wanted the Corinthians to reveal where their devotion and affection were focused.

3. Give in Response to God's Grace (v. 9)

The grace of our Lord Jesus Christ is the greatest example for all believers to follow. "Who, being in the form of God, thought it not robbery to be equal with God: but made himself of no reputation, and took upon him the form of a servant, and was made in the likeness of men" (Philippians 2:6–7). Jesus gave up His position and became a human. He was born in poor circumstances, lived a poor life, and died in poverty—all so He may bestow His favor upon us. "In whom we have redemption through his blood, the forgiveness of sins, according to the riches of his grace" (Ephesians 1:7).

4. Give According to Your Ability (vv. 10–14)

Paul urged the Corinthians to complete the collections for the poor that they had planned a year earlier (2 Corinthians 9:2). The gifts offered should be in proportion to what they were able to give. God does not want us to be burdened by giving that which we cannot sacrifice. Whatever we give, we should do it willingly. "Every man according as he purposeth in his heart, so let him give; not grudgingly, or of necessity: for God loveth a cheerful giver" (v. 7).

When you have given to others, they will help you when you are in need. Paul could be reflecting on the charity of the early Jerusalem church. There was a voluntary sharing among believers in Jerusalem (Acts 4:32–37); everyone shared possessions equally so no one lacked anything. Believers should willingly share with others; we are of one body in Christ. The "material blessings" were to be shared by the Gentile believers in appreciation for the "spiritual blessings" that the Jewish believers had shared with them (Romans 15:27).

Search the Scriptures

1. What was bestowed upon the churches of Macedonia (2 Corinthians 8:1–6)?

2. Fill in the blank: "Praying us with much intreaty that we would receive the _____, and take upon us the fellowship of the ministering to the saints" (v. 4).

3. Fill in the blanks: "For ye know the _____ of our Lord Jesus Christ, that, though he was _____, yet for your sakes he became _____, that ye through his poverty might be _____" (v. 9).

Discuss the Meaning

1. The Macedonian church was said to be genuine in their giving. How might we be genuine when we give our offering?

2. We live in a nation of abundance. How might the church in this nation be able to bless others out of our abundance?

Lesson in Our Society

The United States is one of the wealthiest nations in the world. Our understanding of rich and poor is quite different from other nations in the world where people live on much less. We know abundance, yet our economy still suffers. The unemployment rate is high. Many churchgoers are unemployed, yet we are still challenged to give generously. Paul exhorted the Corinthian church to do just that. How might those who

have the means reach out to those in your congregation who have needs?

Make It Happen

Take some real time to consider your spending. What might it say about you? Evaluate some things you have spent money on that may be considered frivolous purchases. Think about selling some of those items and using the money to support a missions effort at a local church.

Follow the Spirit

What God wants me to do:

_____

_____

_____

_____

Remember Your Thoughts

Special insights I have learned:

_____

_____

_____

_____

More Light on the Text

2 Corinthians 8:1–14

1 Moreover, brethren, we do you to wit of the grace of God bestowed on the churches of Macedonia.

The Greek word for "to wit" is *gnorizo* (**gno-RID-zo**), which means to make known. The word for "grace" in Greek is *charis* (**KHAR-ece**), which is also translated as "gift." Paul wanted to make known God's gift of grace delivered to the churches of Macedonia.

2 How that in a great trial of affliction the abundance of their joy and their deep poverty abounded unto the riches of their liberality.

Paul said that the trials the Corinthians had gone through had become a benefit to them. The Greek word for the phrase "trial of affliction" is *dokime thlipsis* (**dok-ee-MAY THLIP-sis**), which means test of tribulation. Despite their tribulations, the Corinthians had maintained their joy. The Greek word for "liberality" is *haplotes* (**hap-LOT-ace**), which is also translated as "sincerity" or "generosity." Although the Corinthians had dealt with deep poverty, they had been rich in generosity.

3 For to their power, I bear record, yea, and beyond their power they were willing of themselves;

The Greek word for "power" is *dunamis* (**DOO-nam-is**), which means ability. The word for "bear record" in Greek is *martureo* (**mar-too-REH-o**), which means to testify. The phrase "willing of themselves" comes from the Greek word *authairetos* (**ow-THAH-ee-ret-os**), which means self-chosen or voluntary. Paul complimented the Corinthians on their willingness to serve. He testified that the Corinthians gave above and beyond what they had financially.

4 Praying us with much entreaty that we would receive the gift, and take upon us the fellowship of the ministering to the saints. 5 And this they did, not as we hoped, but first gave their own selves to the Lord, and unto us by the will of God.

The Greek word for "praying" is *deomai* (**DEH-om-ahee**), which means urgently pleading. *Paraklesis* (**par-AK-lay-sis**) is the Greek word for "entreaty," which is also translated as "exhortation." The Corinthians almost begged Paul to receive the gift that they were giving. The Corinthians also wanted Paul to accept the fellowship of ministering to the saints. The Greek words for "fellowship" and "ministering" are *koinonia* (**koy-nohn-EE-ah**) and *diakonia* (**dee-ak-on-EE-ah**), respectively. *Koinonia* means community, communion, or joint participation; *diakonia* means serving. The Corinthians not only wanted to continue communicating with Paul, but also continue helping Paul in any way possible.

In this verse, Paul continued to emphasize how the Corinthians had gone above and beyond expectations. The phrase "not as we hoped" actually means "beyond our hopes." The Corinthians gave themselves to God first, and then they gave their money to Paul. They even gave their money "by the will of God." The Greek word for "will" is *thelema* (**THEL-ay-mah**), which means pleasure. The Corinthians pleased God with their giving.

6 Insomuch that we desired Titus, that as he had begun, so he would also finish in you the same grace also.

Titus had encouraged the Corinthian church to give in the first place. Paul hoped that Titus could encourage them to keep giving. The Greek word for "desired" is *parakaleo* (**par-ak-al-EH-o**), which means to encourage or exhort. The word for "finish" in Greek is *epiteleo* (**ep-ee-tel-EH-o**), which is also translated as "to fulfill completely." Paul was urging Titus to encourage the Corinthians to fully complete their giving.

7 Therefore, as ye abound in every thing, in faith, and utterance, and knowledge, and in all diligence, and in your love to us, see that ye abound in this grace also.

The Greek word for "abound" is *perisseuo* (**per-is-SYOO-o**), which means excel. The word for "utterance" in Greek is *logos* (**LOG-os**), which is translated as "word." *Spoude* (**spoo-DAY**) is the Greek word for "diligence"; it means earnestness. Paul said that the Corinthians had excelled in their faith, speech, knowledge of the Word, earnestness, and love for Paul and Titus. However, Paul wanted to make sure that they excelled at the grace of giving as well.

8 I speak not by commandment, but by occasion of the forwardness of others, and to prove the sincerity of your love. 9 For ye know the grace of our Lord Jesus Christ, that, though he was rich, yet for your sakes he became poor, that ye through his poverty might be rich.

The Greek word for "commandment" is *epitage* (**ep-ee-tag-AY**), which means decree. The word for "forwardness" is *spoude* (**spoo-DAY**), which is the same word used for "diligence" in the previous verse. Paul was not making a decree that the Corinthians must give more, but he wanted them to have the chance to prove the sincerity of their love.

Paul also reminded the Corinthians of the unselfishness of Christ in order to encourage them to remain unselfish as well. Paul said the Corinthians "know the grace of our Lord Jesus Christ." The Greek word for "know" is *ginosko* (**ghin-OCE-ko**), which means to be sure of something. The word for "grace" in Greek is *charis* (**KHAR-ece**), which can be translated as "favor." Christ did the ultimate favor for the Corinthians, and all of us, by leaving His throne in heaven as King of kings and coming down to earth in the form of a child. Despite His eternal royalty, Christ came to earth as a baby born in a manger, who grew up having to work as a carpenter. Ultimately, Christ made the ultimate

sacrifice by allowing Himself to be crucified on the Cross, to accomplish salvation for all who are in Him. Christ's poverty made us rich in grace and mercy.

10 And herein I give my advice: for this is expedient for you, who have begun before, not only to do, but also to be forward a year ago. 11 Now therefore perform the doing of it; that as there was a readiness to will, so there may be a performance also out of that which ye have.

Paul gave the Corinthians his advice on what to do with their giving. The word for "advice" in Greek is *gnome* (**GNO-may**), which means counsel or judgment. The word "expedient" comes from the Greek word *sumphero* (**soom-FER-o**), which means profitable. The word for "be forward" in Greek is *thelo* (**THEL-o**), which means determined or willed. Paul wanted them not only to continue to give, but also to continue to be determined, just as they had been a year earlier. The Greek word for "perform" is *epiteleo* (**ep-ee-tel-EH-o**), which means to finish. Paul challenged the Corinthians to finish their giving. He said that just as there was a readiness and determination to give before (the word for "will" is the same word used for "be forward" in the previous verse), the Corinthians should be determined to finish their giving according to what they had to give.

12 For if there be first a willing mind, it is accepted according to that a man hath, and not according to that he hath not.

Paul reminded the Corinthians that they could only give what they had. He emphasized the importance of the right attitude in giving. The Greek word for "willing mind" is similar to the word for "readiness" in verse 11. *Prothumia* (**proth-oo-MEE-ah**) is the Greek word used in this verse, and it can be translated as "forwardness of mind" or "readiness of mind." There is a definite theme of willingness to give within this text. The word for "accepted" in Greek is *euprosdektos* (**yoo-PROS-dek-tos**), which means well-received. Paul suggested that the proper attitude in giving is more important than the amount being given. He said that the gift is well-received according to what the Corinthians were able to give and not according to what they could not give.

13 For I mean not that other men be eased, and ye burdened: 14 But by an equality, that now at this time your abundance may be a supply for their want, that their abundance also may be a supply for your want: that there may be equality:

Paul did not want to put the entire burden on the Corinthians to do all of the giving to the ministry. He also didn't want the Corinthians to give so much that they suffered from not having enough for themselves. Paul knew that others needed to give as well, but he believed there should be equality in giving. The word for "equality" in Greek is *isotes* (**ee-SOT-ace**), which means "equity." The Greek word for "want" is *husterema* (**hoos-TER-ay-mah**), which means lack. Paul said that the Corinthians should be able to meet the lack of others now so that in the future, if the Corinthians were ever in lack, others could help them. Since Christians shared supplies in times of need, this is entirely possible.

Sources:
Blue Letter Bible. BlueLetterBible.org. http://www.blueletterbible.org/ (accessed December 2, 2012).
Craig Evans, and Stanley Porter, ed. *Dictionary of New Testament Background.* Downers Grove, IL: IVP Academic, 2000.
Richards, Lawrence O. *The Teacher's Commentary.* Wheaton: Victor Books, 1989.

Say It Correctly

Intreaty. in-**TREE**-tee.

Daily Bible Readings

MONDAY
Treasure in Heaven
(Mark 10:17–27)

TUESDAY
The Measure of Your Gift
(Luke 6:34–38)

WEDNESDAY
Giving in Love
(1 Corinthians 13:1–7)

THURSDAY
Show Proof of Your Love
(2 Corinthians 8:16–24)

FRIDAY
Sowing and Reaping Bountifully
(2 Corinthians 9:1–6)

SATURDAY
God Loves a Cheerful Giver
(2 Corinthians 9:7–15)

SUNDAY
A Wealth of Generosity
(2 Corinthians 8:1–14)

A

Abomination: A foul and detestable thing

Affliction: Anguish, burden, persecution, tribulation, or trouble

Angels: God's messengers; they are not eternal or all-knowing, and are sometimes referred to as winged creatures known as "cherubim" and "seraphim"

Atonement: To "propitiate" (to satisfy the demands of an offended holy God) or "atone" (being reconciled to a holy God) because of sin

Avenger: One who takes revenge, one who punishes

B

Be Baptized: To dip repeatedly, to immerse, to submerge

Blameless: Irreproachable, faultless, flawless

Blessedness: Happiness, joy, prosperity. It is not based on circumstance but is rooted in the deep abiding hope shared by all who have received salvation through Jesus Christ.

Bless the Lord: To simply speak well of Him

Blood of the Lamb: The blood that Jesus shed on the Cross of Calvary when He suffered and died for humanity's sin

Bowels: The place of emotions, distress, or love

C

Called: Appointed or commissioned by God to fulfill a task

Charge: Admonish, order, command

Chosen: To be elected or selected

Christ: The Anointed One

Commandments: God's mandates; the entire body of Laws issued by God to Moses for Israel

Conduct: Manner of living

Confess: To acknowledge or to fully agree

Consider: To determine, make out

Covenant: An agreement with God based on God's character, strength, and grace; an agreement and promise between God and humankind

Crucifixion: Jesus suffered and died on the Cross

D

Decalogue: The Ten Commandments; the words translated "Ten Commandments" literally mean "ten words"

Desolation: Making something deserted or uninhabited

Disciples: Learners, students, followers

Dominion: Rule or reign

Dwelling place: A location that is a person's refuge, home

E

El: The Hebrew word for "god" or "mighty one"

Even from everlasting to everlasting: "Indefinite or unending future, eternity" (Strong)

Evil: To do "bad, unpleasant, displeasing" things

Evil doer: A malefactor, wrongdoer, criminal, troublemaker

Evil spirits: Messengers and ministers of the devil

Exalt: To raise up; to raise to the highest degree possible

Exhortation: Giving someone motivation to change his or her behavior; it can imply either rebuke or encouragement.

F

Faithfulness: Steadfastness, steadiness

Fear of the Lord: Reverence or awe of who God is

G

Gittith: A musical instrument resembling a Spanish guitar that, in ancient times, provided a musical tune or tempo during a ceremony or festival

Glory: Splendor, unparalleled honor, dignity, or distinction; to honor, praise, and worship

God called: To commission, appoint, endow

God's Bride: The Church

God's own hand: God's strength, power

God's protection: Conveys the idea of staying in God's abode, staying constantly in His presence, getting completely acquainted or connected with Him, and resting permanently in Him

Gospel: "The glad tidings of the kingdom of God soon to be set up, and later also of Jesus the Messiah, the founder of this kingdom" (Strong).

Graven image: An idol or likeness cut from stone, wood, or metal and then worshiped as a god

Great Tribulation: A time of great suffering (Daniel 12:1, Revelation 6–18)

H

Hallowed: Consecrated, dedicated, or set apart

Hear: Listen to, yield to, to be obedient

Hearken: Pay attention to, give attention to

Heart: The place, figuratively, where our emotions and passions exist

Heathen: Literally means "nations" and is used in the Old Testament to refer to the Gentiles, all those who are not a part of the people of God

Holy: Anything consecrated and set aside for sacred use; the place made sacred because of God's presence; set apart from sin

Honor: To revere, value

Hosts: Those which go forth; armies

I

Idolatry: The worship of anything other than God, our Creator

Infidel: One who is unfaithful, unbelieving, not to be trusted

Iniquities: Perversity, depravity, guilt

In vain: A waste, a worthless thing, or simply emptiness

J

Jesus' ascension: Forty days after Jesus' death, burial, and Resurrection, He ascended or went back to heaven to sit at the right hand of the Father (Acts 1:9–11).

Jesus' transfiguration: While on the Mount of Olives with His closest disciples—Peter, James, and John—Jesus changed into another form. His face shone with the brightness like the sun and His raiment was white as snow (Matthew 17:2; Mark 9:2; Luke 9:29).

Just: A word often rendered as "righteous"; that which is right and fair

Justice: Righteousness in government

K

Kingdom of Christ: It is the same as the "Kingdom of Heaven (Matthew 18:1–4); it is where Jesus reigns in "glory" (i.e., in "dignity or honor").

Know: To ascertain by seeing, have understanding, to acknowledge

Knowledge: Discernment, understanding, wisdom

L

Labor: To toil to the point of exhaustion or weariness

Logos (LOG-os): The entire Word of God

M

"Make a joyful noise": A command that literally means "shout"

Manna: Food from heaven

Messiah: The Promised One; the Anointed One

Minister: "A servant, an attendant, one who executes the commands of another" (Strong)

O

Omnipotent: All powerful

Omnipresent: All present, present everywhere

Omniscient: All knowing

Ordained: Established and founded by God; founded, fixed, appointed, or established

P

Parousia (par-oo-SEE-ah): Christ's Second Coming

Path: Connotes an ongoing process of taking dynamic steps toward an expected end

Peace: Denotes "wholeness, quietness, contentment, health, prosperity" (Strong); it is far more than an absence of conflict or problems, but that every part of life would be blessed.

Pentateuch: The Mosaic Law or Divine Law; The first five books of the Old Testament, as well as the Old Testament as a whole, reveal the entire set of legal and religious instructions which God gave, through Moses, for God's people. Terms that are synonymous for "Law" include commandments, ordinances, statutes, legal regulations, authoritative instructions, and teachings.

People(s): Most English versions translate "people" as "peoples." The New Living Translation goes even further: "Let the whole world bless our God."

Power: Boldness, might, strength, especially God's

Prophets: They were filled with the Spirit of God and under the authority and command of God, pleaded God's cause and urged humanity to be saved

Profit: To gain, benefit, avail

Prosperous: To make progress, to succeed, especially in spiritual things. It often did not refer to personal profit. Rather it meant "to move forward or succeed" in one's efforts.

Proved: Examined, tested, and tried

Psalm: A Hebrew title that means "praise"

Purity: "Sinless of life" (Strong)

R

Ransom: To redeem (buy back) from, to pay a price for a person. It is commonly used as a purchase price to free slaves.

Redeemed: Ransomed, purchased.

Refuge: Place of shelter; stronghold or fortress—a place to which we can run when the enemy threatens and be secure; a shelter from rain, storm, or danger

Repent: To change (be transformed) or turn back from sin and turn to God in faith

Righteous: To be declared "not guilty"

Righteousness: God's justness and rightness, which He works as a gift also in His people; refers to the right way to live as opposed to a lifestyle that treats others unfairly or unjustly

S

Sabbath: In Hebrew, *shabbath* means "ceasing from work." A day set aside to worship God.

Sanctuary: A word that means "holy" when used as an adjective. The "holy place" of which David speaks is the tabernacle, the portable temple built under Moses' leadership after the Exodus from Egypt

Salvation: Rescue, safety, deliverance

Satan: An adversary or devil

Savior: A defender, rescuer, deliverer

Scribes: They were secretaries, recorders, men skilled in the law

Secret place: A refuge, place of safety and a covering from all forms of destructive elements that seek to attack or destroy the children of God and to prevent us from experiencing the fullness of God's blessings, peace, and divine providence

See: To behold, consider, discern, perceive

Selah: This Hebrew expression (**SEH-lah**) is found almost exclusively in the book of Psalms. Some believe that Selah denotes a pause or a suspension in singing of the psalm or recitation, and the insertion of an instrumental musical interlude. The Greek Septuagint renders the word *dia'psalma*, meaning "a musical interlude." Still others think that the word *Selah* signaled a holding back of singing and allowed for silent meditation.

Septuagint: It means "seventy," and it is the ancient Greek translation of the Hebrew Old Testament by 70 Jewish scholars.

Servant: A slave, subject, worshiper

Shalom: Means "peace"

Shekinah Glory: The awesome presence of the Lord; His honor, fame, and reputation

Shofar (sho-FAR): Means "ram's horn" and was used in celebration as well as in signaling armies or large groups of people in civil assembly

Soul: Refers to the immaterial part of the human being (what leaves the body when death occurs), or to the whole being—the self, one's life

Stiffnecked: Obstinate and difficult

Strengthen: To secure, make firm, make strong

Strive: To struggle, to exert oneself

Supplications: Seeking, asking, entreating, pleading, imploring, and petitioning God

T

Tabernacles: Literally means "dwelling places," the name of the portable temple constructed by Moses and the people of Israel

Teaching: Instruction in Christian living

Tetragrammaton: Hebrew name for God (YHWH)

Torah: The Law, which means "instrument" or "direction"; the first five books of the Old Testament (Genesis, Exodus, Leviticus, Numbers, and Deuteronomy)

Transfigured: To change or transform

Transgressions: Include sins, rebellion, breaking God's Law

Tried: Smelted or refined, purified

Trumpet: A ram's horn that was used in celebration as well as in signaling armies or large groups of people in civil assembly

U

Understand: To consider, have wisdom

W

Wisdom: "Prudence, an understanding of ethics" (Strong)

Woe: An exclamation of grief

Worship: Bow down deeply, show obeisance and reverence

Wrath: "Burning anger, rage" (Strong)

Y

Yahweh: Many scholars simply use the Hebrew spelling with consonants only, *YHWH*, which is God's name.

Source:

Strong, James. *New Exhaustive Strong's Numbers and Concordance with Expanded Greek-Hebrew Dictionary.* Seattle, WA: Biblesoft, and International Bible Translators, 1994. 2003.

Notes

Notes

Notes

Notes

Notes

Notes

Notes

Notes